THE THEATRE IN OUR TIMES

Other Books by John Gassner

Masters of the Drama
Producing the Play
Our Heritage of World Literature
A Treasury of the Theatre (3 vols.)
English Comedies
Comedies of Molière
Human Relations in the Theatre
Form and Idea in Modern Drama and Theatre (forthcoming)
Twenty-five Best Plays of the Modern American Theatre, 1916-29
Twenty Best Plays of the Modern American Theatre, 1930-39
Best Plays of the Modern American Theatre, 1939-46
Best American Plays, 1945-51
Twenty Best Film Plays
Best Film Plays of 1943-44
Best Film Plays of 1945

THE THEATRE
IN OUR TIMES

A SURVEY OF THE MEN, MATERIALS AND
MOVEMENTS IN THE MODERN THEATRE

John Gassner

CROWN PUBLISHERS, INC.   *NEW YORK*

TO MOLLIE

My constant companion at the theatre
  for more than a quarter of a century—
Who made good plays better and poor ones tolerable

Set designed by MORDECAI GORELIK
for O'NEILL's *Desire Under the Elms*

PREFACE

In a collection of essays, *The Forlorn Demon,* Allen Tate declares that like other literary men he has been an eccentric conducting an unfinished education in public. Whether I, too, am a literary man is less certain than that I, too, have been conducting an unfinished education publicly. And eccentricity has been in my case reinforced by the extremely public nature of the theatre to which I have devoted more than half my life. That my education is far from completed will be sufficiently apparent to the reader from the tentative, sometimes even contradictory, nature of the contents of the book. If I sometimes write as if I were entitled to have my say, the reason is not that I claim more authority than most people in a field full of uncertainties, but that I have spent more time than is usual in floundering in it and therefore can speak from experience. I can chart the course of error, and I can lecture others with considerable authority as a pilot who never reached port.

My reason for publishing this book is my realization that theatre in our times has been in a precarious state, has been alternately buffeted by storms and becalmed, has sprung leaks and collected barnacles, and has carried a cargo on which fortunes have been spent and love has been lavished without any certainty that much of it can be delivered to the muse of history without profuse apologies. The theatre, too, suffers from an unfinished education. Perhaps all that can be said, then, in its behalf, and all I can say in my own, is that much of the zest of existence is associated with the course of an education rather than with its completion. The question that can be raised most legitimately concerning both the author and the stage is whether the process has not been miseducation rather than education; and in the case of the theatre, its survival as an institution is greatly involved with the possibility that its energies have been misdirected.

Although many discoveries have been made in the modern theatre, a living enterprise must make them again if they are to have any effect. Therefore, this book reviews and tries to evaluate many efforts now already categorized in histories of the drama. Discoveries must also be distinguished from a thorough exploration of the terrain. I claim no thoroughness in this book, but I believe I do look closely at some of the territory opened up here and abroad by our playwrights and producers. And since we have completed half a century identified with twentieth-century modernism, I investigate some of the results. The perspective I have adopted for this purpose is the only one available to me. It is an American perspective, although, I hope, not a provincial one. It may not be the most comprehensive, but it is the only one most generally relevant to us in America.

To claim the strict unity of argument that pertains to a single-minded exposition is far from my intention. The book is essentially a collection of essays new and old, although much revised; and the latter originally appeared in publications as diverse as *The Atlantic Monthly, Theatre Arts, The Forum, The Quarterly Journal of Speech, The Educational Theatre Journal,* and *Theatre Time.* I preferred the method of covering the subject of contemporary theatre with a procession of essays not because it is a less taxing procedure than consecutive composition, but because it enables a writer to advance a point without irretrievably committing him to it alone. The ambivalences induced by what the critic observes should not be resolved into dogmas for the critic and blueprints for a theatre invariably created by a variety of temperaments and responses. It is usually the business of the artist to make a single commitment in a single work. It is the business of the critical observer to make discriminations, but it is also his obligation to relate them to the diversity of his field of observation. As for myself, I have found my responses too divided to formulate doctrine, even if I cannot subscribe to mere impressionism in criticism.

Thus, I believe that the American stage is most vital when closest to American sensibility and interest, whatever their shortcomings, but that the European enterprise in theatre provides a necessary perspective and corrective. I also believe that realism and contemporary interest alone can give us a living theatre, but that realism should not limit us to realistic technique or style while contemporary interest should not limit us to commonplace or topical matter and attitudes. I grant the importance of *re-theatricalizing* the modern drama that realism *de-theatricalized,* but do not believe that theatricalism can be the sole end of an art that attained cultural stature in modern times with Ibsen, Strindberg, Chekhov, and Shaw. We must develop or refine dramatic and theatrical forms, but these should not be regarded as absolutes rather than as a means for making drama a more intense or revealing experience. I believe in stylization, but suspect a tendency among stylizing modernists to "style" humanity right out of the theatre in the name of art. I do not expect all good drama to be "literature," but am gratified when it is that, too; I favor literary drama, but require it to be theatre as well. I like to be entertained as much as anybody else, but prefer to be stimulated. I favor excitement, but prefer to be excited into some recognition or to some purpose. My quarrel with many of our effective plays is that they are excitative without being formative. I also favor a critical spirit in the drama, but like the theatre to be intelligent rather than intellectual.

I cannot, therefore, avoid dividing my allegiance or shifting my emphasis whenever the theatre moves too far in one direction, and such fluctuations are better recorded in individual essays than in a tightly knit book-length argument. Nevertheless, the essays follow some pattern indicated in the divisions of the book. They are all intended to pursue the same inquiry, which may be summarized as an investigation of the nature of the theatre in our times, the positions it has held, the direction it has followed in so far as it has had any direction, and the gyres into which it has been driven by a world in which contrary winds have blown most prodigiously.

Some of the chapters belong to history, others to dramatic criticism, still others to dramatic theory. But the book as a whole, as has already been said, expresses one man's search for a relationship to a multiple enterprise that cannot be wholly expressed in intellectual terms but cannot be meaningfully discussed without them. And since this search has occurred in the course of a career that has taken the author almost equally into the fields of dramatic criticism, professional stage production, experimental ventures, and education, the endeavor to make some sense out of the contemporary theatre is probably representative. In any case, I am sure that the book is not so inviolably an "above-the-scene" commentary as to be purely theoretical or historical and is, at the same time, not so thoroughly embroiled in the immediate practicalities of "show-business" and the daily practice of play reviewing as to preclude generalization. A certain degree of conviction, too, has influenced the writing in this volume. It is the conviction that the theatre, for all the waywardness that has characterized its efforts in our century, is a proper subject for analysis, argument, and evaluations. It started out in Ibsen's time as a venture of the modern intellect and spirit, and it is still that, despite the bane of humdrum "commercialism" and equally humdrum "amateurism." Only the conditions under which it has functioned, the methods now available to it, and the lessons accumulated, if not necessarily assimilated, since *A Doll's House* are different.

In closing I should like to express my obligation to those with whom I have been professionally associated in my small part of this venture, although they are too many to be listed individually; to the editors of the publications in which a number of the essays were first published; to the John Simon Guggenheim Foundation which granted me a Fellowship that encouraged me to form some midcentury perspectives; to my publishers and their editors Bertha Krantz and Herbert Michelman. Brooks Atkinson, John Mason Brown, Harold Clurman, George Jean Nathan, Richard Watts, Jr., and Stark Young, who first welcomed me into the cockpit of dramatic criticism two decades ago, also must share in my gratitude whether or not they agree with the opinions expressed in this book. And here I must add the names of my friends E. J. West, whose enthusiasm for some of my pieces implanted thoughts of incorporating them in a volume, and Arthur Colby Sprague, with whom I have had many delightful conversations about the theatre for a dozen years or more.

Finally, a major indebtedness must be acknowledged to the author's wife, Mollie Gassner, a lady of many talents not the least of which is perseverance. The idea of publishing this book originated with her, and I could not have actually undertaken the project in the midst of an over-committed schedule but for her editorial assistance. I may say that the publishers and the reader, too, are under some obligation to her, since without her vigilance the book would have been more than twice its present length.

JOHN GASSNER

February, 1954

CONTENTS

Part Two: THE SIGNATURE OF THE TIMES

Part Three: THE INCUBI OF OUR STAGE

Part Four: FILM PERSPECTIVES

PERSPECTIVES OF THEATRE

INTRODUCTION:

THEATRE IN OUR TIMES

When the theatre moved toward the midcentury mark at the close of the 1948-49 season, the temptation to make a retrospective evaluation led us into many channels of inquiry. Usually, we emerged from these with loud laments and with scanty appraisals that could not be used for more than journalistic purposes. Nevertheless, retrospective study is the first step toward a perspective. My own review, first hastily drawn up in the issues of a periodical and then amplified, may serve to introduce the present volume. The review is offered as a casual journey of one person thinking aloud about the travail and somewhat less than unshakable faith he shared with many individuals in the American theatre. The perspectives are largely, if not entirely, those available to an observer situated in New York rather than in London, Paris, or Berlin. And if this introduction raises more questions than it can answer, it may serve as a wedge into the subjects explored in other chapters of the book.

I

As we make a rapid inventory of the period from 1900 to 1950, we may be rather amazed at all that has transpired.

We have witnessed the extension of the theatre into related media based on the development of scientific invention. Up to the present century, there existed in the Western world only one dramatic medium, that of the stage for the actor seen in the round on a platform. Our half century saw three new media spring up before its eyes—the motion pictures, radio theatre, and television theatre. The first and the third were given over to the two-dimensional performer who operated on our senses from a flat screen rather than a platform, and the living actor who gave his image to the screen was many miles—in the case of film, often several thousand miles—away from the spectator. This, in short, was a theatre radically different from any hitherto known, in the sense that the actor and the audience had no immediate actual relationship. The living performer of films was a canned image and a voice who did not perform directly to an audience and catch contagion from it. Until the advent of the "talkies," moreover, he was also consistently deprived of the physiological function of speech, with consequences we need not examine here. In radio drama, moreover, he was even deprived of his face and figure and transformed

3

into a voice, while his environment was reduced to a purely auditory
dimension.

What the drama lost by these transformations is too obvious. Made
available to virtually every man, woman, and child, it lost a good deal of
its freedom, especially the candor that it had enjoyed as a prerogative even
under the censorious eyes of the medieval church and the Tudor, Bourbon,
and Spanish autocracies. The literary element vanished in the silent motion
pictures and underwent marked abbreviation even after actors became
talking images. And literature, in general, became debased in all the mass
media; its style was vulgarized and its content drained of challenging or
complex ideas. Nonetheless, the historian who sees things in a large perspective can note gains as well as losses.

He will observe that the experience of environment was never before
so fully realized as on the motion picture screen. The backgrounds that
the dramatists had had to describe in words and that his production associates could, as a rule, only suggest within the narrow limits of stage
scenery, became a major achievement of the motion picture camera. In
short, a new protagonist or antagonist was fully born in the present century—the physical environment. By comparison with the cinema, the social
problem theatre of the nineteenth century, which attributed so important
a function to the factor of society and topography, was in veritable infancy.
That frequently the camera was employed only to falsify realities, as in
most Hollywood pictures, is merely an example of misuse of a medium
that could give such ample visual realization to background as the early
Griffith films, *The Birth of a Nation* and *Intolerance,* the von Stroheim
film *Greed,* the better Westerns and war films, not to mention such foreign films as *Paisan, Shoe-Shine,* and innumerable documentary pictures.

Nor did the visualization have to be literal, for it soon became evident
that photography, with its angle shots and montage, could be as expressive
as any poet's language. It could even go to the extremes of expressionist
distortion that appeared in *The Cabinet of Dr. Caligari.* Even with respect
to literary style, the historian can note some improvement as well as deterioration, since the camera tended to reduce dialogue to essentials and
to prune it of persiflage and rhetoric. There was hardly any point in letting
a character describe at length what the photographic "shot" conveyed so
much more vividly than words, or in allowing an actor to expatiate on his
feelings or the state of his soul when a close-up of his face showed in an
instant what he would have had to explain at length. In any case, screenplay dialogue, for all its lack of distinction, was vastly more tolerable than
the absurdly turgid writing that proliferated on nineteenth-century English and American stages until the 1880's.

Radio drama, incidentally, held remarkable possibilities for the poet, and it is not the fault of the medium but of commercialism that these were largely unrealized. When Archibald MacLeish wrote *The Fall of the City* and *Air Raid,* Alfred Kreymborg, *The Planets,* and Norman Corwin, *On a Note of Triumph,* it became plain that the lowly medium could become an effective instrument for poetry and good rhetoric.

The drama in the twentieth century assumed many masks and, if we grant, as we must, its omnipresence in the mass media, entered every nook and cranny of the Western world. In this sense, far from shrinking, "theatre" grew enormously. Far from receding from the consciousness of the common man, it assumed a larger hold on him than ever before in the history of the world. It was available in his immediate neighborhood; all he had to do was to round a street corner and there was a neighborhood motion picture house. If he turned a knob on his radio set, he could have audible drama in his living room. With the coming of television, he can now get visual drama, too, just as effortlessly. Playwrights and actors, moreover, found new kinds of employment for their talents. Nor can it even be said that this involved falling from some high estate, for the average actor or playwright, indentured to cheap entertainment and infantile melodramas throughout the greater part of the history of the stage, has not stood on any particular eminence.

Only the so-called "legitimate stage," the stage trodden by the living actor seen in the round, suffered a diminution. Yet this was not always the case when we consider the enormous subscription audiences of the Weimar Republic's *Volksbühne,* and the size of the "little theatre" movement in the United States, augmented at different times by the amateur social theatre groups and the Federal Theatre of the 1930's. And there was even some gain in whatever shrinkage did occur at different times and in different places, so long as totalitarian suppression was not in force.

It has not been sufficiently observed that the mass media based on modern photography and electronics drained off a good deal of the dross that the legitimate stage would have otherwise surely presented and for which it would have received the consent of large audiences, as it did in the nineteenth century. Since the eighteenth century, the bulk of dramatic output had consisted of sentimental comedy, transparent farce, and "thrillers" of murder and crime detection. When film and radio made this type of drama their own and purveyed it at a fraction of the cost of a theatre ticket, the professional theatre lost most of this trash and was forced to rely on drama of a higher quality. Although it cannot be said that playwrights and producers have been able to deliver material that meets elevated standards with any great frequency, the fact remains that much drama that would have been acceptable in 1850 is no longer acceptable in 1950.

The limitations of the stage in our time are obvious enough. Its doldrums and shortcomings are caused in the West by economic anarchy, high costs, and lack of opportunity for the young dramatist and actor to learn their crafts. Yet it is difficult to escape the conclusion that the stage in the twentieth century became a notable medium for intellectual discussion, psychological analysis, social conflict, and experimentation in theatrical and dramatic art—more so, indeed, than in many periods in which the "legitimate" theatre met with virtually no competition from other forms of entertainment. Its only major defeat occurred when poetic drama virtually disappeared as a popular form of playwriting. If the drama of the century made less progress than did the modern novel, the reasons lie in the superior adaptability of the novel and the simpler conditions faced by the novelist and his publisher. Joyce could write *Ulysses* and *Finnegans Wake,* for instance, without considering actors, production possibilities, and the physical theatre; and his publishers could bring out these books without paying theatre owners, actors, and technicians, and without being obliged to have half a million paying customers within the first fiscal year in order to defray expenses and make a profit.

Even the hastiest of reviews will reveal a degree of vitality and accomplishment for which no apologies are needed, and this much must be conceded in spite of our having failed to uncover another Shakespeare or Sophocles. All of Shaw's major pieces, except *Candida* which had its first production in 1897, fall within the century, as do the plays of Galsworthy, Barker, Maugham, and others. The combined work of the English writers overshadows anything written for the stage in England from 1700 to 1890. Ireland, which had no drama to speak of before 1902, contributed the masterly folk art of Lady Gregory and John Millington Synge, the poetic plays of Yeats, the fantastic ones of Lord Dunsany, and the dramas of St. John Ervine, Sean O'Casey, and Paul Vincent Carroll. In America, by a generous stretch of critical standards, we may discover perhaps two or three acceptable plays before 1900 as against the work of O'Neill, Anderson, Howard, Rice, Behrman, Wilder, Green, Hellman, Odets, Williams, and Arthur Miller. All but four or five of the masterpieces of the Russian theatre belong to the century, as do all the significant plays of the Spanish theatre since the seventeenth century and of the Italian theatre since Goldoni's times. A noteworthy part of the French drama since the age of Molière and Racine comes after 1900 with the work of Pagnol, Bourdet, Claudel, Giraudoux, Salacrou, Anouilh, Vildrac, Sartre, and Camus. And if we start our inventory with 1890, it is plain that Central Europe's greatest age of stage drama belongs not to the period of Lessing, Schiller, and Goethe, but to the times of Hauptmann, Wedekind, Sternheim, Schnitzler, Zuckmayer, Brecht, and Kapek. Only the Scandinavian countries experienced a decline after the achievements of Ibsen and Strindberg during the last three decades of the nineteenth century.

To our century, in addition, belong the achievements of the Abbey Theatre and the Gate Theatre of Dublin, the theatrical experiments of Reinhardt, Jessner, and Piscator in Central Europe and of Copeau, Jouvet, Baty, Barrault, and others in Paris. The triumphs of the Old Vic and the Vedrenne-Granville-Barker Court Theatre productions belong to us, as do the full flowering of the Moscow Art Theatre and its musical studio, the *avant-grade* activities of the stage directors Vakhtangov, Tairov, and Meyerhold, the work of the Hebrew Habimah Theatre, and the accomplishments of the Group Theatre.

Acting and staging became arts requiring thorough preparation and design. A new scenic art, rich in theatrical magic and suggestiveness, arose under the inspiration of the Swiss Adolphe Appia and Ellen Terry's son Gordon Craig, and came to fruition in the work of numerous talented scene designers. The miracles of stage lighting multiplied with the advent of the modern electrical switchboard. Choreography, from the achievements of Nijinsky and Diaghilev to those of Tamiris and Agnes de Mille, became a powerful adjunct to the theatre. Musical composition provided new augmentation and expressiveness for the stage in the work of Stravinsky, Prokofiev, Milhaud, Gershwin, Virgil Thomson, Kurt Weill, and many others.

Theatre became more fully aware of style than it had been for centuries. Realism, departing from its late nineteenth-century literalness, became selective and expressive. Symbolism achieved a finesse and range it had never revealed in earlier decades. Ventures of variable value and doubtful permanence but of striking originality ensued after 1910 in a variety of styles carrying such labels as expressionism, constructivism, futurism, and *surréalisme,* until it could be said that at no time in its previous history had the stage displayed such boldness of imagination, such resourcefulness, and such efficiency. In the light of all these developments in drama and stagecraft, it is difficult, indeed, to explain the perennial lamentations that have been bestowed upon the theatre on any other basis than that more has been expected of the theatre than in any other period since the Renaissance. We have been more conscious than in past ages of theatre as a subject. Not more conscious of its importance, and not more conscious of dramatic principles, but of theatrical productions, theatre movements, theatre economics, and the rivalry between the stage and other forms of entertainment.

Nevertheless, there are no signs either here or abroad that the advance noted during the first half of our century will continue unabated in the second half. The climate of ideas and the trends of our social and political life have been more conducive to stalemate or entropy than to progress and invigoration. Valuable plays and productions may continue to appear in both hemispheres, but the impetus for growth and discovery on any large scale seems to have run out, even as it diminished after the first decade of the seventeenth century in England and after the last decade of the same century in France. We shall, no doubt, continue to enjoy triumphs in the theatre by accident of genius and by inheritance from earlier decades of intellectual and artistic fermentation. More than that cannot be foreseen.

We must not overlook the fact that the great progress of the theatre of past decades was floated on successive and commingled tides of hope. We need only list them haphazardly to indicate their enzymic action, which if it has not quite abated has already lost its freshness. I refer to such developments as the democratic and liberal *élan* that inspired hope and suggested new ways of revealing man and his society—the *élan* that infiltrated the plays of Shaw, O'Casey, and others. I also refer to the new psychological interests and psychoanalytic discoveries assimilated into the tissue of much modern drama, with effects on dramatic style and form, as in expressionism and surrealism. And I refer, in general, to the effects of faith in science, the emancipation of women, and the general sway of a questing and critical spirit that became evident after 1875 in the European theatre.

II

The possibilities of either stalemate or progress in the world's theatre, now that it has completed half a century, challenge study. Victories and defeats, achievements and risks, intrinsic values and intrinsic shortcomings must be considered. And one way of making the appraisal is to look at the styles and methods the theatre has followed in this period.

Although it is obviously true that a good play can be written in any style or form, and that effective production is not dependent on any theory of production, the fact remains that drama and theatre have always followed some convention. Theatrical production has always depended upon the kind of theatre area or building in which the play was given, upon the stage at its disposal, and upon means and styles for creating an effect or some kind of illusion of reality. And upon this mode of production, to which the public gives the only kind of assent that matters—temporary submission to the power or charm of a play—has depended the specific character of the plays written at a given time. But for the structure of the Elizabethan theatre and stage, the tragedies and historical plays of Marlowe and Shakespeare would not have the particular vitality we associate with their freely flowing narration, their telescoping of time and place, their descriptive power, and their self-avowals and addresses to the audience in the form of asides and soliloquies.

In our century, however, we no longer have the stability that could give any single convention a long and fruitful period of exclusive or nearly exclusive rule. Conventions of classic drama and staging could last for a long time with only minor modifications. The medieval convention of staging on pageant wagons or on multiple settings of little booths or "mansions" prevailed for nearly three hundred years. The Elizabethan convention of the platform stage lasted some fifty years, and the neo-classic style that succeeded it prevailed in Europe for about a hundred and fifty years. But the theatre of our own century has undergone constant alteration and has followed a variety of patterns. It looks like a mosaic of forms and styles.

The twentieth-century theatre is not to be deprecated for this reason. A succession of stimuli has added interest to the stage, provoked wholesome controversy, and aroused enthusiasms that have given our stage an attractive verve from time to time. It is, besides, rather difficult to imagine that the theatre would have succeeded in commanding attention in an age of rapid transitions and nervous tension if it had settled into a single, undeviating groove of convention. The fact is that the modern theatre has found the successive and simultaneous exploitation of a variety of dramatic approaches absolutely indispensable to its existence. This can be seen vividly enough in the careers of all our major playwrights and of most of the minor writers who have managed to retain our interest beyond one or two plays.

Long ago, George Jean Nathan noted with respect to American playwrights that a distressingly large number of them faded into insignificance after the success of a single piece of writing. Moreover, those who have had a long record of distinguished work have been notably flexible in dramatic composition. O'Neill tried every form of playwriting after his early one-acters. We find him moving from the realistic form of *Anna Christie* to varieties of expressionism in *Emperor Jones, The Hairy Ape,* and *The Great God Brown;* from trim one-acters like *Ile* and *In the Zone* to outsize plays like the nine-act drama *Strange Interlude,* written on the two levels of normal and stream-of-consciousness dialogue, and the trilogy *Mourning Becomes Electra.* Even Sidney Howard, who was entirely at ease with realistic technique, was attracted to fantasy in writing *Madam, Will You Walk,* as well as to a sort of epic form in constructing *Yellowjack.* And Philip Barry, entirely at home in realistic comedy of manners, was drawn to fantasia in such plays as *Hotel Universe, Here Come the Clowns,* and *Liberty Jones.* Robert Sherwood has run the course of sophisticated comedy in *The Road to Rome* and *Reunion in Vienna,* of allegori-

cal melodrama in *The Petrified Forest,* and of the biographical chronicle
in *Abe Lincoln in Illinois.* Maxwell Anderson has shifted from the pungent naturalism of *What Price Glory?* to historical verse drama like *Elizabeth the Queen* and *Anne of the Thousand Days,* to the modern verse
tragedy of *Winterset,* to the verse fantasy of *High Tor,* and to the play-
within-play technique of *Joan of Lorraine.* Even the younger men who
have as yet only a few plays to their credit have been notably restive.
There is, for instance, less difference of content and principle between
Arthur Miller's *All My Sons* and *Death of a Salesman* than there is a difference of style or dramatic form. And the career of Tennessee Williams
has already carried him through highly naturalistic one-acters, realistic
drama, the technique of reminiscence that characterizes *The Glass Menagerie,* the poetically charged naturalism of *A Streetcar Named Desire,* and
the symbolist-expressionistic theatricalism of *Camino Real.*

Across the Atlantic the protean quality of the drama is even more
marked. Gerhart Hauptmann started his fluctuations between naturalism
and symbolism in 1893, with *The Assumption of Hannele,* and the fluctuations became chronic in his case, earning for Hauptmann the derisive
comment that he displayed all "the constancy of a weathervane." Cocteau
ran the gamut of styles from surrealism in *Orphée* to realism in *Les parents terribles.* What a world of difference there is between the Giraudoux
who wrote the elegant "bedroom" treatment of Greek myth *Amphitryon
38* and the Giraudoux who conceived *The Madwoman of Chaillot.* What
a difference between the O'Casey of *Juno and the Paycock* or *The Plough
and the Stars* and of *The Silver Tassie* and *Within the Gates.* One could
have concluded that the man who revealed such overwhelming competence in realism as O'Casey did (and this with a continuous obbligato of
poetic imagination and speech) would have been content to write in the
vein that made him one of the major dramatists of the century. Instead,
driven on by his private *daimon* and by the whiplash of a demoniacal
world, O'Casey turned to forms in which his skill was less secure. He not
which his effects were bound to lose unity and elementary clarity. He not
only turned to expressionistic and allegorical writing but persisted in it
despite a discouraging reception by a public that had praised him unstint-
ingly for his early work.

Perhaps the best example of refusal to be bound to a single dramatic
mode is provided by Bernard Shaw, once the mighty champion of Ibsen
and realism. Shaw's experiments carried him from the compact realism of
Candida to the allegory of *Heartbreak House,* the dialectical conversational drama of *Getting Married,* the extravaganza of *Too True to Be
Good,* and the fantasy of *Back to Methuselah* and *The Simpleton of the
Unexpected Isles.* This "free wheeling" has been apparent even within the

structure and style of single plays. He broke into the third act of *Man and Superman* with the fantasy and conversation piece of the Don Juan dream episode, and wrote a fantastic coda for *Saint Joan,* which is, in other respects, a work of luminous realism. By contrast, that refined craftsman and sober-minded gentleman of the theatre, John Galsworthy, remained faithful to carefully wrought objective dramaturgy, and his reward has been virtually to disappear from the living theatre while his contemporary, whose work was often viewed with misgivings, continues to engage our attention. One ca.i, indeed, sum up the history of half a century of theatre by saying quite categorically that modern playwrights either changed horses in midstream or stopped riding.

The point of major concern is that virtually every mode of playwriting and play production exhausted itself so rapidly that no one among our dramatists had a long period in which he could bring his work in any single style to full fruition. The perfection of an *Oedipus the King* is a culminating point in development along a single line of dramatic form and style. The Elizabethan drama took a long time to reach the elevation of *Macbeth* and *Hamlet.* Among modern forms of playwriting, the only one that has had a long history behind it is realism. As a result we have the perfection of Ibsen's and Chekhov's plays and the continued successful materialization of realism in such plays as O'Casey's masterpieces, Odets' *Awake and Sing* and *Golden Boy,* and Lillian Hellman's *The Little Foxes.* But realism, we must remember, is in all respects a nineteenth-century phenomenon, the product of dramatic and social developments that started long before Ibsen wrote *A Doll's House.*

The present century has *developed* no style, although it has *invented* several styles. If this has not proved catastrophic thus far, it is, we may surmise, only because twentieth-century man's personal outlook is still emotionally rooted in the past. The average playgoer may employ the latest gadgets of modern industry, may travel in stratoliners, and may even respond to the latest antics in painting and "bebop," but he is fundamentally Victorian in his response to emotional complications. He is still basically "bourgeois" in human relations, and indeed modern mass production enables him to gratify the ordinary aspirations of safety, comfort, and convenience more than ever before. All goes well with his middle-class life and aspirations except when an economic crisis or a war blows his house down. That is when he becomes frantic and starts yelling himself hoarse, and his cries echo in the theatre, as they did in Germany after World War I when German expressionism went berserk for a time. Then an adjustment takes place, a calm settles for a time, back goes the twentieth-century man to his *lares* and *penates,* and the theatre reflects his return to "normalcy" with a new crop of realistic domestic dramas and standardized entertainment.

It is no wonder, then, that the greatest artists of the theatre feel isolated. They have looked farther and deeper into the private and public chaos of the century, and their shudder is not easily exorcised by a full larder, by a temporary rise in employment and income, and by a few more factory-made conveniences. They turn to existentialism, to communism, or to the sheer nihilistic despair of O'Neill's *The Iceman Cometh*. They resort to allegory, to rueful fantasy of protest like *The Madwoman of Chaillot,* or to surrealistic escape mechanisms. The most creative spirits become the most disoriented. They favor hybrid forms that are rootless and therefore are incapable of ripening into fruit; or the roots are aerial, so that their best work is merely the sudden exotic blossoming of a rare talent that cannot ripen, as we see in the case of William Saroyan.

There was a time when a period's ablest writers had the greatest or at least a very large following. Their idiom and content were the idiom and content of the public, as in the case of Tennyson, Dickens, and Thackeray during the Victorian period. But this has not been the case since 1914, and not only in the drama but in other forms of art. In much of their work, O'Neill, Giraudoux, Sartre, Yeats, Cocteau, and O'Casey, for example, are at odds with the world of the middle-class playgoer, who has been the theatre's patron west of the "iron curtain." If the rift has been closed now and then, this has been due to extraneous factors, to the sensationalism of the subject, to the unusually attractive theatricality of a production, or to the fortuitous presence of a popular actor in the production. The distance between such playwrights and the majority of playgoers has been bridged at times, but it has been essentially almost as great as the distance between modern poets and the average reader, or between novelists like Joyce and the buyers of novels. When in some special case, like *Death of a Salesman,* a play commands large public assent to something that departs from the realistic routine, it is hailed as a miracle. But when one looks more closely at the miracle, one is apt to find that in spite of its unconventional shape, it has the same middle-of-the-road spirit as its audience, and it follows well-worn grooves of sentiment and sympathy. There is much more rapport between *Death of a Salesman* or *A Streetcar Named Desire* and the average Babbitt than either the playwright or the Babbitt would care to admit. (Neither of these plays is, of course, bad or meretricious because this happens to be the case. I cite these plays merely to illustrate the point that most successful departures from nineteenth-century realism do not depart essentially from its spirit and interest as developed in the nineteenth century.)

Another way of saying what I have tried to set down is to declare flatly that the century has not yet developed distinctive dramatic forms and attitudes of its own except in the isolated "Epic Theatre" of the Brecht-Piscator school. Our Western theatre is moving toward an impasse or declining to a point on its curve where the law of diminishing returns begins to operate. The large number of worthy plays produced within the past fifty years does not alter this fact. The development of other styles and forms and their modifications would alter the situation, of course, and indeed there have been short periods when this seemed to be the case. There has been no dearth of "new" schools of theatre and drama in our time, and its proponents were loud in their annunciations of a new dispensation. Each of these dispensations held out a promise, indeed, and much was expected by its publicists. It is true, nevertheless, that thus far no such expectations were met. Nor, let us note, has the "non-Western" theatre—that which has been under the domination of Stalinist tyranny in the arts—been less vulnerable to disease. Russian theatrical art and drama reached their zenith under the Czarist monarchy, and their most experimental venturesomeness in the nineteen-twenties. Stalinist "Social Realism," in addition to strangulating individuality and freedom, pushed the theatre back to the late nineteenth century and the drama even further back—to the dawn of problem-play moralism in the eighteen-fifties.

Naturalism began to pall quickly in the eighteen-nineties. Its objectivity came to be regarded as cold and forbidding, and its representation of slices of life ceased to command interest. In due time naturalism was vulgarized into the mindless sensationalism associated with Belasco productions and the meretricious photographic detail of Hollywood motion pictures. Dramatic "symbolism," a style that was all nuance and suggestion, was next acclaimed. It served to give design and grace to theatrical production, but proved effete or nebulous as a self-sufficient style. Expressionism ran riot, but within half a decade its tricks of distortion and its vehemence had exceeded the indulgence of common sense. "Constructivism," a mode of bio-mechanical production on skeletal settings that required the services of acrobats rather than actors, enjoyed a brief vogue, especially in Russia, and then was discarded as sterile and factitious. Today we are more apt to find constructivism lending pseudo-modernity to a fashionable bar than to a stage setting. Still later, high hopes were held for so-called "epic production," which used mechanical devices and motion picture slides as means for augmenting the significance and scope of the drama. But the professional theatre, outside of Central Europe, has failed to reveal a single fully satisfactory production in this style since the defunct Federal Theatre's "living newspaper," *One-third of a nation*. Surrealism has occasionally charmed a small group of devotees, as in the case of Gertrude Stein's *Four Saints in Three Acts*. In moderate form, surrealism has even appeared in the Broadway productions of Saroyan's *My Heart's in the High-lands* and *The Beautiful People*. But it proved too exotic for adoption by the theatre as anything more than an occasional tidbit.

The dramatists who attempted new styles could, it is true, give birth to one or two plays that we could greet with enthusiasm, and when these plays are added up they comprise a small body of creditable dramatic liter-ature. But even so, they have been isolated products and constitute no developing line of dramatic style. We do not think of the plays of the Greeks, Shakespeare, Racine, Molière, or Ibsen as aberrancies. But plays like *My Heart's in the Highlands,* Cocteau's *Orphée,* Sartre's *No Exit,* Camus' *Caligula,* and Wilder's *The Skin of Our Teeth* have been nothing more than oddities in the Western theatre. A great dramatic art constitutes a norm and not an aberrancy, a dominant style and not an oddity. Fifty years have passed since the first theatrical season of the century, and the theatre has not yet found a new style to which it could adhere. The twen-tieth-century stage still adheres to a nineteenth-century style that it con-tinues to recognize as old-fashioned and dated but which it cannot discard for lack of anything to put in its place—and this not without having made a number of efforts to develop a substitute. This is the impasse of twen-tieth-century theatre.

III

At the risk of some repetition, let us look more closely at the history of the many theatrical movements, styles, and techniques that experienced exhaustion.

Symbolism, which once seemed to open up so many possibilities when Maeterlinck's *The Blue Bird* and the plays of Verhaeren and Andreyev ruled the theatrical roost, soon came to be regarded as laughably naïve. When Philip Barry nobly attempted symbolism in *Here Come the Clowns* and suffused it with exceptional thoughtfulness and feeling, it was found much too obscure although the parallel it drew in 1938 between an illu-sionist's tricks and fascism was close enough to public concern. When Barry attempted allegory several years later in *Liberty Jones,* his effort was found too transparent and we told ourselves that the allegorical method may have been good enough for the Middle Ages but was rather childish in our own time. Expressionism flared up briefly in Central Europe and collapsed after the dervish dance of its devotees, leaving behind only a few plays like *R. U. R.* and *The Insect Comedy* that the theatre has cared to revive now and then. In France and England expressionism took no root at all, and in America, where it provided a stimulus to the young O'Neill, it proved to be a passing fancy. It was yoked to musical comedy on the one occasion when it enjoyed any success at all after 1930—in Moss Hart's *Lady in the Dark*. When at the present time post-war Germany brings forth an expressionist piece like *Outside the Door*, it proves to be inept in spite of flashes of inspired writing.

"Theatricalism," the style that was supposed simply to evoke the pure joy of play-acting and theatricality, resulted in celebrated productions such as the Vakhtangov *Turandot* and enlivened the staging of many plays, from the Habimah Theatre's *Dybbuk* to the latest theatrical lark (*The Seven Year Itch*). But pure theatricalism did not produce a dramatic composition of any weight either in Europe or America, except perhaps the lonely "jazz-symphony" *Processional* by John Howard Lawson and Thornton Wilder's dour extravaganza on the history of Mr. Antrobus, or Man, *The Skin of Our Teeth*. Nor did the "formalism" so highly prized in the productions of Jacques Copeau at the Théâtre du Vieux Colombier and his successors in Paris (Jouvet, Dullin, and, in a sense, Barrault) give rise to much memorable modern drama. Only Cocteau's *The Infernal Machine,* Obey's *Noah,* and Giraudoux' *The Madwoman of Chaillot* and *Intermezzo* stand out as durable products of the theatre of the Parisian actor-managers. And these plays must strike us in our intellectually un-inebriated moments as mere exercises in playwriting by comparison not only with the masterpieces of the past but with those of our own century—with, let us say, *The Three Sisters, The Cherry Orchard, The Playboy of the Western World, Juno and the Paycock, The Plough and the Stars,* and *Mourning Becomes Electra,* and, of course, *Saint Joan.* "Constructivism" and mechanistic theories of acting, which aroused the interest of the world during Meyerhold's brief rule in the Russian theatre, vanished completely—without leaving a single living play behind. It might be argued that since these styles were essentially theatrical rather than dramatic modes, they should not be judged by whether or not they gave us good plays. Yet we cannot overlook the fact that every vital style of dramatic production in the past yielded a harvest of plays and was justified by this ability to inspire a literature. Without a literature of its own, even the most attractive type of theatre dies of inanition and proves to be only a flash in the dark. The fate of experimental styles in our theatre has been, on the contrary, a quick demise with no progeny to cheat time.

But what about the realism and the naturalism that brought modernity into the Western theatre? Naturalism, in the narrow sense of the term, actually enjoyed no more than a decade of fruitfulness, giving rise to some theatrical reforms in Paris and Berlin and to some plays of more or less lasting value: *The Father, Countess Julie, The Vultures,* and *The Weavers.* It was essentially a reaction to naturalism that instigated a return to romanticism in such plays as *Cyrano de Bergerac* and *Pelléas and Mélis-*

sande. If, in our time, naturalism has appeared in a few successful plays like Sidney Kingsley's *Dead End* and *Detective Story,* it has lacked the mordancies and tang of the original style; *Dead End* was devoted to social reform, and *Detective Story* preached a moral. The only "pure" naturalistic play that won a public in two decades of American stage production was *Tobacco Road!* Realism, of course, we still have with us. It is responsible for most of the plays written here and abroad. Nevertheless, it is obvious to all of us that the instrument that had such a cutting edge for Ibsen became blunted, good enough only for cutting the rancid cheese of commonplace situations or ideas. It lost its value as a scalpel, and those who persisted in employing it for social analysis or for psychological analysis scratched only the surface. Is it surprising, then, that hardly any season reveals more than two or three realistic plays of acceptable quality in New York or London.

For plumbing the depths of the individual psyche, realism was of little avail because the realistic technique, with its "fourth-wall" convention and its absence of poetic dialogue and soliloquy, could present our experience and feeling on only one plane; it could let audiences see only the surfaces that any outsider sees. Realistic drama is preeminently logical, but the inner self is not logical. The realist cannot allow the individual character to expose his inner processes by means of soliloquies and asides, nor is he free to shape the play to suit the character's state of mind. The ordinary conventional realist is in the position of a diver whose hands and feet are bound, and who is deprived of a pipe line through which he can inhale oxygen and communicate with the surface.

What about social reality, however? Society presses hard upon us, it affects many of our important activities, and never before have men been more aware of social realities. The newspapers and books, the Congressional records and the economic reports are full of these "realities." Surely there is enough here for the explorations that the realist can make successfully? He has been at ease, it is true, in dealing with "manners," although not more than pre-realistic playwrights from Plautus and Terence to Molière. The Somerset Maughams, S. N. Behrmans, and Noel Cowards have been very much at ease, indeed, with the modern age except with respect to challenges of intellection and value judgments beyond the sphere of "manners." But can the realistic playwright actually cope with the social realities that have mattered most in our own time? These are economic and political, they consist of intertwined strands of fact so that what happens in one situation affects another, and what happens in Moscow, Berlin, or London determines what will happen in New York, or vice versa. Finance is as complicated a process as any science, and its effect is of paramount importance; and this is also true of agriculture, industry, and

hat constitutes "poetry of theatre" without possessing distinctive
dialogue is *Death of a Salesman*.) And, of course, a poetic play m
e drama *and* "poetry of theatre" or poetic prose drama *and* "poet
theatre," whereas mere fantasy, if poorly written and organiz
he lines of unimaginative "fourth wall" dramaturgy, may be hu
nd actually less "poetic" than a good realistic play.

e have a legitimate basis for maintaining that the modern thea
ered from a lack of poetry, the first and most important c
n is that the poetic idea was usually *willed* rather than natura
n many verse dramas. *Willed* in many senses: As a deliber
n of romanticism, by Rostand, Hofmannsthal, D'Annunzio, a
s a search for the inexpressible or for an ersatz-metaphysics,
ck and others. As that *plus* Celtic idealism, by Yeats; and as t
re general aim of elevating the theatre, by Maxwell Anders
others. More and more poet-playwrights after 1890, aside fr
l inclination to write poetry simply because they were pro
s, wrote poetic drama for some other reason than dramatic
every reason but that poetic drama had grown up naturally,
he Athenian and the Elizabethan theatres. The matter of c
n in our century was not fundamentally poetic, as were
legends favored by the Attic playwrights. The prevailing a
d life in our century were not poetic, as classic and Renaissa
Much Renaissance reasoning, for example, was by analo
s are "poetic" in contrast to modern scientific deduction. C
r modern verse drama—not all, but a good deal of it—
or less forced, as well as esoteric, quality. Drama in v
lly seemed quite convincingly drama for the mass public t
requires. Poetic drama has tended toward aristocratic al
c alienation from common interests, even where in some
t happened to adopt a popular cause, as Yeats adopted I
d as Auden and Spender adopted anti-imperialism and a
the nineteen-thirties. During the formative years of I
Abbey Theatre, Yeats wanted a poetic theatre for an é
ic. Instead, it was a popular theatre that came into existe
. Yeats, it is true, became one of its most devoted lead
ays had little in common with the rustic and, later, ur
ich Lady Gregory, Synge, O'Casey, and other playwrig
people's theatre in Dublin.

eats's early plays (*The King's Threshold*) revealed t
ween poetry and drama which invariably makes its
he poetry is much richer than the extent of the dram
n in a play. That is, when it is apparent, as it is no

commerce. You cannot really speak of social fact without taking into account such matters as cartels, international trade treaties, the balance of trade, and the relation of the pound to the dollar. These and other matters, in turn, determine the business cycle, wages and prices, employment and unemployment, production and consumption. And these, in turn, have a necessary relation to the stability of the home, the happiness of children, and love. "What's happened to love?" sang a musical comedy performer, and the chorus replied, "Economics." There are also such things as class conflict and international imbroglios.

How can the realistic playwright, who often lays claim to importance precisely on the ground of giving us a grip on reality, cope with such a whirligig of facts and relationships? As a realist, he is bound to take a segment of life and render it as the eye of the outsider would see it if he were looking through a peep-hole. He can, of course, allow his characters to discuss the complexity of their problem, but that is unlikely to give us drama that would not be static and tiresome in the extreme. He cannot even give us the pleasure of hearing an extraordinarily brilliant conversation that might compensate for the slowness of the action. Within the strict bounds of the realistic style, a representative clerk or hod-carrier must not speak like Bernard Shaw. If the dramatist, however, desires to exhibit such realities, he is at sea. The alternative to showing everything, which would disintegrate the realistic play, is to show next to nothing. He will tend to content himself with a miniscule situation which may arouse our sympathies but will demonstrate little more than the immediate throb of the moment in a living room. He cannot remain a realist in technique without ceasing to be a realist in the field of modern relations. He cannot "make good" any of his claims to social understanding and intellectual interest. At best, if he foregoes the difficult attempt to write documentary drama which must shatter the "fourth wall" and otherwise violate the conventions of realistic dramaturgy, he is tempted to rely on a combination of political exhortations and some domestic situation.

Against these charges there has been only one answer on the part of a vocal minority. Why bother with facts like these at all? Let us leave these to the sociologist and the economist. "Playwright, deal with the spirit—with essences, emotions, and visions. Your real task is to illuminate the recesses of the heart and to create beauty." And this is likely to be associated with the recommendation that only one kind of drama is worth achieving, and that is "poetic drama."

But even if we discount the important consideration that the theatre must have some relation to the consciousness of its times, there are flies in the ointment that is peddled by the prescribers of poetic drama. One of these is that the poetic dramatist finds his way to Elizabethan romance or to some other remote period and produces only "academic" art no matter how many cash customers queue up in front of the box office. If Maxwell Anderson knows how to write a play with eloquence, color, and theatrical facility in a piece like the recent *Anne of the Thousand Days,* he reaps a golden harvest, as well as compliments from critics as exacting as Joseph Wood Krutch. But the play could just as well belong to the theatre of Schiller's or Tennyson's times. The universal is one thing and the academic is another. But can we say that Mr. Anderson's *Anne* is merely academic? I don't believe we can, so long as we find a good deal of vigor and incandescence in the play. Yet it is plain, I think, that it is the author's talent alone that saves the play from the flatness and sterility we associate with academicism (if it does!), and that, nonetheless, his characters and story have no real contemporary vitality. And surely the same criticism applies to the poetic exercises in spiritual history that have nestled under the shadow of the Anglican Church in England, such as Christopher Fry's *The First-Born* and *The Boy with the Cart.*

IV

It is significant that "poetry" should have become a cant word in the theatre. It became so, in fact, in the eighteen-nineties with the rise of theatrical *Symbolism* under the leadership of the poet Paul Fort, founder in 1891 of the little experimental Théâtre d'Art in Paris, and Maurice Maeterlinck, who was a minor *Symbolist* poet before he became a major *Symbolist* playwright. In past ages, nobody thought of making a special plea for poetry in the drama, for the divorce between poetry and drama was brought about by modern pioneering realism when Ibsen, himself a poet of no small reputation, adopted prose as the proper medium of social drama.

As modern realism advanced, however, many men could come up with no other solution for the theatre's ills than "Poetry." But let us note one plain fact: If we refer to a play written partly or entirely in verse, the period since 1890 has had this kind of poetic drama from Rostand, Hofmannsthal, D'Annunzio (whose *Daughter of Jorio* should not be underestimated), Hauptmann (*The Sunken Bell,* etc.), Yeats, Claudel, Jeffers, Dorothy Sayers, Alexander Blok, Werfel, Toller, Brecht, Unruh, Lorca, Auden, Spender, MacLeish, Fry, and Eliot among others. An age that can show so many poets—several of them extremely talented ones—producing plays does not have to feel apologetic. Nor need it attribute the shortcomings of modern dramatic art to a want of poetry. And if we are willing to extend the honorific term poetic drama to works written in poetic prose, it is difficult to understand what the poetry addicts are complaining about.

An age that, in addition to the verse plays, imaginative prose dramas of Maeterlinck, Strindbe *Dream Play, The Ghost Sonata, Easter, The Bri* Evreinov, Andreyev, Lady Gregory, Synge, O'Ca Sierra, the Quintero Brothers, Vildrac, Jean-Ja Salacrou, Giraudoux, Anouilh, Pirandello, Ros mayer, Billinger, Masefield (*The Tragedy of N* America—O'Neill (in the sea-pieces and othe Odets (surely in *Awake and Sing!*), and Wil much and more to show for sixty years of pl ered hopelessly prosaic. Nor, of course, coul hopelessly literal-minded that possessed such Stanislavski, Tairov, Meyerhold, Vakhtango Piscator, Karlheinz Martin, Berthold Vie Pitoëff, Baty, Barrault, Kvapil, Hilar, Gra rone Guthrie, Peter Brook, Arthur Hopk Clurman, Kazan, Logan, Craig, Pircha Neher, Picasso, Christian Bérard, Robert son, Mielziner, and many others. If we d recall how many of each season's produc we could easily conclude that *rarely in nation so abundantly present.* And if w ness has always preempted a large por we can actually claim for the modern nation that compares favorably with of theatre.

If we are to make sense in appra must base judgment on some basis o of poetry. Let us, indeed, start with some heavenly haven you lift or " adolescents, academicians, pretend Poetry is the precipitate of the ch intrinsic, rather than superimpos attitudes, and aptitude for expre drama, but good drama and goo A dramatic poem, such as *My F* same thing as a poetic play. A cal poetry, a play written in im imaginatively organized to af the shape and sequence of the ground and action, and the s by the author's conception

play t
poetic
be vers
of the
along t
drum a
If v
has suff
sideratio
present
affirmatic
others. A
Maeterlin
plus a m
Eliot, and
the natura
sional poet
cessity; for
it had in t
mon conce
myths and
tudes towar
views were.
and analogic
sequently, o
had a more
has not actua
a vital theatr
ness or esthet
stances the po
nationalism ar
fascism during
drama and the
playgoing publ
with the Abbe
But his verse p
realism with w
created the Iris
Many of Y
divorcement bet
pearance where
conflict and acti

the work of Sophocles and Shakespeare, that the author's prime interest is in the poetry. This was also the case in the early plays of the talented Austrian poet-playwright Hofmannsthal. If Hofmannsthal did not remain one of the many modern poets who are incapable of writing successfully for the stage, he owed his good fortune to associations with Richard Strauss as librettist (*Electra, Rosenkavalier*) and with the folk-Catholicism of Austria which gave vitality to such work as his *Everyman* (*Jedermann*) and *The Great World Theatre* (*Das grosse Welttheater*). And Lorca's respectable contributions to poetic drama in such plays as *Blood Wedding* and *Yerma* drew their sustenance from a continuing tradition among the Spanish people with which Lorca was able to identify himself as man and artist.

Generally, however, such epiphanies were rare among the verse dramatists. More usually, the poetic dramas tended to be effete or bloodless; or they were strained by a resolve to be moralistic and ritualistic. This tendency, most flagrantly present in the work of that great poet Paul Claudel, carried with it the penalty of prolixity and unwieldiness. The modern theatre lost one of its potentially greatest dramatists because Claudel's plays were too cumbersome for general production. Productions of Claudel plays after World War II came several decades after the date of composition. It was too late, then, for the elderly poet to learn by stage experience how to become a truly practical playwright, as Aeschylus, Sophocles, and Shakespeare were practical playwrights. Yeats did not even try to become one at the very time when his talents as a poet and dramatist ripened. His late plays suffered from none of the divorcement between drama and poetry that weakened his early ones, and the poetry was far better, too. Such pieces as *The Only Jealousy of Emer, At the Hawk's Well,* and *A Full Moon in March* reveal a remarkable talent. But, ironically, they are far more esoteric than the early plays which suffered from the young poet's loose romanticism, and they were not even written for production in a public theatre. In fact, much of the symbolist drama after 1890 was conceived as something special and rare, not intended for the common playgoer; and when the reverse was the case, poetic drama was vulgarized into spectacle with the help of Reinhardt in the lavish manner of the *Miracle* production. (Of the vulgarizations by sentiment, usually accomplished by D'Annunzio and minimized by the noble acting of Duse in his plays, we may observe that it ultimately became associated with the vulgar idealism of Italian fascism.)

The recent wave of verse drama in England also had its genesis in a specialized interest—in the promotion of "art theatre" as something distinct from popular theatre and in the development of Canterbury Festival plays. Popular success came to some of these efforts, especially to a few plays by Christopher Fry and T. S. Eliot. Many of the poetic pieces verged on rhetoric as well as sectarianism, but even the best fall measurably below the standard of poetic drama attained in the poetic masterpieces of the past. *The Lady's Not for Burning* does not rise greatly above the level of preciosity of *Love's Labour's Lost,* and is considerably less rich in dramatic characterization and action. And, in view of the decline apparent in later Fry plays such as *Venus Observed* and *A Sleep for Prisoners, The Lady's Not for Burning* was a climax for the middle-aged Fry whereas *Love's Labour's Lost* had been a mere prologue for the young Shakespeare. *The Cocktail Party,* the most theatrically viable of Eliot's plays before 1953, prevailed largely as a Noel Coward comedy of manners and, except in one lifting scene, was deliberately written by Eliot so that the poetry wouldn't be felt as such, which is the same thing as saying that the poetry was not to be poetry. (And, for the most part, it wasn't.)

In one way or another, modern verse drama, I repeat, has been limited in power by the fact that it has been a more or less artificial graft on our stage. Often it has even seemed as if those who decided to write verse plays were doing so as philanthropists. They have, quite frequently, written and talked about their work as though they were professional do-gooders bent upon raising the fallen estate of the stage. They have written essays on the *necessity* of writing poetry of the stage, as Eliot and Maxwell Anderson have done.

Eliot, whose critical faculty is one of the best in the century, put a good deal of common sense into his Theodore Spencer Memorial Lecture *Poetry and Drama,* delivered at Harvard in 1950. Yet the function he allocated to poetic drama was to perceive "an order in reality, to bring us to a condition of serenity, stillness, and reconciliation, and then leave us, as Virgil left Dante, to proceed toward a region where that guide can avail us no farther"—which is hardly, to my mind, the reason why Aeschylus, Sophocles, and Shakespeare wrote poetry for the theatre. (They simply wrote poetry when they wrote plays. They did not make a choice between writing and *not* writing it.) It will be noted, moreover, that, according to Eliot, we are to write verse drama, if we can, not in order to make theatre but to approach salvation, to "Ash-Wednesday" our way to heaven, so to speak.

Maxwell Anderson, who speaks many wise words in the essays he collected under the title of *Off-Broadway* in 1947, now and then writes like a "booster" of morale inside the theatre and outside it—and I doubt that great drama ever got written that way. Great drama was "lifted" by the spiritual and ethical fermentation of an age. Drama as "uplift" is a curious recommendation. It suggests a reformer's zeal to make us "better." A curious doctrine this—that plays are to be written for the soul rather than for the theatre! There is, as Erwin Piscator used to say concerning some poor acting when he was in New York, "too much seriosity" in this view. Surely neither Shakespeare nor Racine entertained it; when the latter did, he retreated to Port Royal and stopped writing plays except for a girls' school.

We may also question the view that we can prod ourselves into writing better simply by writing verse. Eliot, it is true, rejected this view, and could afford to do so since he writes so well. Poetry comes naturally to him, as it did to Hofmannsthal, Yeats, and Lorca. In *Poetry and Drama,* he admits that: "Whether we use prose or verse on the stage, they are both but means to an end." He recommends the avoidance of poetry which could not stand the test of strict dramatic utility. He sets down the rule (somewhat violated by himself, however, in *Family Reunion* and *The Cocktail Party*) that "no play should be written in verse for which prose is *dramatically* adequate." But both Eliot and Anderson are agreed that even the best dramatic prose does not reach high enough. Conceding that the great prose dramatists Ibsen and Chekhov "have at times done things [of] which I would not otherwise have supposed prose to be capable," Eliot nevertheless maintains that they have been "hampered in expression by writing in prose."

Making a concession similar to Eliot's in the case of Synge and O'Casey, Anderson nevertheless rests his case in *Poetry in the Theatre* on the principle that "prose is the language of information and poetry the language of emotion." And Anderson was not the only playwright and critic to write as if the effort to write poetry would give us better dramatic writing. I was myself tempted to support this view in writing an introduction to Stanley Burnshaw's verse play *The Bridge,* published in 1945. I reproduce this particular argument because it expresses an extreme expectation which I shared with many an opponent of humdrum writing:

> . . . Noble themes require noble expression, brilliantly imagined situations demand imaginative speech, to be completely effective. For instance, we have had good reason to regret that the soaring imagination of O'Neill has not had its proper complement in dialogue. He has given us *The Great God Brown, Strange Interlude,* and *Mourning Becomes Electra,* in which dramatic conception and dramatic expression have been strangely at variance. The peacock has a dazzling appearance, but what a rasping sound it makes when it opens its mouth! O'Neill has nonetheless cast a sultry splendor upon our theatre, because he has been a titanic creator even in chains. But what about the minor brethren whose voices do not even crackle or rasp but merely drone—on and on?

It isn't enough that the gift of language has been parcelled out to us grudgingly. We go out of our way to make ourselves tongue-tied. We adopt sloppy rhythms and cultivate threadbare idioms in the name of realism. We make our characters stutter banalities because we are constantly asking ourselves whether John Doe would speak pointedly or eloquently in 'real life' instead of realizing that he ceases to be plain John Doe the moment he becomes genuinely dramatic. We forget that to be truly expressive he must speak as he would speak if he could express himself adequately. How are people to believe his emotional tensions and share them, if his conversation remains color-less and tepid? Has his emotional state had no effect on his articulate-ness? Has he not been transfigured by his dramatic situation? If he has been so transfigured, then no degree of dramatically or poetically enhanced speech can strike us as incongruous. In fact, it is the nature of a character's *response* to experience that is the true measure of his transfiguration.

Worse still, our deliberately fostered verbal stultification must in the end lead to creative stultification, unless we have a highly resistant nature like O'Neill's. Having lulled our faculties to sleep with the bathos of the flattest kind of dialogue, we descend to banalities of thought and situation; we have infected ourselves with the tedium of our own language. The low standard of expression we have set for ourselves, more often than not, depresses the entire level of our expressiveness.

Poetry is the natural antidote for the pernicious contagion from which we all suffer. An inescapable conclusion is that we might try the reverse procedure of stimulating ourselves, of setting a high mark of expression for ourselves. It might conceivably lift the entire level of our creative process, even if it could lead us to excesses and follies. There is a momentum in language for good as well as ill. Characters and situations may be raised by it a cubit or more. Ideas may matter more when colored by imagery and invested with dignity. The actual plot may acquire a significance beyond reportage. The transfiguration of a situation and a statement by poetry (provided it is genuine poetry) must surely lead to the allusiveness and universalization that alone can make spiralling drama out of familiar material and ideas.

Counsel of desperation, no doubt, and as such a summation, I should think, of the lifting-oneself-up-by-one's-bootstraps justification for verse writing which characterizes much of the clamor for formal poetry.

When I came to produce a play independently of my Theatre Guild association, I resisted the temptation to overrate one of the forced or "willed" verse plays of our time only to succumb to the other temptation of overrating a forced or "willed" poetic prose play. It was a revised version of the Welsh folk fantasy *A Comedy of Good and Evil,* retitled, by clamor from my strenuously Broadway-minded collaborators, as *Minnie and Mr. Williams.* The play proved to be too fragile, as I had known all along in spite of Bernard Shaw's assurance that anyone who did not enjoy it was "an idiot." But so have been many other poetic prose plays, whether fantastic, atmospheric, or "folksy," including those which had been successful when first raised to fame by some wave of enthusiasm for "national" or "folk" drama. Some of the best of these, such as Maeterlinck's *The Intruder,* Lady Gregory's *Workhouse Ward,* and Synge's *Riders to the Sea,* were, in fact, one-act plays, fortunately not stretched into full-length ones.

Among the full-length poetic prose pieces, many have had only a localized or provincial vitality. Lacking strong connection with modern reality in subject matter and idea, they belong to Ireland, Spain, the Rhineland, Austria, or Sicily rather than to the Western world as a whole. They made the rivulets of local theatre run more briskly in their time, but they could not enter the mainstream. That has been the fate of many decidedly attractive and appealing plays based on folklore, folk idiom, local customs and manners, or so-called regional theatre movements here and abroad in Latin America, Europe—and India, where Tagore proved to be a cross between Maeterlinck and a Hindu sage. Synge escaped this fate, to some degree, by dint of an ironic detachment that no amount of infatuation with the so-called folk-spirit could dissolve. Historically associated with the Irish nationalist theatre, Synge was nonetheless a fundamentally aloof and lonely man. And O'Casey escaped a folk-playwright's fate by urbanizing and broadening Irish drama.

Even O'Casey, however, reveals some of the afflictions of modern poetic playwrights, whether they have written formal poetry or "prose-poetry." He succumbed, sometimes, to a lyrical rhetoric, however passionate and glowing in his case; to flourishes of sentiment that would have been meretricious in the case of a writer who was less true a man; and to prolixity—that is, the use of more words than are warranted by the gambit of the idea that has to be conveyed. O'Neill was quite an egregious offender in this respect, as were Maxwell Anderson (especially in portions of *Key Largo*) and many Central European expressionists.

Other writers of poetic drama, such as Bernard and Vildrac, made "prose-poetry" equivalent to a sedative and lukewarm playwriting which had only sensitivity to commend it. Others—conspicuously, James M. Barrie—become fey, coy, and sugar-logged. Others—conspicuously, James Bridie—wrote quizzically, so that a fanciful idea combined with teasing

discourse makes up the whole play. Others—conspicuously, Giraudoux and
Marcel Aymé (in the charming comedy *Clérambard*)—married fancy to
urbanity. The results were frequently engaging, but did not make the
drama often more than a flutter in the mind of the playgoer. And this,
in my opinion, is also true of much of Cocteau's and Anouilh's work. The
work of German expressionists often merely whipped up a passing squall
more disturbing to the playgoer's equanimity than thoroughly stimulating.
And, finally, I would say that the "poetry of the theatre" school of playwrights whose ingenious plot or non-realistic structure constitutes the
"poetry" in such plays as Evreinov's *The Chief Thing,* Anderson's *Joan
of Lorraine,* and Molnar's *The Red Mill* often placed a sort of mental
legerdemain in the forefront of playwriting. In one way or another, playwrights were apt to lose themselves in a maze or move into a blind alley
when they set out to conquer the giant Realism and redeem the modern
theatre.

V

It does not follow, however, that the modern theatre or even the
twentieth-century portion of it was a failure. It is more correct to say that
its various limitations became more pronounced as the decades moved toward the midcentury mark. And even so, the fault did not lie exclusively
with the nature of modern drama and theatre. The "entropy" I note elsewhere in this volume was at least accelerated, if not to a considerable degree *caused,* by a variety of crises and disintegrations in Western civilization after 1914—by war, fascist corruption, the Nazi blackout of civilization, the increasingly heavy hand of totalitarianism in Soviet Russia, and
the negativism and intolerance that followed the tide of pre-1914 optimism
and liberal faith.

When we ask ourselves what was contributed during the first half of
the century and the preceding quarter of century which must be added to
the modern post-Romantic age of the theatre, we can draw up a substantial inventory. We can claim a theatre that was frequently fascinating,
if often also humdrum, and a drama for which only a little less than that
can be claimed. And if the verse and prose poets failed to redeem the
stage, there is little doubt that they gave the theatre richly textured and
expressively organized drama. And in the case of Ibsen before our century,
Chekhov at the turn of the century, and Shaw virtually up to World War
II, poetry of a kind achieved successful fusion with the realistic, critical,
liberal drama that was the norm of modern playwriting.

In the inventory we may draw up, it is necessary, in the last analysis,
to regard our century's theatre as an extension of the last quarter of the

last century's stage. Together these periods form the age of modern theatre. If we must draw a dividing line, it should be the year 1914. In the four decades preceding World War I, the theatre was still largely based on a widely held premise of normality—of a stable Western society susceptible of progressive improvement and growth in reason and reasonableness. Since 1914, the theatre has had to struggle against one volcanic explosion after another in Western civilization. It has tended to base itself on premises of anxiety for the day and for the immediate future. These have been premises of a deterioration in values. Specifically premises of a society to be destroyed or preserved by force, or by violation of the principles of critical reason, toleration, and liberalism.

The fact is, however, that, as reflected in the theatre, the pre-1914 dispensation, though gravely imperiled in many parts of the Western world and virtually destroyed in some, managed to hold much of its ground. It lived on as a tradition and it would seem to be that it still lives on in the Western democracies and, we hope, in the memories and dreams of men behind "iron curtains." It may not be as easy to eradicate anything bred in the bone of a civilization as pessimists, pseudo-medievalists, and the enemies of democracy imagine. The naïveté of old-fashioned liberalism, somewhat overpublicized, I believe, in recent years, has required substantial correction in our time. But periodic predictions of the death of civilization have not actually materialized.

As for the specific achievements of playwrights, surely at least a dozen plays of durable quality have come from our country's theatre. As many, if not more, can be picked according to taste out of a list that would include among other plays the following: *The Ghost Sonata, Liliom, The Goat Song, R.U.R., Mother Courage, The Good Woman of Setzuan, The Madwoman of Chaillot, The Flies, Six Characters in Search of an Author, The Passion Flower, Blood Wedding, The House of Bernarda Alba, The Three Sisters, The Cherry Orchard, The Lower Depths, The Dybbuk, The Tragedy of Nan, Man and Superman, Androcles and the Lion, Pygmalion, Heartbreak House, Saint Joan, Murder in the Cathedral, Riders to the Sea, The Playboy of the Western World, John Ferguson, Juno and the Paycock, The Plough and the Stars, The Emperor Jones, Desire Under the Elms, Mourning Becomes Electra, What Price Glory?, Our Town, Awake and Sing!, Abe Lincoln in Illinois, The Little Foxes,* and *Death of a Salesman.* If not all of these would be my choices, they provide choices for someone else familiar with a substantial amount of dramatic literature. And if we join the last decades of the past century to the present, we can add at least another dozen to be taken from a list including *The Vultures, The Fossils, Ghosts, The Wild Duck, Hedda Gabler, John Gabriel Borkman, The Father, Miss Julie, The Bridal Crown, There Are Crimes and*

Crimes, The Tenor, The Marquis of Keith, The Weavers, The Beaver Coat, The Power of Darkness, The Sea Gull, Uncle Vanya, The Importance of Being Earnest, and *Candida.*

This record, for all the severity of my strictures and for all the greater severity of a less complaisant critic than I may be, compares favorably with that of past ages when the theatre flourished—ages when the stage did not have to compete with the mass media but was itself the mass medium for dramatic presentation. Only at the extreme altitudes of tragic and poetic playwriting, occupied for a few decades in Greece, England, and France, were the past ages of the theatre superior. And this superiority is balanced, to my mind, by the modern period's strong position on the plateaus as compared with the peaks. Never before did the theatre bring forth so many intellectually respectable and intensely realized plays below the level of the Mount Everests of dramatic art. If there is any doubt as to this claim, let the sceptic compile a list of the Attic, Renaissance, and neo-classic plays for which one could claim as much or more.

This much is true in any case. For an allegedly decadent civilization (in the opinion of Fascist, Communist, and neo-religious authoritarians), the modern stage was for at least six decades remarkably active—if not in one place during a number of years of cultural blackout, at least in another. The theatre, for all its faults, was never wholly preempted by enervated, academic exercises and the vapid entertainment of fatuous farces and contrived thrillers.

For all the head-shaking of ritual worshippers and idolators of a unity of culture or belief, the theatre and drama were frequently in close touch with modern man. The vogues of Realism and of social drama alone would establish this much. Certainly since the Renaissance, unity was a dream rather than a reality of Western civilization. Men lived and worked out not necessarily ignoble destinies in spite of considerable disunity. And towering achievements in arts, letters, thought, and science came from the "disunified" West. It may be reasonably maintained even that to the pluralistic culture of the modern theatre accrued advantages as well as disadvantages—the greatest being that individuality of creation which distinguishes Ibsen from Strindberg or both writers from Anton Chekhov or Bernard Shaw or O'Casey or Pirandello or Lorca.

It also remains to be proved that cultural unity has had only transcendent merits and no flaws. Even the great Greek drama had many limitations of range, perception, sympathies, knowledge, form, and style—and plenty of awkwardness, too, except in the case of a handful of masterpieces. The "synthesis" that some scholars posit for the Middle Ages gave rise to a widespread popular theatre but failed to give birth to great dramatic literature. Its high-water mark does not rise above, let us say, *The*

Second Shepherd's Play and *Everyman.* As for any unity arbitrarily imposed by fanatical fascism and communism, let the record of Hitler's Germany, Franco's Spain, and Stalin's Russia speak for itself. It is not too much to say, then, that the diversity of a cultural context gave modern theatre a good deal of nuance, vitality, and range.

We may actually speculate whether there would have been so much strong dramatic art in the age without provocations. Had Chekhov not been provoked by the *poshlost* or apathy of his fellow-citizens under the Romanovs, we might not have had *Uncle Vanya, The Three Sisters,* and *The Cherry Orchard.* Had O'Casey been thoroughly satisfied with Southern Ireland we might not have had *Juno and the Paycock* and *The Plough and the Stars.* And had Shaw been able to accept Victorianism, we might not have had—"G.B.S." The times supplied the matter, but also the challenges to these playwrights. The creative rub lies not in finding a congenial milieu, but in shaping something valuable out of one's awareness, dissidence, alienation, or revolt. The uncreative, whether complacent and ready to "sell out" or dissatisfied and unwilling to compromise, can always find convincing reasons for *not* creating.

Filled, as plays were, moreover, with conflicting views and aims which translated themselves into ambivalence or confusions, we should guard against the authoritarianism of critics who consign allegedly confused artists to limbo. The theory that logic is the sole criterion of art is a neo-Aristotelian fallacy, as is the assumption that every work is to be categorized and judged by the degrees to which it fits snugly into a category. That is why I protest elsewhere in this volume against using tragedy as a rigid test of modern dramatic achievement.

"Standards," important as it may be to uphold them, may be used to beat the life out of art as well as children. In either case, the impulse to dominate and thwart may be at work in the disciplinarian. And in either case, we can only too easily rationalize a justification: With respect to modern drama, it is usually the failure of plays to maintain consistency of argument, analysis, or style. I, myself, have taken note of this fact and deplored it on logical and technical grounds, as later essays will show. But consistency or lack of consistency is not all there is to a play (or to any other work that deals with human life), and should not be used as the sole measure. If consistency were that, Shaw would have to be rated considerably lower than, let us say, Frederick Lonsdale. Consistency within a single play, not to say indeed within an entire career, should certainly have made John Galsworthy outlive his great mercurial contemporary, Shaw. Yet the reverse is true.

The ambivalences of the modern theater were not always destructive to values, since a conflict or even ambiguity of values can be more stimu-

lating and more indicative of the vitality of values than a rigorously maintained code or a simple—usually soporific—uniformity. A good deal of
contradiction is needed to ensure an active, viable truth or "order." A
good deal of sin, to ensure active, morally responsible virtue. Values are
made viable by tensions, questionings, reversals, conflicts. Great Catholic
authors in our time—Claudel, Mauriac—understood this far better in
their creative work than the puritanical minds of Irving Babbitt and his
humanist school of criticism, primitive moralists of all denominations,
and doctrinaire Marxists, who frequently violated their own pretensions
to dialectical analysis.

As the anti-confusionists became increasingly vociferous in the thirties,
I felt it necessary to protest against the prevalent school of social criticism.
I wrote:

> . . . I fear that critics of the school are too fond of requiring play-
> wrights to follow some blueprint of social analysis. . . . Something,
> after all, must be left to the intelligence of playgoers and readers. It is
> likewise unnecessary to insist that the hero of a play should be clearly
> oriented toward the problem which he is facing and supposedly solv-
> ing. Life is not like that, as every great playwright has realized. . . .
>
> I am also troubled by the whole question of "confusion" as it
> applies to writers. Contemporary criticism is sometimes relentless in
> ferreting out the confusions of our authors, and there is much to be
> said for the procedure when it illuminates the dynamics of their cre-
> ative processes. But at the risk of being set down as an obscurantist,
> I should like to say a kind word for confusion. . . . The writer who is
> absolutely clear in his point of view and knows all the answers with-
> out fear or hesitation will most likely write tracts for the times; or if
> it is plays that he composes, they may easily remain superficial. The
> fact remains that life is "confused" and confusing, and the great
> writer, who is perhaps the most sensitive film for recording the con-
> flict of principles in the surrounding world, is himself a battleground
> for them. One wonders whether the beauty, depth, and fidelity to life
> in the work of such masters as Euripides, Dante, Shakespeare, Racine,
> Goethe, Balzac, Tolstoi, Dostoevski, and Shaw do not spring in part
> from the confusions which bedevilled them. If they had succeeded in
> settling all problems for themselves, would they have been so restless,
> complex, and human? Finally, the cynic might well ask whether we
> can be so sure that the confusion does not exist in ourselves rather
> than in the object of our criticism; isn't it always the other person
> who strikes us as being confused? . . .

I concluded by suggesting that "there are actually two kinds of confusions which, although they cannot always be distinguished, manifest themselves differently even within the same piece of writing—those which deepen and intensify an author's work, and those which weaken it."

We do not know what the future will bring. We do know, however, what the modern theatre has been—an inglorious yet glorious place, a haven for the mediocre yet a challenge for the talented individual, an ample area for heartbreak but also for exuberance and the taste of triumph. The stage has been a distressing world but also a world of comradeship and ardent recklessness. We in our time and in the generations before us who worked in the modern theatre may have often selected nags instead of steeds, but we ran a race. We often glimpsed a goal, and endeavored to reach it. Our love-hate relationship with the theatre of our time—at least my relationship, but, I am certain, not only mine—cannot obscure these fragments of reality shored against the tide of change.

THE "UNDERGROUND MAN"
AND THE MODERN DRAMA

I

Anyone who ventures to discourse on the subject of profundity in the theatre exposes himself to some ridicule not merely from the practical showman, for whom the raising of the question of profundity in show business is patently absurd, but also from the estheticians for whom the question has appeared to be irrelevant so long as they could make "magic" with stage lighting and scenery. The practical man wants to make money; the esthetician wants to make magic. In either view of theatre, the object is to overwhelm the audience so that it will eat out of somebody's hand, whether he be David Belasco giving us *The Girl of the Golden West* or Max Reinhardt giving us *The Miracle*. Both men tended to become spellbinders, so to speak, though on different levels of theatre. Nevertheless, men of no mean reputation and intelligent playgoers in general periodically ask the troublesome question that may be framed as follows: Must the theatre remain shallow and spectacular, and if that is all that theatre is, does it deserve the efforts, attention, and patronage that presumably intelligent people lavish upon it? We know that Terence framed the question, in more or less these terms, in his Prologues a century and a half before the Christian era; and both Aeschylus and Euripides may well have done so three centuries before his time. When Ibsen and Shaw raised that question during the last decades of the nineteenth century, a major revolution was in the making and the modern drama began to take shape before the eyes of their adherents. When the same point was raised several decades later, there was a minor revolution in America and the modern American drama was born.

A disconcerting uneasiness about the stage must, indeed, be present, with or without affecting the course of the theatre, whenever thinking people concern themselves with the stage. The uneasiness was present not many years ago in articles by Joseph Wood Krutch and George Jean Nathan, in which they tried to explain how they could endure going to painfully empty premieres night after night. Eric Bentley, critic *sans peur* of a younger generation, gave showmen an ungentle reminder that the mind was not a superfluous commodity in the theatre when he published *The Playwright As Thinker* in 1947, and he had been preceded in the nineteen-thirties by critics whose challenge was not less strident although

32

more hopeful. The latter, as we might have expected in the decade of depression and anti-fascist agitation, tended to believe that valid intellectual content began and ended with social and political problems; the best book written by them, Eleanor Flexner's *American Playwrights: 1918-1938,* carried the warning subtitle "The Theatre Retreats from Reality." And the desire to stem any such retreat was, of course, the ambition of the social-minded theatrical organizations of the period, among which the Group Theatre had the least narrow horizons and the most considerable artistry.

No such social interest prevailed in the councils of the Theatre Guild and the other theatres founded a decade or more before. But here, too, there was much awareness of the stage as a vehicle for significant "content." The Theatre Guild, in its great days, *was,* after all, the exclusive American producer of Shaw's plays, a number of which, including the formidable *Back to Methuselah,* had their world premiere under its auspices. Yet even then it was possible for the Guild's ablest director Philip Moeller to express continual dissatisfaction with a life devoted exclusively to the stage. His frequent statement to me was, "Come, John, and admit that the theatre does not provide sufficient stimulation for a keen mind." He himself spent much time on music and immersed himself in the works of Balzac with the same sense of wonder that he brought to many memorable Theatre Guild productions until he fell out of patience with all theatre after 1938. For him and for others who had nourished hopes for a vital dramatic art in the early years of the century, the ideal theatre was one that could engage all the faculties of an adult playgoer and artist.

I have selected the term "profundity" to represent these hopes because it suggests something other than a clever notion or an easily formulated and rigidly maintained "idea"; because it involves the total personality and the total vision of an artist. And I dwell in this essay on the "underground man," with a view to stressing the concept of depth in artistry, as well as for other reasons which I hope to make clear. But it may be necessary to clear up some possible misunderstandings before proceeding with the subject.

In the first place, profundity should not be confused, as it often is, with solemnity. Nor are the earnestness of the moralist and the ardor of the social reformer to be confused with depth. As a result of such confusions, many a hollow tub resounds loudly in the theatre—as loudly as in public life—and is acclaimed as challenging or even sublime art. Many a playwright is likely to inflate himself with seriousness—as a means for soaring above the petty concerns and speech of commonplace playwriting —into the ether of a Marxist or Existentialist *Weltanschauung,* or into the pure empyrean of esthetic mysticism, which turns out to be sophomoric "idealism" transformed into pseudo-religious mysticism, which, in turn, may crystallize, in middle age, into dogmatic "theologism." "Seriousness" becomes equated with a tenaciously asserted political and social view or with some religious gospel superficially comprehended or confusingly articulated, as it was in Eliot's *Family Reunion.*

Seriousness is also equated with "style" conceived as an almost separate entity, such as the writing of verse for the sake of dignity in dramatic art, or with the use of symbolist mystification *á la* Maeterlinck in the hope that obscurity will somehow blossom into significance. As a matter of fact, a plain style need not make for superficiality any more than a florid one makes for profundity. Poetry, needless to say, is something other than window-dressing, whether it appear as a lyric or a play.

Comedy, too, can be profound in a very real sense. And profundity, as Nietzsche well understood in *Thus Spake Zarathustra,* and as every great tragic poet understood perhaps even better long before him, lies at the opposite extreme from moroseness. Comprehensive insight is a "gay science"—a bracing and fundamentally vivacious state of health in the midst of the confusions and *idées fixes* that afflict individuals and society. It is our peculiarly human triumph over disease to be able to recognize a morbid state and to understand its cause. To understand the dangers of the human condition, the ambivalences of our nature, and the contradictions and ironies of our existence is the best way to avoid the shipwreck of the ego and the bankruptcy of society.

As for profundity—that is, a penetrating sensibility and understanding—in the drama, it is a proper concern in the theatre *not* exclusively for the sake of profundity, but for the sake of the theatre. Considering the many exertions of playwrights and other artists of the stage for a period of some seventy-five years, the period of the modern stage to date, we may legitimately inquire how well the modern drama has expressed the tensions and conflicts of the modern world. Only on that basis can we decide whether the modern theatre has fulfilled its potentialities and the expectations of its leaders. And a way of measuring the achievements of the modern drama is to compare them with those of the modern novel. That Dostoevski occurs in this connection will surprise no one, since he stands in the forefront of writers who have confronted the enigma of man with modern penetration and realism. He had the facility of expressing himself in terms which most truly represent the conflicts and contradictions of modern life and the crises in Western civilization—crises that are ultimately moral and spiritual, as well as psychological and social. Moreover, his great novels are constructed dramatically. They are not panoramic epics that commend themselves by their extensiveness rather than intensiveness, so that a comparison of modern drama with his novels cannot be dismissed as a wild irrelevancy.

Dostoevski contributes the term that most comprehensively covers an area of modern interest that challenges playwriting. Taken from his *Notes From the Underground,* the term Underground Man may be used as a metaphor for the hidden, unconscious or semi-conscious, personality, both individual and collective, increasingly investigated by modern psychologists and artists. By taking cognizance of this underground personality or, as Thomas Mann has called it, this "dark underside" of man, many modern writers became significant to us.

Great literature, of course, never ignored the complexity of human nature or overlooked our potentialities for evil and destruction. But modern literature, aside from exploring the subject more clinically and arriving at a special explicitness in expressing it, has made it a central concern; *Oedipus the King,* for example, presents an objective phenomenon, a man's discovery of how he was entrapped by circumstances, rather than a subjective experience. Modern literature has, in fact, gone further and acquired the very shape of the unconscious processes it has expressed, as we may note from the various uses to which interior monologue and the "stream-of-consciousness" technique have been put. To a degree, the Underground Man has given modern writing *form* as well as content. Whereas *Ulysses* owes its flow and style to Joyce's highly individual matter and response, *Oedipus the King* is constructed along the objective lines of Greek tragic form. This is equally true of other Greek plays, such as *Orestes* and *Hippolytus,* no matter how much "depth-psychology" we may be inclined to attribute to each work. *Hamlet* may be considered the most "psychological" play of its age, but the dramatic form of this tragedy is typically Elizabethan, whereas every previously employed dramatic form became transformed in such modern plays as Strindberg's *The Dream Play* and *The Ghost Sonata* by their author's subjective interest.

As Dostoevski was himself the first to show us, too, the Underground Man theme ranges well beyond the mere psychological interest of *Notes From the Underground.* Among his later novels, *Crime and Punishment* engrosses our attention with the comprehensive conflict between Superman ideology and ethics; *The Possessed* revolves around a subject of vast political import; *The Brothers Karamazov* may be described as an allegory of man in his totality. The "underground" man is not just the private individual, but all society. And as such the "dark underside" has manifested itself so distressingly in recent history as to refute the easy assurances of rationalism and liberalism since the eighteenth century, making them seem naïve, if not indeed fatuous. It is, indeed, one of the most challenging features of modern "underground" thinking, whether in work of the stature of *The Magic Mountain* or in some minor novel about a fascistic anti-semite, that it eliminates sharp distinctions between individual and collective disease and between individual and collective struggles.

The Underground Man is nothing less than Man himself viewed as both psychological and social phenomenon; and, ethically, "underground" and "overground" make one entity, just as the hidden roots and the overarching branches make one tree. Recognition of the dark side of the truth about human reality must always posit a bright side—that of the civilized life man creates as a superstructure through his social relations, art, and thought. The dark drives toward chaos and destruction make more imperative the impulse toward the light; that is, toward integration and constructiveness, without which survival would have been impossible for *homo sapiens*. And it is the delicate balance between the darkness and the light that makes humanity's night and day the subject of great literature. And it is mainly the tension of the darkness and the light, culminating in conflict, that constitutes great drama. Out of a perception of this fact, Nietzsche formulated the fruitful polarities of the Dionysian element and the Apollonian when he wrote *The Birth of Tragedy,* and it would not be difficult to find analogues, such as the contrast between reason and unreason or between social moderation and social excess in discussing comedy, too. All such considerations, moreover, have their equivalent in thought and politics, so that nothing human can be considered alien to the theme of the underground and its literary exploitation. We may, for example, frame the idea as a sort of historical dialectic of anti-humanism and humanism, or of "reactionary wickedness" (Mann's phrase) and liberalism. Mann presented it memorably in the struggle between Naphta, the Jewish Jesuit, and Settembrini, the old-fashioned, sentimental Italian liberal, for the soul of "life's delicate child," Hans Castorp, in *The Magic Mountain.* It is the same conflict that underlies the political struggles, large and small, that agitate us today, perhaps no more so than in previous periods of transition.

One could, indeed, trace underground awareness down to "Longinus" and his emphasis on the "sublime," as contrasted with the principle "imitation," in art; to Aristotle and his principle of "catharsis"; and to Plato, among whose observations will be found such statements as that the desires assert themselves in dreams "when the gentler part of the soul slumbers and the control of reason is withdrawn" and "the wild beast in us rages." (So that in fantasy desire "will not shrink from intercourse with a mother or anyone else," Plato added!) Plato's quarrel with artists in *The Republic,* which was surely no simpleminded Purity League raid, came from an awareness of the "dark underside" of reality and art so intense that his ideal of reason could not come to terms with it. That he banished the poets from his Republic of Reason has outraged us, although it has been difficult to charge Plato, of all writers, with philistinism. That he *had* to banish them was a tribute equally to their insight and his own. We may say, then, with little fear of contradiction that underground awareness has always been important, and that when we look for it in modern drama we do not press an arbitrary demand upon the theatre.

II

Dostoevski published *Notes From the Underground* in 1864, and the date is important in the history of the modern theatre because it was also the date of Ibsen's first truly probing play *The Pretenders,* the tragedy of a king who failed for lack of kingliness and floundered with indecisions born of a sense of guilt. Ibsen went on to write three other devastating studies of human confusion and alienation, *Brand, Peer Gynt,* and *Emperor and Galilean,* between the years 1865 and 1873. Six years later, with *A Doll's House,* Ibsen began to create the modern realistic social drama which earned him the title of "father of the modern drama" in works that were usually simplified in interpretation by both their champions and enemies. And, with *Rosmersholm,* in the year 1886, he began to compose the allegedly murky or obscure plays in which he returned to the underground matter of *The Pretenders* in various respects. Several of these works made considerable use of the symbolist elements of atmosphere, suggestiveness, and actual symbols, such as the "white horses of Rosmersholm," the sailor with the "fish eyes" in *Lady from the Sea,* and the "Rat Wife" in *Little Eyolf.* Among these plays, which could be legitimately called "underground dramas," was also the sharply outlined realistic drama *Hedda Gabler,* so that classroom distinctions between realism and symbolism (and likewise between realism and romanticism) only serve to obscure for us the vastly more important distinction that exists at all times between surface-artistry and depth-artistry.

In 1887, with the arrival of *The Father,* Ibsen the Norwegian was joined in the theatre by that demoniacally obsessed Swedish genius August Strindberg, who was inclined to create underground drama whether he wrote naturalistic plays such as *Miss Julie* and *The Dance of Death* or more or less expressionist plays such as *To Damascus, The Dream Play,* and *The Ghost Sonata.*

Between them, the two formidable Scandinavian dramatists Ibsen and Strindberg laid the same foundations for a complex and probing literature in the theatre that Dostoevski established for literature in the library. The drama and the novel could now move forward, so it seemed, in equal partnership. Both were headed in the direction of a realism far removed from the photography of surfaces, redeemed from superficiality and dedicated to exploring the underground of human nature. And both the drama and fiction were also headed in the direction of those depths that both "unserious" commercial art or so-called entertainment and "serious" rationalistic, blithely optimistic liberal and radical reformist art were equally inclined to ignore. In the twentieth century, moreover, it could be expected that both the drama and fiction would gain from the support available to them from the depth-psychology of Freud and Jung, as well as from the new anthropological studies of myth and society inaugurated but by no means exhausted by Fraser's *The Golden Bough.*

Indeed, the entire climate of Western civilization was extremely favorable to the explorations of the dramatists and novelists, as well as, let us not forget, Baudelaire's and Rimbaud's successors among the poets. Not only philosophical thought in many of its ramifications from Nietzscheanism to the latest form of Existentialism, but twentieth-century experience bared many a chasm to our modern artists. Surely, they could not remain pristinely innocent in the twentieth-century world of revolutions, counter-revolutions, and world wars, whose end is not yet in sight. Writers could not fail to observe the crumbling of many a façade of culture erected by previous centuries and fail to hear the crash of long-established values. They could not escape the divisions and anxieties of twentieth-century man; they could not remain complacent "children of paradise" in an age noteworthy for the welling up of barbarism out of ideologies and the abysses of human nature. Progress could no longer be conceived as the inevitable result of universal suffrage, the spread of knowledge, and the education of illiteracy. The young Tennyson's ringing grooves of change could no longer be celebrated with simpleminded complacency—a complacency Tennyson himself was forced to relinquish toward the end of his life. The rift in the lute of Victorianism had become obvious by 1890. The rift in the lute of liberalism on which post-Tennysonian writers had fiddled their harmonics of optimism also became obvious by 1914. Dramatists as well as novelists could emerge from intellectual adolescence, and some playwrights did.

A split, nevertheless, began to appear between drama and fiction in our century. Fiction underwent developments that made it the major literary art of the modern age, while the drama, which had been the major achievement of Sophocles', Shakespeare's and Moliere's times, became an increasingly minor partner. Today, most literary critics no longer find it possible to consider the work of the playwrights with more than a fraction of sober attention that they expend upon the novelists and poets of the century; and the greatest talents, with not many exceptions, have gone into other fields than playwriting.

After writing *Notes From the Underground,* the confessions and speculations of nihilistic man, Dostoevski went on to create the stupendous nightmare tragedies of *Crime and Punishment, The Idiot, The Possessed,* and *The Brothers Karamazov.* Deep called unto deep, and both Strindberg and Nietzsche recognized Dostoevski as the Dante of the modern age. Nor is it only for his psychological penetration that Dostoevski became properly renowned. Important as he is as a psychologist who earned Freud's admiration, Dostoevski is even more important as the *total artist* who not only went into the underground but came out of it. In exploring the abysses of human nature and their threat to the individual, he also understood their threat to society. More than that, he emerged with his dark knowledge more profoundly the humanitarian than he could have become by seeing only the good in man, his scientific progress, and the superficial manifestations of social and political meliorism. By focusing on both the pity and terror of the human drama, he made the pity more manifest and active, and he also made possible a catharsis, a purgation, that pity alone can never accomplish. He rose above sentiment and so carried the novel to the austere heights of tragedy. And, concurrently, he brought into existence the genuine novel of ideas—not the type of novel that merely discusses ideas or problems and gives a novelist a reputation for cleverness or topical importance, but the novel in which characters and ideas are identical, in which feeling and thought necessitously comprise one total reality, as do the good and evil in Dostoevski's world picture.

It is not my intention, however, to expatiate on Dostoevski's artistry here. I cite him here because, more than any other modern writer, Dostoevski set a mark for novelists to aim at after 1880. More and more novelists moved into the underground, studying the suppressed manifestations of man as an individual and as a constituent of society, so that the modern novel, on its highest levels of accomplishment, escaped the superficiality with which contemporary playwriting has so often been charged. The novelists gave us in radically divergent ways a literature expressive of modern knowledge and of modern tensions. And regardless of whether or not they succeeded entirely in any particular novel or in the bulk of their work, they vastly extended the resources of fiction and made the novel an organ upon which it was possible to play all the discords of modern Western civilization. So much so, that I suspect those of us who invested our main hopes and energies in the theatre of often wondering whether we didn't back the wrong horse when we became playwrights, stage directors, play producers, and dramatic critics.

It is true, of course, that along with the development of the novel as art we have witnessed its expansion as a business, which is being threatened only in our day by competition with the movies and television. Unquestionably, the deliberately commercialized novel has been one of the signs of commercialization in all fields of contemporary enterprise. The narcotic-venders, romance-peddlers, shrewd hacks, and the fortunate inno- cents whose mediocrity finds a responsive chord in the mediocrity of readers whom mass-education has made dubiously literate—all these have found novel-writing a benign, and often lucrative, occupation. But my argument is not invalidated, for there have been mediocre and meretricious works in every age and in every field. We assess the achievements of a particular art in a particular time by its best rather than by its worst products, for, after all, the resources of human incompetence are infinite.

It is also true that some excellent novels of the past three quarters of a century have had little in common with the Dostoevskian or under- ground type of novel. One thinks of Hamsun's *The Growth of the Soil,* Reymont's *The Peasants,* and Sholokov's *And Quiet Flows the Don.* But these novels, which possess epic contours, have described ways of life not characteristically modern, although modern realities may be seen imping- ing on them. In the main, it is the underground man, once believed to belong only to primitive stages of society, who is the subject of the im- pressive, modern-complexioned, novels of the past seventy-five years. Whether his clothes and manners be fashionable, as they are in the work of Henry James and Proust, or unfashionable, as they are in the most flagrant of Faulkner novels, the "dark underside" is omnipresent in sig- nificant fiction. The underground man has been the central figure of much of the fiction Henry James devoted to the niceties of conscience overladen with the niceties of manners. He is also to be found in the novels of Joseph Conrad, Marcel Proust, James Joyce, D. H. Lawrence, Thomas Mann, Jacob Wassermann, Franz Kafka, André Gide, and other major writers. He is even present in the materialistic social novels of Theodore Dreiser *The Titan* and *The Financier,* at one extreme, and the profoundly Catho- lic novels of Mauriac. And whether or not their authors were conscious of indebtedness to Dostoevski, although a number of them have been, they have written, in one respect or another, underground novels. Nor should diversities of style, background, or subject matter obscure for us the essen- tial kinship. The novelists have peered into the recesses of human nature and taken note of the forces at war with our pretensions to civilization. They have seen the canker in the rose of our humanity, although the best authors have seen the rose, too. They have looked at reality with unde- luded if not necessarily unvisionary eyes.

Each of the underground novelists presents us with fascinations and challenges that could fill a separate essay or even book. To do justice to such individual works as *Ulysses, Remembrance of Things Past, The Counterfeiters,* and *The Magic Mountain,* and *The Castle* alone would require a major effort on the part of a critic. But that is precisely the point of my invidious comparison of the modern novel and the modern drama. The substance of the truly modern novels is extremely impressive: humanity is exposed so intensively, in such detail and on so many levels of interest that the intelligent reader can be fully engaged by the work. By comparison, the modern drama seems thin and only superficially arresting. Especially when the play is read, and certainly once the theatrical magic of the stage production has receded from the memory, the mind is insufficiently engaged by the bulk of modern playwriting.

For the reader whose recollections of the stage production have grown hazy and, of course, for the reader who never saw the production that first gave the play its reputation, the text of the modern play is a mere wafer of literature. More or less, this must always have been the case, but it is, obviously, more the case in the predominantly prose drama of modern times, which does not have the multi-leveled meaning, the evocative music or magical rhythm, or the rich verbal texture of the plays of an Aeschylus, Shakespeare, or Racine. We exhaust the prose of modern drama too easily as a rule; the prose that we do not exhaust so easily—that of Synge, O'Casey, and Shaw in English, for example—approximates poetry. The theatre always needs poets, and, fortunately, it may get the poet's imagination even without the poet's language, as in O'Neill's work, and the theatre may add a poetic quality of its own in a stage production. It was that kind of poetry of production design or visual effect, indeed, that men such as Appia, Gordon Craig, Reinhardt, and Vakhtangov endeavored to provide. The drama, however, also needs the poet's verbal texture if it is to communicate its fullest potentialities on the page.

However, it would be begging the question to place the blame exclusively on the vogue of prose dialogue. The modern novel is also prose literature, and not all the great novelists wrote distinguished prose at that. Dostoevski himself deplored the quality of his style, and wished he were not plagued by publishers' deadlines so that he could revise his text. His slapdash writing has not detracted from his great reputation. Dreiser's work is impressive in spite of his verbal infelicities and Henry James is a master-novelist in spite of his involved prose. I would register a personal annoyance at Mann's latter-day prose, which I have read both in English and in the original German. Yet Mann's lumbering coyness has never measurably diminished my absorption in his work and my respect for his over-all accomplishment as a writer of fiction. And other readers have been made unhappy by Proust's style or Faulkner's style without denying the eminence of either author. Plainly, it is the totality of experience impacted in novels that has made modern fiction significant to us.

But if style may be of secondary importance, form is not. The novel regarded as a literary form has been extremely plastic and could be adapted to the expression of the multiple and complex interests of the modern age. A playwright is more or less in a straitjacket by comparison with the novelist. We are tempted to believe that this is the case whenever we compare dramatizations of *Crime and Punishment, The Idiot,* and *The Brothers Karamazov* with the novels themselves, or when we compare Kafka's *The Trial* with the dramatization that André Gide made of this novel and that Barrault produced. A profoundly absorbing work was in this case reduced to a series of expressionistic tricks or, at best, to ingenious theatricality—this despite the admirable skill and intelligence of everyone importantly involved in the production. It is to the insignificant and superficial novels that the modern stage has managed to do justice— to, let us say, a *Dodsworth, On Borrowed Time,* or *Point of No Return.*

The length of a novel as compared with the length of a play may have some bearing on the comparative limitations of modern playwriting. After all, we may reflect, no playwright, and certainly no prose playwright, who must make do without the pregnant dialogue of poetry, can be expected to accomplish in a hundred-twenty pages of text what a Dostoevski, Proust, or Mann accomplished in six hundred to two thousand pages of closely packed type. But length alone is obviously not the explanation. After all, Kafka's *The Trial* and *The Castle* are much shorter books, and many novels have been just as long as *The Brothers Karamazov* without deserving to be mentioned in the same breath with it. Nor have modern playwrights refrained from extending the conventional size of the modern play—Shaw in the case of *Back to Methuselah* and O'Neill in such jumbo-sized dramas as *Strange Interlude, Lazarus Laughed, Mourning Becomes Electra,* and *The Iceman Cometh.* That length is not decisive in considering depth is quite obvious. Actually, some of the work with which playwrights have come nearest to the stature of the important underground novelists has been standard-sized or even, in the case of Strindberg's long one-act piece *Miss Julie,* shorter. In addition to citing plays by Ibsen and Strindberg, one could refer to Chekhov's *The Three Sisters,* O'Neill's *Desire Under the Elms,* Wedekind's *The Marquis of Keith,* Lorca's *The House of Bernarda Alba,* Masefield's *The Tragedy of Nan,* Shaw's *Heartbreak House,* Williams' *Streetcar Named Desire,* and Miller's *Death of a Salesman*—all dramas compacted within the scope of a more or less two and a half or three hour production. And I would add the play that to my mind is the greatest of all modern underground plays—Tolstoy's overpowering peasant-tragedy *The Power of Darkness.*

All that I would venture to say, then, on the score of scope is that whereas the length of the composition has enabled some profound novelists to exert their talent with amplitude, and to convey the fullness of discovery and vision, length of composition has rarely, if ever, been of sufficient service to the playwright who has striven for equally significant content. Extreme length has, on the contrary, tended to diffuse and weaken the dramatic force of plays. This was most evident in such plays as *Back to Methuselah, Lazarus Laughed,* and *The Iceman Cometh,* and it was also evident in *Strange Interlude* and *Mourning Becomes Electra.* And plays that have been novelistic in structure have tended to achieve richness of matter at the expense of dramatic interest. In other words, it has been easier for the novelist than the playwright to allow himself the scope that has undoubtedly helped to make *The Brothers Karamazov, Remembrance of Things Past,* and *The Magic Mountain* memorable impressions of the modern world.

The author of works intended to be read is under less constraint to achieve an immediate effect and to avoid overt analysis and explanation than a playwright. He can count upon more patience and also upon more comprehension from a public that can read at leisure and has the written page always in front of it for checking and rechecking. A novelist can distill the content of his mind at a rate determined by his own disposition; a playwright cannot do so without devastating his audience. He must aim for effect. Therefore, he cannot aim for truth as easily, and in the theatre the requirements of showmanship may overwhelm or distort the integrity of analysis and vision.

It is not conclusive to say that commercialism has vulgarized or cheapened the drama without also saying that it has cheapened the novel. It is true only that the process of vulgarization has been more pronounced in the theatre. What must be conceded is, first of all, that it has been more difficult for an unconventional playwright to bring his cargo to market, if for no other reason than that the production of an unusual play is much more expensive than the publication of an unusual novel. And his dependence upon casting and stage production, moreover, may limit the possibility of his having his say in fullness and in his own integral manner. By not working regularly in the theatre, as Shakespeare, Molière, and the young Ibsen did, a playwright fails to acquire sufficient skill to make the dramatic medium serve his intentions; and there has been quite a chasm in our times between the intentions and the execution of many playwrights who seemed to have something worth saying. By working regularly in the theatre, on the other hand, or by developing the knack of getting productions for his plays with ease, the writer runs the risk of becoming so attuned to showmanship that he thinks too much in terms of effects rather than of substance. He begins to concern himself too much with expression through the physical medium of the stage rather than with the substance properly to be expressed in the writing by the classical methods of characterization and dialogue developed to the point of maximum revelatory power.

It is not only of the nineteenth-century follower of Scribe and Sardou that it can be said that no sooner does he think of an idea than he thinks of an *effect*. Especially when forms are unfixed, and they have been extremely unstable in our century, the playwright tends to be diverted both from thought and character-creation whenever he thinks of creating for the theatre. He becomes the slave rather than the master of his medium. When that happens even the most probing and thought-committed dramatist becomes a poseur and trickster or, at best, a pitchman "making a pitch" for his perceptions and ideas.

This became the case almost equally with earnest problem-play writers, with left-wing propagandists, and dedicated artists. I am inclined to believe that only one playwright after Becque, Ibsen, and Strindberg entirely escaped this tendency—the mature Chekhov. O'Neill rarely escaped it, and even O'Casey succumbed to enticements of physical theatre, in *The Silver Tassie,* and to the seductions of "poetry," in *Within the Gates.* Here, as in so much so-called advanced non-realistic playwriting, whether expressionist or symbolist, we had the skeleton for a great human drama, rather than the substantial great drama itself. In *Juno and the Paycock* and *The Plough and the Stars,* by contrast, we had the drama itself. Nor is the quest for "poetry" a real danger when the author is both a poet and a playwright naturally. Lorca escaped entrapment by either "poetry" or "theatre" when he created *Blood Wedding, Yerma,* and *The House of Bernarda Alba,* as did Brecht when he wrote *Mother Courage* and *The Good Woman of Setzuan.* As dramatists, Claudel, Yeats, Eliot, and Fry were subverted by both poetry and theatre because they valued poetry above theatre; and Maxwell Anderson was subverted by poetry because he was *not* a poet. Cocteau, Giraudoux, Anouilh, as well as their superiors Pirandello (except in a few plays, among which *Six Characters in Search of an Author* is the most successful experiment) and Strindberg himself, in some of the work of his last period, exhibit "subversion by theatre." And when Tennessee Williams is subverted by both symbolism and theatricality, as he plainly was in *Camino Real,* we are most unhappily aware of the fact. In comedy, the results are likely to prove least distressing because playfulness accords naturally with theatricality. This is evident, to different degrees, in plays of varying substance such as *The Importance of Being Earnest, The Play Is the Thing, Tonight We Improvise, Blithe Spirit, Playboy of the Western World, Androcles and the Lion, The Madwoman of Chaillot,* and O'Casey's *Cock-a-Doodle Dandy.* Shaw was particularly fortunate in this respect. But, then, most comedies do not invite comparison with the heavy artillery of modern fiction.

The point is that in the novels, even in those of Henry James, one is less conscious of the intrusion of the medium. A reason is, of course, that the fictional form is more plastic or flexible. It yields to the shaping hand of the writer without diverting his attention from the life in the work, and usually (*Ulysses* is an exception, as is, of course, *Finnegans Wake*) without calling much attention to the fact that it is being specially shaped or twisted. One yields to the writing of a Tolstoy and Dostoevski or to the writing of a Proust and Lawrence as one yields to the current of a strong stream. In fiction, besides, the medium is less obtrusive. The medium is language, whereas the medium of theatre is physical—a stage and its properties. In dramatic work a physical medium exists in a tension with the writing, the language, of the playwright.

Theatricality is not to be dismissed, of course. A certain amount of it is necessary and has always been present in the masterworks of the drama. Showmanship, however, can never be allowed to dominate playwriting if dramatists are to achieve the penetration of the major modern novelists. The only showmanship that can be trusted is that which is intrinsic to the content of the work and to the intellect and the artistry of the writer. And showmanship in the case of the producer, director, and actor is always on hand for the produced playwright to divert him from creating with integrity. Showmanship on the part of the playwright's collaborators in the theatre is always ready to assert itself independently of him. Popular actors and energetic directors, such as Reinhardt, Piscator, Elia Kazan, and Joshua Logan, are virtuosi by reason of their giftedness. They contribute a great deal to the success of the play on the stage, of course, and their ministrations are very much needed. But Shaw was right in trying to dictate to them, if only because they are inclined to assert their virtuosity and dictate to the playwright. And, indeed, the ineptitude of most playwriting is an inordinate temptation for them to do so. The playwright and his interpreters are always in delicate balance in the theatre. Chekhov owed his success as a playwright to the Moscow Art Theatre. Yet even Chekhov was aware of an element of danger in his relations with this most scrupulous of stage companies and its great director. Nemirovitch-Dantchenko reported that after the production of *Uncle Vanya*, in which Stanislavski overdid naturalistic effects such as the chirp of a cricket and the use of mosquito-netting, Chekhov declared that he would make a stipulation in his next play as follows: "The action takes place in a land which has neither mosquitoes nor crickets nor any other insects which hinder conversation between human beings." And in the theatre of Stanislavski there was no flagrant commercialism. Chekhov also protested against the tendency of the "Art Theatre" to overlook his comic intentions.

III

If it is obviously unfair to accuse all modern playwrights of having sold their birthright for a mess of commercial pottage, it is also unfair to assume that they have not striven to achieve the depths and comprehensiveness of major novelists. The strenuous, if not indeed overstrenuous, efforts of O'Neill alone would contradict the charge. Playwrights have been aware of a lag between playwriting and modern thought. They have eagerly, indeed overeagerly, ingested Freudianism or "psychology," Marxism or "sociology," and science, both mechanistic and relativistic. (J. B. Priestley wrote at least three plays based on the relativity of time.) Nor is it "content" alone that has engaged their interest. They have endeavored to make the content dictate new forms of dramaturgy, and they have even appropriated the new techniques of novelists and poets. O'Neill borrowed the stream-of-consciousness technique from modern fiction in *Strange Interlude*. The resemblance between the telescoping method of *Finnegans Wake* and that of Thornton Wilder's *The Skin of Our Teeth* was noted; and insisted upon with such persuasiveness by George Jean Nathan that Wilder was deprived of a New York Drama Critics Circle award in 1942. The fantasia of the unconscious and the psychoanalytic "free association" method of Apollinaire and his successors the programmatic surrealist poets have appeared in plays. The "dream technique" has been present in modern drama ever since the late plays of Strindberg, and it became a veritable "delirium technique" in the hands of extremists among German expressionists. Toller, with *Masse-Mensch,* or *Man and the Masses,* and Kaiser, with *From Morn to Midnight,* even acquired international reputations with their experiments.

Dramatists, indeed, have been aware of the imperativeness of "catching up" with modern developments ever since Emile Zola wrote his Preface to *Thérèse Raquin* in 1873 and clamored for a naturalistic drama and theatre. They have drafted programs, plans, and apologies again and again, whether as individuals (as in the case of Strindberg and Pirandello) or as proponents of the modern movements of naturalism, symbolism, expressionism, epic realism *á la* Brecht and Piscator, surrealism, and what not! They have experimented in a bewildering number of styles and forms. And they have been anything but unaware of the necessity of challenging and overcoming a stultifying commercialism in the theatre. Along with critics, actors, scenic artists, and stage directors, such as Otto Brahm, Antoine, Appia, Craig, Reinhardt, Copeau, Jouvet, and Barrault, they have hoped to found and support one non-commercial theatre after another. From Antoine's *Théâtre Libre,* founded in 1887, to the Provincetown

Players in 1919 or, for that matter, to the arena-theatre Circle-in-the-Square group under the talented José Quintero in 1953, theatres have repeatedly dedicated themselves to art and innovation.

Yet the results in playwriting have not been commensurate to the effort. Everybody complains that the playwrights have been failing the theatre, although few of the mourners have explicitly made much of the fact that even our most significant plays have fallen short of the stature of the great modern novels. (Some critics, prodded by Joseph Wood Krutch in the nineteen-twenties, have bemoaned the scarcity of high tragedy in modern playwriting. And, recently, able critics, such as William Becker and Theodore Hoffman, have noted that some of our best literary talents have been absent from the American theatre.) Most play reviewers and play producers would settle for even good second-rate playwrights in no way comparable to a Dostoevski, Proust, Gide, Joyce, or Mann. From a practical—and that is, from a woefully narrow—point of view, I suppose they are right. Nevertheless, I question whether second-rate playwriting is a solution for anything but box-office doldrums. The reason why there have been so few second-rate playwrights is, I venture to say, because there have been so few first-rate ones. (The first-rate are needed to set the pace for the second-rate.) And the same circumstances that have made first-rate dramatic achievements difficult have also made acceptable second-rate ones sparse.

Decade after decade, the ambitious playwright could well envy novelists as he watched his dramaturgy burst at the seams whenever he engaged upon enterprises equivalent in aim to that of major fiction. Prose drama was especially precarious in this respect, but the problem goes beyond the question of prose or verse dialogue, for the seams could burst whether O'Neill wrote prose or Claudel wrote poetry. Nor is it a question of art, in the sense of super-refinement, but of art in the sense of finding appropriate means for expressing the amplitude and depth of the writer's interest and understanding. It was in this respect, primarily, that the novelist could be envied. The novelist could freely shift the angle of his narration or so-called "point of view." He could generally plumb the depths of character and conflict without inhibiting impediments or achieve subtlety and significant emphasis by adopting a restricted but intensive confessional or exploratory "first-person point of view." He could shift his focus, adopt a third-person point of view, and adopt the omniscience of a god with respect to his subject. He could become panoramic or kaleidoscopic when it suited his purpose. He could include the whole complex of a society while also probing into character, as Proust did. He could also address himself directly to the reader in various artful ways, which admittedly could become coy and pretentious at times—as I believe to be the case in some of Mann's work—but which could also express the ramified implications of his theme. The novelist could adopt the method of long interior monologues and follow the stream of consciousness of his characters, as Joyce did, with greater flexibility and sensitivity than a playwright could and without the technical difficulties O'Neill faced in *Strange Interlude*. Once the novelist's powers of observation, sensibility, and intelligence combined with the purpose of creating fiction of major significance, he could move as far and on as many levels as he wished.

Not so the playwright, whose ambitions might have been of the same magnitude in defiance of facile popularity. He was, and still is, hemmed in by the greater objectivity and inflexibility of the dramatic form and by the greater unity demanded by modern dramaturgy; partly by the conventions of the realistic theatre and the peep-hole, picture-frame, box-set stages, which could not be displaced without rebuilding old theatres or building new ones; and partly by the fact that an audience has to be held by a play in one sitting, and that a play has to be comprehended or absorbed in one viewing and hearing if it is to succeed. Also, a stage production must catch on at once, as a rule, if it is to succeed at all.

The playwright did, as I have noted, make a strong effort to adapt the form of drama to his intellectual and artistic ambitions, and he still does, as we can observe in midcentury efforts of Tennessee Williams and Arthur Miller and in a variety of efforts abroad. Nor were they entirely without success. Chekhov and the O'Casey of *Juno and the Paycock* and *The Plough and the Stars* were especially successful in creating fluid and poetic drama without breaking the mold of effective realistic dramaturgy; and degrees of success were attained by other playwrights who did not scrap realistic dramaturgy. Their victories, however, were few or incomplete, and many powerful realists themselves, including Strindberg and O'Casey, arrived at the conclusion that the realistic or naturalistic form of playwriting and the realistic style could not be extended very far.

The alternative was, of course, to break the mold of dramatic and theatrical realism, and it cannot be said that playwrights evaded the challenge. They also found extremely eager and very able collaborators among critics, scene designers, and directors. A good deal of the history of the stage and the drama since 1890 consists of these efforts at symbolism, expressionism, and a variety of other attempts to create more flexible forms of theatre. Interesting effects were achieved, and some fascinating playwriting resulted. We can pick our examples, according to our taste and conviction, from the experiments of the latter-day Ibsen and Strindberg, as well as from the later work of O'Neill, Pirandello, Kaiser, Toller, Giraudoux, Yeats, Eliot, Lorca, Brecht, and Williams.

Too often, however, the modernists have given us the form of drama without its substance, as one critic of expressionism put it. Sometimes, in the case of symbolist playwriting such as Maeterlinck's, they gave us only the atmosphere of drama, confusing a mood with a play and a shadow with life. Too often the modernists became more turgid rather than lucid, as did O'Neill and the German expressionists. They schematized the complexities of human nature and reduced metaphysical questions to bald answers, as O'Neill did in his Freudian and philosophical dramas, and as Eliot has done in his attempts to substitute glib, theologically correct formulations of original sin for the glib formulations of the liberal writers of social drama. Even Pirandello became tiresome and rather hollow when he began to split the ego as mechanically as though he were splitting the atom, and when he confined his view of reality to the single game of whether we are what we are when we think we are. Even Ibsen became obscure when he substituted theatrical symbolism for relentless, explicit analyses of human nature through the action of his well-defined characters. And Strindberg became operatically theatrical and pseudo-poetical in *The Dream Play* and other experiments, although he managed to escape the bathos to which many later expressionists often succumbed. And not to prolong this list of transgressions, let us simply note that many other, perfectly honorable attempts to increase the flexibility of dramatic presentation, such as Evreinov's *The Chief Thing,* Giraudoux' *Intermezzo (The Enchanted)*, O'Casey's *The Silver Tassie,* Wilder's *The Skin of Our Teeth,* and Williams' *Camino Real,* were more or less suggestive of theatrical trickery or artifice. In the avowedly progressive, non-realistic theatre, in short, artifice tended to take precedence over art. And the experimentalists among modern playwrights tended to appear on the stage with their devices showing.

However fascinating modern experiments in theatrical drama may have been, they have not possessed the organic reality of great art; and by the same token, the insistently poetic or imaginative plays of modern playwrights have not captured the reality of both universal and contemporary man. Nor have these "art theatre plays" revealed the reality of modern society, and to the degree that they have failed to reveal it they have usually received less public support than many a "bread-and-butter" realistic problem play such as Galsworthy's *Justice* or *Loyalties.* Charges of decadence and evasion have been leveled at much of the *avant-garde* theatre. Unfortunately, they can be made to stick too often in the case of so-called artistic plays, as can also charges of self-intoxication on the part of their authors. By contrast, the amplitude, depth, and power of great modern fiction has generally stemmed from its informality and naturalness. Even *Ulysses* gives that impression, along with an impression of intense genuineness, once the verbal difficulties are surmounted.

All told, the effort to make drama carry the freight of modern reality by theatricalizing playwriting has not been particularly successful. Since this effort has often been implemented brilliantly by stagecraft and performance, the theatre has sometimes been rewarding for an evening, and for an entertainment. But the underground of man and society has not been penetrated by the playwrights, while even the surface effectively or vigorously disturbed by realistic playwrights has been neglected or prettified by some ardent anti-realists, who have turned out to be little better than poetasters as writers and prestidigitators as theatricians.

It may turn out indeed that they have served the modern drama best with the warning lesson enforced by their failures and shortcomings. In spite of the glorification of non-realistic styles now and then in vogue, it may turn out that realism *is* the most viable form of modern playwriting. I have in mind, of course, a profounder and more flexible realism than that which has been current in the commercial theatres of America and Europe. Modern dramatists' experience with non-realistic forms of dramaturgy since 1890 may enable the playwrights of the second half of our century to use realism in the broadest rather than in the narrowest manner of operation. And the results, provided the playwrights have the requisite substance and the talent, may prove considerably more rewarding than the paradoxical attempts of experimental writers to make the playgoer see more by blinding him with theatrical gold dust. Moreover, the free forms of theatre that have been developed over the years by directors and designers in collaboration with these playwrights of the first half of the century can surely be of assistance to later dramatists. They now have at hand a theatrical medium considerably more flexible than it was at the close of the nineteenth century. It will be necessary only to guard against the temptation to make the physical means, the resources of stage machinery and stage lighting, the master rather than the servant of the stage production—and of the play. It will have to be understood that the playwright's most reliable partner and interpreter remains the actor, for it has been chiefly the latter's collaboration that has made modern playwriting seem less one-dimensional and less woefully arid to its audiences than any considered comparisons with modern fiction would indicate.

TRAGEDY IN THE MODERN THEATRE

I. TRAGIC ENLIGHTENMENT

It would seem as if it were impossible to select a more academic concept than the idea of "catharsis" for consideration. It is encrusted with antiquity and bears the rust of much speculation justly suspect to the practical man of the theatre. The concept is, nevertheless, one of those fruitful insights that profoundly defines what we experience or do even when we do not know what we have experienced or done. And the practical value of the concept to those of us who work in the theatre is that we would be more effective if we knew what is expected of us, knowingly or unknowingly, by playgoers, and if we knew exactly what we were doing while writing and producing plays. Generations of men who have written and pondered upon tragic art have been agreed that Aristotle touched bottom when he declared the effect of tragedy to be purgation of the soul by "pity" and "fear." The Aristotelian formula, supremely empirical, has a dual importance: The spectator is given a definition of his experience when tragic drama is effective, and the playwright a definition of the effect he must achieve by various means when he presents high and serious matter of a painful nature.

Unfortunately, however, Aristotle's analysis was altogether too fragmentary, and his *Poetics* has come down to us in a form that suggests little more than a collection of notes. We do not even know with absolute certainty what catharsis meant to the philosopher and how he thought "pity" and "fear" could actually produce the purgation. The subject has exercised commentators ever since the Middle Ages when scholars seized upon the short passage "Tragedy through pity and fear effects a purgation of such emotions." Each age has added its own interpretation, naturally reflecting its own interests and its own kind of drama. According to sixteenth-century humanists, including the learned Castelvetro, tragedy hardened the spectator to suffering by subjecting him to pity and fear-inducing scenes of misery and violence. Corneille, himself a formidable tragedian, held that tragedy forced the spectator to fear for himself when he observed how a character's passions produce disaster, and that the resolve to rule one's own passions effected the purgation. Others, including John Milton, whose views probably most agree with Aristotle's, took the homeopathic view that pity and fear on the stage counteracted the disturbing elements of pity and fear in the spectator. For the liberals or humanitarians of the

Enlightenment, including the author of *Nathan the Wise,* tragedy purified the observer by enabling him to exercise his sympathies. For Hegel, tragedy reconciled conflicting views, thereby effecting catharsis. And so the interpretations multiplied until we arrived at the view that accords with both the findings of psychopathology and common sense—namely, that catharsis is the effect of the expulsion of disturbing drives within us.

Without adhering to any specific school of psychopathology, I believe that I can safely say that if catharsis is a valid definition of tragic effect (and I believe it is), it means one thing above all: In the tragic experience we temporarily expel troublesome inner complications. We expel "pity" and "fear," to use Aristotle's terms, and the terms are broad enough to cover the most pathological or near-pathological elements—namely, anxieties, fears, morbid grief or self-pity, sadistic or masochistic desires, and the sense of guilt that these engender. In a successful tragedy, we see these drives enacted on the stage directly by characters with whom we can identify ourselves. They are our proxies, so to speak. And these emotions are, of course, aroused in us, and so externalized, in so far as we react with pity, anxiety, and fear to the suffering on the stage.

We must observe, however, that the expulsion of our morbidities would certainly prove incomplete and ineffective if the expelled emotion were merely brought to the surface instead of being fully recognized—that is, understood and appraised—by our consciousness. That something more is needed is evidenced by the whole history of the drama, for the distinction between melodrama and tragedy is grounded in the conviction that mere excitement does not provide the gratifications that fulfill our highest expectations of dramatic experience. Where the excitement emanates plausibly and serves an end beyond itself, there is, we say, tragedy. Where the excitement exists solely as an end in itself, and is accomplished without the operation of reason and its standards of credibility, we have melodrama. If purgation in tragedy were confined solely to the effects of pity and fear, there would be little dramatic distinction between *Hamlet* and *Night Must Fall* or *Angel Street.*

Has it not always been recognized that the superiority of the great tragedies, if we exclude purely stylistic differences (which are not to be discounted, however), has resided in their powerful blending of passion with enlightenment? This is what we mean when we attribute their superiority as drama to the depth of their content, the significance of their conflict, and the relevance of their issues. In tragedy, there is always a precipitate of final enlightenment—some inherent, cumulatively achieved understanding, realization, or recognition.

Having participated in a tragic experience enacted on the stage, we vibrated to the represented passions, observable in the characters but also present in ourselves; passions imbedded in our common humanity, or in our common unconscious, if you prefer the term. We have been enabled to give vent to them; to "externalize" troublesome inner drives, so to speak. They have been *distanced,* too, so that it is possible to weigh and judge—that is, to understand—them. And in this way we have achieved tragic enlightenment.

The passions and their consequences have been distanced, because shown operating in the drama of characters who are not actually ourselves, in spite of our ability to identify ourselves with them. They have been objectified, too, in being given concrete manifestations that we the spectators have been able to observe. And these manifestations have come to us, moreover, in objective dramatic form, in which occurrences have the logical sequence, order, and shape of art. In this process, "objectivity of form" has had for its correlate "objectivity of meaning." Objective correlates have been found for subjective impulses and feelings. Consequently, both the author and his public have moved well beyond pathos. And beyond esthetic response to "form," I would add; for such response, possible in cases of non-tragic drama, too, is not by itself *tragic enlightenment.*

If the process of purgation has been thorough, as it is in the case of true and complete tragedy on its highest levels, the inner tensions have been objectified in a manner that has enabled us to achieve insight into the realities of the human condition and of the world of facts and values in which thought and action transpire. For example, we have observed the laws of cause and effect in operation. We have seen relationships and conflicts exerting a variety of effects in accordance with the possibilities and inevitabilities of life. We have watched the desires and will of men influenced by and at war with such objective realities as the desire and will of other men, the laws of society, the moral sense of humanity, or the moral nature of the universe as understood by the author, who, in this respect, generally represents values more or less commonly held in his world. In the course of the dramatic development we have seen judgments being formed in the play. We have seen ideals violated and reestablished in the action and reaction of men with whom we have been enabled to identify ourselves. And these have been, in a sense, *total* men, for tragic art has given us rounded characterizations, who along with their emotions have revealed their moral values and the content of their intellect—their *ethos* and their *dianoia,* to use the Aristotelian terms.

Tragedy, in short, has given significant meaning to humanity, for the shape of tragedy is profoundly intellectual. The therapy of tragic catharsis could no more be complete and conclusive without intellect than any form of psychotherapy which brings the patient's inner tensions to light without enabling him to understand and master them. If tragedy did no more than objectify the emotions, it would not differ from other kinds of art. Comprehension is necessary if the tensions externalized in tragic form are to be mastered. And it is to be noted, indeed, that dramatic logic and superb articulateness characterize all of the world's tragic masterpieces of the past. *Enlightenment* is the final decisive victory, and the exhilaration or feeling of exaltation we derive from tragedy arises from this triumph of spirit pervaded by intellect. The very elevation or "stature" we have considered essential to the characters of high tragedy is an elevation of intellect—that is, of spirit made supremely conscious of itself by suffering. In tragedy, suffering is never futile, any more than it is accidental. It does not arise without a cause, the discovery of which is an aspect of the enlightenment attained in tragic drama. In this austere, disciplinary art, we suffer in order to understand.

For this reason, moreover, the exaltation and the final peace with which tragedy rewards us are pyramided on reality rather than on opiate romantic reassurances. There is, on the contrary, a profound *realism* in tragic art. I do not believe it is ever romantic art except in superficial respects, for which reason most of our Shakespearean productions, overstuffed and overdecorated in the illusion-mongering post-Elizabethan theatre, have been essentially *sub-tragic*. Tragedy, I repeat, is awareness. It is a full recognition of whatever realities the playwright chooses to represent; it is a keener, more penetrating, and more comprehensive awareness than placid experience makes possible. Tragic drama is too objective a form of representation to constitute a mere "ecstasy." The uplifting experience it provides is not pathological euphoria, not the elation of fancy and flight, in which there is no truth. The reverse is the case: we are elated because we have acquired the strength, for a time, to look truth full in the face. And a full look, or a full awareness, is a full *assent*. If tragedy affords us peace, it does so because it has awakened us, and not because it has doled out soporifics in the form of reassurances and condolences. A tragedian can no more be a sentimentalist than he can be a charlatan.

We may conclude then that neither the exaltation nor the peace of tragedy is mystical. It has an objective frame of reference in the actions of men and the conditions of human rather than supernatural reality. Tragedy is not religion nor a substitute for it. It has been wrongly publicized as such by modern writers who feel the need of religion without possessing the intellectual humility to acquire it. Tragic purgation, no matter how gratifying or ennobling its results, has, in my opinion, a more moderate and mundane basis than religious revelation. Having arrived, through observation and sympathy, at the grace of understanding, which is profoundly "self-understanding," we have successfully passed beyond the bourne of nebulous and chaotic emotionalism, and the process of catharsis has been fully consummated. Through the tragic experience, we have temporarily driven the devils out of our unconscious, so to speak. We have been freed of our demons, because we have not only been enabled to *see* them in operation, but have also come to *comprehend* them. And *knowing* them—and this is the noble temporary illusion that tragedy provides!—we believe we have somehow won control over them.

Tragic enlightenment, then, forms a triad with the Aristotelian "pity" and "fear"—the third necessary element, not noted by Aristotle, in the dynamics of tragedy. It is, moreover, not merely the third element in the process of catharsis but the *decisive* one, because the only factor that masters the expelled tensions is human understanding.

In the tragic action, the playwright brings the dramatic conflict to an end, achieving a stage of rest and a sense of completion. Tragic action, as Aristotle realized and as playwrights evidently realized long before he ever wrote his *Poetics,* is a "complete action." But our own experience as spectators is not completed so long as we ourselves remain in a state of tension and confusion. Even if the tragic character should be brought to a point in the play when he understands his errors and assents to his fate, it is still necessary for *us* to assent, which it is possible to do only with our intelligence.

No matter how well the action or the main character's destiny is resolved, the anarchic forces, the "pity" and the "fear," evoked by the tragedy cannot by themselves establish a suitable inner equilibrium. Only enlightenment, a clear comprehension by us of the forces involved in the struggle, an understanding of cause and effect, a judgment on what we have witnessed, a frame of mind that carries us above the riot of passion can effect the necessary equilibrium. It is not enough to have seen the tragic character put his house of disorder into order. We must put order into our own.

Had Aristotle pursued his investigation of classic drama closer, I like to believe he would have surely arrived at some such view himself. The author of the *Nicomachean Ethics* and the *Politics* could not have failed to discover the decisive role of enlightenment in the purgation afforded by the tragedies of Aeschylus, Sophocles, and Euripides. To adopt Nietzsche's terminology from *The Birth of Tragedy,* Greek tragedy imposed the Apollonian world of light and reason upon the Dionysian world of passion. The Apollonian element in the plot and verse of the plays, including the great choral passages, ordered and so mastered the Dionysian emotional disequilibrium. I believe the same point can be demonstrated in Elizabethan tragedy, in the work of Corneille and Racine, and in later tragedy.

II. "ENLIGHTENMENT" AND MODERN DRAMA

When I first considered the tragic principle of Enlightenment in 1937, in a piece written for the now defunct *One-Act Play Magazine and Theatre Review* (it gained some currency, and a revised statement of my views subsequently appeared in the American supplement of the 1947 Crown Publishers edition of Barrett H. Clark's *European Theories of the Drama*) I intended to propound a view, perhaps naïvely, that could support the efforts of playwrights to present contemporary realities without feeling that they were for that reason hopelessly excluded from the exalted company of the tragedians. And I wanted them to be more aware of the rich possibilities of tragic art than they appeared to be while they were engaged in writing about these realities.

Willing though I had been to extend patience and the best of my understanding to them, I had to consider that they were in danger of reaching an impasse, if they had not already reached it, in presenting contemporary issues solely on the levels of problem drama. On one hand, the social theatre of the nineteen-thirties had begun to slump into a state of moribund repetitiousness, and few of its playwrights were fulfilling the promise we had found in their early strivings. On the other hand, those few had given enough indications of a bent for so much more than topicality that the effort to make them aware of a larger reach might not be wasted. Clifford Odets had certainly given such evidence ever since writing *Awake and Sing!* And among members of an older generation, Maxwell Anderson was manifestly, perhaps even too obviously, reaching for the tragic crown after having had his bout with the immediate political scene in his 1933 Pulitzer Prize satire *Both Your Houses.* Two years later in *Winterset,* in fact, he had attempted to perform the very thing I had in mind, namely, represent and express contemporary life and, at the same time, achieve tragic power. I did not believe he had entirely succeeded in *Winterset,* however. He had no sooner faced the substance of his subject, the subversion of justice, in his generally excellent second act than he flew away from it into a world of reminiscent romanticism. *Winterset* became a tragedy less by logic of characterization and theme than by the imposed rhetoric of Anderson's definition of tragedy. The reality of young Mio's pursuit of justice for his victimized father underwent a false transfiguration into grandiloquent assertions concerning the power of love and of the dignity of man by the tragic lovers Mio and Miriamne and by an extremely voluble member of the rabbinate. And in noting this danger of misconceiving tragedy as an expedient for flight and as a springboard for evasion, I felt a further need of extending my views on tragic drama.

I intended my concept of Enlightenment to assert the possibility of facing reality in the context of a real, rather than legendary or romanticized and sentimentalized, world. I wanted to say in so many words that a play can be, *in its time,* both social drama and tragedy.

I did not know in 1937 that Maxwell Anderson had also begun to struggle with the concept of Enlightenment, although I never, of course, believed that my view that tragedy had to have meaning had been foreign to playwrights ever since Aeschylus entered the theatre. Anderson, following the "tragic gleam" in 1938 with a "compass," as he put it, arrived at a theory similar to mine, proving that my concern with catharsis and its implications did not begin and end with critics. Aristotle had noted the powerful dramatic effect of a "recognition scene"—that is, the recognition (*anagnorisis*) of one character by another, in Greek tragedies. Some of these scenes (the meeting of Orestes and his sister Electra in Mycenae and that of Orestes and his other sister, Iphigenia, in Tauris) are known to every educated playwright. But the idea of *anagnorisis,* or recognition, can be legitimately extended to the discovery of hidden facts as well as disguised or hitherto unidentified persons. The discovery that Oedipus makes about himself in Sophocles' tragedy gives us perhaps the greatest tragic scene in all literature. With this fact in mind, Anderson came to realize that "recognition scenes" were also present in post-classic drama. He arrived at the conclusion in his essay *The Essence of Tragedy* that the mechanism in modern tragedy is "a discovery by the hero of some element in the environment or in his own personality of which he has not been aware—or which he has not taken sufficiently into account." And seeking to translate this observation into a working principle of playwriting, Anderson proposed the following formulation: "A play should lead up to and away from a central crisis, and this crisis should consist in a discovery by the leading character which has an indelible effect on his thought and emotion and completely alters his course or action."

Anderson refers further on in his essay to the "spiritual awakening or regeneration" of his hero; and John Mason Brown, amplifying Anderson's views in *The Tragic Blueprint,* further exalts this "fulfilment of self" as a spiritual process so purifying that tragic heroes are "fated to leave this earth spiritually cross-ventilated." It is plain, then, that this view of tragic recognition concerns something else and something more than a boy's discovery of the class struggle and recognition of the need to fight for better warehouse conditions in Odets' *Awake and Sing.*

Maxwell Anderson's stimulating theory of "recognition," however, has dangers and limitations. It might be mistaken for the Victorian Sunday School notion of art as a moral lesson. Enlightenment is dramatically ineffective without the collaboration of "pity" and "fear" in an intense complication of dramatic events, and should not be confused with a simple prescription for action, or a mere realization on the part of the tragic character that he was right or wrong. Tragic enlightenment is an *experience,* not a moral tag such as schoolteachers once looked for when teaching Shakespeare's plays to their charges.

Enlightenment is certainly not knowledge imposed, but knowledge *won.* And this is the case even when the tragedy makes some opinion explicit, whether by the characters, as altogether too insistently in the third act of *Winterset,* or by a Greek chorus. When some judgment is explicit in a successful tragedy, it reflects character, as when Othello sums up the error of his life before stabbing himself, or when Macbeth succumbs to despair on receiving the news of Lady Macbeth's death—which does not, however, prevent him from sallying forth to fight his enemies. Or the moral comment is tragically irrelevant and therefore ironic, as it is when the chorus of Theban senators mouths platitudes while Sophocles' Antigone goes to her death.

The most dangerous assumptions concerning tragic art, however, are those that recommend "ennoblement," "enlightenment," or, in Anderson's case, "recognition" as a spiritual exercise of the highest order. Four assumptions bolster this climactic assumption. They are as follows:

1. Tragedy is an emotional orgy of "pity" and "fear"—an ecstasy, so to speak.
2. Tragedy achieves a cleansing of the soul, a *katharsis.*
3. Tragedy must have universality.
4. Man possesses or attains stature in tragedy, or possesses stature initially and becomes even more exalted in the course of the drama. (With respect to this view, too, it must be noted that Aristotle spoke more moderately than his successors, writing that "tragedy is an imitation of persons who are above the common level" and should "preserve the type and yet ennoble it.")

Since some validity can easily be found in each of these principles, they add up to a considerable claim for tragic art. And when it is pressed forcefully enough, it establishes a formidable standard to which the modern drama that concerns itself directly with the modern world and employs the idioms of our time cannot measure up. It is not certain that even the classics of tragedy actually meet the expectations that can be aroused by the altogether too romantic wording of these claims in our time.

For Edith Hamilton, who does not actually lose herself in beatitudes, tragedy deals with "the only true aristocracy, that of passionate souls." Essential in the opinion of Joseph Wood Krutch is the playwright's belief in "the greatness and importance of men." The tragedian must make "a profession of faith"; he may "not believe in God, but must believe in man."

For Maxwell Anderson, the playwright must so arrange his story that it will prove that men pass through suffering purified, "that animal though we are in some ways, there is in us all some divine, incalculable fire that urges us to be better than we are." And for John Mason Brown, "death, not life" ultimately becomes the "high concern" of tragic heroes "made whole by their suffering" who are "fated to leave this earth spiritually cross-ventilated." Such are the requirements of a school of criticism that, in compensating for diminished views of humanity by modern realism and modern life alike, departs from Aristotle's plainer humanism and may be denominated Romantic Aristotelianism.

An *ersatz*-mystique, suspect alike to social and to religious realists, can be charged against a fetishist overemphasis of "spiritual awakening" and other towering flights romantically predicated for tragedy. The gospel of salvation by tragic art, which makes catharsis an equivalent or substitute for the "dark night of the soul" described by Spain's mystic poet St. John of the Cross, presses too large a claim for the worldly art of the theatre.

Tragedy, in my view, has its own more modest, if sufficient, place in any hierarchy of values, as we may readily realize the moment we ask whether the writing or witnessing of a play ever changed the moral character of anybody and altered the pattern of his behavior. And that place must certainly be defined in less elevated terms if modern playwrights are to bring the freight of their world with them into the theatre. If they fly too high on Icarian wings, the wings of literary ambition, they will drop into a sea of banality in the course of their rhetorical aspirations toward spiritual significance. They would do better to find support in a strongly grounded religion, as the Catholic poet Paul Claudel realized, or in a simple faith, as Tolstoy realized. Otherwise they may give an impression of self-inflation, such as can be charged against Anderson at the conclusion of *Winterset* and not against Tolstoy in the dénouement of *The Power of Darkness,* O'Casey in the last act of *The Plough and the Stars,* Shaw in the trial and execution scenes of *Saint Joan,* or O'Neill in the resolution of *Desire Under the Elms.* Scorn of earth is a *hybris* as dangerous to playwrights as to other persons.

A major confusion is caused, I believe, by extreme, romantic interpretations of the idea that a tragedy must have "universality." The assumption is made that this can be achieved only by escaping from the actual action or substance of a play, from a specific context of reality, into the vast inane of generalizations about life and spirituality. Ibsen and all later realists are accused of a crime against tragic drama for minimizing this view of universality—a view patently flamboyant by comparison with that of Aristotle, who introduced the concept of universality into criticism. "By the universal," Aristotle explained unpretentiously, "I mean how a person of a certain type will on occasion speak or act according to the law of probability or necessity."

Proponents of "universality" have tended to draw up an indictment of modern realistic drama on the grounds of its relevancy. This view encourages confusion and error both in theory and practice. It sometimes leads to the extravagant conclusion that virtually all modern drama that has had any claim to social reality has been unworthy. It has led idealists of the Gordon Craig and "art theatre" school to legitimize only misty dramatic literature such as the plays of Maeterlinck, cultivated naïveté, the masterpiece of which is André Obey's *Noah,* and at best sophisticated versions of myth, such as Cocteau's Oedipus tragedy, *The Infernal Machine.* Only irony, at which Europeans are more adept than Americans, secures some of these plays against banality, for irony takes into account reality by noting contradictions in human behavior and fate. In generalizations, the result is too frequently an academic kind of playwriting that no one can produce, hieratic art which snuggles under the shadow of some great cathedral, or more or less sophomoric theatricality parading as profundity. To different degrees, O'Neill succumbed to the latter in *The Fountain, Dynamo, Lazarus Laughed,* and other plays. Some of the "universalist" efforts—those that are clever if rather less than tragic, those that possess simplicity, and the very few that, like Claudel's *The Tidings Brought to Mary* or Eliot's *Murder in the Cathedral,* are founded on traditional faith —deserve a place in our theatre. But even the best of these cannot ensure its vitality. By comparison with the major plays of Ibsen, Strindberg, Chekhov, Shaw, and O'Casey, for example, they seem either attenuated or remote—or strained.

Surely the theatre in our time cannot subsist on a diet of "universals" untranslated into recognizably contemporary manners, sensibility, and events. Plays such as *The Infernal Machine, Noah,* Fry's *The Boy with a Cart,* and even *Murder in the Cathedral* can be the dessert, but not the main course, in contemporary theatre. Eliot, himself, realized this when he resolved to make the theatre a vocation rather than an avocation. He deliberately turned from *Murder in the Cathedral* to *Family Reunion* and *The Cocktail Party,* in which he tried to steep theology in quotidian reality and to express his Anglo-Catholic philosophy in the familiar terms of English comedy of manners. He arranged a partnership, so to speak, between St. Augustine and Noel Coward in *The Cocktail Party.* His new play *The Confidential Clerk,* which I have neither seen nor read as yet, gives every indication of carrying this austere poet further into the not necessarily inglorious marketplace.

In stage production, moreover, even the older "universal" drama has suffered at the hands of artists whose predilection for universality becomes a case of moral and spiritual elephantiasis. Grandeur becomes the first mark of such universalization of the classics by production art. We see this in the fashionable overproduction of Shakespeare's drama, in which the settings, born of the misty universalism of Gordon Craig, tower over the actors and swathe Shakespeare's intensely immediate human drama in a universal fog. And in acting, the results tend to be the kind of attitudinizing and overprecise elocutionary delivery of Shakespeare's lines that vitiate performances by Maurice Evans and by many German actors who play *"unser Shakespeare"* as though he were Schiller.

I have nothing against "universals," but it seems to me that the only universals favored by those who criticize modern drama and try to flee from its realism into "Art" are *dead* ones. They are "dead" in the sense that the so-called universal recognitions are presented with little or no relation to substantial pressures of contemporary reality. Universals are conveniently removed from contemporary tensions, especially if they are social in character; conveniently, because the generalizations are made without reference to verifiable fact or after observable facts have been discarded. It seems to me, on the contrary, that our theatre has been made more vital by an *All My Sons,* for all its rough texture, than by an *Elizabeth the Queen,* for all its glossy one, just as the theatre of half a century ago was more vitalized by *Hedda Gabler* than by *Francesca di Rimini.*

Universals for universals, moreover, there is for me a greater, intenser realization of humanity's eternal urgencies in Lorca's *House of Bernarda Alba* (in the context of Spanish country life) or in Odets' *Awake and Sing!* (in the context of metropolitan American life) than in *The Cocktail Party* (in the context of English life). The conflict between the arid family pride of Bernarda Alba and her daughters' desire for love has more substantial universality than the conflict that leads to an off-stage martyrdom in *The Cocktail Party.* An indigent Bronx family's struggles in *Awake and Sing!* brings us closer to universality than Eliot's domestic squabbles in "polite" society. Eliot, moreover, resolves these with far less universality of principle than Odets resolves conflicts in *Awake and Sing!* in noting the failure of compromise for the sake of security and the renunciation of narrow values by the son of the family. When young Ralph starts reading his grandfather's books, turns his inheritance over to his mother, and decides to demand "steam in the warehouse"—flat as these decisions may be—he asserts something just as relevant to human life as Eliot's recognition of the power of Grace—namely, ordinary humanity's capacity for selfless idealism or, at least, rebellion against a narrow, grubbing existence. Everything we have called civilization and much that we have called the life of the spirit have emanated from that restlessness and revolt.

As an incipient Marxist, Ralph is little more than a pipsqueak, and the logic of his cheering his sister Hennie on when she walks out on her husband and child is highly vulnerable. Ralph remains on too low a level of awakening for tragedy when he translates his conversion into specifications within the limits of his mentality and of the situations in the play. But in so far as Odets focuses attention on the boy's capacity for spiritual awakening, his vision draws close to that of Isaiah, from whom he derived the title of his play, a gospel much more universal, as well as reliable, than any gospel according to the garden variety of Marxists whom Odets may have followed in 1935. The most serious limitations of *Awake and Sing!* are that the enlightenment of Hennie, when she runs away with her racketeer-lover, is rather spurious, and that Ralph's enlightenment has not been directly worked out by him for us through any action on his part before he arrives at his conclusions and decisions. These seem tagged on to the play as a lesson, as though they were an afterthought or imposed by the requirements of "social significance" for a playwright of the nineteen-thirties, who was expected to provide a "conversion-ending." Ralph has achieved "recognition," to use Anderson's term, more as an onlooker than as the active agent of the drama, and anything that an observer concludes in a play is a moral tag. If this view of *Awake and Sing!* is unjust to the play as a whole, this is because the action of the play as a family study does involve us in an experience from which insight can be gained dramatically rather than by merely subscribing to a conversion ending. And that insight can be greater than that achieved by Ralph and Hennie. It can be the larger vision of their grandfather, who has rejected materialism, whereas they only rejected compromise; or it can be a view of life enforced by the play which demonstrates man's rebellion against pettiness. That the vision or experience is not of the highest order of intensity and comprehensiveness is merely a concomitant of the nature of the play as *drama* rather than tragedy—that is, of a work that mixes modes of drama in order to carry us beyond tragic acquiescence into mundane activism. In the social context used by Odets, that activism tracks the dust of thoroughfares into the tragic theatre.

An absolute distinction between the particular and the universal experience is, in fact, impossible. Immediate realities contain and imply universal ones. Even our most unvarnished economic and political struggles can be related to the universals of desire, anxiety, suffering, and fear of deprivation, pain, and extinction; they can, in the work of a genuine creation, rather than a disguised tract, involve love and hate, loyalty and treason, selfishness and self-sacrifice, honor and dishonor, falsehood and truth, good and evil. And this is only another way of saying that anything we call universal is only a generalization of immediate and specific concerns. Of even "topical" concerns: If we could put ourselves in the place of an Athenian spectator at the first performance of *The Trojan Women,* the Oresteian trilogy, or any other effective tragedy, we would not speak so glibly of universals as though they had no social—or, for that matter, concrete political—relevance whatsoever. In *The Trojan Women,* for example, the issues of "imperialistic aggression" were comparable to the "rape of Belgium" in the First World War, and were just as "topical"— and, of course, just as relevant to personal experience for Athenians. *Richard II,* with its theme of the deposition of a medieval monarch, was "topical" during the Essex Rebellion, and was considered to be such by Elizabeth's government. Universality should not be construed as vacuity in a play. Everything we designate as universal was at one time, and in one sense or another, immediate—socially *and* personally. It couldn't have been universal, indeed, if it couldn't possibly have any immediacy for the playgoer.

The failure of modern plays as tragic art must have other causes than contemporaneity of substance. I would venture the view that a reason for failure will be found in the social dramatist's, let alone the propagandist's, failure to achieve a real tragic catharsis. He fails chiefly because in striving so arduously for an element of "enlightenment," or for the conversion of his characters and the audience to his point of view, he so often substitutes statement for dramatic process. He neglects to effectuate the "pity" and the "fear"—that is, the tensions and the empathy implicit in these Aristotelian terms. Although it is the combination of "pity," "fear," and "enlightenment" that produces tragic catharsis, his assault-strategy makes the frontal attack with "enlightenment" or "conversion" but forgets about the flanks. The unsupported frontal assault soon crumbles, since there is no effective tragic enlightenment when the play lacks compelling human reality. Emotions deeply rooted in character being absent, no rapport has been established between the observer in the auditorium and the actor on the stage except on a basis of superficial agreement or partisanship more or less extraneous to art. That rapport may be lacking for one of several reasons, such as the case-history character of a "problem play" situation, which instantly makes us the observer instead of the participant in an action. This can be the case even when we sympathize with the victim of social circumstance, as we do in Galsworthy's *Justice.* Another reason is the human insignificance of the characters, which is the case when they are insufficiently individualized or used directly for the purpose of demonstrating a point or mouthing a precept. Such characters make only superficial claims on us. They are not compelling enough to draw a response from the depths in us.

We may sum up the case against many realistic treatments of the problems of our time by saying that the plays have moved us a little and informed us a little but have not moved us sufficiently, because they have merely stirred our sentiments, and have not informed us sufficiently, because they have beclouded their argument with these same sentiments. The result has been middling drama that rests on low levels of emotionalism and intellectuality alike. Universality-worship will certainly not remove this deficiency any more than mere inebriation with tragic grandeur will. Only a sufficiently comprehensive view of the dramatic factor of "enlightenment" can help the modern playwright who does not propose to sever his relationship to his times or renounce his intention to have his say about them, and yet aspires to produce tragic art.

Shall we say with one school of literary critics that we have had no tragedies because playwrights stopped writing poetry? This cannot be the case, since there is no evidence whatsoever that catharsis is directly dependent upon poetry. The experience of catharsis with which we are concerned is an experience of theatre or action. It is the result of our observing the doing and the suffering of a thing. It is not primarily a matter of language (surely Martha Graham can effect a catharsis without uttering a word), and Aristotle, in his clear, if somewhat pedestrian or mechanical, fashion, was surely more sensible in treating the language of tragedy separately, almost as an embellishment, than some "New Critics" who consider language in the drama as an end in itself, as though it were lyric poetry, and interpret a play by explicating the lines of verse. Aristotle, who considered the plot, or *mythos,* paramount and the language of a play secondary, had more theatre in his bones than all critics who treat tragedy exclusively as poetry. Besides, it should be evident that the exalted language must come from *something* in the play, from the characters. That is, from incentives to great poetry in their circumstances and frame of mind. Shakespeare, not to mention Sophocles, can instruct us on this subject.

Next, we may consider whether we can concede the point made by Joseph Wood Krutch, and by those who have borrowed from his book *The Modern Temper,* that tragic art has been virtually extinct because the modern sceptical and scientific outlook has reduced man's stature. Mr. Krutch argued ably and eloquently. But it is not clear that his argument applies ineluctably to the dynamics of catharsis. I fail to comprehend why a character's failure to measure up to the "stature" of Hamlet or Lear must be a deterrent to "pity" and "fear." The case of Willy Loman in the successful American production of *Death of a Salesman* would disprove this assumption. It is precisely because Willy was a common man that American audiences felt *pity* for him and *feared* for themselves. Willy was a sort of suburban Everyman with whom audiences readily established a connection, if not indeed an actual identification.

It does not, however, follow that tragedy itself has been well served by a reduction in the stature of dramatic characters, and Joseph Wood Krutch is not refuted when we maintain that "pity" and "fear" have not been banished from the modern theatre. For the purposes of tragedy, "pity and fear," according to my view, are unavailing unless they form a triad with *enlightenment,* and unless this marriage of emotion and understanding lifts us above the perturbing events of a play. The neurotic is cured only when he is brought out of the nightmare world of his inner conflicts by his recognition and understanding of their nature and source. The sinner is redeemed only after he has understood the true nature of his situation. The neurotic's experience and the sinner's parallel the experience of the tragic catharsis. When a dramatic character lacks the stature to understand reality (and in this respect, the language of the character is, of course, decidedly revealing)—*to understand after he has had experiences that compel understanding,* we are deprived of the possibility of achieving identification on a sufficiently high level of enlightenment.

We may understand the nature of his plight; we may understand why he failed in his human career. But our view becomes too clinical or sociological to provide a sense of exaltation. A physician or a social worker is not exalted in making a proper diagnosis. (And diagnoses in carefully written realistic drama are fairly obvious, too.) The relationship which becomes, then, too much like that of patient and diagnostician prevents sufficient identification for us to make a sufficient ascent for or with the character. We can pity him, as we pity the Willy Loman of *Death of a Salesman,* just as we can make obvious deductions concerning his situation, but we cannot attain sufficient enlightenment through the agency of his person.

Inevitably, I believe, we are driven to the conclusion that there are actually *two* species of enlightenment—one fundamentally *tragic,* and the other fundamentally *non-tragic.* Non-tragic enlightenment may have many values but lacks the decisive value for tragedy of ensuring a true catharsis. We cannot have truly tragic enlightenment when the character's mental and spiritual endowment is so low that he cannot give us a proper cue for vision, or cannot set us an example of how high humanity can vault. In true tragedy, we witness the leap of a human being above the level of victim, villain, fool, or erring man in spite of the individual's being "accident-prone," "evil-prone," or "error-prone," as the case may be in the particular play.

There is reason, then, for stressing the value of tragic stature, for such stature is, of course, a matter of mind or spirit. We must be on guard only against assuming that there is an absolute measure of stature that we can apply categorically to every character. Concerning Miller's Willy Loman, I have been inclined to say that Willy the victim of economics or victim of his own fatuous view of life lacks tragic stature, but that Willy the impassioned man, who is loyal to an ideal of himself and of his son Biff, possesses it. The question is simply whether we find in this second Willy an instance of tragic will or an example of merely pathetic self-delusion.

III. THE SUBVERSION OF ENLIGHTENMENT

Has the element of enlightenment been slighted in so enlightened an age as the modern in which every man, woman, and child has been exposed to a steady stream of discussion and analysis? It has not been slighted. It has suffered a worse fate so far as tragic art is concerned. It has been *misconceived* and *misused,* or subverted. It has been too narrowed down, boiled down to a prescription, or rationalized into a clever idea. Partly as a result of this tendency, comedy has been enriched, middle or hybrid drama (a cross between comedy and tragedy) has been sharpened, and propagandistic drama has been intensified. But tragedy has been debased. Like certain European currencies, tragedy has often been devalued to such a degree that it has lost its character as currency and been rendered worthless. And tragedy has been devalued to the degree to which the element of *enlightenment* has been devalued and become a factor of mere moralizing (in nineteenth-century melodrama), mere social indignation (in propagandistic drama), mere heroics (in revolutionary melodrama), or a mere mixture of pity and analysis—in various degrees of social drama or, for that matter, in psychological drama.

This sorry process started not with Ibsen, as careless critics and historians maintain. That Ibsen possessed a tragedian's temperament is amply shown in *Brand, Hedda Gabler, Rosmersholm, The Master Builder,* and *John Gabriel Borkman.* The decline started when the moralizing and sentimentalizing middle-class dramatists of the eighteenth century began to substitute noble or moral sentiment for tragic enlightenment. The decline was hastened by the romantic playwright who reduced enlightenment to a drum-roll of revolt or idealism. And the devaluation was completed, actually before the advent of distinctively modern drama, by Scribe, who put hokum into both historical costume and modern dress drama, and by his followers, the writers of "well-made" (that is, contrived) problem plays.

Contemporary perverters of tragedy among playwrights, then, are descended from pre-Ibsenite writers. A few of these had philosophical capacities or pretensions. Others were impressive poets, such as Hugo and Schiller. (The latter did write one true tragedy, *The Death of Wallen-*

stein, and one classic imitation, *The Bride of Messina.*) Let us not call all romantic playwrights shallow. But very rarely did they have a *tragic* sense of life. That would have required an awareness of "life's impossibilities," of limitations imposed upon man by the nature of things and by the nature of man, which cannot be poetically dissolved by sentiment or "reformed" out of existence. In the great wave of optimism and liberal idealism which extended from about 1770 to at least 1914, only maverick playwrights could retain the tragic sense of life. Among these Kleist, Büchner, Hebbel, Tolstoy, Ibsen, Strindberg, Curel, Claudel, Wedekind, Synge, O'Neill, Yeats, Lorca, Sartre, and Montherlant come most readily to my mind. And even among writers of this breed, there were a number who were more or less drawn into the orbit of non-tragic serious drama by the lodestone of "idealism" and social criticism or of "psychology."

Let us consider *Ghosts* more closely as an example. And *Ghosts* is worth considering, because Ibsen's triumph with it was so signal that a respectable and significant *genre* of "non-tragic tragedy"—plays tragic in many respects but not quite tragedies—became possible in the modern theatre. We cannot maintain that *Ghosts* fails to generate "pity" and "fear." Only the low-grade quality of the element of enlightenment that pervades this play prevents it from achieving a thorough tragic catharsis. What Mrs. Alving (and through her experience the player or reader himself) has learned in the course of the action is too closely and concretely linked to the possibilities, by no means remote or difficult, of social reform. Consequently, the dramatic conflict in the work does not engage us profoundly enough for tragedy. Nor does the "enlightenment" or "recognition" won through the dramatic experience in *Ghosts.* To reduce the argument to some simple formulation of idea is not entirely fair to the protoplasm of a play in which characters are as alive as they are in *Ghosts.* But both friends and enemies of the play offered formulations, and the play itself encouraged them. And to discuss the "ideas" in it is to discover that the enlightenment it can provide as a dramatic experience lacks the perspectives of high tragedy, even though Ibsen's symbolizing faculty and use of irony lifted his play above the lower levels of didactic drama. The dramatic experience and the "ideas" intrinsic in *Ghosts* are one essence, so that if the ideas engage us on a certain level the experience must, too.

Shall we take the most comprehensive practical view—and a practical view is enforced by Ibsen himself. In that case, we would describe the "enlightenment" not too facetiously as a realization that a narrow education and morality provide poor preparation for a successful marriage for a girl, and that wives should not return to rakehell husbands despite the demands of convention—for if they do, the results will be distressing. All this has considerable importance to the sociologist or educator who believes that here is a situation that needs, and is susceptible of, improvement. But it means precisely nothing to a true tragedian, for whom human bedevilment and human destiny are infinitely more complicated and less calculable. *Ghosts,* like so many otherwise valuable modern plays, can provide analyses and challenges, and these may have a practical value. This may be called *practical enlightenment.* But *Ghosts* does not provide a sufficiency of *tragic enlightenment,* and the play as a whole remains greatly on a level of mundane considerations.

Ghosts is, therefore, incompletely tragic, in spite of its often insufficiently noted, but very estimable, tragic atmosphere, its tragic Mrs. Alving (who has the "stature" of a tragic heroine, in the sense that she suffers intensely and is attaining emotional depth), and its poetically, as well as realistically, established tragic theme of the domestic Até or Alving family curse. Brooding, intense, bitter, and ironic, *Ghosts* definitely is. Tragic, in any thorough sense of the term, it is not. Nor could it be, so long as the decisive complications and revelations rest, in one way or another, on some easy conclusion, such as that catastrophe in Mrs. Alving's life could have been avoided by sex education at home and at finishing school and, later, by a divorce or permanent separation between the Alvings.

Let us look still more closely at the logic intrinsic to the play. It is not the logic of high tragedy, but the logic of the sociology and medical science of a particular period. "Had Mrs. Alving been a less frigid bride and young wife, her husband might have found satisfaction in the home" is one way of formulating the precipitating factor in Mrs. Alving's fortunes. If this is correct, then how easy it all seems, and how inconclusive is the argument in so far as we try to relate it "tragically" to human nature and destiny—to "life's impossibilities," so to speak. The argument concerning the failure of conventional morality cannot be considered an iron-clad one even in the light of plain realistic considerations of human behavior and its incalculability. Does it necessarily follow that Mr. Alving would have been faithful to Mrs. Alving had she been a successful product of one of our progressive schools, or an unblushing bride? All we can say is that, accepting Ibsen's views, the probability of a happy marriage would have been greater. Another way to formulate the problem is to declare that if Mrs. Alving had refused to return to her husband, she might not have passed venereal disease on to her son Oswald. Yet there is surely the possibility that she might have returned to Alving and *not* transferred the disease. An alternative between tragedy and a thorough physical checkup suggests itself in *Ghosts,* and this is a patently absurd notion to the tragic sense of life that views the reality of man, morality, and fate in an infinitely harder light.

IV. THE DEGREES OF DRAMA

Still it must be noted that there have been in the modern theatre degrees of failure to attain tragedy, and degree is a decisive consideration in matters of art. There is, for example, the merely moralistic play, and this genre, whether represented by Lillo's late eighteenth-century play *The London Merchant* or a play by Channing Pollock, is low indeed by any standard, not to mention that of tragedy. On a par with the moralizing piece is the purely sentimental one, of which *The Lady of the Camellias* is the classic example. And the variants of sentimental drama are many; we have even had admixtures of sentimentality and hard-boiled naturalism, such as Hauptmann's *Hannele*. Then there is "thesis drama," which has given considerable content to the theatre of a year or a decade. Problem plays were and can still be stimulating in proportion to their penetration into the realities of character and environment, as well as to the integrity of their dramatic logic. Thesis drama can attain the high level of *Justice* as well as the low one of Brieux' *Damaged Goods*. And there is the "naturalistic" play in which the fact of a situation is allowed to speak for itself. If the "slice of life" is not presented merely as rank sensationalism, it can win our respect as a transcript made more or less meaningful by the values and judgments implied or exposed in it. A naturalistic play may be nontragic and yet fairly engrossing. And if a play, whatever the style or subject, evokes "pity" and "fear" on some level of intelligent interest, it can ascend as far as the foothills of tragedy.

In that case—and I would cite as examples *Ghosts*, Hauptmann's *Drayman Henschel*, Gorky's *The Lower Depths*, and, in spite of its clinical character, *A Streetcar Named Desire*—the play rises high in the order of "serious drama." It may not be called strictly a tragedy and yet possess a tragic quality. Certainly more than just a "slice of life" or a "problem play," it acts upon us as near-tragedy. We might perpetuate an oxymoron on behalf of such a drama and call it "tragic non-tragedy." This last-mentioned genre, whatever we choose to call it, has been especially abundant in the modern theatre, but it would be a mistake to assume that it first arose in the nineteenth century. Euripides' clinical drama *Orestes* and the Elizabethan play *Arden of Feversham* are early examples. Better still, we might call these and other plays, such as *Hedda Gabler*, *The Father*, and *Death of a Salesman*, "low tragedy" in order to signify a distinction between them and the rare indisputably "high" tragedies of the modern theatre, such as *Saint Joan*, *Desire Under the Elms*, and Lorca's *Blood Wedding*.

The distinction is not based on the quality of the language in the plays, although obtrusively weak language would constitute a disqualification for both high and low tragedy—or for any sort of drama. And a contrast between prose drama, to be considered "low," and verse drama, to be considered "high," tells us too little about the essential difference in tragic power. In my view, the distinction is fundamentally one in the *quality of tragic enlightenment*. There is a difference between earth-bound realizations, limited to "psychology" or social situation, as in the case of some plays we could call "low tragedy," and the wide prospect or world-view that permeates such "high tragedies" as *Oedipus the King, Hamlet,* and *Saint Joan.* It is the world-view, whether or not the main character himself completely possesses it, that raises the stature of the tragic hero and that enables him to leave the world "spiritually cross-ventilated" upon his death, to adopt John Mason Brown's phrase. It is the world-view penetrating the author's personality and his play that also gives the hero's language wings for a true flight and justifies poetry in the play as something more than embellishment or convention, if the author can write such poetry. Those critics who desiderate poetry for high tragedy (Leavis, T. S. Eliot, John Crowe Ransom) have urged, I believe, a justifiable aspiration. But we put the cart before the horse if we think that the language comes before the characters, the spirit, and the intrinsic outlook of the work.

In so far as the world-view is omitted, diminished or obfuscated by modern realism, sociology, or psychological science, modern drama cannot at best rise higher than "low tragedy." The characters of the drama may struggle intensely, but their stakes and the author's gambit in treating them are likely to be limited. They may suffer acutely, but they are unlikely to somehow involve the universe in their anguish. That this is true in the case of Ibsen's Hedda or the "Captain" in Strindberg's *The Father* can be only too easily determined by a reading of the text. And even if "low tragedy" characters rise to some degree of understanding or, through their personality and action, enable the spectator to do so, their "recognitions" will leave out ultimate realizations of the human condition or of man's adventure in the universe. Borrowing an intuition from Jung for convenience, we may say that such characters will observe or make us observe every sort of reality except *archetypal* reality. And their *agon* or action will give us every kind of plot but will never approximate the depth and universality we attribute to "myth" but which can be supremely present in plays such as *Hamlet, Macbeth,* and *King Lear,* which are not "myth."

Whether or not high tragedy *can* be created in the context of modern civilization and modern theatre seems to me an academic consideration, because it will be certainly created when the author's vision and his subject meet, as they met when Shaw wrote *Saint Joan.* And that "low tragedy" has been created in the modern theatre can be sufficiently apparent from a review of the drama since the advent of Ibsen.

V. POSTSCRIPT

That is as far as I dare go in elaborating my views without bursting the seams of the essay. I would otherwise have woven several other points into the fabric of the argument.

The first and most obvious point is that playwrights should be exempt from criticism when they obviously did not want to create tragedy for one good reason or another related to their desire to express their age or their anti-tragic outlook upon modern life. This was true of Shaw except when he came to write *St. Joan,* and it is true of Bertolt Brecht. A deliberate attempt to write modern forms of tragi-comedy, "dark comedy," or anti-heroic drama should not only be exempted from criticism because it isn't tragedy but should be respected when it is an intelligently conceived and written departure from tragedy. Among examples to be cited are Becque's *The Vultures,* Strindberg's *There Are Crimes and Crimes,* and Chekhov's *Uncle Vanya.*

It should be noted, too, that Chekhov created his own kind of substitute for standard types of tragedy in all the plays he wrote after *Ivanov,* even if he himself was incapable of defining the type adequately. That he referred to his particular kind of deeply sympathetic, if also ironic and wryly humorous, tragedy of attrition as "comedy" is disconcerting. But defining a work of art is, of course, of small consequence by comparison with the effect of the work. If Chekhov appears to us to be perverse or willful in insisting on the comic character of his work, he is also plainly bent on differentiating it from a stereotype of tragedy, as well as from the indeterminate nature of ordinary thesis-drama. Chekhov did not give us tragedy in the standardized sense of the term. Instead he gave us something else, something uniquely his own, and the results have been found eminently satisfactory. It would be wrong to say that Chekhov tried to write standardized tragedy but misfired. In *The Three Sisters* and *The Cherry Orchard* he wrote dramas of attrition and default, with comic and ironic overtones. And if "low tragedy" is all that he achieved in *The Three Sisters,* then surely our theatre would do well to have more low tragedy of equal calibre. And if Chekhov's definition of *The Sea Gull* and *The Cherry Orchard* as comedies is correct, then our theatre hasn't lost anything either. Nor does the mixture of comedy and tragedy in *Juno and the Paycock,* so astringent and so poignant, leave us regretful that O'Casey did not adopt the grand tragic manner favored by Maxwell Anderson. Obviously, O'Casey found a unique way of expressing his tragic sense of

life in Dublin. An original playwright may carry his originality far
enough to hew out an original form of tragic drama, especially in a theatre
in which conventional forms can have no binding or quasi-ritualistic
claims upon his loyalty.

Lest, indeed, we make tragedy the absolute test of dramatic achievement, we might ponder the words of Karl Deutsch in his introduction
to a recent book by the philosopher Karl Jaspers:

> Tragedy, though rich in truth, is not enough for Karl Jaspers. It
> is a basic aspect of reality, and we can neither deny nor escape it. But
> the experience of tragedy is only one stage in man's process of learn-
> ing. Taken as an absolute, tragic knowledge turns into idolatry,
> whether it be idolatry of images or idolatry of self. Rather, Jaspers
> seems to say, men and women must remain open to the voice of the
> world-wide misery without grandeur that cries out for help, and they
> must seek to transcend the limits that bound their sensitivity and
> their ability to help today. All of us, he seems to say, must seek the
> hard way that continues beyond tragedy.[1]

It seems to me, moreover, that some of the theatre's principal tragedians themselves, Aeschylus (in the Oresteian trilogy), Sophocles (especially in *Philoctetes*), Euripides (in play after play), Shakespeare, and
Racine have not contradicted Jaspers' view; and most modern playwrights
from Ibsen to O'Casey have affirmed it in their plays.

We may well wonder whether playwrights must move heaven and
earth to conform to a pattern of tragedy laid down many centuries ago,
and whether our insistence on tragic grandeur will not give us an academic rather than a living theatre. The criterion of exaltation—an exaltation to be effected by ennobling characters—can be carried too far. It may
be rejected by honest writers more concerned with having their say than
with conforming to blueprints of tragedy. They may suggest that fetish-
ists of high tragedy actually fail to compliment humanity in assuming
that we have to be constantly reminded that we are noble. And they may
well suspect that feelings of heroism, nobility, or exaltation are among
the cheapest experiences available to an individual or a group. Surely,
Hitler's cohorts were not deficient in those feelings when they devastated
Warsaw and blitzed London. The attributes they lacked most conspicuously were the *unheroic* ones of compassion, moderation, and critical
judgment. In the theatre, of course, we have had many instances of ennoblement giving us nothing better than the tawdry melodramas that

[1] Karl Jaspers, *Tragedy Is Not Enough*, Gollancz (London), 1953.

sustained our grandparents' sense of virtue more than they sustained the art of dramatic literature.

Some vision "ample and passionate," to use Joseph Wood Krutch's distinction, is, of course, requisite for tragedy. It is present in all genuine tragedy. Need it be absent in anti-heroic drama? It is certainly not lacking, for example, in *The Sea Gull* and *The Cherry Orchard*. Elevating writing, I would suggest, is a matter of intensity of creativeness rather than of opinions about the character of our species, and there may be nothing the matter with modern drama, after all, that genuine creativeness could not cure. Depressing drama need not eventuate from a view of socially conditioned personality and socially restricted possibilities for the individual, if the author's presentation is sufficiently intense. And other limitations can be noted in the human condition by playwrights without afflicting us with locomotor ataxia. In true tragedy, indeed, as distinguishable from mere romantic flamboyance, there has never been anything but a keen recognition of the bonds and boundaries imposed on us by reality. *Tragic awareness is ultimately an awareness of limits.* Exalted writing is possible even for those playwrights who have not dedicated themselves to exalting man's career on earth.

Since I have referred to modes of drama that depart from the traditional standards of tragedy, it may be useful to remind ourselves that comedy, too, can possess a vision "ample and passionate." Shaw possessed it in our times, as did Aristophanes, with even greater eloquence, in the great age of Attic tragedy. It is entirely possible, indeed, for a playwright to believe that he can serve that vision best by *not* writing tragedy. Comedy also provides a catharsis, although we are unlikely to confuse it with "tragic catharsis." And although the means, too, are different (the "pity and fear" or, at least, the "fear" is absent), the "comic catharsis," too, is virtually dependent upon the perception, recognition, or "enlightenment" precipitated in the course of the comic experience. But the subject need not be pursued further in an essay on tragedy.

I should add, however, that my conclusions on tragedy still leave me dissatisfied, chiefly because I do not know how to give sufficient concreteness to my definition of tragic enlightenment *as a process,* rather than as a mere load of ideas to be accumulated from a play. This is difficult, if not virtually impossible, because obviously no criticism or generalization is the equivalent of a play; and, also, because at the heart of tragedy, which is an essentially poetic form, whether or not it is written in verse, lies the indefinable essence or profound ambiguity of poetry. I could attain a greater degree of concreteness only by the laboratory method of analyzing a dozen or two tragedies in detail, and such an investigation would require a separate book or series of books. For the present, I believe I have only caught a sufficiently clear glimpse of the essence of tragic enlightenment to be able to distinguish it from substitutes such as information and moralization or even social and psychological analysis, all essentially un-tragic and, indeed, anti-tragic in their nature and effect.

A possible unclarity that we may guard against at once, however, can be worded as follows: *Who* is enlightened in tragedy? Maxwell Anderson, in *The Essence of Tragedy,* gives the impression that it is the tragic hero who must be enlightened in tragic drama. That is so, to a degree: Hamlet has learned to understand himself, and is ultimately at peace with himself; Othello realizes at the end that he loved not wisely but too well; Lear lets a profound understanding enter through the gates that let his folly in; and Oedipus learns that destiny's ways are superior even to his vaulting will and spirit. Maxwell Anderson, himself, took care to bring Mio in *Winterset* to that state of grace which Anderson calls *recognition.* Perhaps it can be shown that a good many other tragic characters acquire an understand-ing heart, and a view of their situation, and that they undergo a trans-figuration in the climax of "recognition." Unquestionably, the tragic char-acter rises in our estimation when this occurs. But I believe that the fun-damental enlightenment must be for the *audience,* whether or not the tragic character achieves it for himself—and the heroes of modern "low tragedy," such as Hedda Gabler and Willy Loman, rarely achieve it for themselves to any impressive degree, if at all.

If the tragic characters experience a catharsis, well and good. But it is Aristotle's understanding in the *Poetics,* and it is common sense in any man's book, that tragedy succeeds only if it has effected a catharsis *for the audience.* Just as the "pity" and "fear" must be experienced by the specta-tor, so must the enlightenment. And if this is so, then there is all the more reason for being dissatisfied with moral tags whether spoken by the tragic character or by a *raisonneur.* The audience must be enabled to win its way to some profound recognition not by prescription but by the dramatic ex-perience; and for this purpose, a play cannot have too much *specific* reality, which means contemporaneity rather than an abstruse mythical quality or remoteness of issues.

ARISTOTLE IN ECLIPSE

One way of following the traffic of dramatic art in these times is to note to what degree modern playwrights have tended to depart from the long-established and well-tested principles of drama that we associate with the name of Aristotle. Whether or not Aristotle ever intended to saddle dramatists with prescriptions instead of objectively deriving some conclusions from the plays he knew in his time is unimportant. The fact is that he was given great authority by scholars, critics, and writers. And even more important, he did arrive at perceptions that acutely define the nature of drama in many respects. Whether or not the playwright of post-classic times was aware of Aristotelian theory or heeded it, he made the same assumptions in his effective plays. He assumed that drama was an imitation of an action in terms of action, that its effectiveness consisted in the power of the work to involve the audience emotionally, and that certain means, among which plot is primary, were needed to hold the spectator's interest and absorb him in the life of the story. In the case of high matter, in the elevated art of drama for which Aristotle and his followers employed the single exacting term of tragedy, it was understood, besides, that certain effects were necessary. We were to be moved by the wonder and splendor of the human creature; for which purpose the central figure had to possess stature as a person and had to fall from some eminence, so that we would be moved by pity and fear. These experiences would moreover —by a process that has been debated ever since Aristotle's *Poetics*—purge the soul.

All this is familiar enough matter, which I do not propose to review. Nor do I intend to trace the various ways in which Aristotelian formulations were applied, misapplied, and watered down in the course of theatrical history. My object is merely to note that in our modern drama it has been virtually a necessity for many playwrights to part ways with Aristotle or his interpreters, and that if we are to make any progress at all in our time, we are likely to make more departures from the rules, whose soundness is nevertheless not in jeopardy simply because they are not considered strictly or universally applicable. It is not important to my present purpose or to the drama that we should be departing from an impressive authority whose name happens to be Aristotle. It *is* important that playwrights have felt the need for certain freedoms if they are to be effective in our time.

There are alternatives, you might say—or some ardent anti-romanticist and anti-liberal like T. S. Eliot might say. We need *less* freedom and more authority in our theatre. We need a rooted convention, in order that we may create within the limits established by some accepted dramatic form and style. Liberty within set boundaries proves fruitful. Much freedom can make creative art amorphous, or encourage the artist to concentrate less on essential revelations about life than on novelty, sensationalism, and everything that will catch the eye of the paying customer. The arguments for the value and need of an art restrained by a noble convention can be multiplied. But the trouble with formalism in theatre is that it cannot work very often or very well in the present century, as T. S. Eliot himself demonstrated in abandoning the liturgical and formal pattern of *Murder in the Cathedral* for the loose form of *The Cocktail Party*. In this play, for example, we find a mixture of the polite chatter of British high comedy and poetic mysticism flavored with the doctrine of Grace so that the play might be properly called a synthesis of Calvin and Coward. (The attribution of Calvinism to Mr. Eliot is not quite correct, of course, in view of his Anglo-Catholicism; but his practice of dividing the sheep from the goats, of the elect from the garden variety of mortals, suggests Calvinist doctrine.) Equally significant, too, is the fact that Mr. Eliot made quite a point of his writing the poetry for *The Cocktail Party* in such a vein that playgoers will not notice that it is poetry. Even the most rigorous critic of our "rootless" modern drama has, then, succumbed to the time-spirit and reaped the reward of an undisputed success in the theatre. A formal drama requires a communal sense lacking in modern life, and it is doubtful whether there is anything in our civilization that can make a spiritual community out of a metropolis.

Formal drama that is also genuinely moving and meaningful to its audience is, to some degree, a *rite*. And there can be no rite without believers whose belief is great enough to make them participants rather than mere spectators. The chances of turning drama into a rite again are no greater than they have been for the past fifty, seventy-five, or a hundred years. The medieval communion, or the communion allegedly present in the fifth century B.C. Dionysian theatre of Athens, is impossible in a divided society. Totalitarian state authority is certainly no substitute for real beliefs, especially when it shifts its policies and revises its dogmas continually instead of basing itself on life-long habits of feeling and behavior. In the first flush of enthusiasm, Nazi Germany and Russia tried to make a ritual out of theatre with results that we should be least inclined to admire. And in spite of the increasing severity of the totalitarianism, the rites vanished. Eliot's effort to create liturgical drama in *Murder in the Cathedral* was half-successful at best; it was a sophisticated product, even as Anglo-Catholicism is a "sophisticated" product by comparison with

Catholicism, and Catholicism has enough ritual in its everyday practice not to have to depend on efforts to create rites with new and deliberate artistry. Other efforts to turn the drama into a communion have also been singularly artificial; sometimes purely sophisticated, as in the case of Cocteau's version of the Oedipus legend, *The Infernal Machine,* and sometimes arid, as in the case of Eliot's *Family Reunion.* A ritualistic theatre depends, moreover, on myth to sustain drama. Our would-be ritualists have borrowed myths that no longer possess vitality for the people; or in the case of playwrights of the Irish renaissance at the beginning of the century, they tried to revive national legends essentially at variance with the development of the nation toward industrialism. Protest against this latter procedure is expressed equally by O'Casey's creation of his own allegories and fantasies (*Within the Gates* and *Cock-a-Doodle-Dandy*) and by Denis Johnston's negativistic treatment of Celtic romanticism in *The Old Lady Says No.*

Lacking the basis of consent by belief, the modern theatre has tried to hold its audience by creating a maximum of verisimilitude, of illusion, on the stage. This has been a powerful incentive to the formation of modern realistic dramaturgy and stagecraft, and it is an important reason why in spite of many efforts to create stylized drama (not merely naturalism interpenetrated with poetic mood and feeling, but formally stylized drama, such as expressionism and surrealism), the realistic tradition has held its own against all its critics. It is significant that the most successful style of performance in modern times has been Stanislavski's inner realism, the full purpose of which is to make acting so genuine that it creates perfect illusion. The acting of this kind we have had in America, the acting of the Group Theatre, has followed the same lines of illusion-making. The finest acting in Western Europe, under Jacques Copeau and his successors, was for many years likewise rooted in the superior illusion created by inner realism on the part of the actors; this was apparent even in the case of outwardly stylized and semi-formal productions such as appeared at the Vieux Colombier in Paris.

Yet—and this is the paradox of modern theatre to a degree—the illusion maintained has in most instances been bought at a price that has subverted Aristotelian drama, for which the primacy of "imitation" or illusion was predicated even before the advent of the modern realistic style of drama. Illusion has been successfully accomplished, first of all, by sacrificing heroic art, by dealing with characters whose struggles are ordinary ones and whose disasters are less than momentous, culturally or historically. Little men falling from small elevations or not falling at all, but simply eroding (as in *Uncle Vanya*), have filled the modern scene. The result has been drama of an intermediate type—comic, in the sense that it deals with mundane and commonplace matters, and tragic only in the sense of being serious and sad. Most modern plays fall into this inter-mediate category, for which no satisfactory label has yet been found, so that we have to give it the undescriptive term "drama." Much of our drama has been closer in spirit to the ordinary realistic novel than to the high dramatic art of Sophocles, Shakespeare, or Racine. This has been one limitation of modern theatre, and has deprived it of the highest dramatic flights. This has also been its strength. In order to create a powerful or absorbing illusion, modern drama moved close to ordinary human interests and concerns.

It is also evident that in maintaining illusion without the ritualistic absorption of an audience—that is, by sheer illusion-making rather than by formalizing the deepest convictions of the audience as if it were somehow participating in the rite—dramatists have often won the greatest approval by ignoring the element of *plot* that Aristotle placed even above character-ization when he discussed the drama. Unquestionably, the major bias of the pioneers of the modern naturalistic theatre was opposition to the well-made play of contrived plotting. They favored, instead, plotless plays that would seem reproductions of the unarranged and often uneventful course of daily existence: "slices-of-life," the followers of Zola called this kind of play-making. And what is more important, we are still infinitely grateful when we get an uncontrived drama—namely, a sensitive "slice of life." Even in accepting Lillian Hellman as a powerful playwright, we have had our reservations; we have felt that she plotted too much or calculated effects for theatrical purposes, if not indeed for propaganda. We have called her strongest plays "melodramatic."

Our critics have responded more wholeheartedly, as a rule, to more informal and casually presented pictures of life observed or dreamed up by playwrights, transfigured by a certain degree of poetry and universal-ization, in *Our Town, My Heart's in the Highlands, The Time of Your Life, The Beautiful People,* or *The Glass Menagerie.* It is not insignificant that the most admired American play of the 1949-1950 season should have been *Member of the Wedding,* which is little more than Carson McCul-lers' transcription of her simple novel. The one eventful detail in the play is the death of a little boy. In "plotted" drama, this would have been the consequence and dramatic conclusion of a series of complications; and, in the older well-made play convention, the death would have resulted from an intrigue spun through the fabric of the play. Nothing of the sort is true of *Member of the Wedding,* which manages to be persuasive and re-vealing by being nothing more than a well-observed picture of a girl's adolescence as she grows out of the tomboy stage. And parallel to this description runs another virtually plotless line of interest—the life of the

Negro servant who has cared for the girl. The plot, if it can be called such, is nothing more than the heroine's impossible desire to join her brother on his honeymoon and her brief flight from home when she is prevented from doing so. Ever since Chekhov became a successful playwright, the plotless play, which is usually little more than a string of little occurrences forming a story with a beginning, a middle, and an end, has won the greatest degree of respect and affection. Modern drama has been the result of fundamentally anti-Aristotelian playwriting—largely plotless, meandering, semi-comic, and semi-tragic. This partly explains the esteem in which we have held the plays of Chekhov and the early realistic ones of O'Casey, although we have only deluded ourselves in failing to realize how firmly they are built below the undulation of surfaces.

The other forms of well-regarded playwriting of the recent past have also been intermediate and unplotted. The discussion drama, in general, has been of this nature. "Thesis drama," one of the first carriers of modern ideas in the theatre, was naturally amply plotted; the playwright had to contrive complications in order to demonstrate a point, and this was true not only of the younger Dumas and Augier but of Ibsen and later writers of problem plays. Yet it is well known that even the later problem playwrights, beginning with Ibsen, prided themselves on doing with as little plot as possible and transferring the action to the realm of the mind. For "exposition, complications, crises, and dénouement," the modern writers substituted, according to Shaw, "exposition, complication, crisis, and discussion." Or they threw out most of the "complications" and moved as quickly as possible toward a crisis with the sole purpose of using it as a springboard for discussion, as did Ibsen to some degree and Shaw to a great degree. Even the crisis has been reduced greatly, discussion and revelation through discussion taking the place of almost all other elements of drama, as we may see in such plays as Shaw's *Getting Married* and Sartre's *No Exit*. In Sartre's piece, three characters are placed in an area of hell, which is actually a replica of a drawing room, and here the revelation of the moral bankruptcy of the characters proceeds with slight eventfulness and much conversation.

When playwrights rely heavily on melodramatic action, too, all the evidence points to the subordination of plot either to the slice of life, as in *Street Scene,* or to discussion, as in Sartre's *The Flies*; or to a combination of the "slice" and the demonstration of an idea, as in the action of both *Watch on the Rhine* and Kingsley's *Detective Story*. What was most memorable in the former was the picture of guileless and easy-going American life in contrast to the European struggle against fascism. Present in *Detective Story* was the combined force of the genre picture—the local color of the night-court scenes—and the demonstration that righteousness must not be carried to extremes. We may add here another example: Giraudoux' *The Madwoman of Chaillot* owes its charm less to its imaginative plot than to its discussions and interruptions, of which the "mad" conference of the Madwoman's crack-brained cronies is the best example.

Significant to the highest degree, finally, is the fact that the only dramatic form and style evolved in modern American society should have been the totally un-Aristotelian documentary drama of the "living newspaper." The economic condition of the theatre has not been favorable to the continued composition and production of living newspapers, such as the subsidized Federal Theatre's *Power* and *One-third-of-a-nation.* They require collaborative research and entail musical comedy expensiveness without the popularity of musical comedy. Since people in the theatre are fickle and have short memories, the "living newspaper" has been all but forgotten in professional theatrical circles. But it was surely the one original contribution to dramatic art to be made by our stridently modern life in America. The prevalence of journalistic playwriting is another indication that we are more favorable to immediate fact than to dramatic imagination. And an advance in documentary writing has been apparent in much of the best work of radio and motion picture drama.

Most important as a sign is the continued force of so-called epic drama in continental Europe and the fascination it exerts on some able men of the theatre even in America. "Epic" drama was born in the nineteen-twenties chiefly under the leadership of the German poet Bertolt Brecht. It is still being practiced today, and it infiltrated the popular American stage during the 1949-50 season in the Kurt Weill musical chronicle of love in America, *Love Life.* To a slight degree, "epic style" also appeared in the Kurt Weill and Maxwell Anderson hybrid dramatization, *Lost in the Stars,* though with a sentimental dilution that Brecht, no doubt, would have despised. (Weill was Brecht's collaborator in Germany on *The Three-Penny Opera.*) Every other experimental form developed in our century has had a short life: symbolism, expressionism, surrealism, constructivism, futurism, all had a brief flowering followed by a long winter. If "epic" already has twenty-five or more years of history behind it and shows every sign of a continuing life, the reason must lie in its suitability to the modern interest in society and socially determined problems. Brecht wrote two poetic plays, *The Caucasian Circle of Chalk* and *The Good Woman of Setzuan,* in this country during the war. Since the close of the Second World War, his plays have had many productions in Central Europe, and Brecht has been a very considerable playwright and theoretician there ever since his return from exile.

In theory and practice, the "epic" school of theatre has commanded respect for its anti-Aristotelian approach because its objectivity has precluded the anarchic fulminations and confusions to which expressionism and surrealism have been susceptible. In its logicality, at least, it has been "Aristotelian." But there has been hardly an exception to the rule that our modernist movements since 1890 have in one way or another violated Aristotelian principles of dramaturgy. The symbolists minimized action or dissolved it into moods and imitations, and the expressionists violated unity of time, place, and action and dissolved the boundaries between the objective world and the subjective. The surrealists destroyed not only the dramatic unities but the objective world. And "theatre-for-theatre's sake" theatricalists have often treated the substance of drama—action and characterization—as if it were a football or a toy. Curiously enough, the results in theatre have not been uninteresting, if not entirely gratifying. There is, after all, a difference between chaos and a void. Numerous playwrights and showmen have made the modern chaos colorful, exciting, even stimulating and moving. And the orderly world of "Aristotelian" drama has been splintered even by realists such as Chekhov and O'Casey.

It is by no means certain, however, that men of talent have not been deceived by their anti-Aristotelian bias. To try to match chaos with chaos in art is to succumb to a sort of genetic fallacy. It does not follow that art must be disorderly because life is. The contemporaries of Sophocles and Shakespeare must have considered their world as chaotic as we believe ours to be. If Sophocles and Shakespeare had given us disordered plays to match the disorder of their times, we should hardly think much of them today as dramatists. When Aristotle referred to the drama as an imitation of an action, he could not have held the naïve view that dramatic art must correspond point by point, moment by moment, to action as it transpires on the stage of the world. He could only have an ideal, orderly, and form-giving imitation in mind. Any other view would have been contradicted by his knowledge of the Greek drama. A modern playwright who makes his fantasy as bewildering as the world is actually a naïve imitator in art. He photographs disorder.

Even milder anti-Aristotelian modernism moves toward a *cul-de-sac*. Because many lives are uneventful, it does not follow that art must be uneventful. Because there are no plots in most lives, it does not follow that there is greater art in not having a plot than in having one. Most "static" plays have been as poor as if they had a naïve overabundance of action. Chekhov, it is true, prevailed with a seemingly casual and wayward kind of playwriting, but it is no secret that efforts to write "Chekhovian" drama have been singularly unsuccessful. His imitators have had no difficulty *disintegrating* plays. What they were unable to learn from Chekhov was how to *integrate* them.

DRAMA AND DETACHMENT: A VIEW
OF BRECHT'S STYLE OF THEATRE

I

Since Brecht is a vigorous man in his early fifties and has been a continually developing artist, there is no telling what new paths he may yet traverse. But his work to date is already a cohesive body of drama and criticism exemplifying a special approach to the stage. It has been called by him an anti-Aristotelian approach, because it challenges the value of the principle of unity and of the emotional nature of the drama that Aristotle stressed in the *Poetics*. This anti-Aristotelianism, moreover, is not a negative contribution and an academic interest, because Brecht has turned it into a practice of playwriting, actor-training, and stage direction, as well as into a philosophy of art, distinctly related to a scientific age and its analytical temper, which manifests itself in other fields than the theatre. He has claimed for the theatre the function of demonstration that pervades the mass communication media of radio, television, and the "documentary" film, as well as the industrial and scientific meeting, the sociological lecture, and the various exhibits which society employs so effectively in everyday practice. And like these media, his "epic theatre" has given primacy to neither emotion nor unity, for emotion is, more often than not, an impediment to a successful demonstration; and unity means something else to the demonstrator, who organizes his materials for the purpose of clarifying the subject, than to the narrator who tries to achieve suspense—or to the poet or musician who secures a mood and avoids breaking it.

More than any other dramatist of our age, Brecht has sought to develop a modern dramatic medium for modern social reality. It might be argued, of course, that Aristotle's criteria were intended for tragedy, and that Brecht's outlook, as well as his playwriting, is essentially comic. But since concepts of identification and sympathy have been generally absorbed into comedy, too, since the advent of fourth century B.C. "New Comedy," Brecht is entitled to consider himself an anti-Aristotelian critic and playwright. In any case, needless to say, what matters is not an academic quarrel with Aristotelian formulations but with the underlying assumptions of unity, harmony, and emotionalism in plays and productions which have been made, with or without recourse to Aristotle, in the Western theatre.

Since Brecht has miraculously, and almost against his own judgment or professed policy, functioned as a poet rather than as a journalist, he has laid claims upon more than transitory interest, and his career as a playwright will ultimately have to be evaluated in literary as well as dramatic and theatrical terms. At present, however, he is of particular interest to us not as the literary figure he is (most Americans do not know his plays and poems) but as a playwright-director-theorist who has, on one hand, challenged accepted premises of dramatic art and, on the other hand, proclaimed and exemplified mass-communication demonstration-dramaturgy and stagecraft as the most responsible contemporary reincarnation of dramatic art. This dramaturgy and this stagecraft need not be (and actually are not), moreover, the exclusive property of any specific ideology. There is no reason why the method Brecht has candidly placed at the service of Marxian and materialistic dogma cannot be applied to the propagation of fervently maintained democratic and Christian principles. Democracy and Christianity are also susceptible of demonstration and have problems to present and strategies to consider. In spite of the stress democracy and Christianity place on the individual, they, too, burst the walls of private drama, involve mankind all over the globe in a common cause or problem, and have epic matter to make immediate for our century. There is a good deal of "epic theatre" of demonstration and explication, for example, in Christopher Fry's recent religious play *A Sleep of Prisoners,* a poetic examination of conscience and policy with respect to violence and war, chiefly by means of four disjunctive biblical episodes. Had Brecht chosen to write this play it might have been different in point and style, but not particularly different in technique except for greater clarity. Logic is Brecht's forte, but is one of the less conspicuous virtues of British poet-playwrights, T. S. Eliot included, when they expound religion.

Brecht has viewed the past and present with a twentieth-century mind. His political outlook has always been far left of center, although his left-wing orthodoxy has been questionable even when he has spoken dogmatically. He is essentially an extreme individualist, if not indeed a bohemian artist-intellectual, weaving his way through mazes of collectivist ideals and policies as a poet rather than as a politician. Like others of his time, he has ridden the two horses of idealism and materialism, or of romanticism and Marxism, without any particular sense of discomfort or incongruity. He has also been a moralist of contemporary caliber for better or worse, pondering ethical problems in relation to political realities and expedients until ethics and strategy become indistinguishable in his thought—a dangerous way of thinking mitigated in his case by an essential humanism apparent in his passion for justice and his sympathy for the underdog. For Brecht does not quite succeed in suppressing the human sympathy that he would theoretically banish from the stage, if his theories are construed rigorously. He has endeavored to make drama out of themes and material usually excluded from a theatre dedicated to private emotion. In ways that recall the efforts of Koestler, Malraux, and other contemporary novelists, Brecht has certainly tried to make political reality the center of his art and the springboard of his inquiry into private and public conduct. Even when his main characters themselves have only a hazy awareness of politics, they exemplify the political nature of human existence, and the "human condition" with which Brecht has concerned himself has always been intrinsically a political condition. How Brecht's outlook has determined his form is, however, the paramount question; for his uniqueness as an artist lies not in his content or politics, common enough these days, but in the manner in which he has translated a bias into drama, production style, and dramatic theory.

II

Brecht first attracted attention in 1922 when he was awarded the important Kleist Prize for *Drums in the Night,* an angry and turbulent account of the return of a German soldier to civilian life only to discover how little value his sacrifices have had, and how little sympathy a veteran can expect. Inflamed by the revolutionary situation in post-war Germany, Brecht identified himself with the extreme left-wing groups in the theatre, and harnessing his poetic talent to propaganda, wrote plays intended to instruct the common man as well as the class-conscious partisan. He called the most rudimentary of these pieces *Lehrstücke,* "learning plays," or, more accurately, teaching plays, and the term is loosely applicable also to his more developed dramas, in which he essayed instruction more indirectly. Primarily, however, he broke with representational, "fourth-wall" theatre, with purely affective drama, and with the means, including unity of mood, by which playwriting and stage art draw the spectator into a closed magical circle of experience and induce a hypnosis. Altogether, Brecht imposed on himself the role of a demonstrator employing characters and plot merely as the material and the means of his inquiry or lesson, although the instruction could be oblique. In short, Brecht rejected the technique of realism, a middle-class product ever since Lillo, for the sake of a more functional realism that requires analysis and exemplification. In his work, therefore, Brecht combined expressionism or symbolism with the verisimilitude favored by conventional realists, reinforced argument with a variety of imaginative devices, and launched into satiric and hortatory folk ballads whenever these suited his purpose. He also made much use of music, not only for intermittent effect but for formal structure; and, of course, he rejected the conventional mood-drenched music of romantic pathos, favoring instead a sharp and emphatic music specially provided for him by such modernists as Hans Eisler, Kurt Weill, and Paul Dessau.

One of the first of the *Lehrstücke, The Expedient,* was an analysis of the moral problems faced in political action. The piece was technically an oratorio, with a score by Hans Eisler, and was produced in Germany in 1929. Before long, however, Brecht amplified his dramatic scope, writing full-length plays distinguishable from conventionally constructed drama by their horizontal, chronicle structure and their technique of abrupt scenes and interrupted plot. A good example was *Mother,* his dramatization of Gorky's novel, which traced the rise of social consciousness in a peasant woman. Here Brecht interrupted the plot sequence and punctuated the demonstration with a direct address to the public by means of choruses or "mass chants" which impressed Archibald MacLeish as a means of opening the portals of the theatre to modern poets when the play was produced in New York. In adapting John Gay's classic *The Beggar's Opera,* renamed *The Three-Penny Opera,* for which the late Kurt Weill wrote a memorable score, Brecht made even stronger use of music as a concomitant of commentary rather than as an emotional solvent, actually conquering the romantic musical-comedy field with his new technique. Staged in 1928, with Brecht directing the production himself, *The Three-Penny Opera* became the outstanding musical comedy of Central Europe between the First and Second World Wars. The mordant quality of *The Three-Penny Opera* actually brought it closer to Ben Jonson than to John Gay. A stinging comment on amoral and predatory *laissez-faire* philosophy, which Brecht and his supporters, of course, identified with capitalism, this comedy missed fire when produced in New York. Its influence, however, has been quite apparent in our theatre, in such pieces as *The Cradle Will Rock, Finian's Rainbow, Regina* and *Flahooley* —and in the anti-New Deal *Knickerbocker Holiday,* on which Kurt Weill collaborated with Maxwell Anderson.

When Hitler came to power, Brecht, who narrowly escaped extermination by fleeing from Germany, found even more incentives than before for the composition of the *Lehrstücke* in almost every conceivable form, for now the crisis in the world that was soon to experience the explosion of a second world war added justification to his conviction that a theatre dedicated to sentiment was inadequate. One of the most trenchant of his plays was *Round Heads and Peaked Heads,* produced in Copenhagen in 1936. Here satiric fantastication was most pronounced, as Brecht reduced Hitler's racial theories to an absurdity by means of a grotesque fable. Still more brilliant, although more realistic, was the comedy *Puntila and His Servant* (*Herr Puntila und sein Knecht*) that Brecht wrote in Finland in 1942. Ostensibly writing a folk play about a wealthy landowner and the servant, who, taking advantage of his master's frequent drunkenness, softens his heart now and then, Brecht launched a broadside against the entire Mannerheim ruling class in Finland at that time. Satire, however, was only one of several types of drama written by Brecht during his exile from 1933 to 1945, when he returned to Germany to become the Eastern Zone's favorite playwright and one of its well-regarded directors. (He had a slight ideological mishap in 1951 with an anti-war opera, *The Trial of Lucullus,* originally a radio play, but he revised it according to the latest party-specifications and was restored to favor.) Brecht also extended his "epic" method in three historical plays and wrote, in addition, two remarkable plays that may be loosely called "moralities" or parables.

Sometime before writing *Puntila* and while he was still living in Scandinavia, shortly before the start of World War II, he composed one of the most vigorous historical plays of the modern European theatre, *Mother Courage and Her Children,* a chronicle of the Thirty Years War in Germany recounting the experiences of the promiscuous camp-follower known as *Mutter Courage* (Mother Courage) who makes a profit out of the war but loses all her children in the holocaust. Much may be said about the brutal realism of the writing, the mordant documentation of war—a religious war at that—climaxed by a stirring scene in which Mother Courage's dumb daughter loses her life while attempting to warn a town that it is about to be sacked by the enemy. But the play is greatly enriched by its lyrical components and by the bold variations of mood that project the irony and chaos of the world gone mad with the lust of plundering and killing; especially striking are the ballads interspersed in the text.

Whatever difficulties the play may encounter here, it proved to be one of the most powerful productions in Europe, and it is as incisive as it is exciting. Brecht, it is interesting to note, was disappointed when the Zurich premiere during World War II, evidently a most effective production in which Therese Giehse distinguished herself as Mother Courage, created too much sympathy for the heroine. The press, taking its cue from the death of her three children, called the play a "Niobe tragedy." More interested in emphasizing *"das rein merkantile Wesen des Kriegs,"* the purely commercial character of the war, that attracts Mother Courage to the front and the inability of the comman man to "learn anything from the catastrophe," Brecht made a number of changes in the text for the later Berlin production. A comparison of the Zurich and Berlin texts reveals that Brecht took precautions to eliminate the impression of a "Niobe-tragedy." (Brecht: 9 Versuche 20/21. Frankfurt am Main: Sukrkamp

Verlag vorm. S. Fisher, 1949. Pp. 79-82.) Nevertheless, the dumb daughter in the play is one of the most affecting characters in the entire range of modern drama. And we are at liberty, I believe, to be moved by her plight without violating Brecht's intentions, provided we are sensible, too, of Brecht's effort to make us see her situation in the larger context of the picture he has drawn: the picture of a world in which the very victims of the war are trying to profit by it and share the social responsibility, venality, and confusions intrinsic to the social situation.

Another historical play, *Galileo,* recounts the struggles of the great Italian scientist. It is not merely a biographical drama such as we are accustomed to, but a cool analysis of the problems and state of mind of a man who stands between two worlds and compromises between intellectual integrity and personal safety. The play was too cool, too cold, for a number of New York critics, including Brooks Atkinson, who saw an experimental production of the work with Charles Laughton playing Galileo. It was written with the intention of exposing a situation rather than emotionally involving the spectators; we are not made to sympathize with Galileo but to understand his problem. Instruction is the prime objective of this Brechtian piece—instruction with a view to expounding a historical situation which may repeat itself and therefore must be comprehended. We could embarrass Brecht by applying his exposition to the Lysenko genetics controversy in Russia, and he would, no doubt, be delighted to embarrass us by referring to violations of academic freedom in the United States since the start of the "cold war." But both sides can agree that Brecht's intentionally cold dramaturgy, whether we like it or not, has a special place in modern theatrical art, if due attention is given to the expansion of radio, television, and motion picture documentary or semidocumentary drama. His objective method does seem the most appropriate one for treating historical events. Sidney Howard's *Yellowjack,* which employed the documentary style, would actually be more effective in my opinion if the dramaturgy and style were "colder"; the audience would be less disappointed then because the play isn't "warmer," in the sense of being closer to conventional affective drama. At the same time, Howard's play would have been more lyrical, too, if Brecht had been the author. It is an error to make lyricism invariably synonymous with "feeling"; Brecht, like Aristophanes, John Gay, and W. S. Gilbert, has the talent to achieve "non-emotional" and ironical lyricism.

Brecht's third epic, *The Private Life of the Master Race,* was also an original piece of documentary dramaturgy. Two of its episodes, *The Informer* and *The Jewish Wife,* are profoundly moving one-act plays, and were performed independently during the war. But Brecht would not be flattered by the praise that can be accorded to him on this account. He wrote this play as a cross-section of German life with a view to demonstrating how a nation is terrorized into accepting a dictatorship and launching a full-scale war. Technically, indeed, the play, which I find rather uneven and less than satisfactory because of lacunae in the incomplete published version,[1] is a unique variant of chronicle drama because the episodes are not strictly sequential; that is, they do not comprise a suspensive story, as in a narrative that tells us in a succession of episodes what happened first and what happened next. In the main, each scene is a separate demonstration of some aspect of the Nazi terror. Here, then, is the epic technique not as it appears, let us say, in Homer or in *Henry IV*, but as it could appear in a lecture with slides, each episode constituting a slide to demonstrate an aspect of the subject.

Most appealing perhaps are the two parables Brecht wrote while living in America. *The Caucasian Circle of Chalk*, in which the rights of motherhood are assigned to the woman who cares for a child rather than to the mother who gave birth to it, is both a chronicle and a "morality." Somewhat unwieldy, it is, nevertheless, a good example of the manner in which Brecht deliberately turns even an intrinsically emotional situation into an exposition of attitudes and values. He is the anti-sentimentalist *par excellence* even when his subject is sentiment. The other parable, *The Good Woman of Setzuan*, is, in my opinion, a masterpiece, although it is difficult to produce with sufficient verisimilitude, considering the prevailing taste of our theatre, because the same actress must play both a woman and a man—that is, the heroine's cousin. Brecht, however, has little use for verisimilitude, and would be pleased rather than disturbed if the production violated illusion. He is opposed to illusion-mongering and actually wants his audience to know that it is witnessing theatre rather than life; just as the public watching a demonstration knows that reality is not being photographed but being arranged for the purposes of an analysis. Actions in his type of drama are not intended to represent reality but to explain it and to challenge the critical intelligence of the observer.

Here, as in other plays, Brecht avails himself freely of Chinese theatrical style in which verisimilitude is of no consequence. Although he wrote *The Good Woman of Setzuan* with great charm and resorted to fantasy in bringing several little Chinese deities down to earth parable-wise in order to see how the human race is behaving, his object was to demonstrate a far-reaching point rather than to create illusion. His heroine, a kind-hearted prostitute, discovers that her philanthropy threatens to destroy her

[1] Translated by Eric Russell Bentley, New Directions, 1944. This edition consists of seventeen of the twenty-eight scenes Brecht wrote under the general title *Fears and Miseries of the Third Reich*.

and at the same time to undermine the morale of all the people who depend upon the bounty she dispenses after the gods have rewarded her kindness to them with a gift of money. In self-defense in a hungry world that would easily exhaust her charity without improving the general situation of the poor, she is forced to assume an *alter ego,* and, in the guise of a tough-minded male cousin, she puts all her dependents to work. Before long, however, the momentum of her practical policy pushes her to the other extreme that we might call dictatorship, until the people cry out against the tyranny of the "cousin" and accuse him of having murdered their benefactress. The Chinese gods interfere at last, and order the "good woman" (*"der gute Mensch"*—literally, the good person or the person of good will) to resume her other self. Nevertheless, they assent to her plea that she needs her *alter ego,* and give her permission to impersonate her cousin now and then. There is a sort of sophrosyne in this demonstration of how goodness must be practical and strong but not so "practical" as to take advantage of human helplessness and play the dictator. The sophrosyne at the core of this presentation of the problem of good and evil in social action determines the style and tone of the work. Here, too, Brecht effects a "cooling off" of the drama by means of a quizzical tone, lyric interruptions of the plot, and an "angle of vision" that tilts the picture of life with sardonic emphasis. Brecht, who can be a master of eloquence, knows that "coolness," too, can be a sort of rhetoric—if not an Aristotelian rhetoric of *persuasion,* then a rhetoric of inquiry or analysis. The method is Socratic or, more accurately, Silenic.

III

Brecht is in all respects a rebel against Aristotelian and post-Aristotelian esthetics. Although Aristotle was the son of a physician and himself a biologist, he relied on illusion and emotion when he considered dramatic art. Brecht, who was a medical student, is consistently the surgeon; and this not only in his plays but in his ballads, that often vary eloquence with a sudden flatness, with a lapse into caustic colloquialism, and with an eighteenth-century rationalistic sharpness. He is given to pouring cold water on his work whenever it threatens to become overheated. His "epic" theory of drama and stagecraft is a protest against the priority of feeling and the principle of identification in drama. He does not allow feeling to preempt the field of observation, nor does he want us to get into other people's skin, lest we fail to observe them, assess them, and draw objective conclusions.

Brecht is the most anti-tragic of modern artists, not excluding Bernard

Shaw; and for the same reason that Shaw was anti-tragic except in *Saint Joan*—that is, because Brecht has unlimited faith in the perfectibility of man, the effectiveness of rational inquiry, and the power of men to improve the "human condition" by concerted action. It may be interesting to observe, in fact, that the great ages of high tragedy are not notable for any strong conviction that mankind is committed to progress and capable of it, that improvement is a social rather than individual problem, and that it can be effected by materialistic rather than spiritual means. Tragic art is neither "liberal" nor "radical," in the Western sense of either term since the Renaissance or, at least, since the ultra-optimistic eighteenth-century Enlightenment that promulgated the belief in unlimited progress of mankind on earth. The tragic sense includes a hard truth, harder than anything the tough-fibered Brecht accepts—namely, a sense of "life's impossibilities."

Brecht also abides by the principle of naturalistic objectivity in spite of his rejection of naturalistic technique. One might describe him as a lyric Henry Becque, if we waive the fact that Brecht has favored epic expansion of the drama whereas Becque sought dramatic compression. Brecht, one should add, exercises great economy in building scenes and writing dialogue and lyrics; the expansiveness he requires is of the Elizabethan variety—that is, free-flowing, multifarious, and multi-scened action.

Brecht favors a type of dramatic composition that projects the various facets of man's life in society without accepting an obligation to abide by any strict unity of time, place, action, mood, and style. His plays often have the extensiveness of an Elizabethan chronicle like *Henry IV,* and as much variety of action and tone. One scene may convey a realistic picture and another may take the form of a discussion or a narration; or there may be no scene at all, only a song or recitation. But the episodes, combined with narrative and lyrical passages, and augmented with pantomime, dance, projected slogans, signs or placards, slides, and even motion-picture sequences, if necessary, all following one another in rapid succession, may form one big tumultuous play somewhat in the manner of the "multiplicity novels" of John Dos Passos.

The result of this horizontal dramaturgy is "epic drama," according to Brecht. Since he also takes an analytical view of reality and institutes an inquiry or demonstrates his argument with every conceivable device, his epic style serves the purpose of social realism, and the most accurate term for his type of drama is "epic realism." Foregoing the esthetic advantages of a complete synthesis by tone or mood (the ideal since the nineteenth century of both the conventional realists and the art-for-art's-sake symbolists), Brecht concentrates on the diversity of a problem or situation, because the interrelationship of many facts and forces comprises its social reality.

Brecht, moreover, has proposed a theoretical basis for anti-emotionalism and evolved measures for ensuring that the theatre will not "put the audience in a trance and give it the illusion of witnessing natural, unrehearsed events." Accordingly, he has propounded a principle of *Verfremdung,* or "alienation." The scenery may be realistic, but only partially so; the stage may have enough realism to establish a background for the demonstration, but the scenery should be skeletal or incomplete. Since the audience should not be drawn into the play to such a degree that it loses its ability to stand outside the events, verisimilitude should be restricted and the fourth-wall convention should be violated. Since the audience should not be placed under a spell, the scenic designer should avoid the use of the mood-drenched, atmospheric pillars and planes of the symbolist Appia-Craig school. Nor should the Brecht-trained actor lose himself completely in his role as does his Stanislavski-taught colleague; Brecht's actor must be sufficiently outside the "character" to serve as a "demonstrator." It may be said that the performance should be, at one level, a perpetual "aside" or comment. By these and other means, Brecht expects the stage production to combat the playgoer's tendency to lose himself in illusion. Brecht is convinced that the stage can be interesting and entertaining without creating illusion—rightly so, I believe, though it does not of course follow that only "epic theatre" can be interesting and entertaining. Brecht believes all along that the theatre must be "entertainment." His plays contain much broad humor, raffish wit, and fanciful argumentation, and the stage production he favors must never be a routine and bloodless affair. It must be sprightly and alive; it can be rousing, too, and need not be devoid of emotion, provided the emotion does not blunt the point to be made and is not so thoroughly or so long sustained that the playgoer ceases to be a spectator or observer capable of arriving at an objective judgment. Sustained empathy can produce a stupor rather than the mental alertness that Brecht requires of his public; complete identification with a stage character impairs objectivity and lulls the reasoning faculties to sleep. The playwright and the stage director must therefore draw the playgoer out of the magic circle of illusion and abbreviate or neutralize the possibilities of empathy.

According to Brecht, an Aristotelian catharsis through pity and terror, possible only when we succumb to dramatic illusion and identify ourselves with the characters, is not a desirable experience. When we are thoroughly purged, there is no longer any necessity to evaluate a situation realistically or take action against the evils we have witnessed. The epic style must "awaken his [the playgoer's] energy" with its demonstration, no matter how quizzical (and Brecht is often whimsical rather than dutifully didactic) and must require decisions of him. This the production will do by distancing dramatic experience and breaking the hypnotic spell that realists and symbolists alike cast upon their audience. By bringing into the drama such devices as choral commentary, song, and narration, Brecht intends to achieve a distancing and spell-breaking, "alienating" effect. These interruptions of the action are expected to awaken the spectator just as he is settling down comfortably in his seat to enjoy the story and lose himself in an emotional narcosis.

No one, then, has gone as far as Brecht in banishing Aristotelian pity, terror, catharsis, unity, and illusion as paramount dramatic values. He prides himself upon reflecting the scientific and analytical spirit of modern society, as well as the specially materialistic dialectic of Marxism. From this orientation he derives his "modernity" as well as his challenge to a theatre which no matter how realistic in details, no matter how attached to verisimilitude, remains wedded to eighteenth-century "sentimentalism" *á la* Diderot and Steele so long as it fails to utilize the demonstration techniques of the mass-communication media or of the "living newspaper" form introduced by the Federal Theatre of the nineteen-thirties—a form that owes something to Brecht's experiments with the "learning play," or *Lehrstücke.*

It may be maintained, indeed, that generally the contemporary theatre is pseudo-realistic rather than realistic, and too rarely supplies the alternative of imagination and poetry. By itself this alternative would be "premodern" and unsatisfactory to Brecht, although he has supplied more genuine poetry himself than most contemporary playwrights are capable of writing. Nothing, indeed, is more remarkable in Brecht's career than that he should have been able to satisfy two contemporary needs at the same time—to extend realism and invigorate it, on the one hand, and to promote a theatre of imagination and poetry on the other hand. Imaginative drama and realistic drama are supposed to be the opposite poles of theatrical art. Brecht has resolved the major dichotomy of the modern stage in his own work and has proved that it need not exist.

T. S. Eliot made an attempt to resolve the contradiction between realistic and poetic art in *The Cocktail Party,* but only by eroding the boundaries between reality and fantasy, by functioning as a Symbolist; and Symbolism is fundamentally a nineteenth-century *fin de siècle* phenomenon. Christopher Fry resorted in *A Sleep of Prisoners* to a conventional dream technique that goes back to the Middle Ages. Brecht would probably dismiss such efforts as obscurantist. In one way or another an attempt at a synthesis has been made ever since the advent of modern theatre—by Ibsen in his last plays, by Strindberg in *There Are Crimes and Crimes,* for example, and by Chekhov, Synge, O'Casey, and others—generally, however, by eliminating the boundaries between prose and formal poetry.

Brecht keeps his prose and poetry distinct; as he must, indeed, if he is to remain true to his objective of avoiding any sort of magic of realistic illusion or of symbolism.

As an illustration, we may consider a simple play, *The Private Life of the Master Race.* Here we follow the travels of a German Panzer tank across Europe, from the time when it participates in Hitler's early victories up to the time when it bogs down in Russia and faces defeat. The epic pattern appears in the extensive sequence of episodes, each dealing with a different soldier who was impressed into the service of the military machine and ultimately found himself a member of the tank division: an "Aryan" physician who had had a Jewish wife, a man who had been spied upon by his own child (or so he feared), a disgruntled worker, and so on. The play as a whole constitutes a vivid picture of how an entire nation was enslaved by fear, espionage, "Aryanization" of the professions, and subversion of the law. Considerable suspense is built up in some of the individual episodes, but Brecht deliberately writes a discontinuous text unified only by the theme, the device of the Panzer crew weaving through the drama, and the formal pattern. The suspense ends with each episode, and the story of each section is not continued into the next scene, since suspense must be avoided, according to Brecht, lest it engross the spectator too thoroughly and hypnotize him.

Some of the scenes, such as *The Jewish Wife* and *The Informer,* are admirably realistic. But the work as a whole is stylized and theatrical. It alternates between little dramas and lyric passages consisting of the singing of the Panzer troops and a commentary roaring out of the darkness. Signs and slogans are flashed before us at the beginning of each scene, the scenery is skeletal, and the sound of the Panzer rolling along serves as a prelude to each vignette. The effect is terrifying, and emotions are stirred in different segments of the drama. Yet the overall impression is that of a vivid demonstration of a social situation; the play is a lesson in the strategy of power and terror. It is not merely history—in the sense of a report on past events—but an analysis intended to sharpen our sense of reality and our faculties for acting our part in a vital situation or avoiding a similar fate. The play possesses poetic power, but not of the kind that dissolves our awareness of facts, policies, and procedures. The poetic parts of the play separate the dramatized events and project or essentialize experience. Nor are we allowed to feel sorry for anyone or to identify ourselves with anyone for any length of time; after fifteen minutes at the most, we are carried to the next point, the next demonstration. Brecht called this work a documentary play. A document it is, although not in the pedestrian sense of the term. *The Private Life of the Master Race* is a document with wings.

Not the least attractive feature of Brecht's work, indeed, is the evident tension set up between poet and scientist, fabulist and social realist, the man of feeling and the social thinker who writes with detachment. We sense that the artist has forced his way through a maze of difficulties; he has overcome the resistance of the grain of the wood or the hardness of the marble or bronze. His writing, moreover, indicates that Brecht is not actually proposing to adulterate the drama or reduce it to factual writing. His work suggests that even if the theatre should heed Brecht, if "epic" dramatic style as envisioned by him should prevail, it could remain art rather than mere documentation, and literature rather than merely another variant of educational "visual aid" programs.

The Brechtian technique and idea, as noted earlier, have indeed found some equivalents even in America, where he has never had a successful professional production. (I would refer here to Paul Green's anti-war play of the 1930's, *Johnny Johnson;* the Lerner and Weill chronicle of marriage in American history, *Love Life;* the "living newspapers," *Power, One-Third of a Nation, Spirochete, E = Mc$_2$*; Green's dramatization of Richard Wright's *Native Son;* Blitzstein's *The Cradle Will Rock*. I do not, of course, mean that these are simply imitations of Brecht's work.) The "epic style" crops up in many quarters without either critics or playgoers being aware of it. Brecht's influence, then, continues to radiate. Mathematics has gone beyond Euclid, physics beyond Newton, medicine beyond Andreas Vesalius and Lister. In Brecht's work as a playwright, stage director, and critic, the drama is moving beyond Aristotle, and without annihilating esthetic values either in playwriting or in stage production. The possibilities of argument concerning the merits of his plays and theories are large, but the stalemate in contemporary theatre justifies at least enough interest in this "non-Aristotelian" approach to further inquiry into its possibilities and encourage undogmatic experimentation with epic realism.[2]

[2] Brecht has presented his theories in a number of essays. Among these, the most accessible résumé is *The Alienation Effect,* translated by Eric Bentley, in *Actors on Acting,* ed. by Toby Cole and Helen Krich Chinoy (Crown Publishers, New York), pp. 281-285. Previously published in *Theatre Arts,* XXXIII (January, 1949), pp. 38-40, under the title *A New Technique of Acting.* This essay includes a significant definition of the purpose that underlies the "alienation principle" in acting. "Since he [the actor] does not identify himself with the man he presents, he can see him from a particular, chosen standpoint, can reveal his opinion of him, and bring the spectator, who also was not invited to identify himself with the character, to criticize him." (Page 284.) This approach achieves the "historification of everyday life" that Brecht considers the main feature of his epic theatre.

This essay should be compared with the essay by another epic director, Erwin Piscator, *Objective Writing, op. cit.,* 285-291. Unlike Brecht, Piscator has not written original plays, although he has collaborated in adapting novels such as *The Good Soldier Schweik* and *An American Tragedy.* As stage director in Germany, Piscator even demonstrated the possibility of using "epic" staging for romantic, expressionistic, and naturalistic plays such as Schiller's *The Robbers,* Toller's *Hoppla, wir tanzen,* Gorky's

In Brecht's work and in "epic" drama in general, we find the fusion of all the elements that have figured in recent theatrical history. It is objective drama even when it turns to a legend and launches into poetry. "Epic" is realistic in its outlook, for it takes a cool, objective view of the human scene and the problems it poses to the individual. Yet "epic" also solves the problem of getting away from the narrow realistic play structure that allows us to present only a small, generally subjective picture—and realistic subjectivism in our theatre has been long impoverished. The possibilities for imaginative drama are wide open in "epic production," which *projects* dramatic matter instead of reproducing it literally. Choral passages, lyrics, narrations, symbolization, motion picture techniques, slides, and other visual aids to comprehension are combined here with other scenes that may imitate action more or less as it would occur in "real" life. The poet and the lecturer, the creator of parables and the realist, the fantasist and the statistician mediate their differences in epic theatre.

If "epic" theatre has a future, as well as a past, this is because it leaves boundless opportunities for the play of imagination and provides an outlet for the dramatist who wants to create poetry and theatrically stylized art *without* escaping from modern life into the void of fancy or the vacuous areas of sentimentality. If "epic" drama has appeared on Broadway only in the guise of a musical comedy, Weill's *Love Life,* the reasons may be that our theatre has been insufficiently trained in stylization and is averse to lessons of any sort. "Epic Theatre," however, is the closest approximation of a dramatic rite that is suitable for modern urban and industrial civilization in that it has the qualities of an illustration and explication of facts and ideas.

In fact and in theory, "epic realism" drama has been the most anti-Aristotelian type of drama developed by Western civilization, and its chief

The Lower Depths, and *What Price Glory?* Between 1940 and 1950, Piscator also demonstrated the "epic" style of production in New York, at the "Studio Theatre" of the New School and at the President Theatre. His application of the epic style to *King Lear,* with Sam Jaffe in the title role, was singularly unsuccessful. But a moderate epic staging of Sartre's *The Flies* by Paul Ransom under Piscator's supervision proved extraordinarily effective; and a production of Robert Penn Warren's *All the King's Men,* the play Warren wrote before writing his Pulitzer Prize novel, was highly provocative if rather inconclusive.

Two other illuminating essays by Brecht available in English are: 1) *A Model for Epic Theatre,* translated by Eric Bentley, in *The Sewanee Review* (Summer, 1949), in which Brecht describes his theory of acting-technique; and 2) *A Little Organum for the Theatre,* translated by Beatrice Gottlieb, in *Accent* (Winter, 1951), pp. 13-40, in which Brecht elaborates an esthetics for our "scientific age." The *Organum* is not always easy to follow, but it is stimulating.

The best expositions of Brecht's plays and theories in English by someone else are by Eric Bentley in *The Playwright as Thinker* (Reynal and Hitchcock, 1946), pp. 250-72, *The Private Life of the Master Race* (New Directions, 1944), pp. 117-136, and "German Stagecraft Today" in *Kenyon Review,* XI (Autumn, 1949), pp. 630-648.

proponent, Brecht, insists upon his heterodoxy. He has no use whatsoever for "unity," for epic drama is written to be comprehensive and to take into account the diversity of the social reality and the variety of forces that impinge upon the individual. More than that, Brecht has made it plain that the object of epic drama is to abolish not only "illusion" but the subjection of the spectator to an emotional orgy by means of sympathy and identification with the characters of the stage, who can, nevertheless, be considerably individualized; that is, they need not be puppets of society in being representative, nor need they be the author's mouthpieces when their attitudes and actions are sufficiently revealing. The disjunctive structure of epic drama, the interruption of the action by comment, the continual cooling off of emotion, and the truncation of plot just when it promises suspense and a neat little story—these are means intended to prevent the playgoer from becoming engrossed to such a degree that he cannot think clearly and arrive at a perspective. Even the acting is to avoid drawing the spectator into the orbit of illusion. The public must be reminded that the play is a demonstration upon which it is to base conclusions to be effectuated by action in the outside world. And the scenery, too, is expected to prevent emotional immersion. Lest the playgoer lose himself in a scene that is a complete replica of a room, Brecht will not allow us to see more than fragmentary scenery. "Pity" and "terror" are disavowed by Brecht as ideals, because they can be achieved only by steeping the public in emotionalism. "Catharsis" is discounted, because Brecht's object is not to purge us of tensions but to make us aware of the conditions under which tensions arise. Besides, catharsis is supposed to be a complete discharge within the boundaries of the theatre, whereas the aim of the epic demonstration is to prepare us for discharging the understanding we have acquired from the play into life outside the playhouse. Here is theatre for *extroverted,* non-subjective drama, as contrasted with introverted, subjective realistic, symbolist or expressionist drama, yet drama with poetry.

To what extent this or any other style of non-Aristotelian playwriting will give us great drama cannot of course be determined. We have gained much freedom for experiment. By its fruits shall this freedom be tested.

CONSERVATISM IN THE THEATRE

As we rounded out fifty years of twentieth-century theatre and some seventy-five years of modern theatre, we found ourselves wondering in the early nineteen-fifties whether a period of dramatic art of such long duration was not in danger of disintegrating. Modern theatre had already lasted as long as the great Attic stage, and it had already enjoyed a longer life-span than the Elizabethan and vital French neo-classic drama. Two global wars, anti-humanist eruptions of totalitarianism, and a continual war of principles in art, as well as in society, had often jolted dramatic art out of its grooves, toppled it on its sides, bruised and battered it, stopped it in its tracks for years, and forced it to move ahead at an unsteady clip. It could not be assumed, however, that the era of modern theatre is over. Curtains had been rung down on a free theatre throughout Europe from time to time, and the production record of the American professional theatre had been shrinking steadily, and yet drama unmistakably modern continued to be created. If the new playwrights who arise now and then are not the giants we think they are in our first moments of unguarded enthusiasm, they do, nonetheless, suggest that not all modern drama has hardened into academicism or turned to slush.

It is in a period when everything still hangs in the balance, when we oscillate between sound and unsound theatre, that it becomes useful to look to the health of our dramatic art. And one pertinent point to consider is whether we have anything to conserve, if not to enlarge and advance; and experimental efforts that diversify and sometimes invigorate our art should not divert us from a glance at our accumulated resources and from the consideration whether these are not being too heedlessly written off, wasted, or misused.

For all the enthusiasm that has been lavished on plays in which nuance and mood exceed characterization or in which snippets of observation are more dominant than plot, as well as for all our faith in expressionistic experiment or interest in Brechtian epic creation, we should be very much on our guard. There is an anti-dramatic tendency in the exaltation of mood into a dramatic absolute. The disdain of plot by playwrights is often not the concomitant of any passion for ideas such as Shaw expressed, but a weariness of soul or laggardness in the realm of conviction. Those who have nothing to say or do not care to say anything definitely can easily take refuge in a mélange of titillating pictures. To refrain from creating a plot may be actually a means of evading intellec-

97

tual responsibility, for plot need not be a fabrication for the purpose of stunning an audience but a means for enlightening it. In creating plot, Sophocles shaped a story in an *Oedipus the King* or *Antigone* in order to demonstrate a point. There are many able or cultured playwrights for whom the denigration of plot is a justification for avoiding commitment to a point of view. And Brechtian epic theatre, as well as other modernist styles, can mask an incapacity or a disinterest in investing the drama with the dimensions of human life.

All the varied experiments of modernism, moreover, can prove antidramatic in proportion to their anti-humanism. Drama is fundamentally action; otherwise there would be no point in writing a work intended to be acted out on the stage. And all action is fundamentally human action; otherwise there would be no point in using living actors. Drama is drama to the degree to which it constitutes cohesive, meaningful action involving human characters, regardless of what other gratifications may be provided by the play and the stage production. Our modernists must be warned to *conserve the drama* whatever else in the theatre they may not choose to conserve. And it follows that they will conserve humanism, too, if they heed individuality, for dramatic values have always been associated with it. Great drama coincides with a view of life that postulates for man a high degree of individual identity, sense of direction and responsibility, and capacity for making decisions as well as resorting to action with a total personality.

Conservatism, to my mind, is no better than the values it tries to conserve. Therefore, there are many kinds of conservatism and we must appraise them differently. Conservatism after 1850, for example, was dedicated to preserving a theatre that had lost the spirit of vital romanticism, that favored a makeshift pseudo-realism, that spun webs of intrigue without truth to life and truth to spirit, and that allowed actors to substitute their own harlequinade for the words of the playwright—even when the plays had the integrity of Henry Becque's *The Vultures* and *La Parisienne*. Such conservatism, indistinguishable from chicanery, had to be deplored, and was rightly challenged by Becque, Zola, Ibsen, Antoine, Stanislavski, and other pioneers of modernism. Also the conservative orientation of Broadway in our own day displays a disposition favorable to standard musical comedies or revues and to banal realism. It is only proper that creative writers and directors should scorn the "Broadway" point of view which knows only one objective—that of putting on a profitable show by pandering to the lowest common denominator of taste for live entertainment.

We have also encountered in our time a politically determined conservatism. In Nazi Germany, for example, the conservative point of view dismissed all modernism as decadent, tried to turn the clock back to Sardou and Scribe, and destroyed the humanism of the theatre along with its experimentalism, with the result that a dozen years of Nazi rule brought Germany not a single play we can respect. At the midcentury point, moreover, the most commonplace theatre was to be found in the Soviet Union. Under Stalinism, a theatre once renowned for its vitality even under the far from encouraging rule of the latter-day Czars, and a theatre that aroused the wonder of tourists during the early post-revolutionary years, gradually became stultified. There arose, indeed, the anomaly of an ultra-conservative theatre in a country that has prided itself upon being the most dynamic in the world. The results have been distressing. Soviet plays have been largely utilitarian in spirit and theme. Creative imagination has been strangled in Russia by so-called Socialist Realism, and by the inability of its dramatists to feel free to express their individuality and personal convictions. They may find their craft profitable, and they have economic security so long as they toe the mark and address themselves to the average mentality as determined by Communist Party lines. Playwrights had more freedom of self-expression even under the benevolent or inefficient monarchies of the past than they have had for years in the Soviet state. And the Communist Party line beyond the borders of Russia is also "conservative." It is niggling, witch-hunting, narrow. It bites even the hand of the artist that is held out in a handshake. It demands obedience to dogma and policies, and it denounces every individual deviation as a form of "bourgeois decadence."

Conservatism can prove just as arid, of course, anywhere else than in Russia and under any other dispensation when it enforces orthodoxy and represses freedom of expression. I have not heard anything particularly encouraging about the Spanish theatre since the death of Lorca in 1936. And I do not rule out the possibility that our own drama could lose its buoyancy and critical spirit under similarly repressive conditions that were to impose hypocrisy and time-serving upon playwrights,

The conservative point of view that has been and is likely to be fruitful is of a different complexion from that which I have described above. It pertains to dramatic art itself and to the fundamental values that constitute the tradition in drama that has hitherto commanded our respect and admiration. I refer to standards that have prevailed in the art regardless of change in the art and in the society in which it was created. Much dramatic criticism in modern times has been impressionistic, and a paragraph would hardly exhaust the tribute we can pay to its merits or the justification we can find for it. Criticism that has insisted on "standards" has, on the contrary, often possessed a narrow heart and a narrow mind, whether or not these standards have been neo-classic with their rule of the "unities," moralistic in the arterio-sclerotic manner of that Victorian American critic William Winter who fought Ibsen, or dogmatically Marxist. It is not, therefore, with the intention of standardizing the drama or dramatic criticism that I would refer to ruling concepts or practices the preservation of which seems to me essential to the continued vitality of the modern drama.

The first of these principles must be humanism in the broadest sense of the term. If the drama loses its concern with man as an individual, it surrenders the main source of its significance as art and as a communion. All qualities we look for in a play stem from the individualization of the characters—good dialogue, interesting complication, dynamic force, and human significance. This is a platitude, but I am not ashamed to repeat it because individuality has been under a cloud for a long time, not only in totalitarian countries but in the democracies. Realism won its early triumphs in the work of Becque, Tolstoy, Ibsen, Strindberg, Chekhov, and others, because its practitioners never lost sight of the individual in spite of their concern with society. But the tendency of latter-day realism has been to subordinate him to the social realities which actually lose most, if not all, of their reality the moment the individual fails to hold the stage.

In the various stylizations of drama, this danger of suppressing or depersonalizing the human being has been equally manifest, if not more so. Mechanization vitiated expressionism and expressionistically slanted drama. It even deprived the latter-day modern masters of some of the interest and power we had a right to expect of them. O'Neill, for example, overindulged in the schematization of characters and plays. Nina's "three men" were created primarily to represent man the father, man the husband, and man the lover in *Strange Interlude;* and the Electra and Orestes characters of *Mourning Becomes Electra* were confused with Freudian complexes. From *The Emperor Jones* to *The Great God Brown, Dynamo,* and *Lazarus Laughed,* O'Neill's plays would suffer to different degrees from a schematization of men and ideas. There was a great overflow of dramatic tension and energy in all his work, but this is not to be confused with a flow of life when he became Freudian or metaphysical. In all the plays O'Casey wrote after *The Silver Tassie* one could always note an abundant stream of feeling, but even feeling is no substitute for the complete man when O'Casey rode a poetically bedizened argument too hard, as he did in *The Star Turns Red.* Feeling, like thought, is only one of the attributes of the human being, and one of the confusions of modern liberalism has been this tendency to make feeling or intellection or social responsibility the sum total of humanity. This mistake was not made by Shakespeare or, in our century, by Chekhov. O'Casey is the chief exception among our living ideological playwrights. Even when passion for an ideal jolts his writing, he steers us into the channels of humanity; he remains a poet while others merely cavil. O'Casey has very rarely succumbed to his politics, whereas too many social-minded playwrights have.

The fault is not only in liberalism, "Socialist Realism," stylistic experiments that reduce man to an automaton, and psychological drama, where the neurosis is confused with the whole man. The flaw is also in the poetic drama, whether written by MacLeish (in the depression drama *Panic),* Yeats, Auden, Spender, or Eliot. Least pardonable, indeed, is error on the part of Eliot who leans toward Catholicism without possessing the catholicity of the leaders of the Church, who understood that man is man and not a faceless entity or a single attribute. The understanding to be found in St. Augustine's *Confessions* or the philosophical existentialism in arguments against Platonism by St. Thomas Aquinas is not present in either *Murder in the Cathedral* or *The Cocktail Party* in spite of Eliot's attempt to achieve theological correctness. In the former, the characters are generalized out of existence whether they be the women of Canterbury, the priests, or the knights. Even the personality of Becket is more hinted at than realized. In *The Cocktail Party,* the sheep are categorically divided from the goats, and in this lies the prime limitation of this ably written drama: The characters remain sheep and goats instead of rounded people. The commonplace individuals have no real dimension and none was attributed to them by definition, and the heroine turned saint loses all dramatic reality and becomes a subject for conversation. How differently created are the many characters of the dramatic masterpieces, whether written by Sophocles or Shakespeare or, for that matter, by Racine, Ibsen, and Chekhov! Nor should we slight the true Catholic drama of the middle ages when we recall such simple examples of humanization as the *Brome Abraham and Isaac,* the *Second Shepherds' Play,* or the Noah plays.

The truth is that everything, including the psychological and the religious interests that should enlarge the human reality of our drama, has tended to reduce or truncate life. Conservatism is needed to conserve the human being in the play. If an understanding heart has not been entirely absent in contemporary playwriting (it beats in O'Casey's *Juno and the Paycock* and *The Plough and the Stars,* in Paul Vincent Carroll's *Shadow and Substance,* in Odets' *Awake and Sing!,* and in a number of other plays), it has been in frequent jeopardy regardless of the political, moral, or poetic convictions of the dramatists.

Concurrently, a genuine conservatism should help us to clear up a variety of confusions without which completely effective humanization is virtually impossible. The greatest of these—and, indeed, the confusion that contains *all* seeds of confusion within it—is sentimentality. It takes shape whenever there is no fixity in culture and thought. It has assumed many shapes in our century, and it insinuates itself into some of our best plays.

There is the radical form of sentimentality which assumes that all men are free from "original sin," that they are at heart all good and are corrupted only by social forces beyond their control. Great drama has a hard core; too much modern drama has had a soft one. An insufficient understanding of moral responsibility, a willingness to shift responsibility from man to something called Society or Capitalism, a readiness to respect all complaints and to countenance the whimpering self-indulgence of individuals who never knew the value of discipline and endurance—all this has limited the work of even talented dramatists.

Awake and Sing!, for example, would have been a better and a more enduring play if it had occurred to Clifford Odets that his heroine's complaints that she is frustrated have little basis in reality. If Hennie is a victim of middle-class society, then we are to assume that society owes a girl as many love affairs as she desires in addition to the right to palm off her illegitimate baby on another man, to leave him when she comes to an understanding with her lover, and to go off in search of a dubious romance with nary a thought for the infant she brought into the world. Hennie's brother, who cannot marry the girl he loves because his impoverished family needs his income, has a better case, and we can surely sympathize with him. But Odets might have reflected that we are all compelled to make renunciations, and that this is not a special circumstance of middle-class society but of life itself. Odets might reasonably have asked himself whether men have not been called upon to make sacrifices under any other form of society, not to mention Russian communism. When Hennie, moreover, "awakes and sings"—that is, runs away with her lover, bearing with her the blessings of her "awaking" younger brother—the tone of the writing is curiously rapturous. Only the force of Odets' playwriting and the sentimentality that passes for liberalism could have prevented intelligent critics from discovering the callowness of this resolution.

It is also questionable whether some sympathy was not misplaced in the same author's *Golden Boy.* Here it is understandable that the young hero should have turned from violin-playing to prize-fighting, and that he should have been coarsened by the profession. To want to escape poverty is a strong motive, and to pursue the conveniences and pleasures that are invariably overrated and overpublicized in a materialistic age is normal behavior. But Odets, reflecting, although also transcending, a concern with materialism almost equally well distributed among left-wing adherents and Babbitts, dissolved the play in too much sympathy for young Bonaparte's pleasure-seeking. Worse than that, Odets weakened the force of his argument by stressing the artistic sensibility and promise of the boy. We are expected to feel a special pity for him because his creative possibilities were destroyed by his prize-fighting career—a career he chose as a profitable alternative to playing the violin and probably remaining poor. Since when, we may argue, has life had to be easy for the creative spirit? Since when has talent insisted upon favorable economic circumstances in order to persist in its aims; and when has it *not* been called upon to resist the temptations of the world of material success and power? When has it not been called upon to reject, to use Thomas Mann's apt phrase, "the blisses of the commonplace"? *Golden Boy* has its merits, it is true, but it would have been made of more endurable fibre if its author's moral understanding had been stronger. Even Arthur Miller's *Death of a Salesman,* in spite of the critical intelligence displayed in the play, may lead us to wonder whether it is not charged with more sympathy than the traffic will bear. I should be more certain of transcendent merit in *Death of a Salesman* if Willy Loman, for whom the playwright has claimed tragic importance, were more man and less dolt, and if he gave more evidence of the noble qualities that Willy's wife attributes to him.

It would be unfair, however, to confine our criticism of sentimentality to the writers of social drama. That commodity has not been absent from the Canterbury Festival plays of English poet-playwrights any more than it has been absent from many Kaufman collaborations in which the breezy pseudo-sophistication of the nineteen-twenties was liberally sprinkled with sugar for the public palate. The debunking Kaufman collaborations passed for cynicism, but only their deliberate sentimentality is cynical. Writers of psychological drama also became sentimental in various ways, ventilating personal despairs, as O'Neill did in romanticizing the loss of faith in *Dynamo,* or Williams did in blazoning the sorrows of a neurotic Magdalen in *A Streetcar Named Desire.* Great drama does not dissolve in an author's self-pity or in pity for a failure of nerve; it strikes a *balance,* and it does not confuse *empathy* with *sympathy.* O'Neill, Odets, Miller, and Williams, being men of talent, were able to transcend, to a degree, the limitations of the sentimental points of view. But what about writers whose talent is less sturdy? When these flounder in sentiment, they invariably go under, and the age encourages exaggerated tender-mindedness. It is surely significant that so many contemporary plays have been written about children, whose moral responsibility is slight, while there is not a single instance of a play having been written about a child-hero by the master-dramatists of the past. Even *Romeo and Juliet* is no true exception; whatever their actual age, Romeo and Juliet are not children in their passion and speech.

True conservatism in the theatre need not, of course, favor any single style or form of drama. Nor do I maintain that we should legislate on the subject-matter or political beliefs of playwrights. A sensible conservatism is needed, and badly needed, in the contemporary theatre for something more important—for sound appraisals of human behavior for a sound application of values to democratic sympathy. It is also needed as a solvent for disruptive elements in our theatre, such as the tendencies to substitute a spotlight for a good speech and to display a sequence of telegraphic scenes instead of presenting fully realized actions. A play, in spite of the ruling passion for speed, is not a bicycle race. Dramatic conservatism cannot tell us too often that drama is a form of poetry—that its mental and emotional movement lies largely in its language. And this language must possess expressiveness, force, and nuance: It must not be a mere lever to action, but an action itself—an action of the mind and spirit that can be contemplated long after we have become familiar with the story of the play.

Dramatic conservatism, finally, cannot stress too strongly in this day of motion pictures, radio, and television that scenes in the drama are not fragments of story-telling to be got over as quickly as possible, but *experiences* to be fully savored. If a number of Shakespeare's scenes have a brisk, cinematic quality, these are at least justified by their poetic force and by the epic sweep of the action of the entire play, as in *Henry V* and *Antony and Cleopatra*. The short scenes of third-rate writing in much modern writing have, as a rule, only one purpose—namely, that of propelling an action that the author was incapable of expressing with more intellectual and emotional density.

The nature of the stage is such that it enables a writer to present life as an experience. A *story* can be told sketchily and with great speed, as the films have shown us. An experience is something to be absorbed and assimilated. We are so busy in our era with getting things done that we tend to overlook the fine art of experiencing life. Neither commentary nor story-telling is the essence of the timeless art that allows the living actor to enact his human nature and his destiny in the immediate presence of his fellowmen. And for that reason, theatrical conservatism would conclude today, we should not be summary in dismissing realism unless we can be sure that we are getting a sense of the substantiality of life from the differently styled types of drama.

IBSEN IN THE
CONTEMPORARY THEATRE

A recurrent problem important to creativity and progress in the theatre has been that of assimilating its geniuses. The English stage has had this problem for centuries with Shakespeare, and has never quite assimilated him, as multitudes of abortionate blank verse drama from Dryden's day to our own have made sufficiently evident. France faced a similar difficulty with Racine, and even "the battle of Hernani" was only a dubious solution. Hugo's success was followed not by a succession of dramatic poets but by the trite tribe of Scribe. The poetic fires were banked when Racine's reign was over, and even Rostand could supply only firecrackers in their place—poses instead of passions, sentiments instead of desire intensely at war with reason.

We have a similar problem today with Ibsen. After seventy-five years, the modern theatre still has not succeeded in coming to terms with the "father of dramatic modernism." Those who consciously rejected him either died of pernicious anemia, as did Maeterlinck and Andreyev, or never attained the full growth to which their talent entitled them. Those who accepted him, without understanding or being willing to understand him, made themselves into pinchbeck replicas.

Only the playwrights who remained true to themselves, or borrowed from him only that which they could make their own, attained true stature. But to cite the fortunate case of a Shaw, a Chekhov, or an O'Casey does not make the Ibsen problem less exigent. None of these men found a following; in the main, they were and remain *sui generis*. Ibsen's followers, on the contrary, still populate the theatre. Indeed, virtually all the serious English plays are watered-down Ibsen. The French existentialist flock, with Sartre as its bellwether, drinks Ibsenism spiked with a metaphysical brew; and this brew is, incidentally, from the same Kirkegaard "Either-Or" distillery that Ibsen patronized as long ago as the eighteen-sixties when he composed *Brand* and *Peer Gynt*. And in America I can find only three active playwrights whose work entirely escapes Ibsen's libations—Thornton Wilder, who doesn't write plays frequently enough, Saroyan, who writes them too frequently, and Maxwell Anderson, who has been more at home with Schiller and the Elizabethans for some twenty years.

It is difficult to exorcise Ibsen from the contemporary theatre, and it is precisely for this reason that men who entertain high expectations for the drama have concentrated their fire upon him. His influence has irked them whenever they have dreamed of liberating the theatre for imaginative art. A struggle against Ibsen has been going on, indeed, ever since the eighteen-eighties, and as it is likely to continue for some time, it may yet go down in theatrical history as its Hundred Years War. One does not have to be Nostradamus, however, to predict that, like most wars, it will settle nothing of consequence. One reason is, of course, that the only thing that settles anything in art is genius, from which all finalities—whether those of a Mozart or a Shaw—come. But another cogent reason for the inconclusiveness of the struggle is that the battles are waged over false issues. Actually, it is not Ibsen but an imaginary Norwegian Old Man of the Sea who has been riding herd on playwrights, weighing them down with commonplaces and turning their marrow into water.

Although I don't know how the argument on behalf of the real Ibsen and for the benefit of modern playwriting can be pursued in less than a book-length essay or without repeating previously made observations, I believe some points can be singled out for stronger emphasis than they have generally received. It may be to the point to say in summary fashion that, historically considered, his work was a culmination of middle-class civilization and of middle-class drama. He was the only powerful European dramatist to present the middle-class in a habitat that preserved it virtually unmixed with dissolving ideas or attitudes while himself remaining detached and critical. Ibsen is a classic writer because he expressed a way of life fully crystallized and entirely representative. He was also able to present it with the intensity that major dramatic art always brings to its subject.

It is to be noted that if Ibsen, beginning with *Love's Comedy* and ending with *John Gabriel Borkman,* shows this life crumpling or becoming untenable, he shows that to be the case *from within.* If he dramatizes a conflict, it is invariably a "palace revolt," rather than an invasion, and it is a struggle resulting from inner compulsions rather than from superimposed ideologies. This, too, accounts for the intensity of his work by comparison with plays turned out by both the sophisticated cosmopolitan and the class-war writers. In their work, the conflicts are essentially so weak that they must lead to comedies of manners, such as Maugham's *The Circle* and *The Constant Wife* and Barry's *Holiday,* when the situation is cosmopolitan, or to external action and even melodrama when middle-class life is challenged by proleterian writers and allies who have declassed themselves, as no Ibsen character ever does or really could.

No playwright was ever less "sophisticated" than Ibsen, a fact noted by Henry James, who would have an eye for such things, when he dubbed him "a provincial of provincials" and called his art a miracle "because it is the result of so dry a view of life, so indifferent a version of the comedy of things," or referred to the plays as "lamps burning in tasteless parlours, with the flame practically exposed." No playwright was ever less "proletarian" either, in spite of his having favored socialism for a time. (And what is socialism, after all, except the bourgeois aspiration of the working-class!) Ibsen's careful financial investments, love of decorations and decorum, sense of guilt, methodical ways of working, and Protestant moralism only substantiate a fact amply evident in his plays once he abandoned imitative romanticism.

Ibsen wrote nearly all his important plays, beginning with *Brand,* in foreign capitals. But except in *Emperor and Galilean* and the penultimate act of *Peer Gynt,* the subject is small-town Norwegian life. Even Norway's capital, Christiana, was in his time a small provincial town. Nature itself—mountain, fjord, or sea—is subverted to the uses of moralistic notation, as in *Brand* and *Peer Gynt,* or matrimonial adjustment, as in *The Lady from the Sea.* The snow-covered slopes facing the former tycoon John Gabriel Borkman standing in front of his prison-house merely climax as small-town a story of narrow life as it is possible to conceive. Ibsen's *leit-motifs* rarely stray from the theme of the soul fettered to the ferris-wheels of suburban opinion or behavior, and soul-anguish is all the greater for this. The effective metaphors in the plays are middle-class conceptions or poetic extensions of these, such as the poisoned springs of a health resort or the white horses of Rosmersholm that symbolize conscience and retribution!

Most obviously, too, when Ibsen turned to his contemporary world, he, a poet with a national reputation, abandoned poetry except in his early effort, *Love's Comedy.* He did so, besides, without compromise; that is, without recourse to the poetic colloquial speech of the countryside that Synge found so rewarding. He adopted the unflavored language of the middle-class, even in his best late symbolist plays. How he nevertheless charged it with drama, how he perfected urban prose dialogue as the new dramatic medium can be observed even through the veil of William Archer's Victorian translations and more clearly in the three Una Ellis-Fermor translations recently published by Penguin Books. (German translations are still more effective, which may help to explain the fact that the mature Ibsen won popularity first and most extensively in Germany.) Prose, thanks to him, became to modern dramatists what blank verse had been to the Elizabethans and rhymed hexameters to the French. Bringing to bear upon his chosen *milieu* by means of his chosen prose medium the powers of observation and analysis for which he is justly renowned, he gave the fullest realization to the realistic view inherent in middle-class drama from its beginnings—beginnings that can be traced as far back as the guild plays of the Middle Ages displaced by aristocratic Renaissance drama "tragical-comical-historical-pastoral."

Ibsen, moreover, climaxed the long ascent of this realistic theatre by the most single-minded concentration on the theme of individuality and struggle for self-realization to be found outside the literary scope of romance. In fact, Ibsen was an explosive figure in his day precisely because he took individualistic doctrine at face value. The really troublesome iconoclasts and rebels are not those who introduce absolutely "different" ideas but those who take accepted, taken-for-granted values so seriously that they ask us to live up to our professions. Only persons who take religion seriously can become heretics! Ibsen fought the battle for individualism to which the middle-class was dedicated not only by its beliefs but by its historical role in Western European civilization. It is also to be noted, of course, that he spiritualized the middle-class idea of self-realization; or re-spiritualized what had been already well affirmed by the French declaration of the Rights of Man and by our own Declaration of Independence in favor of "life, liberty, and *the pursuit of happiness.*" But it is still more significant that, as I have noted before, he dramatized the need and struggle for self-realization *within* the strictly middle-class society. He was the realist *par excellence,* since he encountered a society instead of escaping from it. And he was the dramatist *par excellence,* since he observed the struggle where it existed most intensely rather than in cosmopolitan circles where it is apt to be less exigent. If Ibsen's plays, indeed, can strike anyone as dated today whereas they were considered too modern in their own day, a major reason is that the truly parochial society, insulated from the world of mixed social intercourse and relaxed values, has been disappearing. The struggle for individual self-realization in terms of liberation from convention is no longer a primary concern—or so it seems to influential dramatic criticism, which is always metropolitan.

"The author nevertheless arrives at the dramatist's great goal—he arrives for all his meagreness at intensity," Henry James said of him. And Ibsen was able to write classics of middle-class life and sum up its essence, its humanity, because he possessed that intensity—in combination with mastery of the narrow dramatic form natural to his matter. The "actuality" of his plays is the result of creating individuals completely in the round. An exceptional empathy enabled the historian Egon Friedell to describe the ultimate reality of characterization that makes realism most valuable in Ibsen's work. In the brilliant cultural history, *Kulturgeschichte der Neuzeit,* which is a better introduction to the drama than most books written exclusively on the subject, Friedell wrote that Ibsen's characters give the impression that they are merely paying him a visit: *"dass sie eigentlich nur bei ihm zu Besuch sind."* They come from somewhere outside, spend some time in his play, and then leave it. They were alive before the play started and live on after the show is over. One also finds it possible to learn more about them, as about real people, by forming closer relationships with them; that is, the more often one reads the play the more one knows about its characters. But, as Friedell notes, *"Ganz auskennen wird man sie niemals"*—we shall never get to know them completely.

Ibsen shows us a great deal—as if he were a mere photographer. But a good deal of the reality lies in the shadows of the picture. The main character's self-analysis and confessions do not tell all, just as the opinions of the secondary characters have only partial validity. For all his analytical prowess, Ibsen foregoes definitions of character even when he seems to be defining it. There are always possibilities left unexhausted, and even points of fact, such as the paternity of little Hedwig in *The Wild Duck,* are left uncertain—as they are apt to be in life. When asked whether the disreputable Engstrand of *Ghosts* had not deliberately set fire to the orphan asylum, Ibsen replied that "he didn't know but that he wouldn't put it past him!" Moreover, all important Ibsen characters, when Ibsen is at his best, reveal themselves piecemeal, disclosing not only to us but *even to themselves* facets or abysses of their character, capacities for action or reaction they did not seem to possess or didn't know they possessed previously. Character in Ibsen, as in Shakespeare, is not a thing but a process, and this is to a large extent, in Ibsen's case, the secret of the dynamic quality of plays so slightly dependent upon stage intrigue and overt action.

Considering all these qualities, how can we deny that Ibsen recreated life itself in his realistic pieces and consequently created a true *criticism of life.* (I am inclined to sustain this claim even for plays of his Romantic phase, such as the memorable historical drama *The Pretenders* and, of course, *Peer Gynt,* and for plays of his late Symbolist phase, such as *The Master Builder, Lady from the Sea* and *Little Eyolf.*) Considering also that the middle-class is extremely representative humanity—there is the bourgeois in all of us, as there has always been, to reckon with!—Ibsen's art, for all its "meagerness," is universal art. Ibsen is the past master of those who arrive at universality through the particular and local realities.

If conclusive evidence is needed, one will find it in his characters. Solness, the ubiquitous master (whether business man or professor, craftsman or artist) past his prime and dispirited, jealous of upstart youth yet infinitely, fatally, attracted to it; Mrs. Elvsted, the eternal woman, and Hedda, her eternal counterpart; *The Wild Duck's* Hjalmar Ekdal, omnipresent weakling and average self-indulgent man; and the Ekdals' incubus, Gregers Werle, whose story Friedell called *"die ganze Leidensgeschichte des tragikomischen Menschheitsapostels,"* the Passion of the eternal tragicomic reformer-meddler whose well-intentioned efforts invariably cause trouble—these are all universal figures in spite of their provincial background. If the richness of the characters and, therefore, of the plays is not as evident as it should be on our stage, this is not so much because Archer's translations are so poor as because our performances are poor. This would seem incredible because Ibsen's roles seem so distinct. But they are also complex and subtle. Without, indeed, scrupulously studying the text of *Hedda Gabler* as one would study an orchestral score, and with the same knowingness a musician must bring to his subject, one will never quite know how much has been lacking in any American presentation of *Hedda Gabler,* for example, since the late Emily Stevens' performance in the mid-twenties.

That Ibsen prevails as a dramatist through his characters has been apparent ever since the recession of the specific issues that collected a veritable *Schimpflexikon* of diatribes against Ibsen as a home breaker and immoralist. Nora, for instance, may have been taken as a heroine of the movement for feminine emancipation in seeking experience outside her doll's house that would entitle her to citizenship in the world, but it is clear as daylight that her reasons for leaving her husband were deeply feminine. In not offering to save her from arrest on a charge of forgery by taking the blame on himself, he had failed her as a lover; therefore, he had failed her as a husband. Yes, there is "discussion" in the plays, as Shaw noted, but it interpenetrates their action instead of being superimposed, and it does not subordinate characters or diminish their reality. The "idea" emanates in many instances from the intensified life of the drama as steam naturally rises from a boiling kettle. The resolutions of the plays, besides, are not actually resolutions, except where, as in Hedda's or the "master-builder's" case, a fateful career comes to an end. Did Nora find the realizations she sought, did Mrs. Alving administer the lethal pills to her son, did Mrs. Elvsted and Tesman ever reconstitute Lövborg's book? We shall never know. The demonstration of the "idea" has already occurred in the flux of a life displayed before us and is not dependent, as a rule, upon the solution of a problem or a final action. Every point concerning Hedda as a failure has already been made before Ibsen has her put a bullet into her lovely head.

It is important, finally, to realize that Ibsen not only refrained from doling out panaceas, but revised the views that streamed through his plays. He did so from play to play, and sometimes within the same play. If an "emancipated" outlook was good for Nora, was it good for the heroine of *Rosmersholm* or for Hedda? If Hedda was sophisticated and Mrs. Elvsted was naïve, who was nevertheless the freer woman? If the free, idealistic woman can be as creatively useful as a man, how is it that bold young Hilda encompasses the destruction of the master-builder Solness? If it is important to take out the skeletons from society's closets, is it also good for Gregers Werle to take them out of the Ekdal closet?

For a writer who seemed to be Europe's chief merchant of categorical imperatives, Ibsen was, we must remember, a remarkable relativist. Ibsen the most labeled man in the theatre, defies labels. Shaw maintained that the Norwegian play-maker created the "drama of ideas." But this means something only if we realize that Ibsen was, to adopt Edmund Wilson's apt term for Shaw, a "triple-thinker."

On close inspection, a qualification must also be made concerning the notion that Ibsen's "natural" technique affords some sort of dispensation from dramaturgy or, more importantly, from creative arrangement and patterning. In starting a plot close to the catastrophe of a play, he achieved concentration on the most challenging and intensely revealing moments of a life. In this respect, he worked as a "dramaturgist." In finding correlative symbols for characters and situations, he worked, at the same time, as a poet. As a matter of fact, and contrary to superficial generalization, his contribution to modern playwriting is not that he raised his wand and with one swish displaced the midcentury "well-made play" of the French school of Scribe. If this is true, especially after the writing of *A Doll's House*, it is so not because Ibsen brusquely dispensed with such elements of the "well-made play" as suspense, revelations and discoveries, *confidants* and *raisonneurs,* and even intrigues, but because he transposed them into another key—the "key" of the human symphony. For example, Gregers Werle carries on a good deal of sleuthing in *The Wild Duck,* but he does this as a neurotic character sublimating itself by "idealism" rather than as a professional sleuth and intriguer. Something comes from his sleuthing, besides, that is intellectually provocative and humanly significant.

Ibsen was not fool enough to believe that a play should *not* be contrived, for every work of art is contrived. He was not a naturalist in either practice or theory. Contrivance is present even in his most austerely written plays. In *Ghosts,* for example, why should the fire at the orphan asylum erected in honor of Alving occur after the pastor dissuaded Mrs. Alving from insuring it and before Mrs. Alving reveals that her marriage was a failure and that her servant is Alving's illegitimate daughter, after which his legitimate son Oswald reaps the harvest of hereditary venereal disease? Here the long arm of coincidence is plainly employed for ironic-symbolic purposes. Why, in that model of realistic dramaturgy *Hedda Gabler,* should Lövborg be in town and Mrs. Elvsted turn up exactly on the day Hedda has returned from a honeymoon abroad, and why should Lövborg lose his single manuscript in the street, Tesman find it, and Aunt Rina's death take Tesman out of the house conveniently so that Hedda may burn the book? The point is that contrivance in Ibsen's best work not only has results different from those turned out by thrill and sensation factories but that it is a product of something other than play carpentry. Ibsen in much of his work is actually functioning as a poet or "maker."

Where does this disquisition carry us? And to what useful purpose nearly half a century after the playwright's death?

It has not been my purpose to extol his virtues but to situate them in the modern, specifically contemporary, theatre. Their pertinence can be summed up as follows: In the first place, the writers of problem plays, whether reformist or radical, are not his heirs, but Augier's and Dumas *fils'*; that is, they stem from a type of drama that Ibsen's major work superseded. The problem-play authors are mistaken, in short, if they think they are swimming in the stream of the modernism whose floodgates were opened by the Norwegian Proteus. Secondly, the writers of social drama in general have not learned their lesson from him, because they have put society first and the individual last in their plays. Our social realists have too often dramatized a condition, whereas for Ibsen the condition was crystallized in the revealed individual. Or they have dramatized the "idea" rather than the person. Writers of character drama, moreover, have not been materially different. Rather than the character itself, they have tended to present the "idea" of a character. They have been pseudo-Ibsenite vendors of problems and character-studies, and I suspect that the main reason for their failure is that they try to emulate Ibsen without understanding him.

The average playwright is either tethered to the commonplace, workaday world to such a degree that he describes it without the critical probing with which Ibsen roused the moribund nineteenth-century theatre; or he is capable of wielding Ibsen's surgical instrument but has only the shadow of a patient on which to perform the operation because the middle-class world has only a shadowy reality for him. The conformist tends to be a dullard; the non-conformist, a sleight-of-hand artist.

Ibsen achieved a synthesis between description and analysis and became a *total* dramatist. His imitators are usually only half-dramatists. If an Arthur Miller, treading in his footsteps, wins respect with an *All My Sons* and admiration with a *Death of a Salesman,* it is because he, too, is able to achieve a synthesis. But the contemporary theatre rarely encounters an Arthur Miller or the Odets who wrote *Awake and Sing!* Either the playwright bogs down in his *milieu* or he leaves it for a show-business mentality or for a sophisticated orientation that separates him from his subject matter, and for a would-be realist the results are attenuated or schematized playwriting unless he has a bent for comedy.

It is true, of course, that the cosmopolitan temperament can lead the playwright to experiment with non-realistic styles; and, occasionally, considerable success attends the effort in America and, more frequently, on the European continent. The break with middle-class drama has sparked many an anti-realistic movement in the theatre. But altogether too frequently some core of life has been missed by most anti-realistic writers. That was not the case when Ibsen himself turned to symbolist stylization after his middle period of realism. Except in his very last play *When We Dead Awaken,* written with failing powers, he managed to precipitate a substantial experience even when his more or less symbolist plays suffered from elusive thematic development and nebulous intimations. There are areas in such plays as *The Master Builder, The Lady from the Sea,* and *Little Eyolf,* not to mention *John Gabriel Borkman,* when the characters reveal themselves to us in depth and with intensity. In all these instances —such as the "master-builder's" relations to the younger generation and the conversations between husband and wife in *Little Eyolf*—Ibsen was not writing with his head alone. He remained naturally and deeply in the midst of life even when he entertained "ideas." Too many later playwrights suffered from "experience in the head," just as too many moderns, according to D. H. Lawrence, have suffered from "sex in the head." Ibsen did not belong to their company. If he has been accused of being too "bourgeois," we should be grateful that he invited this criticism. Perhaps he would have been less the playwright if he had been less the bourgeois. Perhaps it is true that he does not belong to our age on either side of the "Iron Curtain." If this is so, however, it is *our* misfortune, rather than his.

HENRY BECQUE:
THE MORDANT VIRTUOSO

At a time when good writing for the theatre is at a low ebb in most countries, not excluding our own, it may be well to return to the fountain-springs of the modern drama, which are now so muddied by the demands of commerce. And in returning to the sources we could do worse than glance at the struggles of Henry Becque, the one founder of dramatic modernism who is least known in America although James Huneker acclaimed him, Ashley Dukes translated him, and his plays found a place in all the influential theatres of Europe. Today, when showmanly cleverness is still too often a substitute for true penetrativeness in the theatre, there is still more lip-service to his principles than actual observance of them. To remember Becque is to recall how difficult it has been and still is to maintain playwriting on the high level to which it was raised by him and others in the eighteen-eighties.

In remembering Becque, moreover, we are forced to give some thought to the entire question of salvation for the theatre through departures from realism. Blame for the pinchbeck nature of much dramatic writing is often placed on the triumph of the realistic technique, whereas Becque's plays, perhaps even more than Ibsen's and less only than Strindberg's, would expose the absurdity of the charge. It was precisely against meretricious theatricality that modern realism ranged its heaviest batteries, and the vacuity of much that passes for realistic drama here and abroad is the very antithesis of Becque's work as well as that of the pioneers who were his contemporaries. The proposal to discard realism so often voiced by faithhealers of the stage incorporates one fallacy: The imaginative or poetic style of drama with which they intend to displace realism can also play us false, and humbug is humbug no matter whether it wears the trappings of poetry or the sack-suit of prose, the homburg of fancy or the straw hat of suburban realism. When the play is dramaturgically unsound or unconvincing, the deception does not succeed for all the prestidigitation of fanciful and stylized playwriting.

Becque's battle for sound, objective theatre was won at the end of the nineteenth century and then lost in a flood of "Maeterlinckéd" sweetness without light, buried in Reinhardt spectacles, and distorted by expressionistic subjectivism that produced no results comparable in value to the objective workmanship we got in the best plays of Chekhov and O'Casey, for example. The theatre had just rounded out half a century since Becque died, and yet the victory he gained for objective revelation, without tasting more than thin slivers of its fruits himself, had to be won all over again in spite of the recent appearance of a few good plays by Tennessee Williams and Arthur Miller.

It was Henry Becque's ironic destiny to be neglected while he was laying the foundations of French dramatic realism and then to be unable to complete a single long play when the theatre finally caught up with his art. In the eighteen-seventies, Émile Zola was thundering precepts in prefaces and searching for saviors of the French stage. His eyes lighted readily enough on the de Goncourt brothers, the novelists who shared his credo of "naturalism" and authors of a wretched play, *Henriette Maréchal*. He even glanced appreciatively at himself, writing some half-dozen plays as exemplars of stage realism. Zola looked in every direction except that of Becque. When the dramatist later came to write his memoirs, he would, remembering Zola's indifference, remark glumly that "the dog barks and the caravan passes."

Upon graduation from the old Lycée Bonaparte, Henri-François Becque, the son of a lowly government clerk in Paris, first found employment in a railroad office. But influenced by a maternal uncle Martin Labize, who had collaborated with the famous Labiche on a comedy, the young man turned eagerly to the theatre. From clerking at the Chemins de Fer du Nord he moved to a small position in the chancellery of the Legion of Honor and then to the household of the Polish diplomat Count Potocski as tutor and private secretary. Here came his first opportunity to emerge as a writer, the Count having introduced him to a young composer Victorien Jonçieres, for whom Becque wrote the libretto to the forgotten opera *Sardanapale* in 1885. In the same year, Becque also became the drama critic of the newspaper *Le Peuple,* and in 1886 he had the additional good fortune of seeing a little farce produced successfully.

Encouraged by this first taste of success, the no longer so very young author resolved to rely solely on his literary labors for a livelihood, and the decision was to cost him nothing less than a lifetime of embittering experience with producers and critics. His zeal for the theatre carried him so far into recklessness that he produced his first full-length play, *Michel Pauper,* at his own expense in 1870. He was rewarded for his pains with a resounding failure, and his next attempt in 1871, *The Elopement,* fared no better. Twice defeated, the playwright returned to the chancellery of the Legion of Honor and, from there, graduated to a stockbroker's office, where he remained for several years. Some measure of success came to him in 1878 with the reproduction of a short play *The Shuttle,* and, in 1880, with *The Virtuous Women,* which ultimately found its way into the repertory of the Comédie Française. But neither play greatly improved his financial condition, and his temper was sorely tried by failure to obtain a production for his first masterpiece *The Vultures (Les Corbeaux)*, written in 1877. It took him five years to win a hearing for the play, and its acceptance by the Comédie Française was only the prelude to a protracted struggle with the directors. Stubbornly rejecting all demands for changes in the text that would turn it into a "well-made play" of intrigue, Becque finally saw *The Vultures* on the stage in 1882 exactly as he had written it. But the disparity between his objective picture of middle-class life and the artificial style of stage production then in vogue gave him at best a qualified success. The hisses that greeted the play were as loud as the applause of the progressives in the auditorium, so that the premiere threatened to become another pitched battle like the "battle of 'Hernani' " half a century earlier, when romanticists had fought classicists on behalf of Hugo's romantic melodrama. Nor did Becque gain enough prestige at the time to be able to place his next play *The Parisian Woman (La Parisienne)* on the stage without first encountering humiliating rejections. The first production of this notable comedy in 1885 created a sensation without actually giving the author the success he deserved, and the Comédie Française, which condescended to present *La Parisienne* five years later, nearly turned a masterpiece into a fiasco with its inept staging methods.

When we look at the first of Becque's two masterpieces today, we are apt to find *The Vultures* almost as unique in our practical theatre as it was in the theatrical world between the years 1877 and 1882 when he tried to get his play produced. Although the theme seems familiar enough because we are accustomed to seeing business ethics criticized on the stage, we shall, if we are sailing in the weather of Broadway or West End theatrical production, consider Becque's dramaturgy altogether too simple, bare, and naïve. An American producer reading the play in innocence of its authorship would consider it the work of a promising young author who still "doesn't know his way around," for this is what the producer will find: He will read a first act that starts the play altogether too soon with a picture of the homelife of the middle-class Vignerons. The mother flutters about contentedly and the genial father dotes on his three daughters and makes them sing a *chanson* before he departs to keep an appointment. The pretty daughter Blanche looks forward to marrying a young man of good society; another daughter is absorbed in her study of music, and a third girl Marie is inconspicuously involved with nothing in particular. (When is the action to start, wonders the producer?) The house gradually fills with visitors, including Blanche's young man and the latter's aristocratic mother. They are just starting to celebrate Blanche's engagement, when a physician comes in to announce that Monsieur Vigneron has died of a heart-attack. And now it is really the turn of the producer to shake his head sadly. Why doesn't the inexperienced author manage it so that Vigneron will die on the stage—perhaps overexcite himself at the festivities and collapse in full sight of the audience? This is always good theatre, whereas the offstage death is untheatrical. The author would waste his breath if he explained that the first part of his act is a slice of life, and that he has no reason to turn Vigneron's death into a holiday for the box-office customers.

What follows is that Vigneron's business partner Teissier, his lawyer Bourdon, an architect, and a number of petty cheats proceed to pluck the helpless family. It is especially plain that the family's lawyer and the business partner are acting in collusion. Yet once the methods of the scoundrels are revealed, the playwright makes no effort to make a stage plot out of their rapacity, for the kind of plucking the Vignerons get is a routine matter that proceeds in a perfectly untheatrical, legalistic fashion. Instead of making an exciting thing of the business intrigue, then, the play turns to the personal complication of the impulsive Blanche, who gave herself to her fiancé only to learn that his mother refuses to countenance the marriage without a substantial dowry. And here, too, our hypothetical showman is bound to be disappointed. He would expect a pathetic scene between hero and heroine, but it is only the mother, who has gone from place to place to ascertain the Vigneron family's financial condition, who calmly tells Blanche that the marriage cannot take place. Becque, moreover, has no sooner held out the appetizing dish of an illegitimate pregnancy to the public than he austerely removes it from our sight. The girl's condition is quickly absorbed by the over-all dramatic development, which has in the meantime caught up with her sensible sister Marie, who has attracted her father's rascally partner Teissier.

The aged vulture proposes marriage and Marie, aware of her sister's condition and of the helplessness of the family, accepts him. Blanche's problem will no doubt be settled now one way or another, and the playwright does not even tell us this, because he is not interested in untying all the knots of his story simultaneously, as is so often the case in the theatre and so rarely the case in life. Teissier arranges the marriage through his lawyer Bourdon, and strangely enough it is this second swindler who most effectively protects Marie's interests by making her insist on a settlement of one half of Teissier's fortune. Becque has again disappointed the conventional showman by not writing a scene showing the reformation of the advocate. For Bourdon, according to his "realistic" view of life, it was absolutely right—a Darwinist law of nature, so to speak —to rob the Vigneron nest when the father-bird was gone. Now it is equally right for Marie to pluck Teissier, for nature has placed an old man at the mercy of a young woman. *The Vultures* resolves itself as if Becque had dispassionately observed a law of nature working itself out in the decline and restoration of the Vignerons' fortunes. Yet nothing could be more ironic in tone and more devastatingly satiric than this exposé of how "social Darwinists" act and think. And the more indifferent Becque is to the amorality of his characters the more thoroughly he exposes them as the vultures they are.

Becque's virtuosity in refraining from virtuosity is even more remarkable in his second masterwork *La Parisienne*. This comedy does not even have a "resolution," for Clotilde Du Mesnil, who has been betraying her husband at the beginning of the play, simply continues to betray him at the end. Nor does *La Parisienne* actually possess a "crisis." There is never any question of Clotilde's being found out; the husband is a complacent individual who misses the lover's company more than the wife does. There is much comic conflict, it is true, in the first act, but it is between the woman and the lover, and it quickly disappears when Clotilde simply drops him, only to take him back toward the end of the play when she has herself been dropped by another lover. The blasé second lover, who has furthered her husband's political ambitions at her request, quietly informs her that he is leaving for the country. Neither for him nor for Clotilde has the breaking up of the relationship assumed any critical proportions. Recriminations are for people who feel intensely, whereas the point of Becque's comedy is precisely that nobody is capable of intense emotion in this Parisian *milieu*. Nobody, that is, except the first lover Lafont, and he is merely ridiculous, since he claims the proprietary rights of a husband to her fidelity. Without a real crisis and resolution, with hardly any exposition, and without inserting a single bout of wit or a single prurient line Becque managed to write one of the most brilliant —and amoral—comedies of all time.

La Parisienne is full of irony, unconscious in the case of the characters; but the most ironical thing about it is that Becque's aloof observation of life should make the play pass for one of the most cleverly written pieces of the theatre. When the late A. B. Walkley, a critic not given to unconsidered enthusiasms, saw Mme. Réjane play Clotilde in London in 1901, he marveled at "this whiff of sulphur combined with *odeur de femme*," and called the comedy "diabolically clever." "It purports to have been written by the late Mr. Henri Becque single-handed," he added, "but I suspect Old Nick to have been at his elbow, an unseen collaborator." Yet this effect was the result of nothing more than the author's pretense of acting as the part of life's amanuensis. The play begins, as Walkley noted, with "one of the most complex hoaxes ever devised by a playwright." We are led to believe that Clotilde is engaged in a lengthy conjugal brawl with a jealous husband, until she calls out *"Prenez garde, voila mon mari"* and we know that the man is her lover. But the hoax is life's trick on the characters, for the comic and realistic point of the illicit relationship is that usage has made it indistinguishable from the unromantic state of marriage. As a romance, prolonged adultery is a highly overrated experience, and the jealousy of her lover proves as boring to Clotilde as would have been the jealousy of her husband. Becque's main achievement, however, was that his tenacious veracity should make Clotilde so monstrously immoral without turning her into a monster (she is patient, reasonable, considerate, and congenial), and so amusing without giving her an ounce of humor to flaunt before the public. Like Joyce's Molly Bloom, she is nature unadulterated by the sense of right and wrong.

Becque needed a theatre capable of giving life to his characters instead of dipping them into greasepaint and thrusting them out into the footlight area in order that they might hurl their lines into the auditorium. The entire point of the dramatic treatment in both *The Vultures* and *La Parisienne* was, after all, the revelation of moral turpitude in the society of his time through the natural conduct of his characters. They are drawn as people who consider their questionable morals above reproach, they regard their conduct and sentiments as norms of the social level on which they thrive. Both the humor and the indictment in Becque's two masterpieces arise entirely from the discrepancy between what his characters think of themselves and our judgment of them. The little foxes of *The Vultures* (and Lillian Hellman's *The Little Foxes* strongly recalls Becque's play) consider themselves merely realistic businessmen when they cheat a widow and three orphaned daughters of their inheritance. Clotilde in *La Parisienne* believes herself to be a devoted wife to her husband, for she wins him political advancement through her infidelity, and she considers herself so proper a person that she can seriously reprove her lover for his lack of religion. Unconscious irony can go no further than the conclusion of *The Vultures* when Teissier, the most ravenous of the rascals, proceeds to drive off the other vultures after winning Marie in marriage and remarks: "Since your father's death, my child, you have been surrounded by a pack of scoundrels."

To let the actor play up to the audience and address his remarks to it instead of to other characters, to push him out of the scenery that frames the room in which the action is supposed to take place, to allow him to declaim his lines with exaggerated gestures—these were the unpardonable sins that the conventional theatre committed against Becque and other realistic dramatists. A major upheaval was needed in theatrical art to make the revolution in playwriting effective. The revolution was started by André Antoine when he founded the Théâtre Libre in 1887, and it is not surprising that Becque rallied to Antoine's support. It was this pioneering actor-manager who gave *La Parisienne* its first distinguished production in 1897, with Mme. Réjane playing Clotilde to his Lafont at the Théâtre Antoine, founded two years before Becque's death.

With the triumph of the new naturalistic stagecraft, Becque finally came into his own. But by then Becque was depleted of his creative energy. He wrote nothing of significance after 1885 except two short pieces, *The Start (Le Depart)* and *Widowed (Veuve)*—the former a sketch of a shopgirl's induction into vice by a respectable employer who discharges her for refusing to yield to his son, the latter a sequel to *La Parisienne* which shows us Clotilde widowed at last but otherwise unchanged. Three other one-acters written in the year 1877 were trifles, and *The Puppets,* an exposé of the world of finance started fifteen years earlier, was left unfinished at his death. Admitted to the Legion of Honor in 1886, lionized in society for his acrid wit, invited in 1893 to lecture in Italy where his plays had become popular, he nevertheless remained poor and lonely. His admirers racked their brains for ways of stimulating him to create more masterpieces, and Antoine even lured him to Brittany for a summer's vacation to induce him to write again. A fire that the solitary man started in his bedroom with a lighted cigar caused him a severe shock, and he had to be placed in a sanatorium by friends. He never recovered. His death on May 15, 1899, was a deep blow to the men of the theatre who honored his forthright struggle to modernize the French stage.

Writing in 1905 about Becque, James Huneker declared that *The Vultures* was "the bible of the dramatic realists." Yet, unlike Zola, Becque never propounded any formula of Naturalism for playwrights. He did not even evince any marked enthusiasm for Ibsen, and the only realist who affected him was Tolstoy, whose peasant tragedy *The Power of Darkness* impressed him greatly. With curious inconsistency, probably for personal reasons of gratitude, he maintained a life-long admiration for Victorien Sardou, whose theatrical contrivances Bernard Shaw once dismissed as "Sardoodledom." In writing a preface to *The Vultures,* Becque dissociated himself from the Naturalists' fondness for sordid drama and from their pet doctrine of heredity. He wrote: "I have never entertained a great liking for assassins, hysterical and alcoholic characters, or for the martyrs of heredity and victims of evolution." He distrusted any sort of legislation for dramatists, declaring, "there is no law and there are no rules; there are only plays which are so different that no generalization is applicable. . . ." Concerning his encounters with conservatism in the theatre, he maintained merely that there were no conventions that originality could not displace, that "the history of art is nothing but the history of struggles between original talents and routine-bound minds."

All that Becque intended to do was to set down reality without distorting it for the sake of theatrical expediency. In confining himself to a segment of life, he seemed to say, "Make what you will of it, this is how people behave in our time and place, this is how they think, and this is how they speak." He dispensed with tricks of the trade, such as artificially emotional or scintillating "big" scenes and act-endings that brought the curtain down with a bang at the expense of naturalness. Like Strindberg, when the Scandinavian playwright came to write his remarkably compact one-act dramas, *Miss Julie* and *The Creditors,* Becque pruned his plays of all inessentials at a time when witty conversations, *ex cathedra* preachments, and declamations were considered the indispensable machinery of any theatre that expected to attract an audience; against this kind of dramaturgy, Becque declared that drama was the art of elimination. He endeavored, moreover, to release a natural flow of action which would make it impossible for the parts of a play to be differentiated mechanically as "exposition," "climax," and "dénouement." In a play like *The Vultures,* which suffers from some prolixity, and in the more brilliantly executed, if more narrowly Parisian, comedy *La Parisienne,* it is Becque's sharp observation that stands foremost. Unlike Ibsen, he did not quite rid his work of occasional asides or soliloquies, but these do not materially detract from his realism. It is the integrity of the conception and the writing of both plays that has preserved them, and it is integrity, for which there has never been too much regard in the theatre, that explains the influence this dour playwright exerted on the formative modern drama. From the ideal that he set for dramatists, there have been, regrettably, more descents than ascents, and this is as good a reason as any for remembering him half a century after his death.

At this time, especially in the American theatre, there is, however, an equally good reason for giving some attention to his two masterpieces, and that reason must strike us as a paradox if we still adhere to a naïve view of realism as a mere transcription of life. Becque had the gift of making a transcript look like a travesty, or if you will, a travesty look like a transcript. The "naturalness" of his dramaturgy and writing, which made it possible for him to set down reality in such a matter-of-fact manner, was in his case an instrument of satiric comedy. To treat the behavior and thought-processes of his vultures and amoralists as perfectly "natural" was the most powerful method he could have adopted to outrage us and make us consider them monstrous. The result is travesty achieved by naturalness. That is, the logic or consistency of these characters makes them exaggerations or caricatures. Conversely, for Becque to present such monsters of iniquity as perfectly natural specimens of the human species and of society is tantamount to directing his satire at the species and society. What, in other words, are we to think of the human race and of human society if Becque's amoralists are to be regarded as normal people!

It will be seen then that Becque used "realism," or "naturalism," far from naïvely. Unlike many later playwrights up to our own time, he was not the slave but the master of the realistic mode of playwriting coming into vogue in his day. He was a creator when he adopted the role of a transcriber, whereas many a playwright who succeeded him was a transcriber while adopting the role of a creator. Becque brought a distinctive, tart, and quizzical temperament and a nimble mind to the modern theatre. His astringent essays in *Souvenirs d'un Auteur Dramatique* and *Études d'Art Dramatique* also enforce this opinion. With these qualities he gave a unique comic style to naturalism, a style simultaneously "natural" and grotesque. One might call it a sort of expressionistic naturalism, without expressionistic fantasy and structure.

One can find this style, which is a quality of creativeness and urbane intellect, variously present in the work of European playwrights. It ferments in the plays of Carl Sternheim, barely known in America; in Hauptmann's *The Beaver Coat* and *The Conflagration (Der Rote Hahn)*; in Wedekind's *The Tenor;* in Granville-Barker's *The Voysey Inheritance;* in Pagnol's *Topaze,* Jules Romains' *Dr. Knock,* Crommelynck's *The Magnificent Cuckold,* and other French and Belgian pieces. In America, this kind of writing has not prevailed, unless we can ascribe it to *Tobacco Road,* where it is more salacious than tart, and to Edwin Justin Mayer's *The Children of Darkness,* where it is bespangled by romanticism. Other borderline cases may occur to us. But for the total charge of naturalistic irony and the full blast of boreal comedy, which American playgoers don't seem to be able to relish, we must go, first of all, to Henry Becque. We are, of course, under no particular obligation to like what we don't like. But the maturity of Becque's mind and the tempered steel of his spirit will remain a challenge to playwrights and a reminder that naturalistic playwriting can become a thoroughly creative act. Perhaps his denial of interest in Naturalism as propounded in France during his time, along with his favorable opinion of Sardou, will not seem egregious perversity or blindness on his part when we realize that he was not a simple purveyor of "slice of life" dramaturgy even while seeming to be just that. Becque, to conclude, was one of those pioneers of modern drama who, along with Ibsen, Strindberg, Shaw, and Chekhov, possessed true individuality and a rare power to shape reality while pretending to photograph it.

SHAW AS DRAMA CRITIC

Not the least important facet of Bernard Shaw's historic career was the dramatic criticism he contributed week by week, from January, 1895, to 1898, to *The Saturday Review,* a weekly edited by Frank Harris in his palmiest and most sober years. It is no secret today that the three-volume compilation of Shaw's reviews entitled *Our Theatre in the Nineties* is the most considerable body of dramatic criticism in the English language. Shaw, of course, never ceased to be a dramatic critic, as the prefaces to his plays prove, but it was as the author of *The Saturday Review* articles that he had the greatest significance as a galvanic force in the English theatre. It was in these pieces that he dealt with the immediate problems of the theatre and concerned himself regularly with the play in production as well as in print. His reviews, combined with his pro-Ibsen polemic *The Quintessence of Ibsenism,* published in 1891 (enlarged in 1913), are not Olympian judgments uttered after the battle for dramatic modernism in the English language. They are, on the contrary, themselves maneuvers in a decisive campaign. Considered as such, they prove doubly remarkable —remarkable for their direct effectiveness, on the one hand, and for their permanent value, on the other.

Shaw's occasional errors of judgment and exaggerations were a neccessary part of his showmanship, as well as a calculated risk based on the conviction that nothing save shock-therapy could rouse comatose humanity. But the sense behind his nonsense becomes more apparent with the years. His criticism, seen in perspective, is found to have been a creative force rather than a carping pettiness on the part of an uncreative observer of other men's failures. And his emphasis on the intellectual element in the drama stands out as the most seminal contribution to dramatic theory made in modern times. One way to understand Shaw's dramatic criticism is to consider the circumstances under which it was written.

That play reviewing was an adjunct to his own playwriting was important to his work as both critic and dramatist. Shaw's reviews not only provide an ambidextrous case of one writing arm supporting the other, since his discussions cleared the field for his own plays, but of one playwright feeling enough kinship to another—to Ibsen—to work up a personal passion in championing a new dispensation for modern drama. By the time Shaw stopped reviewing he had already written seven plays, among them *Candida, Mrs. Warren's Profession,* and *The Devil's Disciple.* More than most drama critics, Shaw knew what he wanted contemporary playwriting to be—because he himself was providing the example. Moreover, he was not at all reluctant to identify his interest in his own plays, still neglected in England, with those of the modern drama as a whole. Ninety years had elapsed between the production of *The School for Scandal* in 1777 and the première of the first remotely modern English drama of the nineteenth century, "Tom" Robertson's *Caste*. Another quarter of a century had been consumed in productions of ignoble farces and melodramas before Oscar Wilde, Henry Arthur Jones, and Pinero breathed some life into the British theatre. Even in the nineties, moreover, British modernists were more of a hindrance than a help to the triumph of the genuine modernism represented by Ibsen's realistic plays. As Shaw was to point out, they were merely fobbing off the complaisant public with a pretense of daring, while actually purveying conventional sentiments. Important as it was to discredit the old-fashioned farces and melodramas and Sardou's vapid "well-made plays" of intrigue (dismissed by Shaw with the epithet "Sardoodledom"), Shaw considered it still more to the point to prick pseudo-Ibsenite trial-balloons of realism and "new ideas." Shaw knew that London would give anything to acquire the comfortable feeling that it was up-to-date without having to accept a transvaluation of values, or even a moderate diminution of conventional beliefs.

Arthur Wing Pinero was England's most popular substitute for Ibsen in the nineties, and *The Second Mrs. Tanqueray,* produced in 1893, was considered the most advanced British play because it presented the marriage of a gentleman to a woman with a past. Here was so-called *realism,* especially when it turned out that the woman's stepdaughter was on the verge of marrying Mrs. Tanqueray's former lover. To Shaw, however, it was obvious that Pinero had merely contrived a situation that would restore the equipoise of Victorian moralism. The marriage of the gentleman and the lady-with-a-past would be shattered by the coincidence of her daughter's engagement to the one man to whom Mrs. Tanqueray could not be a mother-in-law. Mrs. Tanqueray would be suitably punished for her past sins by the deft arm of dramaturgic contrivance, and the respectable public could breathe freely again. Shaw exposed both the artificiality of such playwriting and the conventionality of the mind served by it. He was willing to grant Pinero a fair talent for fiction and stagecraft, provided one did not mistake the author for a member of the vanguard when he was actually only "a humble and somewhat belated follower of the novelists of the middle of the nineteenth century . . . who has never written a line from which it could be guessed that he is a contemporary of Ibsen, Tolstoi, Meredith, or Sarah Grand." When Shaw had the occasion to review another Pinero play, *The Notorious Mrs. Ebbsmith,* the drama of a woman agitator's disillusionment, he seized with special glee on Pinero's *coup de théâtre* and bid for reputation as a daring modernist. Although the entire review is a masterpiece of close reasoning and critical sharpshooting, his examination of the climax is so cogent that it obviates the necessity of citing other examples of his war against pseudo-Ibsenism.

Being a master of the art of criticism even in summarizing a play, Shaw prepared the groundwork for his assault in his description of the climax. The once unhappily married Mrs. Ebbsmith reaches the peak of disillusionment when the man who proposed to become her partner in agitation against the evils of conventional marriage proves to be interested only in her sexual attractiveness.

"In pursuance of which detestable view," Shaw wrote, "she puts on an indecent dress and utterly abandons herself to him. A clergyman appears in this crisis, and offers her a Bible. She proudly pitches it into the stove; and a thrill of horror runs through the audience as they see, in imagination, the whole Christian Church tottering before their eyes. Suddenly, with a wild scream, she plunges her hand into the glowing stove and pulls out the Bible again. The Church is saved; and the curtain descends amid thunders of applause."

Refusing to join in that applause on the grounds of implausibility in the supposedly daring action, Shaw next proceeded to the kill: ". . . to introduce a woman—whose one misfortune—her unhappy marriage—can hardly by any stretch of casuistry be laid to the charge of St. Paul's teaching; to make this woman senselessly say that all her misfortunes are due to the Bible; to make her to throw it into the stove, and then injure herself horribly in pulling it out again; this, I submit, is a piece of claptrap so gross that it absolves me from all obligation to treat Mr. Pinero's art as anything higher than the barest art of theatrical sensation. As in *The Profligate,* as in *The Second Mrs. Tanqueray,* he has no idea beyond that of doing something daring and bringing down the house by running away from the consequences."

The "Mrs. Ebbsmith" review is a perfect example of the Shavian tactic of reducing the logic of a play to absurdity. For the salient feature of Shaw's dramatic criticism was its frank, indeed flagrant, destructiveness —in the interests of reconstruction on new foundations. The clamor for so-called constructive criticism is, more often than not, merely an appeal to the critic by the timid and the vulnerable to hold his fire. Shaw would have considered himself derelict in his duty if he had done so, for his essential constructiveness lay in his destructiveness. He did all he could to badger the managements, including Sir Henry Irving, into producing truly modern drama, chiefly the plays of Ibsen. His best recourse was to demonstrate the vacuousness of their ordinary offerings, and the spuriousness of the plays they presented as extraordinary. The alternative of Ibsen drama, the worth of which he had already demonstrated in the company of Archer and others, could be made all the more attractive by his destructive method. "Exhibitions of magnanimity," he wrote, "are not the business of a critic any more than of a general in the field; for both alike, the pursuit is as important as the victory." He aligned himself with the most eminent of dramatic critics, Lessing, who had been described by Heine as "not only cutting off his victims' heads, but holding them up afterwards to show that there were no brains in them."

That Shaw ultimately won his battle is a matter of record. He won it with the help of an abatement of Victorianism, for which irresistible social pressures were more responsible than he. Within a decade after he stopped reviewing plays, the English theatre belonged to his plays and those of Galsworthy, Barker, St. John Hankin, Barrie, St. John Ervine, and other post-Victorians, although it is doubtful that all of these could satisfy his exigent mind. But Shaw was correct in complaining that his efforts were unappreciated. In his valedictory article he asked half facetiously, "Do I receive any spontaneous recognition for the prodigies of skill and industry I lavish on an unworthy institution and a stupid public?" He might have asked more seriously whether his argument was actually understood. London did not know what he demanded in his criticism any more than it knew what he was trying to say in his plays, and it is not at all certain that students of the theatre are clear about it today.

Although he called himself a realist, it was something other than a facsimile presentation of life that he demanded. It was certainly not the realistic technique of prosaic authenticity, the fourth-wall convention, and photographic detail that he sought to establish in the theatre. He was as enthusiastic over a poetic drama such as *Peer Gynt* as over *A Doll's House*. He was impressed with *Ghosts* not because a playwright had dared to present the fact of venereal disease or heredity on the stage, but because Ibsen had challenged conventional thought. He was just as pleased, later on, when Ibsen expressed his challenge symbolically rather than realistically in plays such as *Little Eyolf* and *When We Dead Awaken*. Realism for Shaw was penetration rather than photography. It was original thinking rather than strict adherence to make-believe verisimilitude, which merely substitutes the commonplaces for old-fashioned stage trickery. If there is a new realistic dramaturgy in Ibsen, as Shaw was quick to perceive, it is a consequence of an interest in ideas so great that it excludes plot contrivance as a means for holding our interest—simply because something far more important is holding that interest.

The "new technical factor" in the dramaturgy championed by Shaw the critic (in the revised *Quintessence of Ibsenism*) and exemplified by Shaw the playwright is "discussion." "Formerly," Shaw explained, "you had in what was called a well-made play an exposition in the first act, a situation in the second, and unraveling in the third. Now you have exposition, situation, and discussion; and the discussion is the best of the playwright." Protest as we might that discussion is not dramatic (which it is not, of course, when mediocre playwrights indulge in it) and that art should not be didactic, Shaw insisted that "an interesting play cannot in the nature of things mean anything but a play in which problems of conduct and character of personal importance to the audience are raised and suggestively discussed." The new type of drama was to be differentiated from the old "through a conflict of unsettled ideals rather than through vulgar attachments, rapacities, generosities, resentments, ambitions, misunderstandings, and so forth." And it is in this respect that realism or naturalness is important, since the old devices of intrigue, coincidence, accident, and theatrical sensations can only obviate or confound an intelligent grappling with ideas. Just as surely as bad money drives good money out of the market, so pinchbeck intrigue and violence would drive the intelligence out of the theatre. And Shaw's vaunted "moral passion" was fundamentally passion for intelligence. Since, moreover, the discussion play could succeed only if the spectator could identify himself with the characters, it was imperative to discard those unreal characters and improbable circumstances which the public could be induced to accept only by lavish and ingenious use of dramatic and stage trickery.

What makes a character "real" is a question that Shaw, so far as I know, never actually answered, or even properly raised. All that can be deduced from his writings is that he believed himself to stand on sure ground whenever he found the characters in a play by Sardou or Pinero to be unreal. They were that whenever their motivation was strained, their actions subordinated to plot contrivance, and their reasoning fallacious while their authors presented that reasoning as logically tenable. It is also plain that the characters' reality was enriched for him in a play whenever they settled down to discuss a subject of concern to them, as was the case in Ibsen's work. It may be said that Shaw, who had no great interest in the creation of character for the sake of mere characterization (Aristotle and he occupy common ground on this subject), was the first dramatic critic to restore the intellect to a place of importance as one of the components of characterization. The way a character thinks was for Shaw an intrinsic element in the definition of character. And the way an action "thinks"—that is, presents a mode of thought or stimulates one— was for Shaw an inherent component of action. When it is noted that his interpretation of Ibsen gives us Shaw in place of Ibsen, we are overlooking the point that it was Shaw's final tribute or criticism to consider the elder dramatist's plays mirrors in which a good mind could see reflections of itself. And in this respect Ibsen's critic was also telegraphing to us that his own view of "realism" was far removed from mere verisimilitude-worship or worship of "fourth-wall," "peephole stage" technique.

Once the question of "realism" is cleared up, we are, indeed, in a position to achieve a proper perspective on all matters that are trouble-some in Shaw's program for modern dramatists, including himself. It becomes plain, for instance, that the factor of "discussion" is anything but an anti-dramatic device to his way of thinking and writing. It is anti-dramatic only when a hack dramatist stops the physical action of his play to deliver an argument or preachment. Discussion, as a general intelligence permeating a work and determining its course, moves *with* the impetus of the play instead of moving *against* it or standing in its way. Shaw de-scribed the ideal of Ibsen and post-Ibsen dramaturgy as "the introduction of the discussion and its development until it so overspreads and inter-penetrates the action that it finally assimilates it, making the play and discussion practically identical." How this could be done no one was able to demonstrate better than Shaw himself. His later praise of Chekhov is evidence of his realization that the "problem" element can exist as well in the matrix of the human element as in debate. In *The Cherry Orchard* he found "the sentimental ideals of our amiable, cultured, Schumann-playing propertied class . . . reduced to dust and ashes by a hand not less deadly than Ibsen's because it is so much more caressing" and because "nothing more violent happens than that the family cannot afford to keep up its old house." Nor did the discussion drama, as envisaged by Shaw, entail the vending of the pat solutions and panaceas we associate with the so-called problem play of sociological and topical playwrights.

The quintessence of his notion of Ibsenism was, as he plainly stated, "that there is no formula." It is enough that the intelligence has been allowed to discover and light up a human problem; that, in short, the theatre put us in a state of mind for examining a crisis and exercising our reason on it. Shaw's own plays often leave us in a state of animated, tin-glingly sharp suspension. It does not matter even when the tongue-in-cheek solution that he places at the end of a play, as in *Major Barbara,* is one so patently inconceivable as that the world will be saved by efficient manufacturers of war munitions. The outrageousness of the proposal is only a further provocation to thought.

To Shaw, besides, the intellectual drama was not in conflict with imaginative and poetic drama. If he did not appear to respond to the call for theatrical magic propounded by Gordon Craig and Max Reinhardt; if he was less than impressed with the symbolist and neo-romantic play-wrights, such as Maeterlinck and Rostand, it was not because he was in-sensible to poetry and imagination. He merely found it unnecessary to fight for a theatre devoted to these qualities, since it had been long in existence, and since the new poetic playwrights gave no evidence of being able to improve upon his favorite poet-playwright, Shakespeare. It is also possible that Shaw suspected the magic-makers of obstructing the progress of Ibsenism. Nevertheless, since irradiation of the mind was his prime concern, he did not hesitate to prescribe for the modern dramatist not only "a forensic technique of recrimination, disillusion, and penetration," but a "free use of all the rhetorical and lyrical arts of the orator, the preacher, the pleader, and the rhapsodist"—which covers considerably more territory than prose, realism, and naturalism. He found part of this prescription in Ibsen; the rest he compounded himself out of elements congenial to his temperament. Moreover, he followed the prescription fully, as one can see in the Don Juan dream-episode of *Man and Superman,* the fantasy of the *Saint Joan* epilogue, the allegory of *Heartbreak House* and *Back to Methuselah.* Shaw wielded his critical lance not to enslave the modern drama to any one style, but to free it from every impediment to the full play of mind and spirit.

It was not the only campaign of liberation that Shaw undertook, for concurrently he attempted to liberate Shakespeare from his admirers. Here, too, he succeeded, though again not so single-handedly as he professed to believe when he concluded in his valedictory that "When I began to write, William was a divinity and a bore. Now he is a fellow-creature." When Shaw waged war against the uncritical worship of Shakespeare which he called Bardolatry, he became subject to misunderstandings to which he himself gave currency. It was generally, but erroneously, held that he considered his own plays superior to Shakespeare's, whereupon the cries of outrage could be heard round the world. Employing his familiar device of arousing awareness by gross irritation, Shaw accomplished what he set out to do. He helped to bring Shakespeare back into the theatre where he belonged, a Shakespeare unobscured by the Romantic criticism that acclaimed him the peerless sage of the world who was better read than produced; a Shakespeare-the-playwright who needed no improvement but rescue from the dismemberment and rearrangement long practiced by later playwrights and actor-managers. Shaw carried his campaign *for* Shakespeare as the supreme poet-playwright, and *against* Shakespeare as a substitute for the authors of the modern drama of ideas, well into the twentieth century. But all save a negligible part of his Shakespearean criticism, and the misunderstood "Better Than Shakespeare?" part of the preface to *Caesar and Cleopatra,* is to be found in his writings during the nineties: in *The Saturday Review* articles and in the letters to Ellen Terry. All that is necessary is to piece his comments together, balancing depreciations of Shakespeare as an intellectual and a spinner of often trashy plots against appreciations of Shakespeare as an artist. When this synthesis is made by a man who knows both literature and theatre—as it has been made conclusively by Professor E. J. West in "G. B. S. on Shakespearean Production" and other essays—the evidence is incontestable: Bernard Shaw proved himself one of the great Shakespearean critics.

He set the tone and exposed the point of his criticism in his very first *Saturday Review* article, entitled "Poor Shakespeare!" (1895). Reviewing a production of *All's Well That Ends Well,* he insisted that the ear is the sure clue to Shakespeare. Only a musician could understand the play of feeling which was the real rarity of the early works; they would have died long ago "in a deaf nation." The moral point of view in them was conventional and secondhand, no matter how finely expressed, and the borrowed ideas were not on a par with "the original criticisms of life" present in the later works. Then Shaw proceeded to deliver one of those decisive insights that come only from men who are equally sensitive to literary and dramatic artistry: "Even the individualization which produces that old established British specialty, the Shakespearean 'delineation of character,' owes all its magic to the turn of the line, which lets you into the secret of its utterer's mood and temperament, not by its commonplace meaning, but by some subtle exaltation, or stultification, or slyness, or delicacy, or hesitancy, or what-not in the sound of it. In short, it is the score and not the libretto that keeps the work alive and fresh." Then, taking note of the tendency of the times to mutilate and then overproduce the plays, to smother them in splendiferous scenery instead of letting the language prevail, he attacked the players and playgoers of his generation as being for the most part "deaf as adders."

"Their appreciation of Shakespeare," he declared, "is sheer hypocrisy, the proof being that where an early play of his is revived, they take the utmost pains to suppress as much of it as possible, and disguise the rest past recognition, relying for success on extraordinary scenic attractions; on very popular performers, including, if possible, a famously beautiful actress in the leading part; and above all, on Shakespeare's reputation and the consequent submission of the British public to be mercilessly bored by each of his plays once in their lives. . . ." The more the manager departed from the old platform stage for which Shakespeare wrote, the more money he spent on lavish elaboration of the stage picture, the greater the imposture; even though few had the hardihood to do anything but praise the manager, the actress, and the Bard, and "sincere people who do not know what the matter is [and he might have been thinking of Charles Lamb as well as of contemporaries] begin to babble insufferably about plays that are meant for the study and not for the stage." Actually, "such crown jewels of dramatic poetry as *Twelfth Night* and *A Midsummer*

Night's Dream faded into shabby colored glass" in the manager's purse.

Then Shaw went on to indict the scenery of the production on the double charge that it was bad enough to destroy all illusion, which would have been better served if the simple stage directions of the text had been printed on a placard and hung up on a curtain; and that, as usual, the play had been "pulled to pieces" in order to enable the scenery to do its damage to stage illusion. Shaw also delivered a blast at the prissy expurgation of the text out of consideration for "the most pestiferously prurient person" in the audience, and added a particularly apt objection to that powerful enemy of Shakespeare, the "elocutionist" who instead of "sensitizing his artistic faculty to receive the impression of moods and inflexions of feeling conveyed by word-music . . . devotes his life to the art of breaking up verse in such a way as to make it sound like insanely pompous prose."

Four months later, in reviewing an amateur production of *Macbeth,* Shaw declared facetiously that it was one of his eccentricities to be old-fashioned in his artistic tastes: "For instance, I am fond—unaffectedly fond—of Shakespeare's plays. I do not mean the plays of actor-manager's editions and revivals: I mean the plays as Shakespeare wrote them, played straight through line by line and scene by scene as nearly as possible under the conditions of representation for which they were designed." Then he used the occasion to denounce all other Elizabethan playwrights, for whom he entertained a blind if explainable aversion; and to lecture contemporary playwrights, including "Mr. Pinero" and "Monsieur Sardou," wishing they could learn from *Macbeth* how to write a play "without wasting the first hour of the performance in tediously explaining its 'construction'!" "They really are mistaken," Shaw concluded poisonously, "in supposing that Scribe was cleverer than Shakespeare."

Toward the end of the same year, 1895, reviewing a production by William Poel's recently founded Elizabethan Stage Society, he again offered sound instruction to Shakespearean actors, denounced Sir Henry Irving's acting versions while complimenting his performance as Macbeth, and reiterated a preference for simplified staging. In 1896, Shaw continued his quarrel with the Shakespearean actors of his day, remarking among other things that the famous actor-manager Beerbohm-Tree wanted only one thing to make him an excellent Falstaff, "and that is to get born over again as unlike himself as possible"; and he continued his controversy to the very end of his journalistic career.

Shaw's animadversions against Shakespeare's shortcomings are well known. He was infuriated by any evidence of his favorite poet's potboiling proclivities. His indignation after seeing a production of *Cymbeline* could make him declare that he knew of no eminent writer other than Homer whom he could despise so entirely after measuring his own mind against his. In reading such diatribes we are apt to overlook Shaw's many tributes to Shakespeare, such as the qualifying statement that he has "outlasted thousands of abler thinkers, and will outlast a thousand more." But it is not Shaw's appreciation of Shakespeare, which is obvious today, that matters. What matters is the sensibility and knowledge Shaw brought to the plays and their acting possibilities, along with his success in rescuing the "bard" from the "bardolaters."

A notable example of criticism illuminating dramatic writing and acting simultaneously, and it is an elementary lesson for dramatic critics even today, is Shaw's treatment of the part in *Richard III* where Richard mesmerizes Lady Anne after having murdered her husband. According to Shaw, Sir Henry Irving, in the role of Richard, ". . . was a flat contradiction, not only of the letter of the lines, but of their spirit and feeling as conveyed unmistakably by their cadence. . . . If we are not to have the tears, the passion, the tenderness, the transport of dissimulation which alone can make the upshot credible—if the woman is to be openly teased and insulted, mocked and disgusted, all through the scene as well as in the first 'keen encounter of their wits,' why not have Lady Anne presented as a weak, childish-witted, mesmerized creature, instead of that most awful embodiment of virtue and decorum, the intellectual American lady? . . . But how could she [the actress Julia Arthur] play to a Richard who would not utter a single tone to which any woman's heart could respond? . . . Richard, after playing the scene with her as if he were a Hounsditch salesman cheating a factory girl over a pair of second-hand stockings, naturally could not reach the raptures of the tremendous outburst of elation beginning

'Was ever woman in this humour wooed?
Was ever woman in this humour won?'

One felt inclined to answer 'Never, I assure you,' and make an end of the scene there and then."

Other examples of close observation of this order abound not only in Shaw's Shakespearean criticism but in his comments on Mrs. Patrick Campbell, Bernhardt, Duse, Elizabeth Robins, and Janet Achurch in modern plays. Little effort is needed to establish Shaw as one of the ablest judges of acting, especially when one notes his ability to differentiate between the actor's and the playwright's contribution to a role, his distinction between good acting and a pleasing personality, and his attention to the voice as both a musical and a characterizing component in a performance.

Shaw prevailed, besides, with the gift without which no criticism is effective—namely, his formidable talent for communication. Nor did his determination interfere in the least with his inclination to be entertaining. His reviews must have provided more entertainment to his readers than many now virtually forgotten plays upon which he performed his harlequin's dance. Dullness in the subject is never an excuse for dullness in journalism. Practiced orator that he was, moreover, he possessed a power of modulation given to few writers who harangue the public in print alone. He mixed vituperation not only with laughter, as we should expect, but with double-edged compliments to his victims, disarming confessions of bias, sly apologies—and gallantry to the ladies of the stage. He alternated a teasing pianissimo with his fortissimi, a procedure he may have learned from his favorite composer, Mozart. Shaw, in short, was as wily a magician when he reviewed plays as when he wrote them himself.

We shall not have another drama critic like him. Even if the miracle of gifted critics and prose masters does occur from time to time, the criticism cannot be the same, for the provocations can never be duplicated. Shavian criticism was a special phenomenon of the twentieth century aborning in the nineteenth. It was the product of a collision between this unique period and the equally unique personality of Shaw, concerning which the last word has by no means been spoken. The sparks scattered over a wide area of the theatrical world, but they were not dissipated as so much merely bright dramatic criticism has been dissipated in our time. The Shavian sparks started a steadily burning fire in which much of the old dramatic rubbish was consumed, and in which a new dramatic art was molded for England and America.

SAINT GEORGE AND THE DRAGONS

I. SHAW AT NINETY

On July 26, 1946, Bernard Shaw achieved one of his laudable ambitions for mankind. In *Back to Methuselah,* which he wrote as a mere stripling of sixty-five, he concluded that human beings would simply have to live longer if they were to achieve any sense. Being an inveterate optimist then, he saw no insuperable impediment to extending the life-span by several centuries; and being a practical man, he must have resolved to set an example.

It is true of course that a mere ninety years falls considerably short of his Lamarckian ideal. But since our notion of longevity is quite moderate, we celebrate his ninetieth birthday as another Shavian feat, and perhaps he will grant us his indulgence. It is certain, however, that the tongue that has served him as his spear would make short shrift of us if we were so inept as to reckon his years by simple arithemetic. Life without moral passion, he noted long ago, is nothing; life without usefulness even less than nothing. If his faith in the perfectibility of man has been immense, if evolution has been almost mystically assured in his credo, he has been relentless in insisting upon the imperativeness of personal will and exertion. For our latter-day Saint George, faith and works have been inseparable.

One of the most inspired conceptions of the Middle Ages was the identification of sainthood and knight errantry in the same person. The original Saint George and his contemporary counterpart are both products of this ideal. Shaw has combined personal austerities with zeal for the fullness of earthly life; one of the first dragons he hunted down, while we were yet unborn or still in our swaddling clothes, was Victorian morality. He has been a great humanitarian and no one in our time has been so tenderminded, whether the subject of his protest was slums and sweatshops, war, and the competitive system, or vivisection and "the slaughter in the butcher's yard." (Physicians, too, have been among his real and fancied dragons.) Yet he has been the arch-enemy of sentimentality, and has even entertained the feasibility of liquidating useless members of society. He has disdained materialism, but has been a shrewd bargainer in the marketplaces. He has been a fiery opponent of competitiveness (he even invented a system of lawn tennis in which the players were penalized for winning!), but few men of our times have been so aggressive or so impatient with weakness.

Everyone who has tried to affix a label to Shaw has been confounded at one time or other. "Karl Marx made a man of me," he declared in his later years, yet much of his thinking, especially in his plays, has been undoubtedly non-Marxist. He has rejected much in Marx, including the cardinal doctrine of the class-conflict. He has been a self-proclaimed Fabian socialist and yet has evinced the greatest scepticism of parliamentary politics, pointing out in *The Apple Cart* that no matter which party wins the elections it was always capital, "Breakages, Ltd.," that ran the country. He has been a champion of the masses and of the ideals of democracy, and yet he has also worshipped at the shrine of the Nietzschean superman.

What shall we make of this man or phenomenon? It is a question that puzzled Max Beerbohm even before Shaw turned us into whirling dervishes whenever we tried to follow his gyrations. The irrepressible Max drew a cartoon in 1914 entitled *Life-Force, Woman-Set-Free, Superman, etc.,* in which Shaw was shown bringing a package of clothes to Georg Brandes. *"What'll you take for the lot?"* asks Brandes. *"Immortality,"* is the answer. *"Come,"* says the alert critic, *"I've handled these goods before! Coat, Mr. Schopenhauer's; waistcoat, Mr. Ibsen's; Mr. Nietzsche's trousers—"* *"Ah,"* replies Shaw, *"but look at the patches."* Yet it is certain that the cartoonist missed the full import of his point by not taking Shaw's reply seriously. The "patches" have made all the difference between a borrower and a great man of letters, and it is also a matter of considerable importance that it was Shaw who wore the clothes. Much that would have looked like tatters on another wearer was plate armor on the man who came to London as the self-styled upstart son of a downstart Irish father and proceeded to map out the prolonged campaign that has occupied his years.

The dragon he has tracked down and slain countless times has assumed too many shapes for any one man to destroy it with finality. Shaw's very ideals—Fabianism, Marxism, feminine emancipation, the cult of the superman, and so on—have had a curious way of turning into dragons in our century. He reached the peak of despair in the early thirties: In *On the Rocks* he was ready to acknowledge the failure of the masses who had been the supreme article of faith with liberals and radicals ("Yes; they always break the wrong windows, poor fellows"), and when he came to write *Too True To Be Good* in 1932 all Europe was the subject of his funeral oration. Employing the voice of the clergyman character Aubrey, he announced that The Western World was "damned beyond salvation." Yet he knew he would have to go beyond negations, as he always did, and as he has continued to do: "Is No enough? For a boy, yes; for a man, never . . . I must preach and preach and preach no matter how late the hour and how short the day . . . ," to which he added, "The author, though himself a professional talkmaker, does not believe that the world can be saved by talk alone." The truth of the matter is that it is easy to know what to make of Shaw, once we recognize the fact that the world's dragons are many and the saintly warriors few. Shaw has always fought to make right reason and good will prevail in the maze of the modern world. Only his divagations need explaining, and this it not difficult, considering the nature of the world through which he has pursued his knight-errantry.

Let us consider the itinerary: Shaw was intellectually cradled in the nineteenth century when individualism and self-realization were progressive ideals, when Ibsen's emancipated woman was a passion for intellectuals, and when Nietzsche's clean-spirited superman formed a welcome antithesis to hypocrites, philanthropists, and the philistines of the bourse and the sweatshop. Discovering the contradiction that an individualistic society may abort real individuality, he turned socialist, under the miscellaneous influences of Henry George, Karl Marx, and the Webbs. He joined the ranks of the parliamentary semisocialists only to find that evolutionary socialism moved in devious ways and brought dubious results. He pinned new hope on revolutionary socialism only to find that the masses of Europe were apt to succumb to totalitarian counter-revolution, and this led him to look hopefully toward any iron-fisted pseudo-saviors who might knock some sense into people. Had he not earlier glorified their prototype in *Caesar and Cleopatra* with a Caesar whose clear mind triumphed over the political mess-makers? Bumbling had always been the cardinal sin in his doxology. Then, of course, came the disillusionment with the Mussolinis and the Hitlers who quickly proved themselves misleaders rather than leaders, and so G. B. S. came back to an earlier belief in revolutionary socialism to which he has clung with a tenacity that is more suggestive of desperation than of youthful ardor and conviction.

Charging the protean demon of the twentieth century was an inhumanly difficult experience, and he had his lance broken many times. The exertion was also enervating, and so it is not surprising that he who started out with a simple eighteenth-century belief in the nostrum of reason should have wavered on the way and even leaned on the crutch of a Bergsonian *élan vital* that would ensure man's salvation in spite of man's feebleness. Nevertheless, intellectual oscillations which would have discredited smaller men cannot discredit Shaw; certainly not the *creative* Shaw who has nearly always had a way of holding disparate particles in a luminous solution of comedy and exhortation. Nor can it discredit him as a man of his times and adventurer that he could not cut a straight path through the twentieth-century jungle. The tall, bearded gentleman of the Olympian brow and voice is disqualified only from playing God. It is the one limitation to which he will have to submit at last. Much as it may irk him to be deprived of a role he would have enjoyed adding to his diversified repertory.

The above-printed paragraphs were my small tribute in 1946, given here in order to illustrate one response to Shaw in a time of grave crisis when the Shavian spirit was in danger of being extinguished. That danger will be a recurring one, I fear, in our century. It is likely to make our continued appreciation of Shaw an affirmation, come what may.

Bernard Shaw did not celebrate his ninetieth birthday. It was celebrated for him. Like pilgrims of old, the literati flocked to the shrine of Ayot St. Lawrence, drawing a light shaft from G. B. S.: "They've come to see the animal just because he's ninety." Their adulation made him remark: "All my life affection has been showered on me, and every forward step I took has been taken in spite of it." Perhaps he had forgotten the first forty years when he was incapable of earning a living by writing, as well as the decades when he was indulgently dismissed as a clown. During World War I, he lost many friends for his anti-imperialist stand and was roundly denounced by his old friend Henry Arthur Jones. In the post-war years, he outraged the Tories by his championship of Soviet Russia; in the pre-World War II days, he outraged a new generation of radicals by having kind words for Mussolini and treating Hitler too gently. He was irritated with the fumblings of the Labor party, disgusted with the stupidity of the masses who didn't know where their best interests lay and were willing to let strong hard-hearted men have a fling at cleaning up the mess that parliamentarians had been unable to remove. And in each case he left himself open to considerable and not always amiable criticism. Perhaps, however, he had not forgotten these days but was merely keeping his tongue in his cheek.

It is true that he had never lacked a small circle of friends who loved him whether or not they agreed with him, and among these could be counted great contemporaries like Gilbert Murray, Beatrice and Sidney Webb, and H. G. Wells. It is true that tributes to him for this or that accomplishment or attitude had never been wanting. Some praised his wit; some his style. And an increasing, though still small, number of critics were even willing to concede that he was a good playwright. Some people even liked his politics, when he remained in one spot long enough for them to know what his politics was, or when they were unimaginative enough to believe that they *knew* his politics. Now, at ninety, he could be liked by everybody, a fact that must have disturbed him considerably, especially since he couldn't stop the love-feast. He could be loved now because he was a personality, "a character," and the world loves a character, especially once he is more or less removed from the field of battle.

Unfortunately, he could also be praised now by the experts, since there wasn't a subject touched by him which he hadn't illuminated or at least stirred up in the cauldron of his mind. Admiration for him could be concrete as well as general. In New York, the birthday party given in his honor at the Waldorf-Astoria heard from the experts, from literary, dramatic, and music critics; from the Theatre Guild which had produced him in America; from Dodd, Mead and Company which had published him and now promised to re-issue all his work, and from his fellow-playwright, Maxwell Anderson, who read an intelligent essay. The one discordant note came from Henry Seidel Canby of *The Saturday Review of Literature* who still didn't believe that Shaw was a good playwright and doubted that his plays would live on.

The birthday was also the occasion for Dodd, Mead and Company's release of a book, a *Festschrift* entitled *G. B. S. 90,* edited by S. Winsten. It gave an appraisal of aspects of his life and work, perhaps not altogether inspired but far more detailed and considered than the birthday oratory. It included pieces by J. B. Priestley on Shaw as a social critic, J. D. Bernal on Shaw as a "scientist," C. E. M. Joad on Shaw's philosophy, and Dean Inge on "Shaw as Theologian." Whatever else may be said about the book, and some of the classifications of Shaw's genius are rather amusing due to their academic terminology, it can be set down as required reading for this nation's and England's playwrights, to most of whom it never seems to occur that a playwright should be more than merely a playwright —as if plays of any distinction could be written in an intellectual and spiritual void.

It is more probable, however, that the birthday present which pleased G. B. S. most, since it had his indispensable permission, was Penguin Books' publication of *Major Barbara, Pygmalion,* and *Saint Joan.* In these editions of some of his plays and prefaces, he could speak for himself, and no one has been able to speak more lucidly and effectively for Shaw than Shaw himself. Besides, the Penguin editions were intended for mass consumption. Shaw, who never had the slightest patience with the art-for-art's-sake theory, must have been perfectly satisfied to accept the pittance of royalties derivable from twenty-five-cent volumes, so long as these enlarged his public. His life-time ambition had been to be *heard* whether from the Hyde Park soap-box of his youth or from his latest book or latest letter to the London *Times.*

His sanctioning of the Penguin publications can come as a surprise only to those people who have unreflectingly chuckled over the fact that the veteran socialist should drive such hard bargains with publishers and producers and should be such a stickler for royalties. The truth is that Shaw merely maintained that in a money-minded and money-conditioned society, in which everybody tries for the largest possible reward for his work, the artist should not let himself be fobbed off with intangibles. When the "New Deal" Federal Theatre wanted to produce his plays at popular prices, Shaw did not hesitate to give his permission for a nominal weekly payment of fifty dollars. "As long as you stick to your fifty-five-cent maximum for admission," he wrote the Federal Theatre in April, 1937, "you can play anything of mine you like unless you hear from me to the contrary. Any author of serious plays who does not follow my example does not know what is good for him. I am not making a public-spirited sacrifice; I am jumping at an unprecedentedly good offer." It was characteristic of Shaw not to make the W. P. A. theatre project feel that it was getting charity. No one has ever known so well how to help people without patronizing them.

An interesting feature of the Penguin publications is that *Major Barbara* is the screen version of the film produced by Gabriel Pascal in England. I cannot vouch for the authenticity of the story, but it is reported that Shaw, who had spurned all previous film offers, was won over when Pascal, who had come to get his permission to make *Pygmalion,* asked him for the loan of a pound with which to get back to London. If Pascal had told G. B. S. that he had millions in the bank with which to make the picture, it might have gone badly for Mr. Pascal. It went badly for the great Goldwyn who tried to bargain for terms by impressing Shaw with his esthetic intentions. G. B. S. is said to have replied that they couldn't arrive at an agreement because "you are interested only in art, and I am interested only in money."

When *Pygmalion* was filmed, Shaw, who insisted on being his own exclusive scenarist, was obstinate in his objection to adding anything to the original comedy. It was his understanding with Pascal that the play was merely to be transcribed for the screen—without Hollywood "beauty parlour" treatment. He finally consented only to the addition of two scenes. However, for the second film, *Major Barbara,* Shaw wrote no less than sixteen new sequences, although only six of them could be included because of "running-time" considerations. Shaw, who had taken such keen interest in the production of his plays that he had written lengthy stage directions and had often given minute instructions to actors and producers in England and America, began to show the same concern for the proper realization of his work on the screen. The excellence of the *Pygmalion* and *Major Barbara* films amply rewarded his admirable sense of responsibility.

It is improbable that Pascal's far less successful third Shavian film, *Caesar and Cleopatra*—with Claude Rains playing Caesar and Vivian Leigh, the role of the Egyptian strumpet—had the benefit of the aged author's active supervision. Considering the faultiness of the film treatment, one could wish that Shaw *had* kept a watchful place on this project, too. Pascal is correct in writing that "G. B. S. would have been the greatest scenario writer for the screen if I had met him twenty-five years earlier."

In any case, the screen version of *Major Barbara* is the most readable, as well as the most intelligent, screenplay yet published in any country. The best features of the original play and of a remarkable film are combined in the scenario. And, as if this weren't enough for any of us, the excellent *Major Barbara* preface, revised in 1944 to take account of the film version, is included. Like most of the Shavian prefaces, it is a masterpiece of English prose. For its equal, we have to go back to the eighteenth century, to Jonathan Swift, with whom Shaw has so much in common, although the Dublin dean's *saeva indignatio* is transmuted into the more genial passion characteristic of the Shavian method of flailing at human stupidity.

The *Major Barbara* prefatory essay, aptly subtitled "The Gospel of St. Andrew Undershaft," reminds us once more that, in spite of peregrinations around virtually every interest and concern, in any *self-limited argument,* Shaw has always put first things first. This is the secret of simplification known only to men of genius. This is also foolhardy, at times. It gets unusual people into trouble, when it doesn't catapult them to success. For a human being to be so downright logical is sensational, and I am prepared to say that it is this remarkable habit that has made Shaw the great personality that he is. His logic was so direct and sure that it seemed outrageous and absent. He was never a mountebank. He was merely going to the heart of a matter like the eighteenth-century masters from whom he learned—Mozart, Swift, Lord Chesterfield, Voltaire; and like the nineteenth-century leaders—Nietzsche, Ibsen, and Samuel Butler, to whom he pays tribute in the *Major Barbara* essay. Sometimes, we may add, he attained his wit precisely by letting logic have its way; and it is a question whether man's logic is not as productive of comedy as his illogic.

In this preface to his Salvation Army comedy, Shaw starts out with the simple premise that poverty is the root of all evil: "In the millionaire Undershaft, I have represented a man who has become intellectually and spiritually, as well as practically, conscious of the irresistible natural truth which we all abhor and repudiate: to wit, that the greatest of our evils, and the worst of our crimes is poverty. . . ." G. B. S. goes on to show that it poisons the world even for the rich, since all the evils we vainly try to cure arise from the cesspool which Europe failed to abolish. An "economic deadlock" immobilizes social service agencies and reform movements, since these must get their subsidy from "tainted money"; that is, from the wealth that breeds on the poverty of those who have to be reformed or helped. The actively evangelical Salvationists try to "fight the devil instead of merely praying at him." But "they have not quite ascertained his correct address." The rest of Shaw's verbal fugue is a series of variations on the theme; of brilliant musical phrases on crime and punishment, "Crosstianity *versus* Christianity," revolution from above and revolution from below. He describes religious bodies as "a sort of auxiliary police taking off the insurrectionary edge of poverty with coals and blankets, bread and treacle." He flails at the hypocrisy of charity by means of which economic marauders like the philanthropist-distiller Bodger "can always depend on the Salvation Party or the Church of England to negotiate a redemption for him in consideration of a trifling percentage of his profits."

Then there is the action itself, in which Salvation Army Major Barbara experiences these variations in the course of her reformist-idealistic blundering, and is brought back to the main theme of hard economic fact by that great realist, her father, the munitions-king Undershaft. And here lies the final bright cartwheel of Shavian dialectic: he can indict British capitalism and yet make the hero of his indictment an arch-capitalist like Undershaft. This is the secret of comic genius, and, at the heart of it, is common sense so resolutely pursued that it becomes startlingly *uncommon* sense. For Shaw realizes that those who abominate and try to remove the evils of society will never prevail until they acquire as much realism—that is, as much comprehension of economic fact—as the Undershafts.

If G. B. S. had visited our shores on his birthday, he might have seen the fruits of his example on Broadway in *State of the Union* and *Born Yesterday*. He might have derived some gratification from the observation that these plays demonstrated that the only modern way of writing successful social comedy is Shavian. It would not have escaped him, too, that the fruit was still comparatively green. To vary the figure of speech and get to the point, the authors—Messrs. Lindsay and Crouse, and Garson Kanin— can write simple melodies. But only Shaw in our time had been able to write comic fugues which never gave the mind and spirit rest until the final phrase was uttered. The fact is not exactly amazing when we consider that, before him, only two playwrights—Molière and Aristophanes—managed to exhibit the same talent. But their world is remote, and his is acutely immediate. His example, therefore, would serve, if our playwrights would learn from it. But, first of all, they would have to become full-fledged citizens of the comic world, instead of men with a mental horizon often limited to Broadway or reaching no further east than the Stork Club. That, however, would take some thinking and doing.

II. EPIPHANY

I shall always regret that I did not pay Shaw a visit when I was in England during the summer of 1950. I hesitated at first because I feared he would be pestered at that time by members of the tourist invasion and, later, because the state of his health would have made my visit an imposition. I felt some obligation, nevertheless, to make a brief appearance at Ayot St. Lawrence in order to express my gratitude for a favor. The news of his final illness put an end to my waverings; I would never have another opportunity to thank Shaw for his kindness.

The news of Shaw's death filled newspaper columns. His death was an "event." But neither these reports nor the tributes of distinguished contemporaries could quite express the sense of loss I felt in common with men of three generations who owed at least some part of their education to him. Since Shaw had lived to the age of ninety-four, the conventional reasons for mourning his departure were absent. It was not his death that we mourned, but the end of an age kinder and more hopeful than the present. It had been drawing to an end for decades, but we had been less inclined to accept the fact while he had been alive. He was our symbol of Western man's possibilities. Horizons for the century's intellectuals became both narrower and darker with his passing. We think symbolically, and Shaw as symbol had been a light to our understanding and expectations.

The obituary notices buried Shaw, whereas our greatest need had been to revive our culture hero. And, for many of us, such a revival could occur only on the stage. To read his essays and books, good as they are, is not enough. Wrenched out of the context of such life as the theatre can give, his thinking had been merely thinking. As such it was more symptomatic than curative, since its confusions stood out as prominently as those of other articulate men of the age. It was necessary to hear Shaw *speak,* and he could speak again only in his plays. Curiously enough, in the case of so intellectual a writer as Shaw, it was the *life* and not the thought in his work that had mattered most, and that life had largely been a life of "theatre." Not merely the life of his characters, about which there has always been dispute, but the life of intensified and gloriously theatricalized reality, whether depicted, caricatured, argued, or translated into somersaults of wit and fancy. After decades of misapprehension, most of us had finally renounced the fallacy of disapproving or approving his work as mere social philosophy or realistic literature. We had come to realize that neither as philosophy nor as literature did his plays have any unique value except in so far as they became theatre—theatre on the printed page and especially theatre *in* the theatre. That is where an epiphany could be expected, provided his plays were given more than a merely dutiful revival. It may well be that, for years to come, the stage in England and America will owe much of its buoyancy to such epiphanies by Shaw.

The year after Shaw's death, the American theatre provided three epiphanies, the first with the Theatre Guild production of *Saint Joan,* which opened on Broadway on October 4, 1951, the second with the "First Drama Quartet" opening of *Don Juan in Hell* at Carnegie Hall on October 22, and the third with the Lawrence Olivier production of *Caesar and Cleopatra* at the Ziegfeld Theatre on December 19.

The last-mentioned, described elsewhere in this book, was the least satisfactory; and, aside from inadequacies of the production, there are inadequacies of a dramatic nature in *Caesar and Cleopatra* for which Shaw himself was responsible. He had an authentic vision—or, shall we say, mirage—in his portrait of Caesar. ("Mirage" seems to be the proper word, since the Caesar of the play could have existed only in Shaw's imagination, the imagination of a man consumed with thirst for the life of reason.) But *Caesar and Cleopatra* must remain a minor achievement by the old theatrician, because his tricks became too transparent when he lost himself in political intrigue and military adventure, as well as in some anachronistic nose-thumbing at English mores. *Caesar and Cleopatra* is not pure Shaw. It is Shaw *plus* Sardou in the matter of plot; and Shaw *plus* college sophomore in the "cracks" at Brittanicus. *Don Juan in Hell* proved a memorable achievement for the theatre in which it was presented as a "reading" by Charles Laughton, Charles Boyer, Cedric Hardwicke, and Agnes Moorehead. That play is pure Shaw. The borrowed ideas about Don Juan, morality, and creative evolution are transmuted here into an independent creation. The technical feat is also entirely Shaw's. He was the only man who made drama with no more plot or action than is needed to start a play and to end it. Since the producers lived up to this theatrical intention by presenting the dream fantasy as pure discussion, they brought Shaw back without ventriloquy, masquerade, and sleight-of-hand.

I doubt that there is a greater piece of *speaking*—of comparable length —in the English language since the death of Shakespeare. But a still greater epiphany could have been expected from the Theatre Guild revival of *Saint Joan,* for it is in this work that the full range of the theatrician is present on the highest levels of his conviction and artistry. Here he is speaker, dramatist, and showman in complete fusion. Warwick's and the Bishop's tent-scene discussion and Joan's and the Inquisitor's speeches at the trial represent a master of discourse who is also a playwright capable of developing an action with deepening human experience and mounting excitement. Nor is the showman more than one step behind the dramatist here as Shaw traces Joan's tragic career from peasant maid to national liberator and martyr, as he unfolds court intrigue, military action at Orleans, and a trial and execution which pulse with visual and emotional force. That disappointment with the Guild's Margaret Webster production was so keen in some quarters was itself evidence of the power we have found in this play. A comparable production of an inferior play would have been found quite satisfactory. The production was unsatisfactory chiefly because we knew that there was more to *Saint Joan* than Miss Webster and her cast revealed on the stage. *Saint Joan* could have been Shaw's greatest epiphany in 1951. It did not prove to be that. But it had this merit for me and probably for others: We could see Shaw performing a miracle in his own behalf with less assistance than a playwright is entitled to receive from a stage production. *Saint Joan* epitomized the Shaw who was the *artist* rather than the polemicist of the liberal dispensation that is either at an end after centuries of growth or is undergoing major transformations.

The Theatre Guild's production of *Saint Joan* was the third return of Bernard Shaw's masterpiece to the American professional stage. The world premiere of a great sceptic's tribute to faith was the Theatre Guild's production in 1923, more than a quarter of a century before, but time had deprived this work of none of its freshness and relevance. The theatre is an ideal place for affirmations, for in it men and women can gather for communion. *Saint Joan* is all the more remarkable because the man who conceived it had won an international reputation for his frequent playing of the devil's disciple. In his sixty-seventh year he startled the world by revivifying the story of the Maid of Orleans, the savior of France who was burned in the flesh as a heretic and canonized in the spirit centuries later. And it is apparent by now that whenever *Saint Joan* is played, the theatre, too, is revivified, and with it the spirit of man that has so many reasons for becoming periodically disheartened.

Shaw should not have startled anyone acquainted with his previous writings. He had told us often enough that he was in earnest even while he jested. It was apparent, too, that he had always directed his shafts only at false gods, Victorian or otherwise; and his tender regard for "saints," for men and women of exceptional good will and energy, had long been evident. It is surely not surprising that the man who wrote *Androcles and the Lion* in 1912, who declared in *Man and Superman* that the only passion worth having was moral passion, who had created so memorable a mystic as Father Keegan in *John Bull's Other Island* was continually engaged in a search for saviors. He had evinced a special partiality for the savior-superman in politics, and his portrait of Caesar in *Caesar and Cleopatra* had been that of an *Uebermensch* in the field of *Realpolitik*. His search for such superman later led him to exasperatingly benign attitudes toward Mussolini and Stalin; he mistook seemingly strong men for actual good men and, in later years, sometimes he spoke as though he had confused the identities of Saint George and the Dragon. His errors, however, were incidents in that long quest for mainsprings of redemption which had once led him to the early Christians and then to Joan, for in her he found a superwoman in politics (surely not a difficult notion for so ardent an Ibsenite and feminist as Shaw), and a leader in whom virtue and vigor, goodness and intelligence were one. He was in sympathy with all fellow travelers on his road, and he found an especially congenial companion in "Saint Joan."

As every true artist does, Shaw transfigured his subject. He endowed Joan with his own inquiring spirit, his own self-confidence, and his own uncommon common sense. While recognizing her universality, which is ultimately the universality of a species of mankind dedicated to spiritual aims and likely to crop up in any time and place, he made Joan fundamentally modern. Shaw had already indicated in *Androcles and the Lion* and *Caesar and Cleopatra* that his engagement with ancient history was a *modern* adventure, and that he had no inclination to compose that feeble kind of playwriting that goes under the name of "costume drama." To make the "Passion of Saint Joan" further relevant, Shaw, moreover, cast the searchlight of modern interpretation upon her history. He made her the victim not only of the eternal stupidity and moral indifference of men but of the efforts of established institutions to maintain the *status quo* in a changing world. Drastic measures and injustices are most apt to be perpetrated when the old order meets the new. Each strikes the other as unreasonable and dangerous, and whichever has the upper hand at the moment resorts to the faggot and the ax.

Shaw's Joan is sent to the stake as a heretic to the feudal state and the medieval church. The former looks upon her as a proto-Nationalist, the latter as a proto-Protestant and, according to Shaw, she is actually *both* while trying only to be loyal to the State and the Church. In each case, her simplicity is both her glory and her suffering. She has the simplicity to believe that a king should be a king when all the more sophisticated people of her time know that a king is, properly speaking, only a puppet of the feudal nobility, and are content that this should be so. Her simplicity tells her that this should not be the case especially when a divided France is being conquered by England. In her simplicity, she also believes in private revelation. When she hears voices, she knows they must come from a divine source because she has unquestioning faith in a providence that gives direct guidance. Her simplicity gets her in trouble with the Inquisition. Her faith earns her the crown of martyrdom—and canonization. But what the voices whisper is the common sense that her own intelligence approves. Peasant and saint, medieval woman and proto-feminist, pragmatist and believer—the portraits mingle, dissolve, and recombine to produce the human being. No one after the death of Chekhov ever gave the modern theatre a greater example of dramatic characterization. Originality can be accurately attributed to both that characterization and the play that contains it. And originality is precisely the quality that could be expected of a man in whom one could usually find "the right mind cooperating with the finest sensibility, and then freely expressing it," which Herbert Read considers the final condition of literary genius.

The tent scene in which her fate is sealed in a long discussion that is a masterpiece of dialectical analysis does not, indeed, exhaust the power and meaning of the play. The great trial scene, in which Joan prefers death to imprisonment and recovers total integrity, is yet to come. The dream scene of the Epilogue, too, has yet to make its contribution with its mordant and anguished view that dead saints are much preferred to live ones. The tent scene, however, is our best reminder that Shaw's reverence and sympathy were compounded of more durable stuff than sentiment. He remained loyal to the "drama of ideas" which, in his view, was the distinctive quality of dramatic modernism. A unique combination of realism with idealism, or of rationalism with the poetry of faith, makes *Saint Joan* a modern affirmation, as analytical as it is fervent, rather than a genuflection to traditional piety and heroics. Shaw was no less strenuous when he discovered values he could accept as when he found values he had to reject.

It is the athleticism of Shaw's mind and spirit that the Margaret Webster Theatre Guild's production of *Saint Joan* projected most successfully. The spiritual glow that should invest Joan was less conspicuous in Uta Hagen's impassioned and vigorous performance than some of us could have wished. Miss Hagen had shown in past performances that she had at her command a personal grace that would have been highly appropriate in this instance. When Katharine Cornell played Joan about a dozen years before, she wore a personal halo to great advantage. Miss Hagen restrained herself too much, however grateful one could be for *some* restraint, or she was too greatly restrained by her director.

The role of the Inquisitor, played by the English actor, Frederick Rolf, was also shorn of splendor in the production—contrary, I believe, to Shaw's intent when he created a thoroughly humane and spiritual champion of the Church Militant who graces rather than disgraces his faith with attempts to save Joan from the fire reserved for heretics. It was plain from Uta Hagen's performance and from the casting of Mr. Rolf, as well as from the rather skimpy and unimpressive stage settings, that the Theatre Guild and Margaret Webster paid more attention to rationalistic or anti-heroic Shavianism than Shaw himself evinced when he wrote this and some other plays. Or, to be more accurate, the production failed to duplicate Shaw's feat of combining intellectuality with warmth and sympathy, as well as with subtleties of characterization, in telling Joan's story. The most emphatic performances were reserved for such roles as the weak-willed Dauphin, played entertainingly—with a slight cockney accent for good measure—by John Buckmaster, and Joan's formidable feudal enemy, the Earl of Warwick, whose worldliness was admirably conveyed by Andrew Cruickshank.

Although the production gave us less than full measure, it nevertheless exposed the playgoer to the persuasive power of a playwright the theatre honors itself in honoring. So long as the stage makes works such as *Saint Joan* its special province, the "fabulous invalid" will not lack justification. It was a tribute to the vitality of Shaw's writing that a *Saint Joan* production should have been the first respectable success of the 1951-52 American theatre. The first new season of the second half of our century assumed significance on Broadway by means of an alliance with the mind of the great humanist through whom the spirit of free inquiry and the dedication to human progress can be traced back to the nineteenth-century liberalism which gave rise to the modern drama.

III. ANTI-SHAW

Shaw continued to be in vogue both in the United States and England after 1951. But looking about us, we could wonder whether a reaction against Shaw might not be in the making within the present decade. Although I do not believe it will be easy to negate his preeminence so long as his plays are competently produced, sentiment against everything for which he stands has been growing in literary quarters. Drastic revaluations of Shaw are likely to come into favor sooner or later.

Shaw never captured the French theatre, and it is unlikely that he will do so now. The Paris of Molière has not been disposed to find any marked originality in his work. Rightly or wrongly (and, I believe wrongly), the theatre of Giraudoux, Anouilh, and Marcel Aymé can content itself without Shaw in translation. Central Europe, where his plays won special favor, will have to recover an equipoise lost decades ago before it can restore Shaw into pristine favor. Eire seems to recognize only one piece in the Shavian canon, *John Bull's Other Island,* and it is doubtful that Irish criticism will be disposed to turn Shaw into a favorite son of the Republic.

Outside of England and the Scandinavian countries, the one theatre that is likely to remain loyal to Shaw is commercial Broadway. Broadway will be the last stronghold of nineteenth-century liberalism in the American arts if for no other reasons than that it has no suitable substitute and that it is inveterately "middlebrow" at a time when liberalism is mostly a middlebrow preoccupation. Broadway isn't "clever" enough to provide a favorable climate for anti-liberal highbrowism. Broadway is not rationalistic enough to rationalize liberalism out of existence or to rationalize neo-medievalism *into* existence. Broadway also likes "fun," and a good deal of Shavian drama is fun. Also there is no evidence that Broadway is giving rise to a tribe of humorists capable of ousting Shaw from the theatre. Whereas the twenties gave rise to Kaufman and his collaborators, Sherwood, Barry, Behrman, Sturges, Hecht and MacArthur, the subsequent decades were more favorable to the development of serious and rather heavy-handed playwrights. Even with all these factors in mind, we cannot, however, overlook the lines of anti-Shavian assault now forming.

The assault on his ideas as a Fabian will come, as it has always come, from both pro-capitalist and pro-communist quarters. But the intensity of the attack is likely to increase; and that the mélange of his social views, ranging from reformism to semi-fascism, can be assaulted with success is quite obvious. As a social prophet he has been discredited in many respects by historical processes since 1914, and since he advertised himself as a prophet, the temptation to confuse his artistic achievements with his philosophical pretensions is likely to be strong. Moreover, no other man of letters in England, since the death of Shelley, was so completely devoid of a sense of guilt. Today, however, no doctrine carries as much weight with the intelligentsia as the conception of "original sin." Shaw is in danger of being considered superficial and suffering the same eclipse on that account as Anatole France has suffered.

Sooner or later, efforts may be made by some zealous thinkers of a new age to demolish Shaw's reputation on the grounds that he was guilty of the simplemindedness and lack of realism it has been fashionable to attribute to "liberalism." The argument that he was himself impatient with liberalism will be discounted by those who argue that it prepared the ground for totalitarianism—if not of the brown, then at least of the red, variety; Shaw's own perverse Stalin-worship will be cited in the bill of indictment. And if his defenders should call attention to the indisputable fact that the promptings of his critical and reformist spirit are deeply rooted in the history of Western civilization since the Renaissance, his detractors may seize upon precisely that point. They may maintain that it is just *this* that makes Shaw so vulnerable: The disintegration of the West *started* with Renaissance humanism, sceptical and worldly, and Shaw became its prophet, compounding its simples into a brew with which to confuse the generations that came under his tutelage! Since reasoning runs in this direction during our midcentury period, I am not propounding inconceivable charges.

If Shaw could reply, he would, I believe, admit the guilt and revel in it. With Luciferian aplomb, he would probably declare that to confuse humanity—and he could do it with *logic*—was a noble occupation. He would assert that there was no better way to stir Adam out of his mental slumber and moral apathy, wrench him from Abraham's bosom, and send him on the far journey of a quest for independent self-realization in the service of the Life Force, for which the security of a single era and the happiness of a single generation were of little account. The answer would not lack loopholes of logic. Nor would it escape the fallacy of the assumption that anything that serves an historical process, mystifyingly called a historical purpose, is necessarily *good*. But it would be a heroic answer, like all of Shaw's answers. "Learn the art of navigation," he might say with his Captain Shotover, "precisely because the seas are treacherous and the voyage precarious! The one thing humanity cannot afford to do is to hug the harbor."

Shaw also happens to be entirely clear, and a lucid author is unlikely to be a particularly popular subject with the post-1945 intelligentsia which is never happier than when it can play the role of explicator. A writer who does not possess many "levels of meaning" and who makes his appeal to rationality cannot satisfy current neo-estheticism. From this point of view, he cannot be regarded as a poet, and it is "poetry" that is now demanded of the drama—a poetry which is in essence magical rather than directly communicative. Nor is there any difficulty in connecting this esthetic protest against Shavian drama with the fleshly school of popular criticism. By claiming that Shaw denied the flesh and failed to create living human beings, his new critics will be able to disguise their dislike for social drama and their interest in theology and mysticism. The neo-intellectual will be able to conceal supercilious intellectualism by claiming that Shaw's playwriting is not full-blooded, just as it is possible to conceal anti-liberalism by charging Shaw with fascist tendencies. And, indeed, he had these, too; his mind had many chambers, and not everything that took up residence in them was good. And he was not consistently a logician. Although he honored Marx, he actually did as much as any man in England to dissolve Marxism; and although he raged against poverty, he formed no alliance with the poor. What the communist can say, echoing Lenin to the effect that Shaw is a "good man fallen among Fabians," would be a matter of perfect indifference to us. But what anti-Shavian Western criticism can say may carry a good deal of weight, especially when it can come at us as a concern with art rather than with social action.

Also, all the accusations can be well supported by the literati who take

Shaw's characters off the stage instead of leaving them where he put them. Shaw's ideal world of the "Ancients" in *Back to Methuselah,* a world in which emotion has been banished, can be described as the very epitome of an anti-humanist millennium. His great talkers, from John Tanner down to the lowliest discoursers, can be shown to be dilettantes, monsters of nature, or nullities. His saints, including Joan, can be charged as partly notions spawned by a rationalist's brain because they lack "mysticism." His tongue-minded rebels, whether Dick Dudgeon of *The Devil's Disciple,* Blanco Posnet, or Don Juan, and his tough-minded reformers can be called disguised sentimentalists. Even Don Juan can be charged with being sentimental; he is that about man's possibilities. Serious as Shaw was about his proposals for reforming society, he was even more serious as an artist about creating unusual characters. They were not necessarily his mouthpieces, as was often charged, but they were certainly symbols with which he endeavored to create his City of Reason. Nevertheless, the characters he presented as exceptional are vulnerable to criticism, and can be dismissed by anti-Shavian critics as spurious, if not, indeed, as mediocrities. Those who play this gambit will be able to designate Candida as an old-fashioned woman rather than the "new woman"—and a middle-aged flirt at that—and Marchbanks as a romantic adolescent rather than a genius; Tanner as a dandified sub-adult less qualified to be a parent for any child (let alone as ancestor for the superman) than his chauffeur; Caesar as a balding politician rather than a philosopher-king; Undershaft as a hypocrite rather than a philosopher-industrialist; Professor Higgins as a retarded prankster and egotist; Dudebat as a charlatan rather than an artist; Captain Shotover as a senile and alcoholic bumbler; his Joan as a mere conglomerate of the qualities of a saucy maid, a shrewd peasant, and a starry-eyed girl dressed up for sainthood by an irreligious Protestant.

Some of these charges would have some point, indeed, but for the fact that it was Shaw the playwright, not God, who created Shaw's characters. They exist for their author's limited purposes, and they are a function of a particular kind of play-making. They can be legitimately expected to live for us only in so far as they live for theatre. They are not subjects for evaluation of a total personality, which only human beings rather than play-characters possess.

One consideration—and, I believe, a decisive one—is that, except for our criticism of the "Ancients" in the last part of *Back to Methuselah,* Shaw was well ahead of his critics. He himself so characterized these and other exceptional characters as to make them vulnerable on a variety of counts. In giving flaws to his characters, he established their limitations himself. The flaws are generally deliberate creations of his perception of character, his philosophical intelligence and, above all, his sense of comedy.

For it is the business of comedy to note imperfection rather than perfection in man and society; to note imperfection even where merit is also present. The very sanity and depth of comic art consists of such perceptiveness, which is at its greatest where we can approve something, such as the wit of Beatrice and Benedick, the spiritedness of Falstaff, or the integrity of Molière's misanthrope Alceste. Shaw's approbation does not extend to the whole person but to the particular characteristic that interests Shaw with respect to the point he is trying to make. The error in thinking otherwise stems from the fallacy of confusing a delimited character in a play with a whole person outside the play.

A playwright does not create a human being but a stage character whose attributes suggest enough reality to put us in rapport with the stage action; and that reality is relative to the playwright's objective. Even Hamlet is only a dramatic character, which means that he is both *less* and *more* than a human being. Caesar, Tanner, Higgins, Undershaft, Shotover, etc., are also characters whose most human qualities are both less and more than human. They serve an action of Shaw's mind, and their service as the ideal statesman (Caesar), the resister and quarry of the Life Force (Tanner), the experimenter in phonetics and *mores* (Higgins), the exponent of realistic social action as contrasted with palliative philanthropy (Undershaft), the captain whose symbolic ship is symbolically floundering (Shotover) *reduces* them as human beings while *enlarging* them as "characters." Not to realize this fact is to be ignorant of theatre, to succumb to the vulgar view of realism as a duplication of reality. They are alive only in the world of art, which in Shaw's case is the world of comedy of ideas.

The seeming exception of *Saint Joan* is actually no exception. Tragic figure though she is, she, too, is created, not duplicated. She, too, has only the reality that matters in drama—namely, the reality that pertains to the play in which she is present. She, too, is a "character," although a singularly rich one, in a Shavian "drama of ideas." And I would assert that this is simultaneously also a "comedy of ideas," though a "dark comedy," for Joan's tragedy is the world's comedy. She is made to operate in a comic world of self-interest (Warwick's and the courtier's), of blind chauvinism (John de Stogumber's), personal inadequacy (the Dauphin's), and religious dogmatism. Only the Inquisitor's role is entirely free from comic implications. In view of the coexistence of comedy and tragedy in *Saint Joan* (and let us not ignore the fact that Joan herself brings a good measure of the comic spirit on to the stage, in her treatment of the Dauphin, for example), Shaw exhibited dramatic tact in not ending the play with Joan's execution. For all the pathos of the Epilogue, Shaw's ending carries out the comic pattern: the failure of men to live up to ideal principles of conduct is still his major concern. Talk of "modern conceptions of tragedy"! Shaw provided one without our realizing it, just as Euripides provided one with more than one *deus ex machina* in his day without Athenian arbiters realizing it. And the contribution was the same in both cases—tragedy in which the reasoning faculty or the philosophic temperament (Socratic in the case of both Shaw and Euripides) is not overwhelmed by the suffering in the play but reasserts itself.

We may also note that Shaw's Joan, although a tragic character, is not destroyed by her own "tragic flaw," unless her flaring spirit (like Antigone's) is that, but by the self-interest and blindness of her antagonists and fair-weather associates. And Joan, at the same time, is not treated by Shaw as the "heavy," humorless, and inflexible *tragedienne* of standard tragedy, a lightness and levitation being intrinsic in her character before and, to a degree, also after she is tried by the Inquisition. The Shavian élan actually underwent no fundamental change when *Saint Joan* was written.

Shaw, be it noted finally, is himself so fully aware that his "special" characters are "specially" working for his ideas that he reminds us of this fact. He does so by giving them another contradictory or "ordinary" dimension, and by surrounding them with other characters whose main function is to supply the resistance or inertia of life. The evidence will be found in every play of his that merits attention as such. Candida is housewife as well as sybil; Marchbanks, boy as well as genius; Shotover, drunkard as well as sage; Joan, peasant as well as visionary. Also, Candida has her husband Morel and her father to contend with. John Tanner has Ann, who has her way with him and can afford to encourage him to "go on talking," as well as Violet, who puts a spoke in his wheel of unconventionality when he rhapsodizes over the glories of unmarried motherhood. He also has Stryker, the independent and mechanically minded chauffeur, who has little use for his employer's half-baked philosophy. Undershaft, Shaw's Fabian industrialist, is balanced by his conventional wife and by Barbara. *Heartbreak House* has Ellie Dunn to remind us of "reality," and Joan has, among others, the Inquisitor, the common soldier, and the John de Stogumber who goes completely to pieces when she is burned at the stake.

Shaw did not deceive us as to his intentions. He wrote his plays with a sense of balance as if he were saying something to this effect: "The game I am playing occurs in a context of resistant reality even if it is mainly for the sake of the mental exercise afforded by my unique personages that I have brought you into the theatre. If you look sharp and listen intently, you will discover that my invention is itself a token of reality. For *all* thought is symbolic, never the actual thing, and awareness of the world is a symbolizing activity. What we make of the world is always a new and special reality. The little stage in the theatre and the big one outside it do not actually differ. They are both the creations of men. They are both products of fantasy. If the big one claims it is not fantastic, just glance at its behavior—then glance at the little stage that mimics that behavior and that actually is less bizarre. In fact, the superiority of the world of my creation over the world created by the majority of men who are not conscious artists lies in the irrefutable fact that *my* fantasy is more logical and consistent. I am in control of my fantasy, and the non-artists and pragmatists are not. And my explanation is not radically different from that which you might jolly well have received from my peers, Aristophanes, Ben Jonson, Molière—and Jonathan Swift."

The final answer, however, has been given by the audiences that have entered into Shaw's transfigured world for more than half a century and have found it quite commodious. That it is not a lyrical one is irrelevant. There are many worlds, and we inhabit these according to our taste. In fact, we move out of one into the other with considerable facility, for there are not worlds enough to make up the one "real" world we seek to know. Moreover, if Shaw's is not lyrical, it is none the less a poetic one. It is freely invented and created—for a speculation, a satire, a challenge, or a thought. It is, indeed, frequently even fanciful, the work of a playwright who was never a photographic realist.

That it is, in the main, also a nineteenth-century world should not surprise us in the case of a man born in 1856. The element of his playwriting concerned with the cash-nexus in society, beginning with his first play *Widower's Houses* in 1892, recalls Tom Robertson's mid-Victorian plays, such as *Caste* and *Society,* and W. S. Gilbert's non-musical comedy *Engaged.* The Victorians were much concerned with money and the culture pattern in which it functions. There is also a good deal of Gilbert and Sullivan in Shaw's fantastication, and the man who wrote *Arms and the Man* might have written the libretto of *H.M.S. Pinafore* or *The Pirates of Penzance* if he had had any skill at versifying. He was particularly fond of peopling his plays with Pooh-Bahs. Nor is it surprising that he should have remembered Samuel Butler's "Musical Banks," Birth Formulaes, Professors Hanky and Panky, and the Pontifexes of *The Way of All Flesh* in writing plays.

He felt a close affinity to the utopianism of William Morris, which derived from such earlier nineteenth-century schemes of social reformation as Fourierism and Owenism, and he naturally felt closer to John Ruskin's moralism than to twentieth-century estheticism. That moralism included the arts in its gambit, and a moralistic view of art was, of course, well entrenched in the Victorian world, so that even a word-magician such as Tennyson adhered to it. Nor was it absent in the rest of the nineteenth-century world: in the America of Emerson, in the France of those didactic dramatists Dumas *fils* and Augier, and in the Russia of Tolstoy, whose essay *What Is Art?,* maintaining the moral responsibility of art, might have been written by Shaw himself. This view, which did not prevent Tolstoy from remaining a great artist even after his conversion to a heterodox Christian idealism, did not restrain Shaw's fancy and humor.

Shaw's faith in an élite that would keep humanity up to scratch, that faith which the twentieth century was to translate into the rationalized and irrational totalitarianism of the fascist and communist dogmas, was a nineteenth-century growth. It was the age of Napoleonism, and even after the death of the Emperor on St. Helena his ghost had many apparitions, fascinating to men as diverse as Heine and Dostoevski, not to mention Nietzsche. And with or without Napoleonism, the dream of an élite was strong in the period, captivating men on both political and esthetic levels, men as diverse as Arnold and Carlyle, Kierkegaard and Rimbaud. Mechanism and vitalism, or materialism and idealism, were polarized in the age as they always remained polarized in the mind of Shaw, which played equally with economics and the "Life Force." Evolution, the major doctrine of the period, engrossed Shaw, and Optimism, the period's dominant mood, buoyed his spirit until the last decades of his long life. Experiment with ideas, the century's ruling passion, was his own passion, too.

For all his belief in an élite and for all his interest in Marxism, which he fitted into a boiled shirt while others were fitting it into a worker's blouse, Shaw was lower Anglo-Irish gentry and middle class, and in this respect he belonged to the years of his youth and early manhood. Only as a prose stylist does he bear more kinship to other centuries, to the eighteenth and the twentieth; and, indeed, the former hung on in the Dublin of his youth. Social reformer rather than revolutionist, a vestryman for a time who remained bound to the biblical fervors of dissenting Protestantism, businessman with a bookkeeping streak that never entirely left him, ardent bicyclist, faddist, debating-society luminary, man of courtesy and idealizer of women, and man against sex—in these and other respects, he was certainly a scion of the age which he was supposed to overthrow rather than represent. That only representative men effectively challenge their times is both a paradox and a fact of history. Shaw, along with many Victorian rebels, including the Victorian agnostics and atheists, exemplified that paradox. It is perhaps a profounder one than any he himself ever placed on paper.

When Shaw first aroused attention in the eighteen-eighties and -nineties, the age did not realize that Shaw was its child rather than an invading Nemesis or an eccentric from another world. It remained for our century to claim him. Yet these claims will be found less than assured, except in so far as the period from 1900 and 1914 was still an extension of the eighteen-eighties and -nineties. Actually, any differences we have or are likely to have with Shaw as man and author stem from differences between the present age and the past. The breach is widening between them every day. Is it possible that there will come a time when there will be no basis of understanding between them?

Whether or not this proves to be the case, it should not be impossible to understand Shaw. Not so long as there is an understanding of art—and particularly of theatre. We should be able to appreciate him most, indeed, once we no longer consider or care to consider him as anything *else* than a playwright; that is, once we no longer find it necessary to view him outside the theatre in order to view him inside it. At the same time, however, we shall not have much area of agreement with those early critics of Shaw who dismissed him as a mountebank because they considered his ideas unorthodox. We are more likely to disparage them as *orthodox*. Relative to our times, certainly, they are "unmodern"—though I should not justify our feeling superior to him on that account. In paying some attention to economic factors and to man as a *zoön politikon,* as a political animal, he was surely more modern than contemporary critic-esthetes.

His moral view of man can certainly strike us as rather simple. Shaw, who prided himself on his practicality and worldliness, had too little of the world, the flesh, and the devil in him for our diabolical age. He *was* Saint George and *not* the Dragon. As long as the devils do not leave us, or as long as we do not cease to be devils ourselves, we shall be inclined to regard him as actually *naïve*—this man who represented ultra-sophistication for many decades. (As those who go out to slay dragons usually are considered naïve, especially when they expect that dragons once slain will remain dead!) Shaw was not, however, a naïve playwright. We cannot condescend to the playwright in him without proving ourselves as simpleminded in dramatic criticism as he was in his most callow and overconfident social criticism. "Modernity" changes its colors—or spots—too often for us to make a fetish of it. To erect standards of criticism on it is to build on water. "Modernity" changes; art remains.

BERNARD SHAW AND
THE PURITAN IN HELL

As a result of a miracle for which we were indebted to a quartet of excellent actors and an enterprising producer, many thousands of playgoers in New York and other cities made the acquaintance of Shaw's *Don Juan in Hell* for the first time in the years 1951 and 1952. This was more of a miracle than most of them probably realized, and for more than one reason.

Some appeared to be unaware of the fact that the full-length play they saw was only an interlude in a larger play, *Man and Superman,* in which they had previously seen Maurice Evans, Carmen Matthews, and other performers disport themselves several seasons ago. For practical reasons, this, and other productions of Shaw's gay account of a man-hunt by a young lady who knows her mind, omitted the Don Juan episode which makes a full evening's entertainment by itself. Playgoers were enjoying a piece that was long considered unplayable, and that Shaw himself did not insist on having played in productions of *Man and Superman.*

Shaw was not usually so considerate of his producers' difficulties with his lengthy and discursive works, being generally ready to assure them that he knew his business and they didn't, just as he was always apt to tell even the actor-idols of the English-speaking stage how to act. Unlike many modern playwrights, who have had altogether too little competence in the art of stage production (although this has not prevented them from snorting and barking from the sidelines), Bernard Shaw was generally right. But in connection with *Don Juan in Hell,* Shaw was not right. For once, however, in spite of his custom of very blithely advertising his genius, he was too docile or good-natured to realize that he had created better than he himself knew.

These are good enough reasons for reviewing the facts about *Don Juan in Hell.* But there is another reason, too, for telling what must be a twice-told tale to the specialists. How many playgoers, one could wonder, observed that they were witnessing a *religious* play, and, more than that, actually enjoying it? How many realized that this was the most puritanical piece of dramatic literature written in the English language since John Milton composed his biblical tragedy *Samson Agonistes* more than two and a half centuries ago?

Shaw, who masqueraded as the "Devil's Disciple" on so many occasions, played Satan one of the worst tricks ever played on him and out-moralized the most rigid of Puritan divines. Even they did not go so far as to make sex, even with benefit of clergy, a cardinal sin, and to declare marriage to be the "most licentious" of institutions.

The anti-amorist view of the legendary Spanish rake was not new to Shaw when he came to write *Don Juan in Hell* and incorporate it as John Tanner's dream episode in *Man and Superman,* composed between 1901 and 1903. The god-father of that episode was none other than Mozart, for whom Shaw's admiration knew no bounds and to whom he refers in the preface to *Man and Superman* as "that master-enchanter, the master beloved by masters." As long ago as 1887, Shaw published an essay entitled *Don Giovanni Explains* in which Mozart's hero claims he was shamefully slandered by the women he had eluded. The essay made no particular impression, as its thirty-one-year-old author was still barely known in spite of his having published five novels between 1879 and 1883. He was then a year within starting to cover music for the London paper *The Star* under the pseudonym of "Corno di Bassetto" and acquiring notoriety as an impertinent scribbler.

Shaw's status was, of course, radically different when he returned to the Don Juan subject in 1901. He was now the praised and pilloried author of dramatic criticism for *The Saturday Review,* of rousing Fabian as well as pro-Ibsen and pro-Wagner tracts, and of nine full-length plays including such famous and infamous pieces as *Mrs. Warren's Profession, Arms and the Man, Candida, The Devil's Disciple,* and *Caesar and Cleopatra.* He had been badgered for some time by the scintillating gentleman-critic, A. B. Walkley, once his colleague on *The Star* and now play reviewer for the respectable *Times.* Walkley enjoyed Shaw's writing and praised him for providing intellectual stimulation but refused to take him seriously as a playwright. Walkley said Shaw failed to give enough scope to the human emotions and did not budge from this opinion even when confronted by so conventionally written a play as *Candida.* He facetiously insisted on regarding it as a fantasy.

"Mr. Shaw amuses us," he wrote, "by representing a world where conduct is regulated by thought, and men love women, as the civil servant in *Pickwick* ate crumpets, on principle." Ideas, he said, are "two a penny," and our thoughts "mere bobbing corks on the stream of life." By ignoring the non-rational life and "all its subconscious and unconscious elements," Shaw obtained "most amusing results," but, according to Walkley, had not dealt seriously with life.

When Walkley made similar charges some years earlier, he suggested that Shaw ought to try to write a play about Don Juan. Such a character, entirely involved in irrational emotion, would no doubt give Shaw a great deal of trouble. Walkley, of course, did not make the proposal seriously.

He was merely challenging Shaw to deal seriously with the emotions in general and with sex in particular.

No one who reads the Don Juan play Shaw did write, along with the brilliant prefatory letter "To Arthur Bingham Walkley," can seriously believe Shaw wanted to satisfy his critic rather than to put him in his place. But Shaw did meet the challenge—and, as usual, on his own terms.

He met it in *Man and Superman,* subtitled "A Comedy and a Philosophy," and he blandly called it the only real treatment of the subject of sex ever written. It is superfluous to explain in detail how Shaw acquitted himself of the assignment, since he always explained his intentions better than anybody else. But this much should be noted. He reversed the old adage that you can't eat your cake and have it, too.

He ate the cake by composing one of the most congenial love comedies of his or any other time and filling it with delightfully drawn characters. He also made his hero John Tanner succumb to the very "stream of life" in which Walkley took such stock. At the end of *Man and Superman,* Tanner, one of the most intellectual of stage heroes, consents to marry Ann Whitefield and he surrenders to the most irrational of all emotional forces: Sex.

But at the same time Shaw kept the cake by surrendering none of his own prerogatives as a "realist." He dealt with a romantic situation, but he did so unromantically and unsentimentally. John Tanner was the reverse of a conventional Don Juan; he ran away from a woman instead of running after her. Woman is the pursuer, and man is the quarry in this comedy.

Moreover, Shaw not only retained his intellectual cake but multiplied its size many times over by writing the *Don Juan in Hell* interlude, in which Tanner dreams up another Don Juan who does not succumb to women at all and rejects all the blandishments of sex, a Don Juan who could give any Puritan spades in abstinence and moral purity. The real artist-creator, according to Shaw, is a match for any woman bent on creating in her own, more physical way; he is, indeed, the only real match for a woman because, like her, he has a real purpose. John Tanner is a talker rather than a creator, and is, therefore, quite properly captured by Ann Whitefield in the "realistic" plot of *Man and Superman.* But Don Juan, in Tanner's fantasy *Don Juan in Hell,* is a creative spirit; a heavy-weight whereas Tanner is only a light-weight. Tanner is only "Man"; Don Juan is "Superman."

Now, Shaw had some warrant for this anti-romantic and anti-sentimentalist portrait which contradicts the popular notion of Don Juan as an oversexed tomcat. Earlier playwrights, too, had been less interested in Don Juan's philanderings than in his contempt for conventions. In his earliest incarnation as the hero of the seventeenth century Spanish play *El Burla-dor de Sevilla,* he was an "enemy of God." In Molière's famous *Don Juan, or the Feast of the Statue,* he was a cynic who was even more intolerable while playing the religious hypocrite than he was as a sceptic. In Mozart's opera, too, Juan's major attributes are his disregard for conventional scruples, scorn of moral precepts, and flouting of heaven's justice.

Shaw, then, followed an established literary tradition. But with this decisive difference: Whereas his predecessors made a rebel out of the licentious Don Juan by picturing him as an unbeliever and immoralist, Shaw turned him in to a major revolutionist by portraying him as a *believer* and a *moralist.* Once more, therefore, Shaw made a good profit out of the transaction with Walkley. Shaw got himself an ideal expounder of the Shavian principle of the Life Force, the Shavian ideal of the Superman, and the Shavian religion of Creative Evolution.

It is not incumbent upon us to accept the gospel of Don Juan and Shaw with deadly seriousness. It is sufficient, and far more intelligent, to follow it as a metaphorical statement to the effect that strong minds and spirits reject second-rate gratifications, and, for the rest, to enjoy *Don Juan in Hell* for the mental exercise it provides, as well as for the poetic experience of watching Shaw's mind make dazzling gyrations that are visionary as well as intellectual. Shaw's Don Juan carries us imaginatively beyond the present state of the world at which Shaw laughed and thundered for over half a century.

In spite of his activity in politics and in social reform, Shaw knew as well as any clergyman that the world would not be better until individuals were. Don Juan's vision of the Superman is a vision of an improved species of man who would give Shaw the better society for which he agitated as a socialist. He even made Juan envisage the liberation from the flesh in this world that saints envisioned in the next. Juan is aligned with the world's great philosophers and mystics. Like them, he sets himself the goal of penetrating the heart of reality by means of the power of pure contemplation. Using one brilliant paradox after another, then, Shaw performed the miracle of writing a play about sex and turning it into an ultra-religious drama.

A poet was needed before this miracle could be accomplished, and in writing *Don Juan in Hell* Shaw was a poet. But only a keen intellect, capable of making distinctions, could get the fantasia in hell started at all. Declaring it to be his intention to "write the only play on the subject of sex ever written," Shaw started with a sharp distinction between Casanova, the traditional lover, and Don Juan, the traditional rebel, who in Shaw's up-to-date version rebels against everything that limits man's potentialities, including sex itself. Not Casanovism but Don Juanism is Shaw's ideal.

The one concerns itself with illusions, the other with realities. The one relaxes the will or desire for perfection, the other intensifies it until the Shavian hero must reject all illusions—except perhaps the illusion that life can be freed from all illusion.

Casanova would be entirely at home in Shaw's "hell," which is the place of pleasure and illusion. Don Juan can feel at home only in Shaw's "heaven," which is the place of work and reality. Casanova is a romanticist, Don Juan is a "realist," and, as such, must find a purpose in the world and serve that purpose. Like his creator, he has "an evolutionary appetite." The distinction between Casanovism and Don Juanism is the essence of the joke Shaw played on Walkley by complying with the latter's teasing request for a Don Juan play. And, like most of Shaw's jests, it was a serious one.

Shaw, who was often charged with inconsistencies, was, moreover, remarkably consistent in one ultimate respect. He remained as much of a Puritan in writing *Don Juan in Hell* (or, for that matter, all of *Man and Superman*) as he had proclaimed himself to be in *The Devil's Disciple, Caesar and Cleopatra,* and *Captain Brassbound's Conversion* when he published them in 1901 under the collective title of "Plays for Puritans." His *Don Juan in Hell* may not be the "only play on the subject of sex ever written," but it is certainly the most puritanical one. As a matter of fact, he never stopped writing "Plays for Puritans."

The wonder of it all is, of course, that he derived so much enjoyment from his puritanism. Nietzsche, from whom Shaw adopted the evolutionary Superman ideal (but without the "blonde beast" attributes), had called for a *gaya scienza,* a gay knowledge, and then went mad from desperation. Shaw actually possessed *gaya scienza* almost as the birthright of his talent, and never lost his reason—or even his temper.

But there is another wonder in *Don Juan in Hell:* It is a complete drama of discussion rather than of so-called action. In favoring a "slice of life," the Naturalists of the previous two or three decades, with Zola as their bellwether, had called for a drama without plot. They did not succeed in supplying it; but Shaw did.

For other reasons (namely, a passion for ideas and a belief in the theatre as a medium for enlightening the race), Shaw the critic also called for a drama that would be intrinsically "discussion." He claimed his "discussion drama" could find sanction in theatrical tradition and called attention to the considerable success of the preaching profession in holding audiences. He attributed the rise of pure discussion drama in the modern theatre to Ibsen, but with less accuracy than partisanship for both Ibsen and himself. It was only Shaw who succeeded in writing a play that is wholly discussion and yet holds up as theatre. Nobody has been able to duplicate his feat, and he himself was able to perform it more or less successfully only twice, in *Don Juan in Hell* and *Getting Married*. He performed it partially, of course, in virtually every major work, as in the remarkable tent scene of *Saint Joan*.

He demonstrated that a play can be essentially plotless, devoid of external action and yet not be static, whereas it had been held generally that a plotless play was the same thing as a static one. At the top of his form, he showed that thought, too, was action; that ideas, when intensely maintained and refuted, not only activated the stage but made it exciting. Everything depends, of course, upon the intrinsic interest of the ideas and upon the dramatic verve with which they are stated. Discussion as managed by Shaw is made for speaking rather than merely for reading. It has the variety, pace, and sting of effective stage action.

In order for discussion to constitute drama, it must be sparked by some need, intent or passion by the speakers. The playwright must be able to infuse the conversationalists with this motivating element; must create dramatic personalities. They must be capable of feeling, believing, and willing. Don Juan, the Devil, Ana, and the Statue became such personalities.

Shaw, who was willing to get along without "plot," never maintained that a play could be written without "characterization." Actually, Don Juan and the Devil are as memorable stage characters as any in modern English drama. Moreover, they are magnificently "orchestrated," affording sharp contrasts and engendering tensions by their contrasting attitudes. And the Devil and Juan are worthy opponents. There are no easy victories for Don Juan when Old Nick turns social philosopher and blasts the ideal of progress with the historical evidence of man's progress in the art of self-destruction. Don Juan prevails, in fact, only by resorting to a Shavian profession of faith; to a poetical mysticism which only goes to show that even so ardent a rationalist as Shaw was only an inverted romanticist, since he was romantic about "purpose" in the universe and even more determinedly romantic about man's ability to lift himself up by his spiritual bootstraps and become the Superman. Don Juan wins in poetry rather than in argument when the Devil pins him down to facts.

Although it would require a much longer essay than this to demonstrate Shaw's dramatic artistry in detail, it is not too much to say that, intentionally or not, he played a final trick on his friend Walkley, who was partial to conventional playwriting. In the Don Juan interlude, Shaw wrote a play that violated all conventional expectations of what a play should be. Yet the result is engrossing theatre. And the Laughton-Boyer performance has shown us that the play is, in fact, such good theatre that it can be played as a "reading" rather than as a fully staged piece replete with costume and scenery. *Don Juan in Hell* succeeds without any of the illusion-making procedures that ordinary plays get—and fail in spite of.

How cleverly Shaw worked in this masterpiece can be fully realized if we observe how, virtually from speech to speech, and also within the individual long speeches themselves, he provided effective equivalents for external action. Nor did he forget "showmanship" when he wrote the remarkable verbal arias of Don Juan and the Devil. The long speeches require virtuoso feats of delivery very much like the performance of tenors in our opera houses. Good actors rise to a verbal challenge as good singers rise to a musical challenge, and if there were any doubting Thomases at performances of *Don Juan in Hell,* they must have been silenced when the ceiling shook with applause after Boyer's and Laughton's page-length speeches. The "aria," when brilliantly rendered, can be the ultimate in showmanship. Shaw, the former music critic, was not apt to overlook this opportunity.

Moreover, watching for skill in "dramaturgy" we also see that he even organized the discussion in such a way that it agrees with the Aristotelian prescription that a play should have a "beginning," "middle," and "end." It contains, too, the dynamic factors of discovery (or "recognition") and reversal (or "peripety") Aristotle considered essential to good playwriting. There are physical discoveries or recognitions at the beginning when Ana meets Juan and her father in hell, and there are mental and spiritual discoveries, of course, throughout the play. As for "reversals" (which Broadway calls "switcheroos"), the entire play is a "reversal," from the start when the conventionally pious Ana is amazed to find herself in hell to the last minute when she converts to the religion of Creative Evolution. In between, besides, we have such reversals as the presentation of hell as the place of pleasure and romantic illusion, heaven as the place of work and reality, Don Juan as a moralist, the Statue as a hedonist, and all those twists and turns of dialectical discourse that make the play continuously stimulating and delightful.

We need only add all these witcheries of craftsmanship together to realize how devilishly clever was the Irish-born Puritan who made a first-grade Puritan out of Europe's most celebrated sinner. The kingdom of heaven may not be made of such things, but the kingdom of theatre most assuredly is. Shaw may not have redeemed the earth as he would have liked to do, but he redeemed the English theatre; and it can be said, too, that it was the first time in history that the theatre ever derived any benefit from a Puritan.

WHEN SHAW BOILED
THE POT

When *Misalliance* opened at New York's City Center Theatre in February, 1953, nearly half a century after the play was written, an informed critic may well have imagined he heard some of the chuckles in the audience from Shaw himself. And if some of that laughter made the reviewer a trifle uncomfortable, who could blame him, since Shaw seemed to be having the last laugh on drama critics. In 1910, when *Misalliance* was first produced in London at the Duke of York's Theatre, it proved to be an utter failure for Charles Frohman, who quickly scrapped his plan for an English repertory theatre and retrieved his losses with a revival of Pinero's reliable *Trelawney of the Wells*. To be as precise in a business matter as Shaw used to be, a historian would have to report that *Misalliance* ran for only three performances. Even Shaw's friendly successor to the post of drama critic on *The Saturday Review,* Max Beerbohm, had misgivings about the long play which was written as one uninterrupted act, all of it seemingly a debate and a good deal of it delivered by offensive young people. And when seven years later, William Faversham gave the play in New York, with cuts reported by Archibald Henderson to have been as extensive as they were inept, even the generous opinion of John Corbin in the *Times* failed to include more enthusiastic adjectives than "pleasant" and "adequate."

On further study in the newspaper morgue and the library, a critic may derive comfort from the reflection that a colleague, Sir Desmond MacCarthy, who saw the play at the Everyman Theatre in 1924, found it "exceedingly interesting." He actually complimented Shaw on "making discussion so amusing that on the stage it throws most comedies of situation in the shade as an entertainment." Even MacCarthy, however, regarded it only as a "preliminary canter for the far finer *Heartbreak House,*" and voiced the opinion that the author "had not a clear notion where his perceptions in this case were leading him." Before the evening of February 23 was going to run out, New York reviewers were ready to acclaim *Misalliance* as the most stimulatingly entertaining play of the Broadway season 1952-53. They were ready, so to speak, to eat crow for the entire play-reviewing profession. Even if they were to assuage their critical conscience and temper their enthusiasm with the platitudinous observation that the play was not Shaw's greatest, Shaw might well chuckle.

I would submit, nevertheless, that both parties—Shaw's critics as well as Shaw himself—had good reason for laughter at each other's expense; Shaw, because he wrote a farce in *Misalliance* that completely overshadows the thesis that the play was supposed to carry, to judge from the prolix preface he added to the printed text; and Shaw's critics, because their view that the play is solely a discussion is just as fallacious as their opinion that the play succeeds in spite of the fact that it is an extended argument. And I would further submit that if *Misalliance* cannot be regarded as a major work, this is the case not because it is a disquisitory drama, but because the disquisition is not great enough. *Misalliance* is one of the great farces of the English language, along with Jonson's *Bartholomew Fair* and *The Importance of Being Earnest*. It is a few shades less superb a farce than Wilde's contrivance mainly because it is less inventively absurd. It is many shades less distinguished than Shaw's best plays because Shaw the debater and conversationalist was not at his very best here.

Ultimately, it was Shaw the comedian and showman who triumphed in *Misalliance*. Shaw either deceived himself or tried to deceive us—and, I believe, he did both—when he called attention to the "problem play" quality of *Misalliance*. His critics deceived themselves, whether they took him at his word and didn't like the play or they took him at his word and did like it in spite of accepting it as a problem play or thesis drama. If these contentions, moreover, seem paradoxical, may not the reason be that, in the main, Shaw is a paradox among playwrights—not, of course, in the superficial sense that he made paradoxical statements, but that he was himself a paradox. He was a man who came to scorn theatrical nonsense (he disapproved of it even in *The Importance of Being Earnest,* in one of his play reviews) but favored it for himself. He came or pretended to have come to the theatre to propagandize prosily, but became a poet at times, and in such a piece as *Misalliance,* an entertainer. The greatest paradox of his career is, indeed, that the most aggressively earnest of British playwrights should also have been the most theatrical. *Misalliance* is merely an extreme instance, because it is, with *Getting Married* and *Heartbreak House,* the most discursive of his interesting plays.

Nothing perhaps will prove more instructive than a glance at the preface *Parents and Children* he wrote for the published version of the play. That he wrote this preface, like other prefaces, after the first production does not alter the fact that he not only took his prefatory argument seriously, for it expresses convictions he aired repeatedly, but believed that it was the argument of his play. Shaw wrote some prefaces that do not actually accord with the explicit content of his plays. He seized the occasion of publishing a play to compose a more or less peripheral discussion. A conspicuous example is the introductory essay to *The*

Millionairess in which he discusses Mussolini and Hitler. But there is hardly a point developed in the numerous subchapters of *Parents and Children* for which an equivalent point is not present in the actual dialogue of *Misalliance*. Archibald Henderson is not wrong when he declares in his authorized biography that the play itself should have been called *Parents and Children.*

Those for whom the "misalliance" of the title means the misalliance between the rich middle-class and the aristocracy surely miss the dramatic center of the play. The "misalliance" pertains only to secondary matters in the plot contrivance—only in the fact that Bentley and Percival belong to the nobility whereas the Tarletons are a "linen-draperish" family. The "misalliance" that is traced throughout the play and dominates the resolution is the mismating of parents and children. Bentley is a problem to his father Lord Summerhays; Hypatia and Johnny—and the illegitimate clerk "Gunner" or Baker, too—are problems to the bookish businessman Tarleton. And Percival, who ultimately wins Hypatia, is the best-adjusted young person of the lot because he was brought up by "three fathers," which is as good as being brought up by none. It is true, of course, that the play diverges into other matters than parents and children, such as government and democracy, but so does the preface, too. All is grist so long as Shaw does the grinding.

What a difference there is, however, between the preface and the play with respect to sheer vitality of composition. The preface is a disquisition; the play, a work of theatre. There is great writing in the first two-paragraph subchapter, "Trailing Clouds of Glory," on the subject of death, and exquisite briefer passages are strewn throughout the prefatory essay. One remembers such lines as "What is a child? An experiment," "A child is a restless, noisy little animal, with an insatiable appetite for knowledge," "The secret of being miserable is to have leisure to bother about whether you are happy or not," and "A perpetual holiday is a good working definition of hell." Shaw is, after all, our greatest master of English prose since Dean Swift. But let us face the fact that the 126-page introduction to the 106-page play is pretty much of a bore. At least, it is as boring as anything by Shaw could be. But the play, as Cyril Ritchard's City Center production proved beyond a doubt, is anything but boring.

Fortunately for my argument, it cannot be maintained that the stagepiece is lively because Shaw *departed* from the subject matter of "Parents and Children." It cannot be said that Shaw simply let himself go and, like a surrealist, allowed his unconscious to take over when he wrote the play. For all its seemingly rambling discourse, *Misalliance* is not a spontaneous effusion. It is, on the contrary, an exceedingly calculated collection of dramatic materials—of situations and points Shaw had in one way or other used before and was to use again. *Heartbreak House* is anticipated in the picture of aristocratic decay and of family confusions and conclaves; the buoyancy of Tarleton is comparable to that of Captain Shotover; the comic intrusion of the illegitimate clerk with homicidal intentions is well paralleled by the intrusion of the burglar in the later play. The refined sensibility attributed to advancing years in the case of Summerhays (and Tarleton) suggested to Desmond MacCarthy the spiritualization of age presented in *Back to Methuselah*. The eccentric young aristocrat Bentley, whose sharp mind is encased in a frail physique, reminds us of March-banks, and Bentley is mothered by Mrs. Tarleton as Marchbanks was mothered, up to a point, by Candida. Percival, the desirable male, is chased by Hypatia Tarleton as John Tanner is chased by the "mighty huntress" Ann in the earlier written *Man and Superman*. Lina, the Polish gymnast, was to have her equal in physical prowess when Shaw came to write *The Millionairess* in his old age. Lord Summerhays, who ruled a kingdom in India many times larger than England, is a shadowy variant of Shaw's Caesar, the superman of common sense in the field of politics. And Mrs. Tarleton, whose mothering instinct brooks no romantic non-sense about honor and revenge, is Lady Cicely of *Captain Brassbound's Conversion* in a middle-class incarnation. If there is any spontaneity in *Misalliance,* it is that of the showman who fetches everything within easy reach, no matter how familiar to him or to his public, so long as it will provide another turn to the entertainment he is contriving—or, as we say on Broadway, another "gimmick," except that Shaw's gimmicks are often "ideas."

If we knew nothing indeed about Shaw that could not be derived from his wildest farces, we could still be sure that he loved "ideas." He must have truly loved them to play with them so zestfully. And in this he differed from all the "serious" playwrights who couldn't play with them at all. It is questionable whether they (Galsworthy and Brieux, for example) really loved them when they hugged them so close to their bosom that they strangled them. "Problem play" writers have, indeed, never loved ideas; they have only loved problems and solutions. Shaw, of course, also held convictions, but he usually knew how to distinguish be-tween an idea and a conviction when he wrote a play. Ideas, indeed, served Shaw—in *Misalliance* as well as elsewhere—as means for making theatre. He made them prance so mischievously or so poignantly, as the case might be! They prance, in the main, only mischievously in *Mis-alliance,* in consequence of which, along with other factors, the play is a farce—a "farce of ideas."

The old magician, however, had other tricks in his bag which may make us wonder how serious he really was when he claimed for himself, as well as for Ibsen, the "discussion play" as his special province. "Discussion play" usually suggests to us a play devoid of plot, physical action, emotion, and everything else except argument. In analyzing *Getting Married,* Shaw himself made the mistake—or perhaps merely the pretense —of justifying argument as drama by pointing out that the description of a classic play was often called an "argument"; and Archibald Henderson, taking him too seriously, I suspect, pointed out that this "argument" was merely the prefatory description of the plot rather than the play itself. Actually, it should be obvious, Shaw never contended that "discussion drama" shouldn't be theatre. He believed it *could* be theatre, and proceeded to prove his point.

He did so in *Misalliance,* in the first instance, by resorting to sheer physical action as flagrantly as any harlequinade of the *commedia dell' arte* or Punch and Judy variety. In this elementary respect, in fact, *Misalliance* is more farcical than *The Importance of Being Earnest.* Young Bentley throws two calculated fits on the stage, one toward the beginning and another toward the end of the evening—and both quite brazenly. Lina, the gymnast and aviatrix, hauls him offstage, after his second fit, by main strength. Lina also uses six oranges and a Bible for a juggling act, which an actress capable of the feat would no doubt perform onstage rather than offstage. The scene of the illegitimate clerk Baker stealing into the house, hiding in the portable Turkish bath, and bobbing in and out of it to watch Hypatia making overtures to Percival provides more physical farce, as does the intruder's attempts to assassinate his dad and Lina's disarming the frantic chump. Characters threaten each other when they are not actually committing violence, as in Punch and Judy puppetry. The exits and entrances in the play are numerous and some of these, such as the entrances of Percival and of Lina after their plane has crashed into the greenhouse in the garden, are thoroughly theatrical. Characters are constantly dragged on to or hauled off the stage. Not only the ideas, but the characters—the participants of the conversation, if you please—canter about the stage; sometimes in order to demonstrate an idea (Hypatia's pursuit of Percival) or to put a stop to a discussion for which there is no prospect of a conclusion.

In the Ritchard production, this farcical translation of ideas was abundantly evident not merely because the play was briskly staged and vivaciously performed, but because two intermissions were used. Shaw's text, which called for no intermission at all, may easily deceive its theatrically unimaginative readers who cannot sense the physical action in a playscript. Although the original 1910 production in London also had two intermissions, critics, too, appear to have been deceived by the printed version. Why else should they have made so much of the "Sophoclean" structure. Even the less than sedulously reverent Hesketh Pearson, who published "G. B. S." as late as 1942, refers to *Getting Married* and *Misalliance* as "daring experiments in the Aristotelian unities, which Shaw always defended as of cardinal importance." We may note that they were hardly as daring as Mr. Pearson thinks. Strindberg, whom Shaw admired greatly, had anticipated him in the writing of full-length no-intermission— or, if you will, one-act—plays by about two decades with *Miss Julia* and *The Creditor*. Shaw intimidated the critics of *Misalliance* into believing he was austerely dedicated to pure intellectualism and earnestly concerned with keeping audiences attentive to his argument, as though he had momentous matters in mind, when he was actually interested only in keeping the pot boiling.

He never took the play seriously, and considered it a potboiler. If critics had been willing to accept his judgment without secret reservations, they would never have compared it with *Heartbreak House,* found it wanting, and failed to enjoy the farce. And this is perhaps the final paradox of the matter: If they had expected less from the play because it came to them as "discussion drama," they would have found greater value in its matter or, if you please, "ideas."

They would not have looked, perhaps unconsciously, for a closely reasoned and compact argument or thesis. They would have derived gratification, instead, from the contrast between the flagrantly farcical plot and the brilliant lines with which it is studded. "Common people do not pray, my Lord; they only beg"; "Nothing is worth doing unless the consequences may be serious"; "I feel the first chill of prudence. Save me"; "Men like conventions because men made them"; "The strength of a chain is no greater than its weakest link; but the greatness of a poet is the greatness of his greatest moment"; "Good thing the empire educates us. Opens our minds." These lines that Wilde would have been pleased to beget are doubly effective because they jump at the listener out of the nonsense of the proceedings on the stage. The greater the contrast between the sense of the ideas and the blithe nonsense of the plot, of which there is a shameless abundance, the greater the striking force of the intellectual content. This is one way in which Shaw was able to eat his cake and have it, too; to have his say and at the same time make theatre. An idea smothered among ideas may appear flat. But an idea lifted up in the midst of obvious plot contrivances sticks out like a steeple among cottages. And the obtrusiveness of any element in farce, far from being disadvantageous is, of course, advantageous.

Perhaps, however, we should not ride this theory of farcical technique too hard without noting that whenever Shaw wrote plays his discourse usually underwent other transformations that distinguish it from his prefatory statements. His discourse in dramatic, rather than essayistic, form patently benefited from the compression required by playwriting. A point is scored in playwriting, and there is an end to it—until there is an occasion to return to it. And the point comes at the playgoer not solely from the ambience of the author's intention but, as it were, from the tension of the characters. Granted even that the characters in *Misalliance* are not completely round people but animated Jonsonian "humours" (and I am prepared to argue that this is not entirely the case), they are none the less stage figures motivated by notions or obsessions, whims or intentions, for the duration of the play. They have random hankerings if not perhaps true desires, and they invariably give some provocations for action or response *pro tem*. These form a dramatic context from which the dialogue stems, which is not the case in the prefaces in which Shaw expresses his views directly. The verbal fireworks in the play are then theatrical, if not always conclusively motivated, fireworks, and Shaw is no mere expositor. More perhaps than any other play, *Misalliance* disposes of the old canard that he could not create theatre. He met its requirements and his own at the same time. And they were more alike than he himself was willing to concede. His insistence that they were not alike may be one paradox of which he himself was not aware. Or was he?

STRINDBERG AND THE
TWENTIETH CENTURY

It is reported that when the British actor Robert Lorraine read *The Father* to his wife, he found her on her knees before him at the end of the second act, assuring him that all their children were his own and that he was not to believe a single word of the play. That, we take it, was not how he came to appear in Strindberg's masterpiece and make a success of it in 1927, as well as to venture upon the forbidding double drama *The Dance of Death* one year later; but it convinced him that a playwright so alien to English nonchalance had enough dramatic force to spellbind London. We may take it, too, that it was the same demoniacal intensity that enabled Strindberg to triumph over German *Gemütlichkeit* and French *bon sens* in the eighties and nineties of the last century, and to prevail finally even over his own countrymen in spite of the multiple irritations he caused them. He became Sweden's grand old man, a role that actually did not fit him, and that would not have fitted him if he had lived to be a hundred instead of dying of cancer of the stomach in his sixty-third year. The centenary of his birth on January 22, 1949, was a national event in Sweden, and there might have been celebrations in the rest of Europe but for the political weather. The European theatre has been fully aware of its debt to the author of fifty-six full-length and one-act plays from which it drew much sustenance for its two major styles of naturalism and expressionism. It has even tended to agree with his chief competitor, Ibsen, who, although berated by his irascible junior colleague, claimed to work best when he had Strindberg's photograph in front of him, and said, "He will be greater than I."

In America, Strindberg's centenary raised nary a ripple. Although it is possible that some universities in the Middle West took note of the event in their fashion, Broadway was decidedly unmoved. Elisabeth Bergner had been forced to scuttle a revival of *Miss Julie* "on the road" two seasons before. A free adaptation of *The Dance of Death* under the title of *The Last Dance* had fared poorly on the main stem during the previous season, and no revivals of his work were to be seen on New York's stages when his centenary should have been celebrated. (Productions of *The Father* and *The Creditor* appeared considerably later.) No Broadway dramatic critic paid Strindberg the tribute of a column so far as I know, and the one American dramatist who could have been expected to honor him, Eugene O'Neill, was doubtless too taken up with his struggle for health to rush into print. O'Neill had not been niggardly when he wrote that Strindberg was "the precursor of all modernity in our present theatre" and that he remained "the most modern of moderns, the greatest interpreter . . . of the characteristic spiritual conflicts that constitute the drama." This plaudit came, however, in 1924, at a time when O'Neill's Provincetown Theatre was in the Strindberg market, and when our stage was conscious of its European heritage.

Is it possible that Strindberg's champions in the English-speaking world have lost their ardor, and that his influence has faded? I suspect that this is the case, even if it is not so long ago that Bernard Shaw converted his Nobel Prize into a trust fund intended in part to ensure good English translations of Strindberg's work. The Nobel Prize is a substantial sum, but the posthumous beneficiary of it, Strindberg, was too much at odds with the secretary of the Nobel Foundation to win the coveted award himself, although he had sixteen novels and short story collections, seven autobiographies, and nine other books, as well as the plays, to his credit or discredit before he died in 1912. Strindberg's furious genius has certainly not embodied itself in our later dramatists as it did in O'Neill, which may be a pity when we consider the electric power such plays as *Beyond the Horizon, All God's Chillun Got Wings, Desire Under the Elms, The Great God Brown,* and *Strange Interlude* derived from the Strindbergian whirlpool of sex ambivalence and inner chaos. Strindberg himself, moreover, has not had a single conclusive triumph on the American stage. Nor is he likely to have one in the foreseeable future.

Those of us who consider Strindberg not only a major figure in the modern theatre but a still very effective playwright are forced to take up defensive positions, and we are put to some trouble deciding what ground we shall try to hold. We can, for example, fight behind a hypothesis by asserting that Strindberg would come into his own in America if we had the kind of theatre that could produce him well enough, and would not have to operate on the murderous basis of commercial production. We can snipe at the tendency of reviewers to draw their conclusions exclusively from what they see on the stage instead of using their mind's eye. And it is, after all, true that most reviewers, unlike Shaw and Nathan (not to mention Dryden and other departed champions), are too humble, too apt to let themselves be led by stage productions, instead of leading the theatre. Pieces for the theatre, unless they also happen to be durable poems that gratify the reader, have to be constantly reborn in the theatre. Otherwise they cease to be alive for us. That is one of the penalties many plays pay for constituting a public event rather than a private pleasure. If Strindberg's best work had appeared in his novels, there would be less question, even in America, concerning his magnitude and magic.

It is also permissible to doubt that Strindberg's stature can be gauged from the two or three samples of his work in anthologies and scattered revivals. Even if we had superior productions of *The Father* and *Miss Julie,* we should still have too narrow a base for judgment. There were several Strindbergs in his collected works, and not many of his plays would strike us as irrationally anti-feminist and impossibly vindictive. There is *Easter,* as tender a play as any written in modern times, though hardly one of his best. There is the vivid folk-drama *The Bridal Crown.* There are those haunting dream fugues *The Dream Play* and *The Ghost Sonata,* and those mordant comedies *Comrades* and *There Are Crimes and Crimes.* There is that curious trilogy of human error and search for salvation *To Damascus.* And, finally, there are seven or eight plays drawn from Swedish history that make him the greatest writer of historical drama since Shakespeare. Even the large anti-feminist or sex-duel vein in his genius yields remarkable products that have been overlooked. One of these, *Creditors,* concentrates more drama into a single act than many playwrights get into an entire career. Another, *The Link,* is without doubt the most trenchant divorce play ever written.

It is probable, nonetheless, that those of us who are so disposed to argue are wasting our breath and possibly also begging a question or two. We may have to cede Strindberg, so far as America is concerned, to history, where his place as a molder of the modern drama is impregnable. We may also have to yield him to the larger mercies of literary criticism, for which he qualifies with writing, including a series of remarkable auto-biographies, that would be impressive even if not a single play of his were suitable for production anywhere; and to biography, which has found his complex life a continual source of fascination. Regrettable as this may be, since Strindberg had a lively sense of theatre and wrote for stage production, we may have to give him up until such a time as there is a theatre and a public state of mind to vindicate our claims for him as a playwright. He was discovered once during the formative years of our "modern" theatre and he will have to be discovered again. His fate recalls the fate of Stendhal and Melville, who also had to be "resuscitated," and are due for a second resuscitation.

America, it would seem, has been inhospitable to writing that is either strenuously analytical or vatic, and Strindberg's work is generally either one or the other—or both. We have also put a premium on reasonableness, and Strindberg is not reasonable. His judgment on the hostility of the classes and the sexes is warped by his patrician-plebeian origins, his feuds with wives, his suspicion of friends. His best-known penetrations are too hate-directed for our taste. He is nearly always writhing and heaving, and we are likely to agree with the English critic Desmond MacCarthy that "the man who is all struggle may be huge, but he cannot be great." The statement can be contradicted by the evidence of Aeschylus, Dante, Dostoevski, and Melville, but extremism is nonetheless disconcerting. We are the Bernarr Macfadden among nations, and Strindberg is definitely not healthy. We may know that pearls are produced by diseased oysters, but we prefer to dissociate the oyster from the pearl. We cannot easily dissociate the two in Strindberg's work, except in the case of the historical dramas, whose subject matter happens to be too remote for American interest because it is strictly Swedish history. We are also disposed to share MacCarthy's irritation with what he called "the sorrows of a henpecked Bluebeard." Strindberg would serve as a perfect target for Wolcott Gibbs's enviable talent for parody. We favor extroversion, whereas Strindberg is almost always introverted. That which made him so important to modernism in the theatre, his locating of dramatic conflict within the soul, frequently his own, limits his communication with a people that strains mostly outward with all the push of two centuries of manifest destiny. So far as America is concerned, we may say for him what our greatest poetess said for herself, that he is "Too intrinsic for renown."

For all that, the fact of his potency is indelibly present in the text of the plays. It is plain for us to see, even without benefit of the many productions Strindberg has had abroad ever since Antoine gave *Miss Julie* at the Théâtre Libre back in 1892. It is as apparent in plays he wrote in the realistic vein as in those which foreshadowed modern departures from realism; as evident in the plays in which he rejected everything but the climax of a story and reduced drama to a psychological conflict between two or three actors, as it is in the later kaleidoscopic symbolist-expressionist efforts that called for Reinhardt productions.

That Strindberg should have touched the two extremes of modern theatre was no doubt inevitable. He experimented with dramatic art during the periods that witnessed, first, the rise of naturalistic staging in the 1880's and, later, the birth of the Gordon Craig and Reinhardt school of "art theatre." But that quality which is unique about his effort in both directions is that it was not a nod to ruling fashions, but a necessity of Strindberg's personal tensions and of his quest for expression. And this is as important to us as it was to the vitality of his work, because so few of our playwrights write out of their entrails. O'Neill is the only one of our dramatists who has consistently done so.

The pioneer of naturalism, Emile Zola, clamored for a style of playwriting that would be as objective as a clinical report. Strindberg, too, became a "naturalist" in playwriting, but he brought an intensely personal passion into the theatre. Strindberg showed men and women clawing at each other in such pieces as *Miss Julie, The Father, Dance of Death,*

Creditors, and *The Link* with the animus of personal involvement, for which the life-and-death struggle of his first marriage provided both the incentive and the insight. It is not without reason, then, that the work glows with fever, shows a large freedom from the synthetic sociology of "problem plays," and is too immediate for comfort. A good dinner does not sit well on the stomach at such a performance; we cannot remain "objective" when the author was not at least semi-detached from his matter. Strindberg the naturalist is the polar opposite of an English "naturalist" such as Galsworthy, whose objectivity is, as a rule, indistinguishable from the urbane restraint of a country gentleman. The only way to defend oneself against encroachments upon one's complacency is to loathe Strindberg or to dismiss him as either ill-bred or mad. Shaw would no doubt counter that the man was an artist and couldn't afford to be a gentleman. As for madness, it is true that he suffered from delusions of persecution. He once requested a certificate of sanity after a curious correspondence with Nietzsche in which they alternated signing their letters "Nietzsche Caesar" and "The best, the highest, God," and he once voluntarily entered a sanatorium. But an artist may be a species of neurotic who cures himself through externalizing and understanding his conflicts while he is creating, and Strindberg's naturalistic plays are surely products of his lucidity. There are in them no evidences of a clouded mind, but only of a penetrating clarity and a remorseless logic. The difference between himself and less intense writers is that his clarity happens to be a surcharged lucidity.

More than is perhaps realized, it is characteristic of the plays that they distribute justice between their antagonists, take account of the contradictions of personality, and are tinged with humor. Strindberg can be considered humorless only by those who think that a man has no humor if he is not good-humored. Like most good writers, he wrote even better than he knew. He may have wanted to justify the husband against the wife in *The Father,* and the argument tends in that direction. Yet the Captain in that play is as unreasonable as his wife Laura in claiming exclusive control of his daughter's education, and in becoming obsessed with doubts of her legitimacy. The villainess, who is so clever and ruthless in destroying him, is shown to be also stupid and conventionally religious, and she is made as considerate toward everybody else as she is inconsiderate toward her husband. Even in the all-consuming conflict of *The Father,* we find the contradictions that distinguish life from the closed syllogism of argument.

Examples of creative flexibility multiply the more we read Strindberg's work with understanding and imagination. Both *Miss Julie* and *The Link* drive relentlessly to their conclusions; they are, indeed, superb examples of how we could make theatre out of the final flare-up of a human crisis without collecting the lumber of exposition or starting a slow progress of combustion on the stage. *The Link* manages to show the attraction and pathos of a couple suing for a writ of separation as vividly as it dramatizes their compulsive recriminations. They are inescapably people, not the puppets of a misogynist's bias. In *Miss Julie's* midsummer madness there is still room for norms of behavior. The special snobberies of rich and poor, and the very real contrast between the attitudes of servant and mistress, aerate this otherwise fetid tale of debasement.

It is, then, in the fabric of the realistic plays—multi-faceted in spite of singleness of direction, and patterned with keen give-and-take of dialogue—rather than in Strindberg's publicized anti-feminist notions that we find his true genius. His protests against what he called modern gynolatry, against *Doll's House* feminism and fashionable droolings on self-realization for women, may appear as dated as they are extreme. The widening wave of human struggle that he started by casting his pebble into the current of life itself is, however, another matter, and it makes Strindberg's work frequently masterful. Enriched with life in his plays, moreover, the anti-feminist attitude itself acquired more validity and interest than it could possess in any *obiter dicta*. The bias became perception in his drama. It became valuable both as an insulin shot for sugar-logged liberalism in problem plays and as an enzyme for psychological drama. Ibsen himself may have profited from the younger man's stimulus, as *Hedda Gabler* suggests.

Psychological literature was largely the creation of notable romanticists, with whom Strindberg, like Ibsen, had strong bonds. For writing such as Strindberg's we must go back to Constant's *Adolphe,* Lermontov's *A Hero of Our Time,* and the plays of Kleist, Grillparzer, and Hebbel. Strindberg's contribution was, however, decisive for us. Stripping psychology of its gaudy plumage, he fitted it into modern dress. He turned the drama inward without Byronism or romantic ululation. He spoke like a twentieth-century man as early as 1887, when *The Father* appeared. His modernity was more marked than it is in latter-day *Little A* plays about vixens who make Milquetoasts of their spouses; and he was more strenuous, too, than George Kelly in *Craig's Wife,* where the wife is easily given her congé by a not too bright and not particularly impassioned husband. Strindberg's battle of the sexes is between strong equals. The sparks fly upward because there is flint in the colliding particles.

Passion remained with Strindberg to the end, even after he became a disciple of Swedenborg and acquired religious longings. Although the weirdly penumbral writing that he began to turn out with the first two parts of *To Damascus* in 1898 departed from the sharply etched earlier dramas, it does not materially alter our picture of their author. In his "dream plays" he helped to liberate modern drama from the prosiness to which realism had condemned it. How gratifying playful fancy and extravaganza can be in the theatre is something we discover whenever a Saroyan, a Giraudoux, or a Thornton Wilder works his spell efficiently. But Strindberg does not, as a rule, use the theatre merely to be theatrical any more than he is merely fanciful. By comparison with him, they are self-indulgent or "cute." Admittedly, the shadow-play of symbols and figures in *To Damascus, The Dream Play,* and *The Ghost Sonata* is elusive. More than the realistic pieces, these need re-creation by artful stagecraft, for much that seems troublesome in the printed text can yield immediate reality on the stage. Strindberg was not playing charades. His is work of imagination rather than fancy, by virtue of the human anguish pulsing in his marionettes and the passion that pulls their strings.

If their bedlam dance often causes confusion, this is the result of the flickering communicability of the dream technique. One thing is certain, however, we cannot attribute the confusion to rifts in the writer's mind. He wrote these plays during the same period that brought forth his clear chronicles of Swedish history. His choice of a tantalizing style that telescopes time and place, and that splits personalities again and again, was required by what he wanted to express. This became a twentieth-century necessity, as Joyce and Virginia Woolf prove, and the theatre of the past three decades has found determined men like O'Neill, O'Casey, and Dennis Johnston still wrestling with the protean symbolic-expressionist style. If they have persisted in this unequal struggle, we know them too well to charge them seriously with either schizophrenia or wilful obscurantism.

For all his failure to achieve classic outline and wholeness, Strindberg's particularizations are remarkable; and it is, after all, the very point of his expressionist plays that there is neither firmness nor wholeness in our lives. Like the more communicable pieces that preceded them, they exhibit man and society as lacking integration, reaching for it and missing, longing for it and despairing. Both by choice and inner compulsion Strindberg became an uncanny exponent of our century. He is the dramatist of our division.

STRINDBERG: 1950 CENTENARY PRODUCTIONS

Belatedly, the New York theatre, which should have celebrated Strindberg's centenary on January 22, 1949, got around to giving some productions of plays by the master from whom modern dramatists learned more than from any pioneer except Ibsen.

None of the tributes paid on the stage in Manhattan were as satisfactory as the biography The Macmillan Company published on the "bedevilled Viking," Elizabeth Sprigge's *The Strange Life of August Strindberg*. The book went far toward explaining the sources of this playwright's fascinating and yet repelling war with women and the world which made him the parent of modern psychological drama.

The reader of Miss Sprigge's book will come to understand the mainsprings of Strindberg's psychological insight into the war of the sexes and the intense presentation of it in play after play which made him the parent of modern psychological drama. Miss Sprigge tells the story of Strindberg's early fixation on his mother, a servant girl who lived out of wedlock with a man of good social standing until a short while before Strindberg was born. Miss Sprigge traces the course of a childhood marked by deprivations, the greatest of these being his having to share his mother's love with a brood of children and the death of this mother while he was still a youngster. Henceforth, Strindberg was to look for a mother in every woman he loved and lost, but he was to resent being a child to each of them. He compensated his vestigial dependence on women by claiming all the prerogatives of a lord and master in his household. Three marriages and divorces resulted from this peculiarity. The first of these, with Siri von Essen, the wife of a nobleman whom he had taken away from her husband and an actress of some talent who chafed at the domestic bonds Strindberg imposed on her, is told with especial interest by Miss Sprigge. Out of the scandalous struggle with Siri came *The Father* and other plays.

Since Strindberg had other devils than domestic ones to deal with, his case was hopeless indeed. He suffered from delusions of grandeur, which made him turn to alchemy (he believed he had discovered a formula for making gold and that America stole it from him). Worse still, he was subject to delusions of persecution which brought him to the verge of insanity—a fate he feared and tried to stave off after discovering that his correspondence with his admirer Nietzsche was with a man who had lost his reason. The realist Maupassant, whom he esteemed highly, also had to be confined to an asylum. A psychiatrist can indeed have a field day with the biographical data of Strindberg, the best of which were supplied by himself in a series of embarrassingly candid but remarkably penetrative autobiographies.

In fitting Strindberg's work into the framework of his strange life, Miss Sprigge has performed a greater service to criticism than many a critic has done. It would be difficult to find another modern playwright whose work is so decidedly a projection of his inner reality. That Miss Sprigge is able to do justice to her subject is hardly surprising, since she is a competent creative artist herself.

Strindberg spent some time in an asylum and never lost certain symptoms, such as abnormal suspiciousness, belief in the omnipotence of thought, and delusions of persecution. But Strindberg had the power to externalize his inner complications and discharge his unhealthy drives in ways impossible to the insane—that is, in the formal structure of art, in universally applicable penetrations, and in self-criticism. He was, in short, the classic example, along with Dostoevski, of Freud's statement that an artist is a neurotic who cures himself through his work. I am not sure that every artist is a neurotic, and it is safer, I suspect, to say that instead of curing himself, the artist who is a neurotic merely wins surcease from his devils or attains periods of lucidity and mental health through externalization by socially acceptable productivity.

We may take Strindberg's twisted and charged animadversions against women and his idiosyncratic overemphasis of the power of suggestion with a grain of salt, but we cannot dismiss his work as the ravings of a maniac. Nor can we lightly dismiss the plays in which he gave his poetic creativity full sway as fantasist, mystic, expressionist, and folk-dramatist. The author of the romantic *Lucky Pehr,* the great folk-play *The Bridal Crown,* the quizzical "dark comedy" *There Are Crimes and Crimes,* the *To Damascus* trilogy, *The Dream Play, The Spook (Ghost) Sonata,* and *The Great Highway,* was guilty of many excesses. He was not a secure artist, alienated as he was not only from his world but sometimes from himself as well. But he was responsible for some of the most expressive non-realistic drama in modern times. Like every major dramatist he was keenly concerned with the possibilities of the theatrical medium and shaped his plays to make use of its capacity for assuming a variety of forms.

If we except O'Neill's enthusiasm which made him produce *The Spook Sonata* with Robert Edmond Jones and Kenneth Macgowan in 1920 at the Provincetown Playhouse, we may say that the American theatre has evinced no understanding or appreciation of Strindberg's playwriting in any field other than that of naturalistic drama. New York producers have a mortal fear of complexity. Even in coping with Strindberg's naturalistic pieces, however, they can make small claim to anything but modest accomplishments, if any. *The Dance of Death,* Strindberg's two-part drama of the sex-duel, was unsuccessfully presented by the Theatre Guild in its famous pioneering period, in 1920. A butchered version was a thorough failure in the Broadway season of 1948-49. Elisabeth Bergner was compelled to abandon her production of *Miss Julie* "on the road." Jed Harris failed to make good his promise to honor the Strindberg centenary with a "Jed Harris Production" of *The Father.* And two of the playwright's best and most appealing pieces, the divorce-drama *The Link* and the comedy of "equality" in marriage *Comrades,* remain unstaged on Broadway. Even easy Strindberg is apparently not easy enough for a successful encounter with Broadway playgoers.

Still, it was something for New York to have three Strindberg productions—two of *The Father* and one of the long one-acter of domestic conflict and mental suggestion *The Creditor* in 1950. If the full range of his work was not uncovered by any of these productions, some portion of Strindberg's stagecraft and penetrativeness was salvaged. And if none of the productions won the Broadway public's individual allegiance, the reason is that Strindberg plays must be performed superlatively.

A little group that first produced *The Father* at Carnegie Hall revealed its amateur status, but delivered itself of an honest job of work. The production was appealing even when crude, because it did not try to turn the play into a customer-cadging performance. The producers of *The Father* on Broadway could be commended for risking the play in the marketplace and treating the content with respect and devotion, but for little else.

Raymond Massey's direction was not the brightest example of theatrical art available to us. His own performance of the cavalry captain driven out of his mind by his Clytemnestra had shortcomings—less of acting than of personality. Massey is a good and wholesome man who tried to masquerade as a violent and obsessed character, as demanded of the role. One could sympathize with the character portrayed by him, but it was difficult to be held by him. Massey's Captain was too uneven a match for his wife to evoke more than pity in us. And if there is one thing that can be safely said about Strindberg the naturalist, it is that pity is *not* the commodity we expect of his work. The temptation to present Strindberg's male characters as weaklings is great, because many, though not all, of them succumb to feminine ruthlessness. Since Massey also directed the play, his characterization was his sole responsibility. Although he could be blamed for not being able to transform himself into the sort of person he is not, different direction would have either cast someone else in the Captain's role or toned down Mr. Massey's antagonist Mady Christians, who played the wife, and somehow lessened the impression of a pitiable character. Ideally, however, the Captain, who is driven to death by Strindberg's Laura, should have the tragic power to crumble like a colossus in the life-and-death struggle Strindberg invented for him. But it is plain that Mr. Massey and the producers followed the mistaken notion, sometimes sponsored by the anti-feminist author himself, that Strindberg men must be weak. The other male characters, except for a comic commoner (a soldier), appeared to be made of jelly; or rather, had a lean and hungry look, as if they had been drained of much of their lifeblood by vampire women. Nevertheless, it cannot be said that Mr. Massey's performance lacked variety and sensitivity. His direction was intelligent and tasteful, even if deficient in force. And it was a stroke of genius to cast Mady Christians in the role of the Captain's wife, who is driven by forces within herself to destroy her happiness and her man. Nothing Miss Christians had acted here, not even *I Remember Mama,* revealed her greatness as an actress so clearly. She played the part of Laura as though every fibre of her were possessed, and she played, as Nazimova used to do, with every muscle in her body.

It must be recorded, too, that some of the shortcomings of the production are to be laid at Strindberg's door. The reality of *The Father* depends upon an obsession which makes his hero something of a fool and neurotic unless he is played by the most forceful of actors. He is consumed with the conviction that it is simply impossible to establish the legitimacy of any child, so far as the father is concerned. It was also Strindberg's obsession for a time, and he discharged it in the play he wrote.

Strindberg falls short of being one of the greatest playwrights of all time largely because in work like *The Father* he discharged his feelings directly instead of subjecting them to a process of sublimation. Strindberg has too much depth and too little breadth of insight. He needed the wide prospect that a viable tradition, such as the Attic playwrights had, could have given him. It is not enough for an artist to present what is real to him. He must present that reality with due consideration of the degree to which it can become convincingly real to others. The feeling that originated the play must *die* in the play, and then be reborn.

The same shortcomings appear in *The Creditor,* in which a maligned first husband returns to wreak vengeance on the woman who sucked him dry and then made him ridiculous in the eyes of the world. By means of suggestion, he brings out the disillusionment and despair buried in the soul of her second husband and exposes the wife to scandal. But *The Creditor* is an even more remarkable piece of dramaturgy than *The Father*. It is one of the most concentrated plays of the modern repertory.

It shows Strindberg capable of doing precisely what he hoped to do for the drama—namely, to strip it to the bare bone.

It is true that here Strindberg actually fails to carry out what must have been his real purpose—namely, to expose the woman. He does expose her as a vain creature trying to assure herself that she is still attractive by courting the admiration of young men, as a parasite feeding on men's minds and spirit, and as a person who tries to cast down all the men who lift her high lest she realize her own inadequacy. Like other Strindberg women she is bitten with the bug of feminism and adds to the natural ruthlessness of woman the ruthlessness of all people who try to make more of themselves than they really are. She is the victim of the neurosis of success that seized women, according to Strindberg, when they began to try to play a man's role in the world while claiming all the time-honored prerogatives of women in the Western World. But Strindberg's picture of the two men in her life is so repugnant, the one as a weakling and the other as an infernally calculating avenger, that the woman is tolerable by comparison. In a sense, Strindberg "crossed himself" up by trying to match the woman's villainy with that of her former husband.

The performance given by the valiant and capable On-Stage group at the small Greenwich Village theatre, The Cherry Lane, would have been excellent but for a trifle too much youthfulness on the part of George Hill who played the "creditor"—the husband who wreaks his revenge. The second husband, an unhappy artist who has tried to conceal the failure of his marriage from himself, was well played by DeWitt Drury. Beatrice Tekla, who impersonated the wife, revealed herself as an actress of considerable range in voice and stage movement. Miss Tekla is a dynamic actress. If the performers had played together in repertory for a few years and had matured a little more, they might have made *The Creditor* a memorable rather than a merely approvable production. *The Creditor* is one of the many modern plays that belong to a repertory theatre and should not have to be at the mercy of improvised production.

The 1950 productions exhibited the bizarre quality of Strindberg's temperament, although its most extravagant manifestations were left undisclosed. It was sufficiently evident that this temperament intruded too much into his work. It would be absurd to associate the future of our theatre with his upheavals. But in a theatre in which playwrights so often seem totally devoid of temperament his brief reappearance on the New York stage was a reminder that drama is a mode of *expression* rather than of mere observation and sentiment.

THE ANNIHILATORS

I. "THE MACHINE"

"Spectator," says the narrating "Voice" of Cocteau's *The Infernal Machine,* "this machine you see, completely wound up here in such a way that the spring will slowly unwind the whole length of human life, is one of the most perfect machines constructed by the infernal gods for the mathematical destruction (*l'anéantissement mathématique*) of a mortal." The play, first produced in Paris by Louis Jouvet in 1934, then proceeds to present the classic tragedy of Oedipus in a most unclassic manner, and Cocteau's legerdemain continues to endear him to most intellectuals of the mid-century who condescend to take notice of the theatre. Cocteau's "modern tragedy" is virtually a symbol of the anti-realistic dispensation with which the avant-garde proposes to redeem the drama. Unquestionably *The Infernal Machine* requires consideration, along with a number of other plays, as representative of endeavors to give the modern stage a new direction. The "machine" of the play that Cocteau himself has wound up is one of the most perfect that modern playwrights have constructed for the "mathematical destruction" of theatre as an art that affords the illusion of reality.

Whether or not the results are admirable, whether or not the playwright's machine has actually destroyed the life of the drama as thoroughly as the gods' machine destroyed Oedipus, the play sums up the crisis in contemporary drama and theatre. Cocteau, in this as well as in other products of his abundant theatricality, is one of the major annihilators of the realism which first gave us modern playwriting and has also been regarded as the most persistent incubus of the twentieth-century stage. And he is also, despite noble vociferations on his part, one of the major annihilators of the humanistic basis of that stage.

The modern theatre has been in a state of continuous crisis, a crisis inherent in modern culture and exacerbated at different times to different degrees. Today, when that crisis is particularly marked, it is more necessary than ever before to understand its nature, whether or not we can actually master or ameliorate the situation. It is a conflict between humanism and anti-humanist tendencies in the consciousness and strivings of the theatre's artists—tendencies sometimes concealed from the artist himself, sometimes clearly articulated by him. This subject is not, as a rule, the simple one of "content"; not even of the philosophies or ideologies proposed by the writer, even when these are plainly stated in his work. The naïve moralistic view tells us no more about the intrinsic humanism or anti-humanism of art by raising the question of whether the artist is on the side of "good" or "evil" than does the naïve Marxist view which judges the work by whether or not it is on the "right" side of the class struggle, a five-year plan in Russia, or the latest maneuver in the conflict of the communist and the democratic worlds.

The question is one of treatment, structure, *form*. It is the "esthetic" nature of the work that actually crystallizes the moral, philosophical, or social elements that the terms humanism and anti-humanism imply. The writer's sentiments may be entirely on one side of the dichotomy of humanism-antihumanism, but his "form" may be on the other side. Thus the sympathies of Picasso in writing his surrealist play *Desire Trapped by the Tail* may have been entirely humanistic. *Desire* is said to reflect Picasso's distress over the state of France under the German occupation. Picasso's "form," nevertheless, carries us about as far from humanism as any piece of writing can. It is disjointed, uncommunicative in any terms other than irrational ones, and devoid of characters who have some of the fullness of human nature. The artist, considered simply as a human being, may impress us as a civilized and sympathetic person if we know him or know something about his opinions and conduct. His work, precipitated by his deep-seated ambivalences and determined by the esthetic principles he has adopted, may nevertheless be generally desiccated. It may be coldly formalistic art, or even a veritable nightmare of savagery and schizoid phantasmagoria. The reverse can also be true, as I believe is the case with Henry de Montherlant, whose best plays possess a large measure of humanity whereas his opinions outside his creative work were anti-democratic, if not indeed fascistic.

No doubt the creative product can tell us a good deal about the artist that he himself may not know. The buried man inside the conscious man comes to light in the exhuming process of creation. But here I am primarily concerned with the work itself, such as it is; and it is the work that expresses a tendency toward annihilation of the human element in much modernist drama, though rarely as transparently as Picasso's sole venture into playwriting. *The Infernal Machine* is the work of a playwright whose professional experience and attainments are such that neither his representative quality nor the value of the play itself can be ignored. Let us look at it more or less closely.

II. COCTEAU AND "THE INFERNAL MACHINE"

The basis of the play is well known to everyone familiar with dramatic literature. When Oedipus was born in Thebes to King Laius and his wife Jocasta, the oracle predicted that the child would some day kill its father and marry its mother. Jocasta had the infant exposed on a mountainside by one of her men-servants after piercing its feet and shackling them in order to ensure death by making the child entirely helpless. But Oedipus was saved by a shepherd and given to the childless royal couple Polybius and Merope of Corinth, who brought him up as their own son. When Oedipus, who considered them his natural parents, reached manhood he learned what was in store for him from the Delphic oracle and, resolving to avert parricide and incest, left home. During his wanderings, he encountered Laius, who was of course a total stranger to him, and unintentionally slew his father. Shortly after this event, he became the hero of Thebes by ridding it of the Sphinx, by answering the riddle of this man-killing monster. The grateful Thebans made him their king after marrying him to their recently widowed queen Jocasta, who bore him two sons and two daughters. Many years later a plague breaks out in Thebes and in the course of tracking down the unknown murderer of Laius whose presence, according to an oracle, is the cause of the disaster, Oedipus discovers the dreadful truth. Jocasta hangs herself in despair, and Oedipus, horrified by his fate, gouges out his eyes with her brooch.

The subject, perhaps first dramatized in a lost play by the father of Greek tragedy Aeschylus, received its classic treatment in the great play by Sophocles, *Oedipus the King*. Voltaire was one of several writers who wrote an Oedipus play after the revival of interest in the classics during the Renaissance. The French, with their tradition of neo-classicism which gave them their greatest playwright Racine, have been particularly disposed toward creating variations on classic subjects. Even in the present period Cocteau is not the only one to have returned to the subject; Gide made a well-known version, *Oedipe,* in 1931, giving it the premise that happiness based on ignorance must be rejected. But Cocteau's more dramatic treatment is the significant one for our time.

Cocteau came to *The Infernal Machine* as one of the most adept and experienced of the French playwrights who fell under the spell of the anti-realistic theatrical movement spearheaded by Jacques Copeau at the *Théâtre du Vieux Colombier,* founded by him in 1913. It was, significantly, Copeau's closest associate, the actor-manager Louis Jouvet, who staged *The Infernal Machine,* with scenery and costumes by another celebrated "theatricalist" Christian Bérard. Cocteau, moreover, had gone through most of the modernist movements, including *surréalisme*, in France, turning out films (the famous *Blood of a Poet*), ballet, and music hall *chansons*, as well as plays. His collaboration in 1917 with Piccaso, Massine, and Sartre on the cubist ballet of *Parade* decisively launched him on a career of experimentalism. And experimentalism is indeed the mark of the man as artist, as it is of so many of the modernists who, unlike the fortunate master-artists of other ages, have lacked a more or less stable dramatic form serviceable to them for any length of time. His pantomime, *Le Boeuf sur le Toit,* performed in 1920 with the Fratellini clowns (here it was the nonrealistic circus that engaged his interest), was another free fantasia in which the imagination associates itself with modern sophistication. (For example, the electric fans in a dive decapitate a policeman, who, at the end of the piece picks up his head and sticks it on again. . . .) And *Les Mariés de la Tour Eiffel* (translated as *The Wedding Breakfast on the Eiffel Tower*), performed with the collaboration of the Swedish Ballet in 1931, was a third and more elaborate "synthesis of the arts" on a level of fantasy considered surrealistic.

That Cocteau's interest in the abstract arts remained dominant when he turned to classic themes is apparent in his collaboration with Stravinsky on the "opera-oratorio" *Oedipus Rex,* and in his synoptic *Antigone* of the year 1922 which was little more than a sketch upon which Honnegger could fashion his music and Picasso his designs. His *Orpheus,* a Pitoëff avant-garde production of the year 1926, was a fantasy of some depth on the subject of death. And here, too, theatricality was the prime consideration, not merely in the wild plot-invention but in the extravagant use of scenery as the active factor (the "mystery" of a room and window, the fact that the way to the world of death for Orpheus is through a mirror) and the placement of the action high up in the air. It is not surprising, therefore, that Cocteau should have favored a theatricalist approach in another treatment of classic myth, in the comparatively austere *The Infernal Machine*.

Cocteau's freewheeling dramaturgy is apparent not only in the treatment of the myth with modern psychoanalytic details, but in his deliberate use of anachronism (Thebes is pictured as a modern city like Paris and Queen Jocasta is drawn as a more or less Parisian woman) and, above all, in his discontinuous style of presenting the Oedipus story. The spectator cannot settle down to observe an unbroken progression of the plot, as in a realistic play. He is jogged out of any expectations of losing himself in any illusion of reality which he may have ever entertained. An opening narration ("The Voice") gives away the plot and comments on it. No two adjacent scenes are pitched in the same key or shaped the same way, almost as if the author were still attached to his early variety-show career.

His presentation of the story is, in short, theatrical. If here and there, due to the power of Cocteau's writing, it is possible for the spectator to lapse into an "illusion of reality," the narrations between the scenes are sure to remind him that he is in the *theatre* rather than in the midst of reflected life.

The theatrical shock technique starts at once as The Voice sums up the story of Oedipus at considerable length and *baldly* in such lines as "The dead man is Laius, the king of Thebes. Parricide!" and "Be that as it may, Oedipus enters Thebes a conqueror, he marries the queen. Incest!" In a Broadway playwright, for whom no artistic pretensions have been advertised in advanced circles, such flatness would be considered unpardonable by the intelligentsia. In Cocteau's play, the same quality is considered "art." He is commended for putting his cards on the table and for not fobbing us off with "suspense" and "illusion." He is praised for telling us that we are in the theatre. "As if we didn't know," sceptics might retort.

Act One: The ramparts of Thebes are being patrolled by soldiers. The opening scene, like the other scenes, is played on a little platform in the center of the stage. It is surrounded by "nocturnal curtains," to suggest the mystery of the events. All the scenes, moreover, are to be laved, according to the author's directions, in "the livid mythical light of quicksilver"; lest the public miss the point, I suppose, for this play is intended to be mystic and profound—and, of course, "mythical." The night is stormy, but the city people are dancing, "getting tight," and spending the time in "nightclubs." A young soldier is tense and has to be admonished by an older companion, for they are awaiting the ghost of Laius, which has appeared to them on previous nights in order to warn Queen Jocasta and the High Priest Tiresias against impending disaster. They explain it all to the "Chief," their commandant, who is giving them a soldierly scolding for having communicated with the palace directly—all this in the colloquial prose of our day.

Then Jocasta, a slightly giddy middle-aged woman, appears, accompanied by the prophetic High Priest, Tiresias, whom she affectionately calls "Zizi." But she is unsuccessful in making contact with the ghost of her husband; although he is present, no one can see or hear him until the queen and Tiresias depart. It is obvious, then, that the "infernal gods" are preventing him from delivering a warning that would interfere with fate. (That there is solipsism, as well as generally jejune thinking, in Cocteau's play is a point hardly worth making. Nor would it be considered relevant by ardent theatricalists: After all, the old boy is making "theatre," isn't he?) And we are being prepared most insistently for the tragic development of events by "mystery." Everybody steps on the queen's long, red scarf. It is most annoying, she complains. She is surrounded by "objects that hate me." All day long the scarf is strangling her. It catches in the branches, it gets wound up in the hub of a carriage, and so on. "It will be the death of me."— *Irony,* in case there is any lack of it for you in the story of Oedipus: She is going to hang herself with her scarf at the end of the play.— And as if this were not enough preparation, there is the "psychological" approach. The middle-aged queen is greatly taken with the Young Soldier, who is nineteen years old, exactly the age her son would have been if he had lived! And there is the "psychoanalytic" approach: The Queen has dreams. She is standing in the night, attending "a kind of nursling" in a cradle when it suddenly becomes "a sticky paste" which runs through her fingers. It sticks to her and as she hurls it away from her, it flies back in her face, and it has "a kind of mouth" which fixes itself on *her* mouth. Then it "creeps everywhere," and "feels" after her belly and *thighs.* Cocteau doesn't miss a trick; he must be "modern," even if he has to appropriate Freud's entire treasury.

Act Two occurs simultaneously with the above-described action. Oedipus encounters the Sphinx in a remarkably visualized and imaginative scene. (Cocteau is at his best here.) The agents of fate, a jackal-headed monster who is Anubis the Egyptian God of Death and the girl-shaped Sphinx, who is Nemesis or Vengeance, await Oedipus. The Sphinx in her womanly incarnation is tired of killing and is taken sufficiently with the brash young man to want to let him go. She even gives him the answer to the riddle he is supposed to solve. Ungratefully, the commonplace youth who wants the shallow triumphs of a Babbitt of the Heroic Age rushes off and the Sphinx, in the tradition of the Parisian boulevard theatre, is presented as a woman scorned. But he returns for his trophy, for he must have evidence that he has killed the "monster" if he is to be acclaimed by Thebes. Obligingly, to facilitate his destruction, she goes through the farce, which to him is reality; she borrows the jackal-head for Anubis and falls dead in front of Oedipus. Thereupon Oedipus hoists the corpse on his shoulder and carries it in triumph to Thebes, while the Sphinx, the now gigantic form of Nemesis, watches him pityingly.

This ingeniously conceived and well-written scene is as fascinating as theatre as it is devoid of the "illusion of reality." Its high point, for all its depth, is, of course, hocus-pocus. And it is the best illustration we have of the difference between the "theatricalist," who cares primarily about producing effects even when he concerns himself with human destiny, and the humanist whose concern is with man even when he works, as Sophocles did, in a formalistic theatre. Sophocles doesn't even represent the meeting with the Sphinx in his great tragedy; he relegates the event to a brief report, treating the supernatural as the mythical *donné* of his drama. It is the completely human action, revealing the character and the behavior of men in a crisis, that concerns the classical author.

Act Three: Oedipus is in Jocasta's bedroom after his marriage to her, and the major "prop" is the cradle of her child she has always kept there. Tiresias, coming to bless the royal marriage bonds, offends Oedipus with news that auguries of the marriage "look black, very black." Oedipus, scornful of oracles, since he is confident of having thwarted them before with his "audacity," quarrels with Tiresias. But in looking into the prophet's eyes, he suddenly becomes blind; for he is just at the point of seeing that which "the gods wish to keep in darkness," as Tiresias explains before he goes off with a last warning. And the fate theme is further theatricalized by the appearance of Anubis, taking shape from the animal skin spread on the nuptial bed, who mocks Oedipus in a dream. In another dream, he also hears the Sphinx repeating the fearful words of incantation she employed in the previous scene,

"I wind, I unwind, I calculate, I meditate, I weave, I winnow,
I knit, I plait, I cross,"

while Jocasta is tormented by her incestuous dream of the "paste," mentioned in Act One, that makes obscene love to her.

Irony of fate is continually worked into the fabric of the dialogue of the queen and Oedipus. The "cradle" motif, supported with constant references to his loving Jocasta as a son who likes to be taken into her arms, is given the full theatrical "business." One stage direction reads, "He lies across the bed with his head on the edge of the cradle." Later, after trying to shake him out of his sleep, Jocasta puts his head back "on the edge of the cradle." A third stage direction reads, "She lulls the sleep of Oedipus by gently rocking the cradle." The incest theme is worked here for all it's worth. It has psychological justification, of course; Oedipus has unconsciously desired a mother all his life, Jocasta has always longed for the child she disposed of by infanticide. But the concentration on the above-given details in the wedding-night scene is obviously intended to work like a sledge hammer on the audience and also to impress it with *nouveau*-intellectuality.

Cocteau is striving for *effect* no less—*more,* in fact—than the showmen of the mid-nineteenth century theatre of Scribe and his followers which was displaced by Ibsen and scorned by Shaw. But now—ever since the proselytizing of Gordon Craig—all this is done in the name of art rather than under the more honest label of "show business."

Act Three does not lack excellent human touches in the relationship between Jocasta and Oedipus. Nevertheless, they are not the primary interest. "Theatre" is; and theatre is effect, magic, prestidigitation. The illusion of life, no less evident on a heightened plane of expression in the episodes of Sophocles' play than in a play by Ibsen, must make way for a special kind of playing with showmen's "props" and for heavy psychological punctuation marks. Little, if anything, is left for the playgoer or play-reader to discover for himself. Everything is telegraphed to him in advance or spelled out for him repeatedly in an elementary, sometimes quite mechanical, manner. Otherwise there would be nothing for the actor to do except "live" on the stage, and that is apparently supposed to be too simple a thing—and too uninteresting. "Theatre" is the fetish to be served; the "end" of art is to be simply art. That is the extreme to be reached from the perfectly valid point, supported elsewhere in this book, that "reality" insufficiently translated and transformed is neither interesting nor significant on the stage. Cocteau's procedure is tantamount to draining the life out of art in order to achieve art—a case of emptying the bathtub by throwing out the baby.

Cocteau didn't quite do that in Act Three. But to observe how perilously close he came to doing so, we need only turn to the last act. Act Four occurs seventeen years after the marriage. (Jocasta is still wearing the same red scarf for the convenience of the symbolism.) In a manner so perfunctory that a college sophomore familiar with Sophocles' play could have written most of the scene, Oedipus learns that his supposed father, King Polybius of Corinth, is dead. The next minute, he is told by the Messenger that Polybius was not his real father, and that he was found on the mountainside as a baby with his feet tied together. Oedipus reveals the fact that he killed an old man at the crossroads where Jocasta's husband Laius was slain. Thereupon, Jocasta runs into the palace, and, in rapid order, Oedipus discovers that she has hanged herself, learns that he is the son of Jocasta, and blinds himself. All this, to which Sophocles devoted an entire play, happens without any sort of time-lapse in eight pages of print.

It is evident, then, that the man in this crisis is of little account for Cocteau, whereas the *man is the play* for Sophocles. All that transpires in Act Four up to the blinding of Oedipus is merely the last turn of "the infernal machine," and it has to be accomplished in the quickest possible manner in order that Cocteau may get on to his final notion.

The ghost of Jocasta, seen only by Oedipus, comes out of the palace, the long *scarf* wound around her neck. They hold a mother-and-child conversation. He complains of pain in the eyes he has gouged out with her brooch. She tells him, "I will give you a dressing [*sic*] at the fountain," and helps him down the stairs, telling him to hold on to her dress and counting the steps of the platform for him. Accompanied also by his young daughter Antigone, who isn't a ghost, he goes down the steps to leave the city forever.

"Who will admit them?" asks Creon, Jocasta's brother. Tiresias replies, "Glory" will. The point is that Oedipus will become a legend, and if we wish we can elaborate on the idea quite neatly. Oedipus, the victim of so horrible a fate and an example of how the "infernal machine" operates, will achieve a classic *"gloire"* as the subject of men's thought and men's art. It is a distinction vastly superior and, of course, more lasting than the "obscure glory" to which Oedipus aspired in his shallow youth when he wanted to save Thebes from the Sphinx and claim his reward. And, indeed, that conclusion is entirely proper in the play, since Cocteau took such pains in the second act to make him out a Rover Boy.

What is evident, however, is that Cocteau has actually given Oedipus no particular *"gloire,"* since he has invested him with none of the rich humanity that Sophocles gave the character almost twenty-four centuries before. The Oedipus drawn in *The Infernal Machine* is a vainglorious, unfeeling, single-tracked Grade B motion picture character in Act Two, and merely an uneasy, mother-fixated and still shallow bridegroom in Act Three. Sophocles' Oedipus, on the contrary, is a hero-king, a man of keen intellect and of tempestuous but noble spirit. He represents humanity on a plane that does qualify him for glory, and nowhere more so than when he is shown tracking down the truth about himself. Belonging to the aristocracy of passionate souls (as Edith Hamilton would say), Sophocles' Oedipus is great in trying to save his city from the plague that has broken out in Thebes, great in his quest for the truth, great in his suffering. Cocteau's Oedipus is none of these things. He is not a creation of the humanist tradition, as a comparison with the tragic and near-tragic characters of the Attic tragedians, Marlowe, Shakespeare, John Webster, Racine, Ibsen, our O'Neill, and even our Tennessee Williams and Arthur Miller can forcefully reveal.

Cocteau, it is true, has "The Voice" declare just before Act Four that misfortune "makes this playing-card king, in the end, a man." And much is made of this point by Cocteau's admirers. Perhaps Oedipus does become, "in the end," a man. But *not in this play!* In the last act, he is still a nullity. He is given one manly line to speak, "Whether I am the child of the muses or of a common tramp, I shall question without fear, I will know things"—a flat echo, incidentally, of Sophocles' words. But for the rest, he is commonplace before the full discovery of his identity, and he lapses into the role of a helpless child in relation to the ghostly Jocasta at the end of the play. He does nothing and says nothing that could even remotely give him any *gloire*. Any true glory he ever gets will be only passively acquired, for all that *The Infernal Machine* shows of the man. The poets and playwrights, who are not the characters of Cocteau's play, will give it to him by writing about him. This, then, is the play that advanced critics and their followers recommend to us as "a modern masterpiece of tragedy."—This is the play that allegedly points in modern directions, should cue us in the search for new dramatic form, puts all serious American playwrights to shame, and shows up O'Neill as a bungling and blatant tragedian.

That *The Infernal Machine* is frequently interesting cannot be denied. It may even be a success of the theatre—or of a "poetry of the theatre," to use Cocteau's own term. But it is surely a failure of drama as it is a failure of humanism, and it is a failure as drama *because* it is a failure as humanism, toward which it merely gestures. And the play, precisely because Cocteau has skill, can sum up for us the failure of *theatricalism* as a reliable philosophy for high and serious dramatic art; the failure of the highly touted "histrionic sensibility" as a substitute for the less pretentious—in my opinion, far more difficult—business of playwrights and actors to bring characters to a full life on the stage when the subject to be presented is not simply a game to be played or an entertainment to be whipped up. Cocteau, as the annihilator of realism, may have been delightful when playfulness was appropriate to his work and fascinating while working in other media than the drama—in his films, for example. But he is *not* the savior of the theatre that unwary young American playwrights may be talked into considering him, no matter how clever the talk, no matter how cultivated the accent.

I have selected *The Infernal Machine* among Cocteau's plays (rather than his *Antigone, Orpheus, Le Chevaliers de la Table Ronde,* or *The Eagle Has Two Heads*) because *La Machine Infernale* is his most mature non-realistic work and possesses scenes of unquestionable fascination and power. But it highlights three areas of theatrical art frequently explored by him and more or less favored by the modernists to whom a new intellectual generation looks for guidance. *The Infernal Machine* is our best introduction to continental European "art for art's sake" theatre in its twentieth-century incarnation which is animated by interest in myth, mathematical art, and intellectual-theatrical prestidigitation. And the three interests tend to interact in Cocteau's dramatic work as a whole—and to *undermine* it considerably as viable art.

Alienated from the twentieth-century world, deficient in any strong faith in its strivings, and out of sympathy with contemporary man, the Cocteau-type of modernist tries to cast anchor in the myths of the human race. Perhaps he will find fixity, meaning, and purpose there. But first he must rationalize that which is fundamentally sub-rational, pre-scientific, pre-religious, and pre-sociological. Consequently, our intellectual artists often snip off a bit of Freud, a bit of Frazer, a bit of Géza Roheim, and make a dainty pastry of the particles. The pastry becomes "myth," and is supposed to nourish us. It doesn't. It nourishes only the mind, which,

I am told, requires no more energy for a day's activity than can be derived from a single peanut.

The ultimate object of the myth-mongers is to find *symbols* of universal significance. They find the "significance" easily enough, but it is significance without substance. The myth that had once been a part of the life of a people (and such a long time ago!) is now invented or fabricated. The myth that once had been a collective consciousness associated with custom, semi-history, and, above all, ritual, now becomes a private, individual construction. The author, of course, helps himself to the supernatural elements of the myth. But in his work, since he is a modern and sceptical man, the supernatural is a sort of French dressing. The procedure is trivial or frivolous. The author has not gone down to "the Mothers" in mortal anguish and come up shattered by his experience in the darkness of the "Unconscious" or transfigured, like a St. John of the Cross, by the "Dark Night of the Soul." No, he is the same *boulevardier* and *littérateur* he has been before his dabbling with myth. The author has not actually explored the meaning of the ideas associated with the myth—the ideas of life's or the gods' purpose, the ideas of chance, the ideas of fate. He has *adopted* these ideas, as one puts on a costume for a masquerade. They remain clichés in his work because he has added nothing to the words *chance* and *fate* that can be considered revealing. It is to be noted that the word *machine* in *La Machine Infernale* literally means "contrivance" more than "machine"; and that is exactly Cocteau's meaning and evasion. He presents the contrivance with which the "gods" destroyed Oedipus, not the essential nature of fate. The "contrivance" yields literary melodrama, not genuine tragedy, although it is as exemplary modern tragedy that *La Machine Infernale* has been celebrated by its American enthusiasts. I say "American enthusiasts," because French critics of comparative austerity think considerably less well of his work; one of them, Jean Boorsch, charges Cocteau with generally devaluing the suprarational, wasting away metaphysical possibility, and reducing mystery to jugglery.

At most in *The Infernal Machine,* "fate" means that the gods are bent upon destroying a man for no discernible reason, surely a sophomoric idea surrounded by bizarre skulduggery constructed around notions of the supernatural. Notions not believed in, moreover; notions *played* with. Sophocles concerns himself with the tragic *man,* Oedipus, he can understand, not the *trap* of fate he cannot understand and makes no pretense of elucidating. Cocteau concerns himself with the *trap.* The tragic man escapes him; only the Greek boy-scout attains vivid realization in Cocteau's play. But to return to the "idea" of fate, it is plain that Cocteau is pretending to examine the *purpose* of all the confusion and suffering. And what is the purpose? To create a literary figure. A subject that poets may write about in later ages is all the purpose the literary man Cocteau discovers and solemnly presents as his solution of the riddle of the universe.

Cocteau, however, was not an idiot or *naïf* when he wrote any of the plays he based on myth. He was a clever Frenchman and theatrician, perhaps slightly deluded by his own cleverness but able to shift his ground quickly. And he does shift it by constantly reminding us in his nimble playwriting that he stands outside his play as an artificer detached alike from the myth and the characters.

For this purpose, moreover, Cocteau could utilize some more or less legitimate contentions to the effect that we ought to get away from hazy poetry, aim at exactness and "muscle" in poetry, and treat poetry as a mathematics of expression. The next step was to translate this theory of poetry into a theory of drama. Drama could then be viewed as a sort of "living algebra." And what do you build with a "living algebra"? A theatricalized action, invention, or fancy with no real core of character-drama, conviction, and realizations, or a play ultimately justifiable *only* as "theatre." And to create that kind of drama, one doesn't have to care about anything except theatre or art. It is enough to be *clever*. And so the third principle of dramatic modernism enters into playwriting and stage production. One must be capable of performing cartwheels with ideas and setting the wheels of theatrical machinery whirling. It is enough then for the playwright to function as a high-grade prestidigitator.

The historical role of Jean Cocteau has been to give sanction with his unquestionable talent and intelligence to prestidigitational playwriting. Modernism has become more and more identified with it. And I, for one, would have no objection to it if it were not presented as a profound or important contribution to dramatic art and were simply considered showmanship. My only other reservation would then be that although showmanship is very much a desideratum in the theatre, drama is, if not something *else,* something *more* than that. I find myself, then, willing to accept "theatricalism" as almost anything except a formula for creating dramatic masterpieces.

III. PIRANDELLO AND THE "SIX CHARACTERS"

In *The Infernal Machine* it is not the man but the machine—the machinery of the playwriting—that we are most aware of. And since the "machine" of an idea and the machinery of the playwriting have proved attractive to our modernists, intellectual theatricalism is worth exploring further as to its nature and results. The "machinery," I ought to add, is not usually that of contrivance in plotting the action; not the tricky suspense, trumped-up discoveries of lost letters and wills, the down-with-a-bang curtain lines, and other paraphernalia of the "well-made," speciously realistic play in vogue during the nineteenth century. It is, instead, an ingenious way of using the stage theatrically, with or without physical machinery. "Theatricalism" prevails by using the actor "histrionically," with or without ballet, mime, acrobatics, or other kinds of stylization associated with the work of Reinhardt, Copeau, Jouvet, Meyerhold, Barrault, and other imaginative directors. It also employs play-structure theatrically rather than realistically. We are dealing here with demonstrative play-writing in a strongly self-conscious age. The theatricalist play may *deal* with life—every kind of play does that. But the "life" put on the stage is some special "theatrical" awareness of it. "Theatricalists" even favor demonstrating openly, *in the presence of the audience,* how one could or would proceed to make effective theatre with various situations.

Plays directly presenting this interest and employing the "play within the play" technique, have proliferated in the modern theatre. They are not as new as might have been imagined by the first enthusiasts who lauded Molnar's *The Play's the Thing* or Pirandello's *Six Characters in Search of an Author*. The Attic stage had its theatrical spoof in *The Frogs,* the Jacobean stage in Beaumont and Fletcher's *The Knight of the Burning Pestle,* the Restoration stage in Buckingham's *The Rehearsal,* the eighteenth-century stage in Sheridan's *The Critic*. We have had more plays of this kind in our times because we are more self-conscious about the theatre as well as of the other arts. When the play-within-the-play device is a mere convenience, as in the case of Rodgers and Hammerstein musical comedy *Me and Juliet,* or when it is a springboard for sophisticated comedy such as *The Play's the Thing,* nothing in particular is significant about it; we know that somebody is busying himself with show business! But when consciousness of the theatre becomes a violation of realism undertaken "esthetically" and "metaphysically," as a *criticism* of theatre and an inquiry into the nature of reality, we know that we are in the presence of the vanguard. We are in the presence of Luigi Pirandello, one of the culture-heroes of the avant-garde. He wrote three plays, including the impressive *Six Characters,* about the theatre, and he more or less "theatricalized" all his other plays except his early ones, of which *Liolá* is an attractive example. *Six Characters in Search of an Author* is a thoroughly successful play and a rather delightful, as well as oddly moving, one. It is also the classic dramatic presentation of the gospel of theatricalism.

Pirandello was another major annihilator of both the conventional realism and conventional humanism of the theatre—a fact that his nihilistic statements concerning life and society and his much publicized cynicism expressed extra-artistically, superficially, and in some respects misleadingly.

Being a deeper man than Cocteau and a profoundly troubled one, a "man of feeling" actually, Pirandello reconstituted life on the stage with his sympathy in many a play such as *Henry IV* and *Naked*. Also, he never quite lost a sense of closeness to the provincial life of the Sicily of his youth. He was its poet in more ways than one ever since his early one-act genre or folk pieces, among which *Sicilian Limes* is particularly affecting. An appreciation of Pirandello as an artist would have to take many more qualities of his playwriting into consideration than I do here. Nevertheless, his philosophy of theatre, in his case also a philosophy of life, frequently dissolves the stable reality—the very identity—of one or more characters as human beings, and sometimes thrusts the machinery of playwriting into the foreground almost as an end in itself.

This becomes especially apparent when one considers many of his plays; they prove to be mostly variations on a single theme, and the theme itself is a negation of a full reality for people. Masks, impersonations, notions of themselves, personalities invented by the characters for themselves appear frequently on the Pirandellian stage. Even so gripping a play as *Henry IV* becomes unsatisfactory as one stands away from it and as the melodramatic drive of the action ceases to exert its potent spell. The matter in hand, a once mentally deranged man's frustrations and desperation, is serious; it is intensely realized by Pirandello. But ingenuity takes over in the play with the elaborate setting up and carrying out of an experiment by those who visit "Henry IV," with his own planned experiment on his visitors, and with the many twists and turns of the plot. Pirandello's machinery is considerably in evidence here, as elsewhere. Without it, Pirandello would not have as interesting and exciting a play. With it, he has an overcomplicated mechanism.

Six Characters is a more successfully fused play, fully executed, and unified as comedy, though with dark and troubling overtones. Nevertheless, *Six Characters*, too, impresses me as a work more interesting than fulfilling, in the sense of fulfilling the potentialities suggested by the author's own human material. I believe I actually resent his subverting its poignancy in order to give me a clever demonstration about the difference between art and life, theatre and reality. Wrongheadedly perhaps, I feel that the author is cheating. And not only me as a reader, but himself. Why is he afraid to commit himself to his characters? Do they wound him that much?

The point of the work, as any Pirandellian disciple will tell us, lies of course precisely in the fact that the "six characters" were unrealized, and so in a sense their story was unrealized, by the playwright who conceived them. Since *he* couldn't make a play with them, they are going to write the play themselves; they are that eager to externalize their tensions and justify their conduct. Consequently, they invade a theatre in which a manager and a group of actors are rehearsing another Pirandello play called *Mixing It Up.* (Pirandello is urbanely mocking himself.) Led by the Father, a philosophical gentleman greatly perturbed because an unusual experiment of his in human relations worked out disastrously, the main characters try to give the Manager the play they individually see in their relationships. They even act out for him a few brief scenes, mere sketches for the play the Manager believes can be made out of them—a box-office play which outrages them with its factitiousness and conventionality. But they do not succeed in giving him the play they sense in themselves, each character in his own way. Aside from the fact that their author never finished their drama, the play cannot be written because the gap between reality and theatre is too great. The one disturbs the other; the play fails precisely where the words should be heard and the action should be developed. Their life, or as much of it as they can or are allowed to convey on the stage, refuses to yield an effective and clear plot.

Yes, that is the point, and Pirandello not only makes it extremely well but uses it to press home his views on life and art quite absorbingly. But the fact is that he has done much more than that, and that is the final reason why the play can move and stimulate us greatly but at the same time leave us with a feeling of deprivation. He has filled his work with fragments, with *disjecta membra,* of an intense reality to which he leads us to give our utmost attention and concern. They are as follows: An intelligent but confused Man, driven on by the "Demon of Experiment," upon observing an innocent emotional rapport between his humble wife and his equally gentle clerk, first sent the clerk away and then, when she appeared to long for the man, sent her after the clerk. She lived with him until his death, and gave birth to three illegitimate children. She also has a legitimate son, brought up in the country away from his mother, in order that he should grow up healthy and strong, so the Father says. The destitute mother and her illegitimate children were brought by the Father into his house after the clerk's death, the woman's husband (the Father) having met his stepdaughter in a fashionable bordello patronized by him. The stepdaughter, constantly flagellating herself for her disgrace, is also tormenting the Father with her contempt and desires to avenge herself on him. One illegitimate young son, a sensitive and proud lad, is contemptuous of them all, including his mother, who longs for his kindness and forgiveness. Painfully aware of the legitimate son's contempt and of his own anomalous position in the household, he finally shoots himself. We have all this and more—the drowning of the third illegitimate child, a baby girl, the stepdaughter's flight from home after these deaths, and the bitter stalemate of the father, wife, and legitimate son left to lead an unhappy life together. Such is the outcome of a man's compassion for his unhappy wife and his violation of the conventions when he allowed her to follow the man she loved.[1]

Pirandello deliberately adds up all these details, as well as the passions and self-questionings associated with them, only to prove that it is impossible to write a play about them. It is impossible, he proves, to give dramatic realization to reality in general and to the particular reality of these complicated and afflicted characters. For that is what the play adds up to, no scene actually dramatizing any of the events more than sketchily while the manager and the actors engage in discussions and vainly propose alterations. Pirandello, one might say, behaves like a man who offers a starving man a doughnut but whisks it out of his reach on the grounds that it isn't really done. Or that only the hole in it is real. This is one way to describe the sense of frustration which constitutes much of the play's meaning and this reader's or playgoer's final experience.

Pirandello brings us to an impasse in the theatre by demonstrating in *Six Characters* that the theatre and reality cannot actually meet without fatally destroying each other. The strict logic of a thoroughly theatricalist view of the drama can lead only to this negativist conclusion. Whether or not Pirandello intended to go that far, he has written a play to end all plays. Certainly, to end those plays we are expected to take seriously as representations of reality, and to destroy the validity of our losing ourselves in their action as reality, even *pro tem.* So much for such plays as *Oedipus the King, Hamlet, Macbeth, King Lear, Phaedra, Hedda Gabler,* and *The Cherry Orchard.* We have obviously been deluded about the great tragedies of the theatre in believing in their action as though it were reality; and Sophocles and Shakespeare were surely mere pretenders in enabling us to do so. Somebody must be in error. Was it Shakespeare or Pirandello?

In theory, the argument can be protracted indefinitely, even if Aristotle joins the discussion with his principle that dramatic art is an imitation of an action—to which various objections can be raised. (For example, that the imitation is not, after all, the "real" action but an artistic falsification of it, or that the imitation isn't actually an imitation, but a recreation.) But, empirically, we, the simple-minded playgoers and readers, know where we stand on the issue. We crave life and *more* life for the theatre, so much so that we willingly "suspend our disbelief" whenever the playwright gives us half a chance. And, indeed, Pirandello himself has often given us half a chance, if rarely a whole one. Even in following *Six Characters* we are likely to succumb from time to time to an illusion of

---

[1] Divorce from the Father and a marriage between the Mother and the clerk, an unlikelihood in Catholic Italy, does not come up at all as a possibility in the play.

reality. Even though we shouldn't, if logic, especially Pirandello's logic in the play, were to rule us. The theatre would, indeed, reach an impasse if logic had its way. It would be just theatre purged of all human reality—a game for the intelligent, a confusion for the unintelligent, and a make-believe affair to be considered honest only to the degree that it does not make us believe that what the play shows *"is."*

Fortunately, we resist the logic of such a conclusion when we are left to ourselves and are not belabored with theory—as, in my opinion, no play-goer need be. And so do most theatricalist writers and performers themselves violate the Pirandellian principle. Even Cocteau has done so; there are portions of *The Infernal Machine,* though only portions, where we can believe we are observing a real Jocasta and a real Oedipus. Only extreme stylization in the performance of the play could annihilate that impression. Unless the actor deliberately destroys "illusion," density of experience on the stage takes on life. The experience is *present,* therefore *existential.* If intensely realized enough, the experience is likely to be so replete with life that it transcends the stage. This can happen even in formalistic poetic drama. Our response to the major plays of Shakespeare proves this con-clusively. It is actually more difficult to keep some sort of life and illusion of reality *out* of the theatre than to put some sort of life *into* it. One has to work harder, more consciously and with greater skill, to *dehumanize* the drama than to *humanize* it. A platform with people on it (and actors, in spite of what some directors can do to them, are people) is a terrible temp-tation to existence. It begins to assert itself. The results may not always be art, and they are never *good* art without considerable shaping on the part of the actor and the writer. But "life" is on the stage the moment the living actor is on it, and it grows the moment there are also people not deprived of sight and hearing "out front."

There is no great likelihood that theatricalism will actually suc-ceed in destroying human reality in the modern theatre. The resistance of audiences, whether we approve it as natural or deplore it as simply stupid, alone would tend to keep theatricalism within bounds. And kept within bounds, theatricalism can give us intelligent and stimulating theatre. To various degrees, it has certainly attracted most intelligent playwrights in our century. But the tendencies so brilliantly epitomized by Pirandello in *Six Characters* are more likely to give us a diminished modern drama than an augmented one.

The effort to make the drama more interesting by making it less "drama" and more "theatre" (a dichotomy that should never have arisen!) may well devitalize both playwriting and theatre. This has happened be-fore: The great classic drama petered out in the Graeco-Roman world after the second century B.C., making way for the purely histrionic arts of mime and spectacle, with results that ultimately capsized the theatre, too. And a characteristic of decadent Jacobean-Stuart drama was that it became more theatrical than dramatic. If it is the destiny of the modern drama to yield more and more ground to theatricality, it is hardly a fate to be contemplated with delight. And it is hardly a tendency to be encouraged indiscriminately even under the banner of art; even in the enterprise of seeking new forms of dramatic writing. The form without the substance—"the form of drama without the content" was Alfred Kerr's description of extreme expressionist playwriting in the Germany of the twenties—is what we are likely to get in the long run.

IV. EXPRESSIONISM

In earlier ages, theatre and drama have tended to hold on to a style or method for long periods of time, ranging from half a century to several centuries. The result has often been a tenacious conventionalism which has discouraged experimentation, so that the theatre has often lagged behind non-dramatic literature. Matthew Arnold could wonder at the difference in his time between the modern matter readers received from the men of letters and thinkers of his time and the trash they seemed willing to accept from a stage devoid of ideas. Against the dangers of superannuation, however, we can at least set the advantages accruing in some past ages from a long period of gestation and stability. A particular style once had time to develop its optimal possibilities by trial and error and by gradual modification. Actors from Betterton to Coquelin trained in a well-established convention apparently could make it as personal a possession as an old habit and could carry their style to complete refinement. Playwrights writing for a theatre rooted in convention could grow steadily into greatness, as did Shakespeare and Molière, instead of jumping from one style to a radically divergent one long before their artistry had matured.

By 1900 or so, many a performer, who had just learned to round out his art of characterization for the realistic theatre, had to dissolve himself in a mist of poetic implication and become an essence or symbol instead of a person, a figment of dream rather than a multi-dimensional character. When the symbolist "Blue Bird" and "Pelléas and Mélissande" vogue died down, he had to turn himself into a tangible character again. But not for long! Between 1919 and 1925, when German expressionism began to make strong claims upon the theatre, he had to depersonalize himself or change himself into a self-charging dynamo by order of directors like Leopold Jessner and Jürgen Fehling. He struck poses of startling angularity or assumed glowering attitudes; or he shrieked his lines and negotiated flights of steps—the so-called Jessner-steps—at breakneck speed. Had he just popped out of a witches' cauldron he could not have been more spectral, nor could he have sputtered more. Meyerhold, the apostle of "constructivism," made other demands upon the actor, who had to become a "biodynamic" automaton swinging from trapeze bars and performing acrobatic stunts on bricklayers' scaffolds and catwalks in the Soviet Theatre. Another stylist, Tairov, tended to turn acting into a form of choreography, and still another, Piscator, wanted the actor to be simultaneously a character in some scenes, a symbol in other scenes, an objective narrator or lecturer, a *commedia dell' arte* type, and so on.

Among the casualties of our unstable affections has been modern expressionism cultivated before 1914 by Strindberg and Wedekind, widely practiced in Germany after the First World War, disseminated throughout Europe, and adopted in America by *avant-garde* playwrights of the nineteen-twenties such as O'Neill, Rice, and Lawson. It was the one experiment in non-realistic theatre and drama that promised effective transvaluation of modern theatrical values. Expressionistic techniques were employed by playwrights whose motives were anything but superficial. Among them were men like Strindberg and O'Neill, who endeavored to express personal tensions and problems they considered representative of modern man's alienation from his times, rootlessness, and depersonalization. Believing that ordinary realism could properly objectify neither inner experience nor the external world as it presented itself to a troubled mind, they resorted to a fragmentary, constantly dissolving picture of reality. They represented the inner self not as an orderly organism that moved more or less clearly toward well-defined ends, such as winning a girl in marriage or getting on in business, but as a highly unstable compound of promptings and confusions.

The concept of a unified self was a product of nineteenth-century rationalism, materialism, and mechanistic science, and its ideal representatives were the gentleman and the career man of the bourgeois world. The rebels against this society were no different in spirit or aim, since they, too, were set in their ways, confident of their reasoning powers, and secure in their convictions. But what if a career or an attainable goal was no longer considered a desirable objective, what if it could not be pursued or enjoyed by a divided and bedevilled personality? What if the individual's major difficulty was his *not* having a unified self that could look out through a clear pane of perceptions at a clearly outlined world?

The form of plays like *The Dream Play, The Spook Sonata, The Emperor Jones,* and *The Hairy Ape* became a whirl of fragmentary events rendered in short scenes. The plays consisted of situations in which the main characters revealed themselves in facets that failed to harmonize to form a single rounded image. And since the external world was presented as the world formed by the dreamer or the perceiver, it fragmented itself, too; it appeared dislocated, turned out of shape, and exaggerated by the character's state of mind. Characters in a play changed their identity within the same play or acquired abnormal attributes indicative of the protagonist's state of mind or the author's attitude toward society. O'Neill's burly "Yank" in *The Hairy Ape,* for example, hurls himself at the well-dressed citizens coming out of a Fifth Avenue church only to rebound from them because they represent a society to which he cannot belong. Making a fluid subjective private world out of an objective one ordered by conventional perceptions, playwrights even abolished the conventions of time and place by which we normally live in society. The "Officer" in Strindberg's *The Dream Play* changes from youth to middle age and old age with uncanny rapidity. Past and present time mingled freely in expressionist plays: Memory intruded itself into a present situation and not only dominated but altered it, as when Strindberg's "Officer" goes back to his childhood school as a teacher only to find himself a pupil again, unable to do simple arithmetic and humiliated by a schoolmaster. O'Neill's Emperor Jones is bedevilled by memories of his past as he tries to escape from his enemies; and not only by the memory of things he personally experienced as a convict, but by the "racial" fears of ghosts and the "racial" memories of the auction blocks of slavery. Jones was given a Jungian racial memory in addition to his personal memories.

Expressionists found uses not merely for conventional fantasy as old as the theatre but for dream patterns in which inventions of the imagination exist not in the context of our ordinary, stable consciousness, as do the characters in *A Midsummer Night's Dream,* but in the context of a transformed field of consciousness where nothing is stable or rational for any length of time. Expressionists also went beyond ordinary symbolism, which is after all only an extended metaphor by means of which we say one thing in order to signify another. They resorted to symbolism, it is true, but this alone would not have represented anything new or revealing in their work: The conventional Buddhist symbolism in *The Dream Play* is the least striking feature of Strindberg's play. The significant element in expressionism was the "psychological," by which is meant not the simple, mechanistic psychology of the nineteenth century before the work of the forerunners of Freud but the discovery of processes that defy logic or have a subconscious logic of their own. The theatre began to play host to the incalculable processes of "free association," the "stream-of-consciousness," depersonalization, psychosomatic occurrences, strange recurrences of experience, the impression of having experienced before what one could not have experienced (*déja vu*), telepathy, and other psychic phenomena.

Measured by the potentialities of expressionism, Arthur Miller's treatment of Willie Loman's mental state in *Death of a Salesman* is elementary.

Expressionism did not remain confined, however, to matters of private and individual experience. Both Strindberg and O'Neill employed the expressionist technique for social commentary. *The Dream Play* dealt with the failure of society as well as of individuals, and *The Hairy Ape* is far less important as the drama of an individual stoker who went berserk after being snubbed by an heiress than as a tragedy of Man's loss of unity with Nature. Applications of expressionism to social drama gave us, indeed, many of the most challenging plays of the modern theatre, from Wedekind's first assault on sexual taboos in his tragedy of adolescence, *The Awakening of Spring* back in 1898, up to the large number of dramas of social conflict with which the nineteen-twenties abounded.

To dramas of vigorous protest and of revolt the expressionistic technique brought hortatory declamation, nervous dialogue, and high-strung characters, sensational situations, symbols and imagery, and a general air of explosiveness. Ernst Toller, starting with *Man and the Masses,* and other Central European playwrights, such as Georg Kaiser and Fritz von Unruh, wrote a large number of flailing and impassioned plays. For social satire the expressionistic style provided emphatic exaggerations, and the extravaganzas of the satirist brought relief from well-intentioned but humdrum problem plays. In writing *The Adding Machine,* Elmer Rice drew an imaginative caricature of the commonplace Mr. Zero, the clerk displaced by an adding machine whose soul had been so routinized that he found life in Elysium too immoral for an after-life. In *Beggar on Horseback,* to cite another example, Marc Connelly and George S. Kaufman found effective theatrical stylization for the monotony of big business routine. The musical comedy nightmare they invented for a young man about to marry into a wealthy family was a sprightly substitute for a dull, realistic picture of dull life in the machine-age. And when John Howard Lawson resorted to a jazz symphony treatment of life in the nineteen-twenties in *Processional,* the style of extravaganza was more telling than a factual report on that life could have been. As class conflicts came to be viewed with greater earnestness and dogmatism in the deepening economic depression of the nineteen-thirties, expressionism lost status in the social theatre, with the result that the stage was glutted with routine stories of poverty, capital and labor strife, and social workers' case histories. None of these could command half the interest that legitimately pertained to plays like *Waiting for Lefty, Bury the Dead,* and *The Cradle Will Rock,* the writing of which entailed some use of the expressionists' imaginative stylization.

Expressionism made the matter-of-fact reality of the problem play *theatrical.* That was one of the major advantages of employing the technique. It was a highly suitable one, too, for the distortions and intensifications of life produced by political conflicts, such as those that broke out in Germany after the First World War. And the deliberate depersonalization of individuals in playwriting accorded well with the growth of the mechanized mass production and mass consumption world after 1918. Georg Kaiser dramatized his dismay and forebodings in his trilogy *The Coral* and *Gas I* and *II.* In writing *R.U.R.* about the revolt of a robot proletariat invented as a substitute for refractory wage workers, the Czech playwright Karel Capek merely carried the theme of modern mechanization to an ultimate hypothesis. The literalness of strict realism was broken by the expressionists precisely at a time when literal treatments of social reality would have reduced dramatic composition to intolerable mediocrity and boresomeness.

A reaction to expressionism was inevitable, and it was brought on to a degree by the undisciplined practice of its proponents. Their effort "to picture the inside of things without showing their outside," as Galsworthy called it, resulted not only in morbid introversion but in extreme confusion. In many instances it was impossible to distinguish in the plays between a world of wakeful consciousness and the dream world of the characters. Since consistency was not considered either a virtue or necessity, the sequence of events was not always clear. Since the general style was usually strident or hysterical, the action abrupt or insistently repetitious, the tempo breathless, the dialogue frantic or monotonously telegraphic, expressionist plays tended to tax our nervous system. Tricky effects of sudden transformations in the writing and the scenery were employed so frequently that the style tended toward hollow sensationalism. The pursuit of illogic for its own sake by the dramatist or for mere theatricality by his producer became the rule. Mystics and champions of irrationalism invaded the theatre along with purposeful propagandists, satirists, and students of psychology. Empty vaporings by the dramatist and his actors, supplemented by exhibitionism on the part of the stage director and scene designer, discredited and nearly wrecked a potentially fruitful enterprise of the antirealistic modern theatre.

Since the tempo of modern life is so fast that we tend to throw conventions overboard faster than in previous ages, expressionism was never given a chance to cool down and crystallize. There have been no true expressionist masterpieces, as none could have been created until the seething and fuming of revolt and pretentiousness were over. Expressionism could not have matured as an art form until, its novelty disappearing, artists could come to regard it as a norm upon which the only improvement would not be a heaping up of new tricks and sensations, but modulations and refinements of technique, as well as enrichment with thought and human reality.

No reprieve was granted to this revolutionary style of theatre. It had a brief and torrid summer, but never a time of harvest. Consequently, the stage continued to hold on to a somewhat withered realistic convention while reaching out now and then for an exotic hothouse fruit like futurism, constructivism, dadaism, or surrealism which generally proved indigestible and provided little or no nourishment. Ever since the failure of the expressionist movement, men of the theatre have dreamed up cults, regretted the lack of imagination on the stage, cried out against the commonplaceness of realistic plays and productions, and heralded the dawn of a modern poetic drama that has thus far proved illusory. What we have had now and then is a shooting star such as Christopher Fry in England, Giraudoux and Anouilh in France, or Saroyan and Tennessee Williams, whose personal talents are hardly the equivalent of a new day in dramatic art.

It would appear to be too late for expressionism to resume its former place in the theatre, take roots again, and begin to grow organically. Its destiny now appears to be that of an "influence." The seed it developed during its brief season fell far from the parent plant. It began to send up shoots in such alien soil as the fields of musical comedy and musical revue, and it emerged as one sprout among many in a sort of Japanese rock garden of mingled styles of modern theatre. Expressionism suffered the indignity of being impressed into the service of lechery in a George White's Scandals production which painted eyes on the chorines' bosoms and concealed their faces in oversized stovepipe hats. In less dubious examples of musical entertainment, the expressionistic style appeared in some fantastic ballets, such as the notable Balanchine "Slaughter on Tenth Avenue" number danced by Tamara Geva and Ray Bolger. Expressionistic elements also cropped up along with realistic scenes, arguments, and demonstrations in didactic or more or less documentary drama—in "learning plays" and other examples of so-called epic theatre developed in Germany before Hitler by the poet Brecht and the director Piscator. Also, in the documentary lectures known as "living newspapers" created by the Federal Theatre here during the depression. In one example, *Power,* nine masks represented the Justices of the Supreme Court or "nine old men" who had ruled against New Deal legislation. But the range of expressionist imagination was carefully circumscribed in these efforts.

In the borderline case of Moss Hart's *Lady in the Dark,* expressionism was legitimately chosen to represent the vagaries of a business woman's unconscious as she lies on an analyst's couch. Mr. Hart proceeded to make profitable musical comedy extravaganza out of the lady's exhumed memories with the help of the assorted talents of Gertrude Lawrence and Danny Kaye. Later, Moss Hart endeavored to prevail incautiously without benefit of musical comedy sauce in his divorce drama *Christopher Blake.* But the ill success of his venture into a little lad's unconscious was only one more indication, along with the fate of such plays as O'Casey's *The Silver Tassie* and Dennis Johnston's *The Old Lady Says No,* that unadulterated expressionism can expect scant sympathy from critics and the general public. *The Skin of Our Teeth,* as memorable a play as any begotten by the Second World War, only bewildered and irritated large numbers of playgoers when Thornton Wilder telescoped life in the Ice Age and contemporary New Jersey and presented the antediluvian world in terms of an Atlantic City business convention. Nor did Wilder and his stage director Elia Kazan fare better for theatricalizing some scenes as though the object had been to compete with the showmen of the musical comedy stage.

It would seem, then, that expressively stylized imaginativeness has had a vagrant, uneasy career in seventy-five years of modern theatre. The boldly stylized drama of the classic Greeks or the Elizabethans is a thing of the past, and a modern equivalent productive of masterpieces has not yet arrived, if indeed it can arrive within the foreseeable future. Free stylization in serious dramatic art has yet to lay firm foundations in our theatre. It is at least partly for this reason that modern poetic drama in verse has made so little headway. Its best products have been Brecht's plays, which burst into verse only in lyrics supplementary to realistic scenes; Lorca's dramas, which stemmed from a lyrical folk tradition in Spain; and *Murder in the Cathedral,* in which T. S. Eliot was deliberately traditional in a medieval, liturgical manner except when he reverted to modern prose and was consciously Shavian.

Expressionism was the first drastic effort playwrights made to disintegrate realistic structure. Great talent, as well as vaulting ambition, went into the endeavor, and a large measure of modern chaos or of a modern *sense* of chaos characterized it. If the technique of dream formation can teach or has indeed taught contemporary playwrights how to make playwriting more flexible, the fate of expressionism can, nevertheless, also teach them that chaotic playwriting is an insecure foundation for modernism. To shatter the mold of realism is less difficult than to create new forms or a new cohesion. The old non-realistic forms grew up naturally and were based on an assent by ritualism or an assent by custom. And when that was the case, the playwright did not have to bother much with the external form. He could go ahead with the business of filling the outward form with the palpable reality of characterization and action, and of giving shaped, definitive expression to his subject matter, which is intrinsic form—the only kind of form that constitutes art. The Expressionists were the first modernists to concern themselves with the outward form of drama as a paramount consideration. Too often, consequently, they failed to attend to the chief business of a dramatist, that of making sure that there is something substantial and abundantly gratifying to pour into a play regardless of whether its shape is Attic, Elizabethan, neo-classic, realistic, or expressionistic. They confused a convention of play structure with drama, an outer form with an inner intrinsic one. Sterility was the price they paid for concerning themselves so strenuously with the conventions of play structure, which are secondary to the expressed reality that matters in whatever convention rules the theatre of a period. Numerous playwrights employed Elizabethan dramaturgic conventions. Shakespeare is distinguished from them not by his use of these conventions but by the use to which he put them. The danger of *willing* oneself into a new convention is that one is likely to concern oneself almost exclusively with it.

THE REBUILDERS

I. ALTERNATIVES FOR DRAMA

The effort to annihilate the centrality of man and of the illusion of objective reality has been going on for a long time, with or without the accompaniment of a program of esthetic theatricalism. Cocteau and Pirandello merely gave brilliant expression to this trend after 1914, the year from which we may not too arbitrarily date the *contemporary* theatre. The objective, realistic drama which follows the normal sequence of events and natural step-by-step development of character and action, therefore creating an illusion of reality, won intellectual stature and artistic validity with the work of Ibsen between 1879 and 1890. It was supplemented by the efforts of Henry Becque and Émile Zola in France, and by the passionate naturalism of Strindberg in Scandinavia. And it began to prevail on the stage with the pioneering of the "Free" or "Independent Theatres," with the *Théâtre Libre* created by Antoine, *Die Freie Bühne* led by Otto Brahm, the Moscow Art Theatre under Stanislavski. These and similar endeavors in Europe (the American theatre as yet was barely aware of them) now belong to theatrical history. They are intrinsically, as well as chronologically, nineteenth-century events. They constitute the "classicism" of modern dramatic art.

But they had barely begun to crystallize in the test tubes of the pioneers when the counter-effort to dissolve realistic drama was in process. The neo-romantic symbolists began to give some attention to the drama and the theatre as the decade of the eighties drew to a close. And as the *fin-de-siècle* art-for-art's sake movement swung into action in the nineties, the poetic playwrights and their so-called art theatres were busily decomposing the objective, "life-like" art of realism. Their own often narrowly limited, success—that of a Maeterlinck in the drama and of a Gordon Craig in theatrical art—is not the only measure, not even the true measure, of the process. They introduced new standards for writers. They even influenced the realists and naturalists who either modified their writing or adopted the new fashionable mode of mystical half-light, poetic suggestion, and outright symbols. Strindberg himself briefly succumbed to Maeterlinck, and some operatic neo-romanticism appears in even so original a work as his *Dream Play*. Hauptmann left the naturalistic austerities of *The Weavers* for the mixed realism and fantasy of *Hannele* and for the fairy-tale symbolism of *The Sunken Bell*.

Even Shaw, who fought the good fight for Ibsen's realism in the eighties and nineties, fought it, in part, on grounds other than those of realistic dramaturgy and character-building—that is, on grounds of Ibsenite intellectualism. And in his playwriting immediately after his own first play *Widowers' Houses,* Shaw increasingly "theatricalized," Gilbert-and-Sullivanizing in *Arms and the Man,* developing a sort of "farce of ideas" in other plays, and even a sort of "poetry of ideas," which he continued to write with variable success from *Androcles and the Lion* to *Heartbreak House*—or, for that matter, to *The Simpleton of the Unexpected Isles* as late as the mid-thirties of our century.

Nevertheless, it is plain, I believe, that the modern theatre would have quickly died of inanition but for a continual process of chemical recomposition. The modern theatre since the nineties has not been given over to the two questionable alternatives of Maeterlinckian mist and merely humdrum realism; and these are still not the alternatives that face us today. Nor has the contemporary theatre since 1914 been hopelessly divided between the banal surface-realism and a theatricalism utterly drained of human reality. Nor need it be so divided today. A process of rebuilding the sense of reality in the drama or creating some sort of equivalent has gone on simultaneously with the process of disintegration. It has occurred, not necessarily with complete success, in the theatre practice and playwriting of many producing companies and writers throughout the Western world.

It has occurred with such diversity, however, that one simple generalization can tell us nothing. We can understand the process much better by focusing on specific examples, for the best work is always individual. And perhaps the simplest examples are plays, for descriptions of stage productions are notoriously inadequate and unreliable, especially when brief. The text of a play is fixed in print, whereas performance is fleeting; and theories of stage production, though stimulating, do not work out in individual cases quite as planned.

II. STRINDBERG, IBSEN, AND SHAW

We can take as an example a late play by Strindberg. When he carried the process of theatricalization to an expressionistic extreme in such work as *To Damascus* in 1898, *The Dream Play* in 1902 and *The Ghost Sonata* in 1907, he was passionately involved not with mere theatre but with a view of life. More than that, with an experience of life, for he was involved, in every sense, with himself. There was no theatrical dilettantism in his break with the naturalistic style of drama which he himself had carried to a *niveau* and to which he returned whether he wrote another of his sex-duel dramas, the appallingly relentless *Dance of Death,* the superb folk drama *The Bridal Crown,* or his series of Swedish historical plays.

An intense personal charge galvanized "theatre" into life in Strindberg's non-realistic experiments, whether or not we regard them as entirely successful examples of playwriting. I believe we can demonstrate that a sense of reality is exigent and intensely generates dimensioned people, such as the lawyer and the incarnated Daughter of Indra in *The Dream Play.* This, in spite of Strindberg's operatic machinery, and in spite of the fact that normal time sequence is violated, objects undergo transformations, and the identity of characters is dissolved. We can also show how doggedly Ibsen carved out human characters from the start to the finish, and without interruption ("time out taken to play at abstract theatre") even in late symbolist plays such as *Rosmersholm, The Master Builder, The Lady from the Sea, Little Eyolf* and *John Gabriel Borkman.* Whether or not we consider any of these pieces totally successful, we cannot fail to realize that dimensioned characters and not symbols or hints of the supernatural give meaning and power to all the late Ibsen play, except the feeblest of these, *When We Dead Awaken.*

Ibsen and Strindberg are, of course, our classicists: Ibsen, the Sophocles, and Strindberg, the Euripides who begins to break the classic pattern of modern drama. Chekhov is another classicist, and in him the fusion of theatricality and objective dramatic reality is the most natural. And Shaw who attains that fusion less completely is also a classicist of our drama. For Shaw, too, the direct frame of reference is the objective world outside the theatre, no matter how much he invariably remains within the theatre. He belongs to the modern period's Sub-Age of Reason. The Liberal dispensation keeps him from making theatre solely for the sake of theatre. Or for the sake of casting a magic spell on the audience. Even in writing poetically or resorting to fantasy, he is more the Francis Bacon than the Merlin of the stage.

It is not difficult to maintain that many of his characters are Shavian talkers, walking paradoxes, figments of theatre. It is so easy to do so, especially when one overlooks the excellent opportunities they offer for fairly natural acting, that both Shavians and anti-Shavians have seized the opportunity to display their cleverness in ferreting out the "unreality" of Shaw's characters. Since Shaw's talent for theatre was indisputably remarkable whereas many of his opponents used to accuse him of lacking precisely that talent, it is even necessary to bend backward to prove that his bent was theatrical.[1] But it is equally important to realize how often theatrical characters in his plays also possess the density of life of "real" characters. It is not difficult to roll out in behalf of this view a long list

[1] See *Misalliance,* p. 163.

of names—from Morell, Candida, Prossy, and Burgess to Joan and her Dauphin, if not indeed to Newton and Charles II of *In Good King Charles's Golden Days*. In those plays by Shaw that are not completely farcical it is the attitude or arguments of the main characters, Undershaft's, for example, and not their personalities, that are likely to be "theatrical." (And, of course, the same thing can be said of some of the characters of Shakespeare—Iago, for instance—and of other master-builders of character.) John Tanner, for example, is a distinctly recognizable young intellectual, whether or not the opinions he expresses have a shred of validity in our opinion—or Shaw's.

Several other factors ensure the triumph of "reality" as against mere histrionics in the theatrician Shaw. For one thing, Shaw can make characters maintain a point of view with such intensity and work out their beliefs or mere attitudes in a continuous disputation so thoroughly that the ideas themselves create the substantiality of a character—and even the illusion of a *real* event. That is the case, conspicuously, in the *Don Juan in Hell* fantasy, which has the effect of being less fanciful, of being more "real," so to speak, than any five problem plays by Brieux rolled together (except possibly, *The June Bugs* or *Les Hannetons*) or so naturalistic a picture as *Tobacco Road,* which could strike Joseph Wood Krutch as "grotesque" rather than real. For all its "social realism" or sociological reference, *Tobacco Road* is far more fantastic in effect than Don Juan because the sordid picture stands away from us and we are able to disassociate ourselves from it. *Don Juan in Hell,* on the contrary, draws up closer to the characters, if we have any capacity at all for following their argument and enjoying their verve and animus. Shaw's rich argument, indeed, often creates the people more convincingly than the people create the argument. And it doesn't matter at all, of course, if that is the case, so long as the characters somehow come to life for the duration of the play. Whether the character is generated by argument, poetic soliloquy, or action, the important thing is that the character *is* generated.

The playwright cannot, of course, generate the character by any means unless his instinct and the ambience of his interest, combined with his feeling for acting, are such that he makes a world rather than a game on the stage. Shaw's ingrained involvement with the reasoning and analytical faculty amounted to a passion. Some of his critics might say that it was his only passion. Even if this were only a half truth, and I believe it is only that, this passion alone could make human reality possible for him to a considerable degree. An intensely analytical faculty operating on a psychological level (but not submerged as *mere* psychology) enabled Racine, though working in a distinctly formalistic convention, to create a world that transcends mere theatre. This is the case in *Phaedra,* for example, and even in so less obviously dramatic a play as *Bérènice*. An analytical faculty of a different kind enabled Pirandello himself to transcend the logic of theatrical nihilism imbedded in *Six Characters in Search of an Author,* as is the case in his *Henry IV* and *Right You Are (If You Think So!).* Perhaps it was Pirandello himself who made this point most tellingly— he certainly phrased it most economically—when he had "The Father" in *Six Characters* explain to "The Manager" that "Every true man who is somewhat above the level of beasts and plants does not live for the sake of living, without knowing how to live, but he so lives as to give a meaning and value of his to life." That is what Shaw makes his characters do, sometimes comically, sometimes seriously, but always by the intensity of the reasoning. Discourse creates the real world in Shaw's theatre.

That discourse finally derives from an outside world of values. Shaw's continual interest in social questions, which certainly did not make him an infallible prophet and did not give his plays the iron-clad thesis he often claimed for them, did one thing for him. It helped him to build up in the theatre the very world of reality that his theatrical bravura, his fertile invention, and his departures from strict realistic dramaturgy constantly tended to decompose. And it was not merely his observation of people in society that assisted him in accomplishing this, but the discourse that his social interest gave him.

The discourse, above all! It was creatively effective, not because it was clever, as some critics thought, but because it came out of a concern with an objective world outside the theatre. If it had been drawn out of a parlor alone, not to mention a Fabian debating hall, it would have been enough, so long as the parlor-habitués, not to mention the debating club members, had the outside world for their concern. Shaw was, then, quite correct, at least for himself, in prescribing "discussion" as a revitalizing factor in modern drama. It was a continually revitalizing factor in his own playwriting.

III. THE "HISTRIONIC" ART OF ANDRÉ OBEY

Shaw's methods were, of course, uniquely his own. Other writers have had to work differently in accordance with their temperament and interest. André Obey, an excellent if decidedly minor writer, illustrates another approach to playwriting. He deserves our attention here not merely because he has written with charm and grace, but because he is one of the heroes of the theatricalists and, above all, because his playwriting derives from one of the most influential of movements in the European theatre. He worked closely with the *Compagnie des Quinze,* a group of actors carefully trained by the great Jacques Copeau who gave theatricalism its least eccentric orientation and its most reliable basis of histrionic art. Obey was greatly taken with the *Compagnie's* command of rhythm, gesture, mime, dance, and music. Not discourse, but primordial miming, doing, or showing, was the aim of these followers of Copeau. Obey, in other words, was drawn to a theatre which is antipodal to the theatre of ideas or discussion-drama of Shaw, who attributed its origin to Ibsen.

At the same time, however, this was not the eccentric kind of theatre favored by the Parisian bohemians and sophisticates. It was not deliberately exotic, decadent, or spectacular. On the contrary, the *Compagnie* was singularly unsensational, never sensation-seeking. It adhered to simplicity, as Copeau always adhered to simplicity in preferring simple platforms for staging areas and keeping the stage of his short-lived Théâtre du Vieux Colombier in Paris unpretentiously architectural and formal. Copeau was a singularly pure man. His dedicated life, along with his talent as a director, explains the reverence in which he is held and the influence he exerted on more opportunistic and worldly-wise individuals such as Charles Dullin and Louis Jouvet. This student-company, The Company of Fifteen, training in the Burgundy countryside for nine years, led an almost idyllic life before it began to tour in French cities and in other countries. Michael Saint Dennis, the nephew of Copeau and his stage-manager at the Vieux Colombier who became the director of the actors of the *Compagnie des Quinze* in 1930, vividly describes the bucolic life they led in his introduction to the English edition of Obey's *Noah*. The actors of this noted company busied themselves with preparing mimes on simple themes such as the coming of war to a village and the work of the *vignerons* of the vineyards, as well as with performing plays by Molière in the villages.

Obey saw them perform in Lyons before they became officially known as *La Compagnie des Quinze*. He joined them in 1929 and became their quasi-official playwright for a period of three years. It was during that time that he wrote *Noah*. Obey became perhaps the most attractive of those modern French playwrights who have departed from the so-called boulevard theatre in poetic rather than realistic terms. But the most important point to be made about his work is that it is written entirely in terms of the theatre rather than of any moral or literary program, although his work is not altogether devoid of moral sentiment and is certainly not devoid of literary accomplishment. "I thought of the stage," he declares in his preface to *Noah,* "and that was enough." For him "a play is a *thing* of the theatre so strictly . . . so freely-invented for the stage, composed and developed on the stage, subjected to the stage to such an extent that the life, the reality and rhythm of the drama are there before the words which express it."

One may feel the same mode of composition in other plays. I, for example, felt it in Saroyan's *My Heart's in the Highlands* when it was staged by Robert Lewis for the Group Theatre in 1939. (Saroyan had not worked in the theatre; his personality, however, was distinctly theatrical.) But I know of no other example of a playwright not engaged in mere "show business" who has so consciously and tastefully followed this "theatrical" principle of playwriting. What are the results, we may ask, in the case of a true artist? To what extent can we or ought we to exalt the principle of composition enunciated by Obey as the prescription for making modern theatre a meaningful and vital enterprise? Merely to raise these questions is to answer them, it seems to me, when we examine two of Obey's most characteristic creations during the nineteen-thirties, his short play *Venus and Adonis* and his full-length drama *Noah*.

Venus and Adonis is a perfect work of art, and it is certainly "theatre" while we follow the resistance of the sport-loving Adonis to Venus and his death as poetic story and myth. The play as language is extended by a continual series of opportunities for the actors to act as well as speak. The lines of dialogue actually carry the rhythm for the amplifying stage business or histrionic action. Hardly a minute transpires without something being done—and done not by way of plot, but by way of acting. This procedure starts with the first speech as Adonis, entering in a riding habit at daybreak, stretches and calls out "Good Morning" to his off-stage friend Martial, as he looks at his wristwatch and decides it will be a fine day for hunting birds, as he claps his hands and calls for his mare. The ensuing dialogue between Adonis and Martial quickly establishes that Adonis has a neighbor, a lady called Venus, who has transformed the grounds into a veritable garden. In some twenty speeches, only the first of which has any length, there is perhaps only a single line that does not convey the movement of men in a hurry to go off hunting. And the conversation with Zoë, the servant of Venus who tries to shush the men, continues the active preparation for departure. But it would be impossible to give a moment by moment account of the beats of action without reproducing the play verbatim. The piece virtually plays itself on the printed page.

We can stand in admiration before the skill of the author. But only until we start asking ourselves what it is that is being churned up so expertly. The answer is: a Gallic rendition of an older woman's interest in a handsome lad impervious to her usually unfailing charms, quite entertaining and then deepening with the ominous approach of Death in the figure of a slight and well-groomed lady who also has a hankering for "handsome boys . . . careless unfortunately." Adonis, Venus soon learns, has been killed by a boar in the forest while hunting and has disappeared mysteriously "like a vapor." Only a handkerchief tinged with his blood remains. Venus passes it over the ground in front of his house, and behold everywhere anemones, the beautiful white forest flower "with one tiny red spot," spring up from the soil.

Using solely the theatre for a frame of reference, or merely things of the theatre, Obey created nothing more than an acting piece. In the same decade, other writers, in America, wrote such short plays as *Waiting for Lefty, Bury the Dead, Hymn to the Rising Sun,* and *My Heart's in the Highlands,* with frames of references decidedly not entirely the theatre, just as Synge and Lady Gregory, more than two decades earlier, had done. The crudities of the first two plays mentioned place them well below the pure artistry of *Venus and Adonis. Hymn to the Rising Sun* leaves an acrid taste in the mouth. *My Heart's in the Highlands* is frequently awkward, and its language lacks Obey's finesse. But if any theatre in the world, including France where variations on classic tales are traditional, could address itself to more than a coterie public with this piece or sustain itself as a vital institution, I have yet to hear of it. And if the theatricalist ideal had depended on a repertoire of plays of this nature it would have had no effect on the very art of theatre that Copeau set out to reform. Copeau himself started in theatre, in 1911, with nothing less challenging than a dramatization of *The Brothers Karamazov!*

Obey, however, wrote another play, *Noah,* for the Company of Fifteen, just as theatrically adept, just as sensitive to playing values and possibilities, if not indeed more so. And *Noah,* a simple account of the legend of the flood and eligible for children's theatre with the animals of the Ark, can relate itself to modern consciousness in any land. We do not explain the difference between it and *Venus and Adonis* by saying that it deals with a myth, since the subject of the latter play also possesses the quality of myth. There is, of course, a difference in the quality of the myths, for the Hebrew one has no pretty fancifulness; and this does make a difference. But not so much as does Obey's treatment of the material, for he could just as well have spoofed or "poetically" attenuated it—or somebody else could have done so. Nor is it that Obey repudiated "theatre" in *Noah.* On the contrary, his theatricalizing work is thorough. The characters, including the animals, mime their way through much of the play. In the last act, for example, Noah's sons, coming out of the Ark at last, create a veritable poetry of the dance as they celebrate their contact with earth lustily, scrunching into the mud. The treatment that makes the marked difference between *Venus and Adonis* and *Noah* cannot be "theatrical."

The difference is accounted for by two fundamental elements in *Noah*: The first is *dimensioned characterization.* Obey dimensions Noah as the troubled and long-suffering man of good will trying to keep his sons in line, Noah's wife as the eternal mother and housewife trying to mediate between her children and their father and ending up as a pitiably drained and complaining old woman as the youngsters fly from the coop, and Ham as the brash and sceptical young man with a desire to throw off parental domination and assert his own will and energies. The second decisive factor is *intellectual substance*: Obey is reflecting on human nature and the human condition here. Noah's awareness through experience is communicated to us directly through him as a character. And what is he aware of? Quite simply, *humanity*.

Noah observes its workings through his family, noting the fretfulness, the weakness of faith in divine providence, the will to power expressed in competitiveness and fighting, and the drive toward separateness. As the three sons and wives go off to Africa, Asia, and Europe respectively to start the warring races of the world, yellow, black, and white, calling each other, "Chink! Slant-eyes," "Pale face," "Nigger," Noah sees a vulture hovering over the unredeemed world of man. "There's the vulture already," he declares. "It will take a lot of courage." He finds himself on a bare rock, "with a hundred ways of dying," but he assures God, which is his way of assuring *himself,* that he will find a way out "somehow or other." He doesn't understand what it's all about, this sorry scheme of things, and he tells God he's given up trying to understand. But only just one thing: "Be up there a little now and then, will You? Let me hear Your voice once in a while. . . ."

Obey may tell me all he wants about his admiration for the theatre of mime, dance, gesture, and movement. But it will be difficult to convince me that the success of *Noah* as theatre does not owe at least as much, if not a great deal more, to his concern with the extra-theatrical phenomenon of the human species, which is all the "reality" we know intimately and the only reality we need on the stage. In *Noah,* he is not as far from the Shaw of *Heartbreak House* and the epilogue of *Saint Joan* as "pure theatre" enthusiasts might think.

Obey has not been able to go further in the direction of significant drama, although he wrote other plays such as *The Rape of Lucrece,* which has had its admirers. Obey has been a distinctly limited writer, and I believe the major limitation is one of temperament, which is too mild, or of intellect, which is too narrow. He is a minor figure in the modern theatre. But he provides a good demonstration of how the sense of theatre and the sense of extra-theatricality can be fused, with one element drawing benefits from the other. And he is not the only writer drawn strongly to the theatricalization of playwriting who can give us this demonstration. Thornton Wilder has done so on the American scene with *Our Town* and *The Skin of Our Teeth.*

Wilder, who adapted Obey's *The Rape of Lucrece* for Katharine Cornell, has felt the same modernist influence that draws artists away from realism. He may have even felt the influence of Obey, although Wilder has not achieved the perfection of *Noah* in either of his full-length plays.

The Skin of Our Teeth (which also brings the animal and human world together, carries a meaning similar to that of *Noah,* and has a central figure, Antrobus, who bears a strong resemblance to Obey's patriarch) is impressive only to the degree that Wilder has figured the human condition concretely through his everlasting suburbanite family of Mr. and Mrs. Antrobus, their children, and their housemaid-Lilith. It is precisely where *The Skin of Our Teeth* becomes mostly a show, where the histrionic element dominates (in the machinery of the framework and in the Atlantic City convention scene) that the play is most skittish and least truly imaginative. The more theatrically sophisticated the author becomes in the course of an otherwise engrossing account of man's struggle through the ages, the less effective his "theatre" becomes. In this respect Obey was the better artist; he had his theatricality much more under control in *Noah,* as he also did in *Venus and Adonis.*

Our Town would have been merely a coy piece of make-believe if it had lacked the objective correlate of closely represented New England life. The mere idea or emotion with which Wilder started might have given him no more than a one-acter; the mere Chinese-styled theatrical framework of characters on ladders, a mere skit in a musical revue, such as the *Grand Street Follies* in the twenties used to satirize an Arthur Hopkins' *Jessner-treppen* type of Shakespearian production. Wilder's last point concerning the value of life and the importance of savoring it to the full would have been the most banal of banalities without the frame of reference established fragment by fragment in the play—the breakfasts, the soda-fountain courtships, the street conversations, the domestic life of the characters. No amount of scintillation on Wilder's part and no amount of admiration for the components of "pure" theatre would have enabled the play to survive as theatre for anybody but some epheboi of variable age for whom America's plain-dealing playwrights, from O'Neill to Miller, are too appallingly crude to be endured. The tenderly noted commonplaces of the first two acts precipitate the play out of the solution of Wilder's theatricality, and they give it whatever value may be claimed for it.

Both Obey and Wilder, in their best work, more or less recomposed the "theatricalized" drama with the common stuff of life and with meditations on it. If it was not given to them to become major figures of the modern drama, the reason is no doubt that they failed to bring any potent catalytic agent into their composition, such as a passionate temperament or an impassioned intellect.

IV. JOHN MILLINGTON SYNGE:
SYNTHESIS IN FOLK DRAMA

In John Millington Synge and Federico García Lorca, whose play-writing also had its origin in the revolt against dramatic realism, we can observe a similar mediation between drama and pure theatre. They, too, have been anti-realistic vanguard heroes, but they, too, managed to escape dissolution as dramatists. They both started by associating themselves with "esthetic" anti-Ibsenite writing, but moved, how knowingly or not, toward a reconstituted dramatic realism. And they actually accomplished this in two steps. The first one they took was folk-play writing, which gave their work a substantial basis of environment or milieu in addition to mere "atmosphere" and nuance. And taking a second step, they transcended the mere folk-play.

Synge's status in the theatre is extremely variable. He is Ireland's greatest playwright, with the exception of Sean O'Casey, and to a considerable degree he set the pattern of Irish playwriting for half a century. His achievement in the still green field of Irish peasant drama during the first decade of the century has yet to be equalled—and not for any lack of effort on the part of later playwrights. Since he wrote in the English language, Synge also belongs to the English theatre, in which his place is secure as a superb minor artist. He also has a place in our American theatre, as the foster-father of regional drama. In the foreign-language theatres, however, his work cannot yield more than a tiny fraction of evidence for his talent. Both the literature and theatre in his plays lie to a large extent in their dialect, and both the characterizations and situations in his work are too dependent upon Irish countryside ways to carry the full charge of observation, humor and meaning. High tragedy usually speaks a more universal language than comedy. But even the high tragedy *Deirdre of the Sorrows* is not entirely exportable, since the ancient saga upon which it is based was translated by Synge into a peculiarly Celtic mode of feeling and expression. Although a superb artist, Synge is not a world figure in the theatre, because he made himself a national playwright. This, in a country still largely provincial at the turn of the century and barely touched by modern urban and industrial civilization.

Whether or not Synge would have been capable of a larger range cannot perhaps be determined. His reticence, of which shyness was only one component and negativeness was a larger one, makes it unlikely that he would have played a very much wider gambit even if his talent had not been completely lavished upon the Irish National Theatre. He gave no indication of possessing the extroversion and the intellectualism of an

Ibsen or Shaw. On the other hand, Synge was still a young man for a playwright when he died of cancer. At the age of thirty-eight, Ibsen, too, was still only a national playwright, and Shaw was still a fledgling dramatist. It is reported that toward the end of his brief career of five and a half years, Synge was planning a play about slum life, which would have inevitably confronted him with the face of modern Europe from which he had turned when he left Paris for the Aran Islands.

Localization, however, was the first condition of Synge's becoming a playwright at all, because only when he gave up trying to be a left-bank artist at Yeats's advice and returned to his native land to steep himself in the life of the Aran Islanders off the west coast did he find anything to say in dramatic form and a way of saying it. His finest play *Riders to the Sea* derives directly from his visit to the Aran Islands. Like Charles Vildrac and other French playwrights who had no taste for the turbulences of modern society, Synge escaped a sterile bohemianism by fixing his eyes on elemental realities. He became, indeed, one of the first of the modern writers of genuine folk-drama—by which I mean plays about a region which do not merely romanticize the countryside, plays in which the local color is part of the dramatic experience rather than a background for events that with slight changes could have occurred on the boulevards of Paris.

So potent, moreover, is the energizing effect on a writer of getting out of the hothouse literary circles in order to create literature, and of getting out of the theatrical circles in order to create theatre, that Synge was able to make a virtue of the "art for art's sake" penchant that had kept him floundering in a garret. The very estheticism he had favored in vain now became a source of creative strength. The symbolist vogue in the theatre started by Maurice Maeterlinck called for "static drama"— that is, for playwriting without plot but with interior action. Even the Moscow Art Theatre, ever willing to pursue any path leading away from claptrap play-fabrication, responded to the call and produced several of Maeterlinck's early plays. This theory of static drama, though a welcome antidote for melodramatic excess and overstrenuous thesis-writing, led modern playwriting into one of its early impasses. It "worked" in the case of a few short plays by Maeterlinck, notably *The Intruder* and *Interior,* but was patently unworkable in most cases, especially in full-length plays, where atmosphere alone could not sustain interest. Preciousness and pretentious mysticism were the usual results of trying to make stage drama out of twilight moods and nuances. Static drama, strictly defined, was a lyricist's pipe-dream. Its proponent Maeterlinck was himself first a minor symbolist poet. As he continued to sustain and commercialize his mysticism (a mysticism independent of religious institutions and an established theology, which, after all, have the great advantage of possessing objective existence), Maeterlinck became a bubble-headed journalist almost on a par with writers of advice-to-the-lovelorn columns. As a playwright, he either qualified for children's theatre with a *Blue Bird* or for a romantic stage, essentially claptrap, with a *Monna Vanna*. Nor did his talented Russian follower Leonid Andreyev fare better in the long run after enjoying a brief vogue with morbid symbolist plays too spurious to last, with the uncertain exception of *He Who Gets Slapped*.

The fact is that *Riders to the Sea* is the only static drama that has securely outlasted the 1890-1910 period. It is the only true masterpiece that conforms to the prescription for static theatre. Women receiving the clothes of one drowned man and the corpse of another, and a mother keening over her drowned son—that is all the action there is in *Riders to the Sea*.

Nothing by way of plot and conflict occurs. But this play is superb theatre, for each fiber of the composition is life specifically rendered. The characters of this little tragedy of the sea are not symbolist shadows but persons in an environment or a milieu of occupations and customs who had similar experiences with the stormy Atlantic off the coast of Ireland. The characters are so lifelike, and their speech is so much a part of their character, that merely being alive and responding to an off-stage occurrence is action enough. Not to be able to act, indeed, is in their case and in the situation of the play a form of action. We may rightly say then that Synge, starting with estheticism as a young man and never formally accepting realism as a mode of art, is supremely the realist in *Riders to the Sea*.

The play is none the less poetic drama, satisfying another requirement of the esthetic movement of the eighteen-nineties. For one thing, the dialogue is sheer music without being speciously ornamental. And the reason it can be so free from preciosity is that it is founded upon real spoken language, as Synge assured us. "I have used one or two words only that I have not heard among the country people of Ireland," he declared in the preface to the considerably longer *Playboy of the Western World*. No one stated the happy concordance between a poet's aspirations and the realism possible in folk-drama better than Synge when he declared in the same introduction that in the Irish countryside of his day "it is possible for a writer to be rich and copious in his words, and at the same time to give the reality, which is the root of all poetry, in a comprehensive and natural form."

Poetic drama, moreover, materializes in *Riders to the Sea,* as in other folk-plays by Synge and other writers, because the situation and the emotions are elemental. This is particularly true of the sea that hovers as a presence over the play and whose rhythm pulses in the dialogue. The sea, also the efficient cause of the tragedy, is both a natural factor and a functioning symbol of irrational fate. The "crass casualty" Thomas Hardy speaks of in a poem is objectified here as a concrete image. It becomes a satanic anagoge in the speech of old Maurya whose reply to her daughter Nora's statement "Didn't the young priest say the Almighty God wouldn't leave her destitute with no son living" is "It's little the like of him knows of the sea." And the poetic reality is all the greater in that it is found impacted in the life of people concerned with everyday reality. The overtones of the writing are not the transparently willed production of an artificer functioning as poet-playwright. A few matter-of-fact short lines between Maurya's great concluding lament plant the play firmly in the soil in which the poetry grows: the elder daughter Cathleen tells the old man who has come to make the coffin for the drowned son Bartley, "I have a new cake you can eat while you'll be working." Looking at the boards the mother had kept ready for a son lost sometime before to the sea, the old man asks, "Are there nails with them?" Cathleen answers, "There are not, Column; we didn't think of the nails," whereupon another man remarks, "It's a great wonder she wouldn't think of the nails, and all the coffins she's seen made already."

I believe I could prove, too, that the romantic bohemian element present in the art-movement of the eighteen-nineties is made supremely viable in *The Playboy of the Western World* and *In the Shadow of the Glen* (note here the glow with which a roving life is invested), and that the symbolist tendency, including abhorrence of workaday "realities" in the eighteen-nineties estheticism, attains substantial reality in *The Well of the Saints.* By comparison with Synge's bitterly concretized treatment of the conflict between illusion and reality in the case of his old beggars who prefer to return to blindness after their experience with reality, such a piece of mockery as Jarry's celebrated *Ubu Roi,* with which the vanguard theatre in Paris started, is merely scatalogical. By comparison with *The Well of the Saints,* Rostand's *The Far-Away Princess* is a beribboned lollipop, Ernest Dowson's *The Pierrot of the Minute* a schoolboy composition, and the Nobel Prize winner Benavente's *The Magic of an Hour,* with its porcelain characters, a mere exercise.

Nevertheless, Synge transcended folk-drama just as he transcended estheticism, and without doing so he would have lacked whatever extralocal stature he possessed and is likely to retain. Sceptic, fatalist, and detached observer of men's ways, he went beyond transcripts of regional material, and was able to create absolute comedy and absolute tragedy. Whenever we perform his major plays solely as a kind of genre painting, we reduce and routinize them.[1] Of English Protestant descent, he was virtually a pagan in an intensely Catholic country, and a cosmopolitan in a desperately nationalistic environment. And nationalistic Irishmen sensed an alienated spirit in him. The patriotic riot that greeted *The Playboy* is by now a familiar story. The best, though less spectacular, evidence of unresponsiveness to Synge is perhaps the failure of *Deirdre of the Sorrows,* his tragedy based on the most popular of Gaelic legends, to find a secure place in Irish repertory. Synge can hardly be described as a favorite son of Ireland. When he went "upward out of his ailing body into the heroical fountains," as his patron-friend Yeats reverentially described his death, the man with whom Irish drama attained significance received only grudging obituaries in the Dublin press. One newspaper, the *Sinn Fein,* devoted one fourth of an obituary notice to him and three-fourths to an obscure Gallic singer who had led the demonstration against *The Playboy of the Western World* in the Abbey Theatre.

Deirdre was Synge's oblation to Irish national tradition. And in composing *Deirdre,* on which he labored harder than on any of the other plays, writing about twenty versions of the work after September, 1907, he knew he was scaling heights not hitherto attempted by him. All his earlier written plays had been peasant drama, but in this work he tried to express the heroic ideals of the Irish Renaissance. To dramatize the famous legend that also drew plays from Lady Gregory, Yeats, "A.E.," and Stephens, was a challenge he could not take lightly. For Synge, then, *Deirdre* was the last testament of his genius. Synge died on March 24, 1909. By mid-December of the same year, with Maire O'Neill playing the ill-starred heroine, the Abbey was producing the play while Yeats and Lady Gregory watched over the production anxiously, and the première on January 13, 1910, was a tribute to the dead poet-playwright.

Synge's last play has, nevertheless, been less frequently performed in Ireland than one might have expected, and it was virtually a new play to American playgoers when the venturesome Abbe Practical Workshop presented it on December 14, 1949, at New York's Master Institute Theatre. So far as anyone could determine, this tragedy had never been performed in New York professionally. If it is too much to claim that, with the exception of Dorothy Patten who played the nurse, the actors, capably directed by Richard Barr, did justice to this exacting play (even the Abbey Theatre's famous actors did not do so), there was no doubt that the production was an unusual event. Noting that *Deirdre of the Sorrows* was a difficult play to act, Brooks Atkinson recognized it for the "glorious

---

[1] See p. 537.

drama" it is. Synge, he declared, was "the man who could make the English drama dance with loveliness and rapture," and poured "all his love for the greenness of Ireland into this literary and dramatic incantation with its sadness and tenderness and its sorrow over the cruelty of men." And Richard Watts, Jr., writing in the *New York Post,* reminded his readers that the play "provides a most complete answer to those who have wondered whether the author of *The Playboy of the Western World* and *Riders to the Sea* would have continued to grow in stature if he had lived."

Synge appears to have faced a difficult problem. He not only found it necessary to pitch his verbal music higher than he had done in the plays he had devoted to the Irish peasantry, but he had to write the play in a heroic vein that is virtually a lost art in our century. He was actually still at work on *Deirdre* when he succumbed to cancer, and the unfinished state of the final manuscript is apparent in the incomplete utilization of the grotesque character Owen. In a list of characters of the published play, he is described as Conchubor's attendant and spy, but his role is of slight consequence to the plot.

Nevertheless, Synge acquitted himself splendidly of the task he undertook at the suggestion of Yeats. (Apparently, he had long felt drawn to the subject of the star-crossed lovers who defy King Conchubor. We surmise this from the fact that he translated a portion of an eighteenth-century manuscript, *The Fate of the Children of Uisenach,* into English during one of his early trips to the Aran Islands.) He made other Deirdre plays seem tenuous because he wrote as a tragedian rather than as a nationalist.

He was keenly aware of the tangled web of human destiny and disillusioned about the possibility of happiness; he was also resigned to an early death. The irony and pathos of the play came naturally to him. Devoted to simplicity and a past master of a poetic but colloquial Irish dialogue, he also created a Deirdre who is not a stilted legendary figure. He gave her a resemblance to a Wicklow peasant lass until destiny transfigures her into a timeless heroine. Tempering the romanticism of the ancient tale, moreover, he took account of the precariousness of a seven-year-long idyll, during which a man may tire of an obscure life with the woman he loves and, evidently to the distress of some admirers, Synge concluded Deirdre's and Naisi's last scene together with bitter words; the lovers who are about to die separately for their great love quarrel before they part forever. In the midst of a movement which brought Irish writers and the Abbey Theatre's players closely together, Synge remained the somewhat mordant man whose only unqualified allegiance was to his art. "In the arts," as Yeats wrote in his diary, "he knew no language but his own." Only the genius of Synge during the first decade of the Celtic

Renaissance could have mingled nectar and acid, high romance and abrasive realism, in a single play.

In *Deirdre of the Sorrows,* Synge wrote a play which supersedes everything with its own inviolable essence and supplants both realistic observation and the soft seductions of romantic sentiment. In Paris he had once declared, "We should unite stoicism, asceticism, and ecstasy." A better prescription for composing a tragedy could hardly be found, and Synge met its conditions admirably, although the "asceticism"—the restraint he exercised in the treatment of physical passion and sensuous luxuriance— may remain unnoticed while the rich music of his dialogue weaves its spell. A hard truth is served, and nothing is left for tears as the play arrives at the concluding Sophoclean speeches. It can, indeed, be admitted that the range of *Deirdre of the Sorrows* is not particularly wide for the modern mind, but it rises to those high peaks where the air is clear and the light dazzling while so many contemporary playwrights leave us maundering in the valleys.

Other playwrights, in Ireland, Britain, and the United States, escaped from both boulevard and coterie cosmopolitan theatre into folk theatre, but got bogged down in it. They wasted their talent so far as the professional stage outside their immediate surroundings is concerned. Or their talent, quickly desiccated, never sent up more than a few shoots. That is the tragedy of the regional theatre movement of the United States that started with so promising a prospect in the nineteen-tens. The authors of hundreds of short or full-length "little theatre" pieces have all been frustrated by a superfetation of hayseed and phonetic verbiage. Even a rare *Porgy and Bess* and *Green Grow the Lilacs* coming out of "regionalism" did not assure such writers as the Du Bose Heywards and Lynn Riggs the stature they seemed capable of achieving. The exquisite talent of E. P. Conkle has been largely rusticated, and it is very fortunate, indeed, that the praiseworthy persistence of William Inge has brought him out of the company of mere retailers of Midwestern local color.

Paul Green alone achieved stature in a regionalist setting, and this largely by a natural association of local color with issues of a large ambience in the case of *In Abraham's Bosom, The House of Connelly, Johnny Johnson,* the one-act masterpiece *Hymn to the Rising Sun,* and the dramatization of Richard Wright's *Native Son.* Paul Green's fine conscience and good will combined with his training as a thinker (he taught philosophy at the University of California) enabled him to give more than local interest to the Negro and Southern-white life which supplied the base of his writing. And a close study of this highly endowed writer would reveal how much further he could have advanced the modern theatre if more austerity of temperament and art, and perhaps a deeper turbulence, had found place in his work. The austerity in Synge's soul and in his world-outlook, along with a curious uneasiness which could not be appeased by sociology (good sociologist though he proved to be in his early book *The Aran Islands*), made a greater dramatist of him than he would have become as a mere writer of folk-pieces.

V. FEDERICO GARCÍA LORCA

The same course of moving toward folk-drama while assimilating estheticism and, at the same time, transcending provinciality can be traced in the career of Federico García Lorca, who was one of the century's greatest lyric poets and became one of its ablest poetic dramatists. If anything, the temptation of estheticism was greater in his case than in Synge's because he could prevail so much more certainly with it, in so far as one *can* prevail with it. A good poet can carry a good deal of formalism as ballast for his art without foundering. But Lorca was also adept, without bohemian mountebankery, in surrealism, and he began to write plays of some consequence at a time when theatricalist styles were very much in vogue.

Painter, musician, actor, and stage director, as well as playwright, Lorca was obviously more inclined toward the theatrical mode of expression than a retiring man of letters such as Synge was. Had Lorca elected to play at dramatics as a sophisticated game, he could have carried it off with rare ingenuity, and he would have added true poetic sensibility to the performance. Had he chosen, instead, the Copeau-influenced moderate "pure in heart and pure in wisdom" kind of theatrical playwriting we find in Obey at his best, it is probable that Lorca would have succeeded, too. In fact, he revealed all of the above-described qualities supremely in *The Love of Don Perlimplín for Belisa in His Garden*.

To the student of "pure" theatre nothing would be more rewarding than a close study of this play of changing moods and identities as a man of fifty, married to a voluptuous girl, invents a lover for her and kills himself for her, in order to teach her the meaning of love. The lines themselves are movement—lines like Belisa's

> *Amor, amor,*
> *Entre mis muslos cerrados*
> *nada como un pez el sol . . .*
> *Gallo que se va la noche!*
> *Que no se vaya, no!*

for which "Love, love. Enclosed by my thighs, the sun swims like a fish . . . Cock, the night is going! Don't let it go, no!" is surely no dramatic or poetic equivalent.

The décor and the costuming are fantastically theatrical in every respect. Among the theatricalist details provided by Lorca are an extravagantly large bed, five balconies to the bedroom with five ladders hung to the ground, a man's hat beneath each of them!, and Don Perlimplín seated in bed with decorated gilded horns fully sprouted from his forehead. The quick unrealistic shifts of scene and the action, which is entirely histrionic as the husband impersonates the invented, entirely non-existent lover, are especially theatrical. In Lorca's play, all elements are a single essence, so that it is impossible in *Don Perlimplín* to make any distinction between a play-text and theatre, whereas in the usual realistic play, regardless of the relevance of its so-called ideas, the pattern is the clumsy one of separate "content" or word-action and largely supplementary stage business for the actor. (And the same thing is true of most verse drama written from the time of Stephen Phillips to the time of Maxwell Anderson, with *Paolo and Francesco* and *Key Largo* as especially unfortunate examples.) Jean-Louis Barrault and his company could do justice to *Don Perlimplín*. But so unused to this kind of writing are we in America that there isn't an acting company here that could perform Lorca's little play credibly. And Shakespeare's plays, let us face the fact, don't fare any better here, to take the Olivia de Havilland *Romeo and Juliet* and the Katharine Hepburn *As You Like It* as familiar examples, regardless of the fact that the one failed and the other succeeded commercially. We may be less aware of this deficiency only in the Margaret Webster management of Shakespeare's heavier artillery because the dramatic charge is so much stronger, but it was easily apparent in the Paul Robeson *Othello* except when Ferrer's Iago was on the stage. (Fortunately, he was on it often, thanks to Shakespeare's theatrical acumen.) We tend to let the words in a play be one thing, and the theatre in it another.

In his major plays, *Blood Wedding, Yerma,* and *The House of Bernarda Alba,* Lorca retained all the theatrical afflatus I have lamely tried to suggest in the above-made references to *Don Perlimplín.* The fact that it has not been possible to capture that afflatus in New York productions accounts, in part, for the failure of these later plays to get their due credit from audiences and reviewers. Lorca is simultaneously poet and theatrician in his use of a lullaby in the first scene and of a lament in the last of *Blood Wedding.* He is no less effective in the almost Dionysian clothes-washing scene set on the bank of a mountain stream, in the second act of *Yerma.* He is also a formalist, especially in the forest scene of *Blood Wedding* (Act III, Scene I), in which, drawing upon the classic tradition of Spanish theatre, he uses Death and the Moon as allegorical figures to prefigure a fatal duel. Properly played, that scene is true magic, and it can also constrict the heart with unease and tragic pity.

Yet Lorca is so much more than a theatrician in his mature work that he could never be confused with a coterie writer. He is, on the one hand, local and rooted in a people's way of living and feeling that supersedes literary notion-refining and vacuous theatre-mongering. And, on the other hand, he became something more than a mere writer of substantial folk plays; he became a tragedian. We have evidence, moreover, that he was consciously moving away from lyrical drama toward poetic realism in his drama of family pride and frustration *The House of Bernarda Alba.* He was moving, without losing "poetry" or "theatre," toward cosmopolitan analytical drama and social drama when a Falangist firing squad executed him in 1936.

New York reviewers who turned thumbs down on the tragedy when it was staged by Boris Tumarin for ANTA with a cast that spoke and played in several distinct styles will lift an eyebrow at my expressing admiration for *The House of Bernarda Alba.* But they would at least agree, I believe, that the play gave them less an impression that Lorca belongs to his beloved Andalusian countryside than did *Blood Wedding,* staged by the same sensitive but unfortunate-in-casting director for New Stages. Had Lorca survived the Spanish Civil War (he was only thirty-six when he was murdered outside Granada—irrationally, since he belonged to no party), he might have fully entered the stream of modern drama that crosses most frontiers. Edwin Honig, in his excellent little book *García Lorca,* quotes him as declaring to a newspaper, "I hate him who is a Spaniard only to be nothing more. I am a brother to everybody. . . ."

VI. YEATS: THE LIMITS OF DRAMA

Lorca's virtues as a poet-playwright cannot be felt by us. As Stark Young noted in reviewing a 1935 production of *Blood Wedding* under the strange title *Bitter Oleander,* we are not at home with his passion, in which simplicity and glow are combined. We are not attuned to his language, only partially translatable, which is "hot with the variety and multiplication of images, images that are like new bodies, new and convincing presences, or sudden revelations in light, and that are cold with their precision and finality." We have no such difficulty, however, in responding to the language of Yeats, which does not come at us veiled in translation. We recognized him quickly as a good dramatic lyricist when he wrote his flowing early plays, such as his *Countess Cathleen* of the year 1892, his *Deirdre* of 1907, and *The King's Threshold* of 1904. We have no doubt that he is a lyric dramatist of great originality in such later plays, all written between 1917 and the year of his death 1939, as *The Dreaming of the Bones, Calvary, The Resurrection, A Full Moon in March,* and *Purgatory.*

It is no exaggeration to say that although far less influential through his example after 1917 than Maeterlinck was in the eighteen-nineties, Yeats became the greatest and most durable symbolist poet of the drama. Paradoxically, he became that only by virtually exiling himself from the theatre. That is, from the theatre as a public institution. And the paradox is compounded by the fact that more than any other writer in Ireland—or, for that matter, in the rest of the world—Yeats was responsible for the creation of the Irish national stage, and for bringing publicly effective playwrights such as Lady Gregory, Synge, and the great O'Casey into it.

Yeats left the field of folk drama to other Abbey Theatre playwrights after delivering a number of romantic tributes to Irish legend and one graceful nod to Celtic fairyland with *The Land of Heart's Desire* in 1894. Eventually, he gave up writing original plays for public performance entirely, confining himself to the writing of plays intended for production in drawing-rooms. Paradoxically, again, it is only then that he became a powerful playwright. And this fact should effectively silence extreme adulators of "theatricalism" who praise an Obey or Cocteau solely for making theatre without asking *what* they made with theatre, as it should even more easily dispose of show-business addicts who maintain that a playwright cannot be proficient in his craft unless he stays in the marketplace. If that were true, it would be difficult to explain why many playwrights write their most effective plays *before* they have become seasoned showmen.[1] And there have been writers of noteworthy plays, vastly superior, let us say, to the theatrically so experienced Cocteau's *The Eagle Has Two Heads,* whose traffic with any sort of stage was slight—Buechner, Musset, Turgenev, Tolstoy. Some writers never saw their plays on the stage, some never worked with an acting company, some became playwrights while functioning primarily as novelists, lyric poets—or physicians. Theatre knowledge alone could have given Shakespeare *The Merry Wives of Windsor* or *The Taming of the Shrew.* It could not have given him *Hamlet, Macbeth,* or *King Lear.*

Sooner or later somebody will have to whittle down the overblown reputation of modernist theatricalism to size. Somebody will have to put the relationship of theatre and drama on a more carefully considered basis than it appears to have at present in some avant-garde circles. First the old

[1] Maxwell Anderson has yet to excel his early performance in *What Price Glory?,* written while he was still a journalist; Behrman, his early brilliant comedy *The Second Man.* Pirandello reached his peak with *Six Characters,* Molnar with *Liliom.* Synge never equaled the perfection of *Riders to the Sea,* written when he was still a tyro in the theatre. Eliot's *Murder in the Cathedral* is superior, in terms of his poetic aspirations and our expectations from him, to his later work for the stage; it more fully expresses its theme, and with none of *The Cocktail Party*'s question-begging and descent from his poet's pinnacle.

scholars, mostly Victorian, tilted the drama too sharply toward literature. Then the young scholars, mostly avant-gardists (with Brander Matthews as a predecessor whom they would not care to acknowledge), tilted it toward the theatre. My own, apparently old-fashioned, view, is that a dramatist must have something to say that is worth saying and that carries weight, whether in comic or "serious" terms, both on the stage and on the printed page.

Yeats had his say, out of the ripeness of his isolation. More or less isolated even when he became a Senator of Eire, and essentially alone even when he dabbled with others in fashionable supernaturalism, he made both poetry and drama a private experience. In his later dramatic work, and in revising earlier pieces, Yeats was no longer making nationalist gestures in the manner of *Kathleen ni Houlihan,* even when he treated Irish myth and legend. He no longer found the calling of a poet (triumphant in the early and defeated in the later versions of *The King's Threshold*), the passion of nationalism, and the passion of love subjects for lyric rhapsody. He became a fully grown, if also ingrown, complex writer.

Those who know his latter-day plays will rightly remind me that Yeats became a deliberate theatricalist precisely in these works. He constructed many as dance-dramas in the highly formal style of the Japanese Noh plays to which Pound had called his attention. The "Noh" stimulated him to find a short form of drama with which to move out of the professional theatre as the Irish playgoing public became increasingly distasteful to him after the demonstration at the Abbey against *The Playboy of the Western World* in 1907 of which the later demonstrations against O'Casey's *The Plough and the Stars* in 1926 were a painful reminder. Much has been made of Yeats's expressive use of screens and masks, musical accompaniment, dance movement, and theatrical artifice such as the convention of having a secondary character mime, laugh, or speak the protagonist's words while the latter merely dances out the action. The many formal details of Yeats's plays need not detain us here, they are many and beautiful. And they have the fascination of theatre.

The formal presentation also distances the drama for the spectator, surely an appropriate procedure in the case of theatre in a drawing room. At the same time, Yeats's dramatic verse, now as controlled as his latter-day lyrics, no longer came, as in the early plays, in long passages of narcotic verbal music while the action of the play was at a standstill. The poetry had precision; at times, the stabbing punctuation of machine-gun fire. Nobody in our century except Lorca wrote more dramatic verse dialogue and narration, as well as lyrics, for the modern stage. It may be said, then, that his poetry, too, became increasingly theatre-shaped. Rarely have modern playwrights written verse lines for the actor comparable to

> ". . . but here's a work
> That should be done, and that work needs
> No bird's beak nor claw, but a man,
> The imperfection of a man."

or

> "I have heard that a donkey carries its young
> Longer than any beast,
> Thirteen months it must carry it.
> All that trouble and nothing to show for it,
> Nothing but just another donkey."[2]

But the point is precisely that Yeats was able to rebuild the chemical structure of the drama which the symbolist and the theatricalist theatre tended to dissolve. That he did so while becoming more, rather than less, of a symbolist and theatricalist is all the more to his credit. He accomplished this feat in a singularly individual manner that accorded with his particular views, with his "criticism of life," if you will. There is extra-theatrical substance, or engagement with vision and some sort of passion, in his dramatic work. He did not create theatre in a void even if he compressed it into a nutshell. But then the atom is even smaller. In drama, the explosion is the test of power—though it is hardly the test of ultimate value.

"Value!" That is the question for any final judgment on Yeats's dramatic achievement. That the plays were not written for a large public performance is not a conclusive indictment. Neither Ibsen nor Shaw had the large audiences and long runs for their plays Broadway has increasingly required playwrights to have for purely economic reasons. That Yeats's plays are short, and some are extremely brief, does not detract from any excellence to be claimed for *Calvary, A Full Moon in March, The Resurrection,* or *Purgatory.* If length is a consideration for public performance, the plays can be given as curtain-raisers or after-pieces, or several of them can form a single Yeats program. That some of them are not easy to follow in detail is certainly no fair test of their merit. Although it is true that they need explication (they have begun to receive it), they should not prove essentially obscure in performance. If I believe that Yeats carried his plays and the modern drama into a blind-alley, my reason is that his writing tended toward abstraction, the correlate and perhaps cause of which is Yeats's negativism. There is no more than half a life to his characters.

I am not troubled, as some Irish and English writers are, by the violence and the sadism or sado-masochism in these plays, for which psychological

[2] *The Herne's Egg* in: *The Collected Plays of W. B. Yeats,* The Macmillan Co., 1953, pp. 427-428.

explanations have been offered. Men are killed with curious abandon in *The Herne's Egg* and its heroine Attracta is raped by seven men in one evening. The swineherd suitor to the queen in *A Full Moon in March* is beheaded after offering her a night of love so that "she shall bring forth her farrow in the dung," and the lady stains herself with the blood trickling from the head. And in *Purgatory*, a parricide stabs his son with the same knife with which he had long ago slain his father!—In the first place, the violence is often symbolical of some idea, such as that, to quote Eric Bentley on *A Full Moon in March*, "our wintry and saintly virginity must descend into the dung of passion." In the second place, the action in the plays is distanced by formalistic devices when it isn't actually off-stage.[3]

The violence is not objectionable in itself. But it is a symptom of the negativism that overcame Yeats, who, for all his activity, resigned from his country and his century, if not indeed from the world. This was a personally conditioned act, although we may also regard it as a continuation of the withdrawal or introversion of the art-for-art's sake *"décadence"* of the eighteen-nineties. Shaw, it will be remembered, fought it strenuously. Yeats, a member of the *fin-de-siècle* coterie of that decade, was galvanized into action by the nationalist movement in Ireland. He never belonged to it deeply, however; he was appalled by its activism, an activism that divided him from that long-loved revolutionary amazon Maud Gonne, and he retired into his private visions as the struggle in Ireland became exacerbated after 1914.

Much information has been printed about Yeats's flight into the spirit world, and there is no need to recapitulate it. The relevant point here is that Yeats set out to represent "soul" states rather than people on the stage. His plays were short because he had a dramatist's tact or sense of strategy; he must have sensed that his interest in the inner life, more abstract than psychological, required economical expression. He took some story, mostly from legend, and extracted an essence of idea from it. He turned a story into an extended, more or less activated symbol. That is as far as he would go. Artistic integrity would not allow him to blow up the idea into a ramshackle plot for a full evening's performance.

As he stated in *The Irish Dramatic Movement*, he aimed at achieving an "activity of the souls of the characters." But an "activity of the soul" is one thing and a character is something else. Yeats never fails to express the former, but only here and there, as in his portrait of a roistering an-

---

[3] Since there is less formalistic distancing in *Purgatory* than in other plays by Yeats, and since the stabbing is an on-stage action, this play has been considered too horrifying. I shared that reaction on first reading it, but no longer do so. On further acquaintance with the little piece, I found myself fascinated rather than horrified.

cient king in *The Herne's Nest,* does he more than outline a person. Characters, especially if they are the protagonists, are usually either abbreviated almost out of existence or refined into a symbol. In *The Poet in the Theatre*[4] Ronald Peacock correctly points out that Yeats departed from the convention of drama to be found equally in Sophocles and Shakespeare. Yeats tended to throw away the lifelike experiences from which spiritual or intellectual experience emanates, and gave us only the latter. Drama became for him mainly a way of externalizing his fantasy world—chiefly, an abstract world. He dealt largely not so much with humanity as with symbols of humanity. At the opposite extreme we have drama, such as Shakespeare's, so identified "with the life of emotion and action of passion and will, that it seems to have nothing to do with symbols of any kind, but directly with 'life.'" I know of no better description than Peacock's of the kind of playwriting also to be found in Ibsen and Chekhov. To seem to deal directly with life is *realism,* regardless of the dramatic structure and the prose or verse employed by the author. It is this that constitutes the simple humanism of dramatic art. It was too rarely present in Yeats's plays.

I believe Mr. Peacock errs when he suggests that Yeats's kind of playwriting points toward the future. Yeats's poetic work for the theatre after 1918 is *sui generis.* Yeats wrote that the drama is "an energy, an eddy of life purified from everything but itself." His statement is acceptable only as a sort of "theory of limits," as an ideal that the drama approaches. As an aim completely *achieved,* such drama would annihilate the work of Sophocles, Shakespeare, Molière, Racine, and Ibsen alike. A play that is only an "energy," like a play that is only an "idea," is not a play at all, but only a Platonic archetype. (Or, if you will, a Cheshire Cat's grin without the cat!) Yeats himself gives us more than an archetype, more than a mere energy, in his work. He left out of many plays, however, so much of "the life of emotion and action," so much that we associate with natural human motivation and behavior, that the work seems abstract. The substantiality of life is sacrificed to its abstract significance. *Substance* is sacrificed to *essence.* Not entirely, it is true, but to a great degree. To too great a degree to allow the drama to serve as an expression of the age and a mirror to nature. "Nature" can be an abstraction in modern physics, as it is in geometry, but this is not natural as human beings experience it. And it is for viewing nature as existence rather than as essence that we are drawn to the stage.

It will not surprise me if Yeats's plays come to be regarded as the extreme limit of dramatic art rather than as a starting point for modern

[4] Harcourt, Brace & Co., 1946. See pp. 116-128 on Yeats.

playwriting. If the aristocratic Noh play form became the extreme limit of dramatic abstraction in the Orient, it is reasonable to assume that Yeatsian drama will serve no more than as a limit in the Occident. As for the general public and the critic who does not make the niceties of the art his avocation, who can reasonably blame them for not recognizing Yeats as a fully equipped playwright rather than as a dramatist *manqué*.[5]

Was he also a thinker *manqué*? There is sufficient reason to believe so. Rarely self-indulgent with respect to his profession as poet, he was altogether too self-indulgent for philosophy. He liked to dramatize himself as the sage as well as the artist, as the plunger into profundities as well as the high priest of beauty, and he had the gift of charming others into believing or half-believing him. He had a free-wheeling speculative disposition, which is hardly a substitute for disciplined thought. "We were the last romantics," he himself declared in speaking of lost friends. He was content to make himself into a Parzival type of innocent for the sake of poetry and a sort of poetic wisdom woven into the fantastic cosmic scheme of *The Vision,* given, it is said, in *automatic* writing through the poet's wife. Whether or not he took absolute stock in his "gyres" and "phases of the Moon" as the secret of the universe, he made much ado about them, and he was apparently a ready victim of spiritualist chicanery.

His faith in the enduring perfection of the "artefact," of the work of art, is the least questionable of his beliefs. But he was not content to consider the poet as a "maker," he insisted on his also being a *magus*. The poet, moreover, was to become the seer not by looking outward at the world as Shaw did, but by looking inward—into a Jungian world of the unconscious where the archetypal racial memory and human wisdom presumably preside. Many of the later plays—*A Full Moon in March* is an example—deal with "archetypal" fantasies of the unconscious. In this respect, he was cousin to the surrealists as well as to the earlier symbolists. The archetype rather than that of which it is an archetype became for Yeats the prime subject for drama.

[5] Yeats's prose plays after the first decade of the century, *The Player Queen* (on which William Becker has published an excellent study in the *Sewanee Review*) and *The Words Upon the Window Pane* may be to some degree exempted from my analysis. The former, published in 1922, may seem obscure to the inattentive, but it does develop an action in terms of characters whose thought and behavior have some direct context of "reality." In *The Words Upon the Window Pane,* published in 1934, the main character, the ghostly Jonathan Swift, is never on the stage, he is merely a voice interrupting a séance. Far from being a defect, however, Yeats's exercise of restraint here is tactically right. Potent irony is present in the contrast between the tragic eighteenth-century Dean and the shoddy twentieth-century clients at the séance. The moving conversations between Swift and his Vanessa are annoying interruptions to all but one of the living characters. The incandescence of Yeats's scorn for the second-rate in life makes for life in this short drama.

I believe it is a poverty of subject matter that ultimately limits Yeats's distinguished artistry. We are wrong to separate content from form, it is said. But I am old-fashioned enough to say that his content, though occasionally fascinating, is insufficiently rewarding; that he gave us "form" without sufficient substance. It will probably be the occupation of our literary exegetes for many a year to disprove this charge. But a plenitude of discoverable subtleties does not necessarily amount to enough substance for a vital, meaningful theatre. For realization on the stage, the matter of a playwright must develop a distinctly rewarding *gross action* as well as *refinements*. None of the plays the world has considered great since the *Agamemnon* of Aeschylus has consisted of just "implication" or just "symbols."

Perhaps Yeats pushed his philosophy in symbolic shapes so far into the foreground of the plays because he had so little else positive or capable of being activated to offer. He was far more fortunate in the poems of his maturity. The idea symbolized by images in his non-dramatic poetry is not only usually concrete, often superbly so, but altogether ample for the short compass of the composition. (Only when the image is also an esoteric "emblem" for Yeats does it create difficulties for the uninitiated reader.) But an image, I venture to say, cannot ever sustain a play.

Arland Ussher[6] writes from Dublin that Yeats "seemed to build an art out of his rejections," that he "chose the dying world for text," and that "Yeats was always for good and ill, a little outside of time and space." One can hardly consider these attributes, if Ussher is right, the best equipment for a dramatist. Not even as alternatives, in my opinion, to the too facile affirmations and adaptations to the world of time and space we may properly debit to many American (and also many European) playwrights.

VII. MAXWELL ANDERSON: THE POET IN SHOW BUSINESS

It may be instructive to conclude this review of attempts to reconstitute modern drama on an imaginative and poetic basis by considering an approach that contrasts sharply with that of Yeats. We might call it the non-hermetic approach, and Maxwell Anderson may be chosen to represent it, even more than Christopher Fry. Anderson has been at work for a longer period of time, having started his playwriting career in the early

---

[6] *Three Great Irishmen*, The Devin-Adair Company, New York, 1953, pp. 104, 112, 107. It is noteworthy that in *Calvary* Yeats makes Judas boast to Christ "and now You cannot even save me," and Lazarus complain, "You took my death, give me your death instead. . . . You travel towards the death I am denied." (*Collected Plays*, pp. 292, 290.)

nineteen-twenties. His first poetic tragedy *White Desert* came in 1923; his first successful one, *Elizabeth the Queen,* in 1930. He has had five more or less unqualified successes in the field of verse drama as against one or two by Fry. All his playwriting has been directed, moreover, at the commercial theatre, whereas Fry has often written for the experimental little art theatres and the church. The American author does not even hesitate to arrange a match in *Winterset* between high tragedy and gangster melodrama, and for nearly two acts, the wedding proceeds almost smoothly. We may call Maxwell Anderson the poet in show business. He has proved adept enough to qualify for that title.

It is a derogatory one, when used by the literary snob, though I don't know why this should be so, since Shakespeare was also thoroughly engaged in show business as actor, shareholder, and playwright; Molière even more so. It is not show business *per se* but the quality of the playwriting written for the marketplace that matters. When that quality is at its best, show business is a glorious enterprise rather than a meretricious one. And Anderson's aspiration for the theatre, which he once called the "phoenix of the arts," became as exalted as anyone's early in his career.

Is the drama to be exalted above everyday experiences, the commonplace life of the machine-age, the bourgeois or proletarian characters of the realistic drama? Anderson has the same high aims as the neo-romanticists of Rostand's calibre, as the devotees of myth or legend, and as the reworkers of classic themes. He wrote three plays about Elizabethan royalty (*Elizabeth the Queen, Mary of Scotland,* and *Anne of the Thousand Days*); he paid his respects to legend with the ghosts of Henrik Hudson's crew in *High Tor;* he reworked the *Medea* theme, giving it a New England background, in *The Wingless Victory.* Shall we say that this is hardly enough, that the plays must have implications for modern man? Anderson is unfailingly obliging. He has drawn parallels to and lessons for our times in a Valley Forge play and a Rudolph of Hapsburg one (*The Masque of Kings*) and a Saint Joan one (*Joan of Lorraine*), and a *Journey to Jerusalem* whose subject is the young Jesus of Nazareth and the revolutionists of his times, and a *Barefoot in Athens,* whose hero is Socrates. The struggle for political power (the Elizabethan plays), the question whether revolution is good or bad (*The Masque of Kings*), the need for racial tolerance, the challenge of free inquiry—one or more of these and other "social problems" have agitated him. And as if this were not enough, he has treated contemporary situations directly. The springboard of *Winterset* is the Sacco and Vanzetti case of the twenties. *High Tor* shows a young man defying the age of the machine and its predatory representatives. *Key Largo* deals with the dual subject of the Civil War in Spain and the struggle against gangsterism in Florida, U.S.A., *Candle in the Wind* with the French underground during the German occupation, *The Eve of Saint Mark* with America's participation in the Second World War.

But does Anderson break up realistic dramaturgy and employ "new" —that is, non-realistic—forms of drama? Does he use the theatre expressively or imaginatively? It would be a great comfort to be able to say that he doesn't do so at all—a great comfort, that is, to those who do not want to enroll a "commercial" playwright in the corps of modernists, especially if he happens to be an American. And, of course, the litmus paper test consists of determining whether the playwright makes his drama "theatre" —as if any successful playwright, whether Shakespeare or Dion Boucicault, Sophocles or the authors of *The Front Page, You Can't Take It with You* and *Life with Father,* didn't!

The fact that Anderson has been able to play rings around most of the rather tautological "drama for theatre" advocates ever since he wrote *What Price Glory?* is so obvious that it does not have to be established. That he has sometimes used the theatre lamely has been the result, variously, of the hazards of the trade, poor plot, didacticism, or declamatory verbosity in writing verse. When any or all these errors were conspicuous, the particular play failed and Anderson *pro tem* ceased be successfully "commercial," which is the fate of every showman when his sense of showmanship has left him. And if this answer is too general to satisfy the inquirer, it is not difficult to establish Anderson's readiness to depart from realistic dramaturgy.

An example is the pseudo-Pirandellian technique of *Joan of Lorraine,* in which the story of Joan is presented through the staging of a play about her, the protests of the leading actress that she doesn't understand the play, discussions with the director, interruptions of the narrative sequence, and so on. *Joan of Lorraine* is a play about a play, and a performance about a performance, with intellectual irruptions, and nearly everything that should qualify its author as a *bona fide* "theatricalist" playwright. The historical plays are rather routinely constructed, but even in these we can find "stylization" in the use of soliloquy. *Anne of the Thousand Days,* in particular, has soliloquies as a frame for the play. Anderson even uses them in counterpoint, where Henry VIII at one end of the stage speaks his piece and Anne Boleyn at the other end (in the Tower of London) has her say about their love and marriage. In *High Tor,* fantasy crops up in the critical situation and affects the decisions of the main character, and *The Eve of Saint Mark* contains a dream sequence that relates a soldier at the front with his family on the farm.

Without even elaborating on the author's use of music and the non-realistic conventions of music-drama in *Knickerbocker Holiday* and *Lost in the Stars,* we can say that, except for avoiding surrealism and outright expressionism, Anderson has employed every avant-garde device at some time or other. Proving, I should say, that there is nothing easier in dramaturgy than a departure from realistic structure! Even otherwise incompetent playwrights, I know from my professorial experience, can play tricks with the time sequence, give a play a narrative frame, interrupt the objective course of events with dream sequences, write soliloquies, suspend the laws of cause and effect, and introduce a play within the main play. All these assignments are easier to accomplish than to create a number of truly dimensioned and believable characters, write good dialogue, establish a strong and convincing climax—and, not least important, have something to say. I imagine that Mr. Anderson has regarded the formal stylization of a play as the *elementary* part of his task. It is noteworthy that although he has often commented on dramatic art, he has not discussed any of the theatrical devices he has employed in his plays.

Anderson, in short, has found no difficulty in utilizing the modernist methods of decomposing realistic dramaturgy. Moreover, unlike some rampant modernists, he has been able to attract a general audience rather than a coterie. He has prevailed in the contemporary theatre, such as it is, and not on its periphery. He has been able to develop distinctly communicable plots and creditable characters, and to speak quite relevantly to the ordinary playgoers of our time. He has "rebuilt" the drama and at the same time put it on a paying basis. His has been the pragmatic approach, which has also been the Christopher Fry approach in *The Lady's Not for Burning* and *Venus Observed,* the Anouilh-Fry approach in *Ring Around the Moon,* and, to a degree, the Eliot approach in *The Cocktail Party.* The truth is that there has not been a single element in modern theatricalism that could not be imported into the commercial theatre and turned into ready cash. Only genius cannot be imported.[1] Yes, the modern drama has been rebuilt without difficulty, and large audiences have accepted liberties taken with realistic dramaturgy without blinking an eyelash. I recall Stark Young saying to me at the "second night" of *Our Town,* "Isn't it remarkable how quickly one adjusts oneself to a stage convention!" Experience, especially in so eclectic an age as ours, proves this point conclusively.

There is, however, no proof that any particular style of drama or theatre guarantees the creation of masterpieces, or of even satisfactory work. And Maxwell Anderson sustains the point as well as anyone else in our times. We do not have to go as far as to maintain that he never wrote a better play than his realistic war comedy of the year 1924 *What Price*

---

[1] We may recall the profitable use of expressionism in Moss Hart's *Lady in the Dark* and, earlier, in *Beggar on Horseback*—or the successful use of Cubism in window displays—or *surréaliste* dance in a "girlie" show.

Glory?, although I myself subscribe to this view. Nor do we have to labor the obvious fact that *Joan of Lorraine,* his most theatricalist play, is inferior to plays written by him in a more conventional form, and certainly to *High Tor* and *Winterset.* The point of any evaluation of Anderson's poetic plays—verse plays, high tragedy, fantasy, or *poésie de theatre,* to use Cocteau's label for imaginatively and theatrically built drama, is simply whether their quality has measured up to both Mr. Anderson's aspirations and to general expectations concerning the value of poetic theatre.

Whether a positive or a negative judgment is rendered, it must be based on specific qualities of execution, concerning which I propose to say nothing that has not actually been advanced before. Mr. Anderson has proved that he can write with eloquence and *brio,* but it is also true that his verse is generally undistinguished. It is, as a rule, flabby versification, less than remarkable in imagery. Prolixity, too, often substitutes for cogent, final statement, and rhetoric does the work usually better accomplished for poetry by associated images. In other words, the playwright is conventionally poetic. He also tends to conventionalize tragic characterization. He is at his best when he gives his heroes and heroines their "tragic flaws," as in the case of his Elizabeth, Essex and Anne Boleyn, for Anderson is realistic about human nature, as he is also about society in general. But he is considerably less wary whenever he feels obliged to "redeem" characters for a tragic climax. He allocates to most of his tragic figures the standardized romantic gestures: Essex, in *Elizabeth the Queen,* goes to the executioner's block in preference to some day dethroning the queen he loves, while Elizabeth is ready to share her throne with him. Mary of Scotland dies in order to assure the throne to her son James. Mio, in *Winterset,* renounces the possibility of clearing his father's name and allows the gangster Trock to escape arrest in order to protect Miriamne's brother. An inspirational view of tragic characterization usually asserts itself in this poet-playwright's work.

Anderson tends to be quite effective when he writes in scorn and anger. He has large sympathies, and he can create robust humor. But except for revealing the mixed motivations of characters, which he does well enough, he has tended to pump his heroes and heroines with the conventional pop of heroism, whereas Yeats, who deals with characters more remote than Anderson's, refrains from conventionalizing his tragic characters. Magnification rather than illumination is Anderson's way of treating tragic character, as if he were bent upon grafting grandeur on to the theatre as virtually the sole means of saving it from commonplaceness. As in versification, so also in tragic characterization Anderson has functioned almost as if he believed that a poetic playwright is a decorator of speech and a decorator of souls. He has not been the first anti-realist of the modern stage to inflate and gild the drama since the advent of *Cyrano de Bergerac*. But Rostand's play is, fortunately, a "heroic comedy," as the subtitle reads, rather than a heroic tragedy. It makes clever use of a theme a friend of mine described as a struggle between the "pose" and the "nose." Anderson has tended to present the pose *as* the nose; that is, to make the pose the equivalent of reality. He is certainly not the worst offender among neo-romanticists (there is always D'Annunzio!) in allowing his *dramatis personae* to posture, for he does give dimensions to characters. His Henry VIII and Anne Boleyn, for example, are quite well realized, and his success with these characters, greater than his success with his royal theme, is reflected here and there in *Anne of the Thousand Days* in improved versification. Anderson, to my mind, merely exemplifies the dangers of making a vocation of dramatic *uplift* as a means of superseding modern critical realism, to which he himself contributed vigor in the twenties with *What Price Glory?, Saturday's Children,* and *Gods of the Lightning.*

And here it is, indeed, that noble aspirations can automatically translate themselves into dollar-and-cents show business. As the vogue of historical romances and the Hollywood filmings of these indicate, the public *likes* to be uplifted. When that *frondeur* among modern playwrights Bertolt Brecht gives the public a hero such as Galileo in the play of the same name, a hero who generates critical appraisal and is also self-aware, the complaint one hears is that Brecht is "cold." The audience wants to be made "hot," for isn't Galileo a hero of history. And if he is a hero, why does Brecht take him off his pedestal and fan him with the breeze of critical examination. By commonplace convention, the hero must stand above the public and continue to glow. Sex is allowed him only because sex invariably generates warmth.—A more valid criticism of *Galileo* would be that Brecht didn't realize that his characterization of the Italian scientist was already "cold" enough. Therefore he made it colder by overloading the cooling system of "epic" machinery. Brecht doesn't always know when he is already sufficiently "cold," just as Anderson doesn't always know when he is already sufficiently "hot." Brecht sometimes tries too hard to *instruct,* just as Anderson tries too hard to *uplift.* Certainly, as rendered in the Charles Laughton ANTA production of 1947, the devices for framing and pointing up Galileo's story tended to suggest a sort of progressive-school project for problem children who couldn't be made to interest themselves in the topic without theatrical frills.

In Anderson's case, whether the tragedy has no excessively long furbelows, as in *Elizabeth the Queen,* or has them, as in *Joan of Lorraine,* we can too often note that he is *willing* poetry, exaltation, or ingenious theatre. The work rarely flares up spontaneously, the author does not usually appear to be writing out of a core of fire, as we feel Yeats, as well as Lorca and O'Casey and O'Neill, often do. We feel, rather, that Anderson is an educated man trying to do well by the drama, by himself, and by the audience. Both the artist who wants to supersede humdrum realistic playwriting and the man who does not forget that he is in show business —and the two meet in Anderson's career—are *willing* the art and the commodity value.

He has, it is true, genuine convictions concerning life, society, and politics, as well as concerning dramatic art. He has often spoken out boldly. He spoke out against reckless revolutionary action in *The Masque of Kings,* against fascism in *Key Largo,* against the suppression of intellectual freedom in *Barefoot in Athens.* In his early life he lost academic positions because of tenaciously held beliefs. He is an independent man of good will, and as such entirely deserves our respect. But convictions are not always the same thing as integral passion or vision in art. In our time, O'Neill and O'Casey have often given the impression that a play had been wrung out of their marrow. In the main, Anderson does not even give the impression that his poetic plays have come out of an inviolable sensibility.[2]

As a tragedian, he has certainly seemed *self-elected* rather than *fated.* He seems an epigone of the noble brood that flourished during the classic ages of high tragedy, and the numerous Shakespearian echoes in his plays support this judgment. And so does his verse, which seems less generated by a flame of original imagination or vision than acquired by the reading of good literature, as we would expect from a former college instructor and a notably civilized man. Even his noble rage, in the second act of *Winterset* and here and there in other plays, is not enough to cancel that impression concerning his poetic afflatus. In his efforts to create an inspired theatre, the wheel turns full circle round instead of moving forward. Maxwell Anderson has been a good man to have around in the American theatre, but he, too, has been unable to lead us into the Promised Land of reconstituted dramatic art.

[2] Noticeably, in the first scene of *Winterset* when Trock, the gangster, speaks ill-fitting blank verse.

THE PRODIGALITY
OF SEAN O'CASEY

I

Of the three giants of the new English-speaking theatre, Shaw was released at last from the world of fools to which he played a schoolmaster in vain, and O'Neill, worn down to the semi-paralyzed skeleton of the fine figure of a man we knew, merely lingered to remind us that Fate *is* the ironist he always claimed it was. Only O'Casey is left us from the triumvirate of our theatre, and there is much comfort in the realization that his last play *Cock-a-doodle Dandy,* published in 1949, had more dramatic sinew and vitality than anything written by him since *The Plough and the Stars* a quarter of a century ago. It is no small irony, however, that a theatre very much in need of a breath of greatness is ill at ease whenever the wind blows from the English countryside where Ireland's greatest surviving writer lives in exile. Virtually an exile from the English-speaking theatre as well, O'Casey proudly waits to be invited into the shabby temples of Broadway and London's West End, and he signals to us with play after play that we can have him solely on his own terms. Such independence being most unusual, and also extremely disconcerting when money—money for stage productions—is involved, he enters only the portals of theatrical enterprises poor enough to be able to afford integrity.

Meanwhile the professional theatre deludes itself into believing that it recovers greatness whenever it plays host to synthetic poetic drama. It feels especially virtuous, for example, when it can point to Christopher Fry's *The Lady's Not for Burning,* a play that is, after all, written not only in polysyllables but in extremely clever verse. The professional theatre discovers that it can be more or less at ease with Christopher Fry. A bright talent such as his should always be welcomed, of course, but I suspect that West End and Broadway are not averse to it because it suits their drawing-room mentality. Fry's talent titillates the stage instead of disturbing it. T. S. Eliot's *The Cocktail Party* gets Broadway's and the West End's nod for similar reasons. Its desiccated, if cadenced, philosophy of acceptance ("resign yourself to the fact that you aren't much of anything unless a special Grace has singled you out as one of the elect"—a tinkle of theology after the nature music of St. Francis and the heroic tolling of Loyola!) suits a desiccated intelligentsia. As for the rest of the audience, it can derive pleasure from the very expertly written cocktail conversation

240

with which Eliot occasionally makes Noel Coward look like a dilettante in the art of impolite high comedy.

In such suave company as Fry's and Eliot's, O'Casey seems graceless and devoid of manners—a lumbering giant on whom a dress suit would look like armor. Nor can we expect that the expansive Mr. O'Casey will be considered a proper companion by the current vanguard of New Critics that greatly prefers concentrated, sometimes indeed, constipated, souls and minds whose enigmas invite endless explication. Everybody who is not decently veiled by one or more of the "seven types of ambiguity," is naked in the eyes of the new Alexandrian savants who make and unmake literary reputations among the elect. Such nakedness is considered unseemly, so that for one "new critic" of the prim new literary generation *Death of a Salesman* seemed virtually on a par with Edgar A. Guest's lullabies to Main Street. Nor, to be sure, is O'Casey apt to win support from the contemporary reconstructed "liberals" who exert a literary influence. They have recently discovered "original sin," while O'Casey remains optimistic concerning the essential human being. They mortify themselves with the reflection that the "idea of progress" to which they once clung was a naïve notion inherited from the simple-minded eighteenth-century philosophers, whereas it is evident that O'Casey would rather be naïve than dead.

O'Casey's reputation is not being sparked by any vanguard group. His friends, at least in America, are to be found among "unenlightened" journalists who have a drop of romantic idealism in their veins, and among those "unenlightened" critics who believe with Paul Verlaine that the way to make art is to take "literature" and "wring its neck." (O'Casey, in fact, is always at his worst when he forgets to perform this indelicate, but necessary operation. He forgets perhaps because, as a son of the Dublin poor, he came to literature with difficulty and late in his life.) His champions are individualists among drama critics such as George Jean Nathan, Richard Watts, Jr., and Brooks Atkinson who wear no critical corsets and can therefore follow him in his rugged ascent and enjoy the heady climb.

We must make some allowance, it is true, for the stage that has been remiss in accommodating him, for a number of his plays after 1926 were ill-timed. *The Star Turns Red* came out in 1940 during the Soviet-Nazi pact when communism's stock had dropped sharply in the Western world. His milder *Red Roses for Me,* a recollection of the Dublin Transport Workers strike of 1913, appeared in 1943 when a flareup of conflict between labor and capital was altogether too dangerous to the war effort to be tolerated. On the surface, *Cock-a-doodle-Dandy* is indiscreetly uncomplimentary to the Church of Eire. Perhaps the chief example of poor timing was the appearance of *Purple Dust,* an uproarious travesty on the

British, when England was enduring the blitz and was facing Hitler alone.

It has been O'Casey's fate, indeed, to be always pushing his skiff of talent against the current. Not one of the plays with which he won his early reputation at the courageous Abbey Theatre of the nineteen-twenties followed popular sentiment. Let us face the fact, then, that circumstances involving O'Casey's views as well as the resistance to them have been anything but favorable to his career as a playwright. It would be as futile, however, to wish that O'Casey were other than he is as it would be to remonstrate with him that his avowed religion, communism, is an egregious error and blinks at reality. It is an essential part of his genius to let the chips fly where they will. He is a man of passion, for one thing, and can write only as he feels without considering circumstance or consequence. His entire life is involved in his playwriting, as his remarkable autobiographical volumes since *I Knock at the Door* in 1939 tell us. And he is not the first man of genius whose claims as an artist can be validated without commitment to his politics. We have accepted Balzac without Royalism, Dostoevski without Pan-Slavism, Shaw without Socialism.

Political barriers, moreover, have been lifted in the case of a number of his plays without their making headway in the professional theatre. A production of *Purple Dust* has been possible since the end of the Second World War without offending taste or sentiment, and there has never been any political reason in England or America why O'Casey's masterpieces *Juno and the Paycock* and *The Plough and the Stars,* as well as *The Silver Tassie* and *Within the Gates,* should not have had first-class revivals. There could have been no serious political obstacles to a West End or Broadway production of *Cock-a-doodle-Dandy* or *Red Roses for Me* after the war. And on the symbolical level established by their imaginative quality, all the plays since O'Casey's realistic period in the nineteen-twenties have been quite acceptable. Theoretically, if not actually, in England and America we are all against what O'Casey is against—injustice, oppression, narrow-mindedness, and life-denial. And we are all in favor of what O'Casey affirms—freedom, self-fulfillment, beauty, love. More than any living playwright, indeed, O'Casey is substantially the minstrel of St. Paul's message of charity, of *caritas* or love.

Barring the difficulty of doing justice to his work with haphazard casting of the roles which makes amateur productions inadequate, the real problem of producing O'Casey's plays is a problem of understanding his genius. Our spiritually diminished theatre in a spiritually diminished world cannot quite assimilate his particular verve—cannot even adjust itself to it. His alleged and real faults of rhetoric, wordiness, and sentiment would be less formidable in a theatre like the Elizabethan that was vigorous enough to contain them and even make a virtue of them. His excellence—his wild humor of words and farcical action, his vast anger, and his vast love—threatens to burst the confines of a small-spirited theatre such as we mostly have in London and New York. The fermentation of the wine seems too strong for the pint-sized bottle.

II

We need to understand O'Casey's genius better before we feel confident that we can cope with it in the theatre. In appraising O'Casey we too often alternate between a study of "the political and social aspects of his plays," the main concern of Julius Koslow's *The Green and the Red,* and numerous other writers' able if random enthusiastic appreciations of O'Casey's humor and sympathy. Neither approach is to be deplored, for the social scene is indubitably important in his work and his spirited writing is conducive to enthusiasm in anyone who does not wear sheet-metal over his heart. But the effect of either approach is not altogether helpful.

A nebulous enthusiasm merely makes well-intentioned producers hope to stage his plays but does not lead to a production. Neither the producers nor his backers know what to make of most of the later plays once it is necessary to go beyond the initial pleasant state of admiration. It is one thing to fall in love with a girl; it is another to know how to live with her. And the other procedure, that of sociological appraisal, confuses matters; it disposes individuals to favor and disfavor the playwright on shallow premises. Except in some of his expositions, O'Casey is not a sociologist. As a social thinker, moreover, he is often fugitive and he offers no careful or consistent analysis. *The Silver Tassie* presents the griefs and ironies of war rather than an investigation of its causes. Who is responsible for the plight of the "Young Whore" in *Within the Gates*—society or a drunken mother and a young priest who succumbed to the flesh? And in what way is society responsible for the miseries of Juno's household because her "paycock" Captain Boyle is a shiftless drunkard and her son Johnny a traitor to his associates? We must answer largely in the negative, unless we go *outside* the play and write the social tract that O'Casey did not. O'Casey offers a feeling about the incendiary situations of *The Star Turns Red* and *Red Roses for Me* instead of a blueprint. Even in *The Plough and the Stars* he does not, as a sociologist, go beyond noting the condition and the human contradictions of Dublin's poor during the Easter Rebellion.

Those who want sociology for the theatre are not likely, in fact, to derive much real satisfaction from his work. (I have seen no reports of an O'Casey vogue behind the Iron Curtain!) Nor, unlike Shaw, has he ever claimed to be a dramatist of ideas rather than of feelings and experience. His "ideas" are implicit in the flow of life with which he floods the stage, and in his anger and sympathies. He has never actually employed the methods of discursive reason unless it was to poke sly and rueful fun at the expense of those characters who spout ideas but soon contradict their professions, as do Jerry the "Labour" humanitarian, who lets down Mary in *Juno and the Paycock* on learning that she is carrying another's child, and the Socialist covey in *The Plough and the Stars,* who plunders stores with the rest of the slum-dwellers during the Rebellion. Among those who consider O'Casey primarily a "social dramatist," one group demands a place for him in the theatre on a basis on which he is sure to disappoint expectations while another group denies him his rightful place on the same grounds. The Dublin Gate theatre's leader Michael MacLiammoir, as Koslow reports, proclaimed that the plays deal so largely with a social condition that they could with advantage be read before the Dail and the Dublin Corporation. It is important to know what this playwright is not. It is even more important, of course, to know what he is.

The manifest fact is that O'Casey is a baroque dramatic poet in a largely trivial and constricted theatre given over to neat construction and small-beer feeling. He is as baroque, as lavish and prodigal, as were Marlowe, Shakespeare, Jonson, and John Webster. He belongs to the spacious days of the theatre. And since he will not make himself smaller for anything as inconsequential to him as material success, the theatre will simply have to be made larger if O'Casey is to have his rightful place.

We must remember that he nourished his talent, unregulated and undiminished by formal schooling, on writing and theatre that afford elbow room in all directions. The former hod-carrier brought himself up on Shakespeare, and in an Irish environment (not the environment of the bluestocking and arty circles of Dublin) in which the gestures of life were broad and the speech torrential. And the Abbey Theatre that he knew in his youth, the theatre of Synge's plays and Lady Gregory's peasant farces, breathed an ample spirit and played a wide gambit of lyricism, humor, and emotionalism. The broad effect of sentiment and action was also inherent in the non-literary theatre with which he was acquainted—in Dion Boucicault's *The Shaughraun,* in which he performed at the Mechanics' Theatre, for example. The long haul of language and idealistic sententiousness was also present in the writings of John Ruskin with which he educated himself, as well as in the rhetoric of the Irish nationalist Home Rule and working-class movements in which he participated. Rebellious in his harried youth and losing job after job as a result of his independence and temper; steeped in his youth first in the Gaelic League, then in the bitter transport strike of 1913 and in the Irish Citizen Army led by Jim Larkin and Jim Connolly, lined up against a wall and nearly shot during the Easter Rebellion, O'Casey had a turbulent initiation into art. Art for him has always been the core of a conflict, the center of a conflagration.

O'Casey was nearly forty when he became a produced playwright. He was formed as a writer neither by educational institutions nor by the theatre but by a turbulent life equally remote from the academy and the stage. It has never been possible to subjugate him to either institution. Nor could he accept the rule of any established dramatic form. Realistic group drama suited his needs in *The Shadow of a Gunman,* family drama in *Juno and the Paycock,* mass drama in *The Plough and the Stars.* His passion forced him to adopt expressionism in *The Silver Tassie* and choral drama in *Within the Gates.* Rather simplified drama was his natural mode in *The Star Turns Red* when he polarized the world into revolutionary and counter-revolutionary factions. A lyrical realism was proper to his elegiac mood when he commemorated the great Transport Strike of 1913 in *Red Roses for Me.* A turbulent fantasy was the inevitable choice for his desire to assert the claims of nature against cowardice in *Cock-a-doodle-Dandy.* Its magical cock, with the crimson crest flowering over its head and the "look of a cynical jester," is the suitable symbol for the magic of life that invades the haunts of village puritanism.

Neither in tragedy nor comedy can he be circumspect, cautious, or calculating. His artistry remains pure self-expression and spins everything out of his emotion and immediate observation. And in self-expression he is of necessity intense whether he feels compassion or anger, whether he scorns cowardice and hypocrisy or celebrates the joy of life, whether he buries the past or salutes the future. The danger in such intensity is self-evident and is sufficiently apparent in his plays, especially in those which lack the restraint of the realistic technique. He is the natural man, who is apt to run to excess. He is sometimes too intoxicated with the gush of words and mastered by sentiment, though not by sentimentality. He is apt to see things only in terms of right and wrong, black and white. He is apt, like Dickens, to rely on caricature rather than portraiture, as in *Purple Dust.* He is sometimes hortatory rather than suggestive in simplified situations of plays such as *Within the Gates* and *The Star Turns Red.* He is particularly unsuccessful when he writes formal verse, which requires a long apprenticeship and an arduous discipline, instead of relying on the natural poetry of his prose. Beginning with *The Silver Tassie,* his structural sense, so sure in the early days, leaves him at times when the surge of passion or fancy overpowers him in stylized drama. When this is the case, the results are apt to be the morality-play quality of *Within the Gates* or the repetitiousness and overelaboration of some later plays.

To employ these strictures as an excuse for not warmly welcoming O'Casey's genius into the theatre is rank hypocrisy. Perfection is rarely found in the drama or any other literary form except the short lyric. In the theatre, moreover, many an imperfection can be glossed over and sometimes even turned to advantage. Many a piece of dubious dialogue has been ably transformed by the actor's art. Tempo, stress, change of pace, patterns of stage movement, the stage picture, lighting and music—all contribute to the dramatic effect of a play. Obviously stagecraft has little justification if its contribution goes no further than mere transcription of the dramatic text. Obviously a stage director can make no valid claim to artistry if his work is limited to playing traffic-cop to a group of actors. There is no reason to withhold from O'Casey the benefit of stagecraft when it is lavished so abundantly on inferior playwrights.

III

Where there is fire and heat, there is also apt to be smoke. We cannot have an O'Casey or anyone of comparable rank among dramatists without incurring risks, and without understanding what must be transferred to the stage, namely, his prodigal creativity. Except in the field of high comedy and not always even there, as both Shakespeare and Ben Jonson prove, the genius of English drama is baroque and romantic. It subsists on excess, on a wide circuit and free navigation with full sail. O'Casey's work is conceived in the grand manner. It belongs to the great tradition. O'Casey is true to it. Our contemporary theatre is not. That is the crux of the problem.

To understand O'Casey for the effective purpose of theatre, then, is tantamount to understanding the prodigal nature of his art and making the most of it while channeling off or transforming the waste-products. This is to understand, in the first place, that his work is theatrical and must be given elbow-room for its fancifulness, free passion, and Rabelaisian humor. A scene such as the magical storm in *Cock-a-doodle-Dandy* in which all the cowards and hypocrites are having their clothes blown off and barely manage to hold up their trousers has to be played for all it is worth. So played, it will be seen to be what it really is, the dramatic humor of the Elizabethans and the novelistic humor of Fielding and Dickens. We must also understand that O'Casey makes the "theatricalist" theatre the condition of his playwriting. When he abandons the realistic technique, he makes one unalterable demand, namely, the right to let the play alternate between fact and fancy, verisimilitude and exaggeration or intensification, without regard to *literary consistency*. The only consistency he accepts is *theatrical consistency*. And why not, if we realize that theatre is theatre and neither life nor a photograph of life?

By the same standard, we must acknowledge his rhetoric as *theatre,* and we must accept it. To want to dispense with his verbal splendors and fury is equivalent to trying to reduce an orchestra to a single piccolo; even to wish it thinned out to chamber music dimensions is an error. His larynx is his orchestra. Volume is inherent in it. To object or to want to compromise on this matter is tantamount to saying that one doesn't want an orchestra because the kettle drums are played too loud. His dramatic fervor, fully rendered by his assertiveness and truculence, cannot fail to excite anyone not an icicle by nature or training. And rhetoric, too, we must realize, is part of the genius of major English drama, as is the lyricism of which he is also master. In spite of the prevailing peephole, picture-frame stage, O'Casey, especially in his post-realistic period, writes for the platform for which most of major English drama was written. Nor will it do to insist too nicely on a distinction between "good" rhetoric and "bad" in his case, since the only truly bad rhetoric stems from insincerity, of which this playwright seems constitutionally incapable.

O'Casey, moreover, works in the great tradition when he makes arias out of his anger and love and lets the music preempt our attention in some long stretches of writing. There are celebrated sections in Shakespeare that are essentially arias and are best rendered as such. When this is not done, as was the case in the rendition of the Queen Mab speech in the recent Olivia de Havilland *Romeo and Juliet,* an audience does not have to consist of poetry lovers to sense that some precious magic has departed from the play.

The champions of Naturalism and modern drama, from Emile Zola down to Bernard Shaw, were tireless in scorning plot-filled playwriting as mere dramatic trickery, and soon the medium of motion pictures arose in our century to serve as the ideal vehicle for the Scribe and Sardou type of plot-spinning action. But something had to fill the vacuum in drama left by the banishment of plot-intrigue. Zola wanted the vacuum filled with "slices of life," Shaw with the intellectual content he called "discussion" or "drama of ideas." In his early work, O'Casey filled the void mainly with the "slice of life"; in his later, stylized dramas, mostly with the swirl of verbal music under and over the situations.

As in a quartet or a symphony, the tempo, pattern, and feeling of the music *are* the drama in these passages in O'Casey's work, and to overlook this musico-dramatic effect is to overlook a considerable portion of the vitality of O'Casey's, as of Shakespeare's playwriting. His characters are often found "lilting," by O'Casey's own stage direction, because lilting is a function of his dramatic expression. Very probably O'Casey aims at this effect and finds his procedure entirely proper, if not indeed *imperative,* for a dramatist. My conclusion that he relies a good deal on music was confirmed, I thought, in a letter I received in 1950 from Mr. O'Casey. I believe I am violating no confidence in referring to his comment on Sartre and the existentialist atheism of the Orestes drama *The Flies*. Mr. O'Casey thought that he would "rather be free from Sartre than free from the gods." The latter could, at least, *"sing a song."*

O'Casey, too, sings a song, and it is always the same song of human love and of reaching out to the beauty in the world and in the human soul, regardless of evil and conflict. He retains a heroic positive stand among the loud Nay-saying and the small Yea-saying playwrights of the contemporary scene. Not a mystic, he does not propose to transcend the world but to transmute it through the power of his faith in man, which is his music, and through the power of his anger and challenge, which is his rhetoric. For all this magnificent assault on the failing heart he needs his full voice and his firm, often jaunty, stance. And to this end he employs many strategies of the imagination and the stage, the chorus, the harangue, the black and white characters, the changes of light, the effect of sound and wind, the mood of the seasons, the striking symbol, and quick transitions from fact to fancy, from the commonplace to the transcendental, and from the farcical to the sublime. And so he moves back and forth, and up and down, mightily disconcerting both the lover of orderly realistic procedures and the esthetic logician and precisionist. He disconcerts them with both his dramatic-lyric poetry and the theatrical poetry encompassed by the stage picture and the stage effect. All this, combined with the compassionate and sardonic observation of character and environment which first brought him fame, makes him the not easily classifiable playwright whose large claims are made upon the total man in his audience and upon the total resources of the theatre.

O'NEILL IN OUR TIME

I

For some years now I have felt that the most distressing aspects of the current American theatre are its easy conscience concerning neglect of O'Neill's plays and the apparent indifference with which he is regarded by the young. There would be less reason for dismay if the neglect were a decision of intelligent criticism or, better still, if O'Neill had been supplanted by one or more playwrights of comparable stature whose idiom happened to be more "modern." Such, however, is hardly the case. The representatives of a younger generation than O'Neill's who have been incisively critical of him have had too little influence to stand in the way of professional revivals of his work or to set the young against him. Nor are the young actually set against him; perhaps they are even vaguely impressed when they read his plays—which is never the same thing as seeing them, since "theatre" even more than "drama" was his special endowment. They are merely lackadaisical in accepting his significance; his importance to them appears to be more a matter of academic fiat than of enthusiasm for his published work.

As for the displacement of O'Neill by fresher talent, it is true that a few newspaper reviewers in the nineteen-thirties, notably the late Burns Mantle, ventured the opinion that the glory had descended upon Maxwell Anderson while others placed O'Neill's laurels on the fiery young head of Clifford Odets. And more recently a few have supported the candidacy of Arthur Miller and Tennessee Williams for the honor. Yet it must be apparent that no one has arisen in two decades to take O'Neill's place. When the work of the aforementioned playwrights is reviewed, can more be said than that it is possible to set against his substantial output of drama one single play by Anderson (*Winterset*), one by Miller (*Death of a Salesman*), and perhaps two pieces by Williams, *The Glass Menagerie* and *A Streetcar Named Desire*? Most English and American playwrights who have made an impression since O'Neill delivered *Mourning Becomes Electra* in 1931 remind me in some respects of the neo-classic playwrights who succeeded the "noble brood" of Shakespeare and his fellow-Jacobeans after 1660. They are usually free from the marked awkwardness of the giants, but they are not giants.

As O'Neill, wasted by disease, a thin shadow of himself after 1947, could no longer supervise any productions of his work, and as it appeared that his vast projected cycle of "possessors dispossessed" would be left unfinished, he began to belong entirely to history even before his death six years later. But he had revealed so much of his old vitality in his last new production, *The Iceman Cometh,* on Broadway in 1946 that it was difficult for us not to think of him as still an active contemporary, and we were disinclined to relinquish him to posterity. We had the same feeling about him, the same desire to treat him as a working writer, when we were disposed to criticize *The Moon for the Misbegotten* as a play he should not have allowed to be published but continued to revise like any other functioning playwright. Only the special "off-Broadway" City Center and "ANTA" productions of *Anna Christie* and *Desire Under the Elms* suggested the process of exhumation associated with "revivals." Only the fate of these plays in midcentury America seemed to "date" him, albeit unjustly. *Anna Christie,* sufficiently well received despite a poor production, was transferred to Broadway and lingered listlessly there for a short run. *Desire Under the Elms,* excellently staged by Harold Clurman, revealed an old master who could still overpower new audiences. Yet the play remained an off-Broadway exhibit; for some reason, no one ventured to display this grimly conceived tragedy among the marketable gewgaws of the Broadway showshop. And even the non-commercial community and educational theatres throughout the country were more inclined to welcome the latest Broadway "hit" than O'Neill's masterpiece. With few exceptions, both the commercial and non-commercial stages seemed dedicated to a trivial spirit to which O'Neill had always been a stranger.

With others, I feel sorry for the new generation that has been deprived of the opportunity of experiencing his kind of theatre, of the element of discovery or rediscovery in it, and of the reaching out, or even the fumbling for, greatness that his work represented. As for those of us who grew up in the theatre of the nineteen-twenties when he became our major dramatist, it can be said with certainty that he served us as a symbol of our trust in the greatness and splendor of our theatre's future. We are not necessarily blind to his shortcomings and only pardonably nostalgic when we recall the sense of exaltation that suffused us with the appearance of many of his plays. We cannot help feeling that a mighty presence has receded from our somewhat bleary view. Our mood cannot but be elegiac. We feel the force of what Rupert Brooks wrote in his youthful book on the late Elizabethan playwright John Webster, to whom contemporaries referred as "crabbed Websterio" very much as some people declare O'Neill to be crabbed. Like Webster, O'Neill seems to us a receding titan, "the last of Earth," even if he occasionally merited the reproach Bernard Shaw leveled at Webster when he called that sultry dramatist of extreme passions a wax-works showman—a "Tussaud laureate."

It is difficult to recover for the young our original rapture, which in many instances perhaps has diminished even for us. Although the American theatre, no doubt, has as many youthful enthusiasts and aspirants now as it had in our green years, their hopes for the theatre as a temple of art are, with good reason, considerably more temperate. We were just building a new stage that would accommodate the aims and achievements of the men who founded the modern drama and theatre in Europe. We came somewhat late to this dispensation of modernity, it is true. But our sense of discovery, transforming itself at that time into exploration and settlement, was exhilarating. And in practice we saw ourselves—and chiefly in the mirror of O'Neill, the Provincetown Players, and the young Theatre Guild—as pioneers of "art theatre" in the Western hemisphere. We were celebrants, if not indeed practicing priests, of springtime rites by means of which we tasted the bread of Naturalism and the wine of Symbolism for the salvation of our souls and of theatrical art. It is difficult as well to engage the young in our pristine interests. We sought self-expression while present concerns are properly with survival. We wanted to be free artists whereas the young of the present period, again quite understandably, want to strike roots in a profession—and as quickly as possible. We despised security whereas they, very sensibly, seek it and count themselves fortunate if they can find it. We *left* our homes whereas they want to *build* homes. We wanted to "live dangerously." They, on the contrary, have had their fill of recent danger since the start of the Second World War and are most directly affected in a world that is again turning into a holocaust.

We were, in short, romanticists, and O'Neill—whether he wrote technically realistic or expressionist dramas—was a romanticist with us. The young of today are, by comparison, realists, and O'Neill's metaphysical gloom and dismay may strike them as curious and extravagant. He may strike them as a man tilting at windmills in a self-induced nightmare while they have to push against barriers and barbed wire put in their way by others than themselves. In 1912, the notable Spanish man of letters Miguel de Unamuno wrote *The Tragic Sense of Life,* which had considerable vogue here in the early nineteen-twenties. He made anguish of the soul a condition for rising above the uninspiring life of modern society and declared an insatiable thirst for transcendental truth to be the heroic fate of man. The Salamancan professor concluded his farewell to the reader of the book with the sentence: "And may God deny you peace, but give you glory!" It seemed like a good prayer to our generation of rebels against Main Street complacency and materialistic values. One rather suspects that today most people would gladly forego the "glory" and settle for the "peace"—if they could have it.

II

Primary for O'Neill was a cosmic anguish. It was anguish over the inscrutability of fate and over the search for the faith he personally lost in abandoning Catholicism and that others had lost in abandoning the various religions into which they had been born. The twist of the tragic rack on which our Eugene O'Neill placed both his dreamers and his materialists—whether in *Beyond the Horizon, Desire Under the Elms, The Great God Brown,* or *Days Without End*—was loud in the theatres where his plays were performed. The rack could be love and life frustrated by possessiveness or twisted into hate by failure, lust, or environment. The rack upon which he stretched his characters could be past life and the sense of devouring fate—Chris Christopherson's "old davil sea" in *Anna Christie*. The torment could come from man's sense of being separated from nature and not yet attaining complete humanity, of not "belonging" in the universe, as in *The Hairy Ape;* or of not belonging to either the old supernatural god and the new scientific god represented by the machine, as in *Dynamo;* or of not belonging to oneself and of not quite belonging to any all-fulfilling love, as in *Strange Interlude;* or of wanting to belong, incestuously, to a forbidden object, as in *Mourning Becomes Electra*. Wherever the tension came from, the suffering blackened man's horizons in O'Neill's dramas while the worshippers of material comfort rode the crest of optimism under Presidents Harding, Coolidge, and Herbert Hoover.

O'Neill cast a weird shadow on the easeful life, on money-bought comfort and specious consolations. He stood stonily unreconciled in the land of plenty and promise. He was heroically saturnine. When he smiled for more than a fleeting moment in his plays, it was mainly to smile to scorn the American Babbitt he incarnated in a Venetian one, the Marco Polo of *Marco Millions*. Not until 1933, in recalling the beginning of our tragic century in *Ah, Wilderness,* was his smile genial, steady and conciliatory to life and to a father-image. His major theme was man's disorientation, man's bedevilment from within and from without. O'Neill made himself the dramatist of ironic Fate and of the psychological tensions Freud's interpreters and misinterpreters were then communicating to us in books and lectures. And the young and the brave of the nineteen-twenties found exhilaration in his confronting the bitter "truth" for them so stalwartly—even if many of them were more inclined to make parlor palaver rather than drama out of it, unless they made melodrama out of it by drinking themselves into a frenzy during the years of the "noble experiment." The important point, of course, is that O'Neill made strong drama and exciting theatre out of this "truth." He took for his masters the Greek tragedians of fate, to whom he ultimately paid the tribute of imitation in *Mourning Becomes Electra,* and Strindberg, the Scandinavian dramatist of man's division and search for reunification, to whom he also paid the tribute of imitation in *Welded* and *Strange Interlude.*

O'Neill was not unaware of society and its effects, I hasten to add, although neither his anti-political nor his leftist critics have cared to concede this fact. Surely his ironic romance *Marco Millions* made an explicit reckoning of the era of Prosperity and of the mounting stock-market. His "hairy ape," the stoker Yank, was Worker as well as Man. The society he presented in *The Hairy Ape* with the slumming heiress Mildred Douglas and the spats-wearing automatons of the Fifth Avenue Easter parade scene had what the leftists of the nineteen-thirties called "social significance." He also took sharp notice of racial discrimination and slum life in *All God's Chillun Got Wings,* of poverty and prostitution in *Anna Christie,* of grinding and narrowing impoverished farm life in *Beyond the Horizon,* and of the loneliness and sorry satisfactions of sea-faring men in the *S. S. Glencairn* one-act cycle. The tensions produced by New England patriarchal authority and the struggle for land figured in *Desire Under the Elms.* Brahmin family pride, joy-denying puritanism, and mercantile possessiveness were the correlates of the love drama and incest tragedy of *Mourning Becomes Electra.* "Problem plays" alone found him indifferent.

Deny it who can! O'Neill, who contributed to the Socialist "Call" in his early days of journalism and who mingled with the political vanguard of liberals associated with the Provincetown Players, was a social critic of sorts. And more important to art is the fact that he rendered life and speech in his realistic plays authentically. He did not abandon colloquial dialogue until late in the nineteen-twenties, and then only for good reasons —and he returned to it in 1939 with the writing of *The Iceman Cometh.* He depicted environment scrupulously. And he was virtually the first serious American dramatist of any standing to bring characters from all walks of life on to the stage, noting their origins of race and background with sympathy and understanding. It would not be difficult to sustain the point that he gave us social pictures and socially conditioned, if not altogether socially determined, actions with greater credibility and vitality than most "social dramatists" of the nineteen-thirties and since then. He is, indeed, historically important as the first American to make naturalist art prevail on our stage.

Nevertheless, he was not a "naturalist," and struck out, in fact, against the belief that mere transcriptions of life were the province of art. He fused naturalistic detail with symbolist mood, suggestiveness, and symbol. And taking his cue from his admired Strindberg, he resorted to the "expressionist" dramatic style of distortion of action, speech, and scene, as in the weird calvary of his Emperor Jones through the jungle and in the Fifth Avenue scene of *The Hairy Ape*. Tireless in his search for theatrical means of projecting the inner life and the metaphysical idea, he used interior monologue—speech on different levels of consciousness—in *Strange Interlude,* and he experimented with masks as a method of dramatization —with partial success in *The Great God Brown* and with virtually none in *Lazarus Laughed*. He even employed monologue in one highly effective scene of so realistic a comedy as *Ah, Wilderness,* and he split the protagonist of *Days Without End* into two characters who had to be played by two actors. This constant, if not indeed always satisfactory, experimentation, is actually another important feature of O'Neill's work. It was his role to open all the stops of theatre art in America, and we have reason to be grateful to him.

The well-known restiveness of his personal life had its correlate in his restiveness as an artist which made him seek new forms of expression even after succeeding in one particular style; and the unpredictability of his style added to the excitement that his playwriting brought to an increasing number of playgoers. To contend that this tendency to shift the artistic base of his work prevented O'Neill from completely perfecting himself on one basis is legitimate. To protest that he should not have done so is absurd. He acted under creative, as well as psychological, compulsion in the flux of his life and in the flux of the transitional civilization apparent in both drama and fiction after 1914. He entertained extremely high expectations for the theatre which the success of motion pictures and radio, as well as high production costs, had not yet dampened for the profession; and he had high, sometimes recklessly high, ambitions for himself as a dramatist. In *Strange Interlude* and *Mourning Becomes Electra,* as well as later in *The Iceman Cometh,* O'Neill even violated the sacred right of the playgoer to discharge his obligations to the stage in two hours and a half of theatre attendance. He resorted to epic dimensions, taking some risk of introducing elephantiasis into playwriting. *Strange Interlude* acquired some of the qualities of a large impressionist or expressionist novel. *Mourning Becomes Electra* brought back the spaciousness, if not the imaginativeness, of the Aeschylean trilogy.

He also aspired to the estate of a poetic dramatist, and he rightly sensed that his artistic necessity and the requirements of his matter and point of view would be unfulfilled unless he became one. Whether he succeeded is debatable. It is a strongly held opinion that he lacked "language" equal to the reach of his non-verbal powers. This was noted with particular justice in the case of *Mourning Becomes Electra*. Granted the validity of the charge, it is none the less possible and only right to modify and moderate it. As long as he wrote about common life—of sailors and farmers and social outcasts—he managed his language securely, often with strong effect, sometimes with poetic overtones appropriate to his subject. When he set out to be deliberately poetic, he failed—sometimes embarrassingly. When he turned to middle-class or upper-class society, he missed fire in those parts of his plays in which he tried to generalize a feeling or an idea. Yet it may be conceded that even then he could achieve a poetic effect of low degree through the full rhythms of his sentences, if not through cadences and imagery.

If my memory serves, he was once referred to as a "prose Shakespeare." His plight, apart from personal reasons of insufficient endowment and of insufficient control over slang and colloquialisms (as in the constant harping on "pipe-dreams" in *The Iceman*), was due to the modern division between prose and dramatic poetry—a large subject which cannot be explored here. If, because of his turbulence and reiterations of an idea, he also appeared to lack "taste," it is questionable whether he really lacked it. It is sufficiently present, for example, in *Ah, Wilderness;* and it is difficult for me to believe that I am the only one who found an adequate substitute for it in *Desire Under the Elms,* in my opinion his best play. He simply did not bother about "taste" or balance when the surge of conflict and anguish was strong. Those who press the charge of want of "poetry" in the man should be reminded, moreover, that he got his "poetry," as other modern playwrights have done, not from verbal beauty but from the breadth and reach of his imagination, mood, or feeling, and, especially, from his theatrical—at times exaggeratedly theatrical—sense. If he was not felicitous in creating verbal poetry, he often created a "poetry of theatre"—this in effects of which a few examples are the tom-toms in *Emperor Jones,* the firemen's forecastle and the Fifth Avenue nightmares of *The Hairy Ape,* the mask and transformation effects of *The Great God Brown,* the evocation of the farmhouse and land in *Desire Under the Elms,* and the Greek colonnade, the chanty refrain, and Electra-Lavinia's tragic closing of the doors upon herself in *Mourning Becomes Electra.*

O'Neill did not become the full-fledged tragic poet he evidently aspired to be. And want of language was only one reason. Another was his tendency to set up abstract personalities and issues, as most conspicuously in *Dynamo* and *Lazarus Laughed,* or to schematize characters and deprive them of possible range—this in order to develop a psychological conception or an argument. This tendency can be found in *The Great God Brown* and even in *Strange Interlude* and *Mourning Becomes Electra.* Perhaps he took ideas *per se* with too much of the seriousness of those who have only recently discovered "ideas." He sometimes took these in too simplified a form, and in too rarefied a form for drama—an error not committed by Sophocles and Shakespeare, though committed by other dramatists of distinction such as Euripides and Shaw under the pressure of an "intellectual" climate. He also tended to give a passion a bear-hug instead of an austere embrace, which is the more usual way with master-tragedians. And one may reflect, finally, that he did push too furiously toward catastrophic consummations and drive his characters too hard toward their destiny, thereby eliciting the charge of writing melodrama rather than tragedy. On this score, however, it must be said that he had company among the late "minor Elizabethans," who also piled horror upon horror. He bore, in fact, a resemblance to them in his susceptibility to extremes of passion, will, and affliction, as we may note in John Webster's *The Duchess of Malfi* and John Ford's *'Tis Pity She's a Whore.*

I believe that O'Neill wrote tragedy of a naturalistic-poetic kind in *Desire Under the Elms,* and that he approached, if he did not quite reach, the altitude of high tragedy in *Mourning Becomes Electra.* Generally, moreover, if he failed to write tragedy, as he plainly intended in much of his work, he achieved a noble tragic mood—and this in a context of exciting drama. I believe this will be found to be the case in such plays as *Beyond the Horizon, Anna Christie, The Hairy Ape, All God's Chillun Got Wings,* and *The Iceman Cometh,* regardless of what faults can be ascribed to them. And if the quality of his mind prevented him from securing a maximum of meaning from many of his plays, he at least secured a maximum of tension—which is or contains a meaning of some sort not lightly to be dismissed in the kind of theatre we have had since 1914. He was hardly ever as sharp as Strindberg in scoring his points, and he lacked the agility of a Pirandello in dealing with them. But he was virtually the only American playwright to confront ideas on more than an elementary level and to wrestle with them "tragically"—heroically. He often set loose a mighty smoke with his fire, and consequently the fire was obscured, especially when it was the fire of an idea. But the smoke came from dramatic heat, and it created an atmosphere of dramatic feeling and conception which few other American playwrights have been able, or have seemed disposed, to create.

THE ELECTRAS OF
GIRAUDOUX AND O'NEILL

Whenever a playwright has particularly strong designs on fame he exhumes the Electra theme of classic antiquity and makes something more or less new out of it. Jean-Paul Sartre's existentialist treatment *The Flies,* in which Orestes takes precedence over his sister, expressed the philosophical and political concerns of the Second World War period. Hugo von Hofmannsthal's *Electra* expressed the more purely esthetic ones of the turn of the century. If we are concerned with the perspectives of modern playwriting, however, we would be well advised to glance at Giraudoux' *Electra* and O'Neill's *Mourning Becomes Electra,* and it doesn't much matter with which play we start. Although Giraudoux' play came later, in 1937, whereas O'Neill's was produced in 1931, there is no evidence that the French playwright was influenced by the American. The differences between the two works are, on the contrary, so marked that they enable us to make a special case of the difference between European and American playwriting in our age, the one usually acknowledged to be razor-edged and trimly styled, the other emotion-fraught and realistic. It must be said that the rapier stands here in sharp contrast to the bludgeon.

If invention, "wit," and grace made plays, there would be no doubt in the mind of a critic as to which one should be the better work. Giraudoux' play would be considered the "artistic" triumph, since it is ingeniously wrought, written with finesse, and neatly circumscribed. I have maliciously used the cliché "artistic" employed so often by that great but cumbersome American man of letters Theodore Dreiser, directing it at two kinds of playgoers not usually bracketed together: at the immature art-lover gratified by anything that does not conform to an expected apparition, and at the critic whose judgment is refined to such a degree that the intensity of life in a work is of secondary importance to him. Members of the latter's tribe are likely to treasure *The Golden Bowl* of Henry James as if it were the jeweled Chalice of Suger or Cellini's gold and enamel salt cellar while discarding the "inartistic" Dreiser's *Sister Carrie, The Titan,* and *The Financier* as so much cheap pewter. They are likely to deplore the American "cult of experience" as misguided, if not indeed barbaric. They are of the fellowship of those fastidious commentators who found Miller's *Death of a Salesman* "strangely lacking in a sense of either pity or of illumination" and "a very dull business, which departs in no way that is to its credit from the general mediocrity of our commercial theater. . . ."

(*Partisan Review*) or "a miserable affair," "trite and clumsy," and proceeding with "unrelieved vulgarity" from "cliché to stereotype" (*The Hudson Review*). Yet who can deny that the shape of a drama, the mode of expression, and the form of the dramatic presentation are important considerations. A proper value judgment cannot be made without them.

Jean Giraudoux was an extremely urbane writer equally adept at turning out superior bedroom farce such as *Amphitryon 38* and piquant fancies such as *The Madwoman of Chaillot* and *Intermezzo,* the latter known on Broadway in the Maurice Valency translation as *The Enchanted.* Although *Intermezzo* is actually the more brightly conceived and adeptly executed of the two, it is *The Madwoman of Chaillot* that has impressed itself upon the American public as the epitome of Giraudoux' type of sophisticated poetic drama. Our playgoers were decidedly enchanted with this wry fantasy about the liquidation of predatory French "operators" by a lovably mad countess who lures them into the maze of Parisian sewers with the promise of oil below the city's pavements. It was a unique work in a theatre clogged with mediocre realistic traffic. Giraudoux' language when he wrote fantasy does not translate well, and it was pruned in the American adaptation of some of the largesse of poetic extravaganza. Even so, however, it was evident that neither his ultra-refined inventiveness nor his sense of irony need be lost on American audiences. But Giraudoux, a professional diplomat, was at the same time seriously concerned with the problems of France and Europe, and the full stature of this writer is discoverable in other plays than his fantastic comedies, charged though these be with scorn for materialists. He was also more of a moralist than he would have been willing to concede, if one may judge from Countess Aurelia's exclamation after disposing of the speculators, "My poor cats. What a bore for them if humanity had to be saved every afternoon." In *The Trojan War Will Not Take Place,* written in 1938, he provided a rueful treatment of the coming of the Trojan War as an analogue to the imminence of the Second World War; and his *Electra* expresses a long-standing concern with the futility of revenge, which was also the subject of his very first play, *Siegfried,* written after the First World War.

The revenge of Electra for the murder of her father is an especially austere subject because it involves matricide on the part of Electra and her brother Orestes. It is a subject for tragedy, and Giraudoux tinges it with his own civilized abhorrence for violence even in the name of justice. At the end of the play, death comes to the great city of Argos because its leader Aegisthus, along with the queen Clytemnestra, is slain by Orestes at the urging of his sister Electra. The Corinthians who were on the move against Argos throughout the action have entered it, and they are murdering the people in the streets. Civil war has also broken out, so that the Argive people are killing each other—"innocent people are killing each other." The city is on fire, and one of the Furies who have followed the events remarks, "That's the light Electra wanted with her demand for truth." Electra can only reply desperately, "I have my conscience, I have Orestes, I have justice. I have everything." A second Fury tells her, "You've not slept for seven years because of a crime other people committed. Now you're the guilty one." Her crime has caused many more deaths than Clytemnestra's; it wrecked Electra's father's city as well as destroyed her brother's happiness.

Giraudoux had a clear and unifying point of view, and no one can doubt that he has made the classic subject an effective vehicle for his idea. The idea has surely not grown out of the author's concern with characters independently of any rationale of argument. His art, no matter how great our estimation of it, is at the opposite pole from that of Ibsen in such a play as *Hedda Gabler* or of Chekhov in *The Three Sisters*. In these works, the dimensioned characters would possess reality if they did nothing more than breathe; one feels oneself to be in the midst of life with them. It is not too much to say that in the writing of Giraudoux' *Electra*—only somewhat less than in the composition of his *Madwoman of Chaillot* (or, for that matter, of Cocteau's *The Infernal Machine*)—the intellectual process has been primary. Only in the course of sketching the play as an intellectual construct did Giraudoux, it would seem, give his main characters the attributes of human beings.

Electra has no more dimension as a human being than is afforded by her desire for revenge plus brief details of remembering her baby brother's fall on the palace steps and her meeting her father once on his return from Troy. Orestes, returning from a long exile at the age of twenty, is an instrument of her vengeance with no more dimension than suggested by some poignantly vague childhood memories, some reluctance to join his sister in hate, and a feeling of bitterness toward his mother Clytemnestra who sent him away. Clytemnestra is given a few recognizably human touches when she meets her son and appeals to her estranged daughter for sympathy. In one detail, an argument between Clytemnestra and Electra as to whether the latter pushed the infant Orestes and made the mother drop him (this twenty years after the episode!), Giraudoux fully materializes human beings in his play. For the rest, Clytemnestra's humanity is simply asserted, though very well asserted, by explanations on her part. And Aegisthus is entirely tailor-made to fit the point that Electra's implacable pursuit of justice is a great evil.

Conveniently and without developed motivation, Giraudoux brings him on the scene as a miraculously altered person after having looked down on the city from a hill. An unscrupulous and self-indulgent man who has committed outrages as regent has suddenly been transformed into a king dedicated to saving his country and capable of doing so. He must have been transformed solely for the argument: If Aegisthus had remained unchanged, his assassination by Orestes would not have been a great misfortune. Moreover, he arrives full of admiration and love for Electra, although he has hitherto tried to dispose of her rather cavalierly. If there is irony or pathos in the fact that she should be instrumental in his death, this *motif* is secondary to the point that Electra's exaggerated sense of justice only makes her bitterly charge the Greek gods with "hypocrisy and malice" for changing "a parasite into a just man, an adulterer into a husband [for Clytemnestra], a usurper into a king." I believe we can agree with her when she cries out, "They can't transform a criminal into an innocent man." But Giraudoux, busying himself with his argument, obviously cannot afford not to transform the criminal.

In O'Neill's *Mourning Becomes Electra,* Ezra Mannon returns from war with changed perspectives and a yearning for his wife's love, only to be poisoned by her. We can be deeply moved by this scene, but only because Ezra appeals to us there as a human being. Ezra Mannon is, so to speak, existential here, and if there is irony in his fate at this point, it is relevant solely to himself as a human being. O'Neill is not in the least concerned with proving that Ezra's wife should then and there have renounced her adulterous love for his cousin David Mannon, for O'Neill makes Ezra and Christine exist outside a framework of argument. There is also a much stronger reason for Ezra's change of attitude than for the Greek character's. Ezra had not just climbed a hill; he had fought in the Civil War and seen men die around him.

If there were any doubt concerning Giraudoux' distinctly different purpose, which is the purpose of the intellectual functioning as playwright, the framework of his *Electra* would confirm it. The classical Furies are present throughout, as observers at first, as objectified disaster and punishment at the end. Moreover, the action of the play is *theatricalized* instead of rendered as action that would transpire normally under the given provocations and conditions. A particularly striking example of theatricalization is the fact that in a single day, the wedding day of Aegisthus and Clytemnestra during which all the stage events transpire, the Furies, represented in the first scene as three little girls, become with preternatural rapidity grown women. They grow simultaneously with the evil of Electra's revenge. The stage direction of the last scene reads: "The *Eumenides,* who are [now] exactly the same height and figure as Electra." A character discusses the "girls" in the first scene. "If we ask who they are," he declares, "they pretend they're the little Eumenides. And the horrible thing is that they grow and get fat as you look at them. Yesterday, they were years younger than today. . . . See how her eyelashes grow." They have known much about Electra, they claim, "even before we were." They refer to the childhood episode suggestively, saying, "Electra amuses herself by making Orestes fall out of his mother's arms."

A beggar, of whom it is said at first that he may or may not be Jupiter ("the priests don't want to be asked"), prowls through the palace grounds mysteriously. It is he who confirms Electra's suspicions that her mother and Aegisthus murdered her father Agamemnon. He does this immediately before the dénouement in one long formal speech (he alone, of course, saw everything), at the end of which Orestes goes out "vengeance-bent," "sword in hand," saying, "Don't stop, Beggar. Go on, tell them about the death of Clytemnestra and Aegisthus." And the Beggar, now certainly divine Jupiter, without budging from the scene, supernaturally enacts the role of a messenger in Greek tragedy. About a dozen speeches later, a cry is heard and the Beggar recites the murder of Aegisthus and Clytemnestra on the balcony of the palace.

A bird, too high up in the sky at first to be identifiable, has been hovering over Aegisthus and hasn't left him since sunrise (Scene 7). As Aegisthus refuses to chain Electra and orders Orestes to be unbound (Scene 8), the bird is reported to be coming down, and the Beggar calls out, "Look, it's a vulture!" Giraudoux did not hesitate to theatricalize events even at the cost of a cliché.

Between the two parts of the play, Giraudoux placed an Interlude entitled "The Gardener's Lament." The speech delivered by this character (borrowed from Euripides) who was briefly engaged to Electra runs to about eighty closely packed lines addressed to the audience. It starts as follows: "I'm no longer in the running [that is, no longer Electra's fiancé]. That's why I'm free to come and tell you what the play can't tell you. In stories like this the people won't stop killing and biting each other. . . ."

In the scene preceding the Interlude, therefore the curtain scene of the first act, the supernatural beggar, quite definitely a god here, also delivers an address to the little Eumenides who are watching Orestes and Electra sleeping. It is a long explanation, mixed with ironic commentary, to the effect that Electra told the truth in maintaining she had not pushed the child Orestes—"She's unadulterated truth, a lamp without a wick. So if she kills, as seems likely, all happiness and peace around her, it's because she's right. . . ." And since he has spoken in the presence of the audience as well as of the young Furies, he says as he walks away, "But all you who remain here, be quiet now. This is Electra's first rest and the last rest of Orestes." Giraudoux, it is obvious, takes pains at a high point of suspense to destroy the illusion of reality. The audience is reminded twice—first by the Beggar and then by the Gardener—that it is participating in "make-believe"; he lets the audience know that it is participating in a demonstration of an idea. Giraudoux' *Electra,* then, is structurally theatricalized drama, not actually remote, except in the superiority of the content, from a Salvation Army lecture in which a convert describes his misdemeanors.

It is *one* kind of drama; more radically "theatrical" than even expressionist drama, in so far as Giraudoux does not maintain the fiction that his unrealistically presented picture is the fantasy or dream-formation of a character in the play. Expressionism is "subjective"—in the sense that reality is drastically exaggerated and distorted to *match* somebody's state of mind, whether he be a character in the play[1] or the author himself.[2] In *Electra,* on the contrary, we have *objective,* quite detached, make-believe. The play is candidly theatricalized with a view to establishing the objectivity of the events as simply theatre. The audience is given illustrative action rather than a pretense of reality: In this kind of advanced "theatricalism"—decidedly more advanced than fantasy and than subjective drama —the author may go so far as to make his play an illustrated lecture, as Bertolt Brecht has done in his *Lehrstücke*—"teaching plays" that used to be called "learning plays" in America during the thirties. An American variant was the "living newspaper" introduced in the New Deal days by the Federal Theatre as dramatized journalism. Giraudoux, of course, is imaginative rather than factual in his play. He works with characters, symbols, poetic emphases, fantasy, and brilliant *coups de théâtre.* He is as full-fledged an artist in this tragedy as he is in his fantastic comedies. It is possible to appreciate his *Electra* as provocative drama, though probably more easily in France than on Broadway. The quality of the dialogue and the monologues alone can be a source of considerable gratification. And (a matter rarely minimized by a critic in search of a reputation) it is interesting to write about Giraudoux' tragedy.

Much more so, I believe, than to write about *Mourning Becomes Electra.* That this is any test of merit, however, is greatly to be doubted, as is the notion that the non-realistic form by itself makes a play better than a realistic one—or *vice versa.* We must start merely with the fact that

---

[1] The composer-hero of Kaufman and Connelly's *Beggar on Horseback,* who dreams of how routinized his life will be if he marries a wealthy Babbitt's daughter: "You take our money and you lead our life."

[2] Various gradations: Strindberg's *The Dream Play* and *The Spook Sonata,* Elmer Rice's *The Adding Machine,* and O'Neill's *The Hairy Ape.* In some expressionist plays, the fantasy is presented as *both* the character's and the author's subjective creation. In Ernst Toller's *Masse-Mensch (Man and the Masses* in the English translation by Louis Untermeyer) the German Revolution of 1918 is rendered partly as Toller's nightmare view of an uprising of the masses and partly as the heroine's nightmare in a prison-cell.

Mourning Becomes Electra is a substantially different kind of drama from the French play. This is the case not because it is constructed, or "structured," in a realistic pattern. O'Neill, who demonstrated a strong partiality for non-realistic styles of theatre in earlier plays such as *The Emperor Jones* and *The Great God Brown,* constantly admonishes the main actors of the play to adopt masklike expressions, and he employs a naturalistic chorus of New England townspeople in each part of his trilogy. O'Neill is also a conscious theatrician in his use of atmosphere as well as of symbolic detail. (He assigns a symbolic function to the doors of the house, for example, in the last scene of the play.) More than that, he drives hard for parallels. His Electra's situation at the end resembles her mother's at the beginning of the trilogy. His Orestes, who desired his mother, later (now that she is dead) desires a mother-image in his sister Lavinia. And this Electra, who desired her mother's husband in obsessively loving her father, the Agamemnon-Ezra of the play, unconsciously also wanted her mother's lover, David Mannon, the Aegisthus of the drama. O'Neill wrings a special schematism out of the Freudian psychology he applied to his Electra and Orestes. His scheme is decidedly more theatrical than natural, and it becomes a rather transparent pattern of play-making in the third part of the trilogy. Nevertheless, O'Neill uses theatrical means merely to punctuate the illusion of reality, not to puncture it. And one may credit O'Neill with some sort of tact or dramatic strategy that he did not indulge his stylizing inclinations much further in a work that already carries a surplus of passion and of melodramatic action.

The essential difference between the two Electra plays is that O'Neill concentrated on the story for its own sake, which means, in a sense, for life's sake. That must be one reason why he turned the fifth century B.C. Greek characters into a nineteenth-century New England family and supplied a suitable background of economic interests (the Mannons are in business, not the king-business), folk-life, and folk-idiom. Without stinting on the universality of the passions, O'Neill made the Oresteian legend a local American experience. So much so, indeed, that the dialogue rarely rises to the demands of the drama's passion, giving cause for disappointment to his admirers and satisfaction to his detractors. Working as a part-time naturalist, he has tried not to let the characters step out of their local habitation and exceed the limits of their power to articulate feelings and thoughts. His writing generally stays as far away from literary distinction as it is possible to keep it and still convey intense actions and responses through dialogue. Only the pulse of drama is in the dialogue, not the cadence; only the structure, not the superstructure. Whether or not it was a mistake on O'Neill's part to remain on this level of language, and whether, in view of his limited talent for verbalization, he could have successfully engaged language on a higher level, is hardly a question requiring special gyrations from dramatic criticism. We can simply note that he did not or could not write more memorably, and we are surely in the right when we consider this limitation a serious one.

That it is not, in the opinion of some of us, a disastrous one is due to the extreme density—and intensity—of the experience set down in *Mourning Becomes Electra* as relentlessly as in a Dreiser novel. The density cannot be established without reprinting the entire long play, for it is a cumulative experience that cannot be demonstrated by means of short quotations. (It is always easier to quote O'Neill to his detriment than to his credit.) O'Neill worked additively rather than in flashes of genius as did Giraudoux. He had to pile detail upon detail in building his monumental drama. Although some condensation could be desired, he had to make his play long in order to make it substantial.

The intensity of the play, too, cannot be described by fragmentary means. It is possible to point to such details as his Electra-Lavinia's behavior when her father is with her mother in front of the house and in the bedroom (Act III, Part I), or to the macabre atmosphere generated just before the Christine-Clytemnestra's lover David Mannon is slain by O'Neill's Orestes, Orin. It is not possible, however, to formulate adequately the tension when Christine meets her son, when she is with her returned husband in their bedroom and poisons him, or when she receives the news that her son has killed her lover. Moreover, these are all *acting* scenes rather than fundamentally *speaking* scenes, as is the case with some of the most impressive portions of Giraudoux' *Electra*. I very much doubt that the post-1930 generation of playreaders or playgoers can form an adequate impression of the sheer power of the play when Alla Nazimova, the Christine of the Theatre Guild production directed by Philip Moeller, was on the stage.

Nor is it simply the quality of the acting the play receives that makes the difference. The acting possibilities are *in* the play rather than outside it for anybody who knows how to look for them in texts for the theatre. O'Neill laid the foundations for something more than a superimposed virtuoso performance. That foundation is laid layer by layer in a sequence of revelations, concealments, externalized tensions, and final open conflict. The things done or stated in the final minutes of climax of scenes or acts are things grown in the womb of each portion of the play like a canker. The playwright is not in a hurry here merely to "put across" an idea; the idea in *Mourning Becomes Electra* that human beings can be driven to take desperate measures by the "Oedipus complex" is far from profound and could have been expressed much more economically. But O'Neill refuses to short-circuit the *experience* that constitutes the tragedy. With respect to this kind of playwriting—fundamentally akin to that of Sophocles, Shakespeare, Racine, the mature Ibsen, the early O'Casey, and Chekhov—talk about "esthetic distance" and about "form" for the purpose of ensuring it can become irrelevant mumbo-jumbo good enough only to cast glory on professors of English and their graduate-school students.

The playwright could not afford to be ostentatiously brilliant in treating the situations and characters. He could not obtrude upon the latter without annihilating their immediacy as initiators and sufferers of the action. If O'Neill had annihilated that experience, he would have had no play whatsoever, for he has little else to offer. His Freudian scheme, when considered by itself, is tiresome; his criticism of the sterility of materialistic New England Puritanism, oversimplified. (The subject has been better treated by American novelists ever since Hawthorne began to write.) Experience, as O'Neill's dramatic instinct must have told him, can only be *grown,* and so he grew the Greek legend as human reality on his stage moment by moment, feeling upon feeling, deed upon deed. Shakespeare did the same thing with his good and evil harvest in *Hamlet, Macbeth, Othello, King Lear,* and *Antony and Cleopatra.* If the results are so much more varied, so much richer, so much more gratifying in all respects, this merely measures the difference between the greater playwright and the lesser, and between the world's greatest poet and an American prose-writer.

For O'Neill the sowing and the reaping are, in the main, the slow, methodical work of a day laborer. But he *completes* the labor, he does not circumvent it. And in view of his utter involvement in the story of the madding Mannons, he could rightly feel, I believe, that showing them in simple, sequential action was all that was necessary and desirable. There was already enough puppetry forced upon the characters by the intensity of the passions with which he had endowed them for him to dangle the strings of another, subsidiary of puppetry—namely, the craft ingenuities of formalistic playwriting. Moreover, such strings are by intention, if not indeed of necessity, plainly in sight of the audience. Cocteau and Giraudoux dangled them conspicuously in *The Infernal Machine* and *Electra* respectively. But to do so in the case of *Mourning Becomes Electra* would have been tantamount to undoing the direct realization of the story O'Neill took such pains to achieve. For better or worse, he had to let the play make a simple equation with life rather than work out a dramatic calculus. That is exactly what he did—and it is the equation of whatever merit or greatness we attribute to the work.

Which Electra play we prefer is a matter of taste and a question of expectation—that is, of what we expect from a drama on the particular subject, or perhaps of drama in general. I could not even attempt to adjudicate the rival claims of taste and expectation without courting the labor of a lifetime and the risk of folly from the start. For myself I can only report that Giraudoux' play interests me more, but that O'Neill's overpowers me. If I venture farther, it is only to suggest that American playwrights in search of new forms of dramatic expression can learn more from the example of Giraudoux than from that of O'Neill. But they would be well advised to be on guard lest they have only the puppet-strings, intellectual or theatrical or both, to show for their exertions. Even Giraudoux ran that risk, and, for all his exquisite intelligence and skill, did not entirely escape its consequences. His Greek supernatural machinery, which provides good stage effects, telegraphs cleverness to the audience, whereas O'Neill's plain-as-daylight, if fevered, action is self-contained. Giraudoux faces the Greeks one moment and the rest of mankind the next moment, but in neither case can we forget that a scholar-gentleman is holding the stage and arranging the lecture for us, whereas in O'Neill's case we may feel that the Mannons themselves are forcing the issue blindly and insistently, although his cumbersome stage directions can give the contrary impression.

T. S. ELIOT: THE POET
AS ANTI-MODERNIST

I

It is my belief that until now[1] Eliot has not proved to be a playwright of more than slight and uneven accomplishment. Scholars and critics have been concerned with his plays disproportionately, mainly because of his standing as a poet and critic, and to no small degree because his work has provided rich opportunities for explicatory allusion-hunting and the search for parallels between lines in his plays and lines in his poems. Eliot has been and will continue to be a rewarding subject for discourse on literature.

Although much talent has been manifest in his dramatic work, his legitimate place in the theatre thus far would be small but for considerations that carry beyond his actual achievement in the two fragments of *Sweeney Agonistes,* the liturgical drama *Murder in the Cathedral, The Family Reunion,* and *The Cocktail Party.* The fragments contain the consistently best dramatic writing of which he has been capable until now, but they remain little more than exercises for amateur groups.

Murder in the Cathedral is probably the most successful modern religious drama, with the possible exception of Paul Claudel's less controlled but more richly characterized drama *The Tidings Brought to Mary.* I omit the one play that towers over both Eliot's and Claudel's plays, Tolstoy's *The Power of Darkness,* because I use "religious drama" in the narrow sense of more or less *liturgical* drama. And in doing so, I have simultaneously defined the limitation of *Murder in the Cathedral.* It belongs more to the church than to our theatre, as Eliot himself realized when he wrote the play for a Canterbury Cathedral festival in 1935.

The Family Reunion is, to my mind, an utter failure in spite of the presence of remarkable writing in the text. Admiring critics of the author have variously noted his failure, none better than C. L. Barber in a *Southern Review* article reprinted in the volume *T. S. Eliot: A Selected Critique,* edited by Leonard Unger. Moreover, they are all pushed into a classroom seat—even Mr. Barber, who lost himself in psychoanalytical speculations toward the end of his study—by Eliot himself. His comments on the play in his 1950 Theodore Spencer Memorial Lecture *Poetry and*

---

[1] *The Confidential Clerk,* seen later, has not changed this opinion.

Drama constitute a model of candid and down-to-earth self-criticism. This leaves us with only one play that is viable in the modern theatre, *The Cocktail Party,* first produced at the Edinburgh Festival in 1949 and successfully presented in London's West End and on Broadway. A slim harvest for the eighteen years between 1935 and 1952, even if we grant that *The Cocktail Party* is a masterpiece—a description I cannot quite allow, and not allowed by some of the author's closest students and staunchest admirers.

Any other playwright with as little to show for nearly two decades would not be considered a significant figure in the theatre. Yet Eliot has been considered, and to my mind rightly considered, such a figure. Not on the grounds of his "literary" importance, for André Gide, who wrote more plays, has not been regarded as significant in the theatre in spite of his having had a literary reputation at least the equal of Eliot's. The reason for our paying so much attention to Eliot is that his work represents the most definite break with modern playwriting that has, nevertheless, been a completely *modern* endeavor rather than a retograde activity.

Other writers who broke with the modern theatrical mode or modes did so in one of two ways. Some playwrights entrenched themselves in some area of the Western world not yet conspicuously industrialized and urbanized, such as southern Ireland and Spain, becoming, in a manner of speaking, folk dramatists. John Millington Synge and Federico García Lorca (I might add the young Yeats) are the outstanding representatives of this school. A second group of playwrights beat a retreat to romantic, largely historical drama. Rostand is the most celebrated of the early anti-modern romanticists, although his spicing of the heroic element in his plays with irony indicates that his was no naïve return to chivalry. Claudel is another romanticist. Although he is not that in his use of "psychology," he is romantic in his full-blown rhetoric and frequently turgid plotting. Maxwell Anderson, especially in his historical plays, is another romanticist, although he spices his writing with salty language and gives "realism" its due, now and then, when he treats sexual and political involvements.

Eliot does not retreat to folk drama or to historicity for the purpose of romance. (Even *Murder in the Cathedral* represents no such retreat. The play is anything but a romance, and the history of Becket is not recalled for reasons of historical interest.) Yet more than any other playwright for whom more than local and evanescent distinction can be claimed, Eliot represents a turn in the tide of modern drama. Acutely conscious of the failure of so-called modern values, of anarchy in society and in men's souls, he has turned against the progressivism that distinguished modern drama at its inception and that has formed the dominant mode of influential modern playwriting. In doing so he has profoundly battered the world-view and disposition of the so-called Liberal Doctrine, contradicting its several ideals or illusions—the idealization of Individuality, Will, Reason, and Instinct.

The modern theatre has been predominantly the resultant of the forces of Protestantism, democracy, rationalism, materialism, and science, whether mechanistic or vitalistic, and whether pre-Freudian or Freudian. The modern drama was largely the creation of the liberal Protestantism of the Scandinavian countries, through the endeavors of Ibsen, Björnson, and Strindberg, abetted by the social criticism of Protestant British authors such as Shaw and Galsworthy, the social-mindedness of Russian playwriting, the "scientific" orientation of Zola and Hauptmann, the German-trained but also free-thinking metaphysical disposition of Pirandello, and the scepticism of French writers.

Eliot strenuously opposed each of the fetishes of these modernists and their successors as a playwright as well as a poet and essayist. Individuality, unredeemed by self-sacrifice, expiation, and acceptance of a burden of guilt and of one's human limitations, has received short shrift from him. Reason he has exposed as a broken reed. Instinct, regarded by most modern playwrights as a subject for clinical study or as a justification of revolt against convention (against "Victorianism" in England, against "Puritanism" in America), has been regarded by Eliot as a source of sin and spiritual darkness.

Social reformation, in the liberal's sense of the term, has been a matter of no consequence for him, whereas it has been of consequence to most playwrights since the advent of Ibsenism. His object has been to *"redeem the times."* Indignation, more or less socially directed even by psychological dramatists such as Strindberg and Wedekind, has been the ferment in much of the playwriting that has kept the modern world in view. And this indignation has presupposed the needlessness of human wrong and the possibility of correcting it by social enlightenment. (Only in his last religious phase did Strindberg depart from this view.) But Eliot had predicated failure from the start: To live without redemption is to live under the cloud of "original sin," and to make even a satisfactory life for oneself without sanctification is merely to make the best of a bad bargain, which is the destiny of the worldly Chamberlayne couple in *The Cocktail Party*. Much modern playwriting has been explicitly or tacitly rebellious, whereas Eliot's has been explicitly or tacitly predicated upon an acceptance of one's "burden." In this respect, all positivist modern drama has been romantic in spirit even when the style was ultra-realistic, and the symbolist poet Eliot has been perhaps the modern theatre's only consistent anti-romanticist.

In challenging the liberal dispensation of modern drama on so many grounds, Eliot has been amazingly thorough even though it has increasingly become his ambition to succeed in the commercial theatre, and he may make more and more concessions to it with new plays as he becomes an expert playwright. It would be a mistake, however, to leave his work at the level of content and ideas. A quality of writing, consisting of both style and treatment of character and action, is involved in this departure from the main line of modern playwriting. And Eliot demonstrates this fact more conclusively than anyone else.

Claudel, with whose views Eliot is more or less in accord, does not do so as distinctly by any means, because there is much that is both baroque and romantic in his writing, just as there is a warmth, even a fire or heat, in it that Eliot lacks. (Eliot talks a great deal about tradition, but he is a parvenu intellectual religionist by comparison with Claudel, who is deeply rooted in the Catholic tradition that accepts, pities, and enfolds sinful humanity.) English followers of Eliot who write religious drama create as yet in too routine a manner, echoing not only Eliot but Elizabethan and romantic poet-playwrights. The best of England's new authors of verse plays, Christopher Fry, is a buoyant—and sometimes in *The Lady's Not for Burning,* a delightful—romanticist, when he is not a more or less routine festival-play-monger. Yeats, when he wrote his *Plays for Dancers* and *Purgatory,* was more original than any of these writers, and I believe that he was also more original in his last plays than Eliot himself. But Yeats did not operate in the field of modern non-esoteric theatre at all in his last work, whereas Eliot's inclination has been to do so ever since he wrote the pungent realistic dialogue and characterization of the *Sweeney Agonistes* scenes.

If it appears that his new play *The Confidential Clerk* successfully accommodates itself to the prevailing modern mode (and that accommodation started with the writing of *The Cocktail Party*), this only means that Eliot has realistically resolved to try his skill in the medium of commercial theatre. It does not mean that Eliot's *distinctive* approach to the drama has run in any of the fixed grooves of modernism.

II

There can be no doubt that Eliot has partly achieved and partly pointed toward a reorientation of modern drama in modern terms that other playwrights have not had in view with anything equaling his clarity and decisiveness. To understand this neo-modern quality, however, we must first consider the quality of writing from which Eliot indicates a departure, whether or not he has actually succeeded in departing from it or succeeded in writing good plays. Perhaps Shaw's playwriting is the best example, since Shaw subsumed virtually all the ideas of the Liberal

Doctrine and many of the qualities of playwriting that have adhered to it since Ibsen's middle period.

If Shaw's work radiates one quality more than any other, it is a certain blithe confidence in life generally and in the goodness or good will of human beings, particularly. This is the effulgence we cannot deny to his work, not even to the mordant early plays *Widowers' Houses* and *Mrs. Warren's Profession* and to such works of the close of his career as *The Apple Cart, Too True to Be Good,* and *On the Rocks* in which he succumbed to some despair for Western civilization. So imbued was his spirit with the optimism of the nineteenth century and the rationalism of the eighteenth that he could turn from these plays to such insouciant exercises as *The Millionairess* and *In Good King Charles's Golden Days;* this, in the years of fascist rule many of us regarded as the very nadir of Western history. Nor should we overlook that singularly unsatisfactory play about Hitler's challenge to Europe, *Geneva,* in which his blithe spirit seemed the epitome of aged boyishness.

Youthful confidence, even carefreeness, never seemed very distant from Shaw, except in *Heartbreak House* and *Saint Joan,* just as middle-aged sobriety, if not indeed premature old age, never seems to leave T. S. Eliot. To a sage of the ancient Eastern world the classic Greeks seemed happy children. Shaw exuded both happiness and youthfulness. In spite of all the social criticism imparted by his work, he was generally bubbling with the joy of life—which means, of course, that there were large tracts of life that he tended to ignore.

There are areas of darkness that Shaw barely recognizes in the characterizations and actions of the plays. Nobody is really evil in Shaw's play-world. Even in *Saint Joan* an outrage against humanity is perpetrated by everything but inherent evil in mankind. By weakness (the Dauphin), by stupidity or obtuseness (John de Stogumber), by rational self-interest (Warwick), by principle (the Inquisitor, a character drawn with remarkable sympathy), but not by profoundly evil men. There are no Iagos in the Shavian cosmos. Shaw's war with society is not with indurated villainy, but with stupidity. Shaw is singularly *pure*. Eliot, on the other hand, is profoundly aware of sin, though, I believe, mainly as an abstraction. He seems to be aware of little else except its complement, the necessity of redemption.

Consequently, Shaw works out human destiny in the light even when he takes note of cloudy weather for humanity, and Eliot works in a darkness even when he treats the English salon-world of comedy of manners in *The Family Reunion* and *The Cocktail Party*. The *tone* of the writing differs profoundly, as if Shaw and Eliot were living in different worlds.

The difference in tone is apparent in Eliot's work from the beginning of his dramatic writing in *Sweeney Agonistes,* if not indeed in snatches of dialogue in *The Waste Land.* His informal dialogue (informal, though in verse) contains much mimicry, and mimicry in Eliot's writing tends to be ironic and deprecatory, as though he either despised or condescended to the speakers. The opening of the first *Sweeney* fragment, if not indeed most of the text of both fragments, may be cited as an example. Dusty and Doris, two girls who would not qualify for a girls' seminary, are speaking in alternate lines which go as follows:

> DUSTY: How about Pereira?
> DORIS: What about Pereira?
>   I don't care.
> DUSTY: You don't care!
>   Who pays the rent?
> DORIS: Yes, he pays the rent
> DUSTY: Well, some men don't and some men do
>   Some men don't and you know who
> DORIS: You can have Pereira
> DUSTY: What about Pereira?
> DORIS: He's no gentleman, Pereira ...

Even the lighter mimicry of the first scene of *The Cocktail Party,* so amusing at times when Julia and Alex rattle on, bears a contemptuous implication. A spiritual void is implicit in such lines as

> Do tell us that story you told the other day, about
>   Lady Klootz and the wedding cake.
> —And how the butler found her in the pantry, rinsing her
>   mouth out with the champagne. I like that story.
> I love that story.
> —I'm never tired of hearing that story. . . .
> Am I a good mimic?
> —You are a good mimic. . . .

Eliot purses his lips, so to speak, whereas Shaw takes deep and hearty breaths and speaks out like a good fellow who enjoys a spat or a flight of hearty rhetoric. Shaw employs proportionately much less mimicry, and there isn't a drop of malice in it, as we may note in the querulous lines assigned to Eliza in the Covent Garden vegetable market before Higgins has turned her into a lady. And nothing in Eliot's writing suggests the ease and humorous benevolence, the token of a generous and genial spirit, to be found in her father Doolittle's speeches in Act V of *Pygmalion:*

> It ain't the lecturing I mind. I'll lecture them blue in the face, I
> will, and not turn a hair. It's making a gentleman of me that I
> object to. . . . Now I am worrited; tied neck and heels. . . . When
> I was poor and had a solicitor once when they found a pram in

the dust cart, he got me off, and got shut of me and got me shut
of him as quick as he could. Same with the doctors; used to shove
me out of the hospital before I could hardly stand on my legs, and
nothing to pay. . . .

Eliot, too, jests at times, but he does so wryly, and the jest usually
turns sour. A good example is Harry's comments in *The Family Reunion*
on an accident to his brother John:

> A minor trouble like a concussion
> Cannot make very much difference to John.
> A brief vacation from the kind of consciousness
> That John enjoys, can't make very much difference
> To him or to anyone else.

It turns out that Harry, who has delivered himself of these neat lines,
wasn't really jesting, as he explains:

> If he was ever really conscious,
> I should be glad for him to have a breathing spell:
> But John's ordinary day isn't much more than breathing.

In the first part of the speech Harry is sadistic; in the second part, a prig.

Eliot himself later realized that he had made him one: "My hero now
strikes me as an insufferable prig," he declares in *Poetry and Drama*. But
the tight-lipped quality is present everywhere in Eliot's treatment of
modern people, even where it attains poetic elevation. When the writing
isn't saturnine, it is cryptic, stern with judgment, or with a Sinaitic quality of command in the intonations. The lines are coldly formal, or coldly
ritualistic, even when sympathy is intended, as in the words for Celia's
departure on her spiritual quest:

> She will pass between the scolding hills
> Through the valley of derision, like a child sent on an errand
> In eagerness and patience. Yet she must suffer. . . .
> Watch over her in the desert
> Watch over her in the mountain
> Watch over her by the labyrinth,
> Watch over her by the quicksand. . . .

We need only listen to Joan's last speech in Shaw's play to note the difference in tone:

> I could do without my warhouse; I could drag about in a skirt;
> I could let the banners and the trumpets and the knights and
> soldiers pass me and leave me behind as they leave other women,
> if only I could still hear the wind in the trees, the larks in the
> sunshine, the young lambs crying through the healthy frost, and
> the blessed church bells that send my angel voices to me on the
> wind.

And, as Eliot's disciples, the New Critics, would be the first to maintain, a difference in the texture of the writing is revelatory of a difference in other vital respects—in the spirit and meaning of a work.[2]

The differences in characterization, rendered by the action as well as dialogue, are equally striking. Shaw always shows the surface, even when he draws complex characters; that is, their complications are invariably externalized. Nothing about the characters is hidden or left unexplained or at all unclear to themselves, as in the case of Eliot's Harry, Lord Monchensey, who doesn't know why he feels guilty, cannot explain his feelings to the other characters, and never arrives at an explanation that is objectively valid. Shaw's people, even when in error, are adequate for the purpose of making a good and full life. All they have to do is get rid of their prepossessions, ignorance, or self-indulgence, and think out a course of action. Eliot's people, without spiritual guidance, are never adequate for any sort of life. They may become adequate for a spiritual quest, as in the case of Celia Copplestone. Either that, or they are adequate only for the diminished life considered proper for people of inferior spiritual endowment such as the Chamberlaynes of *The Cocktail Party*.

Even when Eliot's characters are defined as socially active, as Becket is in promoting the claims of the Church against the claims of the state, and as Celia Copplestone is in ministering medically to the natives of Kinkanja (both, by the way, *offstage actions*), they are extracted from social reality by their author, who is concerned primarily with their personal salvation. They are entirely adequate, indeed, only to their death, and the movement of the play that carries Becket and Celia along is only toward a certain kind of death. They must die to the world in order to live fully for Eliot.

Often Shaw seems to be having a buoyant amateur's affair with life, as his treatment of character shows so well, whereas Eliot has a tired, dis-

---

[2] That Eliot's lines concerning Celia would be designated as formal poetry and Shaw's as prose-poetry is not a conclusive difference. Eliot himself has considered it deplorable for people to make a fetish of verse "if that means they are prepared to enjoy the play and the language of the play as two separate things." Nor would there be much distinction as to "poetry" between the passages by Eliot and Shaw if the eye of the reader saw Joan's lines on the page, as follows:

> I could do without my warhorse
> I could drag about in a skirt
> I could let the banners and the trumpets
> And the knights and soldiers pass me
> And leave me behind as they leave the other women
> If only I could still hear the wind in the trees
> The larks in the sunshine
> The young lambs crying through the healthy frost
> And the blessed church bells that send
> My angel voices floating to me on the wind.

enchanted relationship to it. If Shaw may give us the impression of being too young, Eliot gives the impression of being too old. Shaw sometimes behaves as if he were too inexperienced, Eliot as if he had experienced everything and that everything was worth nothing. Eliot is constantly hinting, if not indeed saying, that human beings are patients with more complications of disease than they can ever realize without illumination from a supernatural source that alone fully knows the extreme morbidity of their condition. The veteran Fabian playwright seems to be a breezy and easily satisfied diagnostician; Eliot, a relentlessly profound one. The cures Shaw proffers look like the nostrums of a street-corner pitchman; Eliot's, like the prescriptions of a glum Harley Street physician who disdains placebos even when the patients are clamoring for them. Shaw seems to be having a good time of it while plying his profession; Eliot, a very bad, or at least very lean, time of it while plying his. The one man seems over-exhilarated by his realizations; the other, somewhat numbed by his.

The styles of the two different kinds of playwriting reflect—or rather, express—these distinctions, too, as do the respective structural patterns. Shaw's plays invariably possess an air of informality, if not indeed improvisation; Eliot's are formalistic. *Murder in the Cathedral* is mainly compounded of chorus, litany, sermon in the manner of a seventeenth-century doctor of divinity (Bishop Lancelot Andrewes), and a formal apologia by the knights who assassinated Becket. *The Family Reunion* consists of formal speeches, a semi-lyrical interlude, and a chorus of the Eumenides, Harry's private, voyeuristic furies. *The Cocktail Party,* the least formalistic of Eliot's pieces, incorporates the ritual of confession, a conclave of guardian angels, and a eucharistic rite in the middle section. Shaw's playwriting is prose triumphant—always directly communicative. Eliot's medium is formal poetry, allusive, elusive, and wrapped in mystery even when the writing is admirably precise. Shaw cockily tells all; Eliot is restrained and enigmatic. The former rattles on conversationally, and his eloquence has the quality of a harangue. Eliot often intones, and his eloquence takes the form of ritualistic incantation. Eliot, the formalist, necessarily allows prose-poetry only a secondary place. Poetic drama, for him, must be verse drama. He does not explain his predilection on a formalistic basis, but the very fact that he casts even banal speeches into verse in *The Cocktail Party* indicates his bias.

In *Poetry and Drama,* he considers versification to be necessary as a sort of preparation for the passages of true poetry in a play. But his technical reasons are unconvincing in the case of *The Cocktail Party.* His possibly less than conscious motive is an inclination to restrain dramatic writing, even as he is bent on placing restraints upon human nature. And the necessity of restraining it follows logically from the premise of original sin as held by a fastidious man who has been more fastidiously British than the British, as self-exiled Americans are likely to be.

There are, indeed, significant implications in his views on the use of poetry in the theatre. Poetry is needed to catch the unnamable, unclassifiable emotions and motives. It is to reveal that part of life on the fringe of consciousness that "we can only detect, so to speak, out of the corner of the eye and can never completely focus." It is to express the feelings that we are aware of only "in a kind of temporary detachment from action." The aim here is the opposite of that kept in view by the modern playwrights whose object was to bring social and psychological reality into focus. These writers would have considered an ideal of "detachment from action" the very mark of failure. Eliot's divergence from their aims is nowhere better expressed than in the concluding sentence of *Poetry and Drama* in which he considers the function of art. That function is ultimately one of "eliciting some perception of an order" that may bring us "to a condition of serenity, stillness, and reconciliation" and then leave us, "as Virgil left Dante," to proceed where non-spiritual guidance "can avail us no farther."

Eliot's kind of playwriting, then, holds in sight the polar antithesis of the kind of drama with which we associate the success and failure of the modern theatre. Nor is the contrast with Shaw confined to Shavian dramaturgy and the related dramatic art of Ibsen and post-Ibsen realism. Even when Ibsen, in his post-*Rosmersholm* period, concentrates on character drama or steeps his work in atmosphere and symbolism, he keeps his dramatic style and form largely analytical and rationalistic—and, for the most part, also socially directed. And the same thing is true of Chekhov's otherwise radically different kind of playwriting. Even its rich counterpoint is mundane, in the sense that Chekhov stays entirely within the world of human interests and relations. Even psychological drama, fathered by Strindberg and furthered for good or ill by Wedekind and O'Neill, is ultimately rationalistic drama. Although the subject is irrational human behavior, everything is considered explainable—and is more or less explained. Eliot stands for non-psychological drama; there are things in life that cannot be explained, and Eliot is never more exalted in his poetry than when he is also enigmatic and hinting at an ineffable mystery.

Late in life, Strindberg, like Eliot, became concerned with spiritual reality and aware of the need of redemption. In order to express his more or less religious content, however, Strindberg destroyed a formal picture of the world with his expressionism instead of imposing, as Eliot desiderates, "a credible order upon ordinary reality." He became an artistic as well as a religious heretic of the Gnostic variety, and in this respect loosened the artistic and religious bonds that Eliot attempts to tie tighter.

Far from making the drama more orderly when he tried to put order into his life, Strindberg made his dramatic composition anarchic. And this is exactly what has happened in the case of nearly all the experimental anti-realistic playwriting we have had from *Ubu Roi,* written by Alfred Jarry in 1888, to the latest surrealistic mélange. At the most tasteful level of such writing—let us cite Giraudoux' *Intermezzo* and *The Madwoman of Chaillot* or the Anouilh-Fry *Ring Around the Moon*—there will still be found an indulgent, free-wheeling artistry in the style, plotting, characterization, and viewpoint. The afflatus is more Shavian than we first realize in the case of this kind of poetic or fanciful writing.

One way or another, the non-realistic playwriting of the modern stage has exemplified a riot of artistic as well as social individualism, checked somewhat in the case of some French writers, such as Cocteau, Anouilh, and Giraudoux, only when they made adaptations of classic drama—and not really even then. Consider, for example, even such a comparatively orderly piece as Cocteau's "Oedipus the King" variant *The Infernal Machine,* not to mention his *Orpheus.* Cocteau, who based his play on the most classical and thoroughly tragic of Greek dramas, is exuberantly improvisatory while moving toward the tragic dénouement, as well as strongly "psychological" in treating the Oedipus-Jocasta relationship. He is an intellectual anarchist in a large part of *The Infernal Machine,* as well as an unreformed rationalist in resorting to Freudianism. Not so Eliot. Starting with thematic suggestions from Euripides' satyr-play variant, *Alcestis,* the most comic of Greek tragedies, Eliot makes *The Cocktail Party* a morality drama which is neither exuberant, in spite of comedy of manners in the first and third acts, nor rationalistic in spite of the role of Sir Henry Harcourt-Reilly as "psychoanalyst." The uniqueness of his role lies, indeed, in the fact that whereas his patients expect rationalistic or scientific treatment at his office, they receive only moral and mystic ministrations. The fascination of his associates, the "guardians" Julia and Alex, comes from the fact that their urbanity is simply a masquerade by spiritual powers.

III

Ultimately, of course, we must come to the question of how much or what kind of gratification can be derived from Eliot. Without question, his work calls attention to the looseness and indiscipline that have been characteristic of modern drama both in its content and style. Eliot's writing has been incisive, disciplined, and tight. Yet it seems to me that in trying to operate as a dramatist without the qualities that have distinguished characteristic modern playwriting in one way or another, he has lost a great deal that makes drama a gratifying art; and it is likely that a school of writing strongly leaning in his direction would reveal the same impoverishment regardless of the literary talents of the writer. The result may be improvement in literary quality and retrogression in dramatic quality. Eliot will not redeem the modern theatre. What he has lost and others are likely to lose may be described as a quality of exuberance, passion, and human interest. In the process of seeking to redeem mankind, Eliot, more often than not, appears to have lost humanity in the plays he wrote before *The Confidential Clerk*.

I am concerned here only with the dramatic consequences of this loss, which can be merely covered up by the actors who perform in his plays. It was their contribution that counted strongly in favor of *The Cocktail Party* in the New York production which had Alec Guiness playing Sir Harcourt-Reilly and Irene Worth playing Celia. (The actors' contribution was less marked in the London production I saw in the summer of 1950. With Rex Harrison playing the doctor more lightly, and Celia being played with more brittleness than in New York, *The Cocktail Party* seemed to me considerably attenuated.) The moral implications of Eliot's loss do not concern me here directly, although, as I am not the first to have noted, he has leaned toward the Antinomian heresy which makes moral action of small consequence to salvation. At least, his interest in morality is scanty at the same time that his interest in religion is intense. He has favored perhaps too great a leap from ordinary mortality in his pursuit of religion for dramatic purposes. Even his great talent has not been able to bridge the distance he has put between himself and mortality in his most austere moments of illumination—sacramental moments which like the esthetic ones of his master Mallarmé carry too heavy a load of ambiguity. Moreover, he has tended to hew too closely to the words of the Spanish mystic St. John of the Cross which Eliot printed as an epigraph to *Sweeney Agonistes*: "Hence the soul cannot be possessed of the divine union, until it has divested itself of the love of created beings." It is very much to be doubted whether a playwright can afford to follow the same procedure.

If Eliot himself has not generally gone quite so far, he has gone far enough to divest dramatic art of much of its customary warmth and fire. This was not the case when the great Greeks, Shakespeare, and Racine wrote poetic drama. And he has also nearly divested playwriting of exuberance, on the one hand, and tenderness on the other. There is brittle humor in the dialogue *of The Cocktail Hour* (he out-Cowards Noel Coward in Act One), but there is singularly little zest or joy in the play

—and also less tenderness than it could profitably use. It is not surprising that he should have been quite successful in writing comedy of manners, a field in which detachment brings rewards, but he fails his characters when they need sympathy rather than bright chatter in their dialogue, as in the scene in which Celia's death is reported. He achieves poetry of some magnitude in that act. During the greater part of the play, when he is rendering human relations, his verse dialogue is only precise. His writing glows least when it makes direct contact with humanity. There is irony indeed in the fact that Eliot has thus far invaded the popular theatre with success only by scuttling a large portion of his most valuable cargo—namely, his distinguished poetry.

Thus far in his work for the stage, then, Eliot, whose highest ambitions for mankind transcend the world and the flesh, has brought too narrow a heart to the spectacle of human life. His achievement as a playwright has been limited by this defect. It appears in the resolution of his plays no less than in the developing action; human beings don't seem to matter much as persons. Becket disappears as a human being in the last part of *Murder in the Cathedral,* and long before then he was already a personage rather than a person. Harry, Lord Monchensey, has no true resolution in *The Family Reunion* for his sense of guilt, mainly because the play is pyramided on a dramatically non-existent situation—a deceased father's passing desire to destroy Harry's mother and Harry's own ambiguous guilt. It is curious that the father's homicidal intentions should be treated in *The Family Reunion* as decidedly more important to Harry than the strong possibility that he drowned his own wife. That action, whether it ever occurred or was merely desired by Harry, was a burden on his conscience. But Eliot seems to dismiss this question, as if the murder of a woman were a small matter. (The "Antinomian heresy," or is it simply a constriction of the heart, justified for Eliot by the greater, theological importance of inherited guilt?) It is no wonder, then, that there is nothing else by way of a resolution in Harry's drama than his leaving his mother, which will probably result in her death, and his following the Furies for no purpose other than perhaps a vague search for an indefinable something. Celia Copplestone does not appear in the resolution of *The Cocktail Party.* Once she is dismissed by Reilly with the words, "Work out your resolution with diligence," to which he adds the *consummatum est* reserved for the mystic sacrifice—"It is finished"—Celia ceases to be a person in the play. A rather cavalier disposal of a human being, especially in the case of the most appealing and human character of *The Cocktail Party!* The rest of her life, which came to a horrible end in a native insurrection, is only a report introduced rather whimsically by the "guardians" Julia and Alex.[3] Eliot is done with her as a dramatist as though she would have embarrassed him with her continuing humanity and human action. Reilly declares that she suffered excruciatingly:

> I'd say that she suffered all that we should suffer
> In fear and pain and loathing—all these together—
> And the reluctance of the body to become a thing.

But she has no actual dramatic reality for Eliot, and perhaps could not have such reality for him, once she became, as Eliot puts it mystically, "part of the design." And hardly have the Chamberlaynes received the report of Celia's death than Julia and Alex go off jollily to a cocktail party at "The Gunnings'" (suffering apparently can mean nothing much to the supernatural "guardians") while the Chamberlaynes get ready to receive their own cocktail party guests with an exchange of compliments and chit-chat between husband and wife.

As for the marital difficulties of this couple, these have had a resolution in the third act. They are at last mildly contented with each other and can continue their social life amicably, which is hardly a resolution for which it was worth bringing supernatural agencies into play. *The Cocktail Party,* which starts off with an amusing and incisively written first act and attains to a good deal of distinction in the second act, has no third act to speak of. In an excellent article,[4] Robert G. Heilman correctly calls *The Cocktail Party* a "tragedy manquée." The potentially most dramatic character has been lost to us in a "design," while the main comedy-of-manners characters, Edward and Lavinia Chamberlayne, have nothing to do but demonstrate their acceptance of their lot as second-class citizens of Eliot's stratified cosmic society.

How, indeed, could there be strong personal resolutions, the crowning

---

[3] For an introduction to the subject of a woman's martyrdom, I know nothing so distastefully heartless than the following conversation between Alex, the "guardian," and the Chamberlaynes:

> EDWARD: And meanwhile?
> ALEX: Meanwhile the monkeys multiply.
> LAVINIA: And the Christians?
> ALEX: Ah, the Christians! Now I think I ought to tell you
>   About someone you know—or knew . . .

It is not as if anyone would dare accuse Mr. Eliot of bad taste. But it is to such a pass that one is apt to come in trying to fuse the mode of trifling comedy of manners with high tragic matter.

[4] *"Alcestis" and "The Cocktail Party,"* Comparative Literature, Spring, 1953.

segment of a play from which all other segments derive their justification and fully charged life, if drama is based on a rejection of life? And, more than that, upon a certain degree of anaesthesia with respect to it even when the playwright is as keenly alive to the art of writing and as responsive to an other-worldly call as T. S. Eliot is? Too much insistence on a dichotomy between this world and the other tends to blur the reality of the world for which the theatre rather than the theological seminary is the proper means of expression. Too much insistence on a dichotomy between worldlings and the elect tends to depersonalize both—the women of Canterbury *and* Becket (except in the excellent scene with the Tempters), the earth-bound Chamberlaynes *and* the heavenbound Celia. There is not enough substance in the persons of the play. Desiccated drama, as in *The Family Reunion,* and essentially truncated drama, as in *The Cocktail Party,* would seem to be the inevitable consequence in the theatre of a conviction that the world of men and women not yet "possessed of the divine union" (which Eliot, who insists on the dualism of matter and spirit, calls "the phantasmal world") is something either to endure as best one can or to get out of. And desiccation is also the price of as much frozen intellect and formalism as he has favored in the course of disenchantment with the modern world and the liberal dispensation.

A playwright cannot expect to diminish the density of the life we know without also diminishing the density of dramatic characterization and human action. Even Strindberg's tremendous dramatic power suffered such a diminution beginning with the *To Damascus* trilogy when he started diminishing the world by treating it as "illusion." Eliot has already revealed so much talent for playwriting that it would be regrettable if he were to continue his practice of hobbling it with theological fiats to himself as well as to audiences. He was considerably more relaxed in *The Cocktail Party* than in *The Family Reunion.* Perhaps he will unbend further in new work for the stage he has invaded with his formidable intelligence. Like forced affirmations, forced negations can seriously hamper a playwright. If he makes short shrift of the human world, he is very likely also to make short shrift of the theatre.

SCHISM IN ENGLISH THEATRE

A trifurcation of the modern drama and theatre into distinctively English, Irish, and American branches has long been noted, and this development was until recently considered entirely advantageous. It indicated a welcome diffusion of dramatic art through the significant sectors of the English-speaking world and an even more welcome capitalization on the diversity of their cultures. Recently, however, doubts have arisen, especially among a new generation of critics. It is a question today whether the consequences have not made the respective dramatic art of England, Ireland, and America deplorably provincial, deprived it of universality, and encouraged—by a species of inbreeding—the hypertrophy of native tendencies within each nation. These doubts are inspired by a legitimate restiveness in the face of each nation's shortcomings in stage production and playwriting, as well as by a bias in favor of a cosmopolitanism attributed to western continental Europe and denied to the English-speaking world, at least so far as the theatre is concerned.

The inevitability of a cleavage in English-speaking theatre, however, can be established with little difficulty, and it can be argued that the cultural basis of this division has been so genuine that both the advantages and disadvantages have been virtually ineradicable. The fact is that, for better and worse, the growth of modern drama in English has been concurrent with the cultivation of national attributes. Divisive forces which began to operate in the eighteen-eighties gradually diminished London's status as the sole theatrical capital of the English-speaking world, which has now had three theatrical centers in London, Dublin, and New York for the greater part of the century. Playwrights, managements, critics, and students must start with this fact, whatever their judgment and practices may be.

I

The development of a modern American theatre was not solely an adjustment to the modern world in general but a reflection of social realities in the United States. With the advent of Bronson Howard, whose labor-problem drama *Baron Rudolph* appeared in 1881, and of James A. Herne, whose *Margaret Fleming* appeared in 1890, America began to develop playwrights who could make some claims to modernity. The age of dependence upon English and continental European drama was drawing to a close, and American writers began to take into account the realities of the American scene. The theatre was invaded by the problems of class conflict, political corruption, and trusts and "trust-busting" which reached a climax during Theodore Roosevelt's administration. Even the genteel Clyde Fitch could not resist the now popular role of the man with the muckrake when he presented his exposé of modern politics *The City* in 1909. And these problems, to which we must add those of racial conflict, treated in Edward Sheldon's *The Nigger* in 1910, appeared in a cultural context too distinct to be identified with the matter of English drama. In such plays as Bronson Howard's *The Henrietta,* Charles Klein's *The Lion and the Mouse,* inspired by Ida Tarbell's exposé of the Standard Oil Company, and Edward Sheldon's *The Boss,* moreover, the treatment, too, was distinctive. The writing had a rough grain of surface realism instead of the varnish of urbane manners present in English social drama not only in the plays of Pinero and Henry Arthur Jones, but even in most of the work of their successors, including Bernard Shaw.

The age of dependence of the American theatre also began to end with the literary vogue of a conflict peculiar to America—namely, the struggle against Puritan conscience and the mores associated with it, a subject treated only twice with any distinction in England, in *John Ferguson* and *Rutherford and Son.* William Vaughan Moody's *The Great Divide,* first offered in 1906 under the title of *A Sabine Woman,* was more appropriately retitled in 1909 than perhaps the author himself realized: Moody had in mind a geographical and moral "divide" between Puritan New England and the "Wild West." But his play, no matter how timorously offered, was also a "divide" between the Victorian and post-Victorian theatre in America—a fact that became also evident in Eugene Walter's *The Easiest Way* in 1909, Jesse Lynch Williams' *Why Marry?* in 1914, and many a later American play. O'Neill was still taking note of "Puritanism" in such plays of the twenties and the thirties as *Desire Under the Elms, Mourning Becomes Electra,* and even *Ah, Wilderness!*

The "melting pot" aspect of American life, intensified by successive waves of immigration before 1914, affected the tempo, temperament, and idiom of our cities. Modern American comedy became charged with an exuberance and irreverence that increasingly distinguished the humor of the American stage from that of English comedy of manners. Resting on previously laid down strata of frontier humor, American stage humor may even be said to have developed a case of elephantiasis. The rebelliousness and pseudo-sophistication of the Babbitt-baiting era of Prosperity and Prohibition combined with urban, melting-pot irreverence to give America the nose-thumbing drama of which the comedies of George S. Kaufman and his collaborators are the chief exemplars.

A process of extroversion has continued in the field of American comedy to the present day, so that today most English comedy of manners seems unavoidably mild to the devotees of *You Can't Take It with You* and *Born Yesterday*. Graceful and ultra-refined comedy, such as the Anouilh-Fry *Ring Around the Moon,* strikes our ordinary play-going public as effete. The American stage management that is influenced by the success of a play in London is likely to make a grave error in importing the piece to Broadway without giving thought to national differences in humor rarely overcome except by superlative acting on the part of popular performers. Our humor has tended to spill out of the drawing room into public places: into the market place of America's luxuriantly exotic businesses such as Hollywood and Tinpan Alley, or into the forum of socially exigent ideas—which may explain, in part, the continued vogue of Bernard Shaw's plays in America. Even the superfine high comedies of Barry and Behrman usually took some notice of social, and even political, conflict.

Neither boisterousness nor traffic with social drama, however, is incompatible with puritanism, sentimentality, and romanticism; and neither is the realism of verisimilitude. Boulevard drama has usually been found too salacious for the American stage. Fractious and rough-grained adults, such as the swaggerers of *What Price Glory?* and *The Front Page,* usually receive an accolade from the American dramatists on the principle that unmannerliness is a mark of manliness, candor, and ingrained decency. Children of the *Junior Miss* pattern receive considerable coddling in American comedy; English writers would "put them in their place," whereas American playwrights, reflecting perhaps the extraordinary indulgence of the American parent, give them full sway in the home and the school. And the "common man" either ignored or patronized by the English theatre— or candidly presented as "common"—is usually treated on the American stage as the salt of the earth whose hearty virtues are transcendent and whose idiosyncrasies are lovable. Other American treatments of the little people present them as greatly tried individuals whose faults are caused by their milieu and are compensated by some extraordinary capacity for endurance or devotion. The same common man who is a comic or tragic hero to Americans will, more likely than not, seem a vulgarian to English playgoers. If the latter take to him, it is usually because the characters match English stereotypes of American character.

Above all, it is *detachment* that the American theatre lacks and is least responsive to. It has not responded favorably to this quality in native products such as Edwin Justin Mayer's "Restoration" comedy *The Children of Darkness* and Dalton Trumbo's *The Biggest Thief in Town,* which succeeded in London after failing on Broadway; and it has been unresponsive to English and continental European plays of notably detached or ironic texture. Under no circumstances must the heart of the playwright appear to be cold because his mind is clear.[1] New York was positively resentful of Christopher Fry's "Matron of Ephesus" verse-comedy *A Phoenix Too Frequent,* with which he first won England's plaudits. Henry Becque's masterpiece *La Parisienne* was categorically rejected in New York, and Strindberg's ironic masterpiece *There Are Crimes and Crimes* still has made no dent whatsoever in the American theatre. Neither have the comedies of Carl Sternheim, the crass sex plays of Wedekind, and the plays of Bertolt Brecht, who has deplored emotionalism in the drama on principle and avoids it in his own work. Luigi Chiarelli's *The Mask and the Face,* the classic of the Italian "grotesque" school of drama of which Pirandello became the master, failed twice on Broadway—once in an expert Somerset Maugham adaptation and Theatre Guild production. The Theatre Guild, which started out in 1919 as a cosmopolitan and sophisticated group, nearly wrecked its incipient career by producing Benavente's ironic *commedia dell' arte* piece *The Bonds of Interest,* and found it expedient to curb an early partiality for ultra-intellectual writing.

Although successful American comedy often has been irreverent, it is rarely mordant or loftily detached. One may even contend that the irreverence is a product of rather good-natured exuberance. It has rarely been the product of any marked animus or antipathy; it is certainly not Swiftian. The usual procedure, most notably in the long successful Kaufman school of playwrights, has been to take some bold and resounding steps toward satire and then, just as loudly, to retreat to a hastily improvised position of geniality. The classic example of this Sabine method of dramaturgy may well be Kaufman and Hart's *The Man Who Came to Dinner,* which consists of two acts of satirical exposé and a third act in which the authors allowed their egotistical Alexander Woollcott character to redeem himself by ridding his secretary of her rival in a love affair. This ending, effected

[1] There is no resistance to plays in which a character is ironical or in which the author's irony results in a conclusion favorable to a noble person (*The Constant Wife* and *The Lady's Not for Burning*) or to youth or love, which must be served at all costs by the American arts, as it is also well served by *The Circle* and *Private Lives.*

Is Shaw, whom many critics have accused of coldness, an exception? Without debating Shaw's temperature, one may say that the plays with which he succeeded on Broadway were not cold and were usually played more "warmly" than he would possibly have desired. *Vide: Candida* (Miss Katherine Cornell's performance would have pleased the most ardent Candida-maniacs), *Saint Joan* and *The Doctor's Dilemma* (with other "warm" performances by Miss Cornell), *The Devil's Disciple* and *Man and Superman* ("warmth" from Maurice Evans), and *Pygmalion* ("warmth" from both Lynn Fontanne and Gertrude Lawrence).

by the farcical use of a mummy case, was not hit upon by the authors until their play was already in rehearsal. . . . Satire has existed on Broadway only conditionally. "Satire," Kaufman once declared, "is what closes Saturday night." Kaufman had in mind the failure of pure satire to outlast a week on Broadway, for there was no dearth of "debunking" after 1920. But Kaufman and his colleagues managed the feat of being cynical and sentimental at the same time.

If any comic tradition is assignable to the respective theatres of America and England, it may be said that American humor has tended to be Jonsonian whereas modern English humor has a kinship to the style of Congreve and, more generally, Sheridan. Philip Barry, S. N. Behrman, and Robert Sherwood, it is true, may be cited as major exceptions to this rule. But even they have been less consistently blasé and disengaged than their British cousins, the Lonsdales, Maughams, and Cowards of the London theatre. Broadness and a flamboyant vigor, often combined with plebeian self-assertiveness, have generally characterized American comedy and farce since the First World War. Rebelliousness, even in high comedy of manners (as in Barry's *Holiday* and Behrman's *Biography* and *End of Summer*), has both leavened and neutralized American stage humor. And when the humor has been tart, as in the comedies of Lillian Hellman and in Garson Kanin's *Born Yesterday,* the author has been aggressive rather than urbane.

This is the same extroversion that has appeared in serious American drama, not to mention melodrama since *The Bat.* (Many a melodrama successful in England has been considered too mild or too leisurely on Broadway.) Realism of environment has been carried to great lengths in such characteristic plays and stage productions as *Street Scene* and *Dead End.* Social criticism in the American theatre, as contrasted with social criticism on the English stage, has been crusty and violent rather than temperate and reasoned, as in Galsworthy's plays from *Strife* to *Loyalties.* Denunciations have been frequent and sweeping, and affirmations have been loud, if not indeed thunderous. This tendency was especially present in the so-called drama of social significance epitomized by the early plays of Clifford Odets and other playwrights of the inflammatory nineteen-thirties. Even simple social sympathy and compassion for life's misfits have been lavished freely by American playwrights. Arthur Miller's *Death of a Salesman* is a veritable summation of democratic sentiment on the American stage. William Saroyan won a reputation in the early nineteen-forties with a benevolent attitude toward his "beautiful people"—i.e., the common man, often a derelict or a misfit—that no British critic could regard as anything but extravagant.

American psychological drama has not been noticeably more restrained. Questions of taste aside, the important fact is that American psychological drama has been emphatic and outspoken, if not, indeed, "crude" by British standards as represented in Mordaunt Shairp's *The Green Bay Tree*. England's response to the Freudian afflatus was moderate by comparison with O'Neill's forays into psychology in such mammoth dramas as *Strange Interlude* and *Mourning Becomes Electra*. Tennessee Williams has displayed the same tendency to blow up the diseased psyche for inspection and to inflate the bowels of compassion. Philosophical drama, too, has revealed extroversion and overemphasis. The results have been either disastrous, in such turgid dramas by O'Neill as *Dynamo* and *Lazarus Laughed,* or turbid and inconclusive, in such plays as *The Hairy Ape* and Philip Barry's *Here Come the Clowns*. American playwrights have been least successful, indeed, whenever a subtle dialectic was required of them.

Beyond question, the ambition of American drama has been to *point* up, rather than to suggest, a conflict or idea; to overwhelm rather than to stimulate the playgoer discreetly. And it is also characteristic of American élan that the playwrights' artistic ambitions should have carried them to frequent and extreme dramaturgic experimentation. No traditional dramatic form has held their allegiance for long, and they have not been content to capitalize on carefully stored up resources of style. It is characteristic of the American theatre that Arthur Miller should have switched from the stringently realistic form of *All My Sons* to the expressionist one of *Death of a Salesman* within a year; that Elmer Rice, most famous for the realism of *Street Scene,* should have written *The Adding Machine* and *American Landscape;* that adherents of standard comic structure such as Kaufman, Moss Hart, and Philip Barry should have entered the fields of expressionism and fantasy; and that America's foremost dramatist O'Neill should also have been virtually the most "experimental" of twentieth-century playwrights.

II

Since the differentiation of Irish from English drama is well known, there may be less need to dwell on it. The differentiation was inevitable in view of Ireland's conflict with England. Ireland began to develop a national literature, both dramatic and non-dramatic, during the eighteen-eighties in the very teeth of national despair as a consequence of Parnell's fall from power. The political struggle, temporarily stalemated, was transformed into a cultural struggle, and the Irish Literary Theatre, which opened in 1899, in the Ancient Concert Rooms of Dublin, was conceived as an instrument of insurgent or, rather, resurgent nationalism. Significantly, this theatre opened with William Butler Yeats's *The Countess*

Cathleen, which celebrated an Irish noblewoman's sacrifice of her soul for the sake of her people.

It should be added that Irish patriots, made hypersensitive by both nationalist and religious zeal, were no more grateful for Yeats's early tribute than for such later well-intentioned efforts by Synge and O'Casey as *The Playboy of the Western World* and *The Plough and the Stars.* But it is hardly necessary to prove that the theatrical movement in Ireland was an intensely nationalistic manifestation. That the texture and subject matter of the plays written in southern Ireland have been extremely regional, whether the plays be rural or urban, is quite obvious. The outstanding exception is Joyce's play *Exiles,* in which one of the characters speaks for Joyce himself in declaring: "If Ireland is to become a new Ireland she must first become European." Joyce ranged himself on the side of Ibsen as early as 1900 when he praised *When We Dead Awaken* in *The Fortnightly Review;* and, as Harry Levin has noted, "His cult of Ibsen had kept him aloof from the Irish Literary Theatre."[2]

In dissociating itself from England, the Irish theatrical movement went so far as to try to dissociate itself from European cosmopolitanism in general and from dramatic naturalism in particular. The classic statement on this intentional insularism is contained in Synge's preface to *The Playboy of the Western World,* in which the reference to "Ibsen and Zola dealing with reality in joyless and pallid words" is especially significant. The dissociation was so important to Synge that he made a second disavowal of European realism in his preface to *The Tinker's Wedding.* Protesting here against the problem plays of Ibsen and German writers, he affirmed that "we should *not* go to the theatre as we go to a chemist's or a dramshop, but as we go to a dinner, where the food we need is taken with pleasure and excitement." In "the greater part of Ireland," he exulted, "the whole people from the tinkers to the clergy, have still a life, and a a view of life, that are rich and genial and humorous." That a great deal of Irish drama reflects Synge's observation on the possibilities of a distinctive drama in Ireland is well known, and this is especially the case in the almost virgin field of peasant drama first tilled in Ireland by Lady Gregory and by Synge himself.

The dissociation from urban realism and thesis drama was itself a sufficient dissociation from English drama at the turn of the century. It was intensified, moreover, by a favorable attitude toward the symbolist movement in France, especially on the part of Yeats. Neo-romanticism, which made little headway in England, was closely linked to nationalist

2 Levin, Harry, *James Joyce: A Critical Introduction* (Norfolk, Conn., 1941), p. 22.

stirrings in the formative years of the Irish theatre, as Yeats was to recall in his 1934 Preface to *Fighting the Waves,* where he stated that "Irish imagination fled the sordid scene" after Parnell's party "gave itself up to nine years' vituperation." "Repelled by what had seemed the sole reality," Yeats added, "we turned to romantic dreaming, to the nobility of tradition. Ireland drew solace from the contemplation of a heroic past while rationalism and sociological liberalism, yoked to realistic dramaturgy, were the main means by which the English theatre liberated itself from Victorianism. For better or worse, a good deal of Irish playwriting has remained loyal to the main configuration of the "Celtic Renaissance"—that is, to the folk spirit and to romanticism, as well as to a sort of romantic anti-romanticism which makes rueful reference to the passing of a noble tradition in Ireland, as does Denis Johnston's expressionist drama *The Old Lady Says No!*

It has been especially difficult for talented playwrights living in Ireland to deviate from a nationalistic strain in view of the incomplete realization of Eire's political aspirations. And it would appear that these playwrights have had to forego an international reputation in the effort to achieve a local one. Moreover, Irish playwrights living either at home or abroad have been sensible of a special advantage that accrued quite naturally to the Irish theatre. The Irish theatre was the scene of a remarkable fusion of naturalism and symbolism, for Irish drama could represent the realities of common life and yet attain the symbolist virtues of poetic dialogue and suggestive atmosphere. This was, indeed, the essence of Synge's achievement in such plays as *Riders to the Sea* and *The Playboy of the Western World* and the kernel of the message in his famous preface when he maintained that in Ireland "we have a popular imagination that is fiery and magnificent, and tender." For playwriting Synge could prescribe dialogue that "should be as fully flavored as a nut or apple" because it was more or less the kind of speech that came to his ears from the Irish peasantry. He could find substance and stimulation for the transcendence of art in the very life he observed. Art and life, poetic drama and realism, were not disjunctive or antipodal in the Ireland he celebrated. So fortunate a synthesis, which was denied to most European prose dramatists, could hardly be renounced lightly by an Irish playwright who hoped for an enduring reputation. That he could also be trapped into mere folklorism or into fancy sentiment by the seductions of Irish charm was realized by few Irish playwrights.

At the same time, however, it is apparent that the development of modern drama, both in its general and in its specifically British manifestations, promoted divisive tendencies in the English-speaking theatre. Naturalism, with its emphasis on environmental realities and on colloquial speech, encouraged the rise of local, if not indeed provincial, drama. Henry James astutely noted the presence of "a bare provinciality" of life in Ibsen's art. He called the fascination of Ibsen "charmless" on the occasion of the 1891 London production of *Hedda Gabler*. But James came to consider Ibsen's provinciality quite ingratiating when he discussed *John Gabriel Borkman* six years later (in his February, 1897, "London" letter) and observed that "the bareness and bleakness of his [Ibsen's] little northern democracy is the source of half the frugal charm that he puts forth." Realism and naturalism intensified the localization of drama omnipresent in Ibsen's work—even in his early romantic plays, we may add, since we must not, of course, overlook the celebration of local color in romantic literature.

Nor should we overlook the contribution of the symbolist movement. Concurrently with reviving abstraction or allegory such as appears in Andreyev's *The Life of Man* or in Hofmannsthal's *Jedermann,* symbolism favored the use of atmosphere. Maeterlinck, especially, made atmosphere a major component of the drama, and Adolphe Appia and Gordon Craig gave atmospheric effect a position of primacy in stagecraft. Symbolist atmosphere did not long remain simply symbolic. It became largely associated in the theatre with environment as "local color," the stock-in-trade of much Irish and American regional drama. Even symbolism, then, localized playwriting and so helped to accentuate national strains of theatre. And neo-romantic partiality for the world of saga and legend certainly contributed to the differentiation of Irish from English drama in Deirdre and Kathleen ni Houlihan and Cuchulain plays.

In England, specifically, we find, after 1875, a strong domestication of dramatic modernism and an intensive development of native dramatic elements that actually made English drama more "English." Much has been made of the continental influence in England, and there has been a great deal of stress in histories of drama on the struggle between the Ibsenists and anti-Ibsenists in the eighteen-eighties. But it is possible to overestimate the triumph of international modernism in England. British insularism, noted by Shaw in the eighteen-nineties, did not disappear after the British theatre "accepted Ibsen," and traces of it are to be found today, even in poetic plays in which the authors aim at universality. The ideas in Eliot's plays, for example, have come wrapped in English upper-class manners and Anglican doctrine. The new poetic drama in England, except for a brief flurry of left-wing social dramas by Auden and other poets between 1935 and 1940, has tended to be localized as Anglican liturgical drama, mostly in the Canterbury Festival plays. The one Canterbury Festival play that possessed a truly broad humanistic base was Christopher Hassall's rather static and restrained *Christ's Comet*.

Hassall's prosody, however, is conventional, as is that of other British poets. It is a mark of Eliot's poetic originality that he broke with the tradition of Elizabethan blank verse. The general persistence of this tradition, from the time of Stephen Phillips to the present, is another example of the modern English playwrights' disinclination to deviate from tradition; an ear attuned to Shakespearean cadence is likely to remain full of echoes. It may be charged against Maxwell Anderson, indeed, that he has chosen to play the schoolmaster in his efforts to create verse drama in America. America would have had more plays in verse, perhaps, if Anderson, the chief proponent of poetic drama on Broadway, had been as obedient to American rhythms in composing verse as he and others have been in writing prose dialogue. Anderson has generally employed a loose iambic pentameter in his poetic efforts which is neither good blank verse nor an autonomous meter. Playwrights in America who have favored other verse patterns than the iambic pentameter have been few—the but slightly known poetic dramatist Etore Rella, who has missed having a Broadway production several times, and Archibald MacLeish, whose depression-period drama *Panic* was produced by the short-lived experimental Phoenix Theatre of New York in 1934 and whose two radio-plays *The Fall of the City* and *Air Raid* have been the American broadcasting networks' major contribution to dramatic literature.

There has been, of course, an even stronger tradition in the English theatre—"comedy of manners," in the specific English sense of drawing-room comedy. That playwrights such as Wilde and Maugham should have clung to that tradition is not remarkable. Their manner coincided with their subject matter, as well as with their intentions. Coward's response to the post-World War I period was chiefly one of beating a hasty retreat to the drawing room but tracking some *bad* manners into it. For many other playwrights, from St. John Hankin to Dodie Smith, the drawing room has been a natural habitat. But it is worth noting that even Shaw's Fabianism did not expel him from the urbane company of writers of comedy of manners. Shaw's very belief in the preeminence of "discussion drama" kept him tethered to this English style of drama. Although Shaw was an effective soap-box orator, on becoming a dramatist, he often preferred an oration within the walls of a well-appointed house. His socialism in the plays was designed mainly as "socialism for millionaires." The point being made here is hardly original; it has been made, in one way or another, by Eric Bentley in his *George Bernard Shaw* and by Francis Fergusson in *The Idea of a Theatre.* Fergusson traces the drawing-room pattern in Shaw's plays up to *Heartbreak House,* describing *Major Barbara,* for example, as a "parlor-game," and adding that even in *Heartbreak House* "the life of the play is still the making of epithets and in logical fencing."

The domination of drawing-room drama is observable, too, in the case of Shavian efforts by other writers, such as Granville-Barker and James Bridie. The prevalence of proverbial English caution is not less pronounced in the domesticated naturalism and thesis drama that started in the days of Pinero. The scholar Gilbert Norwood summed up this trend in 1913 when he classified playwrights of the stamp of Pinero and Jones as "pseudo-advanced" and complained that "Ibsen's influence upon them has been too intermittent or slight for them to break with dramatic Victorianism."[3]

Moderation has been both the virtue and the vice of English dramatic realism—so much so that a recent play such as Aimee Stuart's *Lace on Her Petticoats* could affect the midcentury British public as stirring social drama while seeming almost ludicrously tame to American playgoers. *Lace on Her Petticoats* belongs to the diminished tradition of English social drama which John Galsworthy brought to its peak. The judicious Galsworthy of *The Silver Box, Strife, Justice,* and *Loyalties* was the authentic voice of the English social theatre. That his moderation, now often regarded as tepidity, and the comparable restraint of the authors of *The Corn Is Green* and *The Winslow Boy* could carry conviction is attested by the success of these works when transplanted to America. But a wide gulf has lain between these reasonable expressions of social conscience and the turbulence of social passion on the American stage. The distinction was most evident when comparisons could be made, both in text and stage production, between American social drama represented by *Waiting for Lefty* and *Stevedore* and the strongest depression play of England in the thirties, Ronald Gow and Walter Greenwood's *Love on the Dole.*

Except for some romantic poetic exercises and for some favoring of fantastic drama, chiefly by James M. Barrie, British dramatic writing has been temperate and rationalistic by comparison with American, not to mention Irish, playwriting. It is as if British playwrights had never quite left the Augustan Age, whereas American playwrights had never renounced a national strain of romanticism—a romanticism observable in the American frontier and in the democratic spirit of taking the side of the common man, as well as in both Populism and Transcendentalism. The parallel between the respective metaphysical strainings of Melville and O'Neill may not have escaped the notice of students of American literature.

The erosion of social stratifications in America and the frequent consciousness of class distinctions in England even under trying economic conditions may also account, in part, for the greater urbanity of English drama, as well as for the snobbery that permeated even England's most

---

[3] "The Present Renaissance of English Drama" (1913), in *Euripides and Shaw, With Other Essays* (Boston, 1921), pp. 64-65.

notable war drama *Journey's End,* a play produced as late as 1929. Although there are pitfalls in any attempt to determine the causes, it may be said with some certainty that distinctions between the English and the American theatre (*and* the Irish theatre) were sharpened by the very fact that the English drama retained its "English" qualities even more tenaciously after the First World War than it seemed to be doing between 1894 and 1914 when the campaign against "Victorianism" was being waged by Shaw, Granville-Barker, and the Manchester School of playwrights of industrial England.

An enrichment in the substance and the style of drama has undoubtedly accrued from the multiplication of streams of playwriting in English. But it has also encouraged the cultivation of national weaknesses in the respective cultures of England, Ireland, and the United States, and weakened, if not indeed undermined, the foundations of professional dramatic criticism. A confusion of critical standards becomes evident whenever a mild and trivial English drama is overrated by English critics or an overstrenuous American play is overpraised by New York critics. And the confusion is particularly conspicuous in the curious partisanship long present in Dublin criticism—a partisanship that often glorifies mediocrity and denounces everything written by Sean O'Casey. Mr. O'Casey has compiled a veritable *Schimpflexikon* from the Irish press in his autobiographies and in the correspondence he has maintained with American critics, myself included.

It is no small problem to maintain critical standards when reviewers are lured into extravagant gratitude by local qualities of description, character typing, humor, political attitude, and even mere pace. The praise garnered in recent years by *Call Me Madam* and *Mister Roberts* from New York reviewers and that drawn from London reviewers by *Yes, M'Lord* and *Seagulls Over Sorrento,* a tepid British *Mister Roberts,* may be cited in the evidence. There have been, in the main, *three* distinctly different frames of reference—English, Irish, American—even at the higher levels of criticism. Producers of plays have been confused by this fact. Playgoers are also confused. And it may well be that playwriting in each English-speaking country has also suffered from this mélange of critical standards.

British playwrights might not have been so complacent about turning out tepid drawing-room comedies and watered-down social tracts if they had been exposed to the crossfire of American reviewers. Irish playwrights would not have been so ready to trade in rural charm and Celtic mist if they had faced quizzical English criticism. A dash of English bitters in criticism might still be helpful to Tennessee Williams and Arthur Miller, and it might have proved tonic to the early career of Clifford Odets. It is also possible that the superfetation of imagination and speech noted in a number of O'Neill's plays would have been curbed if O'Neill had confronted English, rather than American, reviewers during the nineteen-twenties.

Granted, however, that provincial judgment is narrow and that dramatic criticism in each country needs correction, should we not sound some warning, too, against an undeviating passion for absolutist standards? Surely we would find ourselves concerned with only a handful of masterpieces and in that case not with the theatre at all, for the stage has always had to subsist on *less* than literary masterwork. The Pisgah view of dramatic literature, too, has its dangers. It may prove dizzying to all but the few critics and their followers who have enough common sense to know when they should come down for oxygen—or the few critics who carry enough oxygen up with them from the lower altitudes of practical theatre.

A denationalization of the drama, besides, could prove at least as debilitating to playwriting as the overcultivation of national traits. As a result of laudable efforts to escape the temporal and the local (the limitations of which cannot be denied in the cases of Irish feyness, English suavity, and American overestimation of raw experience), the aspiring playwright may find himself nowhere at all. He may "universalize" his play out of existence. At the very least, he may run the danger of writing fleshless, if speckless, drama; plays dedicated to the vast inane, instead of to the common world he has experienced. In such cases it would be in order to invoke Beaumarchais' sentence: "Only *little* men are afraid of *little* writings." The "universalizing" playwright would have to be a great poet to escape bankruptcy by inflationary ambition.

There is certainly no indication, however, that the distinctiveness, along with the variously limited character of the theatre in America, Ireland, and England is diminishing. And more than a polite interchange of plays and productions among the theatrical centers of London, Dublin, and New York cannot be envisioned. Their rapport will continue to be the usual one of allies who regard each other with some considerable curiosity and some suspicion.

Part Two

THE SIGNATURE OF THE TIMES

SAROYAN:
THE TIME OF YOUR LIFE

When William Saroyan's celebrated fugue on the futilities and joys of living opened in the fall of 1939, the troubled anticipations of its producers were quickly dispelled. By rights the play should have failed, according to Broadway showmen, since it departed from the rules of playwriting. According to ordinary Broadway playwrights, too, failure awaited the seemingly scrambled improvisations with which a short-story writer violated both practical and academic precepts. The difficulties the Theatre Guild, Eddie Dowling production encountered in Boston suggested a dire fate. Directors were changed midstream and the original setting, an abstract one, was scrapped in favor of a realistic one. And even after the play, instead of being abandoned in Harvard's backyard, reached Broadway, puzzled logicians wondered how illogic and inattention to dramatic action-plot could win plaudits from usually harsh critics. Saroyan, who had proclaimed himself the wild man of the theatre and—with touching candor—also a genius, was now admitted to respectable company (he had a Broadway "hit") while his claims to transcendent merit were wholeheartedly accepted by all but a small minority of the theatre's devotees. In time, the New York Drama Critics Circle and The Pulitzer Prize Committee, long at odds (the Circle had been formed for the purpose of correcting the Committee's mistakes), put their seal of approval on *The Time of Your Life,* voting it the "best play" of the first war-time season.

Actually, the mystery of Saroyan's success was no mystery at all. It was the result of an instinctively arrived at accommodation between two schools of theatre that had been at war with each other during the depression-harassed thirties—the school that made social awareness the primary test of playwriting and the school that would have preferred playwrights to sublimate the times into poetry, fantasy, and abstraction.

Saroyan, himself a depression period writer ever since he wrote about starvation in *The Daring Young Man on the Flying Trapeze,* obliged in the play in a variety of ways. He not only drew a picture of poverty and unemployment with characterizations of an actor and a Negro musician, but painted a backdrop of "social significance" by supplementing the foreground action with a waterfront strike which provided conversation for a class-conscious dockworker and a voluble policeman. (In the thirties it often seemed to a hard-worked playreader that no playwright considered his play complete without a labor strike.) Saroyan ranged himself on the side of the common people, too, by sympathizing with a hapless young harlot, whose fragility was more than adequately represented by that delicate actress Julie Haydon to whom gentle roles were usually assigned in those years. He consigned her persecutor, the Vice Squad detective Blick, to scorn and ultimate assassination by "Kit Carson," an ex-frontiersman with delusions of grandeur—a symbol, no doubt, of the gallant West and the good old American spirit of freedom. Saroyan also had uncomplimentary words for wealth based on economic exploitation, and gave Joe, his wealthy hero who plays the roles of observer, intercessor, and philosopher in the play, an acute case of social conscience. And for good measure the author added that the rich, too, weren't feeling very chipper. His derelict, an Arab with a mouth-organ, summed "it" all up by periodically muttering something to the effect that the world had no foundation "all the way down the line."

There was little doubt that this mélange was frequently refreshing and evocative on the busily occupied stage. And the very fact that Saroyan put virtually everybody except the villainous Vice Squad officer, himself a psychological mess, into the same boat helped to "sublimate" the social content of the play. Here, in other words, there was no evidence of the sharp cleavage between capital and labor favored by the doctrinaire political left. The moral to be drawn from Saroyan's picture, and the moral the author himself explicitly drew, was that life being as full of frustration as it is, we should make the most of our time—"in the time of your life" *live.* Not content, however, with this counsel, hardly novel and surely not so challenging as to suggest any passionate involvement in the conflicts posed by the depression and by the rise of Hitler, Saroyan proved the possibility of "living" by extracting as much courage and spirit from his honky-tonk habitués an anyone could wish. Both the common and the uncommon people of the play were, in one respect or another, marvelously vital, imaginative, or sensitive. "The People, Yes," Sandburg's theme, was also Saroyan's. He had a salve for humanity, which we may denote, according to taste, benevolence or sentimentality. And for very good measure, Saroyan spun a world in which everything was possible: Thus, Kitty the magdalen is redeemed and married, with help from Joe, to Joe's handsome and simple-hearted protégé, and villainy is destroyed when "Kit Carson," using his antique frontier-weapon, stalks the Vice Squad insect and shoots him dead for insulting a lady—to wit, Kitty Duval. No consequences to "Kit Carson" are expected from this act of private reprisal, so much simpler in dramatic fancy than resistance to Hitler's battalions of evil outside the theatre. And since even Saroyan did not allege that the war of good and evil was at an end, he made Joe bequeath his own, unused, gun to "Kit Carson" for further exploits when and if called for. At the end, moreover, a young man who has been telephoning a nurse for a date in vain throughout the play finally gets the rendezvous as a reward for heroic perseverance. And a young hopeful who has been playing a pinball game throughout the performance with surely Jobian patience finally draws an avalanche of nickels from the hitherto obdurate machine to the accompaniment of a dance of electric lights and three American flags. . . .

Curiously enough Saroyan's extravagance, which, coldly considered, is infantile, proved to be quite entrancing; and not merely because all of us indulge in wishful thinking or because, as the cliché goes (and cliché and Saroyan were bizarrely related), there is a child in the heart of each of us, but because Saroyan's bravura carried the day. His bravura had been tender and casual in his first play *My Heart's in the Highlands,* produced earlier in the same year, and it had made that long one-acter a unified fancy. *The Time of Your Life* was disunified and sprawling; it was less completely self-contained than its predecessor. But here, too, Saroyan did not withhold his hand from dispensing the bounty of an Americanized, plebeianized fairyland, and he poured a good deal of robust humor and even some tonic of irony into his largesse.

Saroyan, in short, was able to live in two worlds—those of social reality and fantasy—at the same time. The play, coming as it did at the beginning of World War II which ended a decade during which those worlds had stood miles apart in the consciousness of writers, was a fitting valedictory to the militant social theatre movement of the thirties soon to be memorialized in Harold Clurman's book about the Group Theatre under the title of *The Fervent Years.* It is interesting to note that whereas Saroyan was introduced to the stage by Clurman's Group Theatre with *My Heart's in the Highlands,* in the spring of 1939, the new play presented toward the end of that year appeared under the management of Eddie Dowling, the former song and dance man, and the Theatre Guild, often flouted by militant youth in the thirties as a superannuated and moss-backed institution.

As if to bring an era to a conclusion, moreover, the Group Theatre, the most talented company to follow social consciousness as an article of faith in the thirties, struggled for another season and gave up the ghost in 1941. Henceforth, this prodigy and victim of history belonged to history —as a memory of the best ensemble acting Broadway had ever known and as an "influence" through its directors and actors—especially through Elia Kazan, Harold Clurman, and Lee Cobb, who became variously associated with the emergence of the new decade's foremost playwrights

Tennessee Williams and Arthur Miller. As for Saroyan himself, the decline of his fortunes in the theatre actually became more rapid and marked than that of many less gifted and robust playwrights. Only two other full-length plays by him, *Love's Old Sweet Song* and *The Beautiful People,* and his one-act play *Hello, Out There,* all produced within the next two or three years, won any plaudits.

It would be wrong to attribute his misfortunes as a playwright to the very qualities that first drew attention to him. His breezy style and care-free inventiveness would have continued to sustain him on Broadway, which is anything but unappreciative of gusto and unconventional play-writing. Nor can it be maintained that he was always so unconventional that he taxed the tolerance of American playgoers. It is true that for a short time in a few plays, such as *Sweeney Among the Trees* and especially *Jim Dandy,* he played the extreme *surréaliste* like a hod-carrier carrying a needle. But *Jim Dandy* was widely circulated during the war on the circuit of the National Theatre Conference, the Rockefeller-supported confederation of our most active university and community theatres. And, actually, the plays with which he won his reputation as the most promising new playwright at the close of the thirties were less extreme than press reviews had suggested.

Both *My Heart's in the Highlands* and *The Time of Your Life* made only moderate demands for a suspension of disbelief on our part. Their dialogue was colloquial and clear, and their characters were recognizably human, if eccentric. Their "philosophy," when they had one, was individualistic and genial in a manner traditional in the United States. Saroyan's brassy affirmativeness was that of an American street-Arab, his irreverence that of traditional American humorists. His fancies were moderate, consisting as they did largely of propositions favored in American "low-brow" and "middle-brow" circles—namely, that the common man is the salt of the earth, that somehow things usually turn out well for him, and that he has a high-hearted capacity for endurance. God must have loved the little people since he made so many of them, Lincoln had said, and Americans who approved their great leader's supposition could also approve Saroyan's premises. And the fact that Saroyan presented his faith with whimsy and compassion and that he added a spray of rue to his bouquet for "the beautiful people" endeared him to critics.

The structure of *My Heart's in the Highlands* and *The Time of Your Life,* as well as of several later plays, was actually as realistic as his dialogue; only their premises seemed somewhat extreme and askew. He made no literary allusions. He fiddled no harmonics on the strings of bohemian alienation or left-bank sophistication. By comparison with Apollinaire's *Les Mammelles de Tiresias,* Cocteau's *Orphée,* E. E. Cummings' *Him,* and any number of *surréaliste* and expressionist plays, his work was actually that of a conformist.

The Time of Your Life is a genre picture with a wealth of chiaroscuro, enlivened by the characters who reach out differently for their desires and dreams, and are roused out of various degrees of egocentricity by a conventional enough crisis when the Vice Squad detective tries to intimidate the saloon's inhabitants and jail the gentle harlot "Kitty Duval."

Packed into a "honky-tonk," a saloon that supplies entertainment as well as hard liquor, are a number of people. They are, superficially considered, hopelessly miscellaneous. But they have one thing in common— their burden of aspiration or of frustration or of both. The young marble-game addict, the melancholy comedian, the Negro who collapses of hunger and plays divinely when he is revived, the overzealous comedian, the naïvely persistent young man at the telephone, the prostitute who veils her past in dreams, the sensation-seeking wealthy women married to a comically straitlaced husband, the policeman who detests his job, the frontiersman who blusters and lies himself into a glorious past—who are these and others but waifs of the world, impressing upon us the fact that we are all waifs of one kind or another!

The interplay of these characters, the mere fact, indeed, that they constitute a world, provides cohesion to the play on a level of simple intelligibility. And more cohesion is provided by the central character, Joe. Everything, every event or presence in the play, impinges upon him. He is many things in one, this man who acquired money and sickened of it, who is alone and inscrutably so.

Out of his loneliness and sensitivity he has developed a pity for all mankind and a sense of justice. And having money and time at his disposal, he has made himself a paraclete or comforter of his fellow creatures, giving understanding where it is needed and material help where it is imperative. One cannot attribute supernatural or social leadership to this figure. But as a very human person, he is the catalytic agent of a large portion of the play. He has a mystic prototype in the Paraclete of Evreinov's *The Chief Thing,* and a realistically characterized one in the interfering Luka of Gorky's *Night's Lodging* or *Lower Depths.* Saroyan's honky-tonk, itself, is an Americanized "Night's Lodging."

In its rambling way, *The Time of Your Life* even affords a theme. It is the need to make the most of life, which requires endurance, compassion, and opposition to the enemies of life represented by the vice-hunter and bully Blick. All mankind is pitiful, indeed, in Saroyan's stage world; even the sadistic Blick—who bullies the prostitute and maltreats the Negro who comes to her defense—is a pitiful specimen. And at the same time

Saroyan suggests obliquely that there is a degree of evil that can be overcome only by the application of force. Joe wants to give his gun to "a good man who can use it," and he gives it at the end—to Kit Carson. Compassion and perception, and laughter and pity are fused in Saroyan's play. Nothing is basically vague here, although everything is fugitive. If the work does not come to a single point (and there is no reason why every play must, provided it is richly alive), all its separate points are vividly realized. Only a certain sweet tenderness dissolves them, particularly in a bedroom scene between a simple-minded boy and a broken-hearted young harlot.

We cannot, therefore, say that Saroyan won his early place in our theatre with a really radical departure from American playwriting. On the contrary, he epitomized both its virtues and defects in the plays which gave him a reputation on Broadway. Nor did he lose his place in our professional theatre because he offered a new dramatic form which was cravenly or obtusely rejected.

Saroyan's vogue in the theatre, which he has been unable to recover to date, though not for want of trying, was a casualty of sheer wilfulness on his part. Like so many of us in America, he quite appealingly wanted to remain young forever, and therefore performed canters that did not become his subject matter. He was wont to start themes that required serious application on his part with a view to developing them, but he was too self-indulgent to do more than doodle around the edges. Self-indulgence, however, is the privilege of the young, and not of writers of whom maturity is expected after promise has been granted. Many American playwrights failed to mature, and we may well wonder what it was in our theatre that encouraged an arrested adolescence. Perhaps the indulgent education to be had in our schools gave the playwrights an insufficient sense of discipline. Perhaps the belief that success can be had with little effort made them too balky when hard thought was required. Saroyan certainly made too little effort to *think* things through and *work* things out. If the Group Theatre was a casualty of "history," Saroyan, like other writers, was a casualty of our culture. Indeed, he nearly made a cult out of the flouting of responsibility and discipline. Buoyancy and sentiment proved to be inadequate substitutes for meaning even in his often vital kind of playwriting.

CLIFFORD ODETS: THE LONG
JOURNEY OF A TALENT

It is no small tribute to Clifford Odets that his return to Broadway after eight years of Hollywood peonage should have roused singular expectations. Although these were not fulfilled in 1949 in *The Big Knife,* it was a relief to learn that his talent had not been eviscerated in Southern California, that he retained his capacity for passion, and that he was still a formidable scenewright. If one could drive a team of horses through some of the gaps in his argument, if his writing was charged with subjective perversities and non sequiturs, we had reason to be concerned only over the more obvious presence of faults we had tended to overlook in his earlier work. They pertain to his habits of thought and implicate his virtues as well as his vices. They also provide an indispensable basis for any effort to discover why this gifted playwright has not fulfilled the hopes many of us entertained for him, and why his writing has been so uneven.

More is involved than the tired statement that, like other writers, Odets has suffered from the defects of his merits, that his great passion has led to straining, his moral earnestness to rhetoric, his originality to defections from good sense. All this might be true in the case of the man who lacked the discipline of formal education, and found no equivalent discipline in the theatre or the spirit of the time. It cannot be the complete explanation for a writer who was exposed to Marxist blueprints (which, whatever else may be said against them, do not suffer from imprecision) and the planned productions of the Group Theatre. He should have been better disciplined than those of our playwrights who never had a fixed attitude, or have looked for support in romantic or metaphysical quicksands. Nor is it enough to suppose that his difficulties have been the ordinary ones of not knowing enough and protesting too much, or of failing to distinguish between what ails him and what ails the world. *Waiting for Lefty, Awake and Sing!,* and *Golden Boy* had vibrant intimacy and authentic theatrical ring—even if Odets was speaking for a middle class of which he knew only a small, rather esoteric section, and playing Pindar to a working class to which he belonged only by bohemian adoption. Like other artists, he augmented by perception and intensification what he saw or read. In *The Big Knife,* an environment he had come to know intimately actually produced less gratifying results. In any case it was not for his documentation that Odets was applauded in the nineteen-thirties. If Odets was inwardly tormented and lacked roots, how many modern artists

303

do we know who have escaped private anguish and have not felt alienated? The anguish was transmuted into the compassion and turbulence that distinguished his work, the sense of not-belonging into an aspiring affiliation.

It is not disdain for Hollywood nor great dissatisfaction with himself that mars *The Big Knife,* but a plain case of misty motivation and misplaced sympathy. Odets erred in attributing the corruption of his hero to Hollywood, predicating a prior innocence for his weakling, assuming that his Charlie Castle would be a happier and better person in the legitimate theatre, and overlooking the fact that other stars (including John Garfield, the mainstay of *The Big Knife*) have been able to work both in California and New York. And the unemployed on Broadway must find it curious that Odets should suffer for an actor who has a fourteen-year contract and $3,500,000 thrust upon him. It was almost unavoidable that, considering the nature of his premises, Odets should sound rather frantic and pathetic, and that he should have been tempted to strengthen the frail case of his argument with the kind of melodrama he would be the first to condemn as hokum. To justify Charlie's and the author's loathing, Hollywood apparently had to be villainous enough to try to murder a starlet, and Charlie had to slash his wrists in the upstairs bathroom to prove how frightfully Hollywood had destroyed him.

To assume that the author of *The Big Knife* was simply careless or bereft of sense, since he made his own premises, is scarcely tenable. On the contrary, he deliberately chose Hollywood as a symbol for everything deteriorative and unscrupulous in our society; he returned to the *Golden Boy* theme of how a materialistic, success-worshipping world corrupts the soul. He overlooked the weak character of his hero in his zeal to transfer guilt to society; he made equations without considering whether the terms were right. Everything that can be charged to faulty logic and unreality, everything that can be attributed to subjective causes in the play, is implicated in this allegorizing tendency. Odets was off his guard because his eyes were fixed on the horizon. He picked his own pocket while looking for signs above. He dropped some of the change while transferring his money from the pocket of immediate fact to the fancy wallet of social criticism. No wonder his bookkeeping didn't tally. I think that this has been his habit ever since he came to attention as a playwright, and that it is indurated in his intention of writing plays that will have large meaning. His problem is personal, but it is also representative in the case of playwrights who made social drama their specialty in the thirties and yet tried to rise above topicality or journalism. It is therefore worth considering more closely.

Odets has been a writer of allegories in all his work except the underground drama *Till the Day I Die.* This fact has remained comparatively unnoticed because allegory is no longer a popular form of writing, and its terms generally too vague today when there is no common belief out of which they can rise. Critics have always been less impressed with his conclusions than with his dramatic drive. The allegorical method was an almost inevitable procedure for a man who sought significance for his narration, vents for the explosiveness of his characters, and a function for his poetic and romantic flare. Odets, who could never be content with mere realism—who seems temperamentally incapable of the patient documentation of a Sidney Kingsley—had to transfigure his particulars if he was to write at all.

His early version of *Awake and Sing!,* under the highly personal title of *I've Got the Blues,* had to acquire a social rationale before the play could emerge out of its private chrysalis for the Group Theatre's repertory. A public correlate for personal experience was demanded of writers by the embattled nineteen-thirties, when "social significance" was the oriflamme of art and "the theatre is a weapon" was a slogan. It was a crusty soul, indeed, that failed to look at the signature of things for social implications in the individual's behavior or destiny; and if the writer was a genuine artist it was not impossible for him, as with Auden and Spender, to create poetry of social comment. Social processing could become a way of doing, after all, what the creative spirit has always done—a way of seeing and feeling on several levels at the same time.

Odets found identification with others and release from loneliness in the cohesive life of the Group Theatre, of which he was a founding member when known only as an actor of inconspicuous talents. Individually, and in step with members of the Group, he next made an identification with the radical and liberal elements that had by 1935 cemented a united front against the vultures of depression and fascism. He was presumably sure that his identification was with the entire working class, even if his characters were either unmistakably middle class or else pastiche; in any event this belief, either real or illusory, was an outlet for the love that was in him, as it is in every creative personality. On the social canvas Odets could now draw sketches of class struggle like *Waiting for Lefty* or represent one phase of that struggle—the dissolution of the middle classes which Marxist theory made inevitable and the depression seemed to confirm. The Marxist vanguard proffered numerous keys to individual problems and situations for young writers who wanted to make sense of their experience. Home life was viewed as a miniature class struggle, and intramural revolt was considered a step toward revolutionary consciousness, as it is in *Awake and Sing!* (Orthodox psychoanalysts agree, but call it "maladjustment.") The competitive system, it was held, made dealers in hu-

man flesh out of fairly decent human beings, and its materialism gave
once-unspoiled young people a debased sense of values, as in *Golden Boy*.
Economic insecurity invaded sexual relations and deprived men of the
energy and freedom to love, as in *Rocket to the Moon*. The "Little Man,
What Now" humiliations of the dispossessed and unemployed made them
susceptible to the Horst Wessel song of fascism, or disposed to blind ac-
cesses of violence, as in *Clash By Night*. Homelessness and rootlessness be-
deviled the individual until he struck new roots of social purpose, as in
Night Music.

A creative spirit, of armed vision and a poet's susceptibility to symbolism, could easily multiply such propositions and the symbols that sustained them. Given his start by a theatre oriented to the left when the
New Theatre League awarded him an annual prize for *Waiting for Lefty,*
alternately lauded and scolded by the radical movement and kept on his
social mettle within the Group Theatre, Odets' commitment to allegory
(which was only a perfunctory engagement in *Awake and Sing!*) became
a marriage in *Paradise Lost* and *Golden Boy*. The bonds frayed in *Rocket
to the Moon, Clash By Night,* and *Night Music,* but were still strong
enough to hold him in uneasy marriage. In *The Big Knife* he was still
wedded to morality drama—but more uncomfortably than ever.

Particulars reveal the allegorical design. In *Waiting for Lefty* a taxi-
cab strike became synonymous, among other things, with the overthrow
of economic exploitation, betrayal by labor bosses, poison-gas manufacture,
racial discrimination in medicine, and unemployment in the theatre. The
strike was a prelude; or, as Lenin would have said, a dress rehearsal by an
increasingly class-conscious working class augmented by depressed members of the professions. Both the rigid Marxist and the ordinary labor
leader could raise an eyebrow at Odet's peculiar orchestration of this song
of revolution, in which the trumpets were blown by a doctor, a chemist,
and an actor. Sceptics could also question whether low standards of
living, corruption of leadership, racialism, and military preparations were
exclusively capitalistic indulgences. The over-all effect was nevertheless
contagious theatre, in which no small part was played by the animated
structure of vignettes for the pro-strike delegates' moments of conversion,
and by the inflammatory device of turning the play into a strike meeting
with actors planted in the audience. Sketchy characterizations were not
felt as a shortcoming in this one-acter, and symbol and fact were so
explicitly one that it occurred to neither the author nor his critics to call
Waiting for Lefty an allegory.

Nor was *Awake and Sing!* so patently allegorical that critics could
not accept it as a remarkably vivid story of family life, ignoring the explicit conclusion as a dispensable genuflection to the left. Still, the allegori-

cal texture is present in the play even before the sister and brother, Hennie and Ralph, allegedly achieve a tag-end liberation and enlightenment. The family was treated as the breeding ground of revolt, stalemate was predicated for the wool-gathering father who lacked force as well as social understanding, and anguish and suicide were assigned to the man of good will, the old Socialist grandfather who had allowed himself to be trapped into compromise. The working-class family with middle-class pretensions was wrecked after the mother's unscrupulous effort to safeguard its respectability. The only thriving individuals were the capitalist Uncle Morty and the racketeer Moe Axelrod. The family was presented as a microcosm, as a miniature of the social scene.

In *Awake and Sing!,* Odets already showed the difficulty that was to dog him in all his later playwriting, the discrepancy between the facts he gives us and the interpretation he derives from them. *Awake and Sing!* was neither airtight allegory nor completely integrated drama. On neither count were the relations he expressed completely tenable. It was, for instance, much clearer that Hennie's affairs with Moe Axelrod and a second man were attributable to the libido acting up in an intense girl unmarried at twenty-six than to anything in her immediate environment or "the system." Nor was her free-wheeling premarital behavior a particularly apt example of how society frustrates the working-class girl. Neither was her elopement with Moe after her marriage an altogether well-chosen illustration of liberation. It did not follow either that Ralph's great sorrow, his inability to marry his girl, was more than puppy love, and it made a weak example of frustration by the villain Economics when he was so ready to put her out of mind after his grandfather's death provided him with an inheritance with which he could have located and married her. For Ralph, moreover, to applaud his sister's abandonment of her child and flight with Moe as an awakening does not speak well for his own awakening. As impressionism and as a drama of chaos, stalemate, and fumbling toward self-expression, *Awake and Sing!* was the best piece of new writing of its time, without possessing either inevitability or force of argument. It was probably the intent of allegorizing a particular slice of life that made Odets so cavalier with his deductions and valuations. There is a certain arbitrariness in making x equal $y,$ or in saying that if x equals y and y equals z then x equals z. The mathematician can do that freely because all his work is tautology, his system a closed one; because he deals with quantities, not qualities. A writer is not in that fortunate position; his system is entirely open and his human material is qualitative, unfixed and incalculable. It has been fortunate for Odets that he has sometimes written better than he knew. The characters engendered by his considerable creative impulse have often broken the molds prepared for them by his intellect.

In his next two plays, *Paradise Lost* and *Golden Boy,* the calculations appear to have been present from the beginning, not afterthoughts as in *Awake and Sing!* The first of these was acceptable drama, in fact, only when taken as a poetic parable whose large assortment of catastrophes and blunderings serve an allegorical purpose and represent the social chaos that Odets felt. *Paradise Lost* failed for most people who saw it, since the allegorical scheme used people schematically or symbolically, draining their vitality instead of enhancing it. The symbolism lacked an objective coordinate, except by poetic or Marxist license, when it made Leo Gordon's schematically deviled family stand for the doldrums and errors of the American middle class. The musically talented daughter Pearl, who gets no opportunity to concertize, plays the piano upstairs throughout the Gordons' tribulations, and who finally loses her instrument, is the frustrated artist vainly trying to insulate himself from reality. The bank-clerk son who put his faith in stock-market speculation falls prey to sleeping sickness and ultimately loses his physical and mental grasp. The other son, a glorified Olympic runner who counted on connections to launch his career, is the impersonation of the American ideal of athletic prowess, and he is adrift in the cold world of economic fact; he contracts a weak heart, loses his wife, drifts into crime, and courts death by policemen's bullets. The trustful liberal Leo Gordon loses his business and his home. The desperate partner Katz, who contributed to the catastrophe by stealing money from the business, is the rugged individualist who has no future. He is sterile, and all the money he has taken for the purpose of regaining his potency cannot give him a child. When the Gordon family has to leave its foreclosed home, its situation is "Paradise Lost for the bourgeoisie." These and other symbolic situations comprise a social whole, according to Odets and those whose beliefs he shared. That these disasters should all happen to one single family made the jeremiad look like a fabricated and fulsome play unless viewed as largely allegorical.

In *Golden Boy,* on the contrary, symbolism and fact were sufficiently close, and allegory sufficiently fused with reality, to make it Odets' most successful play. Odets had found in his prizefight saga a fable recognizably rooted in American life, and therefore amenable to allegorical explication. He did not have to employ esoteric detail, to vaporize characterization, to warp reality, to strain simple credibility after starting with the hypothesis that a boy who had the hands and soul of a violinist could become a champion boxer. (Hypotheses at the start, as we have found ever since *Oedipus Rex,* do not destroy conviction, as do far-fetched assumptions in the body of a play.) The drama progressed clearly and relentlessly until the last scene, even if Odets used there a somewhat less acceptable hypothesis: that his hero and heroine, Joe and Lorna, having found themselves and their love at last, decide to commit suicide. Those who cared to trace social significance in the parable could do so without ambiguity, and those who cared only for the personal story and character drama could find sufficient satisfaction on that level. The rise and fall of Joe Bonaparte in the context of the prizefighting business made a self-contained story, and anyone was welcome to make as much as he wished of the playwright's references to the corruption of values by economic insecurity. In *Golden Boy,* Odets was singularly fortunate. Dealing with a piece of Americana for which a common understanding existed, Odets did not have to force too many parallels outside the realistic context of the work. Never again did he light upon another fable that would serve him nearly as well.

His next play, *Rocket to the Moon,* with its simple story of a married dentist's inability to win freedom from an unhappy marriage and to enjoy the love of his secretary, seemed to achieve no more than a minor-key variation on men's ineffectual striving for happiness. Odets found himself in the position of dealing with an essentially undramatic character and a tepid situation, which may explain why the play runs downhill after an excellent first act. He tried to make it run uphill by giving self-realization to the girl. She renounces the weak-spirited dentist who could only nibble at love, and rejects the advances of an old man (and an admirably drawn one) who offers her only financial security. But neither the personal drama nor the gospel of liberation could climb with sufficient conviction. The girl was simply too unimportant for significant or exciting action, and too commonplace a person to represent a theme or ideal. Common sense, moreover, could wonder how she qualified as a man's great love, and how winning her or losing her could be of great moment outside the pages of sentimental fiction. Although written with much sensitivity, as well as with more restraint and balance than any of the other plays, *Rocket to the Moon* failed to advance a promising career at precisely the point where it should have reaped the best harvest.

Thereafter the author seemed insecure, rattled. Personal problems, we assume, and unsteady weather in the Marxist bailiwick as well as in the nation, were unfavorable to righting the keel of his dramaturgy. *Night Music,* with its theme of homelessness in the modern world, was a fugue with variations that went off in too many directions. It proved to be more bewildering than enlightening, although a creative imagination attempted some of its boldest strokes in this work. The allegory was slipshod and the symbolism sometimes miniscule, sometimes obscure. *Clash by Night,* in 1941, emerged as a rather febrile triangle, and again some laudable intentions went by the board, since its author had intended to comment on the sources of violence in the age of fascism by plotting a drama of adultery in drab circumstances. A step by step correlation between the private and the public issue can be shown to be present in *Clash by Night*. But so strained is that correlation that both criticism and public reaction paid no heed to it and simply treated the play as a domestic melodrama.

The Big Knife, finally, demonstrated anew the difficulty of writing personal drama as though it were allegory, and allegory as though it were personal drama. The result was that the play was unsatisfactory on either level of interest. It was not until several years later, when Odets wrote *The Country Girl,* that an allegory of sorts no longer stood in the way of personal drama in an Odets work, and then this efficient play made Odets look like an ordinary writer, though a writer endowed with dramatic talent and a reliable flair for theatre. The author, who had been headed in the thirties for a significant place in the modern theatre, now appeared on the stage with his wings clipped.

Odets can find comfort that his talent is intact, and we may still expect much when matter and the significance he intends for it can meet. It may be unreasonable to expect that he will henceforth take the fact and let the symbol go, for his ambition is of a higher order and compulsive. All the division in his writing, all the breach between intentions and execution, is attributable to that ambition. The largeness of his spirit, as well as his artist's need to impose unity upon the disordered raw material of observation, cries out against easy victories in the theatre. Like other men of original talent, he must do things the hard way or not undertake them at all. Like other driven spirits, he can find no sure middle ground between the sublime and the ridiculous, between exalted feeling and mere patter. He must want either a major encounter or no encounter. Alignment with values, with a critique of society and dreams for it, has been a creative necessity for Odets. It is not a Group Theatre apologist but T. S. Eliot, referring to the interpretation and creation of poetry, who has written that "the surrendering ourselves . . . to some system of our own or of someone else is as needful a part of a man's life as falling in love."

PLAYWRIGHT IN TRANSITION:
ROBERT EMMET SHERWOOD, 1941

A capacity for response more direct than an occasional nod in the direction of one's age has been a virtual necessity in twentieth-century theatre. It by no means assures greatness or even competence in playwriting, but it has provided a measure of significance where talent was present. In America, the responses to the time-spirit were especially frequent and strong between the end of the First World War and the end of the Second. And, given some degree of ability, American playwrights managed to cover considerable ground between journalistic forays and socially directed passion. So much so that responsiveness to current tensions have been as much the preoccupation and sometimes pose of many American writers as indifference has been the preoccupation and sometimes pose of many British writers who wear urbanity as a badge of distinction.

The political involvement of the playwrights of the thirties and of such older authors as Elmer Rice and Maxwell Anderson has been much in evidence—sometimes commendably and sometimes deplorably so. But no one represents this tendency so comprehensibly as Robert Sherwood, and up to the early years of the Second World War his evolution as a barometer of the times was so marked that he is certainly the best example we have had of the writer as citizen. It is so easy to dismiss the treatment of current events as a sign of opportunism on the part of authors that the case of Sherwood can serve to correct an unjust impression. And corrected it should be because, as Sherwood's career demonstrated, American playwrights have often written with more or less genuine concern about their times, taking up temporary positions which a changing world forced them to abandon, and risking refutation of their ideas or expectations.

I reproduce, therefore, the essay I wrote on Sherwood as an *Atlantic Monthly* "profile" at the time when he was most conscious of an obligation to defend a world in which some modicum of civilization might be maintained. Final estimates of "pure" artistic achievement are of less concern here—they were certainly less in 1941—than the record of his development. It belongs to a history of theatre in our times not by fiat on my part but by virtue of the fact that playwriting in America, as also in Europe now and then, has been seismographic to a greater degree since the

First World War than in any previous period. If, moreover, I retain the original fervor with which this profile was written by me in 1941, I do so in order to indicate a characteristic response to Sherwood at a time when he spoke not only for himself but for many members of his audience.

I

Writers have this in common with adventurers: they are both apt to be highly individual personalities and yet manage to epitomize their age —whether by reflection or contrast is immaterial. Among the personalities of the literary world none is more currently conspicuous than Robert Sherwood, and few are more representative of this age both in their revolts and by their conformities. In the theatre he is not only one of the masters of his craft, but the one playwright in the lobby or in the haunts of the after-theatre set who overshadows celebrities of the acting profession without so much as a word on his part to call attention to himself. In the political world he is, barring Archibald MacLeish, the one writer who has found a place both in the government and in the scrimmage line of public controversy. At once a retiring but potent counselor to President Roosevelt and a formidable trumpeter when he comes out in the open, he has become the terror of the isolationists and appeasers in the present crisis. And he is perhaps most significant, in the casual way in which only Sherwood can be significant, as a phenomenon of the liberal mind at work in our day. He has recapitulated, in the various chapters of a very human and natural life, the evolution of an entire generation once considered lost by Gertrude Stein and hollow by T. S. Eliot.

A more modest man could not have been thrust into the foreground of current history. Physically, Robert Sherwood, who stands six feet six or seven inches, is probably the tallest writer in creation, but his simple and retiring character has become proverbial on Broadway's Great White Way. His face seems, at first glance, to have been carved out of New England granite. (Actually he is a New Yorker, having been born in New Rochelle on April 4, 1896.) It is, however, so sensitive that one would be reminded of dolorous things like the voice crying in the wilderness and a prophecy of doom if, measuring the gaunt stalk of body that supports his extraordinarily elongated head, the comic element did not intrude. In truth, Mr. Sherwood bears a striking resemblance to our mental image of Cervantes's Knight of the Woeful Countenance. But that hero was voluble, and Sherwood is famous for his silences, which occur between sentences, words, and even syllables. Then there are also the vaster silences that he spreads over the room when the dinner party becomes conversational. Often it seems his shyness simply prevents him from thinking of anything to say; even Shaw's famed volubility was unable to rouse more than monosyllabic agreement with the sage of Adelphi when Sherwood visited him.

Noel Coward reputedly sized up this phenomenon of reticence by inquiring of the writer's sister, "What is that nine feet of gloom you call your brother?" Mrs. Sherwood's pet nickname for her talented husband is "Old Monotonous." She got the name from an ill-fated race horse that she backed with unrewarded loyalty.

Nevertheless, the subject of this report is greatly maligned, since he is anything but a misanthrope or recluse by inclination. He has, instead, a rich capacity for gayety, possesses a keen sense of humor, and mingles freely in society. His plays, of course, prove conclusively that there is no want of wit in the man. His friendly biographer, S. N. Behrman, reports conversations that would, if more frequent, qualify him for some such title as "the life of the party." An example offered by Mr. Behrman is Sherwood's response at the Playwrights' Company to a colleague who wanted a definition of the word "tenterhooks." "They are," replied Mr. Sherwood, "the upholstery of the anxious seat." In the parlors of his intimate friends he will even burst into song-and-dance, earning a reputation for a Fred Astaire rendition of "When the Red, Red Robin Comes Bob, Bob, Bobbin' Along," complete with top hat and cane. Unlike many authors who need a shack in the woods, he can dispense with rustic atmosphere and primeval silences; his friends will affectionately explain that he supplies the latter himself. Sherwood likes to write in offices, finds stimulation in the bustle of Manhattan, and is fond of its round of parties and night clubs. He has also traveled extensively, and nearly always where he could mingle with the world. He married the former Mrs. Marc Connelly in Budapest, and got the suggestion for the blonde troupers of *Idiot's Delight* from American cabaret performers in that normally exuberant capital; he got his idea for *Reunion in Vienna* while visiting Frau Sacher's rendezvous for aristocracy in Vienna; he went to South America about three years ago, has been to London frequently, and has spent many summers in England on a farm in Surrey.

If he has been only intermittently lively, he has been consistently spirited. There is impulsive Irish blood in his system, from the maternal side, and very good Irish blood at that; he is descended from none other than the famous rebel and martyr of Irish freedom, Robert Emmet. It was the latter's older brother, Thomas Addis Emmet, who established the American branch of the family. A refractory gentleman, he got himself exiled in 1803 to the United States, where he quickly achieved a reputation at the bar that won him plaudits from the formidable Daniel Webster after a trial in which they opposed each other. It is from the equally attenuated and dark-haired Emmets that Sherwood seems to have derived his fighting spirit and resoluteness.

At Milton Academy young Sherwood was accused of setting a building on fire, and at Harvard, in 1914, he lived up to his reputation by reaching the verge of expulsion three times. But he survived, and as an upperclassman found more socially useful channels for his *élan vital* in the Hasty Pudding Club and in the editorship of the *Lampoon*. His parody on *Vanity Fair* in the *Lampoon's* annual burlesque number hit the mark so closely that the veteran editor Frank Crowninshield gave him a position after graduation. The dignity rested rather lightly on his shoulders. When he substituted for the sartorial expert of *Vanity Fair* during the summer he filled his column on what the well-dressed man will wear with some choice fantastication detected by no one but the regular columnist.

It was, however, in more serious manifestations that his vivacity was to leave its mark on American culture and politics. His essential seriousness began to appear in his senior year at Harvard. When the United States went to war with Germany, Sherwood tried to enlist in the American forces. Rejected because of his height, he joined the Canadian Black Watch, a regiment of Highlanders that fitted him out with incongruous kilts. He participated in the defense of Arras and Amiens; he was gassed at Vimy Ridge, and later wounded in both legs. It was not until many months after the war that he could leave the hospital in England to which he had been transferred; his heart was affected, and he was not expected to live long. It was after his convalescence that he joined *Vanity Fair,* and here, too, his exploits were not wholly undergraduate. A confirmed liberal, he championed Dorothy Parker when the magazine dismissed her for writing unpleasant dramatic criticism. In the company of Robert Benchley he resigned in protest, which took courage, since his family had met with financial reverses. After a misadventure on the *Boston Post,* he finally got himself a berth on *Life,* where he began writing film reviews which set a precedent in this new field of criticism by their incisiveness and later earned him the title of dean of motion-picture reviewers. In 1924 he became an editor of *Life,* and held his post for four years until his sharp gibes at prohibition and President Hoover terminated his editorial career permanently.

II

By then, fortunately, he was already embarked on the playwriting career that brought him repute, motion-picture sales, Hollywood assignments, and earnings that in recent years have saddled him with an annual income-tax approximating $100,000. He had ample precedent for art and letters in his family. The women on the Emmet side were painters and sculptors, and the playwright's mother will be found listed in *Who's Who* for her accomplishments. The Sherwood side has favored writing and theatre; his grandmother, Mary Elizabeth Wilson Sherwood, was a successful author, and his father, founder of the Harvard *Lampoon* and prominent in Hasty Pudding theatricals, seriously considered an acting career before he succumbed to the brokerage business. His son began his own literary labors tentatively at the age of thirteen by contributing an essay on Lincoln to a nation-wide school contest.

His first play to see the light was his Hasty Pudding show, *Barnum Was Right,* still remembered with pleasure by contemporaries, and its success no doubt proved to him that he was not unendowed with comic talent. The middle twenties were wonderful years for the purveyors of sophisticated entertainment; therefore, finding himself heavily in debt in 1926, Sherwood tried his hand at a comedy, *The Road to Rome,* in which the amorous wife of the Roman senator Fabius divests Hannibal of his passion for conquest. Produced in 1927, with Jane Cowl and Philip Merivale playing the leading roles, the comedy proved exceptionally successful, establishing him as a writer of witty dialogue and aligning him with the playwrights who affected a Continental contempt for stuffy respectability.

In December of the same year, the fortunate author tried another fling at humor, with a dramatization of a cynical Ring Lardner story, *The Love Nest,* in which a film director's inebriated wife told what she thought of her successful husband. It failed, and for some time—for four years, in fact —Sherwood found himself in the anticlimactic stage of always falling short of his initial triumph. His third play, *The Queen's Husband,* was a trifle, and *Waterloo Bridge,* a melodrama of a doughboy and an American girl in London, missed fire. Another melodrama, *This Is New York,* written in 1930, also proved disappointing.

From this point on, however, Sherwood was definitely on the upswing. Returning to his original penchant for deflating balloons, in 1931 he wrote the brilliant *Reunion in Vienna,* which the Theatre Guild's favorite couple, Alfred Lunt and Lynn Fontanne, turned into an extraordinary success. In this vivid comedy, science was hoist with its own petard when a super-psychoanalyst practically handed over his wife to her former lover as a result of overweening confidence in scientific deduction. The depression having hit the theatre, Sherwood retired to the safer pastures of Hollywood for some years, but by 1935 he was back in New York with another successfully contrived play, the philosophical melodrama, *The Petrified Forest,* for which a sojourn at Reno, which is usually less rewarding, was responsible.

He wrote the play in 1934 during the first four of the customary six weeks of residence, and in January of the next year it was on the New York stage with Leslie Howard playing the part of the suicidal representative of a degenerate era. Although its profundities were imposed on an unconvincing character and plot, the play proved provocative and exciting. Its author—who told Lucius Beebe, in a statement that does not sound wholly penitent, "The trouble with me is I start with a big message and end up with nothing but a good entertainment"—was not particularly satisfied. He attributed his success to his audiences' partiality for "two parts of a highly improbable and sentimental romance." Still he is correct in ascribing the beginning of his career as a serious dramatist to this work; in it he began to give thought to our world's ailments.

He was not entirely reformed in his next play, *Idiot's Delight,* which owed much of its success to Sherwood's comic improvisation around Alfred Lunt, playing an American hoofer surrounded by six blonde chorus girls, and the aristocratic pretensions of a red-headed Russian girl from Omaha impersonated by Lynn Fontanne. For all that, *Idiot's Delight* was a deeply stirring work on what Sherwood in 1936 called the "next world war." His prescience was justified more quickly perhaps than he expected; the Rhineland was occupied two days prior to the premiere of the play in Washington, and the London opening in 1938 was introduced to the British public by the invasion of Austria a few days before.

After a brief interlude during which the increasingly serious-minded playwright adapted the French comedy *Tovarich,* he wrote *Abe Lincoln in Illinois.* He had long been interested in Lincoln's story, becoming genuinely absorbed in it through a friendship with Carl Sandburg which had ripened after the latter phoned him once to compliment him on his motion-picture criticism. Reverence made him put aside what he called his "fondness for hokum in the theatre." This episodic chronicle, which opened in the fall of 1938 with Raymond Massey as Lincoln, paid the tribute of simplicity to a simple man; the public took it to its heart instantaneously, and there is a strong probability of its becoming an American classic. The situation of the world having in the meantime grown even more serious, Sherwood remained on the same sober heights when he set down his latest play after being stirred by the invasion of Finland by Soviet Russia then allied to Hitler's Germany.

He was at the time trying to rewrite his London failure, *Acropolis,* a drama of the twilight of Periclean civilization which bore so many parallels to contemporary currents. But the pressure of the immediate world was stronger; after listening to W. L. White's moving Christmas Day broadcast from the Karelian front, he began feverishly to write *There Shall Be No Night,* merely incorporating a speech from *Acropolis* in the new work. The play, which opened on March 29, 1940, proved to be Sherwood's and the Lunts' greatest success; there has never been a week when the receipts fell below $20,000, and it is still one of the greatest attractions of the theatre. Feeling that this protest against imperialism should reach other sections of the country, the author and the producers sent it on a twenty-eight-week tour in November, 1940. The production traveled over 1,600 miles and visited forty-five cities in nineteen states, as well as two provinces in Canada. A second tour, consisting mostly of one-night stands through the South and the Middle West, started in October and was in all respects more like a crusade than an ordinary tour.

III

Like other men, he returned from the First World War with a changed outlook and some firm convictions. Sherwood discovered some wholesome facts about the community of man in the training camps, trenches, clinks, and hospitals. On one side of him during his convalescence lay an Australian who had been burned horribly by liquid fire; in the bed on the other side he found a South African Jew who was permanently paralyzed by a machine-gun bullet that had lodged in his spine. In addition to developing an intense aversion to war, he became "internationally-minded," was convinced that future wars could be avoided by the elimination of excessive nationalism, and was at first enthusiastic about the League of Nations. But his enthusiasm waned under the influence of the Wilson-haters. "In 1920," he has written, "I confess with deep shame, my first vote as an American citizen was cast for Warren G. Harding. Thus, I did my bit in the great betrayal." His position then was not inconsistent with hatred of war. This hatred he inserted into his plays, as did other fashionable writers of the twenties who vented their disillusionment with cynical vehemence but without much serious attention to the fundamental problem. In *The Road to Rome,* which was typical of his work in the twenties, he delivered himself of such passages as "You say he is cruel. Is there any soldier who is otherwise?" and a jibe at womenfolk in war who "sit at home and talk of the great sacrifices they are making." But the cream of the story lay in fashionable digs at virtue and Babbittism, in gay indifference to national calamity, and in the jest of Hannibal overcome by a beautiful Roman woman and the respectable Fabius saddled with an illegitimate son. Characteristic was the debonair optimism which made Sherwood and his audience believe that a Hannibal could be cured of his lust for conquest by "the human equation," here represented by an evening of pleasant adultery.

Then came the stock-market crash of 1929; and the ensuing years of depression, climaxed by the rise of Hitler, rocked the foundations of the civilized world. Proletarian and pseudo-proletarian writers reacted by adopting Marxist social optimism and activism. Sherwood responded, instead, with a philosophy of despair, harking back to "The Hollow Men" and "The Waste Land" philosophy of T. S. Eliot. Believing profoundly in spiritual values and in the value of individuality, he could not accept either rationalistic science or collectivism as a solution. He set down their methods, in his preface to *Reunion in Vienna,* as a "neutralization of nature" which led to a denial of individualism, maintaining that the disciples of both Galileo and Lenin "are determined to exterminate it and can undoubtedly do so, with the aid of the disciples of Freud."

He saw civilization and its intellectuals as hopelessly lost, deteriorated in their souls and helpless in the face of a world taken over by the uncivilized. The hero of *The Petrified Forest* (which Sherwood calls "my first attempt to write a play about my own country in my own time") is a writer who frittered away his talent idling with a rich woman on the Riviera until, lacking something "worth living for—and dying for," he asks an obliging gangster to kill him. Self-pityingly he refers to his possessing "brains without purpose," and Sherwood, who could not supply him with one, fatalistically ascribed the result to nature. Intellectual man, described as "a vanishing race," thought he had conquered nature with science, and "now there is only world-chaos." "It's nature hitting back. Not with the old weapons—floods, plagues, holocausts. . . . She's fighting back with strange instruments called neuroses. She's deliberately afflicting mankind with the jitters. . . . She's taking the world away from the intellectuals and giving it back to the apes."

In 1941, having found renewed strength of purpose, the author called *The Petrified Forest* "a negative, inconclusive sort of play," but in 1932 its philosophy seemed to him sufficiently conclusive. He was too close to the hollow men and made them represent the whole intellectual world. The only comfort he could find—in *Acropolis,* which he had written just before—lay in the reflection that the world of the Periclean intellectuals did not after all die completely, since it lived in the memory of man. But here, too, his intellectuals—Phidias, Pericles, Socrates—were passively losing the world to the apes.

Sherwood's pessimism reached its climax in *Idiot's Delight.* Today he describes it as "completely American in that it represented a compound of blank pessimism and desperate optimism, of chaos and jazz." If he intends this derogatorily, he is somewhat unfair to himself, since his fatalistic prediction of a second world war is justified by past and present fact. He also had a better case against the intellectual than before, when he showed the pacifistic labor leader Quillery succumbing to war hysteria and the internationally-minded scientist Waldersee returning to Germany to make poison gas instead of fighting cancer. If the play did not achieve any genuine clarification, this was because of shortcomings that its author shared with his generation. He made no strong effort to analyze causes, contenting himself with an incisive portrait of a munitions magnate and vague references to the fact that the war is "everybody's fault" or the result of "God-damned bad management"; and the negativism of the preceding plays still prevailed sufficiently to rule out any positive conclusions other than a "hoofer's" saltily stated faith that "no matter how much the meek may be bulldozed or gypped, they will eventually inherit the earth"— which hardly helps the meek.

Something, however, happened to the pessimist at this time. He found his way back to the roots of American life and drew courage from them. His belief in the common man and in the spirit of American democracy became a white flame as he explored the life of Lincoln. It lighted his way not only to that notable play *Abe Lincoln in Illinois* but to a renewed faith in humanitarian striving and the brotherhood of man. Throughout the formative period of this faith, Sherwood had indeed begun to behave quite unlike his passive characters. In his particular craft, he began an active championship of American playwrights against producers in connection with contractual arrangements, became one of the leaders of the Dramatists' Guild, and in 1937 joined Elmer Rice, Maxwell Anderson, S. N. Behrman, and the late Sidney Howard in founding the Playwrights' Company with the object of putting on their plays independently. His interest also extended to bringing the professional theatre to all parts of the country, by means of an association for which he tried to raise $300,000.

In the larger world, Sherwood was at the same time actively concerned with social problems like slum clearance and municipal housing projects, and in politics he became an ardent New Dealer. The writing of *Abe Lincoln in Illinois* crystallized his growing realization that the intellectual could have both brains and a purpose. He was voicing his own convictions when he made Lincoln tell the townspeople who were seeing him off to Washington, "Let us live to prove that we can cultivate the natural world that is about us, and the intellectual and moral world within us, so that we may secure an individual, social and political prosperity, whose course shall be forward, and which, while the earth endures, shall not pass away."

A year after the play opened, that world was distinctly beginning to pass away, and Hitler's Germany began its triumphant march across Europe. Sherwood's new-won faith, however, stood him in good stead while others who had once been less pessimistic and passive than he despaired and stood idly by. He became aware that in his American chronicle he had told "the story of a man of peace who had to face the issue of appeasement or war." Sherwood went through the same doubts. "It was," he wrote, "a bitter moment for me when I found myself on the same side as the Big Navy enthusiasts."

In the hero of *There Shall Be No Night,* Dr. Valkonen, he retraced the stages of his own transformation, but he did not wait until he could find dramatic shape for his new convictions. He plunged into the battle as soon as he arrived at them, and after reconsidering his impulse to reënlist in the Canadian Army, which would have relegated him to a desk job at his age, became one of the leaders of the Committee to Defend America by Aiding the Allies. He wrote its historic advertisement, "Stop Hitler Now," on June 10, 1940, and paid the initial cost of $24,000 out of his own pocket. (He also sent part of his earnings to the Canadian Red Cross, and he gave $20,000 of his royalties from *There Shall Be No Night* to the Finnish Relief Fund.) With his pen he became the Committee's most formidable propagandist. When Charles Lindbergh's first radio speech called upon Americans to be "as impersonal as a surgeon with his knife" in respect to the plight of Europe, Sherwood's scathing reply in *Time* branded the sentence an insult to the medical profession and rephrased it as signifying "We must be as impersonal as the professional mourner, who doesn't lament the seriousness of the plague, or the number of fatalities, as long as it helps his own business."

He became the leading advocate of Clarence Streit's Union Now proposal at the time of Britain's darkest days, because, as he declared at the mass meeting at Mecca Temple, it would serve notice on Hitler "that the power of the English-speaking world was too great for destruction by wanton bombing of British cities." It was at this critical time, on August 30, 1940, while bombs were rocking London, that he also tried to hearten the English people with a speech over the Canadian Broadcasting Company in which he assured them that America stood by their side in their great trial. It was a bold move on the part of a private individual to promise American aid, and it was made more annoying to isolationists by his denunciation of Messrs. Ford and Lindbergh as machine worshipers who had succumbed to the "degenerative influence of Hitlerism." He became a close, if unofficial, associate of President Roosevelt, whom he admires greatly and supported for reëlection for a third term; he was slated to be Master of Ceremonies at the inauguration when he was stricken with the flu at the White House. Although no confirmation can be had from him, his frequent presence at the White House has been connected with the preparation of several presidential broadcasts, including the declaration of a state of emergency. In February, 1941, there were even rumors of his being appointed ambassador to the Court of St. James's. This proved unfounded, but he did take a confidential flight to London from which he returned last October. When the draft bill was enacted he took temporary charge of the Committee on Education, Recreation and Community Service of the United States Army. He is now First Assistant to Colonel William Joseph Donovan, Coördinator of Information, occupying himself in a heavily guarded New York building with the important matter of short-wave broadcasting to Europe.

There is enough in his diversified activities to occupy two men. The spirited hero of many a fracas since youth finds zest in his work. If he was once one of MacLeish's perhaps too severely taxed "Irresponsibles," there is no trace of it left today. He is also undoubtedly a happier man. Having emerged at last from the Slough of Despond, he is, like his Dr. Valkonen, convinced of the heroic possibilities in man's spirit and of the truth of the unknown Jewish mystic's assurance that "there shall be no night there."[1]

[1] Sherwood returned to the subject of one-world idealism in the season of 1945-46 with a crusading war drama *The Rugged Path*, but without any marked success, and his latest contribution to the theatre has been the modest one of a libretto to the Irving Berlin musical comedy *Miss Liberty*. It may be said, then, that the transition in Sherwood's playwriting was completed more than a decade ago.

PHILIP BARRY:
A CIVILIZED PLAYWRIGHT

Anniversary articles are as painful to write as they are pleasant to contemplate when we discover generous impulses in ourselves. I have thought a good deal about Philip Barry both as a playwright and as a person. Although my relations with him were more professional (during many years of association with the Theatre Guild) than personal, I was sustained by the motive of affection. Not having been on intimate terms with Philip Barry, I wondered at the source of this affection, and I am now at last able to identify it. It was an appreciation of one of nature's gentlemen; and, I may add, the contemporary theatre, insecure and nerve-frayed, has had few of them. As a critic of sorts, I had often found myself in a state of ambivalence, deprecating his too frequent concern with the smart set yet sensing genuineness behind his tinsel and responding to a fundamental grace in his personality and art. When I received the news of his untimely death on December 3, 1949, I was, in fact, rather distressed by the prospect of observing and functioning in a theatre from which Phil Barry had departed.

What I can attempt to do here with some propriety is to situate the man's work in our theatre, and it is all the more important to do this because the only two genuinely critical studies of the contemporary American drama have treated that work with sharp reservations. The books I have in mind are Joseph Wood Krutch's *American Drama Since 1918* and Eleanor Flexner's *American Playwrights 1918-1938*. Both books contain valid points, and Mr. Krutch's are, as one would expect from him, made brilliantly. But even if one accepted them all, it is now necessary to qualify them with an acceptance of Barry's place in the American theatre. The plain fact is that Philip Barry won an honorable place in American theatrical history both as a cultivated writer of high comedy and as an experimentalist.

Let us summarize the bare facts first: After preparatory education in Catholic schools and graduation from Yale in 1919, Barry joined George Pierce Baker's Workshop 47 at Harvard and proved himself one of the brightest of the young men who emerged from that beehive of playwrights. Pursuing a diplomatic career for a time, he clerked in the State Department and in our Embassy in London. He made his debut in the theatre in 1923 with his Harvard Prize play *You and I,* a comedy of marriage which incorporated the then fashionable revolt against the twin careers of marriage and business. His next play, *The Youngest,* a year later, was another comedy of revolt by "the younger generation." It was followed in 1925 by the considerably better comedy *In a Garden,* a clever and graceful piece of theatre centered in the character of a writer who loses his wife as the result of an inveterate disposition to take feelings or human relationships apart in order to examine and manipulate them.

In a Garden is of particular interest because it was the playwright's first attempt to experiment with theatre itself. The central event of the play is the main character's attempt to build a high comedy out of elements of his own life by means of an experiment. In order to free his wife from an early unconsummated romance with another man, he reproduces the garden setting of this romance in their apartment when the former lover returns. The experiment backfires, proving that it is dangerous to toy with human emotions. *In a Garden* was not only an experimental play that first revealed its author's highly theatrical bent, but also the first of Barry's plays to express the quite winning curiosity and humility with which he engaged human nature. This is the civilized approach that remains one of the most lasting of Barry's qualities as a playwright. It argues a certain degree of detached disenchantment. He who plays with people, Barry always contended, plays with fire. The doctrine of "original sin" is present in this view, but its application is comic rather than tragic, and Catholic rather than Calvinistic, since there is a large measure of tolerance for human frailty in it. A good case can be made out, indeed, for the contention that Barry, for all his seemingly rebellious sophistication, was always a true son of the Church. His biblical play *John,* in 1927, testified this, too, with its representation of John the Baptist's incomplete Christianity since he does not quite accept Christ's teaching of forgiveness and human brotherhood.

With *John,* Barry started a long and uneven struggle for non-comic art which culminated in *Here Come the Clowns* in 1938. It was necessary for him to engage in this struggle in spite of his great flair for comedy, because the social surface never represented the whole of existence to his questing and, I always believed, somewhat subdued, perhaps even depressed, spirit. The urbanity in him that gave some critics the impression of superficiality was never the whole of Barry. It was perhaps this very necessity to split himself into two different kinds of writers that expressed his artistic limitations. The comic writer and the psychologist of modern disorientation, the sceptic and the mystic, the society man and the poet did not work together as one artist. He did not find it possible to penetrate deeply enough into the human condition with the scalpel of comic art, although it was the instrument that he handled most efficiently. The reasons are worth investigating in a thorough study of Barry and of modern high comedy such as cannot be undertaken here. Too many of us in modern times have been unable to discharge our tensions or our understanding as thoroughly in comedy as, let us say, Jonson, Molière, and Shaw could; or as Strindberg could in his remarkable play *There Are Crimes and Crimes.*

It is perhaps for this reason, too, that Barry resorted to whimsy and extravaganza, as he did in *White Wings* in 1926—a thoroughly original yet not altogether successful treatment of the difficulties of adaptation to change in the world. Barry, who was certainly not unaware of the process, was more responsive as a playwright to changes of value connected with the revolt of the young during the nineteen-twenties than to major social upheavals and transformations. This may be the reason why the plays he wrote during the Depression period were generally weak until he came to write *Here Come the Clowns* in 1938. His continued treatment of genteel society kept him out of the stream of the Depression period social drama to which virtually all other writers of the generation of the nineteen-twenties, including Anderson, Sherwood, Behrman, Rice, and Howard, more or less responded. When he took account of the rising tide of totalitarianism, his response was allegorical and mystical rather than realistically specific in *Here Come the Clowns*, and theatrical in *Liberty Jones,* whose musical comedy technique seemed to prettify the world situation in 1941. Social changes that involved stridency and physical conflict may have been repulsive to him as a gentleman, and questionable to him as an apparent believer in original sin who had to refer evil to human nature rather than to institutions. He could accept the inevitability of change and ruefully observe the difficulty of bowing to it, as he did in *White Wings.* He could grant the importance of opposing evil, as he did in *Liberty Jones.* He could accept the necessity of strategies of struggle against Germany in 1942, when he produced *Without Love,* the comedy of diplomatic efforts to associate Eire with the Allied powers. But the struggles that actually appealed to his refined spirit were those that effected a change in manners, which made him a writer of high comedy, and that involved personal values in private relations.

It was consequently in the area of high comedy, comedy of manners and private values, that Barry truly excelled, and this was first evident back in 1927 in *Paris Bound,* one of the few domestic comedies of our stage that possessed a truly original idea: namely, that casual adultery is too trivial a reason for destroying a marriage. Here Barry was entirely successful, since he could exercise his comic talent and his knowledge of human nature most concretely in the milieu of the well-bred world that he knew best and in which he was most at home. Here, too, he could reconcile his practiced urbanity, which disfavors a shuddering and solemn view of adultery, with his reasonable conservatism, as well as with the tenets of the Church which frowns upon divorce. *Paris Bound* was completely satisfactory within the limits of a comedy of manners, and all the more remarkably so in view of his limited reliance on epigram in this and other comedies. *Paris Bound,* in which the wife renounces her intention to leave her husband, restored the *status quo,* very much as did Shaw's *Candida,* without any obvious concessions to either sentimentality or convention.

In good stride, Barry next went on to write his loveliest comedy *Holiday* in 1928, signalizing the revolt of youth against the materialistic values rampant during the stock-market boom. *Tomorrow and Tomorrow* in 1931 again combined a certain degree of sophistication with a restoration of conventional marriage by unconventional means, revealing once more a tender regard for persons. And *The Animal Kingdom* in 1932 was another, if not completely realized, *tour de force* of rebellion against conventional values that approached the estate of high comedy with its thesis that behavior is decisive. A wife in this play behaves like the garden variety of mistresses in exercising seduction in order to keep her husband's nose to the grindstone of business while an artistic mistress conforms to the ideal of wifehood by proving herself his loyal comrade. Barry, however, had in the meantime delivered the theatrically skillful, if somewhat nebulous, philosophico-psychoanalytic drama *Hotel Universe* in 1930, and his comic talent became increasingly subdued in some tepid comedies and in his memorable allegory of God-seeking *Here Come the Clowns.* But in 1939, he again gave sway to his talent for imbedding a comic point in considered characterization when he wrote *The Philadelphia Story.* He nearly succeeded in the same manner, although in a strained political context, when he wrote *Without Love,* and in 1945 he theatricalized a psychological situation in *The Foolish Notion* with considerable effect, if with incomplete reality. And in *Second Threshold,* finally, he actually succeeded in fusing his talent for high comedy with his less manageable but very real talent for expressing human anguish.

The Second Threshold, completed after his death by Robert Sherwood, showed a retired statesman mired in a suicidal depression, from which he is saved at last by reconciliation with a daughter who had hitherto disappointed his high hopes in her. The dependency of fathers on their daughters was a deeply imbedded motif in Barry's work; it will be found also in *The Philadelphia Story.* It is the pervading theme of *The Second Threshold,* although the statesman's distress was initially presented as having a more comprehensive, if vague, motivation in the contemporary situation. A divided and somewhat mistily conceived work, this comedy was most appealing as a drama of human relations. These, it can now be realized, weighed heavily on Barry throughout his career, and it is now apparent that he carried more emotional freight than the comic spirit can usually waft on its course.

It is not surprising that he was frequently tempted to abandon comedy. If he did manage to become, with Behrman, one of our two most consistently successful writers of high comedy, his manner, nevertheless, distinguishes him from most European writers of comedy. Their steel is more tempered, their point sharper. They appear to be, at least on the surface, more acute observers of folly because less tender-minded. Barry seems to care too much for his characters to seem as astute as, let us say, Carl Sternheim. He could rarely sting.

When this record is carefully studied, it becomes apparent that Philip Barry was a scrupulous artist of the theatre who faced and assigned to himself the difficult task of standing between extremes—between social satire and vacuous entertainment, between social passion and theatrical tomfoolery, between crass realism and poetic drama. In all respects, he tried to arrive at a reasonable position in an increasingly unreasonable world that placed a premium on excess. Playwriting was much easier for farcical "debunkers" on one hand and for hammering social realists on the other hand than for a writer of Barry's disposition and calibre. He was a moderate among dramatic extremists, and a reflective writer among raucous entertainers. His talent being distinctly comedic and theatrical, he succeeded much more frequently when he was not inhibited by the large measure of reflectiveness and sympathy (and whimsy) that he had at his command. And the same inclination also blunted the edge of his satire and the sharpness of wit of which he was capable, for which reason even his best comedies may not yield their full effectiveness to the reader who does not follow them with a sure sense of how well they played and can still play on the stage.

There is, indeed, no great possibility of our now having other writers of comedy who can command his restrained expertness, and even less possibility of our meeting up again with playwrights who will attempt to effectuate themselves in his kind of moralistic yet refined drama. His talent was unique in this respect. It had, so to speak, one foot in a genteel society still secure and another foot in the quicksilver of society as we know it today. Barry was completely at home in the theatre. It is less certain that he was entirely at home in the world. His art sustained him; it could not integrate him. From this circumstance arose the dissatisfactions registered by critics, as well as the unevenness of his career in playwriting.

From this circumstance, however, also arose the distinctive savor of his writing, its truly civilized taste and its humane considerateness for people whatever their station in life and whatever their errors of impulse or judgment. There was no acid in the composition of his writing in spite of his amused attitude toward the social set so well expressed in Mike's line in *The Philadelphia Story,* "The prettiest sight in this fine pretty world is the Privileged Class enjoying its privileges." Despite such apt observations on the social scene as Dexter's reminder to Tracy in the same play, "You're a special class of American Female now—the Married Virgin," Barry was not truly a satirist. In spite of his ability to write many amazingly well-turned lines in his plays, it was not even wit that he specialized in. His forte was something warmer, a suspension of judgment as a way of life. It is well expressed in *The Philadelphia Story:* in Tracy's jibe at that "pin-feather in the Left Wing," Mike Connor when she tells him, "You've made up your mind awfully young," and in her blanket statement: "The time to make up your mind about people is never." If wit emanates infrequently from such an attitude, and excitement even less frequently, other qualities pertaining to high comedy, as well as to whimsy and fancy, do stem from it—amusement, of course, and also a feeling very rare in our theatre that one is in the presence of a civilized soul. It may not invigorate us, but it puts us at ease and in sympathy with humanity, which is one of the saving graces of Barry's art.

Barry's was a healing art at a time when dramatic art was mostly dissonance. Perhaps Barry felt the need for healing too greatly himself to add to the dissonance and to widen the rifts in the topography of the modern, specifically contemporary American, scene. Whatever the reason, and regardless of the risk of indecisiveness, Barry sought balm in Gilead, found it somehow, and dispensed it liberally—and with gentlemanly tact. It does not appear that the future, at least the immediate future, belongs to dispensers of balm. Nor is it either gratifying or feasible to accept it from most givers, since their manner is apt to be maudlin and their palms are often uncomfortably clammy. It was not the least of Barry's merits, a mark of both his breeding and manliness, that his manner was generally bright and brisk and that the hand he stretched out to others, as if to himself, was as firm as it was open. For all the cleverness that won him popularity and for all his theatrical deftness, his considerateness never failed him, and his tolerance never succumbed to either cynicism or indifference. This is a great deal to find in a contemporary playwright, even if there are also greater virtues to be sought in dramatic writing. The word for this quality of Barry's work on the whole is not easy to find. It is not the word that comes most readily to mind; it is not mere urbanity. "Civilizedness," that state of grace which being inwardly civilized entails, is perhaps the most accurate word for Philip Barry, and civilizedness, regardless of the penalty one pays for it, is to be treasured in the theatre that nowadays rarely makes a virtue of it.

The limitations that have been generally charged to Barry were themselves the consequences of his disposition and the causes of whatever distinction he was able to attain. As the gentleman-playwright *par excellence,* he tended to be too partial to good society, and his partiality accounts for the mildness he exhibited in comedy and fantasy. He was reluctant to shake the foundations upon which stood the charming and articulate people who provided him with comedy. And he either transferred them to the more or less metaphysical world he favored, as he did in *Hotel Universe,* giving more attention to their neuroses than the effort was worth, or allowed their voices to susurrate in the world of moral conflict, as they did in his too gentle religious plays and in the semi-morality play *Here Come the Clowns,* in which the war between good and evil was somewhat too subdued.

It was possible to be decidedly unjust to Philip Barry on these counts, and it appears to me that he was also unjust to himself at times. He did not think well enough of the metier of comic writing that gave him virtually all of his success on the stage, and he pushed hard in directions where his temperament was not advantageous. One did not have to be intimate with him to sense that he felt frustrated, perhaps even irritated. In England, a playwright with Barry's pleasant and profitable endowment would feel tidily settled for life as a comfortable gentleman and a well-regarded member of the tribe of trivial comedy-of-manners purveyors. In America, especially during the strident nineteen-thirties, which was a lean period for him until the production of *The Philadelphia Story* in 1939, Barry was especially vulnerable to criticism and self-criticism.

He would have been discontented in any case. He had both an elfin disposition and a religion-bred sense of damnation that do not easily fit into a drawing room. And he was often aware of the ennui and emptiness of the social set even while giving its members some measure of his own scrupulous humanity. *Holiday* and *The Animal Kingdom* are especially charged with discontent. Nevertheless, it was his burden in life to carry the world of the social set with him, whether or not he entirely approved it. The rebelliousness he introduced into his plays always seemed to me symptomatically lukewarm, as if the author himself could not go beyond a palace revolution.

Even for comedy of manners one could have desiderated a stronger animus than any Barry employed or was perhaps capable of mustering into the service of his playwriting. And for that reason alone, if for no other, most of his work seems to belong to a vanished period—almost the mauve period—of American life and theatre. But the amiable disposition Barry brought into his writing cannot lose a certain grace attendant to his humanity. Without that grace—and it was a grace of mind, too, quite often— both theatre and life could probably go on, but in some state of impoverishment that some of us would regret.

S. N. BEHRMAN: COMEDY
AND TOLERANCE

I

When S. N. Behrman's Maugham heroine, the middle-aged Jane, declares that it is pleasant at last to find oneself in the company of men of one's own age, she has the same feeling that mature playgoers must have in the company of Mr. Behrman himself. The author of *The Second Man, Biography,* and other comedies, including the recent *Jane,* is remarkable in many respects. He is, for example, the only remaining American writer of high comedy and he is perhaps the only consistently brilliant stylist in our drama. But in nothing is he more remarkable than in his ability to make us feel mature.

America's youth, as Oscar Wilde quipped, has been its oldest tradition. Youth has also been our oldest tradition on the stage. There have been exceptions, it is true, but not in a decisive number of our better plays. And the situation has not changed since O'Neill expressed a young man's rebellion and despair and since the Kaufman school back in the nineteen-twenties started upsetting apple carts in a series of theatrical pranks.

Clifford Odets, the white hope of the thirties, was succeeded by William Saroyan. Both energized our theatre, the one with his verdant apostolic enthusiasm, the other with an effervescent optimism that was anything if not naïve. Today Tennessee Williams engages our interest with a young sensibility as Arthur Miller does with a youthful moralism. It would appear, in fact, that our theatre owes whatever excitement it has possessed to a large capacity for rejuvenation. Behrman alone has almost consistently made us feel that youth is a highly overrated commodity to carry around with us.

This is not to say that Behrman has been unsympathetic to green love, to youthful impulse and bright-eyed idealism. The contrary is true. It is merely that in one way or another he has managed to make experience with scepticism, or with a balanced view of life, more attractive, or, at the very least, more tolerable than other playwrights have done. "Middle-agedness" as a state of mind scores some sort of victory or acceptance in Behrman's plays; though sometimes somewhat apologetically as in *Biography* and *No Time for Comedy.* The conclusion in *Jane,* for example, actually requires us to approve Jane's decision to renounce her young husband and his egotistic bedazzlement with elegant society.

329

By contrast, when youth wins in a Behrman play, as it does in his *End of Summer,* its victory leaves a bitter taste. That a young girl escapes the machinations of a ruthless psychiatrist in this play is gratifying. But there is no pleasure in the conclusion that concerns the girl's mother, the central character. In fear of loneliness, the idle rich woman takes up with a young revolutionist, who makes no effort to conceal his cynical intention of mulcting her for the sake of the "cause." Her new love affair is the "end of summer" for herself and her class. The young Lindbergh hero of another play, *Rain from Heaven,* is a decidedly dangerous person who is being primed for a fascist role. Nor are Gilbert Dabney's sentiments and values in *Jane* particularly admirable; Jane is quite right in telling the self-centered young man that, although many years her junior, he is "too old" for her.

Behrman is often made uneasy when the young want to have their way. The starry-eyed Monica Grey who sets her cap for the sophisticated writer Clark Storey in *The Second Man* is left stranded by him when he returns to his mistress and patroness Mrs. Kendall Frayne. By comparison with them Monica is refreshingly wholesome. But it is precisely from her youthful wholesomeness that Clark Storey flees. Her love is so exacting and challenging that it frightens him. Marion's young and single-tracked lover, Kurt, in *Biography* is also too exacting when he requires her to blast the reputation of a political opportunist who had been her lover in her youth.

Anything too demanding or absolute frightens Behrman. At the very least it fills him with misgivings. There has been a "second man" in Behrman perennially temperate and middle-aged; it is as if he had been born old. And therein lies his wisdom as well as his limitation, his humaneness as well as his hesitation at the brink of a commitment to action. Only once did he commit one of his main characters more or less successfully—in *Rain from Heaven,* when his detached hero, Hugo Willens, joins that anti-Nazi underground. And, even so, it remains doubtful whether Hugo, the urbane intellectual, can truly ever commit himself to it. When the playwright-hero of Behrman's *No Time for Comedy* commits himself to renouncing comedy for serious plays about the Civil War in Spain, he is allowing himself to be deluded by a foolish and designing woman and is deluding himself. The warnings of his wife may offend his ego but are proved correct when he makes a miserable mess of the serious play.

Only the commitment to urbanity never quite fails Behrman, and in him urbanity is no simple presentation of good manners. The manners in some of his plays are, as a matter of fact, nowhere as good as in the comedies of Philip Barry. They are not particularly good, for example, in *Jane;* Lord Frobisher's are rude, and Jane's candor is, if anything, formidable.

Nor is it clinical detachment that rules Behrman's plays as it rules Maugham's. In the former, we are apt to find the reverse; there is in a number of Behrman's comedies a struggle for what Sartre called "engagement," and the struggle is represented by a main character; most conspicuously by Kurt in *Biography* and Hugo Willens in *Rain from Heaven*. Jane "engages" herself when she assists the young lovers in her play, and she even "engages" the egotistical individualist Lord Frobisher when she makes him liberate a young woman from a concentration camp. It is an essential part of Behrman's warm humanity that the question of "engagement" concerns him so often. He even agonizes over it, as he did in *No Time for Comedy*. Something holds him back from endorsing ideologies that might require single-tracked action, but it is not the lack of a sympathetic nature.

Behrman's severest critics have tried to explain his wariness as a desire to sit on the fence. A softer judgment would maintain that, like Montaigne and other supremely civilized men, he is simply not an "either-or" Kierkegaard man; his is a state of mind that most people arrive at fairly late in life, and it is perhaps significant that Behrman first became a produced playwright at the age of thirty-four. In Behrman's work only the surface is hard, even in his brightest, most detached comedy, *The Second Man*. In renouncing the love of Monica, Clark Storey does her a great favor. He knows he cannot come up to her expectations and realizes that there is a sceptical and self-indulgent "second man" in himself.

It may be that tolerance was a necessary growth in Behrman's impoverished but friendly immigrant background in Worcester, Mass. The reminiscences he has published suggest that he learned to regard foibles and idiosyncrasies as inherent in the human condition and to accept them as necessary to living among men. The least likable characters in Behrman's plays are the pushers, in good causes or bad, or in no cause whatsoever. Behrman's art is, in the first place, one of making allowances for human nature. He has consideration for *Biography's* Marion Froude who cannot overcome her indulgent view of people even if they are stuffed shirts and political opportunists; for the *End of Summer's* millionairess who would rather attach herself to a ruthless young radical than endure loneliness; and more recently, for that paragon of reactionary yellow journalism in *Jane,* Lord Frobisher. Characteristic in *Jane* is the young radical Peter Crewe's flip remark on learning that Frobisher got a girl out of a Nazi camp that, "comes the revolution," Frobisher shall be allowed to live.

In his work, indulgence toward people is almost synonymous with being civilized. There are dangers in this attitude which can result not only in moral flabbiness but in flabby playwriting. There is a considerable flabbiness, in fact, in his own play construction; and it is not always concealed by his trim and disciplined writing. If he can anger us into saying that the price of being civilized comes too high, he is even willing to admit the impeachment.

He did so explicitly when, outraged by Hitler's terror, he made the refined Hugo Willens in *Rain from Heaven* declare, "I see now that goodness is not enough, that liberalism is not enough." And even without provocation by fascism, Behrman took note of the flaw in indulgence early; in *Biography* when he made Kurt, the frustrated idealist, cry out when his lady-love allows a stuffy politician to go scot-free:

"I see now why injustice and the cruelty go on year after year—century after century—without change—because—as they grow older—people become tolerant of evils. Things amuse them. If the time ever comes when I'm amused by something I should hate, I hope they'll shoot me."

But Behrman has no doubt reflected that the alternative of hate—even if it may be justified hatred—will lead the Kurts of the world to do the shooting, in which case the score would be about the same. Behrman is interested in keeping human beings *alive* and in making do with their shortcomings. It is not always possible, of course. It is difficult to write exciting plays with that premise. But Behrman has never been young enough to believe that one does not pay—and pay heavily—for what one buys. He buys a sense of security, and pays for it in the quality of his plays. Latent in his thought is the feeling that in buying anything else, even a way of life more equitable, we may have to pay an exorbitant price. In society we may have to sacrifice humanity; in playwriting, the equanimity and sagacity he favors so greatly. It is probable, indeed, that a fear of strong resolutions and of melodrama underlies the poverty of stage action and engrossing plot often noticed in his work.

Still if tolerance and indulgence in his work had been unsupported by any other important quality, Behrman would never have become our ablest writer of high comedy. Something deeper than style alone distinguishes him from our many purveyors of light entertainment, including those who have at one time or another made a specialty of scepticism and debunking. That something is his habit of balancing the score. It makes him not merely a judicious but an acute playwright rather than a merely congenial one. He always remains *two* men; one man makes the positive observations, the second proposes the negative ones.

Jane, to cite a recent play, provides many examples: If social success is a desideratum for Jane, the dowdy woman from Liverpool, in the first act, so is escape from elegant London society in the second act. If a young husband seemed attractive to her at first, a middle-aged one seems preferable later on. If Gilbert Dabney, whom she marries, seemed too young for her in the first act, she finds him too "old" for her when he later reveals the egocentric cynicism of a go-getter in business and society. If Frobisher is shown to have too much self-confidence at the beginning, he is shown to have too little later on. Above all, I believe, Behrman wants to be fair and, wherever possible, considerate if not indeed generous. This is evident in the second act; if Frobisher is callous at first, he is grudgingly generous later on. If Gilbert Dabney made a social success out of dowdy Jane, she, in turn, made a social success of him. He liked what she made of him, but she tired of what he made of her; if his snobbish values seemed commendable to her at first, they became detestable later on; if her candor commended her to him when he was a nobody, it proved detrimental to him when he is a somebody. It was an idealist, Peter Crewe, who tried to get a girl out of Nazi Austria by marrying her, but it took the realist Frobisher, a political reactionary, to get her out of a concentration camp.

As Mr. Behrman said to me off-handedly during the Philadelphia try-out, we need realists to clean up the messes created by idealists. But then perhaps we need the idealists to create the situation in which realists will prove useful.

We may conclude, then, that Behrman's art of comedy, including his so-called comic detachment, consists of an ambivalence of attitudes that has its sources in the simultaneous possession of a nimble mind and a mellow temperament. He is, in a sense, "detached," but not by cynicism or indifference. The effect of detachment in his playwriting is caused by the ingrained need to see two sides at once and his keen pleasure in playing one side against the other. The essence of life for him is contradiction. The essence of his thinking about reality—the reality of situations and characters—is, to use an overworked but possibly clarifying word, "dialectical." He has a taste for dialectics. Most writers of comedy, now that Shaw has departed, have not. They take the *status quo* for granted, or they take some principle for granted. For Behrman, who is dynamically American even if his plots are usually more or less static, nothing remains fixed.

"Thesis" and "antithesis" abound in his plays and the comic spirit provides the tentative or temporary "synthesis" in them. It is not always a satisfactory one, especially when Behrman raises social problems intended to be taken seriously. It leaves one in a state of suspension which may be "civilized" but is not necessarily gratifying or sharply challenging as Shaw's comic art quite often is. This suggests a tenuousness in his playwriting that a criticism of his work and its place in the modern drama would have to take into consideration. But before criticizing Behrman's playwriting we must understand its nature, and to do so we shall have to go beyond the usual ascriptions to it of cleverness and urbanity. The same can be said of any writer of genuine high comedy. In Behrman's case they appear in the special context of a divided, sometimes distinctly troubled personality that integrates and reintegrates itself continually in efforts to arrive at an understanding with life which will make it tolerably humane. Occasionally Behrman makes this seem possible.

One may call this the illusion, as well as the small triumph, of art such as his.

II

When a strict assessment is made of Behrman's work, reservations are bound to assert themselves. Most of these are already familiar. The usual criticism is that he is strong in dialogue and weak in plot. It is an inconclusive criticism, since it is by no means certain that he would not deserve as great a reputation and lay claim to as long a life on the stage as even Congreve, if prowess in managing a plot were the decisive consideration. Congreve "plotted" *The Way of the World* miserably; one hardly pays attention to the maze of complications in this play, usually regarded as the foremost comedy of manners in the English language. Nor is there any conclusiveness in complaining that Behrman has some routine work, such as *The Pirate* and *I Know My Love*, on his record. Writers who work regularly for the stage are apt to turn out potboilers for the trade. Behrman has been tempted to do so particularly because his style of writing has fitted the Lunts' style of acting rather snugly. And early more or less abortionate efforts of his, such as *Meteor* and *Brief Moment,* in both of which there is fine writing, do not do him any serious discredit. Every new play poses new problems to its author, and even a good playwright is not always in full command of his metier.

The crux of the matter is to be found elsewhere, not in incompetencies attributed to the playwright but to the complexities of creation imposed on him by his particular bent. It may be said that Behrman has generally attempted to pirouette in the salons of comedy of manners while carrying the burden of a rather weighty social conscience. When he carried no such burden in his 1927 comedy *The Second Man,* he was completely the master of his medium, and everybody was amazed at the maturity of comic talent in the emergent playwright. This does not, however, mean that Behrman was completely at ease with a comedy-of-manners world. The seeds of discontent had already sprouted in him. He made his sophisticated writer-hero say, "There's someone inside of me—a second man—grinning, sophisticated, horrid," and explain:

> I used to sit in a garret and believe in Socialism. It didn't take me long to find out how easy it is to starve on idealism. I had facility, and there is a ready market for facility. I got $5,000 for writing a whitewashed biography of a million-dollar sweatshop owner.

No such rueful awareness of compromise is present in the best comedies of Somerset Maugham, not even in *The Circle* where Lady Kitty and Lord Porteous rake over the sorry results of their elopement. When disenchantment becomes a burden rather than a flag of defiance in Maugham's work—in *Sheppey,* for example, where a man is adjudged insane for giving away his money to the poor—he, too, loses control of his metier. Behrman did not lose his in *The Second Man* because the affair at hand concerned characters—a novelist-sponger, a wealthy mistress, and a brimming ingenue—uninvolved in any large conflicts. Behrman's burden became heavy only when some necessity of his nature forced him to take cognizance of such conflicts. And when he did, he didn't have the advantage of Bernard Shaw's airy self-assurance, as well as confidence in the power of laughter and argument, a confidence considerably easier for a man born in 1856 than for one born nearly four decades later.

Behrman is a writer who in every original play of any importance since *The Second Man* has seemed somewhat deficient in confidence. He has stood frequently on the brink of apology, and in *No Time for Comedy,* written on the eve of the Second World War, he actually wrote an extensive apology, justifying a return to light comedy in the case of a writer who discovered that he could not bring his best talents to the cause of liberty during the long night of fascism. Behrman himself tried to do so, with variable results. He made the attempt in 1934 with *Rain from Heaven,* a worthy but inconclusive play in which he tried vainly to hold on to comedy of manners while the story of an exile from Hitler's Germany exacted a troubled seriousness from its author. And in 1940 he returned indirectly to the problem in *The Talley Method,* a sort of domestic comedy parable on the demands of the times which forced a problem-play seriousness on him without affording him the compensatory intensities of *Rain from Heaven.*

He was more at ease when he turned to the American political scene in *Biography* in 1932 and *End of Summer* in 1936. He succeeded in supplying Broadway with two generally delightful comedies. Even here, however, the seams of comedy seemed somewhat strained. It is surely easier to write uncontaminated comedy of manners when there is no social transition in the making. It is when the alternative of changing a situation is not even being considered by the playwright and his audience that completely detached laughter is most possible. It is then, too, that the flight from the immediate scene we have in romantic comedy, including the pastoral type represented by *As You Like It,* can be in fashion. Also, its opposite, "dark comedy" is likely to have some vogue. But for the writing of "dark comedy" a playwright must have a saturnine temperament absent in Behrman's constitution. In such later comedies as *Wine of Choice* in 1938 and

Dunnigan's Daughter in 1945, Behrman was seriously divided; the comic and the non-comic elements were patently in conflict. My criticism here is not that the author should have used heavy artillery on the forces he regarded as evil—a comedian should not be required to use cannon—but that there was too little bounce and lightness in these later plays.

All of the usual criticisms, then, must be related to the pack of troubles, hesitations, and afterthoughts that Behrman, being Behrman and responsive in his way to an age surely not congenial to comedy of manners, has had to bring with him into the theatre. His invention has been hobbled at times by extra-comedic demands. We may also surmise that his invention would have got out of hand, so that he would have become melodramatically plotty, if he had not clamped the lid down on plot-making after having established a comic situation and found the proper orchestration of characters for it. Had he allowed his keen, if divided, awareness of the larger social scene to dictate plots to him, there is no telling how snarled up the dramatic complications would have become. That is exactly what happened in the original version of his *End of Summer* that I read at the Theatre Guild. I hope I am not betraying a state secret when I say that this draft, before revision, was considerably less a comedy than a melodrama in which the psychiatrist became a thorough-going villain and poisoned the wealthy mother of the heroine after having got his victim to assign control of the heroine's estate to him.

Since, however, even the neatly circumscribed action of an exemplary Behrman comedy, along with its urbane dialogue, lacks the triumphant self-containment high comedy requires, it is plain that even so talented a man as Behrman has found it difficult to allow comic detachment full sway in his work while remaining a responsive man in times of extreme tension. Still, if he had not been so responsive, he would have become just another literate entertainer. That is a role to which he has profitably descended from time to time, but no one possessed of his somewhat pained intelligence and generous spirit could be content with playing it continually. He long ago chose the vastly more difficult and precarious office of civilizer to a theatre divided between ardent, sometimes blind, partisans and gelid, almost equally blind, neutrals. There are surely roles considerably less honorable than Behrman's intermediate one.

SARTRE AND PISCATOR: *THE FLIES*

A 1947 late-season nugget was the Piscator presentation of Sartre's existentialist version of the Orestes legend, *The Flies*—a work that embodies perhaps the most intense and deeply considered view of the problem of freedom to come out of the century's theatre. Sartre's "free man" Orestes has no desire to avenge his father, to dethrone the usurper of the throne of Argos, or to rid his city of its tyrants. Taught by his tutor, the representative of above-the-scene, sceptic intellectualism, the exponent of the "civilized" attitude which tells him, in effect, "you must be a detached observer, you know better than to commit yourself," Orestes feels light as a gossamer. He can cry out, "This is not *my* palace, nor *my* door. . . . These folk are of no concern of mine." Nevertheless, Orestes, too, must commit himself, for the feeling of dissociation has its own anguish. He must respond to his sense of justice, to his fellow-men's need of liberation; he must even sacrifice himself.

Orestes must be able to breathe in a world that is free in order to be truly free himself. He must make his world free, even if he must renounce his freedom on the lower level of detachment. If necessary, he must stain his hands with blood and fill his soul with the memory of deeds that give extreme pain to his civilized and humane sensibility, as did the heroes of the French resistance movement who not only killed ruthlessly but risked the lives of their associates and their relatives. Above all, Sartre's hero is most free when he makes a connection between himself and others. His freedom lies not merely in the repugnance he feels for slavery but in his willingness to affirm by action what he holds by conviction. Man is free only to choose his course of action *deliberately with open eyes* and with indomitable resolve—"to choose his bonds," as Sartre has said elsewhere. The "bond" in the case of Orestes is with his people.

A play that communicates that much thought and fire is surely noteworthy. That it should have come out of France under the German occupation is a tribute to the vitality of the French intellect and spirit, as well as to the mind and soul of its author. That the play, however, should not have received a Broadway production does not reflect favorably upon Broadway, which loses fabulous sums on trash because most producers are unable to detect its worthlessness in advance of production and are astute only in discovering financial risks in a work unmistakably distinguished. Especially distressing is the fact that Piscator should not have been able to finance a Broadway presentation of this work *after* he had publicly demonstrated its worth with an excellent production in his Dramatic Workshop repertory at the little President Theatre in midtown New York. Evidently, the only fact about the play that impressed potential investors and co-producers wheedled into attending the performance at the President was the fact that audiences at a Broadway house would not be allowed to check their brains with an attendant before being seated.

Sartre's existentialist morality piece *No Exit* was cited by the New York Drama Critics Circle as the best foreign play of the 1946-47 season, and it is understandable that Sartre's concentrated moralism should have impressed most reviewers. But *The Flies* is a more absorbing and more fully realized drama than *No Exit,* and it was produced with a distinction that was absent in the Broadway production of the earlier play. Although Piscator's cast consisted of students and faculty members of the Dramatic Workshop, the staging, credited to one of the instructors, Paul Ransom, had an authentic Piscator style. There was no bolder creator in America than Piscator during his stay in the United States from 1939 to 1951, and it is regrettable that Broadway failed to avail itself of the talent of this distinguished exile from Germany. He tended to go to extremes in sociological documentation and in the use of stage machinery, and he tended to dominate his actors more than American directors do. But Piscator brought an intellectually tempered imagination to the theatre, and he never failed to give the impression that the play he directed or produced actually mattered. Theatre for him was always something more than titillation of the senses and sentiments. In his production, *The Flies* seemed to possess both immediate and universal importance. He used his familiar lecture-slide method as a prologue; he resorted to a film "tracer" in order to remind the audience that Sartre wrote the play during Hitler's conquest of Europe. Due to mechanical difficulties, the film was unimpressive, and in his desire to instruct the playgoer, Piscator was somewhat heavy-handed, a fault not infrequently attributed to him. Not even a good film montage, however, would have made the play as significant as its stage reality made it.

The Flies was staged with an economy of means that concentrated attention upon its argument, and with an absence of the antiquarian detail of classical columns and friezes that most directors and designers favor the moment they encounter a classical subject. For Piscator and his associates, the Orestes story celebrated in fifth-century Athenian drama was not a Periclean excursion but a modern morality. If the play was based on old material, it was *pre-historic*. It was a plunge into the primitive archetype that we call legend—that is, into the sources of passion and heroism in human history. Ramps, hollow pillars, and a gruesome statue of Zeus, as far from Periclean art as a savage's totem pole, helped to establish the archetypal nature of the fears and superstitions, the tyranny of "gods" and men, and the exactions of morbid conscience to which Sartre opposed the free mind—the French (and only in this sense, Periclean) mind of Sartre's existentialist, intellectual Orestes who frees himself from these forces and shows his people the way to freedom. Piscator, in short, successfully realized on the stage the same tension of freedom *versus* slavery, or courage *versus* fear, that Sartre realized in his writing.

If Sartre's argument is not invulnerable, it has a general provocativeness and validity as a view of life. Sartre made drama with it, albeit a drama somewhat strained and creaky with intellectualism which "highbrows" would tend to overrate and Broadway "middle-brows" to underrate. Piscator made "theatre" out of Sartre's text. Once the awkward film-prologue was out of the way and Sartre's piece itself began, the action moved forcefully across the stage. The small size of the theatre was never felt as a detriment because the mobile turntable and skeletal setting designed by Willis Knighton varied and multiplied the acting area with every turn. The movement of the "machine-for-theatre" setting was itself an action useful in preventing stasis. The very discussions in the play became a series of *actions* on the shifting acting areas, for Piscator would be the last stage director to accept the popular thesis that the theatre is doomed to be anti-intellectual owing to the limitations inherent in it. Projections on a scrim by John McGrew also extended the range of the stage picture to the audience, and the auditorium itself enlarged the playing space, the front of the auditorium serving for actual action and discussions, and the whole auditorium being used for entrances and exits up and down the aisles by some of the characters. And this overworked procedure, usually awkward and artificial, was actually made more than tolerable in this production by the intimacy of the house. The auditorium was made part of the stage picture by a tastefully imaginative scenic treatment of the side walls. The dramatic action became, so to speak, action and discussion in which the audience was a participant, for the audience seated between the pictorially transformed side walls was within an imaginatively extended setting.

My enthusiasm for this Piscator production, when first introduced into his repertory, was shared by others. But more important to anyone who cares sufficiently about theatre as a means of projecting the written play was the lesson one could take from Piscator in the kinetic use of the stage; in this case, so appropriate to the requirements of the theatre in which it was produced, and so pervasively harmonious with the substance of the play that I do not by any means exhaust the comment I could make on this production. Nor do I pretend that my analysis of it conforms exactly to Piscator's own views. For a long time, while in this country, he hoped to establish a magazine in which approaches to his production style could be described and analyzed, but a publication would have required more financing than he could find. To my knowledge only in Germany in recent years has interest in production analysis found an outlet of this nature—in a volume entitled *Theaterarbeit,* dealing with six productions of the Berlin Ensemble. On Broadway, no particular analysis or evaluation was given to the Dramatic Workshop's treatment of *The Flies.* And in all probability only some of Piscator's students and production associates could now tell us something about the staging and the reasoning that went into it, just as we should have no understanding of many a Broadway production but for the few reports by scene designers such as the account Mordecai Gorelik gave concerning his treatment of the stage for *Golden Boy* as a symbolic prize-fight ring.

Sartre, in his early plays written during World War II, revealed a passionate intellect and considerable talent for translating it into concrete symbols. He made his plays rotate on two axes, around the specific situation and around an idea capable of general application. His procedure, surely not unique in the history of distinguished drama, made him the first stimulating new playwright to emerge in the nineteen-forties. The abstract validity of his existentialist philosophy could be debated and doubted. But he proved himself an effective dramatist so long as passion and a desire to redeem occupied France from apathy sparked his dramatic writing.

In his first play, the long one-act fantasy *No Exit,* his sense of theatre was still cramped and crabbed. He made an artificial case history out of his Dante-like picture of human failures doomed to spend eternity in each other's company; his characters were appalling specimens. There was too little humanity in his denunciation of self-delusion and the individual's dependence upon other people's opinion. ("Hell is other people.") In *The Flies,* he achieved verve and positiveness with a positive, heroic treatment of Orestes' return to Argos, not to avenge his father's death, as in the old legend, but to free his people from tyranny and self-enslavement. Sartre proceeded to raise the question of how man could be free in a deeper sense than that of simply driving Hitler's armies out of France, and he concluded that a man must first make himself inwardly free before he could free himself from the yoke pressed on him by others. The usual, and I believe fallacious, view is that it is the slaves who overthrow a tyranny. Slaves, of course, cannot, because they have been mastered inwardly; they have incorporated the tyrant or the tyrannical system into their psyche.

Sartre's answer in *The Flies,* as in his entire philosophy, is hardly conclusive. It is a moot point whether it is not itself tainted with the virus of such thinking as the cult of an élite, of the leader principle, and of amoral behavior. In *The Flies,* indeed, Sartre is not entirely clear. There is, for instance, a touch of the savior-complex in the dramatic line of Orestes' taking upon himself the city's sickly sense of guilt (because *he* can master the sense of guilt, instead of being mastered by it). He kills his mother Clytemnestra when he decides to commit a greater "sin" than the city wallows in, and he makes the Furies follow him out of Argos. The extreme individualism of "existentialism" is indeed misleading when we confront it in a play about the liberation of a people, for then we come up against the ineluctable fact that the French resistance was a collective effort by many "little" people. "Existentialist" man living unto himself, responsible only to himself, and standing above the ideals or the "morality" of others—if such a man can really exist!—would have been ineffective. He might have proved a great comfort to the Germans, since anarchistic individualism and nihilism are powerful inducements to passiveness.

Nevertheless, what really matters on the dramatic level of Sartre's play is that Orestes is "free" in the sense that he is revolted by the spiritual slavery of Argos. Its self-abasement and wallowing in remorse, so useful to kings and gods, stink in his nostrils. He does liberate the citizens, and leaves them free to choose and create a different life from the one they have led. He performs a necessary act of liberation without emotional hypocrisy. He refuses to accept the bondage of the city's and his own sister's codes of righteousness. He kills, but not for his sister's revengeful reasons. Nor does he succumb to theology as represented by a Zeus who holds man in bondage through superstition, fear, and self-abasement. If some of this doctrine becomes a little complicated in the telling for Sartre, as well as for this reporter, the over-all effect is not merely provocative but refreshing and exalting.

To single out the Piscator production and Sartre's drama, however, for a purpose other than that of reportage, we must set them down as stimulating examples of possibilities rarely explored in our theatre and in the theatre of England in post-war years: possibilities of imaginatively representing exigent issues and testing moral fibre in a broad social context. Only Arthur Miller in America after 1945 seemed to be interested in the areas laid open by Piscator and Sartre. The last playwright of some stature to care about them with any sense of dedication had been Robert Sherwood.

NEW AMERICAN PLAYWRIGHTS:
WILLIAMS, MILLER, AND OTHERS

I

If one had to report to Europeans on new American playwrights after the Second World War what would one say? That was the question I had to answer in 1952 when *World Theatre,* a magazine inaugurated by UNESCO, requested an article from me. Would one report on the many crashing failures Broadway produced? Surely not, since the development of an art is not to be sought at its lowest levels. Would one inform Europeans about Broadway's successes indiscriminately? Hardly, since this would equate playwriting with the state of the box-office till, and since, in any case, many popular plays would have no meaning to anyone across the Atlantic interested in the relevance of our drama to modern developments in playwriting form and style rather than in the question of what kind of theatre yields "hits" on Broadway. These considerations limit the reporter, for only a few playwrights could bear inspection, and among these might be found men whose plays failed as well as authors of Broadway successes. And this is perhaps all to the good even for American critics and playgoers. They should be compelled to ask themselves periodically what the years' bustle can amount to as viewed from the perspective of world theatre, and what the disengaged foreign observer would consider worth noting. This perspective would, besides, enable us to pay attention to the unique rather than the common element in a playwright's striving or achievement which enabled him to stand out from the mass of writers who provide grist for the mill of a theatrical center such as New York. A similar view of the English, French, German, and Italian theatres would tell us what the world theatre of the period has actually amounted to during the early post-war period above and beyond the mere production of good, bad, and indifferent drama. And comparisons could then be made between different countries on the useful basis of different precipitates rather than particles in indiscriminate solution. My own judgment would credit the post-war French stage with the greatest achievement. But I could not rank the American theatre disgracefully low in the scale of values when I assessed the precipitated results in the *World Theatre* magazine. Like every other national theatre, the American stage after World War II had to be tested, to a degree, by the calibre of its new playwrights, and several of these had revealed strivings toward something more valuable—considerably more valuable—than play-carpentry. Two of the new-comers, Tennessee Williams and Arthur Miller, actually and deservedly aroused interest abroad.

Tennessee Williams, who was born in the South in 1914, made a first impression on the stage with his memory-play *The Glass Menagerie* in the spring of 1945, when he was no longer an unseasoned young writer, having had a Theatre Guild production five years earlier that was retired in Boston. Born two years after Williams, in New York City, Arthur Miller achieved importance in our theatre two years after the production of *The Glass Menagerie,* with *All My Sons.* He, too, had gone through the experience of a Broadway production with *The Man Who Had All the Luck,* which expired after a short run in 1944. Miller, whose talent belongs primarily to the theatre, actually established himself first as a novelist in 1945, with the successful publication of *Focus,* a novel about anti-semitism. He first impressed Broadway in January, 1947, with the taut dramaturgy and moral passion of *All My Sons.*

Within two years, then, the two young writers were equally in the limelight, and before long it was difficult to decide who was the more important of the two. Williams, after giving the theatre the mild drama-tization of a D. H. Lawrence story *You Touched Me* in 1946, proceeded to overwhelm Broadway again with *A Streetcar Named Desire,* which opened in New York on December 3, 1947. And Miller made an equally strong, if not actually stronger, impression with *Death of a Salesman,* fifteen months later. The two pieces found large and enthusiastic audi-ences, and subsequently reached an even larger public in generally faith-ful film versions. Miller followed *Death of a Salesman* with a tendentious version of *An Enemy of the People,* and started work on *The Crucible,* one of the two outstanding plays of the 1952-53 season. Williams provided *Summer and Smoke* in the fall of 1948 and *The Rose Tattoo* in 1951. The former, which resembled *A Streetcar Named Desire* in some respects, was a failure when first produced, but became the most acclaimed production of 1952 when staged in the arena theatre of Circle-in-the-Square. And turning to symbolism on a grand scale, Williams expanded an early one-act play of his into the *Camino Real* over which New York buzzed with controversy in 1953.

Between them, the young man from the North and the young man from the South have virtually encompassed the range of modern dramatic art and style, and that is what might interest the European observer espe-cially. Miller represents the social realism that has characterized a large percentage of modern playwriting since Ibsen's middle period; Williams, the effort to transcend realism that started in Europe with the neo-romantic and symbolist reaction against Naturalism. Miller uses lean colloquial prose; Williams writes musically, poetically, and imagistically charged dialogue. Miller exemplifies the theatre of the common man and of more or less collective issues; Williams, the perennial avant-garde theatre of subjectivity and private sensibility.

II

Miller, whose descent from Ibsen can be clearly traced, was rightly designated by Harold Clurman as a dispenser of moral jurisprudence. In *All My Sons,* the conflict between self-interest and social responsibility is developed as a drama of hidden guilt, discovery, and retribution in the manner of *Pillars of Society,* a play which we associate with Ibsen's early technique of intrigue in the manner of Scribe. We don't think well of this kind of contrived dramaturgy, of course, but we draw a sharper line between it and the method employed in Ibsen's later plays, from *A Doll's House* and *Ghosts* to *John Gabriel Borkman,* than is warranted. The difference is essentially one of degree, or, perhaps, of tone. It comes down to a question of whether the work is one of calculation for the sake of the plot or for the sake of idea, irony, or some other interest intended to stimulate rather than befuddle and thrill the playgoer. An incriminating letter brought to light in the third act of *All My Sons,* when it could just as well have been discovered earlier, calls attention to plot machinery. Adventitious occurrences in Ibsen's *Pillars of Society* belong to the same order of contrivance. The burning down of the orphanage in *Ghosts* shortly after Pastor Manders refused to insure the charitable edifice out of conventional piety calls attention to irony. An irony compounded by the fact that the orphanage was intended as a memorial to Mrs. Alving's amorously roving husband! And compounded further as a means of representing the destruction of the entire façade of the Pastor's beliefs and Mrs. Alving's conventional life. The superiority of *Ghosts* to either *Pillars of Society* or *All My Sons* is obvious.

Still, we must realize, too, that the plot contrivance of *All My Sons* (or of Miss Hellman's *Watch on the Rhine, The Little Foxes,* or even *Another Part of the Forest*) does not exist as something isolated from other interests served up by the playwright. In a typical "well-made play" intended to be nothing more than audience-catching theatre, whether it be Scribe's *Verre d'Eau* intrigue in the court of Queen Anne or the latest melodrama, the plot contrivance serves only the plot. In the atypical "well-made play," *Pillars of Society* or *All My Sons* (or a Hellman play), the plot contrivance serves something else than the plot. The argument, the idea, or the author's passion for something *beyond theatre* dominates our interest. We must grant, of course, that the contrivance is esthetically meretricious, since the author has reached out for an easy, obvious way of getting on with his play or idea and resolving it. He has been guilty of distinguishing between means and ends, whereas in every artistic enterprise means and ends or content and form should be truly identical. Nevertheless, we must allow the work a place on the foothills of creative art—as a flawed work that nonetheless has merit. And that is precisely the case when audiences and critics, to whom some intelligence is granted by all but fledgling intellectuals, respond to the work, as they did to *All My Sons,* with excitement and a considerable measure of respect.

Nor is it just the "idea" that commands this respect. In a play such as *All My Sons,* there are elements beyond both plot and idea that engage our interest. Characters are brought to life, an atmosphere or mood is evoked, an environment is presented; and insight into how people feel and think or rationalize is present. The texture and actual aliveness of *All My Sons* consists of the reality of family life observed by Miller; of the reality of Miller's Joe Keller, depicted as a shrewd "little man" with a feeling for family and a sense of cleverly concealed desperation; of Keller's wife, presented as the affectionate "little woman" for whom issues of right and wrong or guilt and retribution are secondary to keeping life going with creature comforts and amiable personal relationships; of the ambivalences of Keller's surviving son, whose filial loyalty is being severely tested when he must inform against his father. In addition, Miller made reality out of the neighborliness of suburban neighbors, and out of various other details, down to a blasted little tree in a cramped backyard which is symbolic of the Keller family's narrow way of life, normal intellectual-moral range, and questionable moral situation. Miller, in short, *created* his play rather than merely contrived it. He presented life, as well as argument, on the stage.

Miller's argument could not, however, be slighted either; it had passion and principle. The war-profiteer Joe Keller, who had caused the death of a number of aviators by supplying the government with defective airplane parts, was depicted by Miller as a "little man" rather than as a stereotyped capitalistic villain. Keller justified his conduct on the grounds that he was preserving his small business for his sons. But the crime is exposed by his own son, and the malefactor, stripped of his sentimental defenses, kills himself. The categorical imperative operates here in a manner that recalls the relentless dramaturgy of the Scandinavian master. Narrow practicality is morally bankrupt and has criminal consequences in the case of Miller's "Consul Bernick," Joe Keller. The latter's paternal love and devotion to his family's welfare are exposed as disguised manifestations of egotism, since he endeavored to secure his sons' interests at the expense of other men's sons. Miller wages war against "Gyntism," whatever its form or its self-justification.

Miller's later slighting reference to his "well-made play" as a conventional exercise should not mislead us into believing that *All My Sons* is completely atypical of his dramatic method. In essential matters, he followed the same course of closely demonstrating his social philosophy when he wrote *Death of a Salesman*. He moved the dramatic action freely from one stage area to the other without making any attempt to set the scene realistically. He combined the realistic technique with the expressionistic, weaving a complex pattern of present and past events, of immediate tensions and recollected crises. But he rooted his imaginatively conceived scenes in common reality; the characters and the background were always recognizably middle-class. The composition of the play held present and past events in a vise of dramatic logic as a misguided man, bitterly disappointed in his life and in his hopes for a favorite son, moved from despair to suicide within twenty-four hours. The man's memories and hallucinations moved erratically over time and space, but they were tied tightly together by his immediate tensions and conflicts.

There was, it is true, no "well-made play" kind of intrigue or crime detection in this chronicle of Willy Loman, the mentally distressed sixty-year-old salesman whose life and errors are weighed in the balance of fate. All the discoveries in this drama are essentially self-discoveries by Willy Loman and the son he miseducated. Yet the play was charged with suspense, since Miller was trying a man for his faults and follies. The fact that Willy Loman shared these with a great many ordinary men, a fact that gave *Death of a Salesman* a good deal of its meaning, was not allowed to exempt him from judgment. Miller scrupulously prepared a trap for his main character, and the trap was nothing less than Willy's entire misspent life of hollow success-worship, false values, and chronic inability to face the truth. Ignoring the importance of integrity and achievement, Willy naïvely thought that popularity gained by windy charm constituted a successful way of life. He acted on this belief, blustered about it, and indoctrinated his children with it. But the verdict of reality is ultimately against this deluded man, and Miller, accepting this verdict as essentially just, renders it strictly. The hour of reckoning arrives inexorably in this drama. "Gyntism" is exposed and punished in *Death of a Salesman* even more relentlessly than in *All My Sons,* in spite of Miller's great compassion for a broken man who had never intended to harm anyone.

Miller has generally been applauded for the balance he maintained between pity and justice. The only non-dramaturgic question that has been seriously raised is whether his misguided salesman is worthy of tragic treatment, and the point is rather well taken. It should not be overworked, however. For very obviously the play is not a tragedy in the grand manner, and Miller did not intend it to be one. He defined his play as the tragedy of a common man rather than of an exceptional hero. Where we can part company with the author is in feeling that his Willy Loman is *too* common. Miller intended to affirm the tragic dignity of an "average" man's refusal to relinquish his ideal of himself as an indispensable and admired person, an independent individual, and the father of a son who has a bright future in spite of objective evidence to the contrary. Miller's *ordinary* hero is *extraordinary* in the passionate manner in which he lives and dies for his dream. Is that dream worthy? We balk at this point to a degree which varies with our background and sense of values.

Whether or not *Death of a Salesman* entirely sustains itself as a tragedy, it expresses a sympathetic and heroic view of realities that reveal a good deal of the life and struggles of a by no means negligible stratum of American—and not only American—society in our times. The very dichotomy of the argument is characteristic of this reality. Willy is a victim, but also a fool. Society, with its overpublicized materialistic values and vulgar view of success, pumped him full of notions. But not all men, not even the suburban neighbor "Uncle Charlie," a character who has no towering mind or aspirations, succumb to this nonsense of success as "show" and glib talk and a state of being "well liked." The point is, of course, that Willy did succumb, and that there are many Willys, as average New York audiences readily believed. This is part of Willy's misfortune. But Willy is also an employee, who has become superannuated. He is ready for the scrap-heap, a fate to which he could not have resigned himself easily, given his character, even if he could have drawn old-age benefits or a pension, any more than Othello could have resigned himself to possessing a wife who is not above suspicion. (Iago could, to a degree. But that is one of the many differences between Iago and Othello.) In other words, Willy is a "social problem" as a discarded employee, and a "human problem" as a personality too big in his feelings and necessary pretensions to be merely a case history soluble by social legislation. The play is both sociological and non-sociological and at least oriented toward "tragedy."

Without continuing this line of inquiry, we can say that Miller, for whatever reasons we wish to ascribe to the author, split his play between *social causation* and *individual responsibility* for Willy's fate. Which causation stands out for us depends upon our bias. Both communist critics and their communism-obsessed antagonists focussed on the social causation. The former complained that Miller obscured the social issue. And he certainly did lessen the importance of social causation by making Willy's folly responsible for his fiasco. Others could complain, and with some justice, that Miller had carried over a left-wing animus from the social theatre of the thirties in presenting Willy as a callously discharged and helpless employee when it was evident that Willy had made a mess of life quite independently. And in *Partisan Review,* Eleanor Clark went so far as to accuse the author of a disingenuous effort to cover up "leftist" tracks by exposing Willy's personal follies and allocating to him a personal responsibility for his misfortunes when, according to her, Miller actually sought to indict capitalist society. Many of us, myself included, however, are inclined to contend that Miller placed the *personal causation* in the foreground of the play. The most obvious proof is that Uncle Charlie, the small businessman, succeeds as a human being in the play, although his life and values have been made thoroughly "middle-class" by Miller. There is nothing in the play to indicate that Willy's choice of a career as a salesman was a social or economic necessity rather than truly a necessity of his nature or of his illusions, granted the existence of a milieu favorable to the latter. The dichotomy of Miller's presentation of Willy's plight is undoubtedly in the play. It is not necessarily a virtue, for it causes some confusion in our attitude toward Willy and in our perception of his situation. Yet the dichotomy is not necessarily as egregious a flaw in *Death of a Salesman* as some critics claim. The dichotomy is actually present in the life and destiny that Miller's Willy exemplifies.

There is a failure in tragic art in the treatment. No doubt of it, for Willy never arrives at tragic insight; he even rejects the insight of his son Biff. But could he have arrived at this insight, which amounts to realizing his (and Biff's) littleness, without losing the heroism—confused and morally intellectually limited though it be!—that gives him some stature? Willy, as characterized by Miller, is constitutionally incapable of giving up his dream. That is his tragedy. It nominates him for the select company of those passionate souls that Edith Hamilton calls the only tragic characters of literature. Whether we are willing actually to elect him to that company is debatable. We can divide sharply on that question, and in casting our vote for or against his election we only reveal ourselves. We reveal our bias, our conditioning, our values, moral or esthetic, or both. And at this point our argument arrives at an impasse, for we arrive at the "dead end" of what we ourselves are, and to expect us to change our vote is to expect us to change ourselves.

III

Without possessing Miller's socially directed attitude, Williams, too, has been concerned with the dream-mechanisms of unfortunate characters who try to create and preserve ideal images of themselves. Like Miller, he regards their delusions with compassionate interest as pathetic defenses against the frustration or shipwreck of their lives. In fact, he is able to create a tracery of fantasy for them with much greater subtlety and grace than Miller, although he is vulnerable to the temptations of bohemian preciosity, as Miller is not. His portraits of women who cannot face reality are masterful. Unlike Miller, however, Williams gives primacy to the psychologically rather than socially relevant facts of each situation. This is the case even in *The Glass Menagerie,* in which an important factor is the economic distress of a family during the depression period. No particular affirmation has ruled Williams' plays; he has been content to remain a tender chronicler of failure, and he has not evinced any desire to prove social causation even when he has made reference to it. The primary factors in all his produced plays, except perhaps *Camino Real,* have been instinct and sensibility. Moreover, if Williams has evinced one paramount conviction it is a belief in the power of the libido to both animate and destroy a human being. In this respect, Williams reveals his kinship to D. H. Lawrence, whom he has admired to the point of imitation. Only in *The Glass Menagerie,* among the full-length plays, does sex play a secondary part, and there we encounter a world of pre-adult innocence (even in the case of Amanda, the mother steeped in her girlish past) which entails failure. There is no particular social passion in his work.

Williams has a bohemian writer's "art for art's sake" passion. It appears to be his only passion, as well as his only faith—the faith of a *fin de siecle* or "Décadent" writer with whom Europeans are considerably more familiar than Americans. The interest of the French in *A Streetcar Named Desire* and *The Rose Tattoo,* which they have acclaimed as a great play, might be explained on the basis that *décadence* is a powerful literary tradition of late nineteenth and twentieth century France. His "estheticism," which has made him unusual and fascinating in the American theatre, has been his main limitation as dramatist, in my opinion, ever since I started following his career in 1940 when Miss Theresa Helburn and I gave him a Bureau of New Plays scholarship.

The essence of bohemianism is preoccupation with the artist's singularity or specialness, which is often the same thing as a sense of alienation defensively exaggerated into exhibitionistic defiance. Williams held this tendency in check and transmuted it into objective observation while writing his dramas of emotionally bankrupted women whom he honestly set down as neurotics. He did not do so in the first produced full-length play *Battle of Angels* in 1940; and his latest play *Camino Real,* produced in 1953, is completely grounded in the cult of alienation, for which "symbolism" has been the favorite technique. These plays romanticize the childlike or "wild" individual. He is a Cajun Robin Hood of sex and artist *manqué* in *Battle of Angels* and an American, "Kilroy," sort of innocent or naif in *Camino Real*. Significantly, the hero of *Camino Real* shares the stage with Casanova, Mlle. Gautier, Byron, and Don Quixote, all literary figures associated with defiance of convention and with romance.

Williams' estheticism, with which the realistic details of his plays exist in a dramatically effective fusion, translates itself in other ways, too. The overdelicateness and fastidiousness of Blanche du Bois form a sharp contrast to her circumstances and her compulsive incontinence; and it is altogether apparent that Williams loves her over-refinement as much as he exposes it. The brute masculinity of Stanley Kowalski also unduly fascinates Williams at the same time that he deplores it. (Kowalski, too, is a "wild" man!) Williams' ambivalence in the play has made playgoers fluctuate between a feeling that Stan Kowalski gives Blanche what she deserves and a sense of outrage when he rapes her during his wife's stay in the hospital, where she has given birth to his child. Different actors may vary the emphasis, but the objective line of action (Kowalski has a right to resent Blanche, but is brutish, and Blanche is both annoying and pathetic) betrays the author's ambivalence. It produces a provocative, but also damaging, ambiguity in the play; damaging to the point of preventing *Streetcar* from attaining tragic magnificence. Another ambivalence appears in *The Rose Tattoo*. There is a sharp contrast here between the erotic obsessiveness of the heroine, who is herself divided between sensuality and concern for her daughter's virtue, and the almost asexual purity of Williams' treatment of the love of the daughter and a young sailor.

A close study of "texture" such as the New Critics of the Ranson-Tate-Brooks school employ so efficiently would, indeed, reveal numerous instances of "ambiguity" and ambivalence on which to base analysis, evaluation, and speculation. I am sure that if Williams had been an English or Irish poet instead of an American playwright who has succeeded on Broadway (how injudicious of him!), he would have already been put through the New Critics' wringer. The results would have been fascinating, if not necessarily as conclusive as the New Critics would have believed, for Williams, like every other professional playwright, has had to consider and yield to many objective facts of stage production essentially unrelated to the subjectivity of the author. Williams' fondness for atmospheric and musical effects is transparent, and his consciousness of dramatic and theatrical form makes him a deliberately "theatricalist" playwright. The theatricalism of *Camino Real* is an extreme example of his concern with non-realistic formal devices. A glance at the stage contrivances he prescribed for the staging of *The Glass Menagerie* (they appear in the published version, but were discarded in part by Eddie Dowling, the director of the Broadway production), reveals a bias for theatrical ingenuity and stylization even in this relatively modest piece of playwriting. Actually, the most affecting scenes of *The Glass Menagerie* are written with sensitive realism. Here and elsewhere, Williams is most convincing when he writes without trying too hard to play the symbolist and the gymnast of theatrical effects. No American or living European playwright is his equal when he modestly confines himself to a realistic rendering of non-allegorical, non-literary characters who belong to a real rather than a poetic environment. But it is apparent that he puts a premium both on literariness and on "art theatre" virtuosity in the use of the theatre's physical facilities. He also likes to play with symbols, to use literary allusions, and like the Pound-Eliot disciples, to embellish the programs and published versions of his books with epigraphs (from Hart Crane and other "alienated" writers). He is Broadway's most dedicated avant-gardist.

Williams' work has been popularly called "poetic realism." It edges over into *theatricalist realism* because he tends toward the symbolist school of writing, and whenever symbolism has to be given physical equivalents it becomes theatricalism. Had he devoted himself solely to poetry he would have been a "symbolist." Fortunately he did not, for he would have been a distinctly minor, perhaps only barely tolerable, lyric poet. The theatre has compelled him to objectify experience, which he can do very well.

Realism still proves highly efficacious and rewarding in the modern drama, and that Williams has known this to be the case is apparent. But he has a theatrical imagination and likes to use it. Williams, moreover, has been suspicious of realism, no doubt because he has seen so much degenerate realism in the form of commonplace playwriting. Probably, too, he has confused realism with naturalism to such a degree that he would have been pleased to do without the realistic technique and style entirely if he had been less strongly ruled by his talent for observation and his emotional closeness to his early environment in the South. He has himself edged over into naturalism from time to time. He did so, for example, in the one-act play *The Lady of Larkspur Lotion* and in the rape scene of *Streetcar*. Naturalism pushes realism over the edge of moderation and good taste and becomes a sensational exploitation of sordid behavior and circumstances. Bohemianism tends to succumb to naturalism even while favoring estheticism, for the bohemian artist is fascinated with "raw life," which he idealizes precisely because he feels more or less alienated from life itself. Sensational pictures of reality satisfy the craving for self-assertion and the desire to defy convention and bait the bourgeois or the Babbitt. In his best scenes and plays, however, Williams has managed realism without excess and with considerable insight, sympathy, and accurate observation. He has treated the lost and the damned with understanding and pity, and has also revealed a capacity for humor compounded of a tolerant feeling for human failure and shrewd awareness of bizarre and unrealistic behavior on the part of his characters.

Williams' symbolist tendencies are often controlled by the requirements of his realistic observation and analysis. He is particularly successful when he uses atmosphere and employs music expressively. Except in *Camino Real,* among his produced full-length plays, he never allows the atmosphere to thin out into a symbolist fog. He may overstress symbolism when he resorts to the civic statue of "Eternity" to signify Alma's virginal idealism or "soulfulness" in *Summer and Smoke,* since these traits are more than sufficiently stressed in action and characterization. But the "symbol" is put to effectively ironic use when it is at the foot of this statue that Alma ultimately renounces her purity. The skeleton, or "anatomy," hanging in her lover's office contrasts "body"—that is, the wild young doctor's physical desire for her—with "soul," or Alma's revulsion against sexuality. This symbol is employed too obviously. But it furnishes the occasion for a strong dramatic scene between the two characters. In *Streetcar,* Blanche Du Bois, the former belle of a Southern plantation reduced to prostitution, has a mania for covering electric bulbs with colored lampshades, a habit that validly expresses her desire to soften reality. The morbidly shy Laura of *The Glass Menagerie* collects glass figurines and occupies herself with them. They represent her own fragile girlhood, but they also fit realistically into the portrait of Laura the lame girl who lacks friends, and the glass animals serve the play admirably and naturally in her scene with the ably drawn gentleman caller. When in that scene her little glass unicorn falls to the ground and loses the horn that made it unique, the event signifies to the girl her wish to become a normal young woman. It would be absurd to ask for a more natural and delicately written episode than this delicately managed revelation—that is, for a more discreetly managed "symbolism."

Except in *Camino Real,* in fact, the underlying fascination of Williams' work, as distinct from its more obvious interest to playgoers, has come from contrasts between realistic and symbolist writing; and from contrasts, too, between the reality of characters and environment, on one hand, and the theatrical deployment of his material, on the other. It may be that this is what casual commentators mean when they refer to him as a "poetic" realist, for they do not, obviously, mean that he writes formal poetry in the plays or that he confines his playwriting to evoking mere nuances *à la* Maeterlinck.

After 1949 Miller and Williams acquired three gifted colleagues. One of these is William Inge, a young writer from the Mid-Western states, whose *Come Back, Little Sheba,* produced in 1950, presented the stalemate of a sensitive alcoholic and his love-starved wife. Mr. Inge's authentic dialogue, economy of means, and ability to make uncommonly revealing drama out of common life have inspired high hopes for him. Mr. Inge was an admirer of Williams' early work. The other two recruits, Truman Capote and Carson McCullers, are Southerners. They received encouragement from Williams, and, like him, they present Southern backgrounds in their plays. Both first attained prominence as novelists, and their respective plays, *The Grass Harp* and *The Member of the Wedding,* were dramatizations of their own work. But the dramatizations were made by themselves and revealed talent for the theatre. *The Grass Harp* had extreme inadequacies and made innocence indistinguishable from idiocy. But this drama about some of life's innocents, who upset the conventions by trying to live in a tree, possessed unusual delicacy and poetic feeling. *The Member of the Wedding,* produced in 1950, was an even more delicately conceived play and was entirely successful. Instead of making a young girl's adolescence the springboard for a conventional plot, Mrs. McCullers gave us a sensitive study of the awkward age of growing out of childhood and groping toward womanhood. Her play became a little drama of life itself —of life's irrational course (in the fate of the girl's little playmate who dies of meningitis), of vague hopes and keenly felt disappointments, and of the essential loneliness of children and adults.

A simple term that may be used conveniently to define a small trend in American playwriting is "poetry of theatre." By this I mean a tendency on the part of writers to use the dramatic medium sensitively and imaginatively without actually writing their dialogue in verse, and without relinquishing their hold on common reality. This style of playwriting, which may also be called a species of "poetic realism," is present even in *Come Back, Little Sheba,* in which the author deals with commonplace characters and facts. (It was present again in Inge's *Picnic,* with some notable, if not always tasteful, assistance from Joshua Logan who directed the Broadway production.) In Inge's first Broadway production, the poetic component was an atmosphere of uneasy quiescence before and after the explosive second act in which the alcoholic man became violent.

Atmosphere was the very essence of Mrs. McCullers' *The Member of the Wedding,* where conventional dramatic action was largely replaced by vignettes representing the temporary companionship of a bewildered girl, an imaginative little boy, and a patient Negro nurse. Atmosphere, moreover, attained symbolic value in Capote's *The Grass Harp,* since the tree-house in which the main characters spent a night represented satisfaction of their desire for freedom and self-realization. The huge tree, which spread across the stage, overshadowed the people below it, making the world of small-town conventions appear small and insignificant. The tree was a visible symbol of the innocents' dream, which was also conveyed expressively by exquisite music composed for the play by Virgil Thompson.

Even Arthur Miller, the social and moral realist, moved toward a poetic form of theatre with *Death of a Salesman,* requiring expressive stage lighting and music, shuttling back and forth between present reality and dreamlike reminiscence, and employing fantasy and symbolism in the case of Willy Loman's shadowy brother Ben, who represents Willy's obsession with "success." In an earlier unproduced tragedy about the Spanish conquest of Mexico, *Montezuma,* Miller wrote a thoroughly poetic drama removed from contemporary life, if related to it by implication. And in *The Crucible,* he did the same thing, once more attempting to write tragedy on a more transparently heroic level than Willy Loman's drama. In *The Crucible,* as well as in *Montezuma,* Miller found an epic subject and tried to give the central character of his Salem witch-hunt history some heroic elevation. The need to write tragedy has been very much present in this playwright's mind. So has the need to write dramatic poetry when the context of the play justifies it. Although he has not yet proved himself a poet in words and may never be able to, he has already sought out those areas of subject matter and those possibilities of theatrical expressiveness that point in the direction of poetic drama. A tension exists in his work between the moral passion and political idealism that propel him toward social drama and the desire of a formative artist to rise to visions of human grandeur, however difficult the ascent.

We may conclude, then, that some of our new playwrights have been striving for maximum dramatic expressiveness short of actually writing distinguished dramatic verse. They have endeavored to give their playwriting a variety of levels of interest by using the theatre's resources poetically even when the life they have represented is externally commonplace and its milieu is prosaic.

A STREETCAR NAMED DESIRE:
A STUDY IN AMBIGUITY

I. AN EVALUATION

Among the new plays of the 1947-48 season *A Streetcar Named Desire* was not only the best but the most indicative of the flexibility of realism. Strongly rooted in the reality of character and environment, and replete with stinging naturalistic detail, this tragedy of a fallen member of the Southern landed aristocracy, nevertheless, abounds in poetic overtones. These are justified, in part, by Blanche's refinement of language. She is well bred and she has had sufficient education to have taught school for a while. Her consuming need, moreover, is to make herself and others constantly aware of her refinement. She is concealing her tawdry past of alcoholism, incontinence, and common prostitution. She is compensating for her fallen estate. Her memories being as unbearable as her present circumstances, she must transform both by building a dream-world for herself. Obviously, this world contains a large measure of self-delusion, as well as a good deal of pretentious public behavior. She makes "poetry," which her cultural background enables her to "activize" in the form of "manners" and to articulate in dialogue. Her drama becomes "poetic drama." Not realistic drama with poetic varnish, but realistic drama naturally and necessitously poetic. How necessitously, we can realize from the fact that her very refinement betrays her by becoming excessive—hysterically fastidious rather than natural. Her manners become mannerisms, and her speech verges on preciosity. As if in atonement, she crucifies herself on a cross of culture. In *Streetcar,* poetic drama becomes psychological reality.

For Williams, in this play, there can be no borderline between prose and poetry any more than there can be between reality and fantasy. This was also true in the case of Amanda and Laura in *The Glass Menagerie,* as well as, to some degree, in the case of Tom the Narrator when he remembers and ponders upon their world, so fantastic in its ineffectual twilight reality by contrast with the realities of the Second World War. (And, like Blanche, Tom is a poet *manqué,* as his narrations prove; though inadvertently, I suspect, since the author of these speeches is Williams, not Tom, and it is Williams who becomes "literary.") Alma's story in *Summer and Smoke* would, later in Williams' career, also make "poetry" as an extension of her life and as a defense against it. The fusion of poetry and prose began, indeed, early for Williams, in *Battle of Angels* and in such one-act plays as *Portrait of a Madonna* and *The Lady of Larkspur Lotion*. The fusion is a necessary one not only in his treatment of character, but in the development of conflict. *Streetcar* establishes a contrast between Blanche's mask of inviolable gentility and the opinion of her that others must form. This fact provides a major conflict in *Streetcar*. Characterization in *Streetcar* is indistinguishable from this particular tension, as well as from that which already exists within her. *Characterization as tension* is undoubtedly the best kind of dramatic characterization. We find it, for example, in *Hippolytus, Hamlet, Phaedra*—and *Desire Under the Elms*.

At the same time, there is an ambiguity in Blanche's situation—or, rather, we have here a series of ambiguities. Placed in opposition to Stanley Kowalski at thé beginning of the play, she is the aristocrat who condescends to the plebeian when she is not actually scorning him. This is compulsive conduct on her part, because she must feel superior to her sister's husband if she is not to feel inferior in view of her helplessness. But her behavior does not commend her to us. She is also an element of disease threatening the healthiness of her sister's relations with Stan. We can be grateful at first when Stan, disconcerted by Blanche, tries to take Blanche down a peg. Yet there is a certain splendor in Blanche's personality—a tragic splendor until the clinical aspects of her character dim it. Her sister avoided shipwreck by compromise—by marrying Stan and by satiating herself at the trough of commonplace gratifications in marriage. Stella is fortunate in this respect, as ordinary people, who have an aptitude for "the blisses of the commonplace," are fortunate. Blanche, on the contrary, cannot renounce her view of herself as a rare individual. Like other tragic characters, she *longs* for "the blisses of the commonplace" but is as incapable of accepting them as she is incapable of courting them efficiently. Tragic characters are "efficient" only in courting, suffering and encompassing their own destruction. Antigone, Oedipus, Hamlet, and Lear are tremendously efficient in this respect. Therein lies their *arête,* their specialness and stature, even when it is wrapped in folly, as in the case of Lear's dotage. Therein lies also their ultimate *hamartia,* or tragic flaw, which is, above all, their inability to recognize, in the words of Keats, that life has its impossibilities.

Thus far the ambiguities are dramatically, indeed tragically, fruitful. Reality is encountered meaningfully when it becomes plain that Blanche comes to a haven to which she will be unable to *decline* and therefore "adjust." She must turn safety into hell, given the necessities of her character. Also, those who can provide the haven must either eject her from it or turn it into hell for her. Overabundant in animal health and devoid of tender-mindedness, Stan must try to eject her; and, failing to eject her, to quarantine her psychologically (by proving her to have been a harlot), because she has brought unease, if not indeed disease, into his home. And her sister Stella must eject her as an insane accuser of Stan, after the latter has violated Blanche. Otherwise Stella could not remain with Stan, to whom she is bound by sexuality, love, and economic convenience, especially now that she has borne a child. Stan must also turn the haven into hell for Blanche as a necessity of his brutish inclinations, which have been inflamed by the sex-duel that has arisen between them—not without necessitous, if perhaps only half-conscious, initiative on her part. And these ambiguities, too, produce "poetry"—as dialogue, character insight, and atmosphere.

Williams, however, not only enriched but muddled his play with his ambiguities; they are at times only *melodramatically* fruitful. He reduced potential tragedy to psychopathology. Blanche's psychological situation, indeed, is already so untenable when she enters the home of Stan and Stella that she should be receiving psychiatric care. Williams, moreover, muddled the social basis for Blanche's drama, which he himself underscored with references to her Southern plantation. The aristocratic family's fortunes declined, it is true, and left her economically insecure; but she could have supported herself honorably as a teacher had she not become a victim of neurosis. Her plight is attributed to the bizarre—and to me specious—circumstance that her husband killed himself after realizing that he was a hopeless homosexual. As the daughter of a Southern "Cherry Orchard" family, she might have become quite credibly ill adjusted to reality by overrefinement and pride. But Williams, unsatisfied with normal motivations, adds the causative factor of marriage to a homosexual which has not been established as inevitable. Nor is it convincing that the young husband's death should have led her to seduce schoolchildren and take up with soldiers in a neighboring camp. *The Cherry Orchard* is pyramided upon normal motivation. Therefore the characters, their failure, and their social reality, or their symbolic value as representatives of a dying aristocracy, are equally believable. In *Streetcar,* in so far as Blanche's role is concerned, only her illness is believable—and even that is suspect, in so far as its inevitability is questionable.

It is also curious how Stan's role changes from that of an opponent who has reason to guard his marriage against Blanche to the role of a brute who in violating Blanche also violates his marriage. And if it is argued that the point of the play is precisely that Blanche, who needs every consideration, is thrust into a brute world that gives her no consideration, then, I say, Williams has destroyed the tragic possibilities of *Streetcar* in another way: He has settled for pathos whereas the ambience of his characterization of Blanche suggests a play possessed of a sharper, more equitable, and harder insight—namely, that of tragedy. I would argue, indeed, that having missed that insight—which is surely a defect or insufficiency in the author's thinking—Williams *had* to turn Stan into a brute. Stan was not a mere brute at the beginning of the play; and, later, he could claim the right to warn his wartime-buddy Mitch against marriage with Blanche because she had been a harlot. But Stan became a brute unmistakably in the rape scene toward the end of the play.

Williams, indeed, seems to have succumbed to a generally jaundiced view of normality by giving the impression that the common world is brutish, as if life in a poor neighborhood and Stan and Stella's sexually gratifying marriage were brutish. That is hardly the case, of course, and Williams himself contradicts this view, here and there, in his picture of the New Orleans Latin Quarter and of some aspects of the sister's life with Stan. But *Streetcar* exhibits a good deal of ambivalence on the author's part. The realist and the esthete are at odds with each other in this play. Enough variation in emphasis is possible, given the individual actor and the individual director, to make different stage productions yield different impressions, if not indeed somewhat different themes. But *Streetcar,* for all its dramatic momentum and surge, is a divided work. Ambiguities split the emphasis between realistic and decadent drama, between normal causation and accident, between tragedy and melodrama. Although *Streetcar* crackles with dramatic fire, it lacks a steady flame. Its illumination flickers.

II. "SPINES" FOR DRAMA

An important question arises. If *A Streetcar Named Desire* is so divided a play, how can it be staged satisfactorily?

The answer is that the unifying impulse and intelligence begin to operate. The director arrives at an over-all meaning or "spine" for the play, and for each of the characters—especially for the important ones. To prove the absolute validity of the "spine," assuming that this were always possible or could be done without endless disputation, is unnecessary. It is necessary only to make enough sense of the play and its acting parts to have confidence that one knows where one is going as a director in guiding the actor, determining the stage business, calling for a certain kind of setting, and so on. Likewise, the actor: the "spine" he finds for his role, with or without the director, is not absolute. It can only accord with the actor's personality and temperament, and with his understanding of the part and of its relationship to the other parts in the play.

"Spine" is an approximation of the meaning of the play and the meaning of the part. "Spine" is relative to the director and the actor, who brings himself to the stage production—and in bringing himself brings also, let us note, his education, taste, bias, etc., to it. It is possible, therefore, for different directors to stage *Streetcar* differently, and for different actors (Jessica Tandy and Uta Hagen, for example, in the same role of Blanche Du Bois) to play the same part differently and, nevertheless, to give it cohesion or logic—provided there is enough intelligence operating in the work, as there is in *Streetcar*.

It is also possible for the same play to be produced differently in different places and times. The important factor is this: if the play makes sense to those who perform it, there is the likelihood that it will make much the same sense to their audiences. That is, if these audiences are in accord with the director's and author's taste and viewpoint, or values. (It was noticed after *Streetcar* had been running for some time on Broadway that audiences, no longer typically a New York playgoing public, reacted to the play as though it were rather comic and prurient.)

In the case of Elia Kazan's production of *A Streetcar Named Desire,* we have the director's notes to himself. (They are reproduced by Toby Cole and Helen Krich Chinoy in their useful book, *Directing the Play,* Bobbs-Merrill.) Kazan told himself that Blanche's "spine" was "to find Protection." Concerning the theme of the play, he wrote: "This little twisted, pathetic, confused bit of light and culture puts out a cry." Then it is destroyed by factors which Kazan described as "the crude forces of violence, insensibility and vulgarity which exist in our South—and this cry is the play." Whether we agree with this definition or not (and I quarrel with both the reference to "in our South" here and to the charge of insensibility with reference to all characters except Stan), Kazan made *Streetcar* matter sufficiently to most playgoers on the basis of this effort at unifying its action.

The critic's function is, of course, to discover whether the play is artistically solvent. Neither the playwright's nor the director's (nor the actor's) definitions may be valid in the critic's opinion—or more than only partially valid. But, then, the critic's function is not that of an agent of the theatre whose business it is to make a play succeed. His business is to evaluate or judge the work rather than put it "across." He is a detached, disinterested party in this respect. For him the "spine" found for the play by the playwright's collaborators in the theatre may *not* pull together the elements of the work that have been left unfused or inharmonious.

The reviewer—in so far as he can be distinguished from the critic— will submit to the spell of the production, if it is an effective one. He is more susceptible, so to speak, to the conspiracy of playwrights, director, actors, and others to put the play "across" on the stage. Moreover, he *should* be susceptible, even when he carries his faculty of judgment with him; otherwise he will be a stick of wood in an audience full of live people. It should be possible (and it is usually possible) to work on his sensibilities with all the potency of theatre craftsmanship. That being the case, the reviewer, like any other responsive member of the audience, also organizes impressions or finds a "spine," which is sufficient to make the play mean something to him—unless, of course, the play or the production is hopelessly disorganized and meaningless.

III. PLAY REVIEW

The result is a "review," and, with all its partial insights, oversights, and hastily formed impressions, it pertains importantly to the work that is being reviewed. The reviewer records the effect that the play in a particular production was able to exert on one impressionable individual. If his impressions are not flagrantly at variance with those formed by most other reviewers or experienced playgoers who saw the same production, his report tells us something about the dramatic quality of the work. In the case of *Streetcar,* a consensus established this much with certainty: It was a stirring and anything but meaningless work, if not indeed a work of genius, regardless of my analysis of its ambivalences or ambiguities and consequent shortcomings, upon which I could have, indeed, enlarged. (The same judgment can be also rendered on *Death of a Salesman,* in spite of an unsuccessful fusion of social and individual causation in Willy Loman's drama.)

The fact that a play could make such an impression is certainly relevant to what the play is, if we can assume that the reviewer was not naturally eccentric or willfully perverse. (Or willfully "superior," out of youthful *hybris* or out of a calculated effort to call attention to himself and his predilections rather than to the play in question!) The fact that the work enabled the reviewer—an individual who has written down his reactions for publication—to discover a "spine" of some magnitude and interest tells us that the playwright and the performers managed to exert a certain degree of power and persuasion.

With this in view, and as an example of two levels of judgment which sometimes more or less coincide and sometimes do not, I reproduce here my very first review of *Streetcar,* almost exactly as it was published in *Forum* magazine and subsequently in periodicals abroad.

When *The Glass Menagerie* opened on a memorable spring evening in 1945, New York critics had the pleasure of acclaiming the arrival of a promising new playwright in Tennessee Williams. On December 3, 1947, when *A Streetcar Named Desire* opened at the Ethel Barrymore Theatre, they made the always welcome discovery that their expectations had been met with indisputable certainty. If, in addition, they cast a backward glance at the thirty-three-year-old author's numerous one-acters of unmistakable distinction, as well as the published text of his full-length *Battle of Angels,* which the Theatre Guild was forced to withdraw after its opening in Boston, there could be no doubt that America had a new major dramatist. When the recording angel writes, he will have Tennessee Williams to add to the good deeds America has piled up for herself in heaven as on earth.

In a stirring and beautiful production directed by Elia Kazan, who has a number of brilliant jobs of stage and film directing to his credit, *A Streetcar Named Desire* emerges as the most moving American play of the past dozen years. It is, moreover, a play that needs no erudite exegesis, no coterie support, no apologetics to make it acceptable.

Blanche Du Bois, a young woman bred on a rich plantation that had gone to seed, arrives at a disreputable quarter of New Orleans to stay with her sister Stella, who has married the rough-hewn Polish laborer, Stanley Kowalski. Blanche is not well; she is extremely nervous and hears strange music when distressed. Her distress increases when she surveys the sordid surroundings, when she observes that she will be sleeping next to her sister's bedroom with only a curtain between the rooms, and when she meets her strange and gruff brother-in-law. She has been a schoolteacher as well as a belle. She exudes the spirit of refinement in her speech and comportment, and clings pathetically to her clothing and furs, mementoes of a life to which her present environment makes a garish contrast. Her sister Stella has an earthy simplicity and sound animal instincts; she is happy with her exuberant and violently virile Pole. But she, poor Blanche, who is in such need of quiet and comfort, has entered the strange precincts of the uninhibited, uncomfortably hearty proletariat. Her delicate scorn and wincing aristocratic superiority cannot be mistaken. One cannot help pitying her, and also laughing at her because the life she affects to despise seems so invincibly alive while her eyes seem fixated on a decadent past. But pity claims priority because her helplessness is so palpable, and because she is so evidently concealing a wounded past. Pity, however, is precisely what she cannot incite in Kowalski, to whom her refinement is both comic and affronting, in whom curiosity about this strange woman becomes an obsession, and for whom her presence is a disturbing element. He had been happy with Stella in a rough-and-tumble manner, and now he must defer to Blanche's delicacy, her nerves, and her disdain of his uncouth conduct and animal spirits.

He begins to unravel her past, thread by thread, from the suspiciousness of her conduct and from chance bits of information. It is not long before he discovers that she had been compelled to leave her home town after seducing one of her boy students, and that subsequently she had spent some time in a disreputable house. This is the woman for whom the slightest indelicacy is a torment! And his suspicions are only too well substantiated by her birdlike attempts at sexual intimacy. Her whole pitiful story unrolls before the audience, which the omniscient author involves in an understanding and sympathy that must remain a sealed book to the elemental and lively fellow who is her brother-in-law. In her golden girlhood Blanche had deeply loved and then married a lovable young man who turned out to be a homosexual and who killed himself when his sense of guilt became unbearable. Her seduction of young students became a compensatory and compulsive measure; and her masquerade of fastidiousness was a necessary defense against the gross reality of her desires, as well as against the sordid world into which she had been thrown.

Blanche, we realize, is pretty far gone after the shipwreck of her ego, but she finds one unexpected straw to cling to—that is, in addition to the delusion or pretense that a wealthy man in Florida is ready to leave his wife for her. The straw is Harold Mitchell, a friend of Kowalski's and an innocent, mother-coddled lad who is strongly attracted to the fey creature. After a few affecting encounters he is even ready to marry her, with his mother's permission, and Blanche is eagerly awaiting him on the evening of her birthday, an occasion that is being observed with cake and candles by her pitying sister. But the suitor does not arrive, and Kowalski bluntly admits that he had revealed Blanche's past to his friend; he wasn't going to let his best friend marry a tart. This is the crisis, and thereafter every event contributes torments to unsettle an already badly jolted mind. Valiantly Blanche continues to spin threads of romantic illusion as an anchor to life, but the last threads are severed when her brother-in-law, whom she has been vaguely enticing, violates her, and Stella reluctantly consents to committing her sister to an asylum. The concluding scene is as heartrending as any one of a half a dozen other preceding scenes. The matron from the asylum knocks her down on the floor when she struggles; the physician from the asylum takes one quick look at her and resolves to salvage her self-respect. He removes his hat, speaks to her in courtly accents, and raises her from the floor. Instantly she radiates pleasure and walks out with him, her head high as if she were following a gentleman who has shown her the extreme courtesy which befits a lady.

I have told this story at some length, but even so the narration is the merest summary. The Mielziner setting, which combines sharp realism with poetic beauty, adds the dimensions of environment to the plot. The characterization is vastly enriched by the performances of Jessica Tandy, who plays Blanche with great virtuosity, as well as conviction, and of Marlon Brando, whose Kowalski is a masterful realization of innocence, animality, and shrewdness. The story itself is many-faceted. And here we may find the true measure of the play's compelling power, aside from the variety and magic of the dialogue. Tennessee Williams has accomplished what is seldom achieved in contemporary dramaturgy; unlike most of his fellow-craftsmen, he has not only built a play well but he has built it with the steel and brick of narrative and characterizing substance.

What *A Streetcar Named Desire* has is the abundance of a good novel. It might have actually been elaborated into a novel, which book critics, with customary enthusiasm, would have hailed as indicative of the combined capacities of a Faulkner and Dostoevsky, without being fundamentally more substantial than Williams' play is on the stage. Life has density in this drama of a woman's tragic effort to clothe her nakedness. (The nearest modern parallel in playwriting is perhaps Pirandello's more cerebral play *Naked*.) The theme is one of the universals of human experience, and it has been managed in a variety of ways by such novelists as Conrad, Dostoevski, Gogol, Flaubert, and De Maupassant. The author's viewpoint combines a sharp sense of reality, a naturalistic fearlessness in the face of what is gross in individual life and society, and a just compassion. The handling of the dramatic elements is remarkably astute, since the author keeps wave after wave of revelation hurtling through the play. He balances humor and pathos as surely as he balances Blanche's illusions and the objective realities. He distributes effects in the right proportions and at the right time (for dramatic writing, more than fiction, is dependent upon the proportion of the parts and the timing of impressions), and plays upon the impressionableness of an audience as a concert pianist plays upon the black and white keys. But what stands out as most contributory to the making of a memorable play is the total effect of humanity seen in the round. This has been unnecessarily left to the novelists by playwrights who think more of construction than of the material with which they are building.

DEATH OF A SALESMAN:
FIRST IMPRESSIONS, 1949

Miller's *Death of a Salesman* is another play that made a strong impression here and abroad, but could be variously challenged by the critical faculty. As in the case of Williams' drama, therefore, I reproduce my initial response to the play; and I set beside that review a second one as an illustration of how a play of its calibre reverberates. Since few plays do, they usually disappear from the memory. Miller's play, whatever limitations may be ascribed to it, is one of the few post-war dramas to which substance and power can be legitimately attributed. *Death of a Salesman* proved itself capable of keeping the critical mind active, concerned, and unstable.

I

The ecstatic reception accorded *Death of a Salesman* has been reverberating for some time wherever there is an ear for theatre, and Miller's is undoubtedly the best American play since *A Streetcar Named Desire*. Now it is two new playwrights of more than provincial significance, Arthur Miller and Tennessee Williams, that America can boast of as part of its post-war contribution to the theatre. Many of us would find it difficult to determine which of them is superior. A decision is hardly urgent at this time, and it is too soon perhaps to arrive at one while they are both still at the starting points of their respective careers. At present, it would appear that Tennessee Williams is the more creative artist but is in some danger of exhausting his particular theme of frustration. Miller is endowed with greater objectivity and comprehension of contemporary life but is limited in verbal talent and drawn toward the commonplace by a moralistic tendency. Williams is the truer poet; Miller, the better sociologist.

In *Death of a Salesman,* however, Miller has managed to rise above the ordinary flatlands of moralization and thesis drama. His play is a consummation of virtually everything attempted by that part of the theatre which has specialized in awareness and criticism of social realities. It is a culmination of all efforts since the 1930's to observe the American scene and trace, as well as evaluate, its effect on character and personal life. Clifford Odets succeeded in this enterprise creditably in *Golden Boy* and movingly, if somewhat dimly, in *Awake and Sing!* and *Rocket to the Moon*. Generally our "social" playwrights' efforts, however, stressed the milieu rather than the character even when they transcended special pleading or political agitation. Miller's achievement lies in successfully bridging the gulf between a social situation and human drama. The two elements in *Death of a Salesman* are, indeed, so well fused that the one is the other.

Death of a Salesman succeeds, in truth, as its author himself appears to have realized, as a character drama and an exceptionally good example of so-called "middle-class tragedy." It follows the fate and final reckoning of a commonplace man in a commonplace environment. It is the kind of play that usually falls decidedly short of tragedy and settles on the lower level of pathos, a drama ordinarily conducive to tear-shedding or sympathetic clucking rather than to exaltation of mind and spirit through impressive suffering. That this is not conspicuously the case in *Death of a Salesman* is perhaps the ultimate proof of its author's dramatic powers.

Other playwrights of his generation could have matched the veracity with which he depicts the world of a traveling salesman and his family. They, too, could have depreciated the success-worshipping commercial traveler's "smile and a shoe-shine" philosophy. Miller alone, however, has made the object of his analysis a breathing man and given him some stature. His hero, Willy Loman, may commit errors and may flounder in illusions like the rest of his clan, worshiping material success and thinking that it is bound to be won by sales-talk and Rotarian chumminess. Willy may believe that you are worth nothing that you cannot sell, and he may instill the same notions into his sons. Willy may have the usual fling at extra-marital diversions that seem to be the custom of commercial travelers on the loose. But Willy is not quite commonplace in his commonplaceness. He maintains his faith, inane though it be, with a tenacity that is little short of heroic, and when it crumbles, the man crumbles with it hugely— at least, as the actor Lee Cobb portrays him.

The ordinary mirage that he follows is made extraordinary by the fervor of the man who is in pursuit of it; there is an element of the sublime in his naïveté! When he falls, we note the toppling of a giant. At the same time, we can reflect that he was no brighter than other giants who figure in fairy tales hardly more fantastic than those Willy created for himself and mistook for the American Dream. There may be nothing remarkable in his disappointment in his sons, for whose vices and shortcomings he is at least partly responsible. Still, disappointment has tragic dimension in his case because he feels it greatly. His love for one of them had been too intense, his hopes for Biff too high. In his relations with them, he is a King Lear in mufti. He is closer to Shakespeare's Lear or at any rate to Turgenev's "King Lear of the Steppes" than he is to Balzac's masochistic vermicelli-manufacturer, Goriot. The truth is that Willy Loman is cast in the heroic mould because he can feel greatly, even if his thinking is bounded in a nutshell. And for this reason, he not only fills the dramatic scene substantially himself, but adds substantiality to his well-drawn wife and sons. They gain substance from the magnitude of his flawed relation to them, the magnitude being in himself.

Miller's technical virtuosity also stands him in good stead. He has a flair for tight construction. By itself only a second degree virtue, it becomes a virtue of the first degree because it gives the author both the assurance and the skill to break the conventional mould of realism. The play shuttles numerous vignettes back and forth in time, but it gives an impression of inevitable cohesion—the cohesive demonstration of a man's mistakes. The play is the summation of a man's life that would normally be presented as a chronicle, a horizontal kind of drama, but it becomes instead a spiralling affair. It starts with Willy Loman returning home instead of going away on another business trip, because he can no longer trust himself to drive a car, and his story ends with his committing suicide in order to leave his family his insurance and to repair his personal failure. His past weaves through the other episodes that carry the drama forward from the initial to the final point. Past and present move forward together, illuminating one another, and mounting in intensity. Reminiscences of Willy's errors as father, husband, and human being counterpoint and explain his present, immediate difficulties with his sons and his employer.

In a production brilliantly staged by the genius among American directors, Elia Kazan, the play acquires some texture of music and the dynamics of a dramatic elegy. Misbegotten dreams that turn into nightmares hurl themselves at the bar of fate in wave after wave on Joe Mielziner's skeletal and many-leveled setting. The production defines areas for acting imaginatively rather than literally. At different times, portions of the space in front of the eviscerated Loman home become a suburban backyard, a Manhattan restaurant, a hotel room in Boston, and a cemetery, with the family and a friend standing by the freshly dug grave of Willy. The lighting and the incidental music by Alex North add nuance and expressiveness to the proceedings. The actors are so maneuvered that their reality as people remains inviolable without contradicting or hampering the free-wheeling quality of the dramatic action. This constitutes modern staging in the highest degree, without pretentious estheticism and with complete persuasiveness.

The actors are exceptionally well chosen. If Lee Cobb's Willy Loman is too heavy-footed and portentous, if he resembles a monolith at times, he nevertheless possesses stature as well as statuesqueness. He is both the "Willie the Weeper" of popular song, staggering in the opium fumes of success-dreaming, and a giant threshing about in a snare of his own making. Set against him is the solid *bourgeois* Charley, the kind but blustering neighbor. He is Willy's Horatio, and Miller·is to be commended indeed for not making Willy stand for the whole of our middle-class life. Howard Smith plays Charley with recognizable humanity and with spirit, and also gives an external portrait that recalls the sensible burghers of Flemish and Dutch painting from whom he and his tribe can trace their descent.

"Happy," played by Cameron Mitchell, is the son who incorporates Willy's *insouciance.* He is one of the many recognizable young men who will be found clerking, philandering, and swaggering, who do no particular harm but also no particular good. Biff, the other son, spoiled by Willy's indulgence, which encouraged him to steal and to expect much from the world because he played football at school, is the dislocated youth. He tries to free himself from delusion, his own and his father's. Having idealized his breezy father, he was shattered in spirit when he found him entertaining a strange woman in a hotel room. His story is almost as moving as the father's, and Arthur Kennedy's Biff is even better realized than Lee Cobb's Willy. Set against both sons is the physically unimpressive Bernard, Charley's bright lawyer son, whom the Lomans set down as a negligible boy because he was studious and scrupulous. In Don Keefer's portrayal of the lad will be found the recognizable features of many young men who do not conform to the ideal of strenuous youthfulness that so often turns out the hollowest of men. The saloons are full of Loman boys while the professions are full of Bernards. Perhaps the best job of acting, however, is Mildred Dunnock's Linda, the Loman wife and mother who understands all and suffers all, the *mater dolorossa* of Brooklyn and of a substantial portion of the rest of the country.

Undoubtedly *Death of a Salesman* is one of the triumphs of the mundane American stage. It moves its audience tremendously, it comes close to their experience or observation, it awakens their consciousness, and it may even rouse them to self-criticism. As a text it is, in many respects, the latest version of *Babbitt.* The subscribers of the Book of the Month Club, which has selected a play for the first time in its history, may put the book on their shelves as an authentic piece of American fiction along with the novels of Sinclair Lewis, Theodore Dreiser, and James Farrell. Whether it is actually the great play that many people believe it to be is another matter. I can only register a general doubt here. For all my enthusiasm, I would not place the play in the same class with, let us say, *A Streetcar Named Desire, The Glass Menagerie, Desire Under the Elms,* or even *The Iceman Cometh.* It is deficient in the poetry, the nuances, the wonder, and the unexpected insight of truly distinguished dramatic literature. Mr. Miller's insights are all expected ones; they are observations rather than discoveries.

For all its merits, *Death of a Salesman* is still *drame bourgeois* rather than genuine *high tragedy*. Mr. Miller's story still possesses some qualities of demonstration by a sociologist and few transfigurations by a poet. The contrast of characters is rather schematic, and the moral obtrudes upon us instead of emerging with shimmering suggestiveness from the contradictions of human nature. Mr. Miller's depths are actually shallows, even if he navigates them superbly. Qualifications are, however, less important from the immediate point of view than the fact that the American stage has *Death of a Salesman* to show for a year's effort and that Mr. Miller himself has surpassed his *All My Sons* in breadth and humanity.

II[1]

By far the most noteworthy contribution of the entire season was *Death of a Salesman,* winner of the Drama Critics Circle and Pulitzer awards, and a success of imposing proportions. The play inspired a triumphant production the equal of which it would be difficult to find in any other theatrical capital, so far as we can tell, except Paris. This drama also climaxed the young career of a playwright, Arthur Miller, whose emotional power and skill would have been received with respect anywhere since the advent of prose realism. As projected in the theatre by Elia Kazan's roughly tender direction and Jo Mielziner's functional design, *Death of a Salesman* impressed most play reviewers as a superb work of art. Broadway superlatives are even more suspect than Broadway pejoratives, and both often conceal as much as they reveal. We must look closer at the play, therefore, if we are to understand its character and its place in our theatre.

The play is not quite the masterpiece of dramatic literature that the enthusiasts would have us believe. It is well written but is not sustained by incandescent or memorable language except in two or three short passages. Moreover, its hero, the desperate salesman Willy Loman, is too much the loud-mouthed dolt and emotional babe-in-the-woods to wear all the trappings of high tragedy with which he has been invested. For modern writers of the school of Molière and Shaw, Willy would have been an object of satirical penetration rather than mournful tenderness and lachrymose elegy. By contrast with contemporary dramatists of a poetic grain like O'Neill, Williams, and Anderson, Mr. Miller has written his story on the level of *drame bourgeois*. Although his intellect denies assent to the main character's fatuous outlook, some commonplaceness attends the sentiments of the writing, the overvaluation of Willy as a hero, and the selec-

[1] Published six months later than the above review.

tion of a bumptiously kind-hearted bourgeois, Charley, as the proper foil for the unsuccessful salesman. Charley is the model of right living because he was practical-minded and made a success of his business, and because his son Bernard married and became a lawyer who is now on his way to Washington to argue a case and takes his tennis rackets along, presumably to hobnob with successful people. No one in the play stands for values that would not gain the full approval of Bruce Barton and Dale Carnegie, in spite of the fact that their philosophy is shown to be invalid for Willy and Biff. The Promethean soul is mute in *Death of a Salesman*. The mind and the spirit that manifest themselves in it are rather earth-bound and not in themselves interesting.

Once these reservations are made, however, one cannot deny that the play has singular merits, that it is often moving and even gripping, that it is penetrative both in characterization and in social implication. It expresses a viewpoint of considerable importance when it exposes the delusions of "go-getting," "contacts"—inebriated philistinism by reducing it to the muddle of Willy's life, which is surely not an isolated case.

Miller has written a play remarkably apposite to an aspect of American life, and the audiences that are held by it and the many playgoers who are moved to tears pay him the tribute of recognition. Their interest and sympathy are engaged by the pathos of a man who gave all his life to a business only to be thrown on the scrap-heap, a householder whose pattern of life was interwoven with instalment plans with which he could hardly catch up, a doting father disappointed in his children, and an American *naïf* bemused by the worship of uncreative success and hollow assumptions that "personality" is the *summum bonum*.

A notable feature of the effectiveness of *Death of a Salesman* is that the author's judgments are not delivered down to the playgoer from some intellectual eminence but stem almost entirely from close identification with the outlook and thought-processes of the characters. This probably explains all that I find intrinsically commonplace in this otherwise powerful play. The playwright is not "outside looking in" but "inside looking out," and at least for the purposes of immediate effect it is less pertinent that he is not looking very far out than that he is so convincingly and sensitively inside his subject. Largely for this reason, too, Miller has also given the American theatre of social criticism its most unqualified success, for that theatre, ever since the nineteen-thirties when it became a distinct mode of playwriting, has tended to be argumentative and hortatory. (One can be argumentative, of course, if the brilliance of a Bernard Shaw infuses the argument with lambent intellection; and one can be hortatory, too, as in Shaw's speeches and Aristophanes' *parabases,* when fervor is not dulled by sociology. But one can hardly posit such qualities for most social drama in our time.) Instead of debating issues or denouncing Willy's and his society's errors, Miller simply demonstrates these in the life of his characters. He confines himself, moreover, to the particulars of normal behavior and environment, and nothing that Willy or his family does or says betrays the playwright as the inventor of special complications for the purpose of social agitation. The play does not even set up a conflict between two distinctly different sets of values, which, as I have indicated earlier, is in some respects a limitation of the work, as well as a merit. Even Charley's view of life which is contrasted to Willy's life is only a sensible conversion of it (it is merely a sensible materialism), and no challenging conversion by a character leads us out of the middle-class world. Willy's son Biff surmounts his father's attitude only in acquiring self-knowledge and resigning himself to being just an ordinary, dollar-an-hour citizen. Arthur Miller, in short, has accomplished the feat of writing a drama critical of wrong values and misguided conduct. It stabs itself into a playgoer's consciousness to a degree that may well lead him to review his own life and the lives of those who are closest to him. The conviction of the writing is, besides, strengthened by a quality of compassion rarely experienced in our theatre. One must be either extraordinarily snobbish or exceptionally obtuse to stand aloof from the play.

The virtues of *Death of a Salesman,* as well as the shortcomings, most of which are not likely to be apparent to most playgoers while the play is in progress, belong to the American theatre. They epitomize its norm of verisimilitude, identification with the *dramatis personae,* and an objectivity midway between sentimentality and European ironic detachment.[2] These are democratic qualities, and the artistry of Miller's work is nothing if it is not democratic. Our most successful and substantial theatre, ever since the early experimental days of the Provincetown Playhouse, the Washington Players, and the Neighborhood Playhouse, has tended to be neither lowbrow nor highbrow; it has been almost inviolately "middlebrow."

There is, nevertheless, a world of difference between the average middle-class drama, so notably devoid of force and imagination, and *Death of a Salesman.* The latter impresses us as a triumph of poetic realism and it holds our attention as in a vise, and how this is possible in the case of a play so confined to the commonplaces of life is worth examining. It may throw light on what our dramatists can do, and often fail to do, with the realistic subject matter and dramaturgy to which they are de-

---

[2] We can find that detachment virtually since *Commedia dell' arte,* if not earlier, and there are excellent examples of it since Machiavelli's *Mandragola* and the comedies of Molière to Becque's *The Vultures* and Carl Sternheim's plays. In the American drama, ironic detachment crops up rarely; it does in Lillian Hellman's plays and has been viewed with some misgivings, as may be seen from the New York reviewers' critical reaction to *Another Part of the Forest.*

voted. It is a question of transmutation within the boundaries of realism, as may be gathered from the fact that there is hardly anything even in the reminiscent scenes, as the play alternates between actual scenes in the present and remembered ones, which is poetic or fantastic. The sole exception comes toward the end when Willy discusses his intended suicide with his elder brother Ben, who is now a figment of Willy's mind. When we call the play imaginative we must distinguish it, in the main, from such pieces as *Emperor Jones, The Hairy Ape, The Skin of Our Teeth,* and *The Madwoman of Chaillot.* Essentially, Miller affirms realism in the very process of transcending it. Most imaginative efforts to surmount humdrum realism in our theatre have either stylized or poeticized their matter. For all its ingenuity, *Death of a Salesman* does not seem noticeably "stylized" and is certainly not "literary."

Most decisive is the transmutation of the story itself, and with this a transformation of the character posited for Willy. An ordinary playwright would have regaled us with a lengthy recital of Willy's misfortunes as a superannuated white collar worker immolated on the Moloch of the business machine once his usefulness had ended. In Miller's treatment this is a subordinate part of the story, the main feature of which is the struggle between Willy and his son Biff, so that the pathos of failure is pitched higher than the sociological level. Miller had the wisdom to justify our concern with his blatant hero by making the wheel of the drama revolve around the one attribute that makes Willy extraordinary without being flagrantly atypical. My criticism that the play overvaluates a vacuous individual requires this important qualification: Willy, who is otherwise so unimpressive, is translated into a father for whom the love and success of his favorite son Biff is a paramount necessity and a consuming passion. He has been made into a dramatically charged father-hero, and as such becomes a heroic figure in active pursuit of the father-son ideal. He may be a fool, but he becomes a monolithic figure of some tragic dimension in this respect. This man who is a failure even as a bourgeois recalls somewhat the obsessed and self-consumed heroes of Elizabethan tragedy. Miller has created an intensification of humanity that lifts the drama above the level of the humdrum.

A second intensification is provided by Miller's over-all dramaturgic method. We are most familiar in our theatre with simple *horizontal* and simple *vertical* play building. The former is generally reserved for chronicles of famous lives and historical events, as in *Abe Lincoln in Illinois, Abraham Lincoln,* and *Victoria Regina.* It has not been employed successfully in American or English treatments of historically unimportant characters, so far as I can recall, except in *Milestones* and *Cavalcade,* and here at least the situations possessed historical importance. The vertical type of progression, however, has been standard in our drama. This type of play starts with some intention or plan on the part of a character, the character becomes embroiled in conflict as he tries to effectuate his desire, and ultimately, in the course of spiraling complications related to each other in accordance with the law of cause and effect, there are decisive consequences. Good examples of this procedure are provided by such comparatively recent plays as *The Little Foxes, Golden Boy, All My Sons, State of the Union,* and *Born Yesterday,* and quite as obviously by many other recent and older plays that have succeeded. Nevertheless, this technique has more often than not only exaggerated the defects of the average realistic play ever since the days of Dumas *fils.* The playgoer has been compelled to follow the unstimulating course of some commonplace individual capable of only humdrum desires and utterance forming an intention, then proceeding to encompass it and encountering opposition in ways that are either expected and therefore humdrum or unexpected and therefore likely to be contrived. It is noteworthy that Ibsen, who intensified the material of realism, also intensified its technique by adopting retrospective exposition and starting his realistic plays close to the crisis of the story. But most playwrights have lacked the highly dramatic feeling and imagination required by this procedure.

The point of attack in *Death of a Salesman* comes very near the turning point of the play. Miller's method is, moreover, not merely effectively vertical but at the same time circular—in the sense that the action starts with an already trapped individual and merely snaps the ring round him. The paramount question we are forced to ask of the play is not the usual "What is going to happen next?", "Will the hero win or lose?" or "How will his plan work out?"—questions to which a commonplace life in a commonplace situation can give only uninteresting answers. The important question, since the hero's fate is sealed from the beginning, is rather "What is really the matter and why?"—a question that points to basic realities. And if we are also bound to inquire "What more is going to happen?" the answer can be meaningful only in terms of answers to the prior question. Willy, a sixty-three-year-old salesman who no longer trusts himself to drive his car, comes back to his Brooklyn home instead of going on his prescribed trip. His sons decide to go into business and the older and more errant one, Biff, intends to ask a former employer, Oliver, for a loan, while Willy resolves to ask his employer for "an inside job." Willy is fired instead as a superannuated employee and Biff does not get a loan, disappearing instead with Oliver's fountain pen because petty thievery has been ingrained in him since boyhood. The disappointed Willy goes home in a distracted condition and kills himself. Out of these meager external materials, Miller has fashioned a comprehensive drama by pushing inward into motives and causes. He has done so mainly by employing a memory pattern by means of flashbacks into Willy's past life which are largely Willy's encounters with his younger and more confident self. The published play is aptly subtitled "Certain private conversations in two acts and a requiem."

Still, the resort to flashbacks is by itself too familiar to be remarkable. Sheer dramatic skill is a third factor in Miller's transmutation of the story of a man who devoted his life to selling instead of creating, of a salesman type described by his understanding friend Charley as "a man way out there in the blue, riding on a smile and shoeshine" who is undone when people start not smiling back. I can only note here approvingly with respect to the flashbacks that each reminiscence springs from a *tension* in Willy. The reminiscence is not hurled at us as necessary information but presented as a compulsive act on Willy's part. In several instances, and especially in the crucial scene in which Willy recalls that his son's failure is largely the result of his having found him with a strange woman in a Boston hotel, the memory scene does not arise at once but crystallizes out of fluid and half-formed thoughts. In addition, it is noteworthy that no recollection is allowed to leave the play in a state of stasis. Not only does the over-all action move a step forward after such episodes, but these are both preceded and followed by bursts of conflict between Willy or the mother and the boys. Miller has, in addition, overcome stasis by a steady climb of discovery and revelation. If it is the nature of Willy to go to his death unenlightened, the son with whom he has identified his destiny wrings understanding out of his own and his father's predicaments, putting pretense aside.

These achievements, in sum, are vastly more important and harder to come by than the highly touted external means employed by the author—namely, the alternation of imagined and actual scenes well distributed and well lit on the stage space, and augmented by eerie off-stage flute music. The dramaturgic means are more effective, too, than attempts at symbolism in such details as Willy's small house being overshadowed by the apartment houses that grew up around it so that he can no longer grow anything in his backyard garden and more effective than the shadowy figure of Willy's elder brother Ben, the adventurer who employed jungle tactics in his pursuit of wealth and came out of the African jungle with a diamond mine in his possession. On closer examination, in fact, we may find Ben, who represents the spirit of social Darwinism or *laissez-faire,* an adventitious figure, theatrically effective but dramatically suspect as a motif. There is little doubt, then, that *Death of a Salesman,* praised though it be as a work of theatrical imagination, is essentially a victory for modern realism.

THE GREAT WORLD,
THE LITTLE STAGE

The year 1943 was a critical one in the Western world, and Broadway was one of the few theatre capitals left where the epic struggle in the air, on land and sea, and in the hearts and minds of men could have been expressed. Only one stage production, the Army Air Force show, Moss Hart's *Winged Victory,* expressed that struggle. Amid the other productions of the new season of 1943, it had scope if not depth, as well as wide emotional range, although a range achieved by the accretion of the many little feelings and actions of many little men, rather than by intensification of a character in whom epic possibilities could be realized, as in Shakespearean drama. And in Hart's play an idea also grew to some proportions of significance, though the idea was large by expansion or comprehensiveness, rather than by virtue of profundity or originality.

In *Winged Victory,* sheer size, the amplitude of the physical production and of the episodic dramatic structure, was decisive. Since greatness in artistic achievement is not the same thing as the magnitude of the means, there could be little doubt that *Winged Victory* was not great drama. Yet for a few hours the theatre suddenly began to matter for those of us who gave ourselves up to the production and allowed it to magnify the small and misty view of the reality of the war which we carried with us far from the war front. We became enlarged as bystanders and vicarious participants. And if some of us were none the less keenly aware of literary standards to which the work did not measure up at all, we still sensed that the theatre was involving us on some level of experience that echoed, no matter how faintly, the thunder of the warring world.

Perhaps we should have responded to *Winged Victory* less strongly if the personnel of the production had not been soldiers themselves, and so had not afforded playgoers a sense of participation. But this is only a superficial explanation. We could participate in *Winged Victory* because it provided a *context* for participation; for although Moss Hart's views in the play were quite conventional, his feeling and range of observation were epic. It is the lack of any possibility of participation by the audience in any large sense that undoubtedly reduces the ambience of theatre in our time. The trouble is that the era of international tensions calls for an epic theatre, because it is only in an epic theatre that participation is possible.

We have a narrow middle-class theatre as a rule, here and abroad, almost as much when the playwright denies as when he affirms middle-

374

class values. Something other than opinions and political professions is involved in art. *Art* is involved in art—that is, *form*. And *form* is an expression not of an opinion, but of a way of seeing things and a way of presenting them. One might say that the form is both the true "idea" and the actual artistic presence of things. In this sense, it can happen that the Southern gentleman-dramatist Paul Green does not create middle-class drama when he writes the Roanoke Island pageant *The Lost Colony* (or, for that matter, when he writes the anti-war play *Johnny Johnson*), but the rebellious Clifford Odets of the thirties does create middle-class drama when he writes *Awake and Sing!, Rocket to the Moon,* and *Clash by Night.* With respect to certain dramatic situations in life and the theatre, the narrow realistic form still proves adequate, as it did in *Awake and Sing!* With respect to a situation such as the Second World War and the vast upheaval of lives it produced, the usual form of drama seemed woefully inadequate, so that our sense of proportion—and of propriety—was likely to be violated. With respect to that situation, the dramatic form of a Shakespearean play seemed a thousand times more contemporary than the form of the average contemporary play. Most World War II playwrights, here and in England, were trying to squeeze big subjects into nutshells. They continued to write middle-class drama (in the formal sense in which I use the term)—middle-class drama in a world that had largely ceased to be middle-class to our temporarily expanded consciousness of reality.

We must understand the difference of effect between *Winged Victory,* which stirred large audiences, and the plays that appeared on Broadway at about the same time and failed to make any sort of impression. The authors of these latter plays were holding on to the limiting forms of the old-fashioned "problem-play."

One play, *Manhattan Nocturne,* for example, dealt with the sorrows of a girl who had descended to prostitution after being abandoned by a politician's son. She was redeemed in maudlin fashion by an understanding novelist whose callous wife had sapped him of his creative energy and divorced him. Stella Adler directed the play, Eddie Dowling was woebegone and humane in it, and a young actress, Teresa Holmes, headed for film stardom, gave a moving performance. That the play was picayune in every respect was obvious even to the ordinary playgoer.

Another play, *I'll Take the High Road,* by the apparently not untalented young playwright Lucille Prumbs, had what is vapidly called "social significance." It purported to be an exposé of a factory owner as a fascist of the Krupp-Thyssen variety. That the author intended to play a large gambit must have been obvious to anyone familiar with the role of the German industrialists in the rise of Hitler and the genesis of the global war. But the author's plot contrivance and characterization had reduced reality to such a petty case of villainy that her argument had little more force than a slap on the wrist. And if her range of imagination and thought limited her to wrist-slapping, she should have had the discretion to select another, less challenging subject.

That she did not do so, however, was not a willful case of *hybris* on her part. She, like other well-intentioned playwrights, was the victim of a pervasive misconception. For about a century, numerous writers for the theatre had tried to catch an eagle by the tail—that is, capture a large and ramified subject by means of a small complication and discussion in the living room of a family. This is what "middle-class drama" amounts to, and has amounted to for a long time, as compared to the soaring drama of Sophocles and Shakespeare, which was fundamentally epic drama. Even more practiced and probing playwrights than Dumas *fils,* Angier, or Miss Prumbs had made the same effort. Among them was the redoubtable John Galsworthy, whose problem plays mattered so much in the comparatively stable English world before 1914 and began to matter less and less after 1925, if not indeed before then. For many modern playwrights, Ibsen had set the example with the prose plays of his middle period. But Ibsen always eluded them, as he has eluded many critics who mistake him for a writer of "problem plays" and miss both his complex analytical and ambivalent faculty and his frugal, ironic poetry.

How much they could have learned, these misinterpreters of Ibsen, if they had taken the trouble to compare *Ghosts* with Echegaray's *The Son of Don Juan,* a Spanish play about hereditary disease, inspired by Ibsenism as miscomprehended by second-rate minds and spirits. In *Ghosts,* an entire world of so-called morality and an entire way of viewing reality are challenged with irony while the consequence of immoral "morality" (immoral, in Ibsen's opinion, because false to nature and detrimental to individuality) is blasted and then buried in its own rubbish-heap. In the Echegaray play, the conventional immorality of a philanderer is conventionally "punished" when Don Juan's son has inherited venereal disease from his amorous father. No intellectual fecundity is involved or needed for this treatment. All that the playwright and his public need to know is that it is sinful to philander (that's the "universality" of the play!) and that venereal disease is hereditary (that's the "modernity" in the play!). Combine the cliché of the moralist with the cliché of medical knowledge, both of which require no original thought or sensibility from the author and the public, and you get Echegaray's *The Son of Don Juan.* Combine the same elements and you get nothing remotely resembling Ibsen's *Ghosts* for anyone who is not purblind.

It has been often said that *The Quintessence of Ibsenism* by Bernard

Shaw has more of Shaw than Ibsen to it. But anyone who concludes that Shaw misrepresented Ibsen for that reason is grievously in error. Anyone may *feel* the effect of genius, as anyone, for example, can be affected by Shakespeare's *Macbeth, Hamlet,* or *King Lear.* But only genius can glimpse the *genius* in a genius, as Shaw did in Ibsen. Those who lack even a particle of genius have long prated about those attributes of Ibsen's work that manifest his skill or talent rather than his genius. Hence they have reduced Ibsen to the level of "problem play" writers, and given Ibsen the title of "father of the modern drama" on the grounds that he has fathered a long line of mediocre realistic plays. A dubious and uncomplimentary paternity intended as a compliment has long been ascribed to the deceptive Norwegian. I can well understand why Brooks Atkinson should dislike Ibsen and his alleged influence. Atkinson dislikes the mediocre caricature that passes for Ibsen and protests against its unquestionably deplorable influence.

Extremely commonplace playwriting has been patterned after the mirage of Ibsenism, which should be called pseudo-Ibsenism. The few playwrights who have escaped banality have done so because they couldn't quite manage to be consistently commonplace even if they had tried hard to be so. Such playwrights in our time have been, in my opinion, Odets, Hellman, and Miller. Such a man, and one who was endowed with a subtler mind than they, was François Curel. But playwrights, both here and abroad in our time, haven't bothered much with Curel; they have preferred to follow the example of abysmally commonplace Ibsenites who were themselves copies of earlier commonplace Ibsenites. In this way, contemporary playwrights ultimately bypass Ibsen entirely and return to their real ancestors, who are Sardou, Dumas *fils,* and Scribe. If that ancestry were attributed to those playwrights who have had an education, they would consider themselves deeply insulted. And if anyone were to "pin" that ancestry not solely on the authors of flat failures but on the authors of successful plays such as Lillian Hellman's *The Watch on the Rhine,* Rattigan's *The Winslow Boy* and *The Deep Blue Sea,* and Miller's *All My Sons,* cries of indignation would reach his ears not merely from the inevitably partial authors but from respectable critics. Whoever made that charge, indeed, would have overlooked certain qualities in the work that give it greater distinction than, let us say, Scribe's *Glass of Water* (*Verre d'Eau*) or Sardou's *Patrie.* It is true enough that these contemporary writers are not in the direct line of descent. But if Scribe was not their great-grandfather, he was surely their great-granduncle! And in any case, they are very far from being Ibsens.

If these authors, not to mention Miss Prumbs, can often succumb to pseudo-Ibsenism (as did Pinero and Henry Arthur Jones in the late-

Victorian period), it is not surprising that the intelligent and experienced Elmer Rice should. He never quite escaped the pseudo-Ibsenite influence in the early plays that gave him his reputation; he merely compensated this defect in *Street Scene* and *Counsellor-at-Law* with other qualities, such as the pathos and the panoramic verisimilitude of the slum environment of *Street Scene* and the sharp character delineation, tart dialogue, and the homeopathic set-a-rogue-to-catch-a-rogue or fight-fire-with-fire, resolution of *Counsellor-at-Law*. But Rice became a *bona-fide* pseudo-Ibsenite in 1943 with *A New Life;* no doubt inadvertently, for he tried to give the theatre an anti-philistine and life-affirming play with his account of the marriage of a young couple in spite of economic difficulties and social barriers posed by the girl's wealthy parents. There wouldn't be much point to recount the plot here and to break a worthy man's failure on the wheel of criticism. What is to the point is the ironic fact that Rice, than whom few playwrights here or in England were more keenly aware of the world struggle and its ramifications, should have presented the season of 1943-44 with *A New Life*. Possibly he regarded it as a symbolic statement of resistance to the spirit of intolerance involved in the world-conflict. Possibly, too, he wanted the play to affirm the love and courage with which humanity could overcome the "forces of Intolerance." But his choice of story was itself a case of pseudo-Ibsenism, as was his technique and style. Rice, no less than Miss Prumbs, reduced a big subject to a little one, not simply because he chose little people, as some pseudo-aristocrats of the critical fraternity would maintain; and not solely because he was unable to make these little people big enough by means of characterization and concomitant dialogue, as can be maintained more soundly; but because, to a considerable degree, he couldn't find or invent a greater fable—Aristotle would have called it a "mythos" and Hollywood producers, a "story"—for his purposes.

Quite a number of modern critics (and playwrights, too, of course) minimize the importance of plot in the drama. What they fail to realize is that plot, too, is a projection of the creator's intellect or "spirit," just as it may also be a projection of his milieu. The commonplace plot-invention of many playwrights may well be an approximate measure of their penetration into reality as artists, although it is possible that this penetration would have been greater if the writer had been challenged more thoroughly by the intellectual and moral climate. This has been the age of soap-opera, and Mr. Rice came close to writing one in *A New Life*. Much of our so-called progressive thinking and the writing engendered by it has been, to a degree, nothing more than *liberal* soap-opera, and *A New Life* was a "liberal" play. Show me the kind of plots an age produces—or adopts and adapts—and I can discover a good deal about the ambience of its spirit. Rice, affected by *Zeitgeist,* as well as also by show-business considerations, reduced a big theme to a little subject, and then inevitably (and quite properly) squeezed it into a little play. No doubt, he could justify his procedure on the grounds that he was drawing a parallel between the little subject and the larger issues of the day. It is even possible that he wondered for a time how we could be so dense as to miss the parallel. But in the theatre, of course, we observe plays, not parallels.

Rose Franken, in the same season, rather surprised some of us. She had previously won success on Broadway with *Another Language* and *Claudia,* two plays notable for the plain, sound observation and verisimilitude with which she rendered the commonplace. *Claudia* had been particularly successful, spiced as it was before its woman's-magazine conclusion by a woman's perception of the kittenish immaturity with which many girls start marital life—usually, we are told, in our middle-class milieu. Her new play *Outrageous Fortune* was compounded of familiar details. But they were so mingled in Miss Franken's problem play that they adumbrated a theme more often treated melodramatically and without depth or dimension in many an anti-Nazi play of the period. Her immediate subject was the problem of anti-semitism as it affects both Jews and Christians and the healing power of tolerance. Unwilling to confine herself to sociological statement, Miss Franken aspired to a magnitude for which few drama critics evinced any great appreciation (surprisingly, George Jean Nathan thought well of the effort) and for the very reason that she had tried to pack too much into too little.

Setting out to add to her incisive picture of a Jewish family's response to prejudice the larger subject of inner insecurity, she succeeded up to a point. The stockbroker, who tried to retire to the shelter of his family, and his wife, who tried to curry favor with the outside world, were well observed, as were the man's old-fashioned mother, who was inwardly too secure to sense prejudice, and a woman of the world who loved life too exuberantly to muddy it with racial animosities. Frederic Tozere, Margalo Gillmore, the Moscow Art Theatre actress Marie Ouspenskaya, and Elsie Ferguson, back on the stage after a thirteen-year absence, gave sterling performances in these respective roles. A sharply etched Jewish doctor and his Irish wife, delightfully played by Adele Longmire, added considerable humanity to the drama. But to encompass the larger theme of insecurity, Miss Franken made the mistake of adding homosexuality and a borderline case of sexual inversion to her plot. The mold of the play simply could not hold that much in solution without producing a brackish colloid of substances that refused to mix. When, moreover, Miss Franken imposed upon her woman of the world the impossible task of straightening out everybody's problem with astute behavior and sage counsel, she came close to transforming a charming character into a cross between Pollyanna and a Miss Fix-It.

In the case of *Outrageous Fortune,* the author attempted to inflate a balloon of limited stretch into a Zeppelin. In the case of many ill-fated war and anti-Nazi plays here and in England the reverse was the case, their authors having tried to compress a Zeppelin to the size of a balloon with tiny stories of fortitude and heroism that were picayune beside the drama of a world at war.

It is a mistake, however, to assume that the stage is necessarily limited to tempests in teapots or parlors, or at best to minor skirmishes. Only the cost of commercial, unsubsidized production on Broadway is limiting, not the insufficiently utilizable or utilized, hence ultimately atrophied, imagination of the theatre's artists. What the Elizabethan theatre could accomplish, the theatre of today can do with even greater visual and mechanical effectiveness. This was amply proved by the defunct, subsidized Federal Theatre's living newspapers *Power* and *One-Third of a Nation* and was proved again in 1943 by Moss Hart's *Winged Victory,* produced by the Army Air Force's Command, with an enormous cast and a large orchestra, for the Army Emergency Relief Fund. It was unquestionably a stirring experience in the theatre, owing to Moss Hart's epic treatment and the Air Force's readiness and ability to comply with the playwright's requirements. These were many, including a sufficiently large body of sturdy actors to convey the impression that our Air Force consisted of something more than a few asthmatic 4F youngsters and middle-aged mimes (which was the case in one short-lived English play about the R.A.F.); and settings by Harry Horner, then Sergeant Horner, representing, in addition to the homes from which our flyers came, the training fields in America and a landing field in the South Pacific.

Winged Victory effectively affirmed an unassuming self-deprecating heroism. The men who were soon to become battle-sobered fighters in the skies first appeared as carefree, exuberant youngsters for whom flying was adventure. The men who defended democracy practiced it in their comradeship; they came from all parts of the country and from all the races and religious creeds that comprise America; and the military system of which they were part was a living organism rather than a machine without a soul. Hart's story was that of a group of young men who went through the training period and the actual fighting with deepening spirit; who existed for us as sons, lovers, husbands, and fathers; who cemented undying friendships, and remained simple human beings under all circumstances. Their story was one of partings, anxieties, disappointments, and death—their own or their friends'. But throughout this epic ran a simple strain of humanity, and it was enlivened with humor that ranged from tender little scenes to the burlesque antics of a Christmas celebration in the tropics at which the men outdid Carmen Miranda and the Andrews sisters.

Brilliantly staged by Mr. Hart himself, with imaginative settings such as Harry Horner also designed for the notable production of Hart's psychological play *Lady in the Dark,* and lighting by the wizard of electricity Sergeant Abe Feder, *Winged Victory* was a magnificent show. Acted with irrepressible vitality by an enormous cast and with sensitivity by many ex-actors, among whom Pfc. Edmond O'Brien, playing a wonderful recruit from Brooklyn, was especially vivid, *Winged Victory* was heart-warming and rousing drama. Like its predecessor, Irving Berlin's *This Is the Army,* Hart's *Winged Victory* was a "show," and the collaborator of many a successful farce-comedy and musical comedy could make it a good one. But paramount even in so bustling a performance as *Winged Victory* was not the action but the underlying reality of those who make action and respond to it. The true grandeur realizable in the theatre resides in humanity caught in the swirl of great events or pitched on the high peaks of passion, as in the Theatre Guild's Margaret Webster production of *Othello,* which was the other major event of the theatre in 1943.

A comparison of *Othello* and *Winged Victory* may seem ridiculous. But it may remind us that a "show," too, can have magnitude, if certainly not of the highest order. There are two planes on which stage drama can triumph over mere pettiness. *Winged Victory,* a work sufficient only unto the day, achieved epic qualities on a horizontal plane by providing a cross-section of a nation in arms. *Othello* attained an epic effect vertically. *Othello,* as realized by Paul Robeson, possessed epic stature as the drama of a strong but simple good man who stalks through a maze of error and passion like a colossus. In him man's capacity for suffering reached an altitude. In his antagonist, Iago, human evil found another epitome; Iago, as played by José Ferrer, was truly a symbol of all that is malevolent and destructive; he was a veritable incarnation of "original sin." Whereas Robeson was monumental, Iago was serpentine; whereas the former was monolithic, the latter was mercurial, mobile. Each performer, who might have been very much less effective by himself, supplemented the other's personality and style of performance. The tension between the two natures of man produced tragedy.

The trouble with a great deal of contemporary art, both in the theatre and in other forms of creation, is that our artists, who are barometers of their age, grew up in decades of negation. Debunking and sophistication were the hue and cry of the twenties, man's capacity for greatness was overlooked, and both his torments and his exaltations were broken on the wheel of psychoanalysis and scepticism. In *The Modern Temper,* published in 1929, Joseph Wood Krutch even announced that the modern life could not yield great tragedy. World events in the early nineteen-forties caused the wheel to turn full circle round. We were ready for a while, here and there, once more to appreciate greatness of feeling, emotion that does not masquerade in flippancies or hide its light under a bushel. But whether the results would be sufficiently genuine and long-lasting could be doubted. The basis for great affirmative drama had not been laid. It had been merely strewn on the stage as a thin layer of soil by some responsiveness to great events. Even this did not happen often enough, as my account of some plays of the 1943-44 season would indicate. And it was evident that the foundations one could lay in this topsoil would fail to sustain any strong edifice of affirmative drama. *The Winged Victory,* like Maxwell Anderson's *The Eve of St. Mark,* was compounded of little emotional fragments made glittering by the splendor of fitful action, instead of being constituted of events experienced profoundly, emotions located in the depths of the individual character, and perceptions arrived at by him in the course of conflict. *Othello,* brought to us in 1943 out of times notable for a more spacious conception of the individual, could well serve to remind us that even great public events do not necessarily yield great drama when the capacity for response is limited. For great events, not to mention little ones, must first be greatly seen, and they cannot be greatly seen unless man is greatly seen, whether in virtue or in vice. We are reminded of the Button-Moulder's complaint in *Peer Gynt* that men are no longer ample for good or ill, in goodness or in villainy. They are only middling people. So it appeared at least in our theatre during a period of tremendous issues, conflicts, and testing.

MORDANCY IN THE DRAMA

Incisiveness has become a rare quality in the theatre. I have found little of it in recent European drama except in the French. If the situation is different in France, the reason lies in the indurated scepticism and intellectual bounce of French culture. The post-war Germans, for the most part, have wallowed in guilt-feelings and apologetics. The English have retreated, for the most part, to their cozy world of comedy of manners with a sort of bland defiance of adversity that is characteristically British. The most literary English playwrights, with the exception of the dour James Bridie, have merely added poetry to their suavity in such pieces as Christopher Fry's *A Phoenix Too Frequent, The Lady's Not for Burning* and *Venus Observed.*

In America, mordant playwriting, present only during the sceptical nineteen-twenties, is especially inconspicuous (and it was saucy, rather than mordant in the twenties). Mordancy, whether bright or saturnine, can be a corrective for flabby theatre. And since it cannot be produced by critical edict or by the simple resolve of a playwright to be cynical or depressed—it can only arise from the quality of his mind or spirit—such writing is usually a sign of a distinctive personality and viewpoint that belongs to talent. The age, however, usually encourages or discourages mordancy. Three productions in 1948 displayed it on Broadway. And, significantly, not a single one of these was initiated in the commercial theatre, although one, the New Stages production of *The Respectful Prostitute,* later went to Broadway and parts west.

With productions of *S. S. Glencairn* and *The Insect Comedy,* the City Center Company of New York gave painful reminders of how far the present theatre falls short of the goal set for it even a few decades ago. O'Neill's sea-pieces suffered from too many stock-company shortcomings in the acting, and only *In The Zone* was performed with complete success. But even in a half-realized version *S. S. Glencairn* revealed the differences between its kind of theatre and a theatre of surfaces. *Mister Roberts* can be cited for contrast, provided one concedes that it is a highly enjoyable and occasionally moving piece of showmanship and that Joshua Logan has staged it with true virtuosity. Its gusty tars are as authentic on the surface as they are amusing and lovable, but they remain sailors and good fellows whereas O'Neill's men are humanity discovered in conflict with its private demons and ironic destiny. Unlike their entertaining World War II counterparts in *Mister Roberts,* the characters come to us neither from the band-box of the theatre nor from some clever writer's surface observation (nor, I would add, from stereotypes of vivacious American or Brooklyn youth) but from the anguish of O'Neill and his sultry outlook. Since they are people rather than stereotypes, their destiny implicates life itself. They have, in short, the highest kind of reality— *poetic reality.*

Genuine creativeness operates by intensification—which implies the presence of a writer who belongs, in Edith Hamilton's phrase, to "the only true aristocracy, that of passionate souls." He is the only artist to be rewarded by the double harvest of reality made "real"—in O'Neill's case this means the sailors and the life they lead—and of reality transfigured into symbol, for only a fully realized thing can epitomize a species or condition. If O'Neill became a major dramatist, it was because he could bring, and temperamentally *had* to bring, experience to white heat. The treatment of the sea is another indication of the difference between plays like *Mister Roberts* and *S. S. Glencairn.* In the former the ocean is a geographical fact; in the latter it is both an environment and an essence. Except in the case of Henry Fonda's playing of an officer who learned to appreciate the common man, the expert Broadway show yielded its all on the stage and exhausted itself, whereas the patently inadequate City Center production could trail the spectator out of the theatre.

The City Center completed its season with a revival of Karel and Joseph Capek's expressionist fantasy *The Insect Comedy.* These Czech writers also belonged, at least for a time, to the aristocracy of passionate souls, and much of their passion was mobilized against the possibility that passion, which must be personal to be genuine, would be regulated out of the modern world. Since *The Insect Comedy,* like Karel Capek's *R.U.R.,* deals largely with allegorized characters, the City Center's acting exhibited no serious limitations under José Ferrer's efficient direction, and this triptych of human folly retained much of its original interest. Since its mordant satire, which the creator of Gulliver might have written if he had favored the theatre, remains as pertinent as ever, the City Center was well advised to resuscitate the play. Only the first-act butterfly scene failed to do justice to the authors; it made men behave like butterflies, which is somewhat embarrassing although true to the playwrights' ideas, instead of making butterflies behave like human beings, which is more tolerable because it does not suggest mincing epicene behavior. The rapacious beetle world of the second act was masterfully staged and acted; the totalitarian ant world of the third act made exciting impressionist theatre.

Our world invites the indictment of *The Insect Comedy* even better than did the world of 1921 when the play was written. The wonder is only that the present period should have failed to bring forth work of a comparable nature. We have as yet had nothing to set beside drama like the Capek's plays, *The Three-Penny Opera, Gas,* and *The Hairy Ape* in content and form. Although good plays and productions are not extinct, our theatre art is, on the whole, retrograde; it clings too often to safe traditional forms, and it fails to confront the post-war era with passion. It should not be necessary to return to *The Insect Comedy* when the present day offers stronger incitements. The excuse that disenchantment is too negative a response—too "defeatist" as left-wing critics are wont to say—cannot quite hold water. Only those who, like the Capeks, cherish humanist values intensely are likely to be disenchanted to the point of expressing a vibrant scorn. The negative stems from a positive; the denials posit an affirmation. A land that has neither briars nor roses is arid; a theatre that yields neither conspicuous negations nor affirmations is devoid of vitality. *The Insect Comedy* could only remind Broadway how flabby the stage has become, how decidedly most of its artists have succumbed to the sin of *accidia*.

One new play on the Great White Way that could be completely acquitted of moral indifference was the Jean-Paul Sartre importation *The Respectful Prostitute* and, as is the case in any effective work, the author's viewpoint was not an ethical addendum but a fabric of writing, for content has little value, just as a noble intention is unavailing, unless it is *achieved content* and gives the play a particular flavor and *élan*. Sartre's drama had tension, verve, and tone.

It would be erroneous to define the viewpoint of the Sartre play as an attitude toward the Negro problem in the South about which the author manifestly knows so little that his treatment of it contains more extravaganza than reality. Real seriousness in this bizarre piece pertains to the seemingly least somber aspect of his work. Sartre has written his play in the manner of Molière, with the sardonic awareness of human inconsistency and with intellectual detachment. He may be on the brink of personal involvement but he removes himself briskly from sentiment, as well as from propaganda. *The Respectful Prostitute* has much in common with *The Misanthrope*. But it also stems from the *comédies rosses* of naturalism, and this makes Sartre's play considerably less ingratiating. Crossing *The Misanthrope* with *Tobacco Road,* Sartre leaves one alternately exhilarated and nauseated.

The Respectful Prostitute is suffused with the irony of a writer whose real subject is moral fibre, the integrity and consistency of the human species. Sartre's prostitute heroine who refuses to testify falsely against a Negro is presented as more moral at first than the society that looks down on her. The son of a Southern legislator has so much caste and family loyalty that, in order to acquit an intoxicated cousin who shot a Negro passenger, he tries to "frame" the prostitute into denouncing a guiltless Negro; and no doubt he believes himself the possessor of sound principles. The heroine resists him, as well as the violence of the police, only to succumb to a suave politician who appeals to her sympathy for the genteel mother of the imprisoned Negro-killer and promises her the good-will of respectable people. Her social and ostensibly moral superiors sense no inconsistency in persecuting the innocent man and double-crossing the woman. The scion of the socially exalted family, who intended only to make her perjure herself, has been inflamed by her and proposes to make her his mistress after having proved himself a cad in his behavior toward her. And his proposal is accepted as if he had conferred an honor on her! The upshot of a social crisis turns out to be nothing but an illicit arrangement between two people whose values make nonsense of civilization— only that and the incidental lynching of another Negro in place of the accused man the heroine hid in her room after finally testifying against him.

Irony is the means, in short, to an "existentialist" exposé of human character and its responsibility for social evil. It is, Sartre appears to say, from such a tangled and frayed skein of personal values that we expect to weave the good society. The failure of society is exposed through the failure of its individuals although the playwright does not fail to indicate that their error is compounded, as well as at least partly caused, by the milieu; personal decisions may never be free but they are of cardinal importance in Sartre's thought. This view takes the play out of the sociological category of the problem play with its simplifications of analysis and its pat solutions. An acid intelligence is being employed in *The Respectful Prostitute* as a solvent. A "resistant flexibility," which Colley Cibber predicated for the critical faculty, manifests itself as Sartre views the world of individual and collective responsibility. The approach is familiar enough in the attitudes of comic detachment. If Sartre's irony rather leaves us suspended in mid-air, the experience is more stimulating than any commonplace exposition of the racial problem has been. If it can be argued that the play is not true to fact, it is true within the autonomous world of Sartre's imagination and judgment on human, rather than exclusively Southern, behavior. He may know hardly anything about the South, but he knows a good deal about the moral condition of humanity and consequently is equipped for composing "dark" comedy.

THE DUBLIN GATE THEATRE

More eventful than generally realized was the visit of the Dublin Gate Theatre on Broadway in February, 1948. A collection of gifted actors under the leadership of the English actor-director Hilton Edwards and the Irish actor-designer-playwright Michael MacLiammoir, the Gate had by then rolled up an impressive list of three hundred productions of new and old plays. What the Abbey Theatre was to the Irish renaissance or Celtic revival of the beginning of the century, the Gate, founded in 1920, aimed to be to liberated Eire. A program note aptly sums up the difference between the aims of Ireland's two major theatres: "The Dublin Gate Theatre . . . . , unlike the Abbey which set out to show Ireland to herself and then to the world, set out to show the world to Ireland."

The avowed purpose of breaking down Irish insularity has understandably produced fewer discoveries of indigenous playwriting talent than revivals of European and American drama. But the playwrights sponsored by the Gate may introduce a new and healthy cosmopolitanism in native playwriting. The stimulus provided by exhibiting continental and American drama in Dublin may usher in a new springtime for Irish dramatists, who will no longer play the role of epigones and walk the treadmill of peasant humor and nationalistic romanticism laid down by the Abbey's founders. Besides, the Abbey has long been in danger of running to seed as a producing company, and it has stuck painfully close to pedestrian realism in the arts of production. When the Abbey first aroused the interest of the English-speaking world, realistic staging had not yet lost its novelty in the English-speaking countries. The early Abbey acting companies, moreover, contained actors whose remarkable talents and personalities easily transcended the most prosaic staging. But those superb artists are no longer playing for Ireland's official theatre; time and Hollywood have decimated the ranks.

The advent of the Gate imparted a new dispensation in the theatre arts; the Gate's staging, scenic design, and lighting are modern, imaginative, and ingenious, while its acting talent appears to have developed considerably, in recent years. Hilton Edwards and Michael MacLiammoir, in particular, would be a credit to any stage. Following a Canadian tour, the distinguished visitors from Dublin descended upon Broadway with a trio of productions, substantiating the rumors of the past decade that the Gate stood in the vanguard of modern theatre art in Ireland.

The first production was Bernard Shaw's rarely revived *John Bull's*

Other Island, a purgative play in which the master's humor is considerable, even if it is somewhat esoteric to those who have no particular acquaintance with Ireland. If Shaw's dramaturgy had equaled his wit and perspicacity, even the casual playgoer would have a very high regard for the play. Such is not the case, largely because *John Bull's Other Island* shows G.B.S. arguing on both sides of the fence. Nevertheless, the delightful Gate production directed by Hilton Edwards proved almost continuously exhilarating after Shaw's slow and discursive beginning. A neat reversal, not unfamiliar to Shavians, demonstrates that it is the Englishman, and not the Irishman, who is the incurable romanticist in spite of the Irishman's carefully cultivated romantic pose and protestations. But the inveterate Fabian and anti-imperialist author of the play lost no opportunity to point out that the English romanticist knows how to convert his sentimentality into pounds sterling. By the time the latter, Tom Broadbent, has relaxed in Ireland he has walked off with the district's richest heiress, has got himself nominated for office, has gobbled up all the available land, and is getting set to convert Irish ruins into a modern hotel for tourists.

The Irish are also ribbed for their cantankerousness, their inability to live at peace with one another, and their own brand of sentimentality, which makes them debauch themselves with dreaming of past glory and with self-pity instead of facing reality. The Irishman cannot be interested in Ireland until you "call the unfortunate island Kathleen ni Hoolihan and pretend she's a little old woman." He "can't be intelligently political." The guide who feeds him miracles or sentimental stories of saints has cathedrals built for him out of the pennies of the poor, while the churchman who teaches him "the sanctity of life and the importance of conduct is sent away."

Nevertheless, Shaw was not only remarkably kind to his native land in this play, but inclined to move toward an affirmation that makes his satirical view of both countries merely the dark side of a vision. He gave the vision to an eccentric Irish priest, one of those mystics for whom Shaw the rationalist had such genuine sympathy, and his words should last as long as the English language itself. Father Keegan, who believes that every dream is a prophecy and every jest an earnest in the womb of Time, holds that there are but two countries: "heaven and hell; but two conditions of men: salvation and damnation." Standing between the Englishman who is so clever in his foolishness and the Irishman who is so foolish in his cleverness, the priest isn't sure which of them is the more deeply damned. He *is* sure of what heaven is like in his dreams: "In my dreams it is a country where the State is the Church, and the Church the people: three in one and one in three. It is a commonwealth in which work is play and play is life: three in one and one in three. It is the temple in which the priest is the worshipper and the worshipper the worshipped: three in one and one in three. It is a godhead in which all life is human and all humanity divine: three in one and one in three."

Tract or no tract, moreover, the play has moments of exuberant comedy, flashing glimpses of character, and even a little pathos. The mélange of the year 1904 is Shavian and there are no better potpourris than those prepared by the latter-day Molière. That the Gate should have revived this profoundly un-nationalistic treatment of national traits indicates the cosmopolitanism of the group.

The Gate's second production, *The Old Lady Says "No,"* by Dennis Johnston, also reflected its valiant effort to resist the temptation to conform to professional patriotism in the new republic which is extravagantly averse to criticism of anything Irish. The play, written in the thirties, is still heterodox in Ireland. In America, it proved to be caviar even to the majority of drama critics. That this expressionistic and symbolic play was somewhat recondite in its allusions may be conceded, without detracting from its brilliance and imaginativeness. An actor rehearsing a romantic play about Ireland's Robert Emmett is accidentally struck on the head, and the rest of the play is a rueful delirium in which he is the Irish hero in many guises searching for his lost love, Sarah Curran, who is none other symbolically than "the old lady," Kathleen ni Houlihan, or Ireland. The quest constitutes a sharp and penetrative contrast between romantic illusion and the Ireland of the twentieth century.

The play is a protest against Ireland's failure in culture, politics, and economics, expressed in terms somewhat unfamiliar to Americans. Yet the same complaint may be generally leveled at the rest of the globe, and the play may be regarded as an Irish version of Eliot's poem "The Waste-Land." It expresses the same disillusionment and sense of defeat. If, in spite of its quality of disenchantment, *The Old Lady Says "No"* is anything but a depressant, the reason lies in the rich theatricality of the play; it is written with verve, imagination, and elasticity. The American theatre has not had its like since the days of *Beggar on Horseback, Processional,* and *The Adding Machine.* That was more than two decades ago, and since then inventiveness has lost much buoyancy in a country that actually prides itself on inventiveness.

Least substantial but most popular was the Gate's *Where Stars Walk* by the redoubtable Mr. MacLiammoir himself. But in this production, too, there were evidences of a critical spirit that Irish nationalism is accused of suppressing, with the result that the Irish "renascence" in the early decades of the century has turned into a Thermidor. Since *Where Stars Walk* is a play of recent vintage, however, the production suggests that this dark view of the cultural situation is not entirely warranted. And those who have proposed it in recent years may also be hard put to it to explain the fact that the Abbey Theatre produced *Red Roses for Me,* Sean O'Casey's transport-strike drama, during the war years, whereas the play never received a professional production in the United States and only a semi-professional one in London by the leftist Unity Theatre. The fact that hostility to O'Casey was registered in the Dublin press does not cancel the fact that his play was staged at Eire's official theatre.

Combining romantic fantasy with realistic irony, MacLiammoir's *Where Stars Walk* scores the point that an Ireland that revels in Celtic twilight and makes a cult of legend would not recognize a legendary figure if one materialized in its parlors. It is only right that the ancient Celtic gods should have reincarnated themselves in a servant girl and an handyman; only for the poor people do the old gods still retain some reality. But it is the educated classes that articulate Irish mythology in literature and theatre, and it is they who are the butt of Mr. MacLiammoir's satire on mediocrity of spirit. *Where Stars Walk* fuses fantasy and reality, as well as romantic pathos and sardonic comedy, and it is a marvel that these elements are joined so well. The play is hardly a work of major dimensions and falls somewhat short of exhilaration, perhaps because the spirit of the comedy is softened by penumbral disenchantment. MacLiammoir's Ireland is a land of "Inspiration, Frustration, and Intoxication." It is, however, also the land where poetry still reveals some degree of vital relationship to the theatre, and that is more than can be said for large tracts of the theatre in our time. Although the Gate did not leave our shores with swollen coffers, it restored some measure of confidence in Dublin's potentialities.

THE HABIMAH THEATRE

Theatrical companies from other nations have visited Broadway from time to time, although not as frequently as one could wish. They are generally welcome, whether they are first-string performers such as Gielgud's troupe bringing *The Importance of Being Earnest* and *Love for Love* or second-string tourists such as Donald Wolfit's ensemble bringing a satisfactory *Volpone* and a tolerable *King Lear*. All is grist to the Broadway grinder, and all the productions seem to be gold from a foreign exchequer for the playgoer who frequently gets little more than tinsel from the local Woolworth establishments. Now and then, too, the public is given an opportunity to catch up with its usually neglected education in the field of dramatic literature. This is less the case when the touring company speaks a foreign tongue. But whether the visit be Barrault's French-speaking group or the Hebrew-speaking Habimah Theatre, last seen on Broadway decades ago, much can be learned at least about the one aspect of theatrical art in which we need special instruction—namely, stylization for serious drama, rather than for musical revues and comedies, in stage production.

Not only playgoers who understood the Hebrew language, therefore, but workers in the Broadway theatre and on its periphery could consider themselves fortunate when the Habimah, brought here by Theatre Incorporated and the American Friends for Palestinian Institutions, took up brief residence in Manhattan in the spring of 1948. Too few *aficionados* were left there to be able to make favorable or invidious comparisons with the Habimah of 1926, and very few remained who did not need a refresher course. The Habimah, founded as long ago as 1917, may be looked upon as an old-fashioned institution in Israel, where it has been the semi-official or classic theatre since taking up permanent residence there in 1931; but its production style remains almost flagrantly young and advanced by contrast with staid realistic production on Broadway. The Habimah retains the fine frenzy and poetic vision of the dramatic modernism that marked the early decades of the century. In our theatre since the last visit of this insistently youthful company in 1926, we have had no greater display of knowledgeable enthusiasm for poetic theatricalism. Moreover, theatricalization by the Habimah was generally something else than theatricalization by French theatricians: it was an intensification of life rather than a display of "play-with-me-at-theatre" intellectualism or artfulness.

I. THE HABIMAH'S *DYBBUK*

Wisely, the company opened its repertory with S. Ansky's folk drama *The Dybbuk,* the play with which the company first won an international reputation in 1922 owing to the production staged by Stanislavski's most talented associate, the short-lived genius of the theatricalist style Eugene Vakhtangov. Although the performance seemed somewhat listless, at the beginning, the twenty-six-year-old Vakhtangov production scheme retained its gratifying form, if not its original energy. And the fable of how a lover's ghost takes possession of his beloved and how she joins him in death after he has been exorcised from her body still lends itself particularly well to the Habimah's acting style.

The play is a folk fantasy, rooted in Chassidic life and legend, heightened by Pickwickian touches of humor and characterization, counterpointed by grotesquerie, and transfigured by romanticism. Within settings unmistakably cubistic in inspiration, the actors ran the gamut of acting art, from unpretentious realism in homely details to Brueghel-like grotesqueness in the dance of the beggars at the rich family's marriage feast. Noteworthy were the expressionistic stage pictures in the Tzadig's, or Saint's, study, and the many stylized movements that regularly projected the myth-making quality of art. Yet with all the stylization, the Habimah never lost sight of the theatre's prime requisite of humanization, the potency of which appeared in sharply made contrasts of wealth and poverty, in the pathos conveyed by the poor student whose childhood sweetheart and fiancée is given in marriage to a dolt, and by the girl who mutely walks the treadmill of tradition which prescribes subordination of personal to parental will. Admirably realized, too, were the dignified humanity of the saint's grief over the rich father's callous violation of justice, the rabbinical judgment that the latter must give one half of his wealth to the poor in atonement for depriving the dead student of his promised bride, and the justice of heaven that unites the lovers' souls in death. An elemental pity suffused the expressive gestures and utterances of the performances. One did not have to understand the modern Hebrew spoken by the actors to be gratified by this production, which made more of the human drama than of the supernatural element of possession of the girl's body by the ghost of the deprived lover who had died of a broken heart. It is in the bearing and acting of the participants that the meaning flowers as theatre. Like other great stage companies, the Habimah proved that verbal communication is not the only, and not necessarily always the strongest, means of communication in the theatre. The Habimah production evoked the dignity of man, and gave even unreason the shining quality of reason; even in superstition, man is not a mere clod when art exerts its formalizing, organizing power.

Not everybody was likely to be entranced with the production of *The Dybbuk*. One could cavil at its leisurely movement, especially in the first two acts, and some playgoers probably missed the excitement and wildness they consider appropriate to oriental folklore. And there are people who simply abominate stylization in art, blithely unaware that society constantly stylizes their manners, responses, and modes of thought just as much—except not so beautifully. For myself I could report that the production was one of the truly gratifying experiences of a theatregoing lifetime.

II. *THE GOLEM*

Although there are many objective tests by which to discover a distinguished acting company, and the Habimah met most of them, it remained nonetheless a marvel for our present, generally unprogressive theatre, that the latest Habimah production, H. Levik's *The Golem,* revealed such distinctive virtues.

There was, for instance, the marvel of Aaron Meskin's performance, the manner in which he conveyed the legendary prowess of the Golem, looking like a preternatural outsized figure while completely evoking the robot-creature's infantile intellect. In this performance, we had formidable physical strength completely at odds with intelligence, and the result was so convincingly eerie that it could keep an audience, as it kept this reviewer, continually in suspense, wondering what the Golem would do next, dreading him, and fearing for the human beings in his proximity. The production added to this evocativeness the dimension of humor; for the Golem imitating human behavior, behaving mechanically as if in a stupor and only faintly comprehending himself and his mission, is as comic a figure as he is a menacing one. And comedy in a play of this sort has a healing or reassuring quality; horror is banished by a reassertion of our humanness, of our capacity for the detached criticism of laughter. Indeed, instead of being thoroughly horrified by the Golem, we could also pity him for his witless flounderings. And we achieve superiority over that which we are enabled to pity, as well as over that which amuses us.

All this was very specially the creation of one actor, who in a previous Habimah production dignified the heroically noble role of David in Calderon's *David's Crown*. Here was acting on a level rarely approximated on the English-speaking stage; not even Olivier's talent can hold a candle to it; he was still only Olivier the acting-school actor in Old Vic per-

formances, whereas one could look close and still not find Meskin in
The Golem, even less than one could locate him in *David.* Nor is it saying
much that Meskin is endowed with a soundbox that can sound like
thunder, because he proved in previous roles that he sounds like anything
he has to sound like (barring no doubt a soprano ingenue). And above
all, because it is plain that transformations like Meskin's have a considerable relationship to company artistry, non-existent where there are no
permanent acting companies and where mere simulation of self is an acceptable form of acting.

Meskin's feat was, however, one miracle among many. Shimon
Finkel's Maharal, the sage who creates the Golem, deserves to be long remembered for his realization of intellectual confidence and Promethean
valor. Zvi Friedland's Elijah the Prophet was as winning a character as
any I have seen, but also bore the stamp of something no ordinary acting
can convey—namely, an essence, so to speak. The characterization was that
of a visionary wanderer, a friend of man, a poet of man's redemption, the
incarnate nature of saintliness. Again the secret of the performance lay in
stylization, of the addition of a formal, symbolizing dimension to Stanislavskian realization of character by the actor. More obviously, but no less
memorably, this style was also present in Zvi Ben-Haim's playing of the
madman Tanchum.

Remarkably expressive, too, were the costuming and make-up of all
the actors, based on the principle that ideally they should represent the
essence of a role. Tadeush, the Inquisitor who persecutes the Jews, for
example, was so costumed in mitre and vestments that he walked the stage
as the very symbol of religious intolerance. In an ordinary Broadway production, the result would have seemed extravagant—or naïve. The settings
had the same quality of symbolization, so that the tower of Prague, the
synagogue, and the home of the Jewish sage could be denoted as "environment *plus.*" The geometric planes and masses were there, in short, not
merely for what they denoted as to place but what they connoted—in other
words, they had a musical as well as environmental function.

Although the modern Hebrew of the play was a sealed book to most
of us, it was plain that in *The Golem* the symbolization in the performance effectively projected the symbolism of the drama. This is no mere
rehashing of a ghetto myth. In essence, it is evident that the play dramatizes man's tragically futile effort to create agents of his will-to-freedom
only to find that they are broken reeds so long as they lack heart and
spirit. *The Golem* is a parable for our age.

III. THE HABIMAH AND SOPHOCLES

The Habimah gave two other productions from its repertory. One was a Hebrew adaptation of a Calderon play, *David's Crown;* and to find this seventeenth-century playwright represented in New York was itself a marvel. It was difficult to work up much interest in David's difficulties with his sons, and it did not seem to one unable to follow the lines of this patently prolix work that the play had any particular merit as more than an academic exercise. But the production itself was anything but academic. Especially stirring was the last stage picture of David receiving the body of the slain Absalom—it was no more than a picture but no more was needed, for David was played by the redoubtable Aaron Meskin who radiated greatness as a man and king whenever he held the stage.

Academicism *was* present in one other production, that of *Oedipus Rex,* staged by none other than the Old Vic director Tyrone Guthrie. It was most curious that this should be so, and critics were justified in comparing the performance unfavorably with the Old Vic production which visited us in 1947. This was the production in which Laurence Olivier, playing Oedipus, reached the zenith of his acting career. Olivier's performance overshadowed Shimon Finkel's Oedipus; Mr. Finkel, as a matter of fact, was more of a Hamlet than an Oedipus throughout the proceedings. Much of the visual movement was commendable, but was only remotely exciting, partly because the stage picture formed by the actors and the chorus was too meager, and partly because the beautiful classic Greek setting drew the action inwards. It is invariably a mistake to wrap a play in a mist when it was written to be projected rather than merely photographed as a picture.

The setting of crepuscular platforms and columns approximated the ideal settings of Appia and Gordon Craig. It was suffused with atmosphere; it expressed the inscrutability of Oedipus' fate (the destiny that singles him out to kill his father and marry his mother), and it possessed the magic desiderated by the symbolist movement in playwriting and scenic art. But all these virtues, which spelled out art in capital letters, did not serve the play anywhere as well as Guthrie's use of actors, such as the treatment of the opening chorus as a primitive Greek frieze, and the work of the actors themselves. Joshua Bertonov's Old Shepherd's representation of extreme old age was especially masterly, and once more Aaron Meskin, this time playing the secondary part of Kreon, gave one of those dimensioned characterizations that make a play of any period and in any style a profound experience that only characterization in a great novel can equal. At the end of the Habimah's repertory, I wanted to go out on a limb as a critic and say to anyone who wanted to listen, "If you want to know where to find the world's greatest living actor, you will find him in the Habimah company."

Oedipus Rex was least impressive, possibly because Tyrone Guthrie, who staged the play, did not share its traditions or quite understand its potentialities. That the performers, too, often kept within penumbral acting areas, could have turned Sophocles' tragedy into a searing experience in spite of the language barrier was evident whenever the individual members of the chorus came together and came forward, forming unforgettable tableaux and projecting some of the pity and terror that Sophocles put into his play. Whenever they were unsubdued by the setting it was plain that the actors were on the verge of materializing for us the world of Hardy's "purblind Doomsters" in which "crass Casualty obstructs the sun." If it is true enough that our peepshow stages make projection difficult, there are still ways of bringing the action outward by grouping and lighting. "Theatricalism" is, of course, capable of great range. During the period of the Habimah's visit, we had an example of purely comic theatricalism in a Molnar revival. In staging *The Play's the Thing* with irreverence toward the fourth wall convention, by toying with the curtain so that it sank halfway twice before it closed the act as the playwright character Sandor Turai speculated on how to end it, Gilbert Miller achieved an easy and felicitous effect. He made a play of artifice arrogantly artificial and therefore amusing. By playing to the audience in this conceived *jeu d'esprit* he made us accept Molnar's contrivances and enlivened the play. Contrivance in the theatre is objectionable only when one tries to conceal it; if the audience detects it against the wishes of the playwright or stage director the result is disagreeable. We have caught him at cheating!— But if we are asked to play the game of theatre with the producer and his cast, we are rarely prissy enough to refuse. We did not refuse in the case of the 1935 Jed Harris production of *Our Town,* because the terms of the game were frankly given to us at the very beginning in the narration that Frank Craven delivered so naturally. Perhaps the trouble with Wilder's later *jeu d'esprit, The Skin of Our Teeth,* started when we are asked to play the game too cutely. Cuteness is one of the dangers of theatricalist style.

By contrast, symbolist staging of the Craig-Appia dispensation is fundamentally disingenuous. It tries to put us into a twilight sleep with its magic of shadows and nuance. It casts a spell the source of which is concealed from us. Symbolism is actually the twin-brother of Realism. Both styles stem from Renaissance illusion-making stagecraft, when illusionists' effects were created by painted perspective settings, cloud machines, colored lights, and other means. The pictorial genius of Renaissance and

Baroque painters was translated into theatrical picturesqueness, and *their* artistry was supremely illusionistic not merely in the use made of perspective and color but of anatomy.

Atmospheric symbolism is merely illusion subjectivized and made indistinct—"suggestive." It is effective in lyric poetry, but far less so in nonromantic theatre, and *Oedipus the King* is, of course, profoundly antiromantic. Even though the mystery of fate lies at the heart of the story, the drama itself, which consists of the tracking down of guilt by the keen will and intellect of Oedipus, unfolds actively, logically, and with intense specificity. The fate of Oedipus may be a symbol of human destiny, but the artistry of this classic tragedy is not symbolist. And symbolist mistiness was, of course, utterly unthinkable in the open-air production of the play—or of *any* Athenian play—in the Theatre of Dionysus or in any other Greek theatre. Symbolism is *inwardness,* theatricalism is *outwardness.* And outwardness is the essential attribute of the Habimah's style of performances which the Tyrone Guthrie production-design frequently defeated.

Outwardness, I would add by way of a codicil, is also the essence of playwriting for the Elizabethan public theatre. Shakespeare—as well as, for that matter, Kyd, Marlowe, Marston, Webster, Dekker, and the other vigorous Elizabethans—has been less well served than the public supposes by "arty" styles of contemporary productions, quintessentialized by the Olivier film treatment of *Hamlet.* By disposition a theatricalist, Orson Welles in the thirties did far better by Marlowe with the Federal Theatre's *Dr. Faustus,* by Dekker with the Mercury Theatre production of *The Shoemaker's Holiday,* and by Shakespeare with the modern-dress *Julius Caesar*—this, in spite of the arbitrary amputation of the text. Anthony Quayle's production of an intact *Julius Caesar* at Stratford in 1950 impressed me as also free from the faults of the symbolist dissolution of Shakespeare's matter and style of dramaturgy, as did also the Stratford production of *Henry VIII.* Only for the romantic comedies is a chiaroscuro style of production warranted, so that I could delight, with other playgoers at Stratford, in the entrancing John Gielgud treatment of *Much Ado About Nothing.* Yet the sharply outlined semi-amateur Piscator production of *Twelfth Night* in New York during the mid-forties gratified me more than the lavishly pictorial Margaret Webster staging of the same play for the Theatre Guild which had the services of such impressive performers as Helen Hayes and Maurice Evans. In the Webster production, the most agreeable performance was June Walker's Maria the maid, because Miss Walker gave a neat clear-as-day theatrical rendition of her acting.

In Piscator's production, as directed by Chouteau Dyer, the theatrical nature of the comedy was directly realizable and constituted a unified experience. The Broadway production interposed two star-actors' personalities between the audience and the play. Each insisted upon displaying a specialized inwardness (combined with outwardness of manner), halting the flow of the comedy in order that they might be individually appreciated as distinct entities, despite the fact that the only entity that matters is *Twelfth Night* if the play is not to be disintegrated into an assortment of fragments. We may call these stars' procedures pseudo-Stanislavskism. Stanislavskism, I believe, will always be more of a hindrance than a help on the stage so long as we have no permanent companies and do have short rehearsal periods, so that the Stanislavskian-built characterizations usually appear lumpy and do not fuse. For this reason, among others, the Margaret Webster productions we have had in this country have never quite served Shakespearean theatricalism adequately. They have consisted of interesting parts comparable to plums in a pudding. This is, indeed, how Romantic and Victorian critics (and actors) viewed Shakespeare's plays, hence the vogue of the "Characters of Shakespeare" type of criticism. The old-fashioned star-system accorded well with this view, and it was not considered outrageous that a Shakespearean actor should surround himself with a local cast in Kansas City or Oshkosh when he toured the United States. He did not offer his public *Hamlet,* for instance, but Hamlet the character-part. There is no surer way to defeat Shakespearean theatricalism.

"Symbolism" and partial "Stanislavskism" have been the two poles of presenting the classics in our time. Neither procedure has been completely satisfying. Even the Habimah company succumbed to the one extreme when *Oedipus the King* was staged by Tyrone Guthrie, proving that the "civilizing," "culture-soaked" British mode of interpreting Sophocles cannot be more gratifying than the semi-Stanislavskian mode of interpreting Shakespeare. Less so, in fact, since Shakespeare's plays are less unified than Sophocles' major work.

THEATRICALISM AND REALISM

I

December, 1952, on Broadway was the month of foreign invasions, and it is no longer news that these were successful. Both the Renaud-Barrault Company from Paris and the National Theatre of Greece covered themselves with glory and made playgoing in New York a rewarding experience. Since the two companies departed by the end of the month, the only question that need concern us now is whether they taught us anything. That they did was quickly apparent, for their respective achievement was a triumph of repertory theatre, even if it is wearisome by now to reiterate the need of a repertory system in the United States. The fact that the Greek company subsists on a national subsidy and the French company does not should, however, remind us that it is possible to have repertory companies without federal or state aid. The Renaud-Barrault company has been decidedly more vital than the state-operated Comédie-Française. The question of how a privately financed repertory theatre could materialize in the United States is an important one. This occurred to many of us as we watched the French troupe go through its well-oiled paces, and it will surprise no one familiar with the economics of our professional stage that the subject remains in the realm of speculation for us.

One question more immediately relevant to dramatic criticism than to financing may be worth raising: how far can the theatricalism that distinguished Barrault's repertory carry us? The Barrault productions that were most satisfactory and constituted the core of the repertory were cleverly contrived pieces, mostly seventeenth- and eighteenth-century classics. The one serious contemporary play produced here, Gide's dramatization of *The Trial,* was only half successful. Exceptions were taken to it in France, and exceptions could be taken to it here. Not only was the drama itself devoid of the emotional density of Kafka's novel and incapable of sustaining its nightmare quality, but the production was "intriguing" rather than truly gratifying. The stage became a toy theatre of rising and dropping curtains and of mostly arch acting, with Barrault thrusting his mimic virtuosity rather than an anguished humanity into the foreground. The performance was undoubtedly "theatre," and there is much more to be said for pure theatre than our devotees of second-rate realism are able to understand. But "theatricalism," too, is not an absolute; its value is relative to the matter in hand, and if there is anything that makes the Kafka story memorable it

399

is Kafka's untheatricality or "matter-of-factness" in the midst of the wild improbabilities of *The Trial*. The improbable is made the probable, if not indeed the inevitable, and this it is that produces the almost intolerable anguish of the work. The production gave us "theatre" precisely when "reality" was needed. The production was incongruously blithe in spirit precisely because it made an almost continual display of "make-believe" and ingenuity out of matter the "reality" of which is more fantastic than any "make-belief" could be. There is no "cleverness" in the novel any more than there is cleverness in the Book of Job or *The Brothers Karamazov,* whereas Barrault's production was flagrantly clever and made me (and probably other spectators) conscious of theatrical "know-how."

My strictures call attention to the fact that repertory is not by itself a guarantee of great theatre. There is, on the contrary, a degree of danger in the idolatry of theatre that develops when theatre art becomes an end in itself; when the incentive to stage production is mainly the love of playing rather than a drive to express an experience or perception. We have to get beyond theatre to get to theatre. I find the same danger in our art-conscious noncommercial theatre, too. Undoubtedly, the standards implicit in my warning can be carried to puritanical extremes. These standards are certainly irrelevant when the play itself is "playful," and Barrault's production of Molière and Marivaux could leave nothing to be desired. But theatricality should not come into play indiscriminately and violate the spirit of a deeply felt work.

The same danger was apparent in Barrault's *Hamlet,* in which the aforementioned theatricalization was also a defect. To judge the performance accurately one would have to know French and English equally well, for the reading of lines and passages is of paramount importance. To deplore the loss of verbal values in the Gide translation is, of course, to lament the inevitable. It is sufficient for my purpose to report the consensus that the visiting company gave us a lightweight Hamlet in spite of, or perhaps because of, Barrault's virtuosity as an actor. The production was striking and interesting throughout, but only striking and interesting. Whether Barrault's particular style is the sole reason for his failure to give us a memorable Hamlet I cannot tell. Perhaps he got as much out of Shakespeare's play as it is possible for the French theatre to extract. Our own theatre appears to have considerable difficulty in making the most of many a European play, so that many a work from Ibsen to Anouilh and Brecht seems wasted on us, although this bumbling provinciality did not seem to afflict us in the 1920's. And on our part, it must be said, we sometimes add the mortal sin of sloth by importing a British translation, as in the case of Anouilh's *Legend of Lovers,* and then merely tinkering with it. The domestication of foreign drama—by means of the production as well as the translation—requires as much dedication to the task as the presentation of a play written in our own tongue. Sloth, however, is the last thing that occurs in connection with Barrault. Whatever he may not be dedicated to, he is dedicated to the theatre, and this saves his repertory from becoming a mere salute to "culture" even when he stages French classics.

That the capacity for dedication to high art is not dead in the contemporary world was even more convincingly demonstrated by the National Theatre of Greece, which gave memorable productions of *Oedipus Tyrannus* and *Electra* in modern Greek. Although Katina Paxinou and Alexis Minotis were noteworthy as Electra and Oedipus (and no one who did not see Miss Paxinou's Electra can have any notion of her consummate artistry), the outstanding feature of the productions was the chorus. In all probability tamer—less mimetic and eerie—than the masked classic chorus in the Theatre of Dionysus, the National Theatre's chorus conveyed a sense of formal grandeur that could greatly enhance our comprehension of the inherent dignity of classic tragedy. To be able to distinguish between ordinary and tragic pathos is of cardinal value in dealing with great and all-absorbing emotion. Mourning truly becomes Electra as played by Miss Paxinou, but the persistence of grief throughout the greater part of Sophocles' tragedy was pathos too greatly compounded even in the dignified accents and movements this remarkable actress knows how to command. The choral movement, however, broke up the stasis of sustained feeling that became rather soporific with its cadences and its rising and falling inflections. It was fortunate, therefore, that the chorus took over Electra's grief. The chorus objectified it, making it a condition of universal humanity rather than the private suffering of an individual alone. In the *Electra* production, the patterns of choral speech and presence were so beautifully and yet so naturally designed that the above-described effect was profoundly satisfying.

The treatment provided an excellent lesson for anyone who would ever have occasion to employ a chorus in a stage production. There was also much provocation in the production to those of us who speculate on the woefully "squashy" quality of much modern realistic drama, in which emotionalism belittles the characters and the subject. No doubt there are many reasons for this—the insufficient stature of the characters, the sociological circumstances of the action, the confining stage setting, and so on. Possibly we shall never recapture the dignity of Greek tragedy. But both dignity and significance would be enhanced by the interruption of the emotional stress of the sufferer and by the transference of the feeling to surrogates of the whole or a part of the community—which is what the members of the chorus are. Modern examples of this device, in plays by Yeats, Lorca, Eliot, and Brecht, have proved notably effective.

II

Theatricalism is a delicate matter, and pontification on it is no more efficacious than an indiscriminate use of its methods. The theatricalism of Barrault was extremely successful except when depth or density of experience was required by the substance of such plays as *The Trial* and *Hamlet.* "Stylization" was so thoroughly assimilated in dramatic reality by the National Theatre of Greece (with considerable assistance from Sophocles, of course) that the playgoer could completely forget "theatre" while experiencing it. That is, the theatrical form became the "form" of life itself as perceived by heightened and selective consciousness of its dramatic reality.

It is more usual, however, to resort to various gradations of theatricalism to conceal or to justify dramatic inadequacy or superficiality. The results were sufficient unto the day in the case of such essentially hollow entertainments as *The Seven Year Itch* and *Time Out for Ginger,* which may well keep the amateur theatre content for many a day after they conclude their New York run. The first-mentioned play is an ingenious comedy enlivened with fantasy. The treatment of the subject, a married man's disgruntlement with marriage after seven years and his speculative infidelities during his wife's absence, is light as fluff. Performed with the facility of highly professional actors, among whom Tom Ewell and Vanessa Brown are outstanding, *The Seven Year Itch* jogs along from sequence to sequence with considerable mummery. Tom Ewell has the properly *distrait* personality for giving the playwright's inventions some anchorage in domesticity as well as a considerable amount of humor. But George Axelrod's play itself is essentially anchored only in the familiar "hooray, my wife is in the country" show-business clichés of domesticity. By themselves, these could never sustain even half an evening's entertainment without a great deal of varied theatricality. Since this was supplied by the author, the stage director, the obliging cast, and the even more obliging stagehands and electricians, the production became *Variety's* favorite "laugh hit." Nobody is made unhappy by it, least of all the practical showmen who are relieved that a Broadway show can still pay off. But *The Seven Year Itch* is an illustration of the uses of theatricalism on the level of *Kitsch,* just as, let us say, Christopher Fry's *A Sleep of Prisoners* or Tennessee Williams' *Camino Real* is an illustrative theatricalism on the level of pseudo-philosophy and "art."

If the success of *Time Out for Ginger* at about the same time seems more meretricious to me, it is because the play starts out with greater pretensions. A pillar of society takes up the cause of freedom of expression.

Since Melvyn Douglas makes an appealing small-town citizen and since the principle of tolerance which he upholds decidedly needs upholding, we settle down, with some surprise and gratification, to an evening of civilized comedy. Before long, however, the play shifts both ground and style to become more and more of a "see how sophisticated the author is" type of football story and an egregious farce. Once the local businessman's daughter makes her school's football team, her "liberal" father's atavism turns him into a raccoon-clad fan reminiscent of a John Held caricature of the nineteen-twenties. The transformation is made even more pronounced by the fact that the author, Ronald Alexander, started the play with a quiet scene between the father and his wife written in an admirable vein of high comedy. *Time Out for Ginger,* in short, is another example of the average American playwright's propensity to start a provocative comedy and then run away from its potentialities. He promises us an intelligent evening and then fobs us with a merely funny one. Once more the formula pays dividends, especially when Mr. Douglas impersonates the John Held caricature of a superannuated collegian and when Philip Loeb, playing the role of the bank president who is the hero's employer, makes quizzical attempts to bring him back to sanity. And the author's sympathy for the football-maniac's family provides familiar characterizations on the level of *Kiss and Tell,* so that his rewards for good citizenship are yet to come when the schools and the smaller communities acclaim the play as "wholesome." But his success will have been won largely as a result of a seemingly deliberate disposal of the best part of his cargo. "Theatre" wafts the playwright's craft into the snug harbor of commercial success only after the play no longer carries any substance.

There is injustice in the fact that theatricalism did so much less for such plays as *Climate of Eden,* Moss Hart's short-lived dramatization of Edgar Mittelhölzer's novel *Shadows Move Among Them,* and Richard Nash's equally transitory social allegory, *See the Jaguar.* These plays had far richer matter and signified more ambitious intentions than the aforementioned farces, but they would have come off better if their authors had been able to dispense with a good deal of their theatricality in favor of simpler developments and greater solidity of characterization.

One difference between our stage and the theatre in England and France, indeed, is the fact that it is the larks that usually profit from theatricality on Broadway instead of the serious works. Even when it is not top-drawer theatre, as in the case of the Bette Davis revue, *Two Is Company,* the ingenuity and variety of the production ensure a run. Although Miss Davis proved herself less effective as a revue queen than as a motion-picture star, there were enough performers and antics to make a "show." But the serious drama got no assistance from showmanship, including

ingenious scenic design, in the case of *Climate of Eden* and *See the Jaguar*.
In the work of Anouilh and other Europeans, on the contrary, the theatrical conception is so inherent and so little in conflict with the matter on
hand that the showmanship, whether the playwright's or the author's,
serves the play instead of merely varnishing and sometimes obscuring it.
I became most keenly aware of this fact at the Comédie Française in the
summer of 1950 when I saw the Gaston Baty production of Eugene
Labiche's hundred-year-old farce *The Italian Strawhat* (*Le Chapeau de
paille d'Italie*) in which a gay wedding procession in search of a runaway
bridegroom unified both play and production from start to finish. The
parade became so infectiously a bacchic release that I soon wanted to join
the merry-makers myself and become almost ritualistically one of them.
I had much the same desire, quite incongruously, while witnessing Barrault's production of *The Trial* while Barrault was looking for justice as
Kafka's hero. Here, too, life had been turned if not into a sport, as in the
Labiche farce, into a weird adventure that we cannot help following almost physically. Theatre is, in one way or another, kinetic in such work.

It was purely a device of showmanship that dominated the proceedings in the successfully imported English comedy, *The Love of Four
Colonels* by Peter Ustinov. The pretty wit that Mr. Ustinov commands
cannot conceal the fact that his subject—the different conceptions of love
harbored by Russians, Frenchmen, Englishmen, and Americans—is of
consummate unimportance, and that the Sleeping Beauty fairy tale that
constitutes the bulk of the plot is fluff served up as an oversized omelet.
But the play was inevitably overrated by the press and the public precisely
because Ustinov, who was expert enough to develop his theme with constant theatricality, integrated his "theatre" into his dramatic action. The
play wasn't one thing and the "theatre" something else—if not indeed
something contrary or obfuscating, as in the case of Moss Hart's and
Richard Nash's efforts. It was possible, therefore, to put the considerable
histrionic abilities of Lilli Palmer, Rex Harrison, Robert Coote, George
Voskovec, and Stefan Schnabel to maximum use. Only a shift from politics to the fairy tale was disturbing, and this was apparently caused by
adaptation of the play to suit the American market. When it comes to
playwriting, the English (and the French) are our superiors in making
the most of a *jeu d'esprit*. Although a Russian by birth, Mr. Ustinov has
earned his British citizenship with *The Love of Four Colonels*.

But we must be guarded in our admiration. For one thing, there are
more significant—that is, more profoundly gratifying—plays than these,
and we expect them from the theatre that gave us Sophocles and Shakespeare. And when playwrights across the Atlantic pretend to give us
such plays, they, too, can be inept. Across the Atlantic, for example, Ter-

ence Rattigan confected a drama of passion in *The Deep Blue Sea* and created a substantial feminine role intensely played by Margaret Sullavan. No one could deny that the play was earnestly intended and that its author tried to dredge up the realities of sexual desire in the portrait of a woman who clings desperately to an unworthy love. But it was only a one-string solo that Mr. Rattigan managed to provide until the last few minutes of the play; and his work bogged down in an inconsequential limbo fringed, on one side, by familiar English domestic drama and, on the other side, by somber theatre. Only the performances—especially those of Miss Sullavan, Herbert Berghof, and James Hanley—gave the play some dimension as human experience. It appears that Mr. Rattigan, who is the London West End's most considerable playwright these days, does not realize how soon a one-note obsessive passion exhausts itself. Too many "serious" modern realists have made the same mistake, but have been rewarded by more or less the same public that supports the heart-throbs in the slick magazines and "soap opera" in America. Nor did the English-bred John van Druten, who is quite adept when he does not try to be "deep," fare better than Rattigan with the religious drama *I've Got Sixpence,* which actually held up less well because discussion (and not of the first order, either) took the place of dramatic action.

American-grown playwriting actually commands a little respect when the playwrights are earnest; especially when the theatre goes in for "slugging" rather than for "miming." And Lillian Hellman is just the person to remind us of this fact. She did in the 1952-53 revival of *The Children's Hour,* the play she wrote in 1934 about the machinations of a neurotic girl who wrecks the lives of two boarding-schoolteachers by charging them with homosexuality.

For all the determination Miss Hellman has always displayed in her playwriting, she knows enough not to harp on a single string. She could have written a "spreading the news" type of drama about the evil effects of gossip, and the result would have become thin gruel. Instead, she involves us with the more challenging theme of the question of justice in a maze of personal complications not entirely convincing but "intriguing." The adolescent Iago's socially well-situated grandmother tries the teachers in her own mind without giving them a hearing, and condemns them to ostracism and economic disaster, since the removal of other children from their boarding-school must bankrupt their enterprise. Has she a right to do so? What crimes are committed—and can be committed in the name of righteousness! And still, in spite of having enlarged the meaning and force of her play, Miss Hellman was not satisfied. She felt compelled, it seems, to go beyond the moral and social challenge, too. Economic disaster becomes secondary to psychological shipwreck. The schoolteachers, who have sued the grandmother for character-defamation, lose their case not because of persecution by the wealthy patrons of the school or by the community, which treatment would have been the typical "problem-play" dodge, but as a result of a fatuous relative's failure to show up at the trial as a witness. Moreover, the loss of the trial, combined with other pressures, opens the eyes of one of the teachers to the fact that she actually does desire her friend sexually and has desired her in the past. And with this knowledge, she cannot live. In this respect, as well as in respect to the normal teacher's loss of her fiancé because he cannot quite drive a suspicion of her homosexuality out of his mind, Miss Hellman achieves a reversal or a "peripety," "Aristotelians" would call it, which enlarges and intensifies the interest of the play. And since this reversal of the expected course of the action makes us focus on character drama and personal complexities, the author once more enriched her drama, which started out as an elementary piece of playwriting and would have been left as precisely that by humdrum playwrights. Yes, Miss Hellman overcomplicates and melodramatizes *The Children's Hour,* without quite escaping dull stretches of dialogue. But here is no genteel playwright with one interminable note or "idea."

Although it is not difficult to discover the flaws in this work, a critic must develop a special resolve to denigrate American drama before he can resist the power of *The Children's Hour,* especially in the throbbing second act. The play is, in fact, more poignantly immediate than it ever was, since the possibility of character defamation is far from an abstract consideration in our time; and the psychological effects of victimization by scandal are traced by Miss Hellman with a relentless pen. Not everything in her exposé is entirely convincing. The highlights of the drama may be Miss Hellman's, but its organization is nearly all Pinero's—entailing some labored exposition and plot contrivance. As we watch the proceedings, however, we experience vibrant and provocative playgoing. Although we know that we are not in the presence of a dramatic masterpiece, we confront a determination and passion from which masterpieces *can* come or from which, to say the least, the theatre derives a challenging quality that no other medium of the performing arts in America possesses to the same degree. For this much alone we may well be grateful, and we may view with some perturbation the fact that the plays written in recent years have so rarely possessed the power that belongs to *The Children's Hour.*

ENGLISH THEATRE: 1947-52

There was a tremendous surge of theatrical production in post-war England, in part with the help of some government subsidies *via* a National Arts Council, which went far toward cancelling the impression that the modern British drama had ended as it had virtually begun with Bernard Shaw. The impression had been created by a continual concert of mild domestic imbroglios and brittle chatter on the stage while the Western world was beginning to go up in flames. That chatter was hardly interrupted by the occasional rise of organ-notes from the political right in the case of Eliot's *Murder in the Cathedral* and some thunder on the left from Auden and Isherwood's anti-fascist revue *The Dog Beneath the Skin* and anti-imperialistic poetic drama *The Ascent of F6*.

England became a busy hive of theatre workers in hamlets as well as cities, and the honey of many an excellent stage production tasted sweet to Americans whether encountered in England by the tourist or in New York by his more sedentary fellow-citizen who patronized the Old Vic, John Gielgud's company, and other companies that visited the United States. It was difficult for me to decide whether I was not more gratified by English productions seen on Broadway than by those I saw in England.

In 1946, indeed, New York playgoers were filled with envy of England on the occasion of a visit by the Old Vic company revived after the bombing of its theatre in the London *blitz* of 1941 when Laurence Olivier and Ralph Richardson joined forces. With John Burrell they brought the Old Vic repertory to greater heights than it had previously achieved, and it was no wonder that post-war England should have taken steps to make the "Vic" the official theatre of the nation. True, their *Uncle Vanya* made little impression in New York—the production was rather too British in timbre and the quiet force of Chekhov's drama, somnolently staged, was lost in the vast Century Theatre. But singular merit pertained to their productions of both parts of *Henry IV,* Sheridan's fluffy but charming travesty *The Critic* in which Olivier played Puff as the epitome of dandyism, and the Yeats version of *Oedipus the King*.

Aside from the general excellence of the ensemble, New Yorkers were not going to forget quickly Olivier as Hotspur and Justice Shallow, and Richardson as Falstaff, to which nothing less than a long essay could do justice. In Richardson's Falstaff we had not only the fat reveler who lards the earth as he walks, but the rogue of indomitable heart who maintains his individuality against the slings of nature and slights of his boon-companions with aplomb. Nor could we forget Joyce Redman's gloriously debauched, rag-doll tart Doll Tearsheet, who moved as if alcohol had dissolved every bone in her body. An indifferent performance of Prince Hal did not cancel playgoers' gratitude. And most memorable was the *Oedipus*. That Yeats's version, which abbreviated the tragedy's great choral odes, made the Old Vic's triumph and the audience's response relatively easy was overlooked.

Never before had a Greek tragedy proved so overwhelming within the memory of American playgoers. And never before had Olivier revealed such stature as an actor as in his playing of the fate-entangled hero of a play that many playgoers were ready, without benefit of a classical education, to regard then as the greatest tragedy ever written. No one present at the performance failed to applaud the deep-throated animal cries with which the trapped Oedipus reacted to the discovery of his incest and his appearance on the stage after that event with the blood-soaked eyes the king had pierced within the palace. Nor could admiration be withheld from Piper's pre-Periclean setting consisting of grotesque statues of the pitiless primeval gods of Thebes. This *Oedipus* was altogether rooted in primal experience and primal consciousness. Nothing so perturbing and so profoundly purging as this Old Vic production had been experienced by playgoers within their memory. After the Old Vic's departure, New York seemed rather empty.

The general conclusion I shared with others after my 1950 visit in England was that the British were developing excellent acting companies, that the actors were far better spoken than actors on our side of the contracted ocean, and that the performances and productions manifested a far greater sense of style than could be found on Broadway. My only reservations were that often the speaking was better than the acting and that some of our own performances and productions exhibited greater vigor and vitality. The conclusion I would have been delighted to be able to share with everyone was that the English certainly knew how to make considerably more use of the English heritage of dramatic literature with their numerous revivals of Shakespearian drama, including *Much Ado About Nothing* and *Measure for Measure,* generally neglected in our own bailiwick, Ben Jonson's *Bartholomew Fair,* Farquhar's *The Beaux' Stratagem* (enchantingly performed), and many other plays.

At the same time, I found it less possible to register enthusiasm for the new British plays, as I indicate elsewhere in this book. The vogue of poetic plays found me pleased but not entranced. The rise of some morally uplifting dramas amidst the kind of comedy of manners at the writing of which British authors are generally adept commanded my interest without quite eliciting rhapsodies from me. It seemed to me that the British drama still showed a stronger leaning toward circumspection than inspiration. Some productions, even in the Shakespearian preserves of England, also left me with the suspicion that the genteel tradition of theatre had survived the war. And if this is a tribute to England's tenacity, it is no great compliment to its theatre. The following notes, however, will record some of my first-hand impressions better than any further generalizations.

I. BRITISH POST-WAR LIBERALISM

An Inspector Calls is one of several plays by J. B. Priestley written under the spur of those liberal sympathies which made this erstwhile sophisticated essayist, novelist and playwright a powerful voice in England's war-time propaganda battles. Priestley continued to be the spokesman for an intensified social conscience and championship of the common man. *An Inspector Calls* is a morality play, in which the author combined his partisanship with a previous interest in time-relativity that had led to the writing of several odd but curiously unstimulating plays such as *Time and the Conways* during the thirties. The mixture of morality and time-relativity in *An Inspector Calls* was a curious compound, but it made the play one of the first products of the new British social "seriousness" to qualify for export.

As is usual in such exercises, the moral earnestness is at some variance with the devices of plot that suggest Sardou trickery, here given a metaphysical turn which may pass for "poetry" in some circles, as a précis will suggest: A police inspector visits a well-to-do English family just as it is celebrating its daughter's engagement to an eligible young man. He has come to investigate the suicide of a poor girl who had been dismissed from a position, had lived on the bounty of one young man, had been the mistress of another, and had been turned down by a social welfare agency when she became pregnant. Under the inspector's quiet but firm scrutiny, the mask is ripped off the entire family and its prospective son-in-law. Each of them, it turns out, has contributed to the girl's misery. None of them is without guilt. When the inspector, who has behaved suspiciously, departs, they check on him and learn that there is no such inspector and that there has been no girl suicide. This is sufficient for all but the younger members of the household to shed their acquired sense of responsibility and return to their complacency—until the telephone rings, and they learn that a girl of identical description has just committed suicide!

For all the quiescence of the action, which does induce some tedium, and in spite of the incredibility of the resolution (the inspector is an indefinably supernatural figure and evidently has anticipated the girl's suicide or Time is playing tricks again for Mr. Priestley), *An Inspector Calls* exerts a mild fascination. If the writing is competent rather than brilliant, mere competence seems appropriate to the story and theme. Brilliance in this case could have struck us as mere flamboyance, although Bernard Shaw could have negotiated the brilliance without suffering disaster. If the moral is being driven home in the manner of a tract, the play is steeped in a social compassion that has the effect of sincerity by virtue of its simplicity and reserve. If the characters are unoriginal, here and there they ring true, and the mysterious inspector, as played by Thomas Mitchell, was quietly disturbing. Somehow, moreover, J. B. Priestley managed to convey the pathos of the never-present suicide admirably. She may be faceless to us but she is never actually remote; nor is the possibility of our own responsibility for the misery of others unreal to us as the play progresses.

Excitement does not indeed seem to be the long suit of the British dramatists, and perhaps it is a silly habit of us constantly to demand excitement from playwrights who have something else to offer. Yet, in a curious way, Terence Rattigan's *The Winslow Boy,* another moral tract, communicates excitement. The play dramatizes the famous Archer-Shee case of a little naval cadet whose father fought his case right up to Parliament when the lad was unjustly dismissed from Britain's Annapolis for stealing. The stubborn fight of the father, odd and covered with the antimacassar manners of the Victorian period, becomes something arrestingly fine. It is the test of the political health of a nation that a case concerning the dismissal of a thirteen-year-old cadet, who is very happy in another school, becomes a national issue. The implications of the play are among the most exciting elements of the story. Although much of the plotting after the first act is too routine to make the play memorable, *The Winslow Boy* holds the attention and the sympathies as many a more original piece of playwriting does not. Perhaps the real reason lies, not merely in the theme, but in the fact that it is projected through characters whose somewhat staid exterior covers a wealth of spirit. There is an appealing contrast here between the usually polite reserve of the characters and their persevering quest for justice. The father is a Don Quixote with an umbrella.

II. ENGLISH COMIC STYLE

For all the increased earnestness that could be noted in the English theatre, however, comedy and the staging of comedy retained an old allegiance in the British Isles. I was particularly struck by this fact in

1950 when I attended London productions of *The Beaux' Stratagem* and the Peter Brook production of *Ring Round the Moon,* Christopher Fry's adaptation of Jean Anouilh's Parisian comedy. (Something in the very air of the English theatre must be favorable to refined and glossy sport, and I readily confess that I do not know what it is. I cannot understand, for example, why I enjoyed *Ring Round the Moon* so hugely in London whereas the virtually identical production in New York's Martin Beck Theatre about a year later left me only moderately—actually, somewhat impatiently—entertained.) New York was given a good example of Britain's prowess in the field of comedy, and could follow a lesson if not actually profit from it, when John Gielgud brought over his productions of two English classics *The Importance of Being Earnest* and *Love for Love.*

Nevertheless, we must guard against making a fetish of English comedy, and so must the British. In many instances, English comedy does not well out of the pure Pierian spring any longer; nor is even the playing of comedy by the British invariably effervescent. A performance of *Tartuffe* at the Lyric-Hammersmith, for example, seemed to me to leave a good deal to be desired, owing especially to a too labored, if highly competent, performance in the principal role. An Arts Club production of *Heartbreak House* impressed me as only a degree or two brighter than Orson Welles's Mercury Theatre production in New York in 1938. In playwriting, I have found any number of efforts, except Coward's *Private Lives* and *Blithe Spirit* (and the former with some reservations) and always excepting the best of Shaw, rather less than unfailing in aplomb or invention. The style, too (and in this respect I include the best of Noel Coward), scintillates very infrequently. And in quite a number of comedies, among which Dodie Smith's are best known in New York as a result of productions of *Call It a Day* and *Dear Octopus,* the infiltration of sentiment recalls the general fate of English comedy since its heyday during the Restoration. *Love for Love,* with its humor out of Charles II's day still intact, could serve as a reminder to the historically minded.

Written by the greatest of Restoration wits in 1695, *Love for Love* has enjoyed continuous critical esteem. With *The Way of the World,* written in 1700 by the same "Phoebus Apollo of the Mall," it marks the peak of the English comedy of manners. Yet it has been decidedly overshadowed on the stage by *The Rivals, The School for Scandal, She Stoops to Conquer* and many inferior plays. The historical explanation is that the English stage suffered a change after the seventeenth century. Puritan conscience reasserted itself after the frivolous interlude of "good King Charles's golden days."

The explanation has not only considerable validity but applicability.

Neither the return of sophistication with Wilde and Shaw nor the brief spirit of scepticism after the First World War has materially changed the rules of entertainment. Comedy in the English-speaking countries is, for better or worse, largely *sentimental comedy*. In England, James M. Barrie proved the success of the formula, which consists of one part acetic acid and nine parts saccharine. Sentimental comedy allows us to roam far indeed, so long as it keeps us on the leash of convention. Barrie's sentimentality was not merely a matter of tears and smiles; that alone would not have assured him success in an age that was shaken by the iconoclasm of Shaw, St. John Hankin, and Stanley Houghton. Barrie presumably also purveyed scepticism, cynicism, and unconventionality. But no sooner had the customer bought the commodity and thought himself in complete possession of it than he found it taken away from him by the "little minister's" sleight-of-hand. A perfect example is *The Admirable Crichton*. The customer thought he was getting a "transvaluation of values" when the perfect butler became master of the island while his employers became his servants. But the old values were neatly restored when the family was brought to England. The butler returned to his low estate and obsequious manner, the employers recovered their high estate, and all was right with the world.

The case of Noel Coward, once considered the *enfant terrible* of the stage, is somewhat more complicated. On the evidence of *Private Lives* and *Blithe Spirit,* Coward would seem to be the exception to the rule of sentimentality. He was regarded as such and acclaimed as a model of daring by the post-World War I generations. Overlooking the *Cavalcade* patriotism, the *Point Valaine* melodramatism, and the tragic banalities in Coward's work, many of us noted his bright and breezy sophistication and called him blessed. We saw the mask but failed to catch the face, which is that of a Harley Street doctor who knows that the old virtues of clean living and plain thinking—home, hearth, exercise, and good diet—are the best no matter how often his profession keeps him in touch with the aberrations. Moreover, whenever Harley Street lets itself go, it is as sentimental as the veriest Babbitt. Coward's fancied sophistication is skindeep. It is an effect rather than an ingrained reality. The champagne is really beer and pretzels. We are fooled because when the clever magician is in good form and is putting on a show he is entirely a showman.

If the show is comedy the mood must be gay, and Coward knows how to be gay without making his audience uncomfortable by assaulting it. That would be bad for business, and Coward is a good businessman. He has convictions, it is true, but they are so close to the average customers' notions of honor, patriotism, and decency that they never startle. He is, indeed, never so bad as when he occasionally forces himself to startle them, when he tries for sensation, as in *Point Valaine*. His forte, when he isn't cutting capers, lies in hewing to the line laid down by respectability. That is why he can be so successful with plays and films like *Cavalcade, In Which We Serve* and *Brief Encounter*. The latter, for example, is an excellent motion picture, and it seems extraordinarily adult in its treatment of a middle-aged romance because it departs from Hollywood's jejune romances. But can anyone imagine anything more favorable to the norms of behavior, the conventions of our morality. Wife eschews an extra-marital romance that threatens to become tawdry and returns to a forgiving husband. Absolutely proper people return to the proprieties after a brief encounter with impropriety. As a stage play, incidentally, *Brief Encounter* was rather dismally maudlin; that is what most of us thought in New York where it bore the title *Still Life*. The film is vastly superior.

In spite of many decades replete with bright hucksters of humor, Bernard Shaw remains the lone heretic, in splendid isolation on the tight little island. The reason for this is, paradoxically, that he has been the only genuine moralist among them. Only a man who like Shaw could insist that all true art must be moral, that indeed life without moral passion is worthless, would have the impulse really to *upset* the apple-cart. Shaw was the only one who didn't like the apples. Being reverent he could follow irreverence to revolutionary lengths. Being inveterately responsible to standards of his own, he could hack away at the mean sensual man's standards with such a cutting edge as to invite the charge of irresponsibility. Only Shaw's heterodoxy was the genuine article because it was his exclusively cherished doxy. And this exclusiveness was the final insult to the other people's doxy.

It might be argued, of course, that in this respect Shaw was himself a sentimentalist. That is surely the case, not only because no sentient man is completely devoid of sentimentality but because humanitarianism and freedom are sentimental conceptions. The greatest heretics are probably the greatest sentimentalists. (A brilliant Jesuit once said to me that he hated sentimentality as much as he hated heresy. Pursuing the argument further, he noted that in causation or effect heresy was invariably a form of sentimentality.) That is also why sentimentalists are formidable. Man without attachment is never dangerous because he is automatically removed from the fields of propaganda and action. He who knows the price of everything and the value of nothing has no incentive. It is indisputable, however, that in his time Shaw was the only British comedian who exploded *accepted* sentiment. If he occasionally upheld convention, as in *Candida,* where the wife remains faithful to her husband, it was for an unconventional reason and purpose. If he doffed his hat to genuine goodness (as in *Androcles and the Lion, The Devil's Disciple, The Shewing*

Up of Blanco Posnet), he did so unsentimentally; and his best people are invariably the most troublesome to the guardians of convention.

Congreve's way—and we return deviously to Congreve—was different. So far as one can tell, he was completely devoid of moral passion and reformatory intentions. Although a sharp observer of the manners of his time, he evinced no desire to correct that which he ridiculed. His was the true Olympian attitude, which he shared more or less with colleagues of the Restoration stage, and there is no better way to thwart "sentimental comedy." If Gielgud's revival of *Love for Love* proved less satisfactory than his production of *The Importance of Being Earnest,* it is because he played Congreve's comedy for sentiment in the sense that he appeared to side too much with the play's lovers, especially with Valentine. As the well-read reader may recall, the main complication in *Love for Love* arises from the fact that the young blade Valentine has squandered a fortune in pursuit of the elusive beauty Angelica and is in danger of being disinherited in favor of his sailor brother Ben until Angelica outwits his father.

In staging *The Importance of Being Earnest,* Gielgud understood that Wilde's farce was to be totally disconnected from reality regardless of the possibility of finding more than a modicum of social satire in the writing. *The Importance of Being Earnest* was a pure farce for Gielgud, and rightly so. The complications are wholly improbable; and the main characters should not be taken seriously for a moment even if they take themselves seriously. Gielgud's course was then clear, and his play-acting was unmitigated by any symptom of emotion. In retrospect, Gielgud's playing of "Ernest" in a vein of comic melancholy may indeed have been less deliberate than it was characteristic of the fine actor who gave us one of the best modern Hamlets about a decade ago. Nonetheless, the effect was inviolably comic. His earnestness in a maze of self-created and wildly composed complications could only make the role doubly amusing. He made Wilde's comedy as fantastically unreal as it is by behaving as though it were real to him. The incongruity between the actual situations and his serious response to them was inexhaustibly funny.

Mediocre productions have presented Wilde's plays not in their own terms, but in terms of the usual amorphous, slice-of-life, smear-of-jam, realism. The audience was invited by such uninspired productions to accept and enjoy the plays as "reality." Since an audience is not ordinarily insane, it could not help noting the obvious—namely, that Wilde's characters were ectoplasmic wraiths, and that his plots were absurd and shoddy. Both as director and leading actor of the Wilde production, John Gielgud knew better than that. He knew that he was dealing with a nonsensical story, and that he had to present it with such aplomb and such impeccable artificiality in its own mannered terms that the nonsense would become gratifying. It has its own consistency, its own shape and texture, its own "life." To realize this one had only to watch Gielgud—infinitely wearied of the vulgarities of flesh, passion, desire, and will—lazily handle a hand-kerchief, lounge about, walk over to greet a character lackadaisically, or pretend to have just returned from the funeral of his non-existent brother. One had only to hear Margaret Rutherford, who played the invincibly snobbish Lady Bracknell, reply to Gielgud's admission that he smokes: "I am glad to hear it. A man should always have an occupation of some kind." Or to hear her rattle on to her nephew Jack, who has said that he knows nothing: "I am pleased to hear it. I do not approve of anything that tampers with natural ignorance. Ignorance is like a delicate exotic fruit; touch it and the bloom is gone. The whole theory of modern education is unsound. Fortunately, in England, at any rate, education produces no effect whatsoever. If it did, it would prove a serious danger to the upper classes, and probably lead to acts of violence in Grosvenor Square. What is your income?" The delivery was cool, detached, imperturbable. The woman spoke like an attitude incarnate rather than a woman who happens to have an opinion or is trying to appear clever. She spoke, behaved as a matter of course, because she *was* the attitude, not a person holding it. That is what really makes the play "artificial comedy."

And the final point that may be made here is that not only do such lines, comportment, and depersonalized existence produce inviolate non-sense—nonsense that is always consistent, that has a kind of mad consist-ency, and is uncontaminated with real feeling—but, paradoxically, *sense*. The result is nonsense on one plane which projects a trajectory of sense in another dimension, the real world. Reality is brilliantly satirized because the actual world, which is supposed to be a world that makes sense, is equated with a world of sheer nonsense as evoked by Wilde's comedy. Just reread the above quotations, and note how upper-class snobbishness is reduced to absolute absurdity by Lady Bracknell's unconscious candor—a candor such as "never was on sea or land" and can only be a desecration and the comic poet's dream. Wilde achieves his comic effect by behav-ing as if the actual world isn't even worth satirizing, just as we don't take the trouble to tell a madman that he is mad because it wouldn't do any good—that is, *it wouldn't make sense* to the madman if we told him he is devoid of sense.

Wilde is taking the insanity or nonsensicality of the world as a matter of course, which is obviously the final insult to the world, or rather to that portion of it which he has deigned to notice. Gielgud did the same thing. Both had "style." In the last analysis, style is a matter of *consistency,* of having a distinct system of relationship between the parts, of containing the material in a closed system, so to speak, and of shaping or transforming the raw material of life more or less so that it will conform to the created system.

Congreve, however, seems to have tripped up our talented actor and director. Either that or Mr. Gielgud was incapable of relinquishing the role of Hamlet! The melancholy Prince was much in evidence in Gielgud's playing of Valentine. This is patently wrong, of course. Valentine's past prodigality, his social intercourse in a "Utopia of gallantry" (as Charles Lamb put it), and his playing madman in order to avoid being disinherited disconnect him from the world of genuine emotion. So does the tone of Congreve's writing, not to mention Congreve's extravagant gallery of absurd characters. Merriment rather than melancholy must be the tone of the production, and the play must emerge as a revel of high society with only one frame of reference—namely, the absurdity of man in an artificial world. Congreve may have fooled Mr. Gielgud, I say, because, unlike Oscar Wilde in *The Importance of Being Earnest,* Congreve dealt with the absurd rather than the impossible and therefore predicated Valentine's love for Angelica on greater reality than "Ernest's" love. But Mr. Gielgud should not have been so fooled. However genuinely Valentine may love his Angelica at heart, he cannot afford to manifest seriousness in his milieu, nor is it true to his character and reputation to do so. Besides, Congreve's game simply cannot be played that way, or it ceases to be a game, in which case it ceases to be a comedy. We can, at most, allow Valentine a few scattered moments of seriousness. We can indicate that there is a real lover behind the mask, but we must do so with the lightest flick of expression, for Congreve's comedy is about masks not faces.

Mr. Gielgud played Valentine as a love-sick melancholiac, a fellow of great nobility but little spirit, a victim rather than the creator of circumstances. This performance cast a pallor on the entire façade of artificial comedy. Angelica, for instance, was played by Pamela Brown with absolute rightness of wit and gaiety, and it is to Gielgud's credit as a director that he did not cloud this superb performance. Yet it was difficult to take pleasure in Pamela Brown's charade while Valentine is so plainly miserable. One kept on wishing she weren't so inviolably clever, for the sake of the poor fellow. Had not breeding interfered, one might have called her a name or two. If Valentine, on the contrary, were played as the man of mettle that I believe Congreve drew, I shouldn't have minded a bit; in that case, lad and lass would be well matched, and I could have settled down to watching the sport that our modernists somberly call the duel of the sexes. Then one could leave sobriety to Valentine's devoted free-speaking friend Scandal, admirably played by George Hayes, enjoying him as the one real person because he is the only uninvolved one as the objective observer of the antic world.

Whether or not my reasoning from my impressions is as tight as a noose (and I intend none for Mr. Gielgud and his company because they still managed to gratify us with civilized entertainment), it was evident that the British, too, do not work with impeccable detachment. That they are nonetheless exemplary in many instances, as in the playing of *The Importance of Being Earnest,* is our gain as well as Britain's. It is in the writing of new plays, such as recent Coward and Rattigan plays, including the latter's *O Mistress Mine* which the Lunts carried to success beyond its merits both in England and here, that we have the most evidence that England no longer belongs to Charles II—nor to that much greater monarch Bernard Shaw.

The conclusion given above received considerable support from one of the most successful British comedies to reach Broadway, the quite extraordinary actor Robert Morley's vehicle, *Edward, My Son.* The play is the portrait of a unique yet representative man who responds to a perfectly natural impulse, the paternal one, but who is far too egotistic to keep it within reasonable bounds. If that were all there is to this play, it would be a minor excursion into humor and pathos. But the authors, Robert Morley and Noel Langley, looked beyond the old-fashioned psychology books that used to reduce all behavior to the common rule of instinct. They saw their character, Andrew Holt, in the context of society and created him as a small businessman, vulnerable to the venal component in commercial enterprises. Threatened by the possibility that his cherished little boy (a projection for the father of his own considerable ego) would remain lame for life unless taken to Switzerland for an expensive operation, Andrew Holt set fire to his business and collected the insurance on it. Success in his initial effort convinced him that ruthlessness paid off and confirmed him in a pattern of behavior that brought him fortune and the peerage. In the course of this dubious career, which enabled him to overindulge the boy, Andrew Holt ruined his son's character and his wife's life. It is only by a ruse that he is deprived of an opportunity to start blighting his little grandson's life, too.

Peter Ashmore's direction of the production, on view in New York after a succesful run in London, was as silken and tensile as a spider's web. It certainly held for an evening of good theatre. Robert Morley's performance was a series of feats; this accomplished actor had tricks of theatricality at his finger tips. Only his uncanny precision now and then gave him away as a stunt artist, and even then his very substantial personality managed to conceal much of the calculated nature of his virtuosity. Peggy Ashcroft, playing his luckless wife, even outdid him in this respect. Although she aged perceptibly during the play and worked up to scenes of alcoholic debilitation that rarely fail to be theatrical in any performance, Miss Ashcroft portrayed an utterly believable human being. Her greatest *tour de force* was her success in making us forget that her performance was one.

Gratification would be an adequate estimate of the English play, however, only if one overlooked its essential character as an almost continual *coup de théâtre* rather than a play which flares into theatre because its life substance is incandescent. Closely considered, *Edward, My Son* constitutes as much of a fabrication for effect as any plot in an old-fashioned melodrama. Its scenes are calculated, its effects timed, and its framework artificial, with Mr. Morley appearing in front of the curtain as Andrew Holt playing narrator and, so to speak, tipping off the audience. It is plain that the authors of the play were actually no more involved in their play than Andrew Holt was really concerned with his own destiny. Cleverness was all!

III. MATTER AND MANNER

It cannot be said on the basis of recent English playwriting that our cousins in the British Isles have been more fortunate than we in recent years. Nevertheless, at least two of the three plays that came from them in the fall of 1949 had their points. Rattigan's *Harlequinade* is something we can charitably overlook. It is a "curtain-raiser" inflated into a futile hour-long farce, although it is no doubt more amusing to the author's countrymen than to us. Home's *Yes, M'Lord* is in the same class, with its references to the life of the landed gentry and to minor political aspects of life under the Labor government. Moreover, its story of how a butler runs on the Tory ticket and a young peer on a Labor Party platform is played mostly for the farcical value of a reversal of situations.

Mr. Home is no Bernard Shaw and does not make intellectual capital and high comedy out of his notion. He has, nevertheless, turned out agreeable dialogue, and he has created an excellent central character-sketch, if not quite a complete character, in the candidate's father, the Earl of Lister who stands above the scene of political conflict as a fox- and rabbit-hunting Olympian. The point of the sketch is that peerage and its privileges have been so long in the Earl's possession that he is blithely indifferent to them. He feels so confident of the essential soundness of England that even radicalism holds no terrors for him. He would no more think of protecting England from new social policies than he would think of promoting them. Peerage and position as Lord Lieutenant make him a neutral among contenders. It is his business to welcome at home whichever candidate gets into office. It's a terrible bore, but it's his duty and that's that. Here, indeed, is a comic idea that can be hatched only in an old country that has weathered much history. A. E. Matthews made the Earl of Lister a character out of some novel by Dickens, which was an added pleasure.

With all these advantages and some humor at the expense of social-climbing Laborites, *Yes, M'Lord* is still something that would be more acceptable in a book by Wodehouse than on the American stage. But it is, nonetheless, more civilized entertainment than our home-baked comedies of middle-class life which lack yeast and are flatter than a Child's Restaurant pancake.

Terence Rattigan's hour-length drama, *The Browning Version,* is a work of considerable poignancy. It is the story of a defeated schoolmaster in what we call a "private" and the English call a "public" school. He has become quite a martinet, and is neither liked nor respected by his colleagues and students. But as Rattigan unfolds the sources of his failure as man and instructor, this Mr. Chips in reverse reveals himself as a profoundly human individual undone by marriage to a nymphomaniacal and vengeful woman. For the most part a "slice-of-life" type of play, it is impressive in its honesty. The author may also be commended for dispensing with the usual local color of a "public school," to which British writers like to help themselves rather generously.

Mr. Rattigan, who hews close to the line of psychological drama, has a knack for making dry-as-dust people we would call "Victorian" intensely alive, as he proved earlier in *The Winslow Boy.* In *The Browning Version* he has, moreover, treated the relations of husband and wife with almost Strindbergian power, particularly in the case of the schoolmaster's wife who boasts of her conquests to her husband. He has been very successful in presenting, as Henry James would say, the misery of the superior sensibility at the mercy of a gross-grained nature. Since the former was ably conveyed by Maurice Evans and the latter by the superb actress Edna Best, the effect was arresting. If Rattigan has achieved no masterpiece, he has at least written a tense and compassionate drama. He has gone far toward becoming a playwright deserving of respect since he started his career on the eve of World War II with the vacuous farce *French without Tears,* the trivial nature of which Mr. Rattigan then justified on the grounds that England on the brink of war needed to be spared seriousness on stage.

It could not be said, however, that this author, along with his colleagues, was now entirely dedicated to somber playwriting, as the above-mentioned *Harlequinade,* his comedy for the Lunts' *O Mistress Mine,* and other light pieces continued to remind us. Not even the trials of the war-period and its less than halcyon aftermath could wean Britain from its allegiance to the urbanities of polished comedy. Not even a Labour Party government could "proletarianize" the British out of the country-house and

London upper-class-flat type of humor, and I, for one, rather like the debonair British theatre for its refusal to wear sackcloth and overalls. A nation that can be simultaneously bland and earnest, and that attends to manners as well as matters in our midcentury world, stands for my ingrained "bourgeois" notion of civilization. More so indeed than the more volatile Parisian view of civilization in *boulevard* comedy.

IV. ENGLISH MORALITY DRAMA

In Christopher Fry's *A Sleep of Prisoners,* it was once more evident that Mr. Fry can make literature out of drama, though it seemed less certain that he can make drama out of literature. A reading of the published play (Oxford University Press) will disclose fine writing, reflectiveness, and fervor, without establishing *A Sleep of Prisoners* as a good play. Most of the merits of the piece were lost on the audience in the church in which the play was staged (it was staged in a church in London, too), partly because it was difficult for the actors to project their lines from the choir of the Church of St. James in New York, and partly because of the discontinuous yet repetitious structure of this symbolic work. Perhaps the play would be more effective if it were presented in an "arena theatre," in which case the verse lines could be more easily followed and the episodes could be both more continuous and better knit together for the spectator. The audience, moreover, could participate in the ritual intended for it by the playwright.

That the rise of a new poetic drama in England is a welcome advent is beyond dispute. Since the American ear is less attuned than the British to the music of words and the turn of the phrases, our audiences are apt to flounder when the meaning is not obvious and when the drama is insufficiently relieved by familiar details such as T. S. Eliot provided with his drawing-room scenes in *The Cocktail Party.* We need a more recognizable idiom for American poetic drama and, perhaps, a different rhythm—probably a trochaic meter. Mr. Fry, in turn, needed a play less composed of didactic fragments from the Bible, or a more vertical kind of drama, to do justice to his exalted aims. His episodes—vignettes of Cain and Abel, Abraham and Isaac, David and Absalom, and Shadrach, Meshac, and Abednego—are in themselves quite good, although overladen now and then with some strained metaphysical writing. But they are not easily held together by the cement of a dream technique by means of which four prisoners of war in a church behind the lines have successive and interlocking dreams in which they play a variety of biblical roles. Nor do the dreams move uninterruptedly toward the author's appeal for new ways of living and defending the Christian ideal. The dilemma Fry examines is perhaps best defined by his own lines:

To be strong beyond all [evil] action is the strength
To have. But how do men and forbearance meet? . . .
But where, in the maze of right and wrong,
Are we to do what action?

The question is a good one, even if Mr. Fry's answer gets lost in a maze of words; and when was it more immediate! It does credit to Mr. Fry, who has here shed some of the puckishness that vitiated his far more successful play *The Lady's Not for Burning*. We want also to credit the British theatre with efforts to create a drama that we can respect as literature and thought. But the commendable effort has still to be thoroughly realized in the theatre. Why and how Ibsen, Strindberg, Chekhov, Shaw, O'Casey, and others succeeded from twenty to seventy years ago is a large question. That they did succeed reminds us that the one thing that cannot be claimed in England any more than in America is progress in modern playwriting.

V. THE GLOSS OF ENGLISH STAGE PRODUCTION

Although there was anything but unanimity concerning the merits of the productions of *Caesar and Cleopatra* and *Antony and Cleopatra,* and although attentive playgoers registered considerable disappointment in this or that interpretation, no one could doubt that the visit of Olivier's company from London in the fall of 1952 marked the high point of the New York season up to the new year. It is difficult, indeed, for a critic to refrain from pointing out that the English theatre enjoys some distinct advantages over our Broadway stage. Not the least of these is the noble breed of British actors who dignify theatrical art by devoting their talents and resources to producing distinguished drama meticulously and tastefully. The English nation regards its theatre as an institution rather than as a horse-race. Its performers are sensible of an obligation to sustain the stage at its highest literary levels almost as a matter of course. The actors, moreover, are able to function as *companies* rather than as itinerant individuals moving from one haphazard production to another, in consequence of which they tend to excel in ensemble. Some of our individual performances, especially in realistic plays of modest literary pretensions, may exhibit greater intensity or vigor. But there are usually superior compensations in England's well-rounded, carefully meshing ensembles such as the one Sir Lawrence brought to our shores. At least I have never seen a professional British performance of a notable play as uneven in casting and ragged in acting as the same season's Broadway production of *Saint Joan*.

An important consideration aside from performance is the fact that no producing organization on Broadway finds it feasible to rotate two plays more or less complementary and yet as stylistically different as Shaw's and Shakespeare's pieces. The Olivier program was a small repertory-company achievement, a token of the British repertory tradition; and the advantages for the playgoer consisted of a sharpening of contrasts, as well as some clarification of their historical basis, which is rather dim to playgoers. Shaw's girlish Cleopatra grows into the mature serpent of the Nile as we watch the two pieces in sequence, starting with *Caesar and Cleopatra*. At the same time, the middle-aged, equable Caesar prepares us for the impulse-ruled Antony in a way which intensifies the meaning of both works—namely, the salutary potentialities of intellect and the destructiveness of infatuation. University theatres and some community theatres in America provide this sort of orientation with some of their programs; Broadway provides none. Also a theatrical season that is a disorderly mélange can never provide the public with an adequate cultural reality in the form of theatre, such as that supplied by English and continental repertories of classics and near-classics. The Broadway playgoer's mind is too full of *disjecta membra* to form illuminating relations, let alone to make those frequent comparisons between different treatments of the same masterpiece which exercise the taste and judgment of audiences accustomed to see plays repeated season after season. It is possible to find Londoners who can recall and actually have jotted down impressions of numerous Shakespearean productions; they can compare stage business and the interpretation of the main roles over periods ranging from several decades to half a century.

That comparisons could be made between Vivien Leigh as the adolescent and the grown-up Cleopatra and between Olivier as Caesar in one play and Antony in another enlivened our playgoing experience at the Olivier productions. And more possibilities were open to those who in previous seasons had seen Katharine Cornell's womanly Cleopatra and Godfrey Tearle's manly Antony in Shakespeare's play, or Lilli Palmer's ingénue Cleopatra and Sir Cedric Hardwick's Caesar in Shaw's version. Thus, Tearle's soldierly Antony suggested more powerfully than Olivier the man whom a designing Octavius would have reason to fear and whose fall aroused awe because Tearle's Antony was one of the pillars of the Graeco-Roman world and not at all the sort of individual who would normally succumb to an enervating infatuation. Olivier's slighter figure seemed somewhat dapper by comparison with Tearle's sturdy frame. He also moved and spoke more lightly and with greater modulation—as is, indeed, natural for so adept a performer; his feet and vocal apparatus seemed better trained for the stage than for the battlefield. Still, Sir Laurence conveyed the mercurial nature of the character more than adequately, and he rounded out the tragic story with numerous bits of well thought out stage business, especially in the scenes with Octavius and Octavia in which Antony is walking a political tightrope.

Olivier certainly also made a better Antony in Shakespeare than a Caesar in Shaw. He effected a considerable transformation of his personality when he played the latter, but the role did not seem quite natural to him. There were occasions, such as the famous address to the Sphinx in the first act, when Shaw's lines sounded far more Shakespearean than Shavian. They sounded altogether too heroic for the self-communion of the weary empire builder drawn by Shakespeare's self-appointed successor.

In Shaw's play, Vivien Leigh was quite delightful at the beginning, and always fetching. More at home in her part than Olivier in his, she translated adolescence into a quality of grace by means of a remarkably flexible body. At times, her stage movement had the controlled vivacity of a dance. There being fewer occasions for so mobile a performance in later parts of the play, Miss Leigh became a more static personality there, and she was generally less effective in her reposeful moments. (I am inclined to consider this a reflection on Shaw's characterization, too. The range of his characterization in the play may be sufficiently wide for his fable, but his portrait of Cleopatra does not supply those depths that make an actor's part as interesting when he is physically inactive as when he is active.) As Shakespeare's Cleopatra, Miss Leigh pulled out all the stops of her talent, and deserved credit for exceptional virtuosity, which extended to her voice, deeper (if somewhat artificially so) than it had ever been when she played Shaw's queen. She even attained tragic elevation at the end, and she played most expertly in the scenes in which she seeks and receives the messenger's reports on Octavia.

If a certain depth was missing in the performance, the reason was that she never quite caught the mature Cleopatra of Shakespeare; this, not for want of adequate talent so much as for reasons of physical endowment. Missing throughout the performance, indeed, was the personality of an experienced seductress capable of intoxicating an experienced Antony. The power of Shakespeare's tragedy of passion lies, after all, in the fact that his lovers are decidedly *not* in their springtime. Actors in these roles should convince us that they are seasoned enough not to yield to a consuming passion if they could *possibly* resist it. There is no other way of projecting superb tension in the tragedy. That Miss Leigh could not make any notable experience of that tension is perhaps the crux of any appraisal of the limitations of her performance.

As for the total effect of these most expertly managed productions, opinions must differ sharply. A middle course between enthusiasm and negation seems to me the most accurate one. Expert stage direction made *Caesar and Cleopatra* an admirably fluid production, a chronicle consistently interesting, and a stage show entirely attractive. In a large theatre such as New York's Ziegfeld, the eye-filling showmanship of the production had practical advantages. Judged in terms of Shaw's intention and best execution, however, the staging would have to be set down as more suitable for Shakespearean than Shavian drama. The play was "over-produced" by the company's stage director Michael Benthall, with the result that attention was too often directed at events rather than at the Shavian idea of the Superman-as-political-leader. As Shaw might have expressed this criticism, the production gave an impression of too much "action" and too little "discussion." The lavish staging also dwindled Olivier's stature as Caesar; he was in competition with the spectacle. A leaner *Caesar and Cleopatra* production would have been more serviceable to Shaw. This, even if Mr. Benthall and his scene designer, the enormously talented Roger Furse, did create some stunning effects interesting in themselves, as when they had characters walking to their destination through the revolving scenery. *Antony and Cleopatra* was even more "beautifully" visualized, with tastefully economical stylization, a group of truncated Roman columns serving to suggest Rome and another group of Egyptian ones with pediments establishing the Nilotic background, except in the scenes set in Cleopatra's "Monument."

In the secondary roles of *Antony and Cleopatra* there was much excellence, with Robert Helpmann providing a thoroughly keen-minded and cold-hearted Octavius (he had also been excellent as Shaw's mercurial Greek merchant Apollodorus), Katherine Blake making a charming Charmian, and Robert Hyde White representing a credibly elderly and ineffectual Lepidus, the third member of the Roman triumvirate. Only Harry Andrews, who played Enobarbus, was inadequate in spite of a suitable stage presence and the general impressiveness of his comportment. His rendering of the notable passages of the role, especially the report on Cleopatra (II, 2), was curiously ineffective, and distinctly below the standard set by Kent Smith's Enobarbus in the 1947 Katharine Cornell production. The over-all effect of the last third of the tragedy left nothing to be strongly desired, I believe. If there could be dissatisfaction with the production as a whole, it could be charged to the preceding parts—the first and second acts of this three-act version, which, I understand, followed the J. Dover Wilson text. For one thing, the tripartite division, though convenient and justifiable, made the "second act" somewhat thin in dramatic substance and impeded the surge of the love-tragedy which unifies Shakespeare's episodic tragedy. The second-act division also gave undue emphasis to the scene on board Pompey's galley (II, 8). There was also a tendency before the last Egyptian scenes toward some lackadaisical and fuzzy action that I cannot explain in production terms and must therefore attribute to the major performances.

If comment on the "Olivier Season" is appropriate in this book, it is because we must guard against attributing infallible artistry to the British even in productions of plays by their two major dramatists Shakespeare and Shaw, names Shaw was the first to place together—and rightly so despite the seeming impertinence. Our own defects in production are not primarily the result of obtuseness on the part of our theatre, but of the conditions of commercial production in New York. Many a fault is glossed over in British productions by well-trained English voices and by the experience of playing in repertory. But faults remain. No doubt they will be ineradicable until Gordon Craig's "super-marionettes" displace living actors and the ghosts of Shakespeare and Shaw come down to stage their own plays.

VI. FROM WEST END TO BROADWAY

In the new season of 1952 there was much interest in the Theatre Guild's production of *The Millionairess,* a legacy from Bernard Shaw's valetudinarian period. Brought to New York after a successful London initiation, the play was entirely Katharine Hepburn's vehicle. Shorn of its brilliant, if perverse, preface, *The Millionairess* is, in truth, little more than just a bright extravaganza. The characters are mainly stage people. Shaw's millionairess heroine is largely an animated notion for theatrical antics, and it is as such that she was rendered by Miss Hepburn, who properly enough only *acted* the part. If she had tried to *live* it, the results would have been disastrous. Miss Hepburn used every physical trick of her mannered acting and, except when her deliberate style cracked at the seams (chiefly at the beginning of the play) as it also cracked in her voice, her breezy performance was extremely expert. It captivated London, and it drew plaudits from the Broadway public as well. It could be enjoyed as a calculated exercise, both muscular and vocal (highly vocal!), or as a *tour de force* of strenuous showmanship. One could wonder only whether there wasn't anything more in the substance of *The Millionairess* than an occasion for this *tour de force.*

It is possible to concede that the play is a poor one for Shaw—and that it is one more example of how much closer Shaw was to W. S. Gilbert than is generally realized. We have here the same "typing" of characters and the same insouciant treatment of plot as sheer contrivance. Shaw may have fancied himself Ibsen's successor, but he was Gilbert's successor, too. He may have expressed contempt for "Sardoodledom" as a critic, but he also favored a brand of Sardoodledom all his own when he came to write some of his plays. But Shaw was still Shaw even in *The Millionairess,* and it is not his heroine's capers that are most rewarding but the conversations that treat the success and failure of money and efficiency. It was not Miss Hepburn dropping blockbusters into the play who did it the greatest service. Much of the time she merely called attention to Shaw's Gilbertian disposition and to the harum-scarum dramaturgy of the last period of his career. It was Robert Helpmann playing the Egyptian doctor, the most vivid foil to Miss Hepburn, who carried the impact of Shaw's literary genius—namely, his wit, wisdom, and articulate compassion. Shaw may have approved of hardheadedness and beguiled himself with notions of supermen and superwomen who knock silly or inefficient people's heads together for the sake of a good society. (Toward Mussolini, Hitler, and Stalin, he brought a sentimental attitude, born of impatience with bumbling and irresolution; here Shaw put himself in double jeopardy—as a political thinker celebrated for his humanism and as an artist noteworthy for his comic detachment.) He may have confused hardheadedness with hardheartedness in some of his later pronunciamentos. But it was his bright softheartedness, not usually to be equated with soft-mindedness, that was always most attractive and most provocative in his work.

In *The Millionairess,* the real spine of the play is his ruthless heroine's *failure,* whether or not we conclude that Shaw himself intended this to be so. Her victories are all Pyrrhic ones, and it is the Egyptian doctor, in whom there is an absence of money-making and power-seeking genius, who emerges as the real victor. He proves himself her match; he is the man worthy of her spirit in direct proportion to the superiority of his moral values or *ethos.* Miss Hepburn could neatly destroy furniture on the stage and a calculating admirer ("Adrian Blenderbland," amusingly played by Cyril Ritchard), but *The Millionairess* is most like a play, rather than an overextended music-hall skit, when Shaw bankrupts his heroine or merely rattles her self-assurance. It is possible, indeed, that the play would have been better served if Miss Hepburn had made more of a woman and less of an overanimated puppet of the flamboyant heroine. This view, however, was a minority opinion on Broadway. In the case of *The Millionairess,* it is not for Bernard Shaw but for Katharine Hepburn that the public went to the playhouse both on Broadway and in the West End in London. And the fact that London generally approved the production and enthusiastically endorsed her performance tells us something about London—namely, that it is no more discriminating than New York.

FABIANISM AND THE BRITISH PLAYWRIGHT

The provocation for the ruminations that follow was supplied by the new 1951 Broadway season's first play, *Lace on Her Petticoat,* by Aimee Stuart, an English playwright. It would be a pleasure to be able to distribute compliments to an enterprise altogether honorable, for this drama about snobbery in the Scotland of the eighteen-nineties should appeal to our democratic sympathies. A story of the friendship of a little aristocratic girl and the daughter of a milliner, the play argues that caste divisions are unnatural and then demonstrates that snobbery, from which the poor themselves are not exempt, erects artificial barriers that wound souls and break hearts. *Lace on Her Petticoat* concludes with the proper spark of self-assertion on the part of the plebeian family snubbed by a marchioness who forbade her daughter to invite the milliner's girl to a birthday party. The milliner marries an outspoken village rebel and goes off to Canada with her daughter and mother. It is understandable that Herman Shumlin, the producer of *The Corn Is Green,* should have been attracted to the play, although it is rather difficult to understand why he should have directed it as if everything in it was worth its weight in gold.

Thereby hangs a moral, incidentally. It is not Stanislavski's fault that "inner realism" often looks so inept when misapplied, but one could wish that American stage directors and actors would look twice before leaping into the "system" at every provocation. One could wish that they would give an audience a little credit for intelligence. It is unnecessary to resort to slow-motion and divorced syllables to convince the public that a child would be miserable over inability to attend her friend's birthday. English actors manage this sort of thing so much better, and we may well be grateful for their rapid speech and pace. They hurdle a good many lumps of obvious dramaturgy and humdrum detail, of which there is a generous supply in England and in this play. More style and less realism may be strongly recommended to anyone producing the average British domestic drama, and even one with "social significance" such as *Lace on Her Petticoat.* The Glasgow-born Mrs. Aimee Stuart, who has turned out some twenty-five plays in as many years of playwriting, has too much lace on her own petticoat, but it is doubtful that even she intended it to weigh as much as filigree in lead.

Still, it is British playwriting that is my real concern in this essay, because *Lace on Her Petticoat* is so typically mild theatre. I might sum up my discontent by saying that English playwrights have suffered for a long time from a bad case of reasonableness and circumspection throughout the century. Always, of course, with the one honorable exception of Bernard Shaw who made a cult of Reason most unreasonably. Apparent enough in domestic plays of the *Call It a Day* and *Dear Octopus* variety, in which reasonableness is made more or less tolerable by displays of idiosyncrasy in a country where Dickens is still an influence, the fault becomes glaring in what passes for up-to-date British social drama. Whether it be *Love on the Dole, An Inspector Calls,* or *Lace on Her Petticoat,* the British social play generally displays a moderation as unfortunate in the theatre as it is theoretically admirable in politics. This is not as a rule apparent to British audiences, who seem to believe that mountains are being moved whenever an ant transports its bolus a distance of five inches.

We might call this typically English phenomenon "dramatic Fabianism." It is said to be a fault of the "problem play" that it is tendentiously lukewarm, and it is true that we can also point a finger at several continental writers of some renown (Brieux, Sudermann, Giacosa, Benavente) and at a few Americans such as Rachel Crothers and Rose Franken. A few Irish and Scandinavian sociological writers have also suffered from low blood-pressure. And the responsibility for introducing problem-play sedatives into the theatre has been placed on Ibsen's shoulders where it doesn't actually belong. This partly because the younger Dumas has been so thoroughly forgotten and partly because the triple-thinking, ironical Ibsen is not well understood by the producers and the public. But it was left for the English really to swallow the depressant and give it complete respectability as a beverage. When a good British company collaborates, as it did in *The Winslow Boy,* the results are favored by American playgoers and prove helpful to the British exchequer. These occasions are, however, exceptional. Even Galsworthy's stock has suffered a long decline, and it is as difficult to intoxicate American college boys with *Loyalties* as with Henry George's case for the single tax.

Apparently the British themselves have been aware that their forte has not been social drama. They wisely multiply what they really are adept at —namely, comedy of manners, and we, too, may be forgiven for preferring Maugham and Coward to the reformed Priestley and Aimee Stuart. For a people notoriously well-bred, the English can be delightfully poisonous in comedy, which is perhaps a way of avenging themselves on their breeding. Even T. S. Eliot, now (if not always) more British than American, succeeded better in *The Cocktail Party* with his Noel Coward brand of Chamberlaynes and chattering guardian angels than with the saintly heroine of that play. It was discreet to remove her to darkest Africa before she became too saintly. Christopher Fry also prevailed chiefly with his wit in *The Lady's Not for Burning,* and it must be said for England that, except in the Romantic and Victorian intervals, English poets have not often made the mistake of considering poetry and wit as mutually exclusive. The trouble with Fry has thus far been that he doesn't know his own strength and therefore overexercises it. He tries too hard to be a wit. He also tries too hard to be a poet, and Eliot, if correctly quoted, was right in saying that Fry will be a better poet when he learns to be less poetical.

Fry, in the company of Eliot and others, seems to me to be also making another mistake in trying to be a religious poet. In order to escape from humdrum domestic pieces and problem plays, British playwrights since the middle-thirties have been placing special reliance on poetic religious drama. Except for the pre-war days when Auden and Spender waved the red flag, literary Britons have more or less equated poetic with religious drama. But I cannot refrain from wondering whether they are not merely forcing Fabianism into a collar turned backwards. Each poetic playwright seems to consider it an obligation to write Canterbury Festival plays. A pleasant exercise, no doubt: morally very commendable, and a good excuse for writing verse dialogue and choral poetry! But except for Eliot—and this only in the single case of *Murder in the Cathedral*—they still have a long way to go before they write a religious piece that is memorable, or even genuine, drama.

If we inquire into the reasons, I believe the strongest is the one that would be least likely to occur to them. Their plays are watery because their religion is. They suffer from *religious Fabianism.* Anglo-Catholicism, as these writers propound it, is undoubtedly an agreeable and commodious religion, but it is not a particularly dramatic one, if judged by their effort. It hardly seems more than a semi-religion on the stage. It is well-bred and well-dressed even when it pays lip service to the fine excesses of faith and sacrifice that the writers seem to know only from the literature of Christianity. Theirs is not the wrestling with the demon, the torment, or the acute ecstasy we know to have been an innate and necessary excess in a St. John of the Cross, a Richard Crashaw, or the John Donne of the Holy Sonnets. Donne had to draw blood from words and Gerald Manley Hopkins had to twist and hammer the metal of his poetry, in order to express the seizures of their spirit. There are no divine seizures in plays such as *The Zeal of Thy House, Christ's Comet, The Boy with the Cart, This Way to the Tomb,* or *The Cocktail Party.*

"Who then devised the torment?" Eliot asks in a superb *Little Gidding* lyric. But it is not easy to find any torment in these plays intended to redeem the British drama as well as to "redeem the times." Eliot answers, "Love"; which weaves, according to him, "The intolerable shirt of flame/Which human power cannot remove." But nobody and nothing can be found wearing the shirt of Nessus contained in Mr. Eliot's reference. Only shirts sold at Selfridge's, or at a more fashionable shop, are being worn. That is the impression to be formed from the plays. And no wonder, since no shirts of flame are being worn by the well-tailored playwrights themselves. I must say that I prefer the rough and crumpled workclothes worn by O'Casey, in whom there is more power of Christianity than in a parcel of proper Festival poets. They are mainly *devotional* rather than *religious* poets, and a religious drama without religion is not more exciting than most merely devotional English poetry. Shaw, to cite a contrasting example, was as undevout a writer as one could imagine when he came to write *Saint Joan*. Yet none of the younger British playwrights has come within praying distance of *Saint Joan*. They have *adopted* a faith, whereas Shaw *struggles into one* in this memorable play.

Neither a great need nor a strong struggle is present in these poetic substitutes for social drama in England, and perhaps a reason for this deficiency and certainly a symptom of it is the playwrights' unfamiliarity with *sin*. They appear to have only a nodding acquaintance with Satan, and they have nothing to repent or transcend worth exhibiting to a public. Any adult member of a Broadway audience could give them spades in his knowledge of turpitude. All we know at the end of this kind of drama is that their authors are against sin and error. But in their kind of theatre we no more experience the sin they are against than the sacred love they are for. It takes a full and reckless man to give himself up to either. As Ibsen's Button-Moulder maintained, it requires strong character to be either a saint or a sinner. For the deadly vices we have to go back in time, to Shakespeare and his colleagues. Or, if we want to stay in our own century, we can go to France.

Do we want to know Pride? It is in the works of the contemporary playwright Henry de Montherlant, and I can do no better than recommend the collection of his plays published by Alfred A. Knopf, *The Master of Santiago and Four Other Plays*. In the best of these, *Queen after Death,* pride pitches drama to the key of vibrant tragedy when a king destroys the woman to whom he confessed his disenchantment and world-weariness. In *No Man's Son,* a father's desire to have his son come up to high expectations results in a struggle that would have been worthy of Strindberg if the boy's mother had been any match for the father. In a third play, *The Master of Santiago,* superiority to a world of calculation and compromise becomes a formidable saintliness which teeters on the borderline between God and the Devil. Nothing for any festival play in any of this, but its scorching heat and its blaze would have been properly noted by Dante and the author of *Dies Irae*. Or is it adultery that we should like to encounter? I should hardly recommend the adultery, as uninebriating as a "country-house" high tea, in *The Cocktail Party:* If the Chamberlaynes' amours represent the dreaded sin of adultery, it is hardly a temptation to anyone not permanently enrolled in Sunday School. It is not even a first-rate betrayal of two people's confidence in one another. You can't betray what is already self-betrayed. Nor can you cheat a person of what he never had at all. (To be fair to Eliot, who is after all a very intelligent man, we must note that neither he nor his supernatural psychiatrist is particularly exercised over the Chamberlaynes' defections from conjugal affection.) If we want the real article, the real passion that makes adultery something more than a footnote to marriage, I recommend that we turn to a truly religious play by a real Catholic poet, to *Partage de Midi* by Paul Claudel. . . .

The point I am trying to sustain is that Britain's devotional poet-playwrights are mainly engaged in fashionable parlor games of levitation in the dual effort to raise themselves to salvation as both believers and dramatists. They do have verve—as verbalists, and as writers of comedy of manners. But this cannot carry them as far as they quite honorably wish to rise. I have not intended, however, to impute hypocrisy to them in noting the low temperature of the piety which they want "to make do." In spite of their maximum zeal, they are, inexorably, epigones in religion; and in spite of their modern idiom, epigones in poetic drama as well. Like the writers of problem plays, they are merely earnest Fabians.

England did produce an exciting playwright who was a Fabian by actual affiliation, which they are not, of course. But Shaw knew the difference between a city councillor and a dramatist, just as the author of *Saint Joan* and *Androcles and the Lion* knew the difference between a churchgoing gentleman and a martyr. There was a memorable fury in Shaw, who was supposed to be the most frigid writer who ever put a show on the stage. His mind and spirit worked by excess, and he upset all apple-carts even when he tried to effectuate reforms or usher in a new order by rational argument and strategy! He was the bull in the china-shop of British theatre, and the pieces are still rattling. We continue to hear them rattle after his death. If we want a British drama on the subject of caste and snobbery, treated by Aimee Stuart, we have no further to seek than the nearest library shelf on which *Pygmalion* reposes. If we want eloquence on the subject of equality or on some related subject, we need only to listen to his Eliza-Galatea telling off her Pygmalion-elocutionist; or to his Major Barbara in despair and Undershaft's rationalizations on the manufacture of munitions. And if we crave the saintliness or ecstasy the new poet-playwrights exert themselves to supply, we can turn to *Androcles and the Lion, Saint Joan,* and Father Keegan's description of his vision in the fourth act of *John Bull's Other Island.*

Both the social realists and the devotional dramatists still look feeble whenever Shaw makes inroads into their territory. Led by something too elusive in temperament, intellect, and talent to be called by any name less comprehensive or ambiguous than his favorite "Life Force," Shaw knew his way about the windings of the social scene better than the realists. And the festival poets, too, including the redoubtable Eliot himself, could learn something from the Nietzschean-Marxian-Bergsonian creator of Father Keegan, for whom there are only two countries, "heaven and hell," and two conditions of men, "salvation and damnation."

"What is it like in their dreams," one might ask, echoing Broadbent, and what have they made of it in plays and in superior Eliot essays on the Christian Society to equal Keegan's answer:

> In my dreams it is a country where the State is the Church and the Church the people: three in one and one in three. It is a commonwealth in which work is play and play is life: three in one and one in three. It is a temple in which the priest is the worshipper and the worshipped: three in one and one in three. It is a godhead in which all life is human and all humanity divine: three in one and one in three.

Father Keegan adds, "It is, in short, the dream of a madman." The epigones, who have rarely written a better passage of dramatic poetry although they are professional poets, will need some of this madness if they are to express saintliness for our time. And the realists will need some of it, too, if they are to make drama out of their designs for an ideal society. A good measure of this afflatus animates *Saint Joan,* not in the abstract assertions but in the calvary of one of Shaw's most vital heroines. A good production of Shaw's play would make most later English efforts to dramatize religious faith seem as embarrassingly half-hearted in religious affirmation as they are surely tepid in dramatic execution.

GOLDEN BOY
AND THE MIDCENTURY MODE

The treatment in 1951 of that fourteen-year-old relic from the thirties, Odets' *Golden Boy,* along with the nature of new American plays when *Golden Boy* was revived, could be viewed as signs of the lassitude noted in other fields than the theatre, too. Whether successful or unsuccessful, the productions exhibited shrinking boundaries of dramatic intellection and imagination. And this conclusion could be drawn not from intentionally meretricious ventures in show business, which would prove nothing, but from well-intentioned, honestly or even "idealistically" directed efforts.

The enthusiastic reception of *Golden Boy* also sustains a point— namely, the difference between the fifties and the now popularly disavowed thirties—especially since the ANTA production staged by Odets himself was decidedly more self-contained or more centripetal than the original Group Theatre production, which had possessed a poetic as well as social fervor that may be described as centrifugal. I employ the term in the sense that the production, for both better and worse, carried the play beyond the confines of case history into "metaphor."

It was significant of the times that in the case of the new stage production, Odets himself drew in his horns of prophecy or, shall we say, his pseudopodia of social idealism. An example would be the toning down of the prize fighter Joe Bonaparte's brother's insistence that he, too, "fights" —as a servant of social justice. Another example would be the terse and pinched performance of the philosopher-neighbor Carp, originally played with an odd tenderness by Lee Cobb in 1937. Carp, in the 1951 production, was a caricature rather than a human being; he was presented purely as an eccentric pseudo-intellectual rather than as a "little man" whose fumbling with ideas is oddly touching. In 1951, Lee Cobb played Joe Bonaparte's father and played him extremely well, but I, for one, missed the poetic softness of Morris Carnovsky, who had the part in 1937; I could believe Carnovsky's passion for music much more readily than Cobb's. Art Smith's fight manager Moody was merely realistic (in 1937, Roman Bohnen played the part more bizarrely, as if the manager were flailing about in the half-light of a confused world) and John Garfield's Joe Bonaparte was more convincing as a professional prize fighter than as a boy with music in his soul.

In the play, as Harold Clurman noted in an introduction to the published text (Random House, 1937), "two worlds are mirrored . . . the artists' world with its humble pleasures, its small but basic contentment, and the business world with its fundamental uncertainty, hysteria." This dichotomy, ultimately a poetic conception, was rarely achieved in the revival by artistry rather than by statement. The theme of the "fiddle" *versus* the "fist" was a metaphorical concept; it dissolved in the cold light of realism. Perhaps this was all for the good, since the "fiddle" had a somewhat specious existence in the play as first produced. The play was more clearly sustained when kept to the level of common realism. But the bizarre half-lights reflected from Odets' play in the original Clurman production made *Golden Boy* something more than a prize-fight story— something more even than "social significance" moralization and veiled allegory. There are perhaps no adequate words for what *Golden Boy* was in 1937. The best description of the impression I had was that of a tilting at Giant Compromise by a Childe Roland who fancied himself a hard-headed realist but was actually an uncompromised idealist whose eyesight was somewhat blurred and in whom only the heart was strong—in short, the young Odets.

Among the new plays, Joseph Kramm's *The Shrike* is another example of realism in the non-affirmative fifties. It is an intense drama of a man's struggle against a possessive wife who has driven him to attempt suicide and keeps him in an insane asylum until he relinquishes all thought of leaving her. José Ferrer's production, as well as his performance in the role of the victimized husband, left nothing to be desired if we are gratified by *Snake-Pit* pathos apparently much favored by the age. Judith Evelyn, playing the female vampire with charged restraint, assisted him ably, as did every subordinate member of the cast. The play invokes our basic insecurities and a view of the world and of our dubious chances in it for more than survival. In its capacity for inducing anxiety, *The Shrike* has a considerable tension which Ferrer did not hesitate to theatricalize. At the conclusion, we also experience vibrations of an ironic commentary on how to get along in the world—that is, by deceit and submission: and we are told that we have no other recourse, a view that would have been scornfully rejected in the nineteen-thirties, which had some strong words for it.

The Shrike, then, proved to be a good example of the quite thoroughly daunted realism of playwriting in vogue in the fifties, with or without sensationalist naturalism. *The Shrike* owed its success to realism in the cruel story, and not to reverberations in the mind and imagination. *The Shrike* prevailed, in the main, clinically and naturalistically, as a case history and a horrifying picture of conditions in an institution. At writing, as well as staging, this type of drama we are probably more adept than any other nation in the world; our writers and producers are sure-footed, lynx eyed, and equipped with talons capable of gripping a paying audience. But when the performance is over, little is left in the case of *The Shrike* but the recollection of a painful experience, followed by a void, or, at most, by agitation over the question of whether the practices of psychiatrists and institutions for the insane are that crass here and now. (Precisely this question roused discussion.) It is otherwise with work such as Kafka's *The Trial,* which not only reverberates in the mind but, for all its profound anxiety-compulsions, is dimensioned heroically somehow through "K's" search for some meaningful vindication in the half-light of humanity's failure.

We encounter a similar limitation in plays such as George Tabori's *Flight into Egypt.* From all the tension bountifully supplied by the playwriting and by Elia Kazan's powerful production in one of the best Mielziner settings, nothing more emerges than the fact that a man is obsessively engaged in getting himself and his family out of shattered post-war Europe, that circumstances have marooned them in Cairo, and that his physical condition disqualifies him from entering the United States. A pathetic story, to be sure, and one that is intensified by his wife's self-sacrifice and his own heroic attempt to overcome the paralysis that loses him a visa; but *Flight into Egypt* says at most that it is a mistake to try to flee from reality. The point is well taken, if maladroitly introduced into the play by means of an Austrian patriot's exhortations. It is, however, the family's struggle with creditors and American officials in a Cairo hotel that pre-empts the author's main efforts and Elia Kazan's directorial skill, as well as some superb acting by Paul Lukas and Giusti Huber. In the final accounting, we can place on one side of the ledger the fact that we have had a harrowing experience; but we have nothing at all to put on the other side. The author was successful only with surfaces or, to remind ourselves of the naturalistic limitation of the play, with a "slice of life"—albeit a spiked one. The journalist in Mr. Tabori, as in most contemporary playwrights, was effective. But the thinker and the poet were underdeveloped in him.

This limitation was also the case with Sigmund Miller, the author of *One Bright Day,* an ably produced problem play reminiscent of *An Enemy of the People.* The action revolved around the problems of a director of a pharmaceutical corporation who discovers that a highly profitable drug contains a poisonous ingredient. The decision to withdraw it from the market is difficult to make and is, inevitably, opposed by other directors of the corporation. The play concludes with Howard Lindsay, who gives a convincing portrayal of the idealistic tycoon, releasing the news that the drug is harmful. One must be a curmudgeon to belabor so well-intentioned an effort, and one must concede, I believe, that the second act is exciting drama and that the theme is intrinsically, if also quite routinely, challenging. Unfortunately, only a "triple-thinker" like Shaw (to use Edmund Wilson's useful term) or an ironist in full command of his scalpel, as Strindberg was in *There Are Crimes and Crimes,* could get himself out of the impasse inherent in this situation. Otherwise, the author must either deliver a blatant denunciation of mercenary behavior or an equally flat resolution in which virtue triumphs. Sigmund Miller created on only one level of meaning. He did not escape, did not appear to have even entertained a desire to escape, from matter-of-fact, if morally approvable, theatre.

In one way or another, we are likely to find the theatre of the fifties buzzing no higher than a beetle's flight. If this is the *Zeitgeist,* and there is too little evidence as yet that the decade is developing a different milieu for the artist, then the "sound" ANTA production of *Golden Boy,* with which I started this brief volley, was pragmatically justified. Playwrights who engage themselves to more ambitious intentions than routine realism will require stout hearts—and, considering the norms of playgoing at the beginning of the fifties, tough hides as well.

A conclusive sample of playwriting, indeed, was the well-written *I Am a Camera,* fashioned by John van Druten with considerable skill out of Christopher Isherwood's Berlin stories. The play competed with *Point of No Return* for honors as the best play of the 1951-52 season and commanded sufficient regard from more or less discreet judges to represent virtually the best that Broadway could do at the opening of its post-1950 career. The subject related to the devastating events since Hitler's rise in 1933 from which we were still trying to recover in the fifties with anything but assistance from Stalin, Hitler's successor as chief trouble-maker for Western civilization; related, too, to the even more immediate—and one may say, universal—question of lassitude and egocentricity while the times challenge awareness and watchfulness. One's disappointment with *I Am a Camera,* regardless of how high a valuation one placed on its nuances, came from the very fact that it was so well rendered a treatment of the theme of moral sloth. The play, for all its well-noted points, suffered from a sloth of its own.

Van Druten's dramatization revolved around a young English writer, "Christopher Isherwood," who tries to absorb life by osmosis in Berlin and strikes up a platonic relationship with a morally questionable English girl while the storm of Nazism is gathering over Germany. The girl herself "fiddles harmonics on the strings of sensualism" while making a pretense at being a night-club entertainer. The demonstration of the times' challenge to apathy is supported by an American playboy, a young German Jew who wins his way out of a morass of deception with some difficulty, and a Teutonic landlady who echoes anti-Semitic canards idiotically. Van Druten's picture of social decadence derived from Isherwood's Berlin stories is packed with revealing moments, and the well-directed performances were excellent. Broadway was justly ringing the praises of Julie Harris, whose virtuosity enabled her to create a memorable character. Unfortunately, however, the play was not truly alive because, except in the case of the secondary Jewish characters, it partook of the stalemate van Druten had taken for his subject.

Mr. van Druten counted on our intelligence to draw the full meaning of the play out of the picture he unfolded for us. Still, he was infected with the very virus of footlooseness that he was exposing. This was apparent in the fact that he followed every twist and turn of his heroine's disorientation, devoting the major part of the play to her, when actually she should have been of secondary importance to the presentation of people's failure to face the great crisis of Germany and the world in the thirties. The "lady" would have been a "tramp" in any society, and she would have been ineffectual even if her morals had been above suspicion. The same stalemate in the dramatic treatment is inherent in the "Christopher Isherwood," the main male character. He is assigned the role of the "camera" or observer from the start, in a prologue spoken by him. But he is made to focus too long on the one personal relation (his relations with the English girl, without any of the claims of passion moreover) that least illuminates the social scene he is "photographing."

In an analysis such as this, the purpose of which has been to show how an interesting play by a literate playwright becomes aborted for want of a strenuous application of spirit which the subject could have fanned into a flame of scorn and anger instead of detached note-taking, something else is apparent, too—namely, the difference between Chekhovian variants of drama and Chekhov's own plays. In the latter, we either have a distinct development, as in *The Sea Gull* and *The Cherry Orchard,* in which a stalemate leads to a catastrophe (and, in the last-mentioned piece, also, one way of life is displaced by another), or we have characters staging an intense struggle against an impasse before suffering defeat, as in *Uncle Vanya* and *The Three Sisters.* The pseudo-Chekhovians make much of the possibility of writing plotless plays (as Mr. van Druten did in a *New York Times* article published in advance of the opening of *I Am a Camera*) but overlook the fact of essential conflict and progression in Chekhov's dramaturgy. *They* try to be artfully passive; *he* succeeded in being artfully active. That is one reason why he was a master-dramatist, whereas they stand at best only on the foothills of dramatic achievement. He did not allow himself to be defeated by the apathy and the stumbling he recorded because he himself remained fundamentally unaffected with negativism.

THE USES OF EXUBERANCE

I have been a staunch defender of the crudity—shall we rather say, the stridency in serious work and the exuberance in light entertainment—that has long characterized American plays and productions since Clyde Fitch ceased to be our most prominent playwright. I have even been reluctant to condemn the crudity I, myself, found overstrenuous. (I like a little barbarousness in the theatre, though a little goes a long way with me.) When George Jean Nathan waxed eloquent over the merits of *Hellzapoppin!,* I could appreciate his enthusiasm without actually discovering the merits he found in that lunatic carnival. Error on the side of the barbaric seems to me preferable to error on the side of gentility, although gentility is less tiresome in small London and provincial theatres than in our own considerably larger or less intimate Broadway houses. Except in rare cases, mostly musical comedy and musical revue specimens, however, the zest has gone out of our plays and productions in the mid-century years. Or if the zest seems present, it seems "put on" for show rather than felt; it appears to be a substitute for vitality instead of being synonymous with it. The tail wags on, but the animal is virtually dead. We continue to make theatre these days on Broadway (and also on most European stages, it seems) mainly by rote, and this is evident in the quality of both plays and productions.

I am not prepared to argue that conservatism is necessarily destructive to the drama; that depends upon the values one tries to preserve and the capacity to translate them into theatre. Nor do I intend to proscribe all caution, provided it is more than a skin-saving policy and is induced by wisdom rather than by fear. And convictions do not recommend themselves to me as ferments in the theatre by their soundness, since there has never been any large agreement on the "soundness" of beliefs or ideas. I am, however, prepared to say that conservatism as it appears today has failed to offer any positive experiences or principles. Not even in the plays of T. S. Eliot does the acceptance of a status quo constitute more than a left-handed compliment to tradition. Mr. Eliot himself appeared to be singularly cool and joyless in salvaging the marriage of the Chamberlaynes in *The Cocktail Party.* He reserved his warmth and enthusiasm for the mystique of martyrdom—than which nothing is more challenging to a settled state of affairs. The truth is that Mr. Eliot is not very successful in the role of a conservative, and his followers are successful in inverse ratio to their feeling for drama. Caution, as it appears today, is also a question-

438

able thing. It is not literary taste and tact but mere absence of attachment to anything, to a dramatic style or to a principle.

There is surely a marked absence of fervor in serious drama such as sparked O'Neill and Odets or of zest in comedy such as effervesced, when last present, in *Born Yesterday*. Nor has much fervor or exuberance been present in our stage productions since such early postwar presentations as *Call Me Mister* and *Mister Roberts*. At best we have had the impeccable virtuosity of Jessica Tandy and Hume Cronyn in *The Fourposter*. Mere strenuousness, as displayed by Miss Hepburn in *The Millionairess,* is, of course, a spurious kind of energy. Even revivals of spirited work of the past have, with the exception of a City Center 1953 revival of *The Male Animal,* lacked the verve of the original productions. If reviewers for our learned quarterlies want to worry about the state of the theatre, here is a situation that really deserves their attention. It is the torpor of our plays and performances and not their "crudity" that is likely to be disastrous to the contemporary professional stage.

"Professionalism" has become joyless and dispirited, partly because the actor's livelihood is in jeopardy if the play does not quickly become that artistic anomaly "a smash hit," and partly because Broadway play-goers are on to the tricks of professionalism except when they are, so to speak, blinded by the "star."

Why the professionalism of foreign companies should have a different effect, I am not competent to say. Perhaps drama spoken in a foreign language and performed with exotic accents and gestures *seems* more theatrical. Certainly, the highly polished Laurence Olivier productions of *Caesar and Cleopatra* and *Antony and Cleopatra* did not impress us with any special vitality. Still, the continental stylized performance, whether the Habimah Theatre's or the Jean-Louis Barrault company's, has generally proved invigorating, and the reason seems to be that this type of performance belongs so completely to the experience of theatre—that is, of performances as performance rather than as photographic imitation.

In the case of the average Broadway production, you may often shut your eyes and not be deprived of any dramatic experience; the words are actually about all you get even when your eyes are open. To be entirely fair, let us say that the actors are indeed performing—but only to the front third of the audience because they are not projecting their roles but merely imitating life. However, acting that is not projection is only half-acting. Certainly, the joy of performance is not in it. And in the matter of speech, too, our professionalism is a maimed art by comparison with vigorous continental styles.

The visit of the Madeleine Renaud-Jean-Louis Barrault company in 1952 served to stress the grave lack of theatrical vitality in our haphazard professionalism. It was not always quite so haphazard, as those who saw many an old Theatre Guild and, later, Group Theatre production will agree. Professionalism was also once not so tired as it is today. When it lacked any perfected style, it at least had accent and bravura, as in many a George Kaufman and Jed Harris production of the twenties and thirties. All these productions expressed some positive approach. The visit of some foreign troupe occasionally reminds us that theatre is not truly theatre and therefore not truly invigorating unless it has a distinctive style; and a distinctive production style is a positive value as contrasted with an amorphous or unaccented production which flares up into theatre only by accident of talent on the part of some individual performer.

In a distinctive style of theatre, there is always present an underlying conviction. No one, for instance, could be mistaken about the presence of a distinctive attitude toward life in a Habimah production—even if one didn't understand a word of the language. In a Barrault production, spectators could sense the presence of an attitude; at least, an attitude toward the theatre as something else than a place for dutiful simulation of the "life" described by an author, which is not the same thing as life in a play. Could they do so in the case of the average production on Broadway today if they were unfamiliar with the language? Can one, in fact, sense a truly distinct attitude even though the language is familiar? I doubt it. That there should be little exuberance in our professional theatre is understandable when nobody seeks any particular kind of theatre or any particular purpose for it or point to it.

For this situation, the playwright is, of course, at least as responsible as his producing associates, and it is an open question who inspires or who deadens whom—the dramatist or the production company and producer. Playwrights used to be excited about something or other and struck sparks on the anvil of their passion or delusion. Regardless of whether they followed realistic or expressionist drama, whether they looked about the social scene or glanced away from it with a will and a way! And they usually floated on a sense of wonder and discovery, even when the things they discovered had been near at hand and were already staples of the modern theatre in Europe. They also engaged themselves recklessly, in the Sartrian sense; even writers of high comedy, such as Barry and Behrman, were "engaged"—to the comic view much of the time and occasionally even to some serious, if not necessarily successfully held, position. If some of our playwrights were engaged to nothing else, they were at least engaged to themselves; they clung to their bias and to their temperament—O'Neill to his sense of alienation and his pessimism, Saroyan to his sense of "belonging" and to his optimism. Today, too many of our young dramatists are prematurely old.

ILLUMINATION BY ROMAN CANDLE

When Truman Capote's esoteric play *The Grass Harp* was approaching its première toward the end of March, 1952, its well-wishers on Broadway were legion. After the première, when considerable tepidity was noted in Capote's play, their number diminished considerably. Even so, Brooks Atkinson raised his powerful *New York Times* voice in behalf of the play, and Richard Watts, another loyal devotee of eccentric dramatic art, veiled his disappointment with compliments to "the beauty and imagination in Truman Capote's dramatization of his own novel." Louis Sheaffer, the *Brooklyn Eagle* critic, and Thomas Dash, *Women's Wear* reviewer, do not report to the town's most intellectual public and could be expected to turn in adverse verdicts on dramatic experiments. Instead they were only a shade less enthusiastic than Mr. Atkinson.

The fact is that Broadway would have been delighted to be able to acclaim Capote as the new white hope of the theatre. Earlier in the season Manhattan's reviewers vied with each other in applauding Mary Chase's witch-comedy, *Mrs. McThing,* with mighty dissent only, I believe, from George Jean Nathan. ANTA provided another esoteric experience by reviving *Four Saints in Three Acts;* and no one has yet ventured to write a key to *Four Saints* that would violate its imperviousness to logic, since its author, Gertrude Stein, took care never to deviate into sense. Yet once more Broadway was ready to be entranced.

A visitor to our shores who wandered into our theatres might well wonder whether there wasn't something wrong with the European idea that America is the paradise of pragmatists, the happy hunting grounds of materialists and super-realists. And if he were intent on informing himself about our recent theatrical past, he might encounter a number of other surprises such as Mary Chase's early extravaganza, *Harvey,* Carson McCullers' *Member of the Wedding,* and the plays of Tennessee Williams and William Saroyan.

Even without reading our comic strips (if you can call that reading) and without plunging into the prose of our latest Nobel Prize winner, William Faulkner, the European tourist would have a hard time reconciling the continental view of America's practicality with its apparent fondness for impracticality and eccentricity.

It is surely significant that O'Neill, the one major writer we have contributed to the modern stage, had been, for better or worse, a restless experimenter. I doubt that any other playwright of comparable stature had experimented so much and so strenuously after Strindberg.

As for Broadway, it must be noted that although it is natural for showmen to be cautious when even a trim little production costs $60,000, they are among the most incalculable professionals in the land. For professionals they are rank amateurs. They will try anything that seems likely to rouse the Broadway playgoer out of his lethargy. Nor do they wait, as a rule, until some off-Broadway little theatre has given them the signal to venture all on a nonconformist play that violates standard structure and whips up a soufflé of whimsy, extravaganza, or fantasy. Productions of *My Heart's in the Highlands, The Time of Your Life, Our Town, The Skin of Our Teeth, The Glass Menagerie, Harvey* and many other off-beat (and sometimes off-color) plays were all initiated by the showmen on Broadway whose venturesomeness often exceeds their good sense, good taste, or intelligence.

Broadway never had a more conservative producer than Brock Pemberton, that good Republican committeeman. But it was Pemberton who produced *Harvey,* not to mention Pirandello's *Henry IV* and *Six Characters in Search of an Author,* which he actually staged twice. Two people further apart intellectually than Pemberton and Pirandello can hardly be imagined. And it was Eddie Dowling, previously known as a "song-and-dance" performer, who produced Barry's symbolist *Here Come the Clowns,* Saroyan's *The Time of Your Life,* and Williams' *The Glass Menagerie.*

The showman is willing, and there are a good many to prod him to "try something different." He is dependent upon the approval of the newspaper reviewers and the regular first night audiences. These have attended approximately seventy shows for ten or more consecutive years. We can calculate that they have seen between seven hundred and one thousand plays. According to my own count, I have attended some fourteen hundred professional stage productions, and I happen to be one of the younger members of the Drama Critics' Circle.

Under the circumstances, we become extremely impatient with run-of-the-mill characters, familiar situations, and "well-made plays." Most of us would gladly check our rationality at the door of the theatre if we were sure to find relief from humdrum stage exercise. We are actually disposed to overpraise the eccentric production out of a sense of gratitude for the relief it affords. While our patience lasted, most of us overpraised Saroyan's fantastications instead of breaking them on the wheel of logic. Since in the theatre you are either underpraised or overpraised, no sensible manager will disregard the chance of profiting from an unearned increment of praise for a daring production. This is a gambler's chance, and a good showman, who depends upon windfalls and accepts his defeats with a sportsmanlike shrug, will take it.

These occasions for gambling, we should add, are generally different from the European plays that depart from realistic norms of playwriting. Plays of this type engendered in America are really spontaneous and fresh —often almost to the point of naïveté. They are truly eccentric, whereas even the wildest fancies of European playwrights are usually not quite that. The European experiments are, instead, evidences of a "movement," or they soon constitute a movement or a school of playwriting. They also come supplied, as a rule, with a program or theoretical base and with a label such as symbolism, expressionism, futurism, surrealism and what not. Unorthodoxy in European art rapidly becomes codified and forms a new orthodoxy. Our last codification transpired in the mid-thirties during the brief heyday of its social drama.

In the American theatre since 1939, the contrary has been true, and writers such as Williams and Saroyan remain lone wolves instead of be-getters of movements. They may have imitators, but they form no schools. We appreciate them as individualists and look to them for novelty. We applaud them for ventilating our drama with their random breezes, and woe to them if we arrive at the conclusion that all the breezes blow from the same direction. We pounced on Williams when he gave us *Summer and Smoke* after productions of *The Glass Menagerie* and *A Streetcar Named Desire,* accusing him of inability to play upon any other string than that of Southern feminine frustration. Then Williams quickly pla-cated us by playing a different tune in *The Rose Tattoo* in which his heroine was uninhibited by virtue of her Sicilian temperament.

Earlier we had grown somewhat tired of Saroyan's anarchic manner of composition, whereupon he supplied a masterly example of disciplined drama, his superb one-acter, *Hello, Out There,* and tried to conform to organized play structure with *Get Away, Old Man;* to his detriment when he allowed himself to be guided by the practical producer George Abbott and lost the fine frenzy of the original draft of that play. Subsequently, in several plays Saroyan returned to his early improvisatory style. But by then it had become a routine rather than a novelty for us, and Saroyan lost the amateur standing that had led us to acclaim him as the hope of the professional theatre.

In short, Broadway, so generally the haven of routine stage art, is actually hungry for uninhibited, if not indeed bumptious, individuality. To a large extent our disappointment with Capote's *The Grass Harp* stemmed from our feeling that he did not go far enough in the direction of carefree improvisation and iconoclasm. He started with some novel eccentrics in his first act and sent them off to live in a tree-house in the woods. But he restored the equilibrium of narrow small-town life by bringing them back to their former life after some humdrum contrivances. He gave them one brief bout with windmills during which most of us liked his misfits well enough; then he apparently did not know what to do with them and ended with a stasis. Had Capote gone further in the direction of excess, we might have followed him gladly. We actually longed for Saroyan to break the stalemate with his bronco temperament and high spirits.

The results of our individualism and tendency toward heterodoxy are complicated. To a considerable extent they determine the character of our theatre for better and worse. The atmosphere of our stage favors the meteoric rise of a Saroyan, Williams, Menotti, Carson McCullers, and others who look at life at a slant, take liberties with dramatic structure and place odd personalities in bizarre situations. Every now and then, consequently, our drama splutters into a blaze of what seems to be genius or at least gives evidence of unusual dramatic vitality. The experience is analogous to spontaneous combustion, and the playwright appeals to us as an untutored artist, a veritable *fauve*.

The effect is apt to be quite refreshing or provocative, if also more unsettling than deeply satisfying. But the passion for spontaneity of *fauvism* has its drawbacks, too. It prevents us from laying solid foundations for our drama. We are altogether too dependent upon these meteoric apparitions, and meteors are apt to fizzle out. While waiting for them to materialize, moreover, we are forced to settle for something else, generally a clod shaped into the semblance of a play. When Broadway can't play for a gambler's highest stakes, it is too apt to play so safe that it favors abysmal mediocrity.

The frequently lamented mediocrity of Broadway production stems in part from too great a dependence upon the fortuitous miracle, the happy accident, in playwriting. And, indeed, also in individual stage performance, since our actors lack the opportunity to perfect themselves in the sort of ensemble that permanent or long-lasting European companies provide. They make up with vigor or unexpected inspiration what they lose from want of finesse and finish.

As for our meteoric playwrights, we consume their talent overzealously and then promptly ask for something else, giving them a feeling of insecurity and discouraging them from improving their artistry and solidifying their values. To be under the obligation of always supplying something new and surprising is a heavy burden for any creative writer. We are hungry only for change, and we make the playwright avid for it, too. Either the playwright succeeds in changing or he is set down as a dramatist who failed to fulfill his promise. It is not surprising that there are so many one-play or two-or-three-play dramatists in America. By making a fetish of change we fail to promote growth. With our idolatry of novelty, we fail to prepare the proper climate for originality. The spectacular takes precedence over the rooted and developed sense of life that is necessary for wholly satisfying drama and maturing playwrights.

Our temperamental instability even muddles dramatic criticism which in turn succeeds in further muddling both playwrights and audiences. We overlook or minimize the lack of true foundations in the play whose glitter or excitement has captivated us. Our critics have no frame of reference for judging plays by unorthodox writers and therefore either fail to make any sort of sense out of their work or indulge in unconsidered rhapsodies over its "originality," "delicacy," or "beauty." The talented young playwright is either disheartened by the opposition he has encountered or encouraged by the applause to deploy only his impulses in composing a play. He is then in danger of becoming the eternal self-indulgent romanticist lost in an egocentric world of uncoordinated inspirations.

When Saroyan made one of his characters repeat, "No foundation. All the way down the line," he probably did not think of his own playwriting career. But the line applies only too well to most of the plays on which Broadway has been inclined to rely for redemption from the very banality upon which producers lavish so much costly attention.

We should by all means welcome the meteor when it speeds across our theatrical horizon, but we must not look to it for a succession of sunlit summers and nourishing harvests. The great periods of theatre were made great not by their eccentric products but by their norms of good drama. Their masterpieces were, indeed, among the most normal plays of the age. *Oedipus the King* was exemplary Attic tragedy in structure, style, and philosophy. *Hamlet* brought to fruition the "revenge play" of the Elizabethan and Jacobean periods. *Phèdre* is a model of neo-classic tragedy, just as *Tartuffe, The Misanthrope,* or *The Learned Women* is a model of neo-classic comedy. Ibsen's and Chekhov's best realistic plays, even when most unique, represented culminations of developments in late nineteenth-century theatre, and the same thing may be said for Shaw's contributions to the modern theatre before 1925. *Awake and Sing!,* too, was a climax rather than a vagary. The theatre in our time, on the contrary, becomes luminous as a rule only when somebody sends a Roman candle into the night. Illumination in our time, here and even abroad, results mainly from random, often eccentric, efforts and is usually tentative.

TWO WAR-TIME AND
POST-WAR PERIODS

I

Since the stage and its playwrights have experienced major upheavals since 1914, these must be considered in any account or evaluation of the theatre in our times.

The First World War need not detain us greatly. In America, it was not productive of any plays much above the level of transparent propaganda, the "Yankee-Doodlism" of George M. Cohan, prosaic pieces of pacifism, and musical entertainments in a style previously in vogue. The war temporarily halted the activity of the off-Broadway "art" movement of so-called little theatres since 1911. Thus the Washington Square Players, which gave rise to the Theatre Guild in 1919, disbanded as its various leaders went into the military and diplomatic services. The base of the American stage before 1917, the year of our entry into the war, had been too low, judged by standards of the modern drama, to encourage literary elevation. That had still to come.

England's travail has the distinction of having brought forth a near-masterpiece *Heartbreak House,* which Eric Bentley has aptly called "The Nightmare of a Fabian." Otherwise there was little to glean from the fiery harvest. Galsworthy, who had expressed himself on mass hysteria in 1914 in the rather crude Boer-war drama *The Mob,* was silent until after the war. John Drinkwater made an eloquent gesture in 1918 toward transatlantic democracy with the chronicle play *Abraham Lincoln.* The prevalent sentiment was expressed in *The Old Lady Shows Her Medals* and *A Kiss for Cinderella* by James M. Barrie, who left pathos only in *Dear Brutus—* and then only for fancy. The sensation of the London stage was *Chu Chin-Chow,* a piece of oriental pageantry with jewel caves and lavish landscapes.

In Italy, the ironic "grotesque" school of playwriting started in full swing with Luigi Chiarelli's ironic imbroglio of the year 1916 *The Mask and the Face.* And Luigi Pirandello, in the same year, provided his first full-length play to win international renown *Right You Are, If You Think So,* or *It Is So! If You Say So.* In Russia in 1915, Leonid Andreyev wrote his most highly regarded, moderately symbolist drama *He Who Gets Slapped.* France was in too precarious a position to sustain much of a theatre, and Jacques Copeau's celebrated Théâtre du Vieux Colombier Company was transferred to New York, with assistance from the American art patron Otto Kahn, as a symbol of Allied Powers amity. In Germany, generally victorious until the year 1918, the expressionist playwrights were having a field day. More than manic results appeared only in Georg Kaiser's 1916 drama of an embezzling bank-cashier's *via dolorosa, From Morn to Midnight.*

The post-war theatre, however, attained a second important phase in the history of modern drama to which no essay-length review could do justice. In England, Shaw reached the climax of his playwriting career with *Saint Joan* in 1923 and composed his most ambitious work in that fantasia of Lamarckism and longevity *Back to Methuselah* in 1921. And even the years of his decline brought forth frequently provocative writing in *The Apple Cart* in 1929 and *Too True to Be Good* in 1932. Galsworthy roused himself in 1922 to write *Loyalties,* in its time a noteworthy treatment of class loyalties, and added *Escape* for good measure. Maugham's *The Circle* and *The Constant Wife* came in 1921 and 1923. C. K. Munro and Milne had their vogue in comedy, along with lesser lights of *savoir faire* playwriting, and Noel Coward, after fluttering on the stage for half a dozen years, reached his proper perch with *Private Lives* in 1930. John van Druten began to make an impression with *Young Woodley* in 1923. Serious playwriting, incited by memories and new prospects of war, appeared in such pieces as R. C. Sherriff's *Journey's End* and Robert Nichols and Maurice Browne's *Wings Over Europe,* the first atom-bomb play, written in 1928.

The Irish theatre had a second renascence with the early plays of Sean O'Casey, the first of these, *The Shadow of a Gunman,* appearing in 1923. Denis Johnston by 1929 and Paul Vincent Carroll by the middle thirties began a modest ascent. The American theatre achieved its majority after 1918 with O'Neill leading a first generation of modern playwrights which included Rice, Howard, Barry, Kelly, Anderson, Green, Lawson, Behrman, and Sherwood. And a second generation began treading on the heels of the first by the middle thirties with the rise of Wilder, Kingsley, Odets, Lillian Hellman, and others.

On the European continent, Pirandello went on to complete mastery of his saturnine kind of dramas. Sceptical concerning realistic playwriting, as well as critical of society and the fixed personality it imposes on individuals, he attained international fame with *Six Characters in Search of an Author* and *Henry IV* in 1921 and 1922. He also wrote other quizzical and tantalizing plays expressive of an original mind and spirit. Until the Pirandellian style of drama became subject to the law of diminishing returns as a result of overexploitation of the theme of "mask" and "face," Pirandello was a major figure in the theatre. In Spain, pre-war writers such as Benavente, Martinez-Sierra, and the Quintero Brothers continued in their old grooves, but while their writing lost more than local interest they were succeeded by one of the most original of lyric dramatists, the poet Federico García Lorca.

France experienced a veritable revitalization of theatrical art with the stage productions of Dullin, Jouvet, Baty, and others. Although domestic triangle comedies continued to thrive on the Parisian boulevards, more or less new playwrights such as Jean-Jacques Bernard, Vildrac, Sarment, Salacrou, Savoir, Pagnol, Romains, Lenormand, Obey, and Cocteau variously dissolved and spiced or poetized realism and experimented with fantasy, expressionist technique, and surrealism. Amidst much tepid or merely eccentric drama could be found many a *tour de force* such as *Topaze* and *Dr. Knock* in comedy and Cocteau's *The Infernal Machine* in tragedy. If the writers did not create masterpieces with their volatile and intelligent writing (I myself very much doubt that even the highly touted Cocteau play *The Infernal Machine* is one), they made the theatre a playing field for civilized artistry. One of their number, Jean Giraudoux, continued to refine and deepen his fanciful and ironic writing well on into the second war period, and his satiric fantasies *Intermezzo* (though unsuccessful in New York when produced in an adaptation entitled *The Enchanted*) and *The Madwoman of Chaillot* (*La folle de Chaillot*) are piquant works of modern playwriting.

Central Germany, agitated by post-war challenges, also developed a stylized theatre under the leadership of Reinhardt, Jessner, Fehling, Piscator, and other imaginative stage directors and their distinguished modernist scene designers. The excesses of pre-war and war-time expressionism were anything but lessened in the post-war period, especially between 1918 and 1923. But even in that frantic age, dramatic art was stimulating. Much could be learned from expressionist writing and play production. Notable productions, such as Jürgen Fehling's staging of Toller's drama of revolution *Man and the Masses* (*Masse-Mensch*) and Piscator's staging of *The Good Soldier Schweik,* an adaptation of the satiric anti-war Czech novel by Hasek, called attention to possibilities beyond peep-hole realism. Leopold Jessner's use of ramps as playing levels, his so-called *Jessner-treppen,* introduced a concept of a dynamic space stage production. It fascinated such visitors to Germany as our own Kenneth Macgowan and Robert Edmund Jones who, with O'Neill, sparked the Provincetown Players.

Among the Central-European playwrights, we may single out Toller, Kaiser, Werfel, and the Capek brothers, leaders of the new Czechoslovak theatre, as writers who used intellect and imagination critically. The poet Bertolt Brecht also got his start in that period with his 1922 prize-winning play *Drums in the Night*. His collaboration in 1928 with the composer Kurt Weill resulted in *The Three-Penny Opera*. Based on John Gay's *The*

Beggar's Opera, this comedy carried iconoclasm and irony to their greatest triumph on the German stage. Brecht's lyrics and Weill's music were the work of genius. And talent also appeared in the work of the Rhenish poet and writer of folk drama and satire Carl Zuckmayer, who first drew attention to himself with his prize-winning comedy *The Happy Vineyard* (*Der fröliche Weingarten*).

It must be noted, finally, that the Russian theatre after 1918 was also enormously energized by its stage directors and acting companies. Less so by its playwrights, whose most durable plays are two early plays of the post-war period, Maxim Gorki's *Yegor Bulychov,* a powerful tragedy of the death of a merchant, and Bulgakov's Chekhovian treatment of the vanishing aristocracy *The Last of the Turbins.* Many of the early revolutionary plays were merely melodramatic and a few revolutionary fantasies were absurd. Later plays, except for some comedies among which Katayev's *Squaring the Circle* became the best known, were more sociological than inspired. It was plain even before the advent of Stalin that the playwrights had become subservient to the totalitarian state. But kindness and dreams of a humane society were present in the plays of the twenties, and the arts of the stage were maintained with fervor and daring.

In the twenties and early thirties, indeed, the theatrical arts in Russia still displayed the modernist trend toward more or less attractive stylization general in continental Europe and begun in Russia under the pre-war monarchy with the advent of the ballet impressario Diaghilev as early in 1899. Stanislavskian realism was challenged, and Stanislavski's Moscow Art Theatre, founded under the monarchy, itself explored changes in style after some years. One of the leaders of this trend was the talented Vakhtangov, whose *Princess Turandot* is still remembered as a masterpiece of stylized stage production. Modernism, which won the admiration outside of Russia, ranged from choreographically styled staging by Tairov to ultramechanistic staging in Meyerhold's most extreme style of so-called constructivism despite which Meyerhold, soon to be a victim of the Stalinist Thermidor, displayed some noteworthy imaginativeness.

II

This, in brief, was the first post-war era of theatre, though enervated later in some countries, and though desiccated in Nazi Germany and in the reactionary world of Stalin. Then came the Second World War, and one by one the theatres of Europe were blacked out, blitzed, or turned to war-time uses.

Not to linger too long on the subject, we may note that the blitzed

London stage struggled valiantly to stay alive, but only Coward's fantastic comedy *Blithe Spirit* rose above the mediocrity and confusion of British war-time playwriting. No playwriting of any merit came out of Central Europe, and very little out of Russia, although its acting companies performed energetically at the front and behind it. Whatever acceptable or able playwriting was done by German writers was done in exile, in Switzerland, Sweden, and the United States. Werfel's tragi-comedy about the fall of France *Jacobowsky and the Colonel* proved successful here in an adaptation by S. N. Behrman. Some good writing was also done in America by Ferdinand Bruckner, Carl Zuckmayer, and Bertolt Brecht, who wrote two of his best plays, *The Caucasian Circle of Chalk* and *The Goodwoman of Setzuan* here.

A German-speaking theatre of some vitality existed only in Switzerland, partly due to the efforts of Werfel's sister Marianne Rieser and her husband. Curiously enough, however, France, recovering from the first shock of defeat and the first rigors of the German occupation, produced the most stimulating drama of the period, as if the French spirit were bent upon reasserting itself culturally as a reaction to political and military helplessness. Plays by Anouilh, Giraudoux, Montherlant, and Sartre, written under the Occupation and tolerated by German authority in Paris no doubt because of their obliqueness of reference, may be counted among the best written since 1914. *The Madwoman of Chaillot, No Exit,* and *The Flies* were war-time products.

The only other theatre to retain any vitality was the intact one of the United States, though the vitality was often questioned, for the fact remains that our playwrights rarely rose to the challenge of the times. Many war and anti-Nazi melodramas were written. These were intellectually superior to the vacuous melodramas of the First World War (and they had to be after two decades of modern playwriting in the twenties and thirties), but little more can be said for them. Among serious plays of a higher order produced between Pearl Harbor and V-J Day, Sidney Kingsley's Jefferson-Hamilton drama *The Patriots* stands out as an affirmation of national unity and a study of historical characters; *The Eve of St. Mark* as Maxwell Anderson's semi-poetic response to the tragedy of war; John Patrick's *The Hasty Heart* as an appealing picture of life in a base hospital; Dan James's *Winter Soldiers* as a stirring panorama of the resistance movement; and *The Moon Is Down* as Steinbeck's tribute to the Norwegian resistance movement.

Lillian Hellman's *The Watch on the Rhine,* which proclaimed the impossibility of isolation, had opened before Pearl Harbor, but continued its run after that event. Miss Hellman's review of "appeasement" or apathy in facing the challenge of fascism, *The Searching Wind,* and the Woodrow Wilson play *In Time to Come* by Howard Koch and John Huston, represented a genre of retrospective drama. *Tomorrow the World*, by James Gow and Arnaud d'Usseau, commended itself as a study of the denazification of Nazi youth. But among seriously intended plays before the last war-time season only Thornton Wilder's extravagant serio-comic review of human history *The Skin of Our Teeth* possessed any marked originality, if we except Saroyan's *The Beautiful People,* which had nothing to do with the war or with anything else other than the author's fanciful view of how people can rise above practical considerations.

Comic writing, for the most part, also rarely rose above the commonplace level of *Kiss and Tell.* The madcap murder farce *Arsenic and Old Lace* represents the high-water mark of war-time extravaganza; John van Druten's sophisticated romance *The Voice of the Turtle,* the further reach of war-time high comedy. In the season of 1944-45 came Mary Chase's *Harvey* and Tennessee Williams' *The Glass Menagerie,* and the war-torn period ended with some pleasure and distinction on Broadway.

The aftermath is still taking shape as this book goes to press. In America new expectations were roused by the emergence of Williams, Arthur Miller, and another young playwright William Inge. England experienced an intensified revival of poetic drama. The French theatre, liberated from German control, continued to show some intellectual vigor. The German theatre, liberated from Hitler, began to revive, but without experiencing any marked renascence in playwriting. In Italy, liberation brought a general revival of cultural activity, much of which, however, flowed into the writing of fiction rather than drama. No remarkable playwriting came out of the Scandinavian countries, which had contributed so much to the making of the modern drama. The news from Ireland, which had enriched the century's theatre, was not particularly encouraging except in so far as the Abbey was striving to right itself in the midst of dissensions and the Dublin Gate was continuing its efforts to foster imaginative or modernist drama. The Russian theatre continued to be active, but was enslaved to post-war Stalinist policy, and playwriting under his intensified and expansionist dictatorship sank to lower levels than ever before.

All that could be noted by 1953 was the fact that the old sources of modern drama were not sparkling as much during the second post-war period as they had done during the first post-war period. The condition of the world was not as favorable to a brilliant recovery by the theatre from the last great holocaust, which many people feared would soon be followed by another. A change in temper could be noted which might result in one or two things within the foreseeable future, even if it were not subject to the effects of another global war or a general cataclysm. Dramatic art would either lose much of the intellectual and artistic venturesomeness which had characterized the modern theatre, or dramatic art would somehow arrive at new achievements with altered attitudes and interest. At present, the latter possibility seems the less likely of the two.

III

The strong difference between the two post-war periods appears to be related to the respective position of the intellectual after 1918 and after 1950. After World War I, the intelligentsia made war on Philistia, as it had done before 1914. After World War II, Philistia began to make war on the intelligentsia. Moreover, the intelligentsia began to make war on itself. One faction tried to hold on to a long tradition of liberalism variously described as nineteenth-century reformism, political "innocence," or naïveté. Another faction was composed of disenchanted and repentant liberals, as well as anti-liberals who favored a more authoritarian tradition. The latter leaned toward the belief that rationalism and confidence in man's ability to improve his situation by social reform were misleading, if not indeed dangerous. More and more, the first-mentioned faction was put on the defensive by the second, as well as by Philistia.

In some countries, notably the United States, the defensive position was maintained with increasing difficulty after the first three or four post-war years during which the liberal wing had taken the offensive with such work as *State of the Union, Born Yesterday, Goodbye, My Fancy,* and *Deep Are the Roots,* plays that attacked illiberalism of a political, social, or racial nature with war-time enthusiasm. The fact that much articulate liberalism had unwarily allied itself with communist-sparked movements during the depression and war periods left it open to suspicion and vulnerable to attack once the "cold war" and the Korean War widened the breach between the West and the East.

The two liberal protests staged up to the season of 1952-53, both by Arthur Miller, were the indirect ones of a slanted adaptation of Ibsen's *An Enemy of the People* and a tragic treatment of the Salem witchcraft trials *The Crucible.* It is significant that Miller's *Death of a Salesman* was severely castigated only in the intellectuals' organs, *The Partisan Review* and *The Hudson Review.* It could be maintained, indeed, that whereas before the thirties liberalism and radicalism had been favored by "highbrows," it had been favored in the depression and post-depression periods only by "middlebrows."

In England, moderation was present in all camps; England was still the citadel of reasonable radicalism and enlightened conservatism. In West Germany, the liberal attitude was negative; it took the form of breast-beating over the conduct of the Germans under Hitler. In France alone was the liberal faction more or less on the offensive, but raggedly so and with various degrees of self-betrayal whether by narrow Existentialism or by shifts to the extreme left, as in the case of Sartre after 1950. In Spain and in the iron-curtain countries, liberalism was evidently entirely silenced or subverted.

The doctrine of Socialist Realism in Russia before the war had spawned a tiresome body of utilitarian drama supporting this or that Five Year Plan and prosaically concerned with such matters as increasing factory production, collectivizing agriculture, and enlarging the output of cement. One of the plays was indeed entitled *Cement*. During the war the patriotic motif overshadowed that of "Socialist Realism," resulting in work inspired by revulsion against the German invaders, by sympathy with the common man, and the fervor of armed resistance. Plays such as Afinogenov's *On the Eve* and the journalist-poet Konstantin Simonov's *The Russian People* acquired a temporary glow, even if they could not elicit paeans from detached dramatic criticism. After the war, the rigors of Stalinist dictatorship and anti-American sentiment sustained propaganda plays.

In the Eastern Zone of Germany, interest in theatre appeared to be vigorous, but all the distinguished plays of Bertolt Brecht had been written before his return to Berlin. No other plays of any conspicuous merit have thus far come from the East Berlin stage, to my knowledge. And there was evidence that cultural control required playwrights to hew to the "party line." Denunciations were heaped for a time upon Brecht himself, hitherto given considerable scope for his epic type of theatre despite the fact it consistently violated the tenets of "Socialist Realism." An opera, for which he had supplied the libretto, was withdrawn. And even more conclusive evidence of the failure of liberalism in "liberated" Germany was the fact that Brecht, an intransigent individualist in his literary career, should have eaten crow publicly.

With respect to its once extremely important intellectual situation, then, the modern drama seems to find itself at the crossroads. Which road it will take, if any, will be determined by developments outside the theatre. Since talent and genius nourish in ways often inexplicable and on ground not usually considered favorable to creativeness, I would hesitate to predict an end to modern playwriting. But only a professional optimist could predict a brave new world of theatre.

Part Three

THE INCUBI OF OUR STAGE

THE FALLACY OF UNITY

A question that never stops plaguing us is why so many plays and productions are dull, and the answers we supply are of course numerous. A question that concerns only the serious critic is why plays that are anything but watertight, so far as their logic of idea and structure goes, somehow manage to succeed; and this not only in the sense that they fill the auditorium but that they please intelligent reviewers. The two questions are in a sense the same, because quite often the dull, unsuccessful plays are manifestly orderly or "well constructed" and logical in argument and demonstration.

Now, it is true enough that plays may collapse because their elements fail to fuse, and this is equally true of productions. All of us can recall musical comedies so conglomerate in substance and style that they left an impression of disorder rather than entertainment, if indeed they left any impression at all. I also acutely remember two non-musical productions that suffered because of disparities of acting style and diction, Robert Turney's *The Daughters of Atreus* and *The House of Bernarda Alba*. But there are far more instances of consistent mediocrity and dullness solidly compounded. For such work Heinrich Heine's comment on a minor poet remains pithily *a propos*: "Uhland's poetry reminds me of Bayard's horse: it has every conceivable virtue, but it is dead." A playwright may be a "thinker" or an expert in propaganda, a versifier, even a poet of sorts, or a master of syllogism. A stage director may be formidably competent, and may reason the parts of his production together so carefully that every stage movement points in the same direction and bears upon the same theme. And yet the parallel to Bayard's horse may be inescapable.

Although we are all agreed that the ideal of drama and of theatre is some sort of consistency or unity, there is also a "fallacy of unity" that has afflicted dramatic art at different times. It has affected the average playwright and producer ever since the advent of realism and the thesis drama in the last quarter of the nineteenth century. It has exerted an influence, in fact, ever since the rise of the "well-made play" when Scribe, not Ibsen, was the lawgiver of the drama. I will not go into the history of the subject, except to point out that both the revolt against Scribe by Ibsen and the revolt against Ibsen by the symbolists instead of making less of "unity," made more of it. No sooner had we turned against the unity of contrived intrigue in the eighteen-seventies than we turned to the unity of "idea," "problem," or demonstration with Ibsen, Galsworthy, Brieux,

and their successors. No sooner had we deprecated Ibsenism and naturalism than we cried up the values of unity of mood and symbol with Appia,
Gordon Craig, and the symbolists. It has always been the other fellow's
unity, not our own, that hasn't been any good!

Now, it is not my intention to prove that any sort of unity, except that
of dullness, is bad. I am concerned only with what I would call the "fallacy
of unity," which is the assumption that if you have unity of plot, idea, and
style you have everything and will automatically achieve drama and theatre. And this tendency will be found everywhere in one guise or another.
It appears in the teaching of playwriting with its emphasis on play construction to the exclusion of virtually everything else. Play-carpentry is
confused with creation. In consequence, too, teachers of drama often fail
to attend to their subject, which is theatre. Consistency becomes the touch-
stone of excellence for them so exclusively that they ignore the texture
through which the play is dramatically and theatrically alive.

I have known instructors who were inclined to banish *Liliom* from
the curriculum because they were unable to reconcile the early realistic
scenes with the later fantastic ones. If only Molnar had presented the latter
as Liliom's dying delirium or as Julie's dream after Liliom's suicide! Since
Molnar did no such thing, his play simply does not hang together for
them, and until it can be made to hang together by some ratiocinative
process or some discourse on dramatic style, they are apt to underestimate
the quality of dramatic or at least theatrical vitality that makes *Liliom*
enchanting. And if teachers ought to have their knuckles rapped, producers should have their heads examined. Few of them fail to make the mistake of giving preference to plays, no matter how flat, that cohere as orderly argument as against the rare poetic fugues and flights of imagination
that cannot be reduced to a formula or a definition. Few producers realize
that the play that defines itself too simply wasn't worth writing in the first
place, and that drama, like poetry, must exist on more than one level of
meaning or interest if it is to exist at all. Few, moreover, are exempt from
the still more serious error of talking or browbeating playwrights into
whittling their work into shape—until they have whittled and shaped the
life and theatre out of it.

Although producers have improved a number of scripts, they have
also reasoned and "ordered" more than a few into dead lumber. I know a
number of plays that had a richer texture and greater vibrancy when they
were optioned by the producer than when they were revised under his
direction. Saroyan's *Get Away, Old Man* was such a play. Another, I
believe, was Sidney Howard's *The Ghost of Yankee Doodle*. And quite
a number of plays were abandoned by the producer as hopeless after the
playwrights had revised them according to his specifications.

Most culpable, however, are the numerous would-be playwrights and the actually experienced ones, such as the author of the recent *Hilda Crane,* who remain tethered to their demonstration of a thesis or premise and seem to care for little else. If they are Samson Raphaelsons, which they rarely are, the dramatists manage to at least vary events and tempo sufficiently to give us some of the variety or light and shade we know to be life and human personality. Usually they create character by definition and situations by calculation. The person in their play represents this or that quality, this or that desire, and no other. The situations in which this person finds himself are invented almost entirely in order to support the definition rather than to make multidimensional life and theatre in support of the idea. To observe the difference between this prefabrication and creative playwriting, we need only recall Ben Jonson's *Volpone,* supposedly a play that makes drama out of character traits rather than out of fully realized individuals. Jonson had a criticism of life and society in view, and intended his comedies as social corrosives. Nevertheless, his vital playwriting gave Volpone qualities and actions beyond the line of duty of demonstrating the theme of unscrupulous greed. Much of the fun in this old comedy lies in the pleasure Volpone takes in his scheming ingenuity. He is *living* his rascality rather than merely executing it. Our playwrights, on the contrary, have been taught to demonstrate an idea by putting the argument together scene by scene. They think they have written a play because they have used plenty of dramatic cement. They pay only perfunctory attention to what is being knit together.

The "fallacy of unity" is associated with another widespread fallacy among would-be dramatists. It is the tacit assumption that "theatre" is a single, one-tracked experience, whose destination is the only thing that matters. Such writers think they can be "playwrights" without first of all being "scenewrights." They write as if they thought they could make whole plays in one stroke instead of creating individual scenes, each vivid and vibrant; scenes that make up a play not only by their relationship in the service of plot and idea, but by the sum of their immediate life. These playwrights use the *planner's* rather than the creator's, the *expositor's* rather than the theatrician's, approach. They forget the importance of the moment-by-moment effect on the audience. They overlook the fact that a play is an unfolding experience, that drama is a process interesting precisely as a process to the spectator, since he views the events only as they succeed each other on the stage. They think only of the final result, forgetting that for the audience each scene and sub-scene, each encounter between characters and revelation, is also a *result* or, temporarily, an end in itself.

You will encounter this jigsaw view of playwriting whenever a novice requests his classmates or friends to suspend judgment until they have heard his entire play, or when a playwright is indignant over the thought that a producer may have turned down his play without reading to the end. He had put the pieces of the jigsaw puzzle together in the sweat of his brow and yet there are people who have had the gall to look at the pieces individually. How can his work be evaluated before it has been read through? What he fails to realize is that plays *are* evaluated piece by piece, from moment to moment, for the simple reason that theatre occurs not at the *end* of a performance but *during* it. George Jean Nathan once declared that one should be able to tell whether a play was any good after reading the first few pages. This statement was taken to be just another instance of bravado by Nathan. Yet our senior critic had scored a point. I don't believe he meant that he would be able to make up his mind to produce the play before reading it through. But he *did* mean that he could decide *not* to produce it on the basis of sampling it. Does one have to consume the whole steak before deciding that it is horsemeat!

Our response to theatre does not support the notion that it is a single experience consisting solely of an end-result. If the end-result is good, this is so not only because the argument coheres (often it doesn't wholly cohere, or the main point of the play continues to be debated for centuries, as in the case of *Hamlet*), but because the scene by scene effect was compelling in itself, as well as mounting in interest and significance. That the experience of good theatre is multiple and continuous can be sustained in the case of every sort of effective drama and production. It is merely less apparent in one instance than in another; less apparent for some of us, let us say, in Racine's plays than in Shakespeare's. The fact is that our gratification depends so largely upon the strength and richness of the successive impressions made upon us that we often send our logical faculties on vacation. We may not check our brains upon entering a theatre, but we are apt to do so after one or two engaging acts.

It is not difficult, indeed, to understand why even an experienced reviewer should grow wildly enthusiastic about a play that could be ripped apart and shown to be logically dubious or even patently unsound. Sometimes the impressions and the general notion he has formed are so strong that even his more considered second review, written a week or so later, shows no awareness of the flaw. And this is a tribute to the power of theatre. In a non-dramatic field, such impressionableness would instantly prove incompetence on the critic's part. The effect of theatre—or, I should say, of a succession of theatrical impacts—also explains why men of the intelligence of a Walkley, Shaw, Joseph Wood Krutch, and George Jean Nathan should have been able to endure hundreds of inane productions without going stark mad. It is the infectiousness of theatre that also explains why certain questionable pieces such as Pinero's should not only have passed muster in their time, but been regarded, for a while, as important contributions. It is even possible to understand how the Victorian readers of Matthew Arnold, John Stuart Mill, and John Ruskin could endure the melodramas of their day. As for critics, they are apt to be susceptible to one set of impressions and intentions if not to another. Shaw himself lost some of his critical acumen when his social enthusiasms encountered the lucubrations of that ministerial fuss-budget of thesis drama Eugene Brieux. On another occasion, Shaw's susceptibility to paradox and dialectic led him to declare anent an unsuccessful Welsh rarebit once produced by me that anyone who couldn't enjoy the play was an idiot! Unfortunately, the fourth estate and Broadway were made up of so many "idiots" that I had to close the production within a week. . . .

Although to a great degree the art of the playwright and his production collaborators consists of an ability to make complete detachment impossible, it is nonetheless possible to practice enough detached criticism to take exception even to quite well-written and ably produced plays. Enthusiasm for, let us say, *The Rose Tattoo*—or even *A Streetcar Named Desire* and *Death of a Salesman*—can be greatly modified upon more or less close examination. It has been observed that the symbolism of *The Rose Tattoo* is extravagant and specious. It is also possible to doubt that the superheated conduct of the Latin heroine is a proper equivalent for the principle of vitality glorified by Tennessee Williams. Concerning *Streetcar*, it is not difficult to maintain that Blanche's unhappy condition is overmotivated to the point of absurdity. It takes some straining to believe that a woman becomes a nymphomaniac because her husband has turned out to be a homosexual and has committed suicide. And if Williams' play is to be judged by its argument, is Blanche a proper test for the quality of mercy, and is Stan Kowalski a proper test of humanity's ability to give or withhold it? Is Blanche, besides, a proper subject for tragic exposition rather than for clinical ministrations? And if we are to test *Death of a Salesman* as a thesis, is it improper to inquire whether Willy's objective situation would have been radically different if he had possessed the self-knowledge his author recommends? Is it improbable that Willy would still have become a superannuated salesman or, if he had used his talent for manual labor, a superannuated worker? And, conversely, is it too frivolous to wonder whether, as the world wags, Willy's measure of obtuseness and success-worship could not have made him rich and respected? The moment we forget that Miller's drama is Willy's particular story and not anybody else's, we can only conclude that some people are both stupid and unfortunate; in which case we may also reflect that other people are stupid but fortunate—which leaves us precisely nowhere.

We can multiply such questions easily enough in the case of these and other more or less effective plays, once we stand away at some distance from them. We may even reason ourselves into dismissing them. Yet much of this logic-chopping would be fairly irrelevant in the face of the impression they made not by their unassailable logic, but by the force of their theatricalization of specific human experience. And, also let us add, by a poetic heightening of the banal in life through a scene by scene expression of some dominant attitude in many instances more felt than scrupulously documented for the public.

What we vitally experience and carry away with us from such plays is a series of related flashes rather than a steady illumination. The more or less blending impressions may be, as in *The Rose Tattoo,* an old woman crazily chasing a goat while neighbors superstitiously avoid her; an earthy, passionate woman boasting of her late husband's virility and keeping his ashes in her room; a truck driver clownishly weeping with frustration after an encounter with a brash salesman, and later having his chest tattooed for the purpose of wooing the lady; a young girl experiencing first love with a gangling sailor incongruously sworn to continence by a mother who is both a devout Catholic and a pagan voluptuary. The sum total of these and other incidents constitutes the theatrical life of the play. If *The Rose Tattoo* fails to make any profound sense and is less than a model drama, it has nevertheless provided a reason for going to the theatre—that is, for going where we can find some semblance of life on a more than usual level of intensity.[1]

The closer the accord between a provocative, well-sustained idea and these rudiments of theatre the better of course. *Streetcar* and *Death of a Salesman* are superior in this respect to *The Rose Tattoo,* just as *The Cherry Orchard,* in turn, is superior to the plays of Williams and Miller. But it is the very rudiments of theatre that tend to be neglected in a good deal of current playwriting, and I find this to be a major reason within the compass of my experience for the poverty of our theatre.

The living drama lies midway between the anarchy of mere impressionism and the *rigor mortis* of mere syllogism. While acting in an advisory capacity on a play some years ago, I found myself between the crotchets of a confident producer and an equally confident stage director. The producer assured me during the rehearsal period that all was well with his play because, with revisions by the author, he had turned it into "a swell yarn." The director gave me equally strong assurances that the wobbly play was saved at last because he had *discovered* "a swell idea" for the play, which he was grafting on it by means of the setting he had

---

[1] And less than two years later Parisians, our alleged superiors in taste, found it profound.

ordered and the direction-pattern he was now working out. The "yarn" had no point, and the "idea" had no dramatic support from the events. The producer quite properly fired the director. But if the director had held the purse strings, he could have fired the producer with equal justification, for the play was doomed in either case.

Today nearly everybody with half a mind has an "idea" or point which he is ready to demonstrate at the drop of the curtain. And among the avant-garde gentry everybody has a "form" ready for use—whether it be verse drama with a ritual pattern *à la* Eliot, an Anouilh "charade," or a Brechtian epic structure. And, like the clinical analysts or idea-demonstrators, these formalist disciples of men who often practice better sense themselves rarely pay attention to what the form should project. They, too, immolate living theatre on the altar of a concept or idea, good or bad, original or banal. Both the realists and the anti-realistic stylizers, the clinicians and rhapsodes, the rationalists and the mystagogues, then, can become equally undramatic for the sake of a concept.

The issue, I conclude, is between dramatic idea and total theatre in such cases! If the importance of total theatre, which is no better than its units, is ignored or minimized, everything may be right and yet nothing lives. The nuances, the sudden epiphanies, the rich contradictions and irrelevancies of actual and imagined life remain unrealized. Only the thematic point or the formal structure is served. It is no wonder, then, that many nobly or honestly conceived plays fail while the public carries its bullion to the first tolerable musical comedy in which unity makes way for piquant diversity.

The problem to which I would call attention, I need hardly add, is neither new nor unique. It has been well understood in English literary criticism at least since Coleridge wrote in his *Biographia Literaria* that a poem affords "such delight from the whole as is compatible with a distinct gratification from each component part." We may paraphrase the statement for the theatre by saying that a *play* affords such delight from the whole as is compatible with a distinct gratification from each component scene. And it is not contrary to our experience of theatre to find that we are often less satisfied with a play as a whole than with some or all its component scenes and sub-scenes, just as we are often less satisfied with a stage production as a whole than with some or all of the performances. At the same time, however, it would be most dangerous to conclude that a play or a production can be satisfactory without the components adding up to an experience that gratifies us as a distinct whole, justifiable and meaningful as a total play and production rather than as a mere conglomerate of miscellaneous scenes and acting bits. Both play and production should be an *ensemble,* of course, not a free-for-all.

EMOTION COMES CHEAP

Mr. George Tabori, a reputable journalist from Hungary now both a playwright and an American, is reported to have taken strong exception to critics of his Broadway play of the 1951-52 season *Flight into Egypt* who said that it failed to develop a tenable central idea. Presumably he would have considered himself more justly treated if he had been complimented on having wrung our hearts with the tense situations and outbursts that he provided with his tale of refugees stranded in Egypt. Why did some critics quibble over the theme of the play or over the question of the validity of escape instead of melting with compassion for his struggling characters—a noble husband, a devoted and long-suffering wife, a brave slip of a lad? Since the play departed from the stage after a short run, it may be less important to sustain Mr. Tabori or his critics than to examine the premise that emotional appeal is the saving quality of a play. I propose to maintain the opposite view not out of a desire to criticize Mr. Tabori, but out of a conviction that serious playwrights, here and abroad, are often deluded by too much cant about the importance of emotion in drama. (Cant inherited by our theatre from the Victorian theatre; and by the Victorian stage from the vogue of sentimental drama that displaced aristocratic Reason with middle-class Virtue in the eighteenth century.)

The vogue of emotionalism has a long history. If one period's idiom goes out of fashion, another rapidly takes its place. The older period's gets laughed at. *Abie's Irish Rose,* for example, was already a subject for laughter in the nineteen-twenties. It seemed hopelessly old-fashioned to reviewers, although its author Ann Nichols and the public thought there was something very modern about stage Jews and stage Irishmen loving each other. The new period's cult seems fresh and daring, and ever so "serious" and enlightened, until it is discovered to have been little more than sentimentality with a new accent. During the nineteen-thirties and the war period, the accent was on sharecroppers, striking factory workers, and victims of unemployment. Or on German intellectuals victimized by Storm Troopers. (Broadway alone got half a dozen failures out of this subject, with the German writer Ferdinand Bruckner's *Races* proving the most acceptable of these.) Or the stress was on French and Norwegian nationals resisting the German occupation; with Gallic gallantry in Maxwell Anderson's *Candle in the Wind,* or with Scandinavian steadfastness in John Steinbeck's *The Moon Is Down.*

Continuing into the nineteen-fifties, the *larmoyante* tradition found an especially convenient peg in "refugee-ism." Gian-Carlo Menotti made such a successful bid for public sympathy in *The Consul* that hardly a reviewer ventured to ask for a few pertinent facts in addition to Menotti's information that some Europeans behind dropping iron curtains wanted to escape to the United States and that the passport system wasn't working to their advantage.

Menotti, however, had a double advantage over Tabori, who had a similar theme in *Flight into Egypt.* Menotti's characters had "priority" as popular victims. They were from some unidentified "iron curtain" country, whereas Tabori's unfortunates came from Vienna before their flight to America was stalemated in Egypt. Menotti, moreover, used the medium of opera, to which no one addresses precise questions, whereas Tabori used the medium of spoken theatre, from which reviewers expect some logic. Although that commodity was apparent here and there in *Flight into Egypt,* it was largely absent where it was most needed—namely, in the theme and its development. Deceived by prevalent notions of "good theatre" as the equivalent of heartbreak, the author made his intelligence defer to his sympathies. The result was a divided drama that moved in opposite directions at the same time, and the reviewers, not having been musicalized into narcosis in this instance, spotted the two-way traffic.

The extravagant peddling of notions about the primacy of emotion has undone more playwrights than can be imagined by those who know only plays staged on Broadway, the West End, or other theatre centers. "Feeling" comes cheap. Any mediocrity can have a throbbing heart and shed an easy tear. It is *thinking* that is difficult. Perhaps that is why so little of it can be found anywhere. There is so little evidence of cerebration on our stage that one might paraphrase William Blake and accuse our playwrights, as well as producers, of crucifying the theatre "with the head downwards."

Emotional orgies belong in soap operas, television thrillers, and Western movies. (And why compete with these anyway, since they not only undersell the "legitimate" show but excel it in dispensing suspense, excitement, and pathos?) It was emotionalism that made the pre-Ibsen nineteenth-century stage so abysmally bad that we deride and burlesque its plays. The only dramatists who survive from that period are the writers who were thinkers—which is not the same thing as merely being a writer of a so-called problem play. One Buechner, virtually unknown before 1900, was worth a quorum of bouncing Boucicaults; one ironical Musset, a dozen melodramatists. We are agreed about that today. We laugh at Boucicault, Scribe, Sardou, Sidney Grundy, and Pinero—often without having ever read any of their work. This makes us feel quite superior to the Victorians. Actually, however, we often gulp down the same nauseat-

ing treacle. Only the vessel in which it is served is different; it has modern
or even "modernistic" design.

In due time, the effects on the audience are the same—nausea. The
cause eludes us as if it were a filterable virus. We detect and balk at sentimentality when the quantity and character of it are unmistakable. But our
playwrights are often clever enough to disguise the bolus; they dip it into
some tough, even obscene, dialogue and action (a seduction or rape
scene), and, presto, we swallow it as though it were teeming with vita-
mins. And our actors are also ingenious; they speak the line not trippingly
on the tongue, but with a chortle or a Marlon Brando grunt and grumble,
and suddenly the play is transformed into the rough diamond substance
of "reality." Consequently, few of us—whether we provide the plays or
view them—realize that we are back in pre-Ibsen, pre-Shavian theatre of
the past century or even sentimental eighteenth-century *comédie-larmo-
yante* theatre.

We even view Shakespeare in terms of that theatre when we produce
his plays; we are modern in every respect when we stage them—that is, in
every superficial respect (unit sets, space sets, platform-*cum*-ramps)—but
smother the "wit" or mind that crackles even in stormy scenes and
speeches: "Take physic, pomp . . . ," "Plate sin with gold . . . ," "I pay
thy poverty, not thy will . . . I sell thee poison, thou hast sold me none."
We still produce the plays, hoping to pile passion on passion in the tragedies or pseudo-tragedies, and sentiment on sentiment in the comedies. We
turn *As You Like It* into an operetta by stringing together all the Shakespearean songs we can possibly use, and sell it to the public with Katharine Hepburn as a "show"; and even the *Shakespeare Quarterly* approves.
Sometimes we don't succeed in "selling" the show to the critics or the
public, but then the *Romeo and Juliet* or *Much Ado About Nothing*
production has to be so distressingly poor that even a television producer
would be revolted.

It is obvious to most people that a plethora of plays that say nothing at
all must destroy a theatre for which, except in the case of musicals, only
a more or less adult audience has been left by the so-called mass-communication media. It is less obvious to writers and producers, however, that
this theatre is not going to be salvaged by the plays with a message about
public virtue that heave with fervor but amount to little more cerebration
than the late Calvin Coolidge's assurance that his pastor was against sin.
Virtuous playwrights and producers are going to continue to retail this
product every now and then in a mood of self-gratulation because they are
treating "significant" matter. Nor are they likely to diverge from the conviction that seriousness is a substitute for brains, and that the only way to
be serious is to be solemnly unsubtle. For even our best or most literary

playwriting makes a fetish of "emotional power," sympathy, and poetic haze. It is this hashish-addiction that confuses even such talented writers as Tennessee Williams and Truman Capote. It certainly confuses dramatic criticism, which in turn confuses playwrights, stage directors, teachers and students of the drama.

Most of these earnest souls do not know what to make of playwrights such as Becque and Sternheim who write with dry irony. And it has been my experience that they read the world's great dramas with such innocence that these works, too, rarely stimulate more than one-level, if not indeed one-note, playwriting. Shakespeare is "beauty" for the innocents; Shaw, "message" or, in *Saint Joan,* noble sentiment. Sophocles is "dignity"; Ibsen, "truth"; Strindberg, "passion." Except in the 1952 production of *Don Juan in Hell,* in which Shaw was mercifully allowed to speak for himself, the "triple-thinker," as Edmund Wilson called Shaw, has recently been turned into a "mono-thinker" by his producers. In spite of Shaw's own protest against the "Candidamaniacs," *Candida* remains for the devotees of "feeling" a paean to a good woman, as the 1952 Hollywood-graced Olivia de Havilland production served to remind us. *Saint Joan* was staged by the Theatre Guild as though its author had dutifully written it for a Canterbury Cathedral festival; *Caesar and Cleopatra,* in the Olivier revolving stage production, as though he had prepared his piece for an historical pageant in Madison Square Garden. Anouilh's *Eurydice,* adapted under the title of *Legend of Lovers,* became a sob-story in a Maeterlinckian mist. Some innocents are bent upon transposing dramatic counterpoint into either a flute solo or a Sousa march. If this trend continues, it will be difficult to distinguish the classics from a television show, except that on television the agony is usually less protracted.

We must grant, of course, that great tragic playwrights have given us scenes of overwhelming emotional force, and that masters of comedy, too, have sometimes been intense. Some of Aristophanes' lyrics are as stirring as anything ever written, and some of his harangues or "parabases" supply a rarely surpassed eloquence. The death of Shaw's Dubedat in *The Doctor's Dilemma* is one of the most moving scenes ever written; Joan's trial makes most modern scenes seem tepid; Captain Shotover's *Heartbreak House* discussion of "navigation" and Father Keegan's "three-in-one" explanation of "what it is like in his dreams," in *John Bull's Other Island,* are more rousing than trumpets. But we are too disposed to overlook the knife-edge quality of the thought that rules—and actually produces—the exultation we feel in these instances. This kind of writing is not the product of a commonplace view of reality on the playwright's part.

What we need, it would seem, is a cooling-off period that would make intellectual maturity a requirement or at least an aspiration for the playwright, as well as for the collaborating artists who put his work on the stage. Let him deal with emotion if he wishes—but dealing with it is not the same thing as succumbing to it and dispensing with logic. Let him express convictions if he has any, but let it be thought that is transformed into passion. A cooling-off process would challenge the playwright to use his brains, if he has any, in working out the contradictions, the multi-leveled reality, and the ironies of the human condition, whether he does so in realistic or fanciful terms. He may then learn to keep the mind engaged in experience—alert and active, not submissive to mere feeling or standardized opinion. His craft-view of playwriting being revised to the point of realizing that he is expected to think provocatively if he is to interest us, he may learn to move toward strenuously attained climaxes, as all master dramatists have done.

He may even learn the art of "cooling off" between portions of a play and so reviving the playgoer as a thinking and judging individual. This is the art that was so well employed by the Greek tragedians and Shakespeare, and that Brecht uses in so intense a play as his *Mother Courage*. The "coolness," of course, should not be a vacuum in which dramatic interest simply dies out, but an occasion for the mind to function.

A great deal of bad conditioning stands in the way of achieving an intellectual rebirth in the theatre. For one thing, we have become too accustomed to mental relaxation in our theatre-going. For another, we suspect any manifestation of intellectual aloofness as snobbery. Playwrights don't understand, moreover, that the effective thinking is not a solid and extraneous chunk of exposition, but the context of the work and its form. The thinking should not be superimposed but integral, and indistinguishable from any other dramatic element. It is content *and* form. It is certainly not the content one can summarize in a few simple sentences for a Board of Examiners handing out licenses to teach in the schools, but a way of seeing and experiencing life. It is not the intellectual *per se* who is involved in the process but the *total man* writing or staging the work. One disadvantage of the emotional dramatics we have overrated so mistakenly is that it exercises too small a part of the playwright's, actor's, and playgoer's personality, as though he were nothing more than a breathing conglomeration of impulses and sentiments.

The theatre, like any other art, may need intensity, but the question is whether only emotionalism can provide intensification. No one has yet discovered a way of determining at what point thinking ends and feeling begins. What we honor as passion is simply intensity, and who shall say that intensity is absent in close reasoning, in sustained objectivity, or in an insistently ironical position.

When there are many ways of attaining the intensification of reality that is as essential to drama as to any other art, there is no convincing reason for relying exclusively on emotion. And certainly there is no reason for assuming that feeling is an infallible means of succeeding in the theatre when it has produced so many failures. An actor who is choked up with emotion gives a bad performance. So does a playwright.

Perhaps our theatre will be more tolerable when all of us—playwright, actor, and audience—learn to keep our distance. (At this point there may be anguished cries from arena-stage theoreticians who have been peddling "circular staging" on the grounds that it promotes "intimacy." But distance in art is not a matter of yards or inches, but of attitude; and arena production can provide as much "esthetic distance," if not actually more, than a performance behind a proscenium arch.) We learn to keep our distance and maintain perspectives as we grow older; and as we become more adult, we appreciate less rather than more intimacy, as well as fewer emotional downpours. Perhaps we shall have a better theatre when it becomes more adult, too. Let the "mass-communication media" cater—as they will, anyhow—to our more infantile cravings!

THE PLAYWRIGHT AND THE CAMERA

No sharper contrast to the practice of much contemporary playwriting may be cited than Shaw's declaration, almost half a century ago (in the preface to *Mrs. Warren's Profession,* I believe), that as for himself, as a playwright, he was definitely *not* a camera. And here, as elsewhere, Shaw proved himself a good deal wiser, both as a playwright and a critic, than most of his colleagues who assumed that realism is the equivalent of photography in writing and stage production. George Jean Nathan scornfully used to call this view of theatre "Belascoism." Still, one can set it down as a sort of axiom that mediocrity never learns from genius. Consequently the tribe of realists who thought of themselves as breathing cameras has increased steadily. Today, there are few realistic playwrights left here or in England who rise appreciably and consistently above the classification of animated cameras.

That the *I Am a Camera* attitude has been catastrophic in the contemporary theatre is only too apparent. (I hope Mr. van Druten will forgive my using his title as a stick with which to beat playwriting.) We have only to look at any recent season to observe the results; and those of us who are in the habit of reading unproduced plays by young writers—plays that are no worse but not very much better than those produced—find the same humdrum reproduction of surface realities their authors like to believe are "mother lodes" of precious ore just waiting to be tapped by an intelligent producer.

Occasionally, of course, we encounter a play on Broadway or in our pile of scripts that may be defined as a fantasy, or an attempt at stylized, non-realistic drama which we might call expressionistic or even surrealistic when the fugue is Saroyan's *Jim Dandy,* a standard Gertrude Stein experiment, or Picasso's ragout, *Desire*—the latter generally turning up in Greenwich Village or on the left bank of the Seine. And their authors would feel very much affronted if they were classified with the "camera" tribe. They have their own special difficulties: sometimes their work is so esoteric they seem to be talking to themselves, or, at best, to an élite of specialists in symbolism. Meanwhile, the rest of us, mere lowbrows and middlebrows, usually reach for our hats and make for the nearest exit. Curiously enough, however, they, too, owe a good deal of their aridity to a misconception concerning the nature of realism. They would not scorn logic and communicability so lightly if it were not for the bugbear of photographic literalness with which realism has become associated. The only difference between the realists' bad playwriting and their own is that theirs is a different kind of badness. Their plays are harder to describe, if you feel you must describe them, but easy to praise as "unusual" if unusualness is your criterion for art.

Yet I am surely saying nothing original or unfamiliar when I declare that there is a good deal of difference between surface-realism and the realism of mind and spirit that penetrates into the heart of some matter. There is photographic realism and there is a realism that recreates and gives significance to reality. Specifically, in theatre art there is, on one hand, the realistic *technique* (call it naturalism, if you will) which makes a virtue of prose dialogue and of near-facsimile reproductions of life as if spectators looked into somebody's apartment. The "fourth-wall convention" assumes that the stage is such an apartment. And, on the other hand, there is realism of the spirit, a way of sizing up life clearly rather than vaguely, profoundly rather than superficially, honestly rather than sentimentally. This is the only true realism and the only kind worth cherishing. It is not dependent upon any particular technique or style, although it may be associated, and since 1875 frequently has been associated, with the conventions of the realistic *technique*.

The most scrupulous *technical* realism, the most detailed photography, may be used, as Hollywood has so often used it, actually to misrepresent and conceal reality. You may be accurate about the contours of every piece of furniture and dress, you may reproduce faithfully every gesture and intonation of characters, and yet lie yourself blue in the face. In short, realistic technique is one thing, and true realism is another. For the sake of the latter, indeed, modern playwrights have not hesitated to abandon the realistic technique altogether or to modify it and supplement it with styles and devices often broadly designated "expressionistic." Ultimately, then, it is the attitude the dramatist brings to life that is decisive, and it is the "camera" *attitude* that is wrong with the current practice of realism.

The fact is that the "I-am-a-camera" tribe does not work in the great tradition of modern realism that made modern drama vital and significant. That tradition was created by men of the stamp of Becque, Ibsen, Strindberg, Chekhov, and Shaw, who brought an inquiring spirit, a penetrating intellect, an original sensibility, and a well-formed individuality into the theatre. Their realism did not consist of making a record for the record's sake, and if they took pains to unfold what purported to be an accurate rendition of social reality or human conduct in an accurately observed, specific environment, they expressed a point of view intensely felt and acutely thought out. We saw the creator in his work, and the mark of his personal "slant" or passion was on that work.

So greatly, in fact, did the chief pioneer realists insist upon the expression of a unique, intensely held point of view that they did not hesitate to deviate from mere realistic technique and even from verisimilitude. The Don Juan fantasy in *Man and Superman* and the Epilogue in *Saint Joan* were written by the man who made himself Ibsen's and modern realism's champion in the eighteen-nineties when he worked as a drama critic in London. Shaw, who called *Heartbreak House* a fantasia and who never hesitated to play at theatre, would not have fought for Ibsen, himself not averse to using symbolism, merely for the sake of making accurate copies of middle-class life.

For a long time critics have deplored the fact that there has been too little tragic art in the modern theatre and cited a number of reasons for it. The reason is certainly not that we have had too much realism, as some writers allege, but that we have had too little of the genuine article; for true tragedy is always supremely realistic in the fundamental sense of the term. It encompasses *both sides* of the phenomenon of man: that is, his magnificence *and* horribleness, his reason *and* unreason, his angelic *and* his demonic nature. Tragic realism consists of this double vision, possessed only by those with unclouded eyes. Moreover, genuine tragedy makes its ascent from the solid ground of a recognition denied to sentimentalists of all persuasions (Positivists and Liberals included) that there are natural limits to human power and human possibilities—a recognition, as Keats called it, and as Father William F. Lynch recently reminded us in the magazine *Thought,* of "life's impossibilities." Today, much of our drama is actually sentimental and palliative rather than genuinely realistic. Our plays, for the most part, are merely dressed up in realistic detail.

The mortal sin, then, of our "camera" playwrights is not at all that they record reality so accurately but that they record it so dimly. Even so competently written a play as *Point of No Return* is only mildly realistic, providing an example of the wishful eat-your-cake-and-have-it-too philosophy so prevalent among us. No remarkable dramatic art has ever been founded on this philosophy, unless it was presented ironically, as in Strindberg's *There Are Crimes and Crimes. Point of No Return* makes Henry Fonda obtain the wisdom of disenchantment and self-criticism, which we are expected to approve, and the vice-presidency of a bank at the same time. The wife in the play, concurrently, is allowed to hammer away at her husband to obtain the vice-presidency and at the same time is allowed to retain the public's sympathy. This is no more than the low-level realism of adherence to the commonplaces of society, "the facts of life" so dear to prosperous but self-pitying middle-aged members of the audience.

A camera is inherently passive, and moral or spiritual passiveness has yet to produce a dramatic masterpiece. It is *a deficiency of attitude* or, at best, a faint-hearted attitude which gives us the "camera" type of play-writing. In weaker plays than *Point of No Return* or van Druten's *I Am a Camera,* no attitude pulsates at all, or the argument, such as the demon-stration in the Anita Loos dramatization of Colette's *Gigi* that innocence and candor will be rewarded with true love and a marriage certificate, is essentially a cliché. It need not be, of course, when a Colette herself views such a conclusion in her novel from the corner of an ironic eye, urbanely implying that there is seduction in innocence, too. But most American efforts at irony in the theatre are lamentably crude or covered with a thick sauce of sentiment.

In most plays, in fact, we are not given an attitude toward life at all, but a theatrical pose that passes for reality only by grace of whatever dimensions of character one or more actors manage to convey, as Audrey Hepburn did, for example, in the aforementioned *Gigi* in the season of 1951-52. The performers often express a marked personality, whereas the playwrights do not. The performers, moreover, can reveal it (if they have it) by their very stage presence, while the playwright can present his claim to a distinctive personality only through the text of his play. A camera has no personality whatsoever.

Reality, at least the only reality known to us mortals, is something organized and made meaningful by *ourselves.* This cannot be the case in the theatre unless two conditions are present: A personality capable of dominating the raw material of art, and an approach to playwriting as a creative act rather than as play-carpentry. At present, the genuine person-alities are too few and the play-carpenters, unfortunately, too numerous.

THE NEED FOR FINESSE

Some theatres have too much finesse, others, too little. The French and English theatres have too much, the modern German and American, too little. Each has the quality of its defects: The French is often delightfully nimble-witted; the English, often fluent and precise. The German theatre, except during the dreadful interval of Nazism, has tended to be intense and inquiring; the American, to be compassionate and breezy. But the defects have often been more conspicuous than the virtues. The French stage has been too clever for its somewhat torrid britches with its endless boulevardism, and too clever, as well, with its cartwheels of intellectual puckishness; the English, too fastidiously superior in comedy and too mild-mannered, if not indeed disengaged, when serious-minded. The German theatre has been inclined to be heavyhanded, overinsistent, and even frantic; the American, to be unsubtle except in rare high-comedic situations.

Obviously, these are broad generalizations; and I do not of course wish to imply that the above-noted merits and defects are not nationally interchangeable in the case of specific plays and playwrights. These generalizations, for example, cannot be applied mechanically to Shaw in England, or to Curel, Lenormand, and Sartre (or to all the work of Cocteau, Salacrou, and Anouilh) in France. And to document my summary conclusions would require an inventory as large as this book. My only reason for stirring up these already troubled waters of national differences is that there has been a notable absence of finesse in important areas of theatre. But for the absence of finesse many once successful American plays, including O'Neill's, would have held up better than they do and would have become a vital portion of an American heritage of dramatic literature. And, I should add, many earnest new playwrights would have an easier time of it in trying to establish themselves on our stage, if they possessed finesse as well as seriousness.

I

An extreme yet not unrepresentative example of *furor Teutonicus,* even without benefit of National Socialist frenzy, occurred immediately after World War I when a veritable pathology of theatre characterized the expressionist movement. Restiveness under the Hohenzollern regime and anarchy after its fall in 1918 translated themselves into a frenzied negation of human values except in the case of a few elevated spirits such as Fritz von Unruh and Ernst Toller. Rebellious sons, for example, were constantly flying at their parents' throats in early expressionist plays whose dialogue sputtered like machine-gun fire. In the first of these, Walter Hasenclever's *The Son,* a son is incited to shoot his father by his friend, who shouts, "Destroy the tyranny of the family. . . . Do away with laws! Restore Freedom." In another dramatic explosion, Bronnen's *Parricide,* a youth suffering from an Oedipus complex murders his mother's husband, and in Paul Kornfeld's *The Seduction,* a young man's revulsion against pharisaism leads him to strangle his sister's philistine bridegroom. Following this act of romantic heroism, he escapes from prison; and injected with poison by an enemy, he succeeds in inducing his murderer to commit suicide. More murders abounded in such dramatic monstrosities as Hanns Henny Jahn's *Medea* and *The Coronation of Richard III,* in which characters were being continually slaughtered, tortured, and buried. Baroque theatre, suitably supplied with frenzied acting by no means banished from the German stage even now, ran riot in modern dress. So genial a German critic as Alfred Kerr, remembering the twenties in the early thirties for the *Theatre Guild Magazine,* reported that "on one occasion a gentleman's liver was cut up and eaten." He could not help exclaiming, "They actually produced that in the theatre. Oh, you know too little of this era in the German drama!" When in one of the early years of Hitler's rise, a character in a play declared that he was tempted to whip out his gun whenever he heard the word culture, he was running true to form not only as a Nazi but as a successor to some of the expressionist playwrights.

Interestingly enough, the first serious play of any popularity in Germany after the Second World War was an expressionist drama, variously translated as *Outside the Door* and *The Man Outside* (*Draussen vor der Tür*). It was almost ridiculously frantic and maudlin with the bitterness of return from the war front. Carl Zuckmayer, the distinguished writer of German folk plays, won a large and deserved popularity with *The Devil's General,* the tragedy of a famous general of the *Luftwaffe* who suffers from a sense of guilt for having given the Nazis his support. Though powerful and in some respects distinguished drama, the play gave its public an overdose of plot and exposé without actually effecting the purge that more economically and astringent playwriting could have provided. And Zuckmayer's next play (*Feuer im Kesseloffen—Fire in the Furnace*) on the subject of war guilt was a veritable opera of villainy, expiation, and redemption. It would appear, then, that except for Bertolt Brecht's briskly written and cool plays, German drama tended to be as ponderous and superheated as ever. So were many stage productions, too, if reports are to be credited.

Even in the production of a so-called fairy-play by Raimund, *The Spendthrift* (*Der Verschwender*) which I saw at Salzburg in the summer of 1950, the lumbering machinery of stage production was singularly pronounced. Among actors in the piece were several with whose work we had become familiar in the United States—Hans Jaray, Oscar Karlweiss, and Adrienne Gessner, whose performances had never impressed us as particularly heavy. But once standard German stage production had its way, the wheels ground heavier and bigger by the moment. The play itself, which had been subjected to emendations and to additions from other pieces by the popular nineteenth-century Austrian author, was heavy-laden with treacle and spectacle. Max Reinhardt himself gave evidence of a similar tendency while he lived in exile in the United States. His spectacular treatment of Franz Werfel's *The Eternal Road* with scenery by Norman Bel Geddes occupied an opera house and consumed a fortune.

II

Of more immediate concern to us, however, is the American scene, on which there has also been considerable overproduction of plays, as well as overwriting and overinsistence on "suffering," or "reality," in playwriting. The Moss Hart divorce drama *Christopher Blake,* which came to Broadway with much expressionistic underscoring both in the text and the production, was an example. Heavy musical productions such as *Mr. Strauss Goes to Boston* and *Magdalena* abounded in the flourishing war-time and post-war Broadway theatre. A recent example (1952) was the Joshua Logan production *Wish You Were Here,* based on Arthur Kober's tender depression-period folk comedy *Having a Wonderful Time.* The musical treatment, which lost Kober's pleasant little play in a subway rush of overstrenuous doings at a Catskill summer camp, was suitably publicized for its full-sized swimming pool on the stage.

More significantly, it became evident in our midcentury theatre that plays we had favored a decade or more ago were mostly in need of some saving grace of wit or finesse, lacking which they did not quite exert the interest the producers had expected to revive. This was evident to various degrees in revivals of Sidney Howard's *They Knew What They Wanted* and *Yellowjack* and O'Neill's *Anna Christie,* although it was difficult to know which was more to blame, the playwriting or the production. (I cannot avoid suspecting "production" in general, since revivals of such plays as *Ghosts, John Gabriel Borkman, An Enemy of the People,* in Arthur Miller's version, and *The Wild Duck* made more or less ponderous theatre as performed.) Comedy and fantasy also seemed to lack sufficient spice. The lack was noted in the Kaufman and Katherine Dayton, in 1952 sixteen-year-old comedy of Washington intrigue, *First Lady*. Too often here the humor seemed to have been slapped on the stage with a floor-brush. As for musical-comedy extravagance, the revival of the once vastly popular political travesty *Of Thee I Sing* seemed after thirty or forty minutes more noisy than entertaining or pointed.

Exceptions can be noted. I would select the Nugent and Thurber play *The Male Animal,* which could still strike us as astringent comedy in 1952, and the Rodgers and Hart anti-romantic musical comedy *Pal Joey,* which was at least as gratifying when revived in 1952 as when first shown on Broadway. But, on the whole, it seems quite apparent that we were quite heavy-handed or indulgent toward heavy-handedness from the twenties to the fifties. Too many of our experienced humorists got accustomed merely to turning on a tap and letting the humor splash out, and this fact is associated with our past theatrical history. It was once easy to be a humorist and even easier to pass for a satirist. The Babbitts were so numerous and their behavior so crass that they were just so many sitting ducks for a playwright; he did not have to aim very carefully in order to drop the bird. Politics still seemed anything but a complex and responsible activity; therefore simple travesties were deemed very clever and pointed. The young popular arts of tinpan-alley, movies, and radio provided an undemanding subject—almost as undemanding as bootlegging. They required little more than burlesque treatment; in fact, they were their own burlesque. Our older humorists, in short, did not have to exercise their imagination and intellect to any great extent and it would appear that the new generation of playwrights is no less unsubtle, since it tries to follow the casual methods of its elders.

In *First Lady* the repartee sometimes crackles, as when a Supreme Court Justice hopes to "fill the shoes" of a former President and the latter's granddaughter replies she is quite sure the Justice can but "of course it was the other end of grandfather that mattered"; or when the lowly ancestry of Edna Best, who played the social-climbing wife of the Justice, is summed up with the statement that "Sam Baker never took a spoon out of a coffee cup." But, for the most part, *First Lady* consists of lame attempts at wit, as when one character says that an army travels on its stomach and her dim-witted interlocutor exclaims, "Isn't it awfully uncomfortable," and the play makes many of its points on a comic-strip level of humor. Surely the authors did not strain their imagination when they drew the portrait of a Supreme Court Justice who never misses the "Snooky Wookums" family radio program; they might just as well have put a mustache on the Mona Lisa. *First Lady* may have seemed political satire in 1935 (and I doubt that it was that even in 1935), but it is devoid of sting at present. In *Of Thee I Sing* no sooner does the amusing selection of Wintergreen and Throttlebottom for political office reach the saturation point in the musical-comedy proceedings than the satire loses its barb and the authors' improvisation becomes subject to the law of diminishing returns. The complications become progressively mere complication rather than dramatically gratifying development. A little cerebration on the authors' part would have been more to the point, especially if it had come from them with less reliance on easily fetched improvisation. This crackling package of irreverence from the year 1931 would have had more theatrical life in 1952 if it had sputtered less and exploded more.

We may be slowly learning from *First Lady* and the once fabulously successful *Of Thee I Sing* that there are limits to the amount of insouciant extravaganza to which a playwright may help himself when his subject requires a satirical treatment. There was a time when our playwrights thought it was enough to be irreverent and tie a can to every cat's tail to prove one's mettle. If this struck us as clever between 1920 and 1935, we may explain our indulgence as due to a sense of relief from a theatre that previously had been merely arch. But nose-thumbing is a childish form of registering criticism, and one grows out of the habit. The truth is that our satire was, for the most part, not actually satire at all but merely farce. And very perishable farce at that, because instead of remaining within the artificial world of improbabilities, as did Wilde when he wrote *The Importance of Being Earnest,* the farceurs pretended to be social critics. As a result, their farce was as incomplete as their satire was infrequent. They were, more often than not, vaudevillians blundering into the field of babbitt-baiting and employing elephantine methods of cacchination. If there is anything we expect of satire, it is that it shall be revealing, and to be revealing a writer must give some exercise to the public brain as well as to the funnybone. If he doesn't, there is a good chance that a later generation, although not at all necessarily cleverer than the author will find him a trifle retarded.

Satirists, be it noted, are also more relentless, they "follow through" more, than the Kaufman school was apt to be. Consider how much more stinging *First Lady* would have been if the obnoxious social climber actually had succeeded in making herself the first lady of the land instead of being defeated by her virtuous rival, who has all the social and moral qualifications, including a grandfather who once occupied the White House and a husband who is apparently a tolerable Secretary of State. But the truth is that we should have taken Mr. Kaufman at his word when he once disavowed satire as a metier with the declaration that satire "is what closes Saturday night." Yet, I trust I am not altogether bilious when I say that it was precisely satire we had a right to expect from him and other writers, because it is they themselves who supplied the elements for that acidulous compound before they added the saccharine and the zanily genial endings.

III

In the field of serious playwriting, the need for finesse is obviously greater, if for no other reason than that it is less likely to occur to a playwright who sets himself the task of representing severe tensions. Our tradition of realism, no less than that of impassioned social drama, was not conducive to finesse. It still is not.

It is significant that when the talented Robert Whitehead, heading the American National Theatre and Academy ("ANTA") production program for the 1951-52 season, selected a single new American play, he chose Emery Rubio and Miriam Balf's *Sunday Breakfast*. It was a work of such "honest" realism that but for a strong sense of duty I should have fled from the theatre after the first act and paid my respects to the nearest pub. Mr. Whitehead was merely doing his bit by the American drama, which has had vigor rather than subtlety to its credit for several decades. A vigor that I am the last person on Broadway to deprecate, let me add, and the first person to defend against supercilious dismissal.

In spite of the acute torment Mr. Whitehead inflicted on me with *Sunday Breakfast,* I am prepared to agree with him that somewhere in this collaboration there was talent. The authors revealed a feeling for human drama, for characterization, and for pathos mixed with comedy. But I fear that in squirming through a considerable portion of the production even philistines in the audience were not entirely unjustified. The cardinal error in deciding to produce *Sunday Breakfast* lay in failing to realize that integrity and unpleasantness are not necessarily synonymous in playwriting. The Decker family of the play may be terribly real, but that does not justify our placing its members on protracted exhibition. The husband is a harassed nitwit much of the time, the wife an intolerable termagant all the time. Their grown-up children "have problems," but this fact alone can hardly endear them to us; and although their neglected little daughter is quite pathetic, she is more legitimately the concern of a social welfare agency than the concern of an audience.

It has been one of the fallacies of the prolific breed of post-Ibsen realists, post-Zolaist naturalists, to assume that it is enough to place a parcel of misfits on the stage and pity them. I can conceive of nothing more frustrating than exposure to a situation about which it would be impossible to do anything, even if one were so inclined, and from which it is impossible to derive any particular enlightenment. This situation is bad enough within the covers of a book, but it is quite intolerable on the stage. Stage production brings the world's lame ducks too uncomfortably close to the spectator and leaves him haplessly at the mercy of their miseries and futilities. Unfortunately, this is the greater part of the experience that ANTA offered us in *Sunday Breakfast* and it was less, rather than more, endurable whenever the authors exhibited some talent and whenever Stella Adler's vivid direction was most in force.

The more meticulously a certain kind of "reality" is reproduced, the more lamentable the effect when the raw material is confused with art. This is an unfortunate experiment, this effort to show the public "the bitter truth" or what passes for a facsimile version of it on the stage in the name of "Art." (It is the reverse of the equally fallacious experiment to serve "Art" with obeisance to "Beauty," which is the fallacy of the Craig-worshiping poetry-mongers and magic-makers of the stage.) It enables every philistine to score his most persuasive argument—namely, that the theatre belongs to "entertainment." And so it does, even though the complacency with which the argument is made and the sense of the argument are equally infuriating. The cure for merely nerve-racking theatre is not, of course, quinine from Minsky's but theatre which enables us to see more, rather than less, of reality and to look into it and around or over it rather than simply at it. The trouble with the "slice-of-life" drama of Naturalists, for whom *Sunday Breakfast* would have been most approvable in 1880 or 1890, is that the slice is usually altogether too small and too thin, as well as malodorous, which is surely not the case in, let us say, *The Three Sisters* or *Juno and the Paycock*. The naturalists who have been accused of sordidness and fatalism have always comforted themselves with the certainty that they are telling the truth. But the trouble with the way naturalists have viewed reality is not that they have gone too far, but that they haven't gone far enough.

If *Sunday Breakfast* had encompassed more reality, we would have *understood* the life of the Deckers instead of merely observing them as writhing grubs. They would have had more reality in their relationships with one another and with the world; their failure would have had more meaningful significance. They would have been more richly alive. Reality, indeed, is sufficient "entertainment" when it is rendered in its fullness and is significantly ordered. Nor will the argument that, after all, a good many lives are arid and pointless hold water. If they are that arid and pointless in a book or a play, they have not really been observed as a penetrating writer observes people whether he be a Dostoevski or a Henry James. If they had been so observed, their life could not possibly have been arid and pointless.

And perhaps it is at this point that playwrights should inform themselves that a play is a play—not "life," but something by its very nature "artificial" in the best sense of the term. It can be "true" only in the theatre. And if that is the case, the play must be thoroughly acceptable to us as theatre. Only then is it possible for the play to be also something besides theatre as well. . . . Like so many honest attempts at transcribing life that fail while some cheap fabrications flourish in the market place like the green bay tree, *Sunday Breakfast* is not yet a play, but merely the preliminary sketch for one. Nor would it surprise me to learn that it has been reworked many times. At this moment there must be at least a hundred writers who are doing the same thing—that is, resketching what is essentially a sketch, because nearly everybody who talks or writes about the theatre mentions "fixing" plays rather than *creating* them. Creating is a bold and whole act of thought and imagination. Until our many playwriting tyros (some of them, alas, tyros for the past dozen years and still "New Playwrights" befriended by flourishing oldsters who advise them to be "commercial") realize this, my sermon and their talent will be equally wasted. I shall become an aging critic-teacher and they, perish the thought, permanently "new dramatists." The question will be, who gets tired first and calls it a day—or a night?

IV

In America, as in Germany, however, the fallacy of seriousness has taken its toll not merely from novices, but from experienced and important playwrights, which may be one reason why the novices have been cumbersome. Over the years, we have had occasion to observe and decry a lumbering earnestness in the work of such writers as Philip Barry (*Hotel Universe, Here Come the Clowns*), Anderson (*Key Largo* and *Truckline Café*), Sherwood (*The Rugged Path*), and Odets (*Clash By Night, The Big Knife*). And surely the playwright most vulnerable to the charge has been O'Neill, virtually from the start of his career to *A Moon for the Misbegotten*. Although *A Moon for the Misbegotten* is by no means the most lumpish of O'Neill's plays (one recalls *Dynamo* and *Lazarus Laughed*), the long awaited publication of this play, which was withdrawn in 1947 after a Mid-Western tryout owing to unsatisfactory casting, left some of O'Neill's most loyal friends considerably disappointed. His very concern with ironic and glowering fate, often a source of considerable power in his work, defeated friendly expectations.

The play is most alive when O'Neill conveys the simple reality of the Irish farmer Phil Hogan and his oversized daughter Josie in a relationship at once amusing and touching. There is a bizarre vitality in Hogan's efforts to hold on to his farm and to marry off his daughter Josie to his educated barfly-companion Tyrone. But in writing this piece, O'Neill was once more absorbed in the *motif* of self-damnation and futility under the less than benign heavens. And, as on some previous occasions, O'Neill made the evil stars swell to the huge proportions of a thunderhead. Josie's fate is determined, to a degree, by the circumstance that she is grotesquely large. Her physical size is treated as a fatality of nature; O'Neill was again grasping for the extraordinary and the grotesque with the object of defining life "tragically."

Lest Josie, moreover, should find fulfillment in love, which would either have eliminated or mitigated the tragic premise, O'Neill presents the one man who is strongly drawn to her, Tyrone, as another kind of freak of nature. For all the human dimension with which O'Neill endowed him, Tyrone is fundamentally a walking definition of failure. A mother-fixated and self-destroying alcoholic, he is presented by the author as one huge Negative. The portrait of Tyrone is another oversized O'Neill abstraction. Since Josie is endowed with the yearnings of a woman, this rustic giantess grows before our eyes into a Positive once she falls in love with Tyrone. But the female Positive, hitherto frustrated by gigantism, is left stranded by the masculine—*and intellectual!*—Negative. (The intellectual in O'Neill, we recall, is often sceptical, alienated, and self-destroying—in short, a Negative.) Modern Despair must be served and the human condition made untenable.

A Moon for the Misbegotten is a frequently moving work on a simple level of realistic drama. If its wordage is reduced for stage production, its tensions will probably combine with its gusty humor to give the play greater attractiveness. But if lack of finesse and overemphasis are detrimental to O'Neill's writing, which can carry heavy freight with considerable if not complete justification, they are likely to be far more damaging to the playwriting of other writers. If our other established writers usually display less conspicuous cases of literary elephantiasis, the reason is, no doubt, that their tendency toward excess is proportionate to their smaller capacity for passion.

THE DANGERS OF THE HISTORY PLAY

The advent of *The Crucible* in 1953, Miller's treatment of the Salem witch-hunt, called attention to a type of drama on which our playwrights and producers may come to rely to a greater extent than in the recent past. I refer, of course, to the historical drama, an ancient and honorable form of literature that has had an uneasy and fluctuating career in the modern theatre. Viewed with suspicion as an academic enterprise or as a deliberate escape from contemporary realities and a return to romanticism, the historical drama has probably undergone less development and has been less favored since the triumph of modern realism than almost any type of play. Nevertheless, its uses, far from becoming exhausted after some twenty-four centuries of Western playwriting, remain undiminished, its hold upon audiences continues to be strong, and the fear that it does not accord with the main lines of modern dramatic art is unfounded. Like any other kind of writing, it may be either abused or used to good purpose, and it may be well written or badly written. But there is nothing inherently wrong with it. Today it may actually recommend itself with renewed force to the writer who wishes to press home a parable for the times or to turn from them out of weariness with flaccid topical realism, or out of an ambition to play the poet in a bedraggled theatre.

The playwright will not have solved the problem of writing a good play, of course, by turning to historical drama, for there are no automatic solutions in art. He will have opened a corridor by electing to treat a historical subject. Where he goes, what he does on the way and what he finds or achieves—all this remains to be determined. No one can chart his course for him, give him an indulgence in advance of his deed, or judge the results before they materialize. All that the critic can do is take note of the possibilities and dangers of the historical play in our age. And that he should feel called upon to do so, as I do, may itself be a symptom of the initial problem—namely, that the merely routine historical play popular during the greater part of the nineteenth century was a major casualty of the process that gave us a modern theatre and drama.

The fact is that in the great ages of dramatic literature, non-comic drama was largely historical. The Greeks who did not make a strict distinction between legend and history or, in any case, treated legend or saga as history for literary purposes, set the first example. Until the decline of the Athenian theatre all tragedies then were "history plays." The biblical matter of medieval drama was considered historical by the men of the Middle

Ages, no matter how much the playwrights domesticated the subject by filling their plays with anachronistic and homely detail. Renaissance scholars went so far as to maintain that all tragedy should be historical, and the practice of the Renaissance, whether in Shakespeare's England or Lope de Vega's Spain, favored the historical drama, the tragedy based on what was presumed to be history, and the romance that, however fanciful (as in the case of *The Tempest* and tragicomedies by Beaumont and Fletcher), wore an aura of historical eventfulness.

The same "historicity" marked the later theatre of Corneille and Racine. Contemporaneity was not considered an indispensable virtue before the vogue of "middle-class tragedy," and, as a matter of fact, the modern theatre, whether or not realistic in aim, has had no iron-clad proscription against historical drama either. That outpost of dramatic modernism the Moscow Art Theatre started its career in 1898 with the production of Alexei K. Tolstoy's *Tsar Feodor Ivanovich.* One of Ibsen's best plays is *The Pretenders,* and Ibsen put great stock in his Julian the Apostate tragedy of early Christianity, *Emperor and Galilean.* Strindberg wrote some fifteen historical pieces, several of which are as good as any of his nonhistorical plays. Shaw used history for three of his best comedies before 1914, and attained the summit of his artistry in *Saint Joan.*

The historical drama fell into disrepute mainly because it was abused by nineteenth-century romanticists and cheapened by disingenuous theatremongers such as Scribe and Sardou. A parallel will be found today in the malpractice of novelists of the fleshly school of historical romance. "Costume drama"—the very term is damning, since it places the emphasis on mummery and spectacle—has also been shunned by playwrights and discouraged by producers because it tends to be costly. But it has been impossible to banish history as one of the legitimate concerns of the stage. And none is more legitimate by long precedent and by virtue of the fact that a sense of the "usable past" is most appropriate to the communion that theatre provides in assembling a public to witness the staging of an event. The only valid deterrents to respect for historical drama have been academic imitativeness and defective artistry.

The imitative, usually pseudo-romantic, mode is easily detected, although astute showmanship may make it "artistic" for the culture-hunter or for the playgoer who asks nothing more than a lavish "show." The author of this type of drama may even entertain honorable intentions; he cultivates a literary subject and style from the "heroic" past for the purpose of writing elevated drama. His is the fallacy of the litterateur in the theatre who hopes to lift himself up by the boot strings of his literary ambition in order to occupy a celestial seat next to the great masters. We might call his endeavor the fallacy of the epigone. And closely related to it, or indistinguishable from it, is the fallacy of artificial spiritualization of one's work and of assuming that elevation will automatically produce significant art. On the American stage, Maxwell Anderson appears to have been particularly vulnerable to the temptation to court greatness by means of academic inflation. Even his very successful Elizabethan plays betray this fact—not through their choice of subject and period, since any subject or period can yield memorable drama, but through strong echoes in characterization and style. One forms the possibly unjust impression that the matter and manner have been assumed by this indisputably erudite showman instead of forced out of him by inwardly compelled perceptions and passions. The result, at its worst, is historical drama that remains simply that. But Mr. Anderson's own ambition actually has been always more exalted and he has intended to write tragedy of high matter and universality. In *Off-Broadway: Essays About the Theatre* (pages 53-54), he states that he wrote his first Elizabethan piece, *Elizabeth the Queen,* after "I had discovered that poetic tragedy had never been successfully written about its own place and time." To compose poetic drama for any reason other than inner compulsion, in an age in which dialogue in verse is not the convention, may seem odd. But Mr. Anderson has written historical plays, now and then, because he wanted to write poetic tragedies.

Maxwell Anderson has also turned to history from time to time—in such plays as *Valley Forge, The Masque of Kings* and *Barefoot in Athens* —for the purpose of saying something about his times. This method is not necessarily dictated by caution or fear of persecution. It can be inspired by a desire to let the imagination support the claims of truth or reason, as well as to provide a perspective for one's contemporaries by making a living present out of the past. Mr. Anderson has always had such considerations in mind, whether he warned us against revolution in *The Masque of Kings* or against reaction in *Barefoot in Athens.* But here, too, the danger of academicism is around the corner if no living passion supports the enterprise. Such passion exists, I believe, in *The Crucible* regardless of any defects with which we may charge the author; it did not, I believe, in Anderson's plays—not because their author was insincere in developing an argument or implication, but because he was too conscious of "literature" (and of show business, I suspect). Verlaine advised poets to wring literature's neck. We may make the same recommendation to playwrights, and especially to writers of historical plays. They need it most because they are tempted to adopt the idiom of the period about which they are writing. The quality of derivativeness in Anderson's verse has long been noted, although it has abated somewhat in recent years; and even Arthur Miller did not escape some stilted writing in *The Crucible* that stands between the play and the playgoer. It is remarkable how simply and effec-

tively Shaw solved his problem in *Saint Joan* by employing the best contemporary English at his command—in other words, the dialogue that
came directly from his engaged intellect.

A great practical problem of writing historical drama in our time is,
indeed, largely that of removing barriers between the present and the past.
When the past in the play is recent, as it was in O'Casey's Easter Rebellion
drama *The Plough and the Stars,* there is no language problem. But as
the action recedes in time, the danger of archaism or derivative literariness
grows. The problem can be solved automatically only in genuine poetry,
for the poet can use contemporary language and speech pattern and still
heighten the effect—as Yeats, Eliot, Auden, MacLeish, Lorca and Brecht
have done in our century.

With few exceptions, the language of the poet-playwrights of the great
periods of theatre was contemporary with the audience for which the
plays were written, and not with the subject matter. Hamlet and Lear
speak as Elizabethans, not as heroes of their respective historical time;
Richard II does not speak the language of Chaucer. Nor is antiquarianism,
except when humorously intended, a fault solely because it erects a barrier
between the plays and its audience. It usually stands between the playwright and the act of creation, as all self-conscious effort must.

When that happens, an extraordinary voltage is required to leap across
the gap between what the playwright wants to express and his consciousness of a borrowed style. In the case of *The Crucible,* the necessary voltage
was supplied by the intensity of Miller's tragic convictions. But that
intensity is rare in contemporary playwriting, and intensity cannot be
deliberately cultivated. In prose drama, moreover, the language itself too
often lacks voltage, so that the passion goes lame precisely when it should
reach a climax. In this respect, even Miller was not entirely successful. He
succeeded at the end of the second act of *The Crucible* when he could
make the mounting stage action of the scene function for him. He was less
successful in the third act wherever the words alone had to carry his dramatic action. If no such limitation can be ascribed to the dramatic ascent of
Saint Joan and *The Plough and the Stars,* the reason is that Shaw and
O'Casey are, in their different ways, supreme masters of the English language. It would be comforting, indeed, if future writers of historical drama
shared their mastery. But since this is an idle hope, let us entertain the
more reasonable one that awareness of the possibilities that still reside in
historical drama will attract to the theatre some poets and some prose
writers who write with distinction in other fields. We hear a good deal to
the effect that the contemporary theatre, at least in America, does not
attract the best writers.

A far more legitimate assumption, I believe, is that some of our best

American writers have found their talents better attuned to the writing of fiction, lyric poetry, and literary criticism than to the making of theatre. They need either more expansion or more condensation than the dramatic form normally allows. But it is possible that they could bridge the gap between their nondramatic writing and the stage if they explored a medium such as the historical drama which is less limiting than the routine topical drama favored by most playwrights.

The greatest barrier to effective historical writing for the stage, however, would appear to be the wide gulf between the authors and the historical figures they must bring to life. Too few playwrights have bridged it. Miller, perhaps because he was primarily concerned with mass hysteria and the lesson of the Salem trials, made a valiant but surely not entirely successful attempt to create character in the round. To his credit it must be said that exertions on his part were evident in the last act of *The Crucible*. But the distance between the playwright and his characters remains unbridged in his play, as well as in other plays. In Eliot's *Murder in the Cathedral,* for example, Becket is *tested* rather than created; in Anderson's *Mary of Scotland*, Mary Stuart is *animated* rather than made real; and in *Joan of Lorraine,* Joan is merely analyzed in the person of an actress-surrogate. How much more of a living woman is made of Joan by the truly analytical, "intellectual," allegedly "unemotional" Shaw!

We are very historically minded in this century, but we are also very provincial, especially in America where perhaps the lack of a classical education prevents us from living with the characters of history. We are also so overawed nowadays by the importance of "trends" in history that we forget the people who made the trend. We also hurry past the dead in too businesslike a fashion; they are not living presences for us, as they were in past ages and as they still are in countries where local tradition is stronger. The past remains the past, whereas it is the business of the playwright to make it the present. To do this, however, it is not history that we must write but character drama. It is not history but character drama that stands in the foreground of the best Athenian, Elizabethan, and neo-classic French drama. The humanist connection with individuals has been wearing thin in our times.

The great drama of the past could afford to be historical because it did not lose the individual. The characters, no matter how remote, were *unhistorical* to the author, in the sense that they were made contemporary by the writer. The vaguer sense of history that prevailed in previous periods did not divide past and present as sharply as we do in our age of accelerated evolution and devolution. And it may be for that reason that the talent for universalizing the characters of literature was more developed and more required then. Aristotle could speak with confidence when he declared that "poetry" (or tragedy, in the context of his *Poetics*) "is a more philosophical and a higher thing than history; for poetry tends to express the universal, history the particular." He went on to explain: "By the universal I mean how a person of a certain type will on occasion speak or act, according to the law of probability or necessity; and it is this universality at which poetry aims in the names it attaches to the personages." For the contemporary playwright to perform this feat of humanization rather than of mere ennoblement of characters in a historical drama would be the final triumph. But he is likely to receive little assistance from the spirit of the age, let alone the spirit of show-business. The writing of historical plays today inevitably challenges all his resources. The critic can do nothing more for the playwright than to sharpen his awareness of this fact, for it is true that mere dabbling in historicity has been outmoded since the advent of the modern theatre and should be regarded as an academic and retrograde exercise. And sentimentality, whether from Anderson or Fry, glittering though it may sometimes be, is surely no substitute, either in *Mary of Scotland* or *The Firstborn,* Fry's Moses drama. The danger of historical drama is that it may become *ersatz* drama. It was never that in the great days of the theatre.

THE MOST DIFFICULT
FORM OF WRITING

I

It is a flagrant understatement to say that playwriting is one of the most difficult forms of writing. It is *the* most difficult. Playwriting represents the triumph of hope over reason, just as play production on Broadway in our time is mostly a socially acceptable sublimation of the gambling instinct.

It may not always have been so, but it is now. A glance at the percentage of failures on Broadway even in the best years will confirm this opinion, and it isn't because our dramatists are inherently less intelligent or assiduous than any other American writers. Although many reasons may be assigned for this, the source of a playwright's pathology is his audience.

Unlike a novelist who can afford to reach a few hundred readers here and a few hundred there, the writer for the stage must collect his public in one place and do it fast. If he doesn't fill a theatre for the first few weeks, he might as well not have written at all. He must capture his audience at once and hold its attention.

Unlike the reader of a novel, the playgoer cannot skip pages of the author's text except by the process of falling asleep in his seat. This is an uncomfortable posture, and the playwright is not easily forgiven. You can be bored to extinction by the Father Zosima episode in *The Brothers Karamazov,* but you will still think it is a great book. If you were bored to the same degree by a commensurably lengthy passage in a play, you would find it disastrous, because you can't erase the offending sequence with a flick of the fingers.

You can't speed up the actors the way you speed up your reading; if the play crawls, you crawl with it. Nor can you put the performance aside, as you put a book aside, and pick it up again after you have recovered from boredom or anesthesia. Once you have been bored with a play, you stay bored. Nor can you turn the pages back; that is, stop the performance and ask the actors to repeat something because your attention has wandered, or to retrace the line of development because it is a trifle too complicated. The play races blithely on, and you are left to pick up the threads as best you can.

Hell hath no fury like an audience bored or an audience confused, and no form of criticism is generally as vitriolic as dramatic criticism. The playwright must make his situations spiral in an ascending order of interest. Unless he is telling a chronicle (and it had better be about a national figure of Abraham Lincoln or Queen Victoria stature—so that the public can care enough, and can fill in what the play leaves out), the playwright must use a vertical structure.

At the same time, he must simplify even if it hurts, even when he is bubbling over with psychological or social complexities that would fill another *Remembrance of Things Past*. The man who writes an adult novel builds according to the laws of multiple motivation. The playwright finds himself compelled to assign a single motive to a character or risk nebulousness and confusion, unless he is a real master of counterpoint like Chekhov. He even has to telegraph the mood and meaning of his drama in advance, to create precisely the expectation he intends to fulfill later on.

Still he can't tell the playgoer much at this point or at any point, since the stage is for showing and not for telling, and the audience is held only when it is kept busy putting the pieces of the play together, discovering things and drawing conclusions for itself. An audience doesn't want to be cheated of making its own observation when characters and actions are displayed on a platform. This is elementary, for the playwright. How to make the playgoer draw the conclusions intended by the writer is the problem, and a most difficult one. He stands frustrated, tongue-tied, unable to explain to the public as a novelist does. No wonder, then, that the playwright often becomes or looks simpleminded instead of simple.

There isn't much time in this two hours' encounter with a public, either, to develop characters and ideas. He even loses time—five minutes after the curtain rises and a minute after each intermission. Until the audience settles down, seats stop creaking, programs stop rustling, he can't allow his actors to say anything significant without the danger of wasted effort. There is intermission trouble, too. As the audience files out into the lobby, it must carry with it a substantial experience that cannot be dissipated in smoke and conversation but which is sufficiently suspended to warrant returning to the auditorium for a bout with the next act. If there are scene changes within the act, the writer's problem is even more complicated, unless he has a fast turntable (which can give him other kinds of neuralgia). Many a play gasps out its life during the intervals between scene changes.

Concerning our present-day audience, moreover, we must note an anomaly. It is a highly selective public, generally sophisticated. It scorns the type of melodrama that proliferated in the pre-modern stage, leaving that commodity to the movies, which can do the job better because films have greater visual resources and faster tempo. It even discounts the time-honored ingredients of plot-making, the tricks of intrigue, eavesdropping, lost letters; all the paraphernalia that bolstered old dramatists. The playwright has to get along in his plotting with long familiar and useful crutches unless he can conceal them under the screen of an impressive theme or under a façade of psychological piff-paff, cosmic significance, and rococo *Weltschmerz*. The theatre's clowns have it much easier than the playwright, and it is a great deal easier to like them and shower compliments on them. They do not weary us with the old tricks so long as they bring a new personality with them. And if they bring an old personality into the theatre, that is gratifying, too. They are greeted as old friends, and they offer an opportunity for the intelligentsia of a new generation to display a tolerance they cannot entertain for the playwright, for the latter commits himself on the intellectuals' literary level, so that they see through him, whereas the clown lives in a world from which their intellectuality excludes them. Everybody in the theatre, indeed, is likely to receive indulgence before the playwright is served with a crumb of mercy.

Finally, the author doesn't even reach his audience, directly, but through interpreters. He writes for his cast in the first instance, and the audience sees his work as in a mirror, darkly or not at all. The same play may look like a masterpiece or an aborted embryo in different productions. This has happened even to *Hamlet*. The playwright's interpreters may become his misinterpreters, and he may not be able to recognize his brainchild. The little monster baptized in the fire of Broadway criticism may not even be his own. But he can be quite sure that Broadway will pin it on him.

II

It has been suggested from time to time (most recently and most intelligently at an Educational Theatre Conference in 1950) that we try to counteract routine playwriting by encouraging and prompting invention, and I believe it would be impossible to disagree even if we applied the suggestion to the professionally produced drama that sets the novice an example and incentive. The very course of a considerable portion of the modern drama is implicated in the problem of inventiveness.

The slice-of-life theory has never actually worked. The positive value of the theory lay in directing the writer toward the realities of character and milieu and away from the purely contrived play-carpentry that Shaw blasted as "Sardoodledom." But no tolerable modern play has ever been written without inventiveness regardless of its other merits. The artistry of modern playwriting lay in shaping a play without giving the impression of catch-penny sensationalism and theatricality. The challenge to the playwright lay in the possibility of his making a planned dramatic fire look like spontaneous combustion. But planned work is *artistry* and not a contradiction of it whether it is work within the convention of naturalness as exemplified by Chekhov or within older dramatic and theatrical conventions. Creation is always both inventive and somehow natural.

Still, inventiveness seems to me to require consideration under the aspect of creativeness rather than as a separate recourse. Stress on inventiveness may jog a playwright out of the rut of a routine plot. When the instructor rouses the student into giving his play a fresh start or a new turn, he may also start a chain-reaction of associations that will lead to genuine creativeness. I grant the possibility—provided, of course, that the young playwright possesses talent and has something to say. But in the final analysis, the fostering of inventions in a play seems to me an act of desperation. It may help to make a play more tolerable on the stage once we are committed to producing it, or once we decide that student plays simply must be put on the stage for pedagogic or other reasons. And on Broadway, too, we try this twist or that in the hope of making a play succeed. Kaufman and Hart, I believe, never quite knew how to resolve *The Man Who Came to Dinner* until they hit upon the device of the mummy-case as a means of removing their actress from the last act and clearing the field for Whiteside's secretary. But if the ultimate objective of playwriting instruction is to develop playwrights, I wonder whether it may not be dangerous to encourage the habit of relying on shifts and strategies, on superimposed dramaturgic twists or last-minute rescue work—that is, on *invention* rather than on *creation*. I wonder whether reliance on inventions may not be short-term wisdom, unless we resign ourselves to turning out hack-playwrights.

The quick results may not be the best, and it may be wiser in the case of the student possessed of talent actually to disintegrate his play with honestly destructive criticism if it can be saved only mechanically; to make him start all over, instead of enabling him to win an easy but essentially hollow success. It may be better to force him to work as an artist rather than as an improviser, and to wait for him to ripen into artistry, even if this means that the instructor will have nothing to show the dean or the trustees in terms of immediate results. When Miss Theresa Helburn and I established the Bureau of New Plays and the seminars associated with it, we were agreed that it would take our playwrights—among whom were Arthur Miller and Tennessee Williams—at least five years before they would come up with a successful play. This was in the period between 1937 and 1940. I believe it was worth waiting for Miller and Williams, and we are still waiting for several others, some of whom have already won some distinction in other fields but have not yet made their mark in the theatre.

The waiting I have in mind is not a purely passive process. We do not of course help the young writer by folding our hands and waiting for experience or life to turn him into a good playwright. I am thinking of the genuinely educational procedure of drawing him out—of asking the right questions about his characters and situations and teaching him to ask those questions on his own. I am thinking of a kind of criticism for which the best description was provided by Colley Cibber when he employed the term "resistant flexibility." That is, bending with the breeze of the writer's intention and talent and yet setting up the resistances of the objective reader and spectator. We can, moreover, be most helpful by making the playwright learn as much as possible about his own play and about his creative involvement in it as an individual. We can get him to know the nature and possibilities of his material, his attitude toward his characters and their situation, his responses as an observer and interpreter of life in its private and social aspects. This knowledge can then determine how he will shape his play and find his form, as well as determine what his emphases will be and where these will be made. When he truly knows his material and intention, he can invent *ab ovo,* so to speak, instead of superimposing invented complications.

Much, if not virtually all, the commonplaceness in a play stems from a staleness of observation and attitude. The writer must therefore be encouraged and helped to get back to the well-springs. And if he learns to do this and, above all, if he learns to look into himself and around himself sharply and individually enough, he will be refreshed and strengthened not only for one particular bout of playwriting but for all subsequent bouts. Also, the stagnancy, or *stasis,* we find ourselves called upon to overcome again and again in a writer's script comes essentially from *stasis* in his thinking and feeling. We can rehabilitate the *playwright* only in so far as we rehabilitate the *man.* What do they of playwriting know who only playwriting know? And in this connection we can address ourselves to the total person—that is, the young person who is making contact with life and reality as well as contact with ideas.

Nor is this conception of our problem necessarily confined exclusively to the higher reaches of dramatic art. A way of looking at things and reacting to them has been just as important in the successful Kaufman pieces as in O'Neill's far-flung designs upon the soul or Shaw's and Ibsen's engagements with ideas and social realities. And a way of looking at things—a sharp and unstatic (that is, dramatic) way of looking, conducive to ingenuity, invention, or effective contrivance—underlies even farces like *Three Men on a Horse, Boy Meets Girl,* and *Room Service.* In the last mentioned instance, the transparent contrivances reflected the very nature of the subject, as well as the attitude toward the subject of shoe-string Broadway production; and the verve of the writing would have been impossible without a particular involvement on the part of the writers. Even when it comes to a question of repairs in a script, it seems to me that the man with the suggestions or the actual repairman is most effective when he brings a particular personality or *élan* to the job.

To expect the inexperienced student-playwright to think up effective ways of "play-doctoring" his own work is to expect a good deal in any case. Such ingenuity comes with experience in the professional play market, which most instructors themselves lack, and if the young writer had this experience he would not be a student. It may be more effective to start him on the way to revision by getting down to the business of rethinking the entire play—its materials, its genesis in the author's intent, and its author's awareness of everything connected with the play and with the requirements of his medium. Everything, including the author himself, is involved in the question of the failure of the play we are trying to save. When we become aware of this fact and act upon it, we, as teachers of playwriting, really become educators rather than play-doctors ourselves; in fact, we become play-doctors with far-reaching or long-lasting effects on the playwright only in so far as we perform the services of an educator. We move into the realm of *creation* in trying to promote invention.

This brings us, I suppose, toward some sort of Stanislavski method in playwriting work, which is no better or worse than the teacher who applies it and the student to whom it is applied. This method, which draws out and guides the creative faculty instead of finding short-cuts for playwriting, requires patience and empathy and an ability to establish a personal relation on the part of the instructor, as well as, of course, patience, responsiveness, and some sort of talent on the part of the student. It presupposes or involves a good deal of elementary knowledge, in addition to endowment, on the student's part. It raises such questions as that of the level of the student's development and the level on which instruction in playwriting can be given. Can it be given, except in special circumstances such as the return of war veterans to college, on any but a graduate school or professional level at all? How much selectivity can we and shall we employ in admitting the candidate into a really intensive playwriting seminar? Miss Helburn and I were able to exercise a great deal of selectivity because we had the entire country's crop of young playwrights to choose from; we selected them for our seminars after having read one or more plays that had made enough of an impression to be submitted by reputable play agencies to the Theatre Guild. The range of selection is necessarily more limited for most instructors.

In spite of the limitations of academic training, however, I believe that we must make every effort to treat playwriting as a writer's and creator's rather than as a mechanic's work. Our first and final task is to bring out the writer in the aspiring playwright. He is already too apt, as a rule, to think of "play-*wrighting*" as a method and a trade, and much in our theatre and society has encouraged him to do so. Much of the most worthless playwriting I have encountered in New York, both professionally and in the course of teaching, has come from two types of writers—the person who, possibly influenced by correspondence-school advertising, comes only to learn the tricks or mechanics of the trade, and the person (generally with some experience in summer stock or radio) who has already learned them. Concerning the former I may say that he never learns them, precisely because he never tries to learn anything else. Concerning the latter, who translates all suggestions into mere plot equivalents, I can only repeat what Heinrich Heine said about a popular contemporary: "Uhland's poetry reminds me of Bayard's horse: it possesses every conceivable virtue —but it is dead."

III

One of the things a new playwright should know is how his scripts are read. Another is how he can may make his play readable. We may also try to fit the shoe on the other foot; that is, we may add that one of the things a producer and his henchmen should know is how to read a playwright's script or, for that matter, just how to read *any* play. There is material in this for a book, and no doubt many people are qualified to write it. As for myself, I don't think I shall write it until I reach my anecdotage, preferably completing it just when I can reach a hand out of my coffin and pull the lid down.

How does a producer or his playreader, if he has one, read a new playwright? It depends on the needs of the producing setup and on the reader's temperament, of course, but in general he is hopeful that he will discover a new Tennessee Williams or Arthur Miller. He overlooks and allows for a great many faults. When these occur to him, he invariably counts on guiding the author toward a successful revision. More option money has been expended on this hope than one imagines. It is too often a vain hope, moreover, partly because the producer himself may be mistaken in prescribing revisions, and partly because the playwright may not be able to execute them even if the producer's suggestions impress him as entirely sound. The producer who knew how to fix every script he liked would be as rich as Croesus, but obviously he is often in the dark as to what will make a play succeed; his best calculations may be upset in production. The playwright's mind may assent to suggestions for revision, but very often he has already done all he could do with his idea and his characters. His revisions will be lifeless impositions on the text. The roots of the revision may simply not penetrate far enough to tap his life-blood. They may have reached only as far as his intellect—which is hardly enough.

The producer's indulgence is simply fabulous, although no struggling young writer will ever believe me. Yet, granting that the manager likes the play and believes that its subject and treatment are not out of the question for financing and success, the fact is that he is too easily disarmed by hope. A "producer" must "produce," and this fact inclines him to overrate plays that suit his temperament, education, and experience, which may favor literary drama or bawdy farces, social drama or "escapist stuff," realism or fantasy. In nearly twenty years of reading plays for the Theatre Guild, Columbia Pictures, and for independent production by myself, I was hopefully kind to plays that I could, and sometimes did, rip to pieces as a practicing drama critic. There is a moral to this: the young playwright should be more merciless toward his play than the producer is, if he wants to succeed. His play is not necessarily right because his producer thinks so, and not even if the director is satisfied with it in the harrassing course of production. The playwright must also remember that a producer may have a change of heart on rereading the play he bought or the revisions he favored and actually initiated. He either loses the first flush of confidence or he corrects himself, and in this he is subject to many pressures: his "angels" raise an eyebrow or keep their fountain pens in their breast-pockets, or the actor he interested turns down the part the manager hopefully reserved for him. Usually these rebuffs are accompanied by explanations or suggestions that shake the producer's confidence in his own judgment.

There are also certain factors in a producer's response to a script which may prevent him from accepting a play. A handwritten script is worse than poison and is rejected just as quickly. This may be unfair and the author may be a genius, but no playgoer will ever get the chance to see his play on the stage. A messy typescript or one full of corrections is not only an annoyance but it suggests that the author doesn't know his own mind. Bravura or at least some show of self-confidence is useful to a playwright. He must fill the producer with confidence in so uncertain a business as theatre. Conversely, the extravagantly pretty *de luxe* manuscript is an abomination; it suggests preciousness and dilletantism. Then there are the plays in which the directions are extravagantly full, leaving nothing to the producer's imagination. The producer wants to get on with the spoken story and loses track; or if the writing interests him, he just skips the directions. When these, moreover, consist of redundancies like—

JOHN: (*with hatred*) I loathe you!

MARY: (*ecstatically*) Oh, I am so very, very happy to see you!

—the reader is apt to drop the manuscript. Plays almost wholly written in phonetic dialect are also painful to read. Even an exciting story and vivid dialogue may elude the reader as he tries to extract sound and sense from the unfamiliar syllables. These phonetic impedimenta also suggest that the author is more interested in authenticity than drama.

Finally, there is subject matter to consider. Fashions change, of course, and we have all seen strike plays, war and anti-war plays, come into or go out of fashion. But if one generalization can be made, it is that the new playwrights had better guard against historical and biographical subjects that are too remote from his country's consciousness of history and biography, that require a hand-picked audience of cognoscenti. A producer will lay an unknown's play aside as soon as he finds that its subject is an obscure rhetorician of the seventh century A.D., or a mighty chieftain in Dalmatia. For the playwright, who may be the possessor of a good style and much learning which he would like to share with us, these protagonists may have more than archaic interest. They may provide a parallel to contemporary events or an allegory on the universal spirit of man. For the producer they only suggest a waste of time and have about the same effect as a well-loaded tsetse fly.

Also, the producer has some reasonable predilections. He likes to be able to follow a story through to its consummation and believes that the public does, too—and he prefers one story to five. He also likes to see the action started in act one, whereas many young writers are merely full of promises for the second and third acts. The producer expects that the background and nature of a situation or character will grow upon him while something concrete is happening, whereas the tyro is firmly anchored to preliminary exposition. He has apparently not heard of such a thing as "retrospective exposition," that is, of holding back information until it takes the form of crisis-produced revelations. Then, too, the producer looks for some turn of events, some *reversal,* before two-thirds of the play are up, because by then he needs, and thinks his audience needs, a fresh stimulus. Many a tyro, having established a situation, goes doggedly ahead on the same line as though he were Grant proposing to fight it out if it takes all winter. In short, the producer looks for interest, whether deeply or superficially attained, whereas the young author strives for substantiation.

This leads us to the main cause of disagreement between the producer and the hopeful unestablished playwright. For the latter, it is too often enough if his events happened or could have happened. How many writers have said to me: "But this is what happened! But I *knew* such a character!" What the producer, on the contrary, wants to know is how interesting is this thing that happened? And ultimately the intelligent producer looks for some final cause or purpose—for *justification*. He is apt to be tremendously unimpressed by the inexperienced playwright's reply that his play is justified, and that both the producer's efforts and the public's attention will be justified, because his play is "life."

The producer, even if he is a lowbrow, actually wants "art," not "life." Whether or not he can formulate his thoughts on the subject or cares to formulate them, he knows that life is not life on the stage until it has become drama. Life in a play has to be made singular even while it remains representative; it must be intensified, shaped significantly and made felicitously articulate. Ordinary life we have about us everywhere. "It comes out of our ears," say the producers. And even the extraordinary situation becomes ordinary when it is pointless or is present only as a yarn. A producer senses quickly, as a rule, whether there is any reason for him to go on reading. When he finishes the play, moreover, he requires it to justify itself even more completely. Has the attention he has bestowed upon it been rewarded? Have the events added up to one meaningful experience or to some unified observation, or has the entertainment any point, instead of being simply an aggregate of disparate stimuli? This is what he expects perhaps more than anything else, whether the play he considers be *Kiss and Tell* or *Death of a Salesman*. He may make an erroneous judgment, but he will make a judgment on this score.

A producer, as a rule, is also prejudiced in favor of a little logic in the script. And mere reasoning, the mere flexing of intellectual muscles in the conversation, is not the logic he tacitly demands in anything but a revue. He looks for a logic of motivation in the character and for logic in the sequence of situations. Like the rest of mankind when it doesn't go berserk, he has some respect for the law of cause and effect. The philosopher Hume said that you couldn't prove the existence of such a law. Good dramatists, being less philosophical than Mr. Hume, have demonstrated its existence since the beginning of the theatre.

OUTSIDE, LOOKING IN

On Thanksgiving Day, in 1952, the National Theatre Conference, at the initiative of its able president Sawyer Falk, departed from its annual tradition of limiting discussion to the theatre. The speakers at the symposium, called "Beyond the Theatre," were the distinguished art historian Alan Dorner, the poet and historian Peter Viereck, and the genial philosopher Irwin Edman, so that the discussion might have been more appropriately entitled "Outside, Looking In." Each gentleman confined himself mainly to his own specialty, but the conclusions he drew or left to be drawn from his remarks were of far-reaching importance to the audience of community and university stage producers, directors, and teachers. The only error in the arrangements for the symposium was the order of the speakers. Mr. Dorner should have been preceded, not followed, by Mr. Viereck, since the latter's subject was the more general one. The only dissatisfaction one could feel at the conclusion of the meeting was that the discords introduced by the discussion were left unresolved because the Conference had to turn to business matters.

I

Mr. Viereck, fresh from the Ezra Pound controversy, gave his side of the literary battle over the Bollingen Prize that had been awarded to Pound two years before. Mr. Viereck, who had taken the position that poetry should not be a coterie product, reaffirmed his opinion, but with some cogent qualifications. Poetry had become altogether too cryptic and difficult, with the result that only the select few had any use for it. Poetry had to be made communicable again, if it was to recover its vitality and its public. This did not mean, however, that modern poets were to strain for the laurels of Edgar A. Guest and make no demands upon their readers' imagination and concentration. It was necessary to mediate between the philistines and the literary snobs, Babbitt and T. S. Eliot, Main Street and the Boulevard Saint-Germain. Mr. Viereck, who had hitherto distinguished himself by taking up the cudgels for common sense, was poet enough to defend *uncommon* common sense—which is the poetry of all great writers from Homer to Robert Frost. In the company of pharisees and philistines, he would actually stand up to defend Pound and Eliot and their minor brethren.

Mr. Viereck's words should have both perturbed and stimulated his

499

auditors. Whether or not he was fully aware of their problems, he had touched upon a question that must concern them constantly. Like the Broadway producer, the off-Broadway man of the theatre must be able to satisfy his general public, which is not more, but actually less, sophisticated than the Broadway clientele. At the same time, however, the off-Broadway producer must remain on good terms with discriminating members of his audience whose influence is out of proportion to their numbers. Influential members of the community or the professors and deans of the university reasonably expect (or should expect) some greater justification for a theatre at least partially dependent upon their support than mere entertainment which can be had inexpensively or at no cost whatsoever from the mass media. The director must, above all, stay on good terms with his conscience. He must survive as a practical showman. But he must also survive as an artist.

How does he mediate between the rival claims of his two necessities? As a rule, he does so by means of a compromise program which gives a popular farce or comedy one week and *Our Town* or *Winterset* (or, occasionally, *The Madwoman of Chaillot*) the next. The fluff draws the paying customers, while the dramatic literature satisfies the higher levels of taste.

There are no mysteries in the management of such a theatre, except the eternal mysteries of how a stage production will turn out and how the audience will respond to it. The producer, who is often also the director, can console himself with the further reflection that it has ever been thus. The theatre has always stood on clay foundations. It has been both a temple for the human spirit and a three-ring circus. Shakespeare, too, had to please the groundlings, and the austere Athenian tragedies were followed by a short phallic burlesque and an extravagant comedy in the same day. Nevertheless, there is one problem that is not easily removed by compromise-programming. It stems from the concept of an "art theatre" that conditioned the creation of community stages in America after 1910. In the early years of our century, there had been no dearth of stage productions throughout the country as a result of the traveling stock-company system. Our so-called community theatres were created under the dispensation of art rather than of commerce, and the founders worked under the magically tinted shadow of Gordon Craig and Reinhardt ideals. No "community theatre" stage director worth his salt can be content to exercise his talent on even the average Broadway drama to which he has to devote the major part of his time. Theatre is the product of the artist and the audience; they can mutually debase each other, as well as their art. For one stubborn poet of the community theatre, such as Jasper Deeter, we now have ten artists who have been turned into administrators.

There is nothing wrong, of course, with having good and sensitive administrators; they are essential to the enterprise of theatre and I believe that the Yale school of the drama is fortunate in having Boyd Smith at its head. A Boyd Smith knows how to draw upon the creative powers of his staff; he brings a warm human understanding to its personal and artistic problems, and he can spare it the difficulties with which the single-minded artist cannot usually cope. Difficulties arise only when the artist has to serve as his own manager and is turned to all intents and purposes into a schizoid character. The skill of the community director is actually quite remarkable. Often, by virtue of staging plays regularly, he is more competent than his Broadway colleague. But the fire of an Elia Kazan—where will that be found? Or the poetry of a Bobbie Lewis directing *My Heart's in the Highlands* or *Brigadoon,* of a Peter Brooks directing the English production of *Ring Around the Moon,* of a John Gielgud staging *Much Ado About Nothing* at Stratford and *The Lady's Not for Burning* in London? In one sense, indeed, the Broadway director is in a better situation than the community director; the business of financing and publicizing the production belongs entirely to the producer or manager and his staff.

The pursuit of "beauty" itself, however, is no simple matter and is not the sole end of a stage production. Beauty is not created in a vacuum, but in the context of matter that is either significant at a particular time or is made significant by the artist for other times as well as his own, by his style and form—which is itself no simple matter because form, too, is not absolute and unchanging. Of the limitations of subject matter in the off-Broadway theatre there is no need to say more than is generally known. Written or unwritten censorship, of course, always contributes to the difficulties we encounter in pursuing an artist's vocation, but the greatest of these are the artist's own limitations and the obtuseness of his public. Treatment rather than subject, form rather than content—in so far as a distinction may be made for purposes of convenience—is the crux of the problem. And since it seems to be rarely understood, the reflections of the other speakers at the Conference were highly pertinent.

II

Mr. Dorner considered the history of art in terms of its evolving forms, and quite simply told his audience that the fine arts had frequently gone beyond Aristotelian concepts and evolved styles expressive of ages different in many respects from the Greek fourth and fifth centuries B.C. I doubt whether the greater part of his distinguished audience of stage directors followed him all the way in his argument. After all, how much visualization is required by our standard one- or two-set plays? Most stage directors, as Clifford Odets once remarked, are traffic-cop directors. He might have added that their "beat" is limited to a single avenue where the traffic can flow only up-and-down and across the thoroughfare. If we doubt the justice of this criticism, let us look at our stage settings and observe the routinized crossings on the stage; at the elementary geometry of the stage picture which most plays force upon directors. The truth is they have not been able to graduate from Euclid, and only rarely have contemporary playwrights let them out of school. Moreover, those who encouraged directors to throw away their copybooks have often been wild-eyed adolescents or charlatans whose expressionism could win little credence this side of the Atlantic. For one Arthur Miller today and one O'Neill two or three decades ago there have been many pseudo-experimentalists who erect their growing surrealist pains or their self-induced traumatic shocks into axioms for artistic practice. We have come to such a stalemate that E. E. Cummings' *Him,* staged as far back as 1928 by the Provincetown Playhouse, seemed the most original American play in 1948 when revived at the same theatre.

Mr. Dorner could have driven his important points home with the assistance of photographic slides. I don't know which slides he would have selected had he been given the requisite facilities, but it is possible to consider several for a start—let us say, a piece of sculpture from the school of Praxiteles, a many-limbed Shiva from India, and a Congo statuette. Each figure sums up an aspect of three different civilizations. Professor Dorner's point can be translated into the history of the different styles in which great or at least good theatre and drama have been created through the ages. Implicit in his learned lecture was the suggestion that dramatic art in our own time has to find its own specially expressive forms.

Now all this would be an acceptable challenge to the stage director if somebody could tell him that a certain style or form is really expressive of the age. But nobody can tell him that; or rather, everybody tells him something different while his audiences too often tell him that the old forms do very well indeed, and that the new forms won't do at all. As a result, he generally settles for eclecticism; he tries this style or that, now a realistic drama, now a fantasy, now a "poetic drama," and now, perhaps, an expressionistic or even an epic-styled play such as *The Caucasian Circle of Chalk* or *Galileo* by Bertolt Brecht. Ours, we can say quite accurately, is an eclectic age. There is perhaps nothing wrong with eclecticism; or if there is, we cannot obviously alter an age as transitional as ours is. But there is one thing very wrong with the eclectic approach forced upon the director. He is unable to develop any single style to its proper degree of effectiveness. Many of his most carefully designed productions and most imaginative projects miss fire.

As a result, the director-producer is apt to be discouraged from attempting production of such modernist plays as *Intermezzo, Blood Wedding, The Skin of Our Teeth* and *The Caucasian Circle of Chalk,* while his audience and the local critics become convinced that these plays have been perversely touted as meritorious by long-haired coteries. After several mishaps, the director may come to believe this, too. And, incidentally, the unfortunate experience is not confined to plays of recent vintage, or, for that matter, to audiences in the hinterland rather than in Manhattan. It is only too easy to conclude after unsuccessful performances of *The Duchess of Malfi* and *The House of Bernarda Alba,* both in Wichita and New York, that John Webster is a contemptible playwright, or that Lorca had better be left to the Latin races. The same doubt spreads to Chekhov, Ibsen, and Strindberg—and to Sean O'Casey, with the result that plays that have been in the repertory of European theatres are rarely taken off the shelves with any enthusiasm. It is significant that the greatest living writer of drama in our language—and who can doubt that it is O'Casey!— keeps on writing plays that receive little more attention from the community theatres than from the West End or Broadway. The one natively developed dramatic form in America was the documentary "living newspaper," which flourished in the thirties. But the living newspaper perfected by the Federal Theatre, thanks to the intrepid showmanship of its national director Hallie Flanagan Davis, virtually disappeared from the stage and was ceded to radio and television.

Style is decisive in dramatic production, provided it interpenetrates each performance as well as every production detail. Broadway as a rule does without it, but compensates with professional gloss. The rest of our theatre also does without style, but can less easily succeed without it. It would be grossly unfair to the community and university director to charge him with neglect of what he considers to be form. Even if he cannot succeed in making it operative in the individual performances of an insufficiently trained cast, he is extremely conscientious of *designing* a production. When the means are at hand, he lights the production excellently and makes good use of background music. He will often resort to drapes, screens, raked sets, settings on several levels, "space stages," replicas of Serlio's renaissance drawings for Comedy and Tragedy, a reconstruction of the Globe Theatre, a seventeenth or eighteenth century apron stage, a *kabuki* stage, and so on. He knows the history of the stage better than most Broadway directors. If he does not quite succeed in turning out a finished recreation of an older play, if he cannot give us a production in any way comparable to the 1950 London revival of *The Beaux' Stratagem* or Stratford's *Much Ado About Nothing,* or to Jean-Louis Barrault productions in Paris, neither can the Broadway producer. And for the same reason: Our actors, as a rule, have no style in their bones and larynx. (I mean this literally: It is through gesture, stance, gait, and voice that true stylization is effected.) But more important to Professor Dorner's and my way of thinking is the fact that neither antiquarianism nor invertebrate modernization and domestication of a play is anything but makeshift style. It does not, it cannot, etch itself into a spectator's consciousness. It is usually only varnish on the play.

Effective style can only come from contemporary consciousness formed by an intense response. It is one thing to render a Greek, Elizabethan, or eighteenth-century play in terms of the theatre in which it originated; accurately, in which case we have antiquarianism, or approximately, in which case we have simple accommodation to the fact that we have no Greek, Elizabethan, or eighteenth-century stage at hand. It is another thing to translate such a play into the vital idiom of our times and location.

The theatre cannot remain stationary when life is in flux. The theatrical artist lives in an unstable time-space dimension. He should not be a jack-in-the-box, popping out at the whim of a finger's pressure. But he should have his finger on the heartstrings—and "mind-strings"—of his world. He should be, in the honorable sense of the terms, a *Zeitmensch*— a "time-man." During the days of the Federal Theatre, for example, Halstead Welles made Eliot's *Murder in the Cathedral* come to life by means of a judicious allocation of lines and movement to individual members of the chorus, by a direct projection of Becket's sermon from a platform, and by forthright treatment of the theatre as a forum for the rationalistic self-justifications of Becket's murderers. The director had taken into consideration the ultimate reality of his time and place—the informality, individualism, and "snap" of American life. The British production, imported by Gilbert Miller later on, presented Eliot's play as a liturgical drama. The scenery was stately, the action was leisurely, and the chorus moved as a group and spoke in unison. The American production was for Americans; the British production for English gentlemen and gentlewomen.

Here again Professor Dorner's thesis becomes clear. At the National Theatre Conference he inveighed against assumptions of an "absolute" of beauty in art. Its worship has always vitiated the fine arts, literature, and the theatre. The proportions the Greeks found beautiful in the late fifth century sculpture expressed their vision of life or attitude toward reality. (And perhaps the only reality we have is our attitude to it!) Therefore, the proportions were "right." They were not "right," however, for the Negro sculptor in the Congo or for the masters who carved the statuary of the Cathedral of Chartres, because these had different visions or views of reality to express. A truly creative age seeks new ways of mastering the chaos of experience and impressions that we call life, and the result, if the age expresses itself successfully, is an optimal style—not "absolute," but effective in rendering a particular attitude or interest or culture-pattern.

To shape something is a master's job, and a master is one who rules his matter instead of being ruled by it. And since matter is refractory whether it be a piece of granite or the living complex of a personality, the master needs the strength that comes from perception and conviction. Conveniences and makeshifts have nothing to do with true mastery, and a master scorns relying upon them; or if he adapts his design to the material with which he has to work (such as bamboo or driftwood, bark-cloth or shell in the South Sea Islands) or to topography, as in the case of Mont Saint Michel, he makes the adaptation itself a form of expression. Mont Saint Michel was not merely set on a crag by the medieval architects, but shaped into a Gothic fortress of faith. It stands for the invincible nature of spiritual belief or, at least, for the Church militant.

But it is only accommodation that seems to dominate the stage "off" Broadway as well as "on" with such rare exceptions in Manhattan as the original productions of *The Glass Menagerie, A Streetcar Named Desire,* and *Death of a Salesman.* And accommodation is just as feeble as the achievement of a meaningless "absolute beauty." We think that we have a new form in arena theatre, for example, which is not yet a *new* style precisely because it isn't yet a *style.* It is in most productions as yet only an accommodation to the economic problem of producing plays cheaply. It may be argued, of course, that it is also a means of bringing the play closer to the audience, of involving the spectator. But few people who favor "central staging" have penetrated to the heart of the question—namely, with what point of view, attitude, or vision is the play being brought closer. The real creative problem is not solved but actually evaded when we indulge ourselves in the belief that a new style has been created by arena theatre. You can have arena theatre or any other kind of theatre, but the real idiom, flavor, and force have yet to be created—and created for each particular production. It is not the convention of theatre adopted by us but what we vitally accomplish within it that is decisive. Mr. Dorner's implicit challenge to the contemporary theatre is equally important to off-Broadway and Broadway stage production.

Mr. Dorner was followed by Irwin Edman, who touched upon the seemingly simple but actually complicated question of what relation the theatre can bear to contemporary thought. Since the answer must come in the first instance from the playwright, it provides the subject for another essay. But Mr. Edman's central point applies to the total experience of theatre. Modern dramatists cannot successfully "catch up" with modern thought, and when they present "new ideas" these are apt to be already well out of fashion in philosophical or scientific circles. J. B. Priestley's dabbling in "time-relativity," as in *Time and the Conways,* is an example. There is, in short, a "time lag" between thinking in the theatre and thinking outside of it.

But this problem only brings us back to Alan Dorner's thoughts on "form" as the expression of perceptions of reality. It may be that our dramatists will never "catch up" with science and philosophy in terms of ideas. But it is enough if they translate human experiences in human terms, in the first place, and, at the same time, give meaning to experience through the signification of their dramatic style and form. We are less likely to care whether the dramatist keeps abreast with the latest ideas as such, if he is abreast with contemporary feeling, response, and consciousness.

This kind of consciousness or form—the style, tempo, tone, and stress of art and the "camera angle" at which an experience is caught—addresses itself directly to us, while the discursive reason in a play may fail to make satisfactory contact with the audience. Often, indeed, a writer's explicit ideas are contradicted by the form and spirit through which he expresses himself. The social ideas of many a so-called or actual left-wing American playwright, for example, may have expressed an accord with collectivism when actually everything beneath the surface was, whether or not the playwright knew it, inherently democratic *and individualistic*. Odets in the nineteen-thirties may have often idealized the "proletariat," and some obtuse admirers and opponents may have called him a "proletarian writer," whereas the real essence of a play such as *Awake and Sing!* or *Rocket to the Moon* was as "middle-class" as a James Whitcomb Riley poem, and the author was actually a more genuinely "middle-class" writer than official champions of Main Street and Rotary. "Idealism," especially in America, has been substantially middle-class in inspiration.

The moral of this is that art is the expression of a total personality in its environment. And another moral is that you cannot catch winged art by sprinkling salt on the tail of its ideas. The *flying* mechanism is located elsewhere.

EXPERIMENTAL THEATRE

There is a strange magic in the adjective "experimental" that implies a glorified anti-philistinism and that warrants the proponents of art movements to be paragons of foresight and courage. The word has been appropriated in this sense to cover a multitude of efforts more or less abortive in our century's theatre. Some are already embalmed in the textbooks, as is Guillaume Apollinaire's *Les mamelles de Tirésias* which titillated Parisians in 1917 with pre-*surréaliste* topsy-turvyism. (The wife in the play, deciding against childbearing, removed her breasts and revealed them to be balloons on that historic occasion!) Some experiments are fondly stored up by the middle-aged in their memorabilia: the Cocteau-Satie-Picasso revue of the same year *Parade;* that farcical jazz-age pantomime *Le Boeuf sur le Toit,* subtitled "The Nothing Doing Bar," in which a policeman was neatly decapitated by an electric fan; and the still more ambitious Cocteau effort in 1926 *Orphée,* in which Orpheus fascinated by a horse, no doubt representing the Muse, receives from it a message the first letters of which spell out the disreputable word *merde* and cause him to be dismembered by bacchantes. In America, too—and in recent years at that!—the young and foolish will cherish when they are old and foolish Saroyan's *Jim Dandy,* the 1948 revival of Cummings' *him* (first produced for the edification of their seniors in 1928), and Picasso's World War II caprice *Desire Trapped by the Tail,* in which five characters in one scene did nothing but exclaim, "Oh, my chilblains, my chilblains, my chilblains!" (The scene is framed by two stage directions, the first reading, "Outside each bedroom [in a corridor of the Hotel Sordid] are the two feet of the room's occupant, writhing in pain"; the second reading, "The transparent doors become illuminated and the dancing shadows of five monkeys eating carrots appear.") We may, indeed, thank our stars that the sweet mystery of youth or whatever platitude we use for transient immaturity will never be lost to our species.

Youth had its fling, of course, in other ages. Let us not forget the young gentlemen who gave us gory *Gorboduc* in 1560-61 and the fledgling Shakespeare who perpetrated *Titus Andronicus.* The difference between our theatre and theirs is merely that our prematurely old century has placed a premium on youth. Everything today becomes old-hat before the hat has been worn long enough to fit the head—if any. And not all the experimentation, of course, qualifies its proponents for the booby-hatch. The 1948 production of *Ballet Ballads,* written by John Latouche to music by Jerome Moross, was gratifying theatre even if it was sparsely attended on Broadway after an American National Theatre and Academy off-Broadway presentation. Something could also be said in 1947 for stylized ANTA performances of Bertolt Brecht's *Galileo,* even if the present writer can report no great enthusiasm for Charles Laughton's undraped torso while he got into his costume as the Italian scientist in the presence of the public; as well as for Piscator's staging in 1948 of Robert Penn Warren's *All the King's Men* (the play upon which Warren based his novel), as well as several other Piscator epic-style productions in the small President Theatre such as Sartre's *The Flies,* Salacrou's *Nights of Wrath,* and Wolfgang Borchert's expressionistic *Outside the Door* (*Draussen vor der Tür*), the first unusual play to come out of occupied Germany.

A proper concern is merely whether the experimentation to which eager devotees of the stage look for salvation can redeem the stage by invention or improvisation. Whenever there is no cultural ground in which individuals bent on creating non-commercial theatre can strike roots, or no need they can gratify except the need to make opportunities for themselves, two things happen: The so-called experimental groups die out, or their unique style, if any, is blandly appropriated and commercialized by those who are in business for money rather than for art. As cubism was appropriated by window-dressers of fashionable shops! And as expressionist fantasia was appropriated by one showman of the thirties for a tasteless revue in which he made his chorus girls wear oversized men's tophats over brassieres on which faces had been painted!

Hopeful stage people have launched new ventures continually during recent decades, and they are likely to make renewed efforts for some time to come. They are not apt to be daunted by public indifference or by economic difficulties that have lamed maverick efforts like theirs before. Whenever their idealism or idiosyncrasy is accompanied by at least a milligram of competence, some hearts, at least, will palpitate with a desire to approve unstintedly. Approbation, however, is given easily enough. What is harder to come by is a perspective that can enable us to clarify a view of so-called experimental theatre at present.

A useful appraisal of mid-century progressivism will first of all realize that if it is somewhat confusing, it is nonetheless important and must by no means be minimized. Next, however, we shall have to consider the fact that the achievement is circumscribed in ways that have been barely glimpsed by the advanced groups that have constituted the closest approximation of an experimental movement in our time. In fact, we cannot even predicate the existence of any such movement without also predicating the condition Sean O'Casey defined as a "state of chassis." Only by lumping together a great variety of efforts with a great diversity of aims and methods is it even possible to describe an alternative at present to what passes for the professional theatre in America.

When the Group Theatre, for example, was founded in the nineteen-thirties, an entire social philosophy, an ideal of collective artistry, and an esthetics of production and acting art were involved in the venture, whereas the enterprises that have come and gone since 1940 have revealed no particular unity of objective. Their one "experiment" has been that of trying to establish stages more or less independent of the conditions of commercial production in a period during which costs have mounted, theatrical investments have become increasingly riskier, alternatives between fabulous success and instant failure have grown fewer, and the number of plays staged in any single season has shrunk steadily. We must understand that since 1940 we have not developed a movement comparable to the "little theatre" or "art theatre" movement that flourished between 1916 and 1925 or to the social theatre that came to the fore during the depression of the thirties; not to mention the earlier enterprises, such as the *Théâtre Libre, Freie Buehne,* Moscow Art Theater and the Abbey Theatre, which gave birth to dramatic modernism in important centers. It is for this reason that it has been difficult to get some perspective on the present avant-garde, so that our picture of its activities is a jumble of detail rather than a true composition.

I

Our survey would have to take account of the repertory theatre established by Eva Le Gallienne, Margaret Webster, and Cheryl Crawford at great expense and effort. Its failure after a few inadequate and two acceptable revivals ended all efforts to maintain a repertory on a professional basis. The American National Theatre and Academy maintained an experimental theatre for a number of seasons with uneven results. Its productions fell into the two inevitable classifications of bad plays and good ones. The former were rightly avoided by Broadway as immature and insufficiently realized; the latter—such as *Ballet Ballads* and Richard Harrity's one-acter *Hope Is a Thing with Feathers*—were acceptable as art but impractical as ventures for the commercial stage. New York City Center seasons under José Ferrer and Maurice Evans provided some non-commercial, along with considerable commercial, low-cost theatre, and an enterprising group calling itself "New Stages" maintained itself from 1946 to 1949 with varying fortunes which mounted highest when the company put on Sartre's satiric piece *The Respectful Prostitute.* The Blackfriar's Theatre, a Catholic organization, gave meritorious productions for a few seasons. Semi-professional groups have come forward sea-

son after season, and a number of these—such as Studio 7, The Inter-
players, and On-Stage—for a while actually provided New York with a
secondary circuit of production. Acting companies associated with metropolitan theatre schools and some universities have enlarged the scope of
off-Broadway production. The press favorably noticed the work of the
Abbe Practical Workshop which gave performances at the former Roe-
rich Museum or Master Institute on Riverside Drive. The efforts of Erwin
Piscator's ten-year-long Dramatic Workshop enterprise, first under the
auspices of the New School and later independently, provided an experimental outlook that deserved considerably more credit than critics gave
it. The Dramatic Workshop actually maintained an off-Broadway repertory system inconspicuously for many years. It introduced new foreign
plays of considerable importance. It served as an outpost of an epic style of
theatre developed by Piscator, the poet Brecht, and the Living Newspaper
unit of the Federal Theatre, using projections, slides, and movies to supplement scenery, and turning the stage into a sort of "machine-for-theatre"
with revolving platforms expressive in some and confusing in other instances. Fordham University Theatre, under Albert McCleery and, later,
Edgar L. Kloten, used "arena style," as have other off-Broadway units
such as Circle-in-the-Square under José Quintero. (But with a transparent
curtain around the central acting area to prevent the audience at one side
of the stage from seeing the audience at the other side during performances.) And the Columbia University Theatre Associates, under Milton
Smith, provided successfully styled and mounted productions of a *kabuki*-
theatre adaptation, the Chinese *Circle of Chalk,* and Elizabethan pieces
such as *Comedy of Errors, Eastward Ho!,* and *The City Madam.*

The off-Broadway efforts of the past decade have been numerous,
indeed, and their number would be multiplied greatly if we took into
account the enterprises in other cities, such as Margo Jones' arena theatre
in Dallas, John Wray Young's Shreveport Little Theatre, Frederick Mac-
Connell's Cleveland Playhouse, and Gilmore Brown's Pasadena Playhouse.
And we may take added comfort from the work of many university and
college players throughout the country. These maintained a long record of
achievement under the leadership of such forward-looking educators as
Hallie Flanagan Davis at Smith College, Curtis Canfield at Amherst,
Sawyer Falk at Syracuse, Mabie at Iowa, Drummond and Albright at
Cornell, Selden at North Carolina, Fagin at the Johns Hopkins, Heffner
at Leland Stanford, and others too numerous to mention.

It is no secret that there has been a tendency in theatrical circles to
discount the interest and value of these efforts which, after conventional
productions have been subtracted from the score, add up to the only experimental theatre movement we have at present. It is an assumption of the

Broadway-minded that no production is of much account unless it finds a home in the Broadway area and remains there at prevailing Broadway prices for half a year or longer. That an experimental theatre is to be overlooked until it ceases to be experimental seems to be the prevailing view in non-academic circles. That there is ample provocation for this attitude can be admitted readily. But this concession must be tempered with the reflection that most professional talent is wasted on sheer trash.

Both in extent and quality the off-Broadway theatre has a record that compares favorably with that of the high-geared gambling enterprise for which the "Main Stem" is a striking misnomer. If we tallied the number of playgoers who patronize non-commercial productions we should find that Broadway can claim a superior record only in the case of a few successful plays, generally vehicles for stars of the magnitude of Helen Hayes, Katharine Cornell, and the Lunts. As for the quality of the drama offered by the semi-professional and non-professional companies, it is true enough that there are altogether too many revivals of third-rate Broadway successes, that there is too much pabulum of the order of *What a Life* and *Kiss and Tell* guaranteed to affront no section of the community and to tax no intellect above the high school level. Nevertheless, the non-commercial theatres actually produce drama of superior quality more frequently than does Broadway, even if Broadway is apt to look like very heaven on the rare occasions when it is both brave and proficient, since acting performance in both student and community productions leaves a good deal to be desired. Granted that the non-professional stage does not give rise to the good plays it produces, the fact remains that the plays do get produced again and again.

Certainly, Broadway after the Second World War did not score up for itself a record better than that of the off-Broadway productions of Sartre's *The Flies, The Victors, The Respectful Prostitute,* O'Casey's *The Plough and the Stars* and *The Silver Tassie,* Cocteau's *The Infernal Machine,* Lorca's *Blood Wedding,* Synge's *Deirdre of the Sorrows,* Strindberg's *Creditors* and *The Father,* Pirandello's *Henry IV,* Robert Penn Warren's *All the King's Men,* and Tennessee Williams' *Summer and Smoke*—to mention only a few of the productions in Manhattan. It is, moreover, questionable whether the quality of the staging had fallen distressingly short of the treatment the plays would have received on Broadway. At least this is true with respect to imaginativeness and sensitivity of presentation. It cannot be said that the little "Studio 7" group that produced *The Father* during the summer of 1949 was less proficient than the Broadway producers of Strindberg's tragedy who were able to engage the services of Raymond Massey, Mady Christians, and Mary Morris. One may reasonably doubt that a Broadway management could have done better by Sartre's *The Flies* than did Erwin Piscator in his small midtown President Theatre. Brooks Atkinson found *Summer and Smoke* more effective on the tiny Dallas arena stage and all reviewers found the play more effective at Circle-in-the-Square in Greenwich Village than at the spacious and admirably equipped Music Box Theatre. Mary Hunter's staging of *The Respectful Prostitute* at the New Stages' Greenwich Village headquarters was in all respects identical with the admirable presentation of the play uptown which sustained itself for a long time at Broadway prices; and New Stages' production of another Sartre piece, his French Resistance drama, *The Victors* (*Morts sans Sépulture*), was stirring.

If for no other reason than economy, the non-professionals have had to streamline their productions, which is all to the good when the acting is satisfactory, and they have been forced to play on small stages. One of the most frightening things in the theatre is the empty space on a big set that has to be filled up with all sorts of stage business not inherent in the play. The actors would be better off if they were placed on roller skates and told to play tag with each other on an expanse of stage as bald as an egg in the case of many single-set realistic plays. I have known at least half a dozen plays on Broadway that were deprived of all possibility of success the moment the actors moved into the set and had to cope with stairs, doors, and furniture. One play that was twenty minutes short of two hours' playing-time during rehearsals lasted two and a half hours once the scenery was put up. As usual, it was not the scenery but the play that was cut—for the obvious reason that it doesn't cost a cent to bluepencil a typescript whereas it may cost thousands of dollars to modify or scrap a set. We may well wonder whether *Death of a Salesman* would have been as well received as it was on Broadway if it had been played within conventional realistic settings. We can be certain that Williams' *Summer and Smoke,* for which Mielziner designed a beautiful setting, would have seemed a better organized play if it had not been necessary to play peek-a-boo with the actors placed at the extreme left and right of the stage in homes near the wings while the center of the stage was occupied by a very pretty picture of a village square and a statue employed only in an unnecessary Prologue and in the Epilogue.

II

An optimistic report on the state of the experimental movement must nevertheless be tempered by multiple reservations. It is, in the first place, not a movement at all, but an aggregate of activities on the periphery of Broadway. That is the cardinal limitation, and from it stem most inadequacies apart from incompetent acting—the lack of distinctive styles of production, the absence of a viewpoint in the direction, and the discontinuous nature of many of the enterprises. The avant-garde that gives us our most progressive non-commercial theatre is not a true avant-garde, because its members have nothing in common except a vague fondness for theatre. There has been no unifying concept of dramatic and theatrical aim, content, and style to mobilize the creative energies that must exert themselves before the off-Broadway theatre becomes truly creative.

Virtually no *new* experimental drama, except the Latouche and Moross *Ballet Ballads,* has come out of the experimental theatre of the past ten or more years creditably. And this is the most devastating criticism that can be leveled at so much theatrical activity. An experimental theatre that does not actually engender an at least temporarily impressive body of drama may have many virtues, may perform many services, but is in essence uncreative. After André Antoine established the *Théâtre Libre* in Paris back in 1887, the experimental theatres in many countries bore fruit in a dramatic literature. Men wrote specially for these theatres, new playwrights unfolded their talents in response to the possibilities of expression introduced by a new stage, and distinguished plays like *The Sea Gull* and *La Parisienne* that failed to receive their just due when produced by conventional or staid theatres were discovered to have significance when revived by the theatrical vanguard. This, by and large, was the history of every previous revolt against the commercialized stage. In America, an "art theatre" movement gave us O'Neill and his generation of dramatists in the twenties. Our experimental social theatre of the thirties fathered Odets, Irwin Shaw, Kingsley, Saroyan, and others. Whom has the aggregate activity of the anti-commercial theatre brought forth since 1940? Surely not Arthur Miller and Tennessee Williams, who owe nothing at all to vanguard groups born since then. What new plays other than *Ballet Ballads* have been introduced to the general public by the special theatres? Only two in ten years, to the best of my recollection: *The Respectful Prostitute,* a French play of less than major importance, and *Anna Lucasta,* which was translated from a Polish-American to a Negro background for a Harlem production!

Surely this is a slim harvest for ten years of coast to coast activity and five years of worthy tub-thumping, threshing and pushing by ANTA. And what is most dismaying is that Broadway has actually beaten its non-commercial rivals to the punch time and again in the competition for creative honors. It is humbling for those who expect so much from the off-Broadway theatre to have to concede that since 1939 when the Group Theatre presented Saroyan's *My Heart's in the Highlands* and Eddie Dowling and the Theatre Guild produced *The Time of Your Life,* virtually every meritorious *new* play that can be regarded as more or less unconventional or original in structure, style, or content has been ground out by the Satanic mills of the theatrical marketplace. *The Beautiful People, The Patriots, The Skin of Our Teeth, Home of the Brave, The Glass Menagerie, A Streetcar Named Desire. Member of the Wedding, The Deep Mrs. Sykes, Death of a Salesman, Harvey, The Iceman Cometh, The Sound of Hunting*—these and other plays, all produced on the sinful "White Way," must put friends of the anti-Broadway movement to shame.

The reason for this reversal of roles which makes Satan look saintly when he is set beside the angels who have elected to castigate him is simple. A new art movement cannot be creative unless it is sustained by some positive belief and vision. And no particular vision has emanated from the various and almost entirely unrelated enterprises that have tried to establish themselves on the outskirts of the professional stage. Men have not banded together to create a new type of drama and production style, as in previous periods. Why this should be the case is a problem for the historian. It is, I fear, an indication of spiritual stalemate in our times. During the war period the general fervor for a democratic way of life was only a surface manifestation, and after 1945 the bickerings of the great powers and disenchantment with all ideologies, if not with the very future of mankind, began to overwhelm or at least depress most of our young writers and producers.

We do not expect pervasive inspiration and conviction from the commercial theatre, and it can often hold its own without these attributes by offering the gloss and glitter of professionalism. When Broadway, moreover, plays host to plays of some distinction, one accepts them with gratitude and pleasure without looking too closely at the event. We derived satisfaction, for example, from some of the personal antics of Saroyan, and from the more restrained but equally individual work of Tennessee Williams. We did not balk at plays like *State of the Union, Born Yesterday,* and *Goodbye, My Fancy* because their liberalism had collected moss for decades. Carson McCullers' *Member of the Wedding* entranced us with its simple humanity even though the "plotless" play was a discovery not of the nineteen-forties, but of the eighteen-eighties. Sidney Kingsley's *Detective Story* did not displease most of us because the "slice of life" that is the chief merit of the play was a seventy-five-year-old discovery of the theatre. Nor did we greatly cavil at *The Cocktail Party* because it stems essentially from T. S. Eliot's Anglo-Catholicism which, as the *London Times* took pains to remind us, was a discovery only for Americans. We have become accustomed to accepting an eclectic, directionless professional theatre in New York, London, Paris, and points east.

It is more than a mélange that is expected of experimental groups. They cannot command the qualities of experienced acting, tasteful and expensive costumes, eye-filling scenery, and smooth delivery that cover up a multitude of sins. Nobody expects this much professionalism or reprehends its absence except in cases of flagrant ineptitude. But we do expect the experimental efforts to point in the direction of provocative ideas or expressive styles of production. And we do look at the whole of a production when no single performance illuminates the entire play. Very rarely do these groups create a style, however, because a production style also needs roots in a culture and cannot feed on itself. Nor do the new groups develop a genuine art of ensemble performance to compensate us for the absence of virtuoso acting upon which professionalism generally relies when it has nothing else to offer. Ensemble art is woefully undeveloped in most off-Broadway groups. Since, in addition, they cannot uncover or develop new plays of unique value, they are unable to prevail with their matter any more successfully than with their manner. And since they have had no esthetic or social cause around which to rally, they have been unable to start a wave of creativity that would give them rewarding plays, production style, and ensemble art.

Only in arena theatre has there been an interest in production style, but generally without any organic relationship to the significance or special value of a play, since most advocates of arena-style or central staging are convinced that *any* kind of play will suit their purpose. The one enterprise that does aim for significance by means of a special form or style—namely, the pageant drama movement started by Paul Green in North Carolina and called by him "symphonic drama"—is not, strictly speaking, "little theatre" dramatics at all.

At present, one must reluctantly conclude that most endeavors to take up the slack in Broadway production and to lift the estate of dramatic art in America face an impasse. There are many well-intentioned groups milling about, but I am afraid they have nowhere to go at present. We cannot blame them, it is true, since they are no worse off than the rest of the population. But their plight is greater because they are really trying to get somewhere. And they deserve our sympathy and whatever help we can give them, because they have the courage and are far from being wholly devoid of ability.

Is it possible, in conclusion, that the sentiments expressed in this article are too extreme? I rather think so myself, because I believe that a certain degree of creativity is accidental and incalculable, and it may happen that here and there we shall encounter a miraculous flowering of dramatic art seemingly for no reason whatsoever except persistence. Sometimes we do indeed blunder into something remarkable in matters of art. It is just barely possible that firmly grounded off-Broadway groups pushing out in different directions throughout the country will give us vital theatre.

ARENA THEATRE

There was considerable rejoicing in the theatre after the spring of 1952 over the success of the arena production of *Summer and Smoke* at the Circle-in-the-Square in Greenwich Village. A play that had aroused great expectations in Dallas when Margo Jones produced it in her arena theatre, *Summer and Smoke* came a cropper when it was brought to New York in the fall of 1948. This despite the enthusiasm of Brooks Atkinson and the approval of that redoubtable critic Joseph Wood Krutch, despite the entrancing, if in my lonely opinion disadvantageous, setting designed by Jo Mielziner for the usual behind-the-proscenium, picture-frame Broadway type of production, and despite some excellent performances, among which Margaret Phillips' playing of Alma was especially noteworthy.

The Circle-in-the-Square revival may not have overcome all reservations concerning Tennessee Williams' ironic drama of frustration, but José Quintero's production made *Summer and Smoke* flare out as quite a distinguished play, presented Geraldine Page as one of the most welcome discoveries of the acting profession in a decade, and gave renewed hope to the off-Broadway theatre. Even if the casting and performance of some of the secondary roles left something to be desired, the Circle-in-the-Square company and its brilliant director, Mr. Quintero, deserved all the plaudits they received.

My visit to the Village theatre was the most gratifying experience of a season's steady playgoing. But I am obliged to Circle-in-the-Square for something more than a memorable evening. The Quintero arena production gave me a glimpse into possibilities of off-Broadway theatre in general and of central staging in particular which I had been reluctant to entertain. Mr. Quintero and his associates almost made me a convert to the opinion that off-Broadway enterprises could stem the decline of the American theatre and that central staging could become an effective theatrical style rather than a mere expedient for reducing the cost of stage production and solving the real-estate problem. I was even inclined to associate some of the possibilities inherent in off-Broadway production with the possibilities inherent in central staging.

Nevertheless, there was a sting in the tail of my conviction, as I am not prepared to endorse either off-Broadway or arena theatre on conventional grounds. I find no particular virtue in the mere mushrooming of little theatres or in the mere resort to central staging. We have had little theatres cropping up again, but their contribution to the American stage has been altogether too slight for many years. They have not given us any memorable plays or productions, they have merely "produced" plays.

We have also had quite a number of arena productions in recent years, but there has been no particular evidence that these represented any distinct advance in the presentation or interpretation of drama. Certainly they have not crystallized any distinct style of production—and by "style" I mean a mode of presentation and interpretation of plays rather than a merely convenient convention of playing in the center of the auditorium. It doesn't matter *where* we put on a play but *how* we put it on—what values we stress and what expressive qualities we establish. My conviction is that the off-Broadway stage could enrich the American theatre by producing a *certain* kind of play and by presenting it *in a certain way*.

The plays I have in mind should fill the gap that is apparent in the repertory of the American theatre. I do not propose to outlaw entirely those trivial exercises of playwriting that entertain the public, although I would suggest that these could just as well be taken or adapted from dramatic literature as from the garbage heap of current or past unliterary, mindless, and tasteless theatre. Nor do I maintain that the little theatres should reject a play on no other grounds than that it was successfully produced on Broadway.

But off-Broadway enterprises will not improve the state of the theatre until they devote a considerable part of each season to plays which the American public, including our potential playwrights, do not ordinarily see. We need in our little theatres interesting Broadway failures such as *Summer and Smoke,* plays that Broadway managements rejected solely because they seemed too special for a sixty- or eighty-thousand-dollar production, gnarled and knotted rather than slick work provided it is gnarled for a more valid reason than the mere incompetence of the author.

The obligation rests with off-Broadway groups exempted from many of the exactions of trade unionism, patronized by educated audiences, and often more or less subsidized by local patrons, foundations, and universities. They should be able to produce what Broadway cannot afford or is too cautious to produce, and we have a right to expect this especially of those who operate arena theatres. Moreover, if arena theatre is as good and real a style as its proponents claim it is, more than a few of the rejected or overlooked plays that pose difficulties for Broadway should come off fairly well.

There are two main views to be considered here: if we allow the claims of those who believe that central staging can be successfully applied to *any* kind of play—serious or comic, "heavy" or "light," "presentational or representational"—then there is no problem whatsoever. It is even possible to contend that some fascinating plays would "get across" better in the small theatres than in the large ones in which a commercial manager must place his production if he is to retrieve the investment. Many a play is more effectively on view in the small, comparatively intimate London theatre than in Broadway theatres, where they suffer disaster after a long run in England. It is possible, too, that a nonprofessional company can present difficult plays better when the actors are not required to "project" their performances as much as is necessary in a theatre seating a thousand or fifteen hundred spectators. If, however, we accept the view of those who believe that only a certain style of drama is suitable—namely, "presentational drama," or drama in which a realistic background is unimportant— there are still enough plays to keep arena theatres busy for many a year.

In both cases, nevertheless, there is a problem of style that must be explored. For one thing, it is very questionable that merely putting on a performance in the center of an auditorium is a "style." Merely doing away with flats that would interfere with the audience's vision and merely ordering the actors to enable every spectator to see them from time to time cannot assure expressiveness in a production. Stylization purely for reasons of expediency is not style; it fails to give specific character to a play.

What we have a right to expect is that a production will give cohesive realization to the quality and meaning of the play, and for this purpose it is necessary to have a ruling concept, tone, and emphasis to which all elements are subordinated. For the little theatres to be satisfied with a perfunctory application of central staging would be an egregious mistake. Nothing can do more harm to the art of staging plays than to turn a stage director into a new kind of traffic cop whose prime function is to be that of directing actors' movements in a centrally located area. I fear that there has been too much talk about developing an arena style of production as if it were unnecessary for the director to achieve a highly individual style for each particular work he undertakes to stage. Expediency as a substitute for true stylization—a method of staging plays merely for visibility and for feasible entrances and exits—was too much in evidence in the New York Edison Hotel productions in 1950. That this was not the case in José Quintero's Circle-in-the-Square production was one of the most gratifying features of *Summer and Smoke*. It was plain that Mr. Quintero was translating or interpreting drama rather than primarily directing stage traffic.

Not every detail of the Circle-in-the-Square production was perfectly realized. But the play existed as an artistic entity and as an autonomous reality on the stage. The scenes were fused in an atmosphere of frustration and anguish. There was a nightmare quality in the action as it moved back and forth across the three playing areas of the rectangular stage surrounded by the audience on three sides—the parlor of the heroine Alma's rectory home, the park, and John's office. Owing to inadequate lighting, probably caused by unsolved technical problems, the production had, in fact, too much atmosphere at times. Nevertheless, *Summer and Smoke* was turned into frequently effective drama when it was atmospherically dissolved and presented as a state of mind and a series of tensions.

Realism of treatment is precisely what Williams' novelistic drama cannot stand, because its reality is subjective. Whether entirely by design or partly by happy accident (due to some inefficiency in lighting technique, perhaps) José Quintero created a special world for the play or, to be more accurate, a special world *of* the play—a darkness, fatefulness, and irony emanating from confused and blindly driven lives. The production telescoped the dramatic action by cramping the stage movement not merely physically but psychologically. Stage movement was compressed by a concentrating darkness, so that it was not action but *tension* that was most manifest in the production. The characters moved within an inner darkness, so to speak; they were shaped by it, never emerging into free and sharply lit space. They seemed to belong to their inner compulsions rather than to an environment beyond and independent of them. The floor of the stage served mostly as a platform for their emotional reality, and, in fact, both the park or town square and Dr. John's office *were* mainly platforms, so that the dramatic experiences were mainly "presented" rather than strictly "represented" in the manner of "fourth-wall" illusionism. Being presented or, shall I say, publicly "demonstrated" rather than "imitated," reality became *theatricalized reality* more than it can be on Broadway; it became a semi-expressionist new and inner reality.

It seems to me that many of the plays we do not have an opportunity to see in America are precisely works that exist in a special world, the world the playwright assigns to the characters as a function of their personality and conflicts or as a projection of his own special view of reality. This is particularly true of some of the most fascinating work of Strindberg (such as *There Are Crimes and Crimes* and *The Ghost Sonata*), Wedekind, Sternheim and the latter-day O'Casey. This is true of even such "realistic" plays as Becque's and Turgenev's; of the mordantly *blasé* comedy *La Parisienne,* and *A Month in the County,* with its world of *longeurs* and "nerves" in nineteenth-century provincial Russia. It is also true of many of Shaw's plays, from *Widowers' Houses* to *Heartbreak House* not to mention later pieces such as *Too True to Be Good.* There is no reason for academically using the conventions of the stage for which a play was originally composed. Arena theatre, using a largely neutral semi-abstract stage, is an excellent medium for staging plays whose essential quality is that of reality filtered through a positive, creative temperament and intellect; plays that express disorientation, alienation, or twilight views of human life; plays that are *creations* rather than imitations.

Such plays, which are not to be equated with mere fantasies, have integrity of the same order as that of a noteworthy poem or musical composition; and it is precisely such plays that we need to see if we are to realize that dramatic composition is distinctive creation—that is, vision rather than photography, essence rather than pastiche. Too many of these plays will remain unseen on our stage as long as producers appraise them only as stories or pictures of action to be considered as more or less literally real. To the producer who does not realize that these works are a world in themselves rather than a picture-postcard of reality, their story must seem incredible, their argument extreme, their action embarrassing, their "idea" bald or exaggerated, their style bizarre or mannered. He fails to understand and appreciate such work because he has become accustomed to expecting stereotypes of reality.

The producer is, moreover, encouraged to adopt this view or use this standardized appraisal because he sees a picture frame the moment he thinks of the stage, and expects to be able to put the play into the frame and then let the playgoer gawk at it as a paying Peeping Tom. Arena theatre, once it is not regarded merely as a novelty, challenges the producer and stage director to renounce the conventional role of picture-framer. If only they understood the intrinsic possibilities of a theatre that has no frame! In some arena productions, it would seem, the director is still directing as if he had a frame. He is incongruously trying to stick pictures into a void that cannot hold them. The result is a muddle—a blur of rotating figures that have no relation to anything but the furniture or the stage props.

Arena theatre, once its semi-abstract quality is understood, may further challenge the director to *interpret* even the most realistic play rather than merely making a tracing of it. There is the possibility, for example, that we shall see a production of *Ghosts* that will capture Ibsen's ironic and nightmarish "Fall of the House of Usher" poetry along with his incisive meaning by contrast with the one-dimensional view of that drama which has resulted in flat productions that have made it look as dated as a furbelow. Seeing or imagining just such flat productions could lead Brooks Atkinson to dismiss Ibsen as a desiccated dramatist, and could make the astute Clifton Fadiman declare nearly two decades ago that *Ghosts* had become invalidated by the discovery of salvarsan. When Mr. Fadiman fired Dr. Ehrlich's magic bullet at *Ghosts* he was seeing another, less incisive and poetic play than Ibsen's. And it is precisely the play that Ibsen did not create that the humdrum theatre has persisted in producing.

It is even possible that arena theatre used for created rather than transcribed life may incite our playwrights to write with total integration and expression of their personality rather than to engage in the vocation of play-carpentry.

Whether or not arena theatres, except in rare and incompletely conclusive instances such as the *Summer and Smoke* production, will accept the challenge of their medium remains to be seen. But the possibility exists, and it opens vistas of a decentralized American stage that will be worth supporting. It may even have an effect on those of us who produce on Broadway, try to write for it, and measure it with professional criticism. Before this can happen, however, the proponents of central staging will have to disabuse themselves of the overpublicized notion that the value of their enterprise lies in its "intimacy," which is not necessarily always the great virtue they think it is.

At least some of them will also have to give themselves a course in play analysis and dramatic theory; they will certainly have to unlearn the facile and routinized understanding of dramatic writing that has been the vogue for many decades. They will have to stop discussing the theme and analyzing characters as though these were "real" people living *outside* the play, rather than *inside* it. And to begin with they will also have to give more thought to the matter of dramatic metaphor in both so-called realistic and nonrealistic drama—this, with a view to becoming adept at *expressing* a play rather than merely *representing* it on the stage.

Only then can they hope to overcome the limitations of arena theatre by comparison with the proscenium stage, as well as to make the most creative use of their medium. And only then will the term *arena style* have any particular significance.

THE LOST THEATRE:
OUR UNUSED DRAMA

I

There is much significance in the fact that the Broadway season of 1951-52 should have started out as a Bernard Shaw season. With *Saint Joan, Don Juan in Hell,* and *Caesar and Cleopatra* as the outstanding non-musical plays, and with a disgraceful collection of new plays as the only immediate contribution by current playwrights except for Maxwell Anderson's honorable if unsuccessful *Barefoot in Athens,* Broadway might do worse than give some thought to its doldrums. Broadway did, and some hopes were raised by the efforts of the New Dramatists Committee under the leadership of Howard Lindsay, who found loyal support from his fellow-playwrights and fellow-producers.

It is not at all my intention to cast aspersions on this well-intentioned effort when I am forced to reflect that quite a number of the "new dramatists" have been "new" for much too long a time and when I register the opinion that playwrights are in greater need of inspiration than of encouragement. (I still believe that inspiration is its own best encouragement. I concede only that inspiration must have its source *outside* the playwright as well as inside him.) I do suspect, however, that Broadway cannot afford to wait until the writers shepherded by Mr. Lindsay or by anyone else regenerate the stage. Faith in the theatre, which entails the willingness of people to invest in it, work for it, and attend its performances in droves rather than dribbles, can be sustained only by stimulating or exciting stage productions. Shaw's plays did more to sustain that faith than a dozen maladroit new attempts at playwriting. There is, besides, more inspiration, as well as instruction, for new playwrights in an acceptable production of a distinguished play than in prizes, lectures, and mutual criticism of each other's playscripts. What playwright worth his salt is not going to be proud of his profession when he thinks of *Saint Joan, Hamlet* or *Oedipus the King?* What writer who is not an incorrigible hack can fail to respond to the power of ideas in the theatre when audiences are held spellbound by Shaw's *Don Juan in Hell.* The fact is that no theatrical season need ever be barren or absurd if the stage is willing and able to avail itself of the dramatic literature that twenty-four centuries have accumulated for it.

Is Broadway "willing"? It is quite willing if a good cast can be assembled, if a star can be found to attract the customers, and if the producer, the investors, and the star can be convinced that the play can run long enough to retrieve the investment. Is Broadway "able"? Yes, if the aforementioned conditions are met, if the stage director understands the play, and if by some miracle the cast delivers an acceptable performance even though the actors have never worked together before and, for that matter, haven't worked at all except in restaurants, Macy's basement, radio, and television. The point is, of course, that Broadway is only half-willing and only accidentally able to make effective use of the dramatic literature available to it. It lacks the economic and esthetic basis for consistently capitalizing on the heritage of world drama.

Any historian of the drama can come up with a long list of plays that qualify for "revival"—a vile word which if applied to other forms of literature would require us to say that a novel, a story, or a poem is "revived" whenever it appears in a new edition. Ever since 480 B.C., playwrights have added their largesse or their mite, as the case may be, to our store of dramatic literature. While Broadway remains as closed to the new material as it is to the old, playwrights are still adding to it here and there; if not in America, then in England, France, Scandinavia, Central Europe, Italy, Mexico, or elsewhere.

The "Old Vic" stirred playgoers to their very roots with a memorable production of *Oedipus the King,* but Broadway did not see another product of Greek genius until years later. Robert Whitehead presented Judith Anderson in Robinson Jeffers' adaptation of Euripides' *Medea.* Broadway did see Anouilh's version of *Antigone,* but it saw only a decadent product of French despair of humanity under the German Occupation: It never even glimpsed the luster of Sophocles' heroic drama of private conscience pitted against tyrannical law. And there are at least a dozen great Greek tragedies and half a dozen delightful classic comedies Broadway has not produced in any form. The merest fraction of Elizabethan drama, including the Shakespearian canon, and of Spanish, neo-classic French, Restoration, eighteenth-century, nineteenth-century, and post-Ibsen drama has ever reached midtown Manhattan under proper auspices; or, for that matter, under any auspices. For many years now our university and community playhouses, with limited facilities and actors often too young and inexperienced for their parts, have done better than that. So have ardent little groups stuck away in Greenwich Village alleys producing such plays as Lorca's *Yerma,* Cocteau's *The Infernal Machine,* and Strindberg's *The Creditor.* But twenty-five centuries of theatre have been virtually lost to the professional stage in midtown Manhattan.

An occasionally satisfactory revival reminds us of the existence of that theatre. The production comes and then goes and is not seen again. Years later somebody else has the same bright idea of doing the same play again because a star is available or because it is possible to import a good production from London. That is the extent of Broadway's awakening to the fact that Shakespeare, Strindberg, or Chekhov wrote an interesting play. It is necessary to reflect, too, that an occasional production is by no means a substitute for keeping the plays on view season after season with the same actors or with other actors, and with the same or with different production styles.

Repertory theatres have been few and short-lived in New York whereas they have had a long history abroad. Their failure in New York has been so well publicized as to act as a deterrent to new efforts. The fact of failure has been accepted, but the possibility of having been able to avert failure has been overlooked. The fact that a humdrum production bankrupted a noble enterprise does not prove that a superb production would have done so. Also, there has been so little originality and taste in production style in our professional theatre that it rarely occurs to anyone that scenery can be effective without being expensive, or that virtually no scenery is needed for a great many distinguished works. What would scenery have done for *Don Juan in Hell?* When a producer does trim down production costs, the effect is that of parsimony rather than creative imagination. Appia, Craig, Copeau, Robert Edmond Jones, and many other talented modern artists might just as well never have lived for all the use that is being made of their vision or example.

Admittedly, this reliance on the classics is the academic approach to the problem. Yet the plays themselves were not academic exercises. If they had been, they would never have become subjects for academic study. Nor do I propose the production of classic literature as the sole occupation of the living theatre. Admittedly, too, some interesting pieces are not for general consumption today. But it is only too apparent that the theatre cannot operate on the theory of producing for the lowest common denominator of taste and intelligence that has nearly wrecked the motion picture industry. Moreover, it is precisely this question of popular appeal that needs further exploration, which cannot be undertaken so long as a play is left on the bookshelf.

It was from a bookshelf that Lawrence Langner picked St. John Ervine's *John Ferguson* four years after publication to give the nascent Theatre Guild its first successful production and to start that organization on a commercially tenable career. Nor is it even sound business to be as "flop-conscious" as Broadway tends to be when it shies away from plays because they failed when first produced or when they were ineptly "revived." To the layman, a play looks as good as its production. Perhaps the most crushing failure Molnar ever had during his brilliant career in

Hungary was the original Budapest production of *Liliom* in 1909. I have heard it said that the lady who favored its author at the time made him promise that he would never write another play like this, and his friendly enemies have said that this was the only promise Molnar ever kept. The fiasco of *Liliom*, however, did not prevent the Theatre Guild from turning the play into one of the Guild's greatest successes in 1921 and from getting a second success out of the work with *Carousel*. That the combined prowess and popularity of Ingrid Bergman and Burgess Meredith could not make *Liliom* successful nearly twenty years after the original Guild production does not by itself invalidate Molnar's work any more than Leslie Howard's failure with *Hamlet* or Walter Huston's failure with *Othello* invalidated Shakespeare's tragedies.

The most gratifying season Broadway has ever had would dwindle into insignificance by comparison with a season composed solely of potential and actual "flops" such as the Oresteian trilogy, *Antigone* and *Oedipus the King, Hippolytus* and *Iphigenia in Aulis, Dr. Faustus* and *Edward II, Troilus and Cressida* and *Measure for Measure, The Alchemist* and *Bartholomew Fair, The Changeling,* and so on down the ages to Ibsen's *The Master Builder* and *John Gabriel Borkman* or almost any other play, and not necessarily the best, by a playwright who had talent and had something to say. Needless to say this is an impractical list for the theatre as presently constituted; the whole season might be a success but every producer in town would go into bankruptcy under present conditions. But is not a theatre that cannot afford to produce important or stimulating drama also impractical? How practical is the practical Broadway setup when nine-tenths of the world's theatre is lost to the playgoer. But for university courses and off-Broadway productions we should soon have a generation that would not even know why the theatre is worth preserving.

Attempts at rationalizing are inevitable whenever no effective efforts are made to remedy a situation. One particularly favorite rationalization is to call a play outdated. There are, of course, many plays that "date." But they are generally plays that were never alive at all. If they succeeded at one time, they were given a semblance of life by something else than a creative act on the playwright's part—that is, by popular acting, eye-filling spectacle, some topical interest, or the cultural immaturity of the playgoing public. But as for plays that were once truly alive, the burden of proof rests on those who would date them—and the conclusive proof can be offered only in the theatre. A creative and economical policy should be based on the principle that no distinguished play is ever outmoded to the creative artist. Something similar may also be said concerning theatrical viability. How do you know whether something that was once good theatre is no longer good theatre until you have given it the maximum benefit of a sensitive and intelligent production. If you do, you may surprise yourself. For as long as I can remember and for much longer, *Richard II* was considered theatrically less effective than *Richard III,* with the result that *Richard II* was rarely produced. But Margaret Webster and Maurice Evans were able to find much more "good theatre" in the last-mentioned play than anybody has been able to uncover in the far more active and dynamic *Richard III* for several decades.

The fallacy of dating plays has, in fact, gone so far that professional people in America are ever ready to date even recent dramatists. O'Neill has been considered *passé* by quite a number of people who are still wet behind their intellectual ears. The fallacy of dismissing a great work of literature is equally rampant. It received a stunning rebuke in London only recently from an impressive production of *Samson Agonistes,* a play that Milton himself had not intended for the stage. I know even redoubtable scholars of the drama with practical stage experience who look askance at the choruses of Sophocles instead of asking themselves the decisive question of how the great literature in those choruses, so important to the dramatic meaning and spirit of the plays, can be transposed into good theatre for our day. In consequence of these and other fallacies the contemporary American professional theatre is one of the most wasteful institutions in human history.

II

How the theatre's heritage can be recovered and also augmented by recent and new American plays, available but unproduced or long delayed, is, admittedly, a problem riddled with difficulties. I doubt that these can be solved so long as huge cities such as New York, Chicago, Philadelphia, San Francisco, and Los Angeles cannot maintain a single professional repertory company year after year. But the one certain way of making defeat permanent or the present situation unalterable is to accept it as inevitable. No flourish of the critic's pen can, of course, alter it, and any practical proposals can be easily discredited by the critic's critics: mostly the experienced practical men who have proved their astuteness, I take it, by losing the investment on play after play by favoring seemingly marketable tripe that proves to be unmarketable while, occasionally, a producer of seemingly unmarketable drama, such as Paul Gregory who presented *Don Juan in Hell,* makes them look ridiculous. Nevertheless, having wrung other people's necks, it is only fair that I expose my own by making some suggestions in a spirit of inquiry and provocation.

Suppose you were a producer who can raise the capital for a single

$60,000 production, not to mention a $200,000 musical comedy investment. Couldn't you pool your resources with one or more producers who can raise equal sums of money? Why should you fritter away all that money on an all or nothing proposition, on a single shot in the dark? Why not, instead, collect a good company and alternate two, three, four, or five productions of known quality, running some plays longer than others as the interest of the public warrants.

QUESTION 1: *Who will want to invest in plays having such short runs as to make a profit impossible and a loss certain?*

ANSWER: Anybody who has any business sense, if he is certain that the repertoire is not for a season but for three, five, or ten years. It is on a long-range basis that most sound corporation investments are made. And would any practical man, if he could help it, prefer to risk his money on the sale of a single commodity rather than on a steady stream of commodities?

QUESTION 2: *Can I lease a theatre on that basis?*

ANSWER: You could if you were in a position to make suitable guarantees, provided of course that the theatre owner learned from the experience of having only intermittently lighted buildings, and were brought to his senses by the refusal of a majority of producers to lease his theatres for single productions. It is not even beyond the realm of possibility that a theatre owner is as interested in good theatre as the most high-minded of American producers. Robert Dowling and Louis Lotito, for example, have as good a claim to respect as anyone in the business of producing plays.

QUESTION 3: *Can I interest good actors in such a venture?*

ANSWER: I don't know the latest statistics of Actors' Equity. But it wasn't very long ago when out of approximately 6,000 professional actors only about 2,000 found employment during a season, and most of them did not play more than a few weeks during the year. Good actors would welcome an opportunity to work continuously, and they would become better actors if they did.

QUESTION 4: *But can I acquire the services of stars who would attract the public sufficiently to make the venture profitable?*

ANSWER: Perhaps you couldn't, although this is by no means certain, since there are at least a few "stars" who care more about the theatre than commercial managements realize. If the managements have found it difficult to snare them, this is partly because the actors were offered unattractive roles in unattractive plays. If the managers have found the stars difficult and exorbitant in their demands, isn't it because they have not been offered any artistic cause? The stars of the theatre have had little reason to establish anything but a cash nexus with the stage.

Among other things, it may be noted that the performer who is sought after because he can ensure a long run is apt to become exceedingly bored after a while. The challenge of playing several roles each year might be welcomed by the first ladies and first gentlemen of the theatre. It might also be a relief to them to play a secondary role now and then instead of always being "top banana," once it was clearly no discredit to retreat from the limelight for the sake of a distinguished production. It would be fun, too, to create a few "character parts" for one's personal repertory. What genuine actor can resist opportunities for make-believe! It would also be restful for some of our best performers not to have to carry a play on their backs night after night.

I shall refrain from mentioning names, but our best actors are not getting any younger. It would be far better for them to husband their energies every few days than to take long vacations that sometimes amount to virtual retirement. A varied artistic diet and short vacations can be pre-scribed to them with an assurance of mutual benefit to the individual and the theatre.

Next point: The managers' notion of stardom when put into practice often proves to be *stardoom*. Since their Hollywood careers will by no means be jeopardized by any reminder from me, I feel free to call atten-tion to the more or less recent debacles of Olivia de Havilland and Ginger Rogers. All that glitters on the silver screen is not gold in the box-office of the legitimate stage.

Finally, it is well to remember that new stars can be made by repertory employment more easily than by single opportunities. The most promising actress may not scintillate in the "simply wonderful part" that has been assigned to her. The reason may lie in her personality, in her mistaken interpretation of the part, or in poor stage direction; and not only may she have been misdirected, but the style of the other performances may have been unfavorable to her own. In the theatre as presently constituted, she may be saddled with one ungratifying, reputation-losing part for a long time, or she may find herself quickly out of work and accepting another ungratifying part out of necessity or overeagerness to prove her mettle.

If Miss Uta Hagen will pardon me, I shall take her as an example. I did not happen to be entranced with her performance as Joan of Arc, and for her sake I should much prefer to see her in certain other parts more congenial to her deliberate style. One of these would be the heroine of Bertolt Brecht's *The Good Woman of Setzuan;* another, the Electra of Sophocles, or Euripides; still another might be Hedda Gabler. To make Miss Hagen's rare merits shine properly, one needs a repertory that would reveal the ample range of her talents.

QUESTION 5: *Would not the spread of repertory militate against the production of new plays and playwrights?*

ANSWER: *By no means in the case of new plays worthy of production.* Today managements produce a good many new plays that should not have been exposed on Broadway at all, especially under the present conditions that require long runs. If such plays are to be produced at all, the only sensible reason is to enable the writers to learn their craft from the production.

I happen to believe that this theory can be driven too far, but this is a separate subject. I believe that if a playwright is intelligent, he does not need a full-scale Broadway production to show him where and how he has erred; and if he isn't that intelligent, he shouldn't be encouraged to become a playwright. As a matter of fact, many playwrights who have had production have revealed no progress whatsoever in their work. America, as George Jean Nathan pointed out many years ago, is the land of numerous one-play writers. They wrote one acceptable play, and all the plays they wrote subsequently were worse rather than better.

In any case, the new playwright can learn from laboratory productions, and laboratory productions with professional actors would be made more possible by the presence of permanent repertory companies.

It should also be realized that the development of repertory companies would not eliminate all independent, "one-shot" producers. Who would prevent me from risking my all on the production of a play by an unknown young playwright if I had sufficient confidence in his script?

Moreover, a repertory company might be just the ideal production unit for a new play, precisely because in a repertory setup the play would not have to run for a hundred consecutive evenings to justify production at all. Actually, the professional theatre would be more accessible to unique talent, more open to plays that producers regard as too "special." Most new plays selected for production today are chosen because they are deemed to be safe bets—in other words, so ordinary that they are expected, generally wrongly, to satisfy nearly every sort of taste. There isn't a producer, I dare maintain, who hasn't rejected better—more substantial, original and honest—scripts than those upon which he has wasted time, money, and even talent.

Finally, it is precisely a repertory company that can ensure the perpetuity of new plays, including those that could not weather Broadway today. Even the so often staid *Comédie Française* has again and again incorporated into its schedule plays that had been at some time or another (in some case a half century or more) too special for the generality of playgoers. That is what happened with plays by De Musset and the difficult poet-playwright, Paul Claudel.

During the season of 1950-51, we had a production of *Billy Budd,* a play so "special" that all the efforts of the critics could not make it pay off financially. Nevertheless, I believe it was one of the three or four most worthy plays of the season, and that it can be stimulating in any season. It is also possible that we underestimated the play, and I should like to see it again, just as it is possible that a year from now Norris Houghton, a man for whom I have considerable admiration, might hit upon ways of improving his original production. A repertory theatre could do worse than incorporate *Billy Budd* into its program, and could produce it with far less anxiety and greater artistry than is usual on Broadway because the life of the repertory organization would not depend upon this single production.

Another play that would qualify would be Edward Justin Mayer's *The Children of Darkness,* if Joseph Wood Krutch and I have any judgment. Still another would be Saroyan's *The Beautiful People;* and still another, Tennessee Williams' *Summer and Smoke,* a play that Williams never succeeded in licking into shape and that was hurried to Broadway chiefly because the citizens of Dallas overrated it in Margo Jones's arena theatre. One month's labor by the playwright and some expert restaging would give us a work of art that could make ninety percent of the new plays of this or last season look miserable by comparison.[1] Very much the same point may also be made concerning plays from abroad that were once produced here without the kind of hit-success Broadway required then and certainly requires now, although they found discriminating admirers. I refer to such plays as Obey's *Noah,* Birabeau's *Dame Nature,* and Giraudoux' *The Enchanted.*

And to these examples one may add distinguished plays from abroad not yet seen on Broadway because their chances of running for months have been correctly or mistakenly regarded as slender. Among candidates for insertion into repertory programs I should consider Montherlant's *Queen After Death* and *The Master of Santiago,* James Bridie's *Mr. Gilley* (which moved me in London but which I should hesitate to risk on Broadway under the most favorable present conditions), Lorca's *Yerma,* Pirandello's *Liolà,* and Bertolt Brecht's *Mother Courage* and *The Good Woman of Setzuan.*

Plays have been written and are being written year after year that New York audiences—and audiences in other cities supplied with Broadway theatre—never see and yet are superior to the trash that is produced. Even if they should not be accepted as masterpieces, these plays would justify the theatre as one of the major outlets for the civilized human spirit.

An addendum: The theatre has had a following that will abandon it

---

[1] *Summer and Smoke* was successfully restaged less than half a year after I published this opinion in the February, 1952, issue of *Theatre Arts.* (See p. 516.)

(that has, in fact, started abandoning it) unless it can prove sufficiently stimulating. It is not a following that demands "smash-hits," which it sometimes actually deplores in spite of what seems to these rather discriminating individuals an extravagantly benign press. It is a following that has not waxed ecstatic over *The Moon Is Blue, Season in the Sun, Call Me Madam, Remains to Be Seen,* and *Gigi* simply because some reviewers have tossed their hats in the air. This body of playgoers does not even demand a completely successful piece of dramaturgy. It does, however, want to derive some stimulation from the drama. It would form the backbone of public support for good repertory programs, and it would even go to see the same play season after season if it were worth seeing, just as art-lovers go more than once to view a painting in a museum and opera-lovers go more than once in a lifetime to hear *Carmen* or *Boris Godunov.* Just as there are art-lovers, so there are theatre-lovers.

If their number has been diminishing on Broadway and in its touring centers, and this in a period of relative prosperity, the reason is that Broadway repels them. At the same time, their number is increasing in numerous towns that have good local university and community theatres, and some have been flourishing in the seemingly most unlikely places for decades. The Little Theatre of Shreveport, Louisiana, under the present direction of Mr. and Mrs. John Wray Young, celebrated its thirtieth year of continuous production in 1952.

LET THE REVIVER BEWARE,
OR, HOW TO KILL A PLAY

I. THE RISK OF REVIVAL

Recommendations of repertory theatre of any sort must always be tempered with one qualification: The productions should be sufficiently satisfactory to revive rather than inter the classics and near-classics. I don't believe the element of risk can ever be removed from the theatre. I don't even believe that it should be removed entirely, as the complete absence of risk would be as bad for the morale of the stage as the extreme riskiness of present-day Broadway. Nor is it particularly good to have a dutiful audience, one that attends performances merely because it is proper to support the classics instead of expressing that conclusive form of criticism which consists of staying away from the theatre. A repertory system that merely promotes academicism cannot ensure the vitality of the stage. The history of subsidized European theatre justifies the fear that a permanent repertory company may become staid and sterile after a number of years. The complaints registered against the *Comédie Française* in pre-war years and the frequent criticism of the Abbey Theatre's shortcomings were largely provoked by the *locomotor ataxia* that often afflicts long-established institutions of art.

This is not to say, however, that only state-supported or otherwise subsidized companies destroy classics. Privately run repertory companies, such as the Old Vic and the Olivier Company which brought *Caesar and Cleopatra* and *Antony and Cleopatra* to New York, as well as our own short-lived American Repertory Company after the war, can also fail to do justice to plays. And individual attempts, such as usually crop up on Broadway, frequently have dismal results, here and elsewhere. The only difference between "here" and "elsewhere" is that when an older play except, as a rule, by Shakespeare fails on our stage, influential newspaper reviewers conclude that the play was unstageable or outmoded anyhow. The play will be put back on the bookshelves then for an indefinite period.

How to reduce the incidence of fiascos in revivals is always a question, and no easy answers can be found, although there is never any dearth of glib post-mortems, to which I propose to add some of mine. I say that they are glib because no outsider can know much about the casting and production problems encountered by the producers, and also because one has to be extremely familiar with the scenes and lines of a play to level detailed and accurate charges. We usually depend upon mere impressions, and often merely rationalize our vague dissatisfactions into judgments. If we are particularly self-confident and write with any force at all, our criticism carries an air of authority, and we acquire an unfairly won reputation for acumen.

Long playing under expert direction, preferably with a longer rehearsal period than the four weeks customary on Broadway, may help considerably. That, too, however, is not an ironclad guarantee. Even the prowess of the Moscow Art Theatre joined with the genius of Gordon Craig in 1911 could not produce a *Hamlet* to the satisfaction of Stanislavski. With characteristic wisdom, the latter looked in the direction of style, concluding that his actors were as yet unable to cope with non-realistic modes of theatre—this in the *fourteenth* season of continuous stage production! Those of us who followed the Group Theatre's work in New York observed a similar deficiency in those productions for which the excellent *Awake and Sing!* style of realistic performance was unsuitable. A conspicuous example was the Group's ragged and now and then lumbering performance of Paul Green's epic-styled satire on war *Johnny Johnson,* suggestive of Piscator's *The Good Soldier Schweik.*

The productions to which I now turn with a view to illustrating the fact that classics *can* be killed or, if not killed, at least lamed were all worthy ones. The producers, directors, and actors to whom I allude uncomplimentarily will forgive me, I hope. I revive their inadequacies or the impression of inadequacy they made on me solely in order to ensure specificity in my analysis. In each case, however, I do not claim absolute validity for my criticisms. These were made on the spot, so to speak, with a view to reporting on the production. Also, one viewing of a production is insufficient as a basis for any reliable judgment on particulars. One hearing of an orchestral performance is also not enough. A considerable element of uncertainty pertains to all criticisms of the performing arts. With these qualifications in mind, I proceed to consider a few case histories. The productions have long vanished. The memory of their failure, however, remains with me as a refutation of any assumption that the theatre can be automatically uplifted by our returning to famous old plays, as well as a warning against the carelessness that creeps into such undertakings. Nor does carelessness appear to be their sole error. Far more decisive is the failure to understand the play with a view to determining how to reveal it to audiences. This is a delicate matter of finding a viable spine and an expressive style for the performance and the staging of the play.

II. THE BERGNER *DUCHESS OF MALFI*, 1946

We could have expected the Paul Czinner-Elisabeth Bergner production of John Webster's early seventeenth-century tragedy, *The Duchess of Malfi*, to be, in a sense, the extreme test of a revival season. How much life would the production reveal in a moribund classic? A number of plays by Shakespeare are comparatively easy to revive because the audience and the critics are familiar with the general content and meaning, the situations and lines. Also, the director, as well as the cast, has a tradition of production and acting to either follow or modify. In short, there is a frame of reference, as well as a degree of convenient familiarity, to help us. Not so with John Webster, a little-known figure from the misty regions that only scholars inhabit. He is one of the so-called "minor Elizabethans" whose characteristic faults of melodramadness and slipshod dramaturgy are used to set off the jewel of Shakespeare's art by bardolaters. But John Webster stands high among the Elizabethans. Men of education and taste have had a healthy respect for Webster's poetic power and nightmare vision, although Shaw dismissed him as a "Tussaud laureate." All this, as well as the fact that Gielgud had revived the play in London, and the knowledge that W. H. Auden had prepared a stage version and that the truly talented Miss Elisabeth Bergner was to play the Duchess, aroused expectations.

It is my unpleasant duty to report that *The Duchess of Malfi* production made the old play look like a mildewed heirloom. It fumbled on every count—in adaptation, in staging, and in acting. If some virtues could be found in each scene, these were not large enough to make the play live again. If a play like *The Duchess of Malfi* can be only half alive on the Broadway stage, it is, in effect, wholly dead for the general public. This may be unfair, but there is no fairness for a play when one is bored, confused, or overcome with a sense of futility with regard to what one sees on the stage. And this was particularly regrettable because henceforth *The Duchess of Malfi* would be set down as rubbish by people who would be unlikely to support or modify their views by reading the play with some application and intelligence.

Concerning the adaptation, this hasty report can only say that while the cutting and transpositions were often made for sound reasons, the play lost much of its suspense, bite, intensity, and build. For instance, the villain, Bosola, lost strong evidence of repentance and reformation. In the original, he decides to save Antonio, the husband, after having killed the Duchess on orders from her brothers, the Duke and the Cardinal. That he should nevertheless kill Antonio accidentally, thinking that the latter is an assassin hired by them to do away with himself, adds to the fatefulness and irony of the tragedy. All this was lost in the adaptation. Gone, too, was the final scene in which the son of Antonio and the Duchess is saved and will inherit the duchy. Gone, in other words, is the restoration of right reason and good will—healing elements in the tragedy. Without this ending, the play remains on the melodramatic level established so excessively in several scenes by Webster's penchant for violence. Instead, we were fobbed off with a trite epilogue, invented or pieced together in the style of a morality play or sermon. If the acting was so often inadequate, a cue for it was given by the adaptation.

Although Miss Bergner reached some noble heights of tragedy in the last act, when she received news of her husband's death and later when she was strangled, she started off in the wrong key. She was arch enough at the beginning to suggest that she was still playing the Venetian *gamine* in *Escape Me Never*. She started the play as though she were just about to embark upon a Noel Coward comedy or *The Merry Widow*. Worse still, she suggested the lusty widow her brother believed her to be rather than the deeply emotional and noble heroine of the tragedy. The scene in which she proposes to her steward, Antonio, was better played, but it carried over the coyness of the first scene. It somehow failed to convey the depth of her love for Antonio and her regard for his feelings as a man wooed by a woman who is his social superior. There was more toying with him than true warmth. In the next scene, in which she is with child and is tempted with fruit by the villain who tries to discover her secret, Miss Bergner conveyed the silly woman, farcing up her part, instead of suggesting the woman who is carrying a child under the benign shadow of a great love or under the cloud of a great fear. Until the final act, moreover, Miss Bergner tended to pitch her voice too high (at the end of lines, I believe), giving an *ingenue* effect that seemed wholly wrong for the part. Even in the last act, she fell short of tragic stature, and lacked sufficient pathos as a whole, though she created some very fine moments indeed. It was difficult to resist thinking of what Katherine Cornell would have done with the part (she might not have acted it, but she would have surely *shown* it); and Miss Bergner's faults were, indeed, regrettable when one considered how accomplished an actress Miss Bergner is.

All this, finally, could only rock the very foundations of the main structure of the tragedy—namely, the story of a noble woman who dared to marry her steward in the face of convention and of her dreadful brothers' wrath. To this theme, our generation should have been able to respond with sympathy. Miss Bergner made it impossible for us to do so. She succeeded only in the final act—and even there, as a result of previous errors, she could evoke only sympathy as a suddenly brave victim of irrational persecution. Ultimately, therefore, the tragedy lost the one strong justification without which Webster's play could only strike us in 1946 as melodrama.

Unfortunate, too, was Canada Lee's interpretation of the villain, Bosola. The fault lay partly with the adaptation, which cut the dimensions of the part. The part was also poorly directed. It was difficult to tell, therefore, to what extent Canada Lee himself was at fault. Actually his performance was vastly to his credit. It showed how greatly he had progressed as an actor, how well he had acquired fluency, flexibility, and ease. But he was not the Bosola that Webster had created. His expression was so benign that I expected him to rush to the aid of the Duchess at any time. There was virtually no villainy in his heart or his features, regardless of what foul deeds were his. Too often he suggested at most a perfunctory gangster rather than the true character. The complexity of this character and the source of his villainy were only faintly realized.

We never got to know the Bosola who has turned cynic because he was a needy scholar and an unrewarded soldier who saw that the entire world fattened on villainy—so why shouldn't he; who cared for no one because he no longer cared for life itself. Nor, owing to cuts in the script, were his efforts to make amends by saving the husband of the Duchess and the ironic failure of these amends (in itself, a confirmation of his earlier cynical view of fate) sufficiently realized. Failure in the case of Bosola is a most serious matter because some of the deepest meaning of the play lies in his part. It illustrates the important fact that the beginning of evil often consists in disillusionment and negation. The cynics, those who have lost belief in the ultimate justice of the world and the value of life, are the most efficient agents of evil governments or evil superiors. Canada Lee's Bosola required an understanding of the play that nobody associated with the production seems to have possessed or at least made effective.

There is no need for further detailed animadversions. Let me note merely that Whitfield Connor's Antonio was an appealing characterization, well executed and well spoken by the actor. But Mr. Connor failed to convey the necessary strength of a character who is underwritten by Webster but even so is endowed by him with superior skill in sport and with courage enough to enter the lion's den of the Cardinal's home—in a scene that was dropped by the adapter. Mr. Connor's Antonio was too weak to be the inciting factor in high tragedy.

The Duke was played with fire but with too much smoke by Donald Eccles; there was too much rant and posturing in an already sufficiently overwrought character. John Carradine's Cardinal had the best acting in the play, but lacked the force and bite for the villainy of which he is one of the prime examples. Here again the adaptation was much at fault, since it dropped his poisoning of his mistress and some barbed lines.

This bill of grievances must, moreover, close with a general disappointment in the direction, which was too scattered as well as insufficiently penetrative in guiding the actors. It failed to consider sufficiently the development and meaning of the play. It also did little to orient a modern audience. It was neither quite theatre-wise for Broadway nor quite poetic and passionate enough for Webster. No doubt, it was also the direction that was ultimately responsible for the lack of atmosphere required by the play, and for the inadequacy of the music. (The alternative to good atmosphere would have been—to my mind, better—a cool, neutrally lit production. The Elizabethans had no Gordon Craig!) All told, the direction was far too uninspired. And Webster without inspiration can look, and did look, too much like a hack melodramatist.

III. *THE PLAYBOY OF THE WESTERN WORLD*, 1946

Theatre Incorporated wanted to perform a service in reviving John Millington Synge's masterpiece, *The Playboy of the Western World,* and there were some revealing moments in Burgess Meredith's performance. But it is curious how well-intentioned and talented theatre folk managed almost to commit mayhem on a superb artist's work. The production was kept uniformly slow, apparently in order to enable audiences to understand and relish Synge's flavorsome peasant dialect. If the tempo was speeded up toward the end, it was done precisely when the director might have taken time to underscore the villagers' *volteface* once the "playboy" Chris knocks his father down in their presence. The theme of the play is "What Price Hero-Worship?" since Chris is a hero so long as he killed his father in a distant county and not in the villagers' own backyard. In a sense, the play is also a rueful account of the development of a boy who must realize at the end that strength lies in oneself and not in the ill-founded admiration of others.

The meaning of the play was largely lost in a literal evocation of folk comedy, which in turn failed to work because of a mixture of acting styles ranging from the genuine Dublin article (in Edith Dunne's and J. M. Kerrigan's performances) to Shubert musical comedy in the costuming and playing of the village maidens. Burgess Meredith was excellent in the first act when he conveyed the weariness and loneliness of the runaway Chris, but he lost much intensity in his role as the youth who basks in admiration and gathers strength at the end. Meredith relied too much on a studied lyricism and was slowed up by the necessity of speaking a dialect which mastered him instead of being mastered by him. The revival was languid instead of exuberant as folk comedy; some of it actually seemed slow-motion humor. Yet for all the muted quality of the performances, the production failed to convey the disenchantment at the core of Synge's comic writing.

Disenchantment! That is, indeed, a true key to *The Playboy of the Western World,* whose very title is ironic. But the quality of irony was hardly in evidence in the production. And once we raise the question of irony, as I suspect the producers, directors, and leading actor did not do, we can understand the production problem they failed to solve. They were misled by the superficial criticism and publicity from which the play has suffered virtually from the beginning. That criticism and publicity, supported by Synge's celebrated preface, have invariably thrust into the foreground the *folk-comedy premise,* according to which Synge patriotically and innocently compounded a rich brew of humor out of the naïve, colorful, "primitive" life of the Irish countryside.

Although the countryside was primitive, Synge decidedly was not. He was fundamentally a sophisticated artist—even a *décadent* one—whose view of life remained sceptical and saturnine; almost Baudelairian, even after he left France at Yeats's suggestion. Yes, he returned to Ireland and steeped himself in the folkways and idiom of Western Ireland and the Aran Islands. But what the artist observes and records as "local color" is never what he *creates.* The reason why most folk-plays rarely have merit and even more rarely possess greatness is because they are the work of writers who *see* the local color and *hear* the local dialect rather than of writers who use what they have seen and heard creatively. Great writers build a more or less autonomous world of art that conforms to a personal, rather than a mere *folk,* view of reality.

Irish patriots who rioted at the Dublin premiere of *The Playboy* on the grounds that the author misrepresented the Irish people came closer to the truth about Synge's work than those who, led by Yeats (who has always impressed me as a great baby as well as a great poet), defended the play. Of course, Synge misrepresented Ireland. Only his motives were different from those attributed to him by the rioters. He was not critical of the Irish, he was critical of the human race. And in being that, he *represented* himself in his work.

Synge's view of reality was saturnine, as anyone could have seen in his very first play *In the Shadow of the Glen,* and as he was to prove later in *The Tinker's Wedding* and *The Well of Saints.* Even his sense of tragedy included a large sense of desperation about the human lot, a negative attitude toward the possibility of happiness. Nothing at all could be done about the tragic situation in *Riders to the Sea.* Man did not cause it and man could not avert it. Nor was a single person in the play itself actively engaged in the tragic action of fate.

For a tragedy of fate, *Riders to the Sea* is at the opposite pole from that greatest of tragedies of fate *Oedipus the King,* throughout which Oedipus is vibrantly engaged in discovering the fatality of circumstance in which he is enmeshed. Oedipus, to put the case colloquially, is "in there," fighting all the time, whereas the characters in *Riders to the Sea* are not fighting at all. The play is truly, profoundly "static drama," the theory for which was laid down by another "symbolist" successor of Baudelaire, Verlaine, Rimbaud, and other *décadents,* Maurice Maeterlinck.

In Synge's last play, *Deirdre of the Sorrows,* it is true, there is much activity, and its main characters are decidedly active to the end. But even here, in a work that may be designated as heroic drama, the decisive factor is Deidre's fatalistic belief that love like hers with her lover cannot last. She courts death for him and for herself by prevailing upon him to return to the king who is insanely jealous of him and will kill him in order to possess Deirdre. This is Synge's special interpretation of the great Irish legend which formed the substance of several plays by other writers. It is Synge alone who insists on the motivation of disbelief in the power of love to hold the lovers together for a long time—and this in the case of two of the most romantic characters in all literature!

What has this to do with the Theatre Incorporated production of *The Playboy of the Western World?* Everything! The work is one of thoroughgoing irony—not only about the general fallacy of hero worship to which I have already alluded, but to all the particulars in the play. When Chris thinks he is telling the truth in reporting that he has killed his father, he is not only deceived, but self-deceiving; he builds himself up on the strength of the wishfully entertained deed. He is viewing himself as a marvel when he reports his "murder" in the village to which he has fled. The weakling has become a hero—because he has murdered. The villagers are entranced with him, and two women, one young and another middle-aged, fight over him—because he has murdered; not merely because he proves himself so successful an athlete in the village sports. And what is it that gave him the confidence that resulted in victory? The fact that he murdered his father, as well as that much has been made of him as a marvel because he did so!

Following his athletic feats, the lad's father turns up suddenly with a bandaged head and robs his son of his claim to uniqueness and glory. Not only Chris, but others feel let down. Just think of it, the boy *didn't* murder his father! And Chris is so desperate at discovering that his father is perversely alive that he strikes him down again! And so active is the wishful thinking, the murder fantasy, of Chris and those who glorified a parricide—a fact that should not be glossed over by explanations of the simplemindedness or "naïveté" of the villagers—that everybody instantly assumes that the father is dead. By comparison with so mordant a development of the theme, the rest of the development of the action is actually mild, although it would be sharp enough for many plays. Because the second "murder" occurred in their own village, Chris ceases to be a hero and becomes a criminal whom they are ready to deliver up to justice. And even here the irony cuts deeper than the mere idea that heroism is relative to time and place, or that one is a hero for doing something elsewhere and a criminal for doing it in our presence. (How many mute inglorious Napoleons must be sentenced to death in the villages of France by judges for whom the Emperor at Paris, Austerlitz, or Jena is a glorious figure!) The deeper irony is that the villagers do not realize that they are guiltier than Chris, for it is they who gave him social sanction for his second assault on his father by glorifying him for his first. No wonder Chris is bewildered rather than repentant when they bind him with ropes. Here, if we wish to labor the moral, is the whole history of mankind in a nutshell—punishment for crimes hallowed as heroism under different circumstances, society putting a premium on murder since the beginning of the primal clan and then punishing those who have been taught and encouraged to kill. Finally, there is the gentler irony that the boy becomes a hero in the eyes of his own father, when the latter revives, because Chris had shown *spunk* in *assaulting* him. Change the word "spunk" to "character" and the irony becomes sharper. Change the word "assaulting" to "trying to kill" and the bitterness of the play becomes fully apparent.

The fact is that *The Playboy* cuts deep. It does not owe its greatness to its mere rusticity. Synge worked on several levels in writing it—on the levels of genre painting and universal observation, folk-comedy and universal satire, conscious behavior and "fantasia of the unconscious." As a result, the work is a system of intense and subtle tensions, whereas the Theatre Incorporated production was a work of little and rather superficial tension. I do not claim that those involved in the production should have followed my analysis to the letter or even agreed with it in every detail, especially since I have made no reference to other nuances. And I have not mentioned the obvious point that Synge dissolved the mordant qualities of his play in a glow of good-natured comedy, providing a healing laughter as well as a cutting one, for he was a poet as well as a satirist. But the production would have been more emphatic and provocative if the producers had sensed the implications that exist on the various levels of the play.

And, for "practical" purposes of succeeding in the theatre with *The*

Playboy, one consideration is even more important. If irony had been more sharply defined in the production—if, for example, the action had been more stylized or given a more keen-edged extravagance—the result would have been very much more comic. The saturnine Synge was a comic genius. The casual, languid Theatre Incorporated production was only mildly comic. My reactions to it, shared by others, were confused—that is, divided into feelings of lukewarm emotion, on one hand, and a sense of comedy, on the other, that came only in brief spurts instead of welling forth with any steadiness or force. As for any glow in the production, it could be found here and there in Burgess Meredith's performance, especially in the first half of the play, but the staging, as well as setting and lighting, had virtually none.

IV. FIND THE SPINE

The ultimate lesson to be derived from the productions of *The Duchess of Malfi* and *The Playboy of the Western World* is simply this: In order to produce a play, especially a distinguished work, we must not be content until we have found its *spine*. By this I mean not a mere notion on which to hang a production but a spine to which every turn of action, every suggestion, and every implication is attached. And having found that spine, we must not rest until all the emphases and the nuances of the performance relate to it so distinctly that we really do have a spine instead of a thin thread from which all things dangle and flap like so many clothes from a clothesline in windy weather.

The spine of *The Duchess of Malfi* which the Bergner production failed to use to the full was defined by Webster himself when he made his Duke Ferdinand, the brother of the Duchess, say,

> "Whether we fall by ambition, blood, or lust,
> Like diamonds we are cut with our own dust."

In these lines we have the essence of high tragedy. They call for integrated drama; for something other than the muddled poetic melodrama that the Bergner production gave except in scattered strokes of inspired performance.

The spine of *The Playboy* cannot be so epigrammatically summarized. It has taken me a number of paragraphs to explicate it, and I am aware that I have been only partly successful in that enterprise. To have succeeded entirely, I should have had to argue out a variety of points and analyzed actions and entire scenes in considerable detail. But this much seems to me clear: *The spine is an ironic statement on the contradictions of human behavior and "society," including the contradictions between consciousness and the fantasia of the unconscious*—in which fantasy of murder as a form of gratification or "glory" is present. In serving that spine only fitfully and vaguely, the Theater Incorporated production gave us only a low-voltage and confused comic experience.

Let us note finally how the texture of distinguished writing communicates the spine of the play. The lines call for various inflections, intonations, stances, movements—and what not—from the performer. Let us listen, for example, to the publican Michael, whose daughter Pegeen has has taken a fancy to the "playboy" Chris Mahon. Michael approves of marriage between them. Irony impacted in contradiction can hardly go further as Synge makes Michael say to them:

> . . . I seeing a score of grandsons growing up like gallant swearers by the name of God . . . (*He joins their hands.*) A daring fellow is the jewel of the world, and a man did split his father's middle with a single clout should have the bravery of ten, so may God and Mary and St. Patrick bless you, and increase you from this mortal day.

Christy, called a liar when his father Old Mahon suddenly turns up in the Mayo village to which Christy fled, remarks:

> It's himself was a liar, lying stretched out with an open head on him, letting on he was dead.

Pegeen, who turns on Christy after he has struck down his father, declares, "there's a great gap between a gallous story and a dirty deed." Earlier, Pegeen had scorned a respectable suitor Shawn as "a middling kind of a scarecrow, with no *savagery* or fine words to him at all." Widow Quin, in trying to get Christy to marry herself rather than Pegeen, says to him:

> Don't be letting on to be shy, a fine, gamey, *treacherous* lad the like of you.

When in Act I, Pegeen wants to know whether Chris, who struck his father with a "loy" or spade, shot his father dead, Chris replies indignantly:

> I never used weapons. I've no license, and I'm a law-fearing man.

And when she asks whether he buried his father, Chris explains patiently:

> Aye. I buried him then. Wasn't I digging spuds in the field?

There is a cycle in studying a play of this calibre. We may move from a full realization of the spine of the play as a whole to that of the spine of the characterizations, and from this to the point of the lines of dialogue;

or we may reverse the procedure, in so far as this is possible, by studying the "texture" of the writing. The resulting understanding of the play may be the same. But in staging it, we must start with an over-all understanding of the work, regardless of how we first arrived at it. If the spine has not been first thoroughly discovered by the director and his cast, the lines will be inadequately rendered. Points will be blurred and either under-played or overstressed. In other words, if the spine of the play is missed, the texture will be lost. And if the weave of the dialogue is poorly con-veyed, then, of course, the spine will be lost, too. In either case, the play will be killed or lamed.

V. THE GERTRUDE LAWRENCE *PYGMALION*

Theatre Incorporated had considerably more success, enjoyed a tri-umph indeed, when it revived Shaw's *Pygmalion* during the 1945-46 season as the first offering of a short-lived career. The difference was largely due to a successful realization of the "spine" of Shaw's comedy in the staging and in several individual performances. The fact that some of these were not as perfect as when the play was given by the Theatre Guild did not matter greatly. It is not perfection but a general rightness of inter-pretation with respect to the central essence of the work that matters.

Gertrude Lawrence's Eliza Doolittle was a thoroughly intelligent performance, brilliant in its virtuosity but also undeviating in its service to the central concept of the comedy, in which Eliza carries two related themes: One is the "flower-girl into duchess" idea, in which a social satire is developed. The other is Shaw's variant of the Pygmalion and Galatea myth, in which the irony of human relationships is uppermost. As the cockney Eliza, Miss Lawrence committed such battery on the King's English that she seemed to undermine what was left of the British empire. When, later, Eliza had been sufficiently trained by Professor Higgins, Miss Lawrence was murderously funny. Externally all lady and exhibiting an acquired pronunciation which a duchess could envy, the reconstructed Eliza wore an air that seemed to say, "You see, I, too, can do it"—which was precisely Professor Higgins' point all along. But, following Shaw's text, Miss Lawrence launched into such unseemly statements in the fash-ionable salon in which she made her debut that she exploded the pretense —her own pretense acquired by education and high society's pretense of culture also acquired by education. Not only did Miss Lawrence maintain a poker-face, so that the outrageous remarks seemed as natural as polite conversation (as if to say that the content of people's minds is the same in every walk of life and only the way it is verbalized shows any differences), but she made each *gaffe* telling by means of her best bravura acting.

So much for the "cockney into aristocrat" notion so brightly and zest-fully acted out—and *spoken out*—by Gertrude Lawrence. With assistance from the rest of the well-directed cast, she even carried the comedy further than the mere idea that the difference between a lady and a flower girl is a matter of dress and pronunciation. The production actually showed the "spine" expressed in Shaw's memorable line to the effect that "the differ-ence between a lady and a flower girl is not how she behaves but how she's treated." Since the fluent Melville Cooper played Eliza's raffishly impertinent father Doolittle, the latter's comments on the implications of "class" also lost none of their point. These, too, belong to the core of this amazingly rich comedy. Doolittle—"if he were a horse," wrote Sir Des-mond MacCarthy, "he might be described as High Spirits out of Social Science"—needs to be played with special verve if Shaw, who liked to see a thing or two under the aspect of Economics but could do so entertain-ingly, is to be properly served.

As for the climactic development of the Pygmalion and Galatea theme, Miss Lawrence spiced her role as a woman resentful of a man's indifference and giving him the cutting edge of womanliness. Her antago-nist young Professor Higgins, the Pygmalion of the piece, was played by Raymond Massey. His performance could be criticized on the grounds that he seemed too strenuous or brash. Alfred Lunt in the same role had achieved self-confidence without brashness, intellectual brilliance and ar-tistic egotism without intellectual arrogance. Massey, who was born a Canadian, was too "American." Curiously enough, his strenuous intellec-tualism made him stiff. Lunt allowed himself to be more rattled than Massey when Galatea became a living woman. Nevertheless, Massey missed none of the central force of the role. He was self-assured and spir-ited. He was able to give force to the speech

> The great secret, Eliza, is not having bad manners or good man-ners or any other particular sort of manners for all human souls;
> in short, behaving as if there are no third-class carriages, and one
> soul is as good as another.

The actor who had been our greatest Abe Lincoln on the stage could give conviction to such lines, and these *belong* to the spine, for Shaw did not write just another British comedy of manners when he wrote *Pygmalion*. He, too, wrote out of conviction whereas the run-of-the-mill writers of comedy of manners have written only with assumed amusement at the human race. Generally, they accept social stratification, whereas Shaw rejected it. They make it a point to differentiate between upper and lower class manners and speech in order to *sustain* social distinctions, whereas Shaw made a special point of *subverting* them. This subversion is indeed the cream of his jest.

Massey, indeed, was more forceful than Alfred Lunt had been, if my memory serves, when he spoke the ringing lines, "Would the world ever have been made if its maker had been afraid of making trouble? Making life is making trouble." The same emphatic playing did have a curious effect when Massey's Higgins, replying to Eliza's complaint that he didn't care for her, declared, "I care for life, for humanity; and you are a part of it that has come my way and been built into my house. What more can you or anybody ask me?" The actor gave more support here to Shaw the moralist than to Shaw the comic writer. Shaw might have approved Massey's emphatic playing at this point, but I could not quite approve. The argument of the Pygmalion-Galatea play seemed somewhat shallow to me at this point.

Also, here, as well as elsewhere, Massey's emphatic playing made him seem some kind of roughneck—as well as idealist—who rides roughshod over human feelings. Yet Massey did not fail the play entirely even here. He did capture the thoroughly Shavian—and feminist—vision of a "modern," self-confident male, as well as egocentric artist, who does not crave the salve of feminine subservience to his ego. We might also call this attitude *"masculinism,"* because implicit in it is the concept of a man who has enough "ego" not to need a woman to expand it for him. If the performance lacked certain nuances, it did not lack understanding. MacCarthy reported that Sir Herbert Tree played the role in 1914 with a "dread of even touching Eliza lest the floods of irrationalism should be released in himself." I did not notice any such thing in Massey's playing, and was grateful that he spared us that kind of nuance.

If plays can be "revived" with at least as much integration of performance, staging, and text, there is a good chance that our dramatic literature will not pass from the stage. Not even from the commercial Broadway stage. Too many noteworthy plays are misused, in consequence of which they may ultimately become *unused*.

VI. THE RISKS REMAIN FOR EVEN SHAKESPEARE AND SHAW

Sceptics may say that for a play to be well produced it must be good enough to start with. No doubt there is some truth to this opinion, but the whole history of the stage refutes it as a generalization upon which absolute reliance can be placed. Without resorting to the obvious fact that many a poor play has been turned into a success, since this fact would require too many explanations, I need only point to the failure of many masterpieces, including *Hamlet,* in the Leslie Howard production in the thirties, for example. Plays such as *Much Ado About Nothing* and *Measure for Measure* were eminently successful in their respective Gielgud and Peter Brook productions at Stratford in 1950. They would have certainly failed if poorly staged, and in New York this would have meant that these comedies would henceforth be considered "poison" by the managements.

In 1948 even *Macbeth,* with Michael Redgrave and Flora Robson in the main roles, failed in New York. Yet the actors were notable figures on the English-speaking stage and Paul Sheriff was one of its most talented scene designers. And *Richard III* and *King Lear* were also failures during the same period. Flora Robson's Lady Macbeth seemed evil incarnate and nothing else. Failing to convey sufficient femininity during the early scenes of the tragedy, unless a nagging disposition is considered sufficient, she made it difficult for us to believe that Lady Macbeth could have disintegrated so much out of a sense of guilt or an overstrained sensibility in her final appearance. Lacking a suggestion of voluptuousness and failing to introduce an element of warmth and spice into her marital relationship, she made it difficult to believe that her hold on Macbeth was a factor in the murder of Duncan. It became difficult also to sympathize with the degree of desperation that Michael Redgrave registered over her illness and death. "Canst thou not minister to a mind diseased" fell flat. And since Mr. Redgrave missed much of Macbeth's sensibility, too, in otherwise justifiably playing Macbeth as a rugged Scottish chieftain, Shakespeare's tragedy became largely melodrama. If this transformation can happen to *Macbeth,* it could surely happen, as it did, to the inferior tragedy *The Duchess of Malfi.*

Nor is it safe to assume that, considering the current vogue of Shaw, his plays cannot be killed in production. At about the midpoint of the century five of his plays proved successful on the New York stage: *Pygmalion, Man and Superman, The Devil's Disciple, Don Juan in Hell,* and *Misalliance.* But five others were less fortunate: *Getting Married, Captain Brassbound's Conversion, You Never Can Tell, Candida,* and *Saint Joan—* the latter in a Theatre Guild, Margaret Webster production at that. (The play, in which Uta Hagen gave a vital interpretation for the most part, had a moderate run but aroused much dissatisfaction.) Nor, for that matter, was the Dublin Gate Theatre's production of *John Bull's Other Island* conspicuously successful in New York in the season of 1947-48. The score for Shaw was then under fifty-fifty.

If even *Saint Joan* could suffer, and if *Candida* could collapse under the playing of Olivia de Havilland and Bramwell Fletcher, as it did in the spring of 1952, how much more easily could the early *You Never Can Tell* fail. After seeing the production brought over from London in 1948,

I reported as follows without attempting to point out all its flaws, but without being able to avoid pointing to fundamental errors in the treatment of that admittedly minor work.

A potboiler by Shaw is a *chef-d'oeuvre* for most of his contemporaries, and it is regretful that the production could not do better by G.B.S. Although Shaw hid his light under the very old bushel of a plot composed of mistaken identities, relying as he did on a story of three youngsters' discovery of their father in the Victorian fussbudget Crampton, enough light comes out of the barrel to illuminate the stage.

You Never Can Tell is a much wittier play than could be realized from the production, and the love affair of the unsentimental young dentist Valentine and the resolutely modern daughter of an early feminist, Gloria, is one of Shaw's zestful inventions. Nor does this early farce lack the heady kind of wisdom that Shaw has been distilling for half a century. We need only recall the little last-act conversation in which the terrifyingly clever lawyer Bohun is asked by Crampton whether he doesn't consider the match between Gloria and Valentine unwise. Bohun replies: "Yes, I do: all marriages are unwise. It's unwise to be born; it's unwise to be married; it's unwise to live; and it's wise to die." To which Bohun's father, the Waiter, adds: "Then, if I may respectfully put a word in, sir, so much the worse for wisdom." It is also doubtful that any modernist spoke so well on feminism as when Shaw made the enlightened Mrs. Clandon remark that "Women have to unlearn the false good manners of their slavery before they acquire the genuine good manners of their freedom." Above all, however, we must reckon up the delight the author has managed to communicate through the confusion of the family reared by a "modern" mother when modernism was rampant, and through the strident conservatism of the father whose Victorian course was charted the moment he learned in childhood that "most things that were good for me were nasty."

The truth is that Shaw wrote *You Never Can Tell* with his own mind but with W. S. Gilbert's spirit. The latter obscures the mettle of the former for people who cannot distinguish between contrivance that results from ineptitude and contrivance deliberately embraced for purposes of *stylization*. Shaw could hardly take Victorian domestic relations seriously enough to write domestic drama in the serious vein of Henry Arthur Jones and Pinero, concerning whose problem plays the vivacious scholar Gilbert Norwood once wrote that they turned the Decalogue into a monologue on sex. There was every reason for

Shaw's electing to turn handsprings with the domestic problem once he was convinced that there were more important matters. If he had had an Arthur Sullivan at his elbow he might have written *You Never Can Tell* as an *opera bouffe*.

That he didn't is perhaps the true measure of the shortcomings of the Guild production which made skittishness and coyness the dominant tone, in addition to turning the testy *pater familias* into a heavy-footed, heavy-witted caricature, which in his case is tantamount to caricaturing a caricature. (It is incredible that his family should ever want him when it finds him.) Only the infallible Leo Carroll was completely master of the play, and his memorable Waiter gave the production a proper balance between comedy of manners and comic opera. Although several other characters were cast well enough (Frieda Inescort as Mrs. Clandon and William Devlin as lawyer Bohun were particularly well chosen), the direction made bouncing dolls of some of them, stiff puppets of others, and generally kept the performers at the periphery of a play rather than inside it. Somehow the Shaw who masqueraded through the production seemed robbed of his virility except when Bohun took the stage. Besides, the overstrenuous naïveté of the production did not accord very well with the serpentine lines of the text after the first act, and the naïveté itself was too plainly pretended to be gratifying.

To conclude, the theatre remains the "heartbreak house" of dramatic literature. The theatre is also the despair of literary criticism when play reviewing focuses, as it must, on what the stage shows the reviewer rather than on what he reads in a book. But efforts must continue to be made to avoid turning the stage into the morgue of dramatic literature. And the effort cannot succeed until it *starts* with the dramatic literature—that is, with an understanding of the written play that cuts deep enough to penetrate beneath the epidermis of the story. Too many producers and directors give the impression of being unable to *read*. In the old days of the actor-managers and the unquestioned star system, this inability or unwillingness to read scrupulously was not as catastrophic as it is likely to be today. The audience was satisfied with a virtuoso performance on the part of a Booth, Kean, Irving, Bernhardt, or Ellen Terry. Today, although allowance is still made for star actors, regular playgoers are less likely to be satisfied with half-production of plays that require *total* production.

AN AMERICAN NATIONAL THEATRE

This is the second time within half a year that I have had the honor to address a convention in the South, and on both occasions, last fall at Shreveport and now here at Chapel Hill, I have been under some restraint. As a visitor from New York, where the professional stage has its location for better or worse, I have wanted to compliment the members of these conferences on the attention they have been giving the theatre. But there would have been presumptuousness in the compliment—especially here. I should be assuming that it is not as natural for you to concern yourselves with the theatre as it is for a New Yorker, when, as a matter of fact, it was the South that first made the theatre welcome in our land, when the Hallam Company, fresh out of London gave *The Merchant of Venice* at Williamsburg, Virginia, in 1750. And it was the South, again—and, to be precise, Chapel Hill—that was one of the very first centers of modern experiment in American folk drama.

I am under less restraint, however, in saying that I am especially heartened by this assembly because it comes in the midst of a controversy I have been waging in *Theatre Arts Magazine* with a school of disillusioned young critics who have written as if they would gladly inter our theatre and all its works, although I am sure they are devoted to the stage and intend to serve it. It has been their contention that we never had an American drama and theatre worth cherishing, and that we shall have none until we learn from Europe. It would follow that we are foolish to want to improve a theatre that has been generically corrupt, and that our folly reaches fabulous proportions when we try to enlarge the scope of the American theatre beyond Broadway. For this would be tantamount to enlarging what is not worth even retaining. Instead of attempting to reach more American audiences, our theatre, presumably, should first contract into a cénacle for self-improvement until it can win approval by a European-trained élite. And instead of striking more roots in American society, our theatre should actually uproot itself. It should seek new nourishment by sending aerial roots across the Atlantic, where they could, no doubt, dig themselves into a left-over existentialist salad in Paris. Although I am somewhat facetious in wording my description of this attitude, I am not exaggerating its tenor. However, it is the counter-theme

An address delivered at the Southeastern Theatre Conference at Chapel Hill, N. C., March 8, 1953, printed substantially as delivered.

(and as such not useless) to the theme to which I take equal exception—namely, the opinion of a considerably larger group which finds nothing wrong with American playwriting and play-production that could not be substantially improved merely by producing more plays in more places.

Like myself, you are engaged, I know, only in a lover's quarrel with our stage. You intend to be more, rather than less, concerned with it. You want to be closer to it rather than further removed from it, and to tend its growth rather than to inter it; and, indeed, you have been doing just that. You want the American theatre to respond more warmly to your desires and hopes for it, and you welcome the exertion it exacts from you. You are in the position of the celebrated Portuguese nun Mariana Alcoforado who wrote her light-hearted French lover, "Love me always . . . and continue to make me suffer." And since I know that the question of National Theatre has been often in your thoughts, I should like to consider the subject in a manner possible only among friends and colleagues who are convinced that we *should* have an American National Theatre, if we can build one. I shall inquire into the nature and possibilities of what we desiderate, not presuming so much to provide answers as to raise questions, of which we all have a plentiful supply.

What do we mean, for example, when we express a desire for an American National Theatre? Are we clear about its nature and purpose when we consider anything more than a central clearing bureau for plays and for theatrical information?

Do we mean a theatre subsidized by the Federal government? We did in the nineteen-thirties and during the war period. Evidently, we no longer do. Or, if some of us still mean just that by a national theatre, how can we possibly expect that it would not be subjected to fatally disturbing pressures against which the only defense would be unmitigated mediocrity. A national theatre should surely be distinguishable from a national morgue.

Even if government subsidy were feasible and likely, besides, what would we have to subsidize at present that could be honestly called an American National Theatre. France can maintain a national theatre and subsidize the Salle de Richelieu and the Odéon in Paris. But, then, the French have had distinguished drama for more than two and a half centuries, and a considerable portion of it is classical—in the sense that it has become the heritage of educated Frenchmen. Truly American drama for which even a small degree of distinction can be claimed is less than half a century old, and none of it, not even a play by O'Neill, has become an essential part of our culture. We have simply lacked dramatists who occupy the same place in our civilization that Emerson, Melville, Poe, and Mark Twain do.

Anomalously, then, the repertory of an American National Theatre would not be American at all. The same situation would prevail, of course, if a national theatre consisted of branch theatres in different parts of the country. That is, if by a national theatre we mean a producing company or producing companies dedicated to the continuous staging of those plays of a nation that can be presented as the national heritage. We can have a "Shakespearean Theatre," and it seems at the moment that we could have a Shaw Theatre, for even an insignificant Shavian contribution such as *Misalliance* is received with rapture. But can we at this time build an *American* repertory? I am certain that each of us could compile a list of American plays we should like to see revived regularly, and perhaps a stage director and a cast extraordinarily talented could give these plays a semblance of classical stature. But this is mere speculation, and it must seem a far-fetched one, indeed, when we realize that even the excellent ANTA production of *Desire Under the Elms* directed by Harold Clurman could receive excellent notices and yet fail to win audiences to sustain a long run. This in a city of more than eight million residents—a population larger than that of any of the Scandinavian countries that keep the plays of Ibsen and Strindberg in constant production!

Nor can we say that we have a style or styles of production in our country so distinctively "American" that we could create a national theatre with specific production qualities or theatrical conventions. A Max Reinhardt production was invariably distinctive, as was a production by a Stanislavski or Copeau. At present, the Jean-Louis Barrault company, with a diversified program of plays from the time of Molière to the time of Kafka and Gide, is in command of styles of playing and staging that give a Barrault theatre recognizable cohesion. But we have had no such distinctiveness in America. The Theatre Guild, in business for thirty-four years thus far, was never able to develop it. A Theatre Guild production has usually had a good deal of polish. But patina is not the equivalent of style. And if the Group Theatre of the thirties did develop a reliable style of performance, it did so mainly in the very limited field of colloquial New York social drama. It exhibited little aptitude for high comedy and poetic drama.

We cannot, then, think in European terms when we speak of a national theatre in the United States. Our arts are too fluid and uncrystallized as yet, and our strength lies in diversity rather than in unity. I am not aware, indeed, that the proponents of a national theatre have inquired much into the fundamentals that can give a theatre any strong claim to permanence or, at least, some significance: It would appear, on the contrary, that all thoughts on the subject have been wholly pragmatic, in a more or less businessman's sense of enterprise for making and selling more commodities. A national theatre has also been viewed often as a sort of pump-priming device in a period of diminishing professional stage productions. Its proponents, it is true, have tried to produce "non-commercial" plays in New York from time to time, turning out many failures and, embarrassingly, a few extremely commercial hits such as *Mrs. Mc-Thing* and *Twentieth Century,* a typical Broadway "revival." But for the country as a whole they have had in view little more than the fostering of more stage productions of a professional calibre and the finding of more employment for the professionally trained Broadway actor. These are, of course, laudable intentions and deserve whatever support we can give them. But they are surely no equivalent of a genuine concept of American National Theatre.

It is confusing to consider the usual view a concept at all! It is not only confusing; it is an evasion to promote one thing—namely, the theatre such as it is but merely expanded and decentralized, which is a practical matter—and then to call it something else—namely, a National Theatre, which implies justification by quality rather than by quantity.

It is not the number of productions but a cultural heritage that makes a theatre "national." It is not year-round production in Paris that constitutes the French National Theatre, but a theatre based on the principles of French artistry and built with the plays Corneille, Racine, Molière, Marivaux, Musset, and other writers associated with French civilization. We shall not have a comparable American National Theatre until we have writers whom we can associate with some crystallized essence or notable aspect of American civilization. We already have such writers in the field of non-dramatic literature. It is to be hoped that, in time, we shall also have them in the field of dramatic literature. But in so far as we can contribute to their rise, we shall do so by other than organizational fiat and organizational means. In so far as such playwriting has shown signs of arising in our midst during past decades, it has done so spontaneously, in the pursuit of progressive and honest theatre by such groups as the Provincetown and the Group Theatre Company, and, to no small degree, in conjunction with the rise of producing enterprises, such as the Carolina Playmakers, that sought to create "regional," rather than vaguely "national," theatres.

We can start thinking clearly of a national theatre only if we think in terms of universal or at least profoundly modern dramatic art or of profoundly national dramatic art. By national theatre we must mean something more than merely "big" theatre. There are no other valid concepts if we are to go beyond the nebulous premise that somehow we shall get significant American plays by the hit or miss method of just producing professionally a lot of plays in a lot of places which have had little or no theatre in recent decades. The only sense I can find in this prevalent attitude is the possibility that these theatres would become centers for local activity. But this can occur to any significant degree only if it starts outside the theatre, in the minds and hearts or will of a people, and not because actors need jobs, because Broadway playwrights want as many productions for their plays as they can get, or because we romantically venerate the idea of a nationwide professional stage.

A theatre venture, whether a localized or nationally organized one, can produce no significant results if it has nothing more than production activity for its object. That is, if it has no end in view that consists of an idea or outlook. A national theatre must die aborning if it has nothing worthy to reflect or express, no sense of shared experience and adventure, no search for a humanistically valid meaning in what a people are or intensely desire to become.

During the formative period of our community "little theatre" movement, at Chapel Hill and elsewhere, this was more or less understood, as it does not appear to be understood to any degree in many discussions of a national theatre today. I believe that at present, and perhaps for a long time to come, we shall have to avoid the European conception of national theatre as a treasure-house of tradition. We have yet to create that tradition through the vital activity of those who can give memorable expression to what America is, whereas the most noteworthy playwriting we have had so far has, with very few exceptions, expressed only an isolated writer's sense of alienation from his people or his society.

There is a danger, of course, in overstressing the regional aspects of theatre. Regionalism can become the featherbed under which dramatic groups may fall asleep with the comforting assurance that they are significant and vital simply because they deal with local manners and folklore and somehow acquire local patronage. And we may actually suffocate if we snuggle under the featherbed so lovingly that we allow no air from the circumambient world of ideas and conflict to reach us.

Great theatre, no matter how beneficially localized, has always been, in a profound sense, *world theatre*. It is for a good reason that drama of lasting interest arose only in the theatres of large and relatively cosmopolitan centers. I believe that this is still a condition for the flourishing of significant drama. The only difference is that today, as the world has been telescoped by the development of communications, even the relatively small city can be reasonably cosmopolitan, if its citizenry does not deliberately close its eyes, ears, and mind. We need the non-regional one-world ambience of ideas and interests for a significant theatre; and if we are to achieve such a theatre, a purely regional interest must be transcended. It was transcended in an exemplary instance at Chapel Hill, as I am told, when the Carolina Playmakers produced *The Good Women of Setzuan* by Brecht, and produced it with an understanding of its stylistic requirements. But, at the same time, we also need the regional interest in order that the one-world ideas or interests may flesh themselves in us, and that they may find expression in new playwriting rooted in our language and mores. We need a national theatre made up of component local theatres dominated neither by the airy cosmopolitanism of a Noel Coward or pre-war Budapest playwright nor by the clod-heavy and stultifying regionalism of rustic, "local color" playwrights.

Thus far there has been altogether too much reliance on making bricks without straw, of making a national theatre with standard Broadway playwriting which contributes nothing to a truly national drama except a certain breeziness which other countries facetiously equate with Americanism. There is a spate of talk about "decentralizing" the professional stage. But how are we going to make a national theatre by simply disseminating a commodity that is no more national than a window-pane? Broadway successes and plays condescendingly slicked up for the special use of amateur groups are the vogue in too many instances of community production, and they can provide nothing more than "show business," which does not even succeed in sustaining Broadway. If an "American National Theatre" is to be created by extending the market for such products of commercialism through increased theatrical production throughout the country, then I say that such a theatre will never be national. Moreover, it will never be worth building with or without subsidy, and with or without an impressive charter!

I would conclude, then, on one hand, that in the United States, since our country is vast and diversified, the concept of a national theatre must include, in every vital sense, the intensified activity of regional groups. And, on the other hand, that these theatres should in no sense think of themselves as provincial and limit their horizons. In the contracted twentieth-century world, this attitude would be as unrealistic as it would be self-depreciating. Today, there is no reason why a theatre in Richmond, Memphis, or Atlanta must consider itself doomed to provinciality. There are no more provinces in our midcentury world. And since we are on the subject of provinciality, I would point out that until we have national classics and even after we have them, our regional theatres need never hesitate to diversify their programs with foreign plays old or new any more than does the theatre in New York, Paris, London, or Berlin. Ideally, indeed, preference should be given to these plays over the Broadway potboilers that local producers favor in the belief that their public prefers a New York hit above everything else. This is, indeed, a provincial attitude —it is the desire of the regional moth for the Broadway star.

There are, however, some sizable flies in the ointment I have poured out in my concept of a *federated* theatre—that is, a national theatre which would be in effect a *federation* of regional groups. We have not as yet developed regional theatrical companies of any size or strength on a level of consistently professional competence. Germany, which became a federated nation only as late as 1870, had distinguished professional theatres in different regions, and their combined, if diversified, activity, produced a national theatre greater and more vital than any single subsidized or unsubsidized theatrical company situated in Berlin or Munich or Hamburg. To act in a theatrical company in Munich or to have one's play produced there gave the individual success and prestige.

It is not enough to solace ourselves with the reflection that each region in the United States has many community and university theatres. This is all to the good, and these enterprises should receive as much respect and support as they deserve. But each region would have to develop genuinely professional circles, in which the actor-member of the company could achieve prestige and a good living, and for which a playwright could write plays with some prospect of being able to support and respect himself as a professional writer.

Professional theatres in the region, located in some large center and radiating its productions into smaller localities, are ultimately necessary for this purpose. And far from hampering the work of the local university and non-professional groups, professional regional theatres may serve as incentives by cultivating the taste for playgoing and by encouraging actors and playwrights to improve their performance. This is likely to be the case when they know that there are professional opportunities near at hand, and that they do not have to run away to New York and rarefy themselves into a special *Luftproletariat* if they want to make a career out of whatever talent they possess.

The creation of theatrical capitals in the various sections of the United States is, to my mind, the greatest challenge to creative will and energy. I would not minimize the difficulties that stand in the way when I consider the difficulties of sustaining honorable professional theatre in New York with which I am painfully familiar. But I am disinclined to say that the difficulties are permanently insurmountable in view of the tremendous strides the South, for example, has made in every material and non-material respect. The present leadership of the South in the field of American literature is well recognized. Is it reasonable to assume that the creation of professional theatre on Southern soil is out of the question? The cultural background and context are here. The vision, too, is not absent; and if it is not already here, it can be created.

The outdoor theatre of the South, indeed, gives strong evidence of vision and enterprise. Radiating from the Carolina Playmakers at the University of North Carolina, pageant-dramas, called symphonic dramas by Paul Green, have captured the interest of many thousands of people each summer. (The attendance record for 1953 exceeded 350,000 paid admissions.) Four of these plays, *The Lost Colony, Horn in the West,* and *Unto These Hills* in North Carolina and *The Common Glory* at Williamsburg, Virginia, express the traditions and convey the history of the region vividly. The productions are ample and imaginative. The plays, although uneven, have epic breadth and constitute a new type of American drama combining spectacle with dramatic action and affording scope for music and choreography. The new form offers scope for great poetry, even if it is not yet in evidence in these plays.

Paul Green, who virtually created this form of playwriting and is the author of *The Lost Colony* and *The Common Glory* as well as other examples of this genre, has here discarded both "Broadway" and "little theatre" to give America a style of theatre commensurate with its spacious spirit and truly epic struggles to build a free and equitable world. The productions make one justifiably proud to be an American; the spirit of Walt Whitman hovers over the stage. And the theatres in which the performances are given, amphitheatres laid out to conform to the topography of each area, provide a welcome relief from Broadway real-estate and the picture-frame stage. We are no longer in the diminished replicas of Renaissance theatre architecture of a Broadway playhouse, which is simply a vestige from a vanished aristocratic tradition (recalled by boxes and balconies), but in an open-air structure that recalls the Theatre of Dionysus, the only true democratic theatre. Gone is the sense of confinement one experiences in a New York or London playhouse. One breathes the air of America in these open-air structures, in which the playgoer may well feel that he is participating in a ritual. Perhaps, in time, the poets of America will be able to lift a powerful voice and express a vision worthy of the nation in these arenas.

These enterprises, which enjoy a good deal of local encouragement, have aroused interest as far south as Florida and as far west as Oregon. Pageant-dramas can be sustained wherever Americans possess or develop a strong sense of communion. Even today the example of the South in this instance can serve to correct the focus that seems so bleary when views of a national theatre emanate from well-meaning but essentially insular planners of "national theatre" located in New York or influenced by Broadway.

It seems to me that the only serious difficulty stems from the present thinking about the subject of a national theatre. We must not assume that it can materialize as a mere aggregate of professional companies producing haphazardly just for the sake of producing, nourishing on the same plays that do land-office business on Broadway, and developing out of no felt need and no sense of community.

The concept of a multiplicity of community theatres held together by nothing more than mere "get-togethers" and amiable correspondence, regardless of how informative, will not carry us beyond the present state of affairs. If the community theatres continue to depend on releases of Broadway successes and on weak plays for which play agencies would like a free "tryout" as far from Manhattan as possible, their activity may remain pleasant and moderately useful, but they will not constitute a national theatre simply because a central bureau counts the number of off-Broadway productions and discovers that there are thousands of them. This is not a concept of national theatre, but arithmetic.

Only a federation of properly rooted regional theatres growing up naturally out of what we already have and out of the needs we feel, rather than an institution conceived in terms of numbers, is the answer for the hunger we profess for a national theatre. It would have to be a theatre unified in diversity, as our nation is unified in diversity. And it would have to rest on the same foundations as our country rests; that is, upon the evolving experience and unfolding civilization of America. It cannot be a gift to the people, but a creation of the people. It cannot be brought to the people, as some well-intentioned friends of the stage seem to believe. It must come from the people—or rather *out* of them.

FROM REVIEWER TO PRODUCER

As an olio and envoi, I offer the following lines exactly as I wrote them on October 10, 1948, in the *Boston Post,* which generously allowed me to say a few words the day before the tryout premiere of *Minnie and Mr. Williams,* a somewhat metaphysical Welsh comedy by Richard Hughes. I had been associated in the production of many plays by the Theatre Guild, as well as by the war-time non-commercial Studio Theatre and by an amateur group in Pennsylvania. But the production of *Minnie and Mr. Williams* gave me my baptism as an independent Broadway producer. If my observations in the *Boston Post* were not exactly new to me, they seemed new in the flux and travail of getting the plays on the boards.

I use the terms flux, travail, and boards accurately, indeed literally. The play, which ran some twenty minutes short the day before we left New York, ran a full half hour too long when it opened in Boston. Owing to the usual union regulations and to other "practical" considerations, which from the point of view of a successful production are almost always impractical, the cast had never been able to rehearse in the set. The expensive set itself, excellent in many respects, had to have the stairway leading to an imaginary upper-story cut down by carpenters almost immediately after it had been erected. Mrs. Josephine Hull, as considerate a lady as any you will encounter inside or outside a theatre, discovered that she could not possibly negotiate so many steps as often and as fast as she was expected to do by the action. A series of narrations painstakingly prepared and presumptuously tried out on guests in my friend Theodore Morrison's Cambridge home and particularly approved, if I remember correctly, by Professor Harry Levin, who was as patient on that occasion as he is invariably brilliant, also had to go. Cut as mercilessly as the lumber of the stairway, the prologue to the act disappeared for another technical reason. Juggle as we might with the lighting equipment, Eddie Dowling, to whom the narrations were assigned, always found himself in darkness as well as half in the wings. As the play became a thinner, as well as faster, waif, it didn't become a better drama. It certainly had been a gayer and more amusing fantasy while we were rehearsing in our seats, off which our press representatives had nearly rolled when Josephine Hull read her lines. And we went to our doom on Broadway with the usual recklessness known as gallantry in show business after dropping some seventeen thousand dollars in the tryout period. For the record let me add that the critics had been understanding, kind, and helpful, and none of the newspaper notices was so written as to drive the public away. But the public stayed away, prompted no doubt by some intuition which made it anticipate the New York notices. We played to a virtually empty house most evenings, and, for some reason best understood by the Shuberts who owned it, we were not allowed to "paper the house" with Harvard's student body which might have given us an opportunity to assess the effect of the production upon a large audience.

The production went the way of all productions; the setting, the way of all stage sets. For reasons of union policy, we could not dispose of it to either the Dramatic Workshop in New York or a suburban college that wanted it, because the lumber would first have to be trucked to Long Island and then "re-trucked" to its intended destination, thus rolling up a double expense. The set was therefore disposed of quite theatrically; it went up in a conflagration on a dumping ground none of us, surely not the scene designer, had the heart to visit. But the words remain—the words of the play and the few words the *Boston Post* allowed me to say. The former still read very well, and the latter, which do not read as well, still have enough truth and relevance, I think, to justify my reprinting them. Here they are:

My first discovery on launching Richard Hughes' *Minnie and Mr. Williams* on the stage was that a critic turning producer is news. (When a producer turns critic it isn't news, because he does the expected thing and criticizes the critics.) My second discovery is that he finds himself in the rather anomalous situation of having to pass judgment on his own product. I tried to wriggle out of this situation by resigning from the New York Drama Critics' Circle, but the other playwreckers refused to hear of such a thing. The president of the Circle, John Mason Brown, declared that they were pleased to find one member on the creative side of the theatre at last. I know that Mr. Brown's words were motivated by a regard for me which I deeply appreciate, but to my anxious ears they sounded like "Create—or look out!" To a critic who has turned producer it is embarrassing to reflect that his colleagues will consider it a professional indiscretion if he doesn't come up with a hit.

One question that has been hurled at me with disconcerting frequency is, "How does a critic feel when he is a producer?" I always reply that he feels just like a producer. That is, he is inhumanly busy, humanly anxious, and—surreptitiously defiant. But there is a question that I have asked of myself—"What does a critic learn by turning producer?"—which seems to me far more difficult to answer. In fact, I hesitate to print even an interim report unless it is clearly understood that my generalizations are tentative.

Producing, you will gather from my hesitation, is an experience conducive to humility, a virtue not generally attributed to critics.

The first thing you discover as a producer is that all your best-laid plans, deductions, and convictions are subject to modification by the human factor. The lineaments of a characterization, the stress or quality of a situation, and the very lines in the play on paper begin to suffer a sea-change into something rich and strange (or something strange but not so rich) the moment one has picked the cast. The transformation goes on throughout the rehearsal period, and the producer can hardly catch up with the play he put into production. He may even have to look twice before he recognizes it. The fortunate producers are pleasantly surprised. The unfortunate ones can only blink, gnash their teeth helplessly, and look for a foxhole.

When we critics pound our victim for having produced such and such a play, it is only fair to consider that it may not be the one he bought for production. But there is no solution for him. If he expected to see in production exactly what he saw in script, he will simply have to invent a way of staging it without actors, a director, a scene designer, a stage manager and a stage electrician. Ellen Terry's intrepid son, Gordon Craig, thought he found a way of dispensing with the actor when he proposed to displace him with a super-marionette, but he would still have had to reckon with the other members of the collective enterprise that constitutes theatre. Until a super-Craig emerges on some as yet undisclosed planet (it will never happen on this globe of ours), a producer will simply have to apply all his intelligence and energy to getting some approximation of the values he wants, count his beads, and put his trust in Providence. He must take chances like the rest of us mortals when he links his destiny with other human beings.

This brings up the question of casting. My cup flowed over when I acquired two of the theatre's best loved and ablest veterans in Josephine Hull and Eddie Dowling, and I believe that I shall be considered fortunate, too, in my choice of young Elizabeth Ross and Clarence Derwent and others in my cast. One of these, incidentally, was pounding a typewriter in my office when Mr. Dowling chucked her under the chin and pronounced her an actress, an accusation that Mr. Dowling and I believe that she is strenuously substantiating. Miss Lee Wilcox will not object, I think, if I disclose her name. But my experience in casting *Minnie and Mr. Williams* plainly contradicts some of my assumptions as a critic for many years.

Along with many of my colleagues, I have always been kinder to actors than to plays—perhaps, the cynic will suggest, because nothing could be worse than most of the plays in which we see them; perhaps also because critics are kinder than is generally supposed. My producing experience leads me to suspect that good actors, especially good young actors, are almost as rare as good new plays. Many youngsters (and a good many of their elders, too) will do for radio, summer and amateur theatricals, and for humdrum Broadway pieces, but it is dangerous to cast them in original and challenging plays. Our shrunken professional theatre lets whatever talent they may have had once rust unused. The solution is not to train them longer, but to give them more employment in a great variety of roles. Joseph Schildkraut complained to me the other day that he found it ironical that his reputation in Europe should have been built on nearly a hundred different productions, whereas his reputation on the American stage is based on no more than five roles in twenty years. If the American theatre fails to develop an extensive repertory system, it will wake up one day to discover that it has virtually no talent, except accidental talent, at its disposal.

I also observed great anxiety among the many actors I interviewed for the production of *Minnie and Mr. Williams,* and it was not any display of artistic temperament but a very mundane, economic anxiety. How can we expect actors to relax and draw upon their inner resources when they know that if they don't land and hold on to a particular part they are likely to be jobless for the rest of the season or longer? Nor can they expect much patience from even the most charitable director when he has to put on a show within four weeks. The director soon finds himself forced to act out their parts for them, and woe betide them if he changes his interpretation, as he is likely to do while the play unfolds during rehearsals; for the play changes right under the director's nose as well as under the producer's. We who sit out in front don't quite realize the enormity of the problem because we haven't watched the struggles of the director and his cast. Besides, not having read the script, we rarely realize how much more talent *could* have gone into a particular part, and I suspect we don't particularly care when mediocrity is about all that a run-of-the-mill part rates in a run-of-the-mill play.

Part Four

FILM PERSPECTIVES

EXPRESSIONISM AND
REALISM IN FILMS

The writer of this chapter must begin with a grave confession. There may be a laudable growth of serious thinking and writing about films, but most of it is giving him more perturbation than clarification. We are all constantly colliding with brilliant lucubrations on the regrettable results of realism, fiction, dialogue and what not in the development of the motion picture. Partisanship has been intense, and it has been equally evident in exclusive, extravagant claims for the documentary film and in wistful regrets that the pure stream of cinematic art was ever sullied by reality. It may be a defect of temperament in me, but I have found myself subscribing to every view at one time or other, without being able to hold any one position exclusively. A steady diet of our fiction films may drive me screaming into the fold of the documentaries, but large doses of documentary film fill me with a sense of aridity; and while I may become surfeited with our usual realistic photography, more than occasional exposure to non-realistic abstraction oppresses me with a sense of futility. But, above all, I am haunted with a dread of sectarianism, lest it overconfine creative talent to a too specialized field and erect unnecessarily impassable barriers between the art film and the popular film. A simplification in the present flux of opinion seems to me highly necessary as a start in the direction of common sense, and I have been wondering whether we may not arrive at it by retracing our steps a little, beginning with the very nature of the medium as it has manifested itself in the period of its development.

Film art, it seems to me, has been from its very inception a schizoid art in a largely schizoid society. This seems to me the cardinal fact about motion pictures. In employing the term "schizoid" I do not mean that films are a lunatic art, although we all know too many manifestations in celluloid that could lead to such a conclusion. All I mean is that film art has a split personality inherently, that a division exists in its nature and has continued to be manifest in its evolution for generic and environmental reasons.

I

Some of the earliest efforts of film-makers, most notably of George Méliès, were "arrangements" or arbitrary creations. They tended to *invent* phenomena, as in *A Trip to the Moon*. The early film-maker not only selected but built the object to be photographed. He could use his camera expressionistically from the moment that Méliès' camera accidentally jammed and transformed an omnibus into a hearse. The discovery of double exposure, slow motion, reverse shots, fade-outs, dissolves and other camera tricks opened up a man-created world almost as fluid and evocative as music, until nothing seemed impossible to the imagination or fancy of the creator.

If anything, these possibilities are now greater than ever; and they are that, not merely for playful gratification, but for a purposive emphasis, comment or viewpoint. The satire of scientific pedantry in the extravaganza of *A Trip to the Moon* marked the beginning of a new art of visual commentary more resourceful than anything that civilization had developed hitherto. Potentially, the film-maker could take his place beside Aristophanes, Molière, Swift, and Voltaire. The best works of Chaplin, Walt Disney, and René Clair were approximations of a procedure that could have led film art to the highest reaches of a great humanist tradition, and this with an economy and completeness of expression rarely possible to the purveyors of literature. So elementary a procedure as Clair's comment on industrial regimentation, when he juxtaposed the prison and the phonograph factory in *A Nous la Liberté,* would have required from a Bernard Shaw a stream of words and dialectical clauses, many of which, we may be sure, would not have hit the mark with anything like the mnemonic force of Clair's photography. Since, moreover, even the ordinary story-telling motion picture profits from expressive abbreviations, juxtapositions, montages, and novel shooting angles, it is plain that there could have been no progress in film art without expressionism. The deliberate truncation, telescoping or distortion of the normal perceptions we call reality is plainly an essence of cinematic art. This has been so *sui generis* because the camera eye is the only eye completely subject to man's creative imagination; and after 1929 the camera's creativeness was to be supplemented by the possibilities of expressiveness on the sound-track. But if this is so, and I have barely scratched the surface of expressionism in films, how is it that popular film-making is in almost every instance anchored to realism?

The average film has reduced reality to a glossy picture-card, but it falls within the style of realism. If it falsifies the commonplace, it does so only by resorting to other commonplaces—mainly, the stereotyped trappings of wealth. It is as literal about a million-dollar economic status as it is about a two-thousand-dollar annual income, except that it confuses the latter with the former. It is as literal about a life of crime or adventure as it is about a quiet family conclave in the parlor. The average film employs the Belasco technique, even when the intention is to subvert realism's original and honorable aim of showing the truth about a man and his society.

As for the superior film, which has truth as its objective, it may present a trenchant viewpoint, such as we find in *Major Barbara* and *The Grapes of Wrath,* but it, too, yields its content only in a series of realistically photographed and arranged vignettes.

Even when our films take the further step of purporting to dramatize an inner situation or state of mind, they reduce the potentially expressionistic element in the story to brief and crudely discrete interludes. Films of this order never get into the inner man long enough or far enough for psychological and poetic realization. *The Lost Week-End,* which was acclaimed the best American motion picture of the year 1945, shows how a chronic drunkard drinks himself into a state of *delirium tremens.* Occasionally the film evokes his inner state, as when the bottles in a saloon magnify themselves in his eyes, but this is no more than a moment or two in the film. The expressionistic *pièce de résistance* comes in a highly touted bat scene, in which the miserable hero sees a bat whirling around the room and killing another rodent on the wall, whereupon the victim of the hallucination collapses. But what an inexpressively photographed sequence it is; how tame, how essentially prosaic. The bat is simply a small animal, such as anyone can see flying about; it maintains a discreet distance from the man who hallucinates it and from the audience that perceives it; it never appears in a close shot, never dominates the view, never enters the magnetic field of the drunkard's psyche. The bat remains a notion or a concept rather than an experience. It frightens the man out of his wits, not because his mental picture is harrowing psychologically or cinematically, but because, by convention, a bat is frightening. By the same token the audience is expected to be impressed because the hero is affected, and not because the audience has been overwhelmed by the hallucination. The camera, as I believe the able director of the film himself complained, was not allowed to enter the man. It remained an observer rather than an experiencer.

We can now return to our question. Here is the seeming anomaly of a richly expressionistic art limited, in practice, to the confines of an antipodal realism. How did this happen, how could it happen, and why has it been not only tolerated but rewarded with the gift of the largest body of paying patrons ever enjoyed by any of the arts?

II

We must not forget that films started with photography, and that the first marvel was that pictures should be seen moving. If one aspect of the nature of film photography was its capacity for arranging and stylizing matter interestingly, an equally inherent aspect was the motion-picture camera's capacity for showing actual phenomena better than any previously developed device. A *New York Times* report of April 24, 1896, which records the advent of film realism, conveys the instantaneous response to this naïve but fundamental form of gratification:

"When the hall was darkened last night, a buzzing and roaring were heard in the turret, and an unusually bright light fell upon the screen. Then came into view two precious blonde young persons of the variety stage, in pink and blue dresses, doing the umbrella dance with commendable celerity. Their motions were all clearly defined. When they vanished, a view of the angry surf breaking on a sandy beach near a stone pier amazed the spectators. . . . A burlesque boxing match between a tall, thin comedian and a short, fat one, a comic allegory called 'The Monroe Doctrine,' an instant of motion in Hoyt's farce 'The Milk White Flag,' repeated over and over again, and a skirt dance by a tall blonde completed the view, which were all wonderfully real and singularly exhilarating."

The schizoid nature of film lies, in the first instance, precisely in the fact that it is equally capable of creative expressiveness and literal representation; and that while the former can be extremely potent and is vastly attractive to the few, elementary representation gratifies the multitude, because it satisfies a more primitive level of sensibility. And if novelty were needed to sharpen a jaded public appetite, the effect was likely to be achieved by wonder-inducing pageantry (hence the success of Cecil de Mille spectacles) and by luxurious backgrounds, especially those inducing identification with the well-to-do in a money-minded world.

Once, moreover, motion pictures acquired continuity, which happened as early as 1903, when Porter made *The Great Train Robbery,* they proved that they could convey a story very well indeed, and they were bound to be held to that achievement, because everybody loves a story. And here again superficial realism was a natural concomitant of development in films, because easily recognizable action, transparent characters, and the most actual backgrounds are necessary to popular narrative. The multitude favored content that accorded with its notion of reality or with its fantasies, which are merely tinsel versions of reality, and responded best to the technique that made narrative most easy to follow. Film narration, moreover, was inevitably conditioned by the fact that hitherto story-telling had been the prerogative of literature, and so the literary pattern intruded into film art long before the development of sound.

The public was conditioned by the arts of the novel and the drama, both of which had been largely realistic since 1870. The film-makers obliged by following the sequence of the popular novel or play. The photographed events had to proceed chronologically, cause and effect had to be scrupulously separated in time (instead of being simultaneous as they are in the poetic imagination), and the telescoping of events or emotions had to be undertaken most gingerly. At most, the chronology was interrupted by the device of the flashback, which was also borrowed from the novel.

Transitions were made so elementary that, when a character was to appear in two successive scenes of action, he had to be shown uneventfully going down a long flight of stairs, closing the front door, hailing a cab, climbing into it, riding down streets or highways of no particular significance, getting out of the cab, paying the driver, ringing a front-door bell, going through it and climbing up another flight of stairs. Even so sophisticated a director as Alfred Hitchcock makes the fullest pictorial use of such a transition when he comes to terms with Hollywood in *Notorious*. When Ingrid Bergman and Cary Grant go on their mission of espionage, they drive to their destination over a beautifully photographed highway which would make an excellent billboard for a Brazilian travel agency. Sophistication in the matter of such transitions normally reaches its peak when the travel shots are steeped in atmosphere to telegraph the next dramatic scene to the audience. Occasionally we skip a number of months or years before starting a new scene, and apprise the public of the fact by flashing differently dated newspaper headlines on the screen. We call this *montage,* bastardizing that noble concept with as literal a procedure as any that man ever discovered.

The advent of the talking picture in 1929 only made it possible to tell a story more fully, and its effect on film narration was to reduce the necessity for photographic expression, since the sound-track could now do a considerable portion of the camera's expository and analytic work. Film plays became even more completely transcriptions of novels and stage plays, and generally the novels and plays selected for this purpose were precisely those which followed the norms of realistic narrative. You don't hear of a *Ulysses* or a *Remembrance of Things Past* having been filmed. The verbal element was, moreover, kept on the most prosaic colloquial level, so as to put the least possible strain on the public ear and make identification with the speaker as easy as possible. Special significance may be attached perhaps to the fact that these developments were most pronounced in the United States, the nation that has had the longest history of dedication to mechanically produced mass-art.

III

It is futile to stand righteously apart from the prevailing condition of films, to flail one's arms under the banner of a pure esthetic of the cinema, to regret that the talking picture ever came into existence, to deplore the fact that motion pictures ever started telling stories like the popular novel or stage play. If they had not done so, they would never have become the most popular dramatic art of the century. After the first flush of curiosity they would have been disregarded by the public, and they would have become the special entertainment of a small élite. And by far the greatest futility attends the pious thoughts of those who grieve for the passing of expressionism and the victory of the realistic dispensation. They are banging their heads against a wall of fact. Descriptive, narrative, and dramatic realism is the major Western tradition of all the popular arts, no matter how overlaid they may be with romanticism and fantastic themes. The differences within the *genres* of popular Western arts resolve themselves largely into gradations of realism, which vary with the conventions and conceptions of reality in different periods. True and complete departures from realism have been few and short-lived, and have rarely engaged more than a small fraction of any Western community. And whatever may be argued concerning earlier periods, it is certainly plain that the industrial trends of the nineteenth and twentieth centuries have all operated in favor of realism.

The question, therefore, ultimately resolves into one of accommodation between the antipodal elements in the film art, between inherent expressionism and inherent realism. Shall, and must, the accommodation be always on the lowest level of aborting the camera's and sound-track's superb potentialities of expressiveness and of adhering to the most pedestrian aspects of realism, as is generally the case in Hollywood and Hollywood-aping practice? Even Hollywood has demonstrated in a few instances that this is not necessary; I cite the example of *The Informer*. If only the commercial studios would give more leeway to the imaginative artist, and if only the imaginative artist, instead of remaining aloof and circumscribed in unassailable purity, would make a consistent effort to take the citadels of commercial production by cunning, accommodation or by flanking tactics! Isolation may ultimately drive the artist to the making of this effort, and the law of saturation may compel the large studios to defer to him to a degree. As the films face competition by television which militates against the continuation of routinized film-making, and as even unimaginative and diffident audiences cannot be indefinitely attracted with the same formula, it is possible that the commercial film-makers will find practical reasons for returning more frequently and more fully to the camera's expressionistic power. Film art will still remain divided in spirit, because this is the nature of the art and of the world it serves, but at least the two parts of the split personality will learn to get on with each other with some semblance of integration.

If realism and the fiction film must remain the matrix of contemporary film-making, it does not necessarily have to be of the most pinchbeck variety. The possibilities of excitement and stimulation in genuine realism have been abundantly demonstrated in novels, plays, and such films as *The Grapes of Wrath,* the best Allied war documentaries, and *Open City.* The factual can, indeed, be shatteringly "expressive," especially with the enlarging, lap-dissolving and angling devices that films employ almost as a matter of course. It is very possible, moreover, to combine the fiction film with the film documentary, so that the fiction may acquire greater conviction and the documentary may prove more attractive. There are already films that fall in the desired direction: *The House on 92nd Street* and *G.I. Joe* have been good American examples. If, indeed, the realism in commercial films were actually realism as practiced by the superior, rather than the inferior, realists in all the arts, there might be less complaining. We bring up the question of expressionism mainly because we are starved for meaningful, stimulating, and stirring work, and not because there is some special blessedness in any particular style of art. As a matter of fact, every style, including expressionism, can be debased and perverted; witness the extravaganza and decadence of most German expressionist drama, which was too often a case of transformed *furor Teutonicus.* For myself I doubt whether I would have endured a second *Cabinet of Dr. Cagliari* fantasy. It is the choice of weak matter and the mealy-mouthed treatment that disgrace realism on the screen.

If, finally, the films must remain linked to literature by the bonds of story-telling and dialogue, this, too, does not have to prevail on the lowest levels of matrimonial bondage. There are good marriages as well as bad. Those who protest that films have become indistinguishable from novels and stage plays tend to overlook the cardinal cause of their complaints. Indistinguishable from *what* novels and *what* stage plays is the real point. Would we complain if a film were indistinguishable in essentials from, let us say, *The Brothers Karamazov* or *Hamlet,* rather than from the treacle of the latest piece of popular fiction or stage comedy? Gratification with Olivier's *Henry V* is evidence to the contrary. And, of course, the same line of reasoning may be followed in answering those embattled few who still place all the blame on the invention of the talking picture. Most of us object, not to talk *per se,* but to the *quality* and use of the talk. We should have fewer protests if the talking were done by a Shakespeare or a Shaw, instead of by prattlers who sound like congenital idiots. Distinguished dialogue, besides, is never inherently anti-filmic, because the best dramatic dialogue is quintessential expression. Only bad dramatic dialogue is anti-filmic. When it is flat, it adds nothing to what the picture could show without speech; when it is pretentious or "literary," it only stands in the way of visual movement or nullifies it. But the mark of good dialogue is precisely that it is neither flat nor decorative.

To sum up: we must accept the fact that the contemporary film will continue to hold both the expressionistic and realistic, as well as the visual and verbal, elements in solution. What we need not accept, and can alter with effort, is the present level of so-called realism, story-telling and dialogue, and the manner in which they are employed. I hold further that, as we lift the level of realism, we shall find ourselves also making the soundest use of expressionism; and that as we raise the standards of story-telling, we shall find that it is less and less antipathetic to the nature of film art, because the richer the content the greater will be the opportunity for cinematic expressiveness. These are such commonplace recommendations that it would seem unnecessary to make them. But the more I read film estheticians the more I am convinced that these conclusions have to be repeated.

THE TIME OF YOUR LIFE
AS A FILM

An example of accommodation to a culture-pattern is James Cagney's film *The Time of Your Life,* based on Saroyan's play. Cagney and his associates could be commended for a painstaking effort to hew to the lines of the stage play, to be true to its content and spirit. Since the play was off the beaten track, Mr. Cagney cannot be charged with trying to pander to the lowest common denominator of taste and intelligence, and the result is an above-average motion picture which can be credited with decent compassion. Yet when all this is granted, it cannot be said that the picture is of the same caliber as the play. Censorship by a "production code," which may be called "self-censorship" but also censorship by fear, makes its demands even on politically innocent material.

In the play we have a young man, Joe, who tries to play the paraclete in a San Francisco honky-tonk. One of Joe's major concerns is the lot of a shiftless and untrained but altogether decent young man and of a fundamentally sweet-natured young woman "Kitty Duval" who has been driven into prostitution and salves her ego with illusions of having once been a burlesque queen. Observing that the two young people are drawn to each other, Joe facilitates their romance and encourages the young man to get a job and marry Kitty. The crisis in the play comes when a neurotic and sadistic Vice Squad official starts to persecute Kitty and is likely to block her escape from a tawdry life. The play is resolved when Kit Carson, an elderly liar who fancies himself to have been a hero of the frontier in his youth, kills the sadist for affronting a lady. Joe hands Kit Carson his own pistol with the implication that a pistol is sometimes useful when the little men of the world must be protected from those who persecute them. This point was particularly meaningful in 1940, when Saroyan's play was running on Broadway, since international gangsterism was in full swing in Europe.

Joe, the rich young idler, had had an unhappy love affair which depressed him and may have driven him to drink. This is the conventional motivation we are apt to find in any play. But he is motivated in the conduct that gives him his *active* role in the play by a sense of guilt concerning his wealth and the manner in which he acquired it. "I *earned* the money I throw away," he says in Act One. "I stole it like everybody else does. I hurt people to get it. Loafing around this way, I still hurt people. I don't know who they are, or where they are. If I did, I'd feel worse." He explains, "I've got a Christian conscience in a world that's got no conscience at all." He has withdrawn into Nick's San Francisco waterfront honkytonk, because he can't do anything that won't give him a bad conscience. He is passive with respect to himself and active with respect to others, aiding those he can.

Joe's motivation was amputated in the film, so that his withdrawal was attributed solely to his having once lost a sweetheart to someone. Since Hollywood's regulations forbid any treatment of prostitution, the motion picture never could make it clear why the villain Blick (Saroyan's Vice Squad officer) is a serious threat to Kitty Duval. Nor was Joe's magnanimity truly realized in the film, since there seemed to be no reason why Kitty needed saving. His furthering her romance with his protégé lost much of its significance and tenderness. And dramatic values were lessened by another concession to the Hollywood code, which frowns upon ever showing the police in an unfavorable light and which definitely forbids the killing of a policeman without fit punishment. Blick, who was the head of the San Francisco Vice Squad in Saroyan's play, was therefore presented as a mere "stool pigeon" whose behavior has no legal sanction or force. When he persecutes Kitty, he does so in an unofficial capacity, which greatly reduces the force of Saroyan's point concerning him. If he were killed by Kit Carson, then it would not be evil authority but a verminous species of neurotic who would be destroyed. In the film, however, he is not killed at all; he is merely thrown out of the saloon, which is a rather tame conclusion after all the fuss made over him. These are some of the ways in which a play which won both the Drama Critics' Award and the Pulitzer Prize became a mild and somewhat muzzy motion picture. It is another example of how the "mass communication arts" stop at the foothills of Parnassus.

Whether this is an inevitable consequence of trying to reach the masses is a question of great moment, since it is popular art that disseminates the values by which a people live. The evil does not reside in trying to reach many people (Greek and Elizabethan drama did precisely that), but in lumping all kinds of people, children included, as a single public. It is one thing to create for a public, it is another to strike an average intelligence that is little higher than a retarded adolescent's and make that intelligence quotient the basis of judgment concerning what we should give or withhold from individuals. This is one way in which the mass entertainment media—ironically, for a society in which individualism is considered the *summum bonum*—"socializes" the people into a composite "mass-man." The Western theatre does not do that, and this is one cogent reason why the stage should be considered an indispensable institution. But this is also one reason why it is a small business rather than big, and why it is desirable for it to *remain small.* Hollywood motion pictures that may be considered exceptions to rule by the lowest common denominator of national maturity have been few, except for a few years during and immediately after World War II, and they are likely to be fewer within the foreseeable future.

An improvement in American film-making will be general only when films are made on a base much narrower than has been customary. Only then will there be less temptation to resort to stereotypes and to iron out bizarre manifestations of imaginative as well as controversial matter. The artistry of the best European films has been possible only in so far as the dimensions of European film-making have been comparatively modest.

It would be easy enough to select many dozens of Hollywood motion pictures more deserving of denunciation than *The Time of Your Life.* They represent an obvious, often flagrant, debasement of taste, sense, and civilized values. But the case of *The Time of Your Life* shows us how even the effort to film unconventional material succumbs to convention, sentimentalization, and emasculation when Hollywood faces only the alternatives of financial failure or unlimited mass-appeal. Only in treating a subject of obviously wide public interest such as the Second World War has Hollywood felt free to use the full potentialities of subject matter and more than a fraction of the large resources of the motion picture medium. As a result, not only Hollywood producers and the general public but even most motion-picture critics in the United States have been "normalized," so that they cannot respond to a *Monsieur Verdoux* without a sense of outrage or confusion. And to be able to appreciate only the "norm" is an almost certain way of not truly evaluating even norms.

THE INFORMER AS A SCREENPLAY

The Informer was made in 1935. It was the high point of the collaboration of John Ford and Dudley Nichols, a partnership of film director and screen writer that was the boast of Hollywood for years. This film has been unequaled as an achievement in American film creation since the advent of the "talkies," except for the work of Charles Chaplin. Even the Second World War, which inspired many creditable pictures, brought forth no American film quite the equal of *The Informer*. The talented collaborators themselves did not succeed in equaling it.

The notion still prevails that the screenplay is of secondary value to the making of a motion picture and that the screenwriter is a mere flunkey whose name need not be mentioned in reviews. If the fact that Hollywood has spent a fortune on the preparation of screenplays does not refute this error, the script of *The Informer* may. It is true enough that a screenplay is only the libretto for the film, just as the written stage-play is the libretto for the stage production. But there is all the difference in the world between a thin and poorly constructed scenario and a rich, well-constructed one.

There are, besides, scenarios that ignore the necessary flow of picturized movement, confine the action and thus immobilize the camera, and reduce visual reality to a few standardized locations and objects. Many Hollywood pictures, even such worthy ones as *Watch on the Rhine* and *Gentleman's Agreement,* have failed to take sufficient advantage of the cinematic medium. Hollywood, which rarely errs in this respect when confecting Westerns and melodramas, has long suffered from a plethora of nobly intended films that look like photographed plays and novels. The screenplay of *The Informer* is perhaps most distinguished by virtue of the screenwriter's creative visualization of his material as simultaneously subjective and objective drama.

Nichols' imagination made full use of the mobility of the camera and of its unique power to pick out significant details overlooked by the cursory eye. Objects in *The Informer* become signs or symbols planted and executed as forms of action revealing the tensions of Gypo, the main character who betrayed his friend Frankie of the Irish Underground to the British constabulary. Nichols' use of photographs of a steamship line poster and a police notice throughout the screenplay is an example of facility in screenwriting. Although it is difficult to tell to what degree any feature of the script is the sole contribution of Nichols rather than of the combined imagination of writer and director, this much is certain: the notable picture directed by Ford had a superb screenplay. In spite of good dialogue, in which respect it most resembles a good stage play, the scenario provides that "succession of everchanging dramatic imagery" that Mamoulian has called "the very essence of film art." And if it were necessary to prove this point further, the evidence is at hand. Remove the dialogue, excellent though much of it be, and the film would still be, in the main, intelligible and effective. Dore Schary has provided a comprehensive explanation of cinematic work in his book *Case History of a Movie*. Among the many points made by Mr. Schary is that the continuity of a motion picture "must be on the screen, not on the sound track." It is also important to have the right words at the right time on the sound track, and as Olivier's *Henry V* proved, it would not hurt the industry if the words had distinction! Especially useful is the reminder: ". . . as soon as a given speech has gone far enough so that the audience can guess the rest of it, the picture cuts from the speaker to the hearer as the speech continues off-scene." Reason: to catch the reaction, to see what "emotional effect that speech is going to have on the character to whom it's addressed." The "action" in *The Informer* consists largely of the betrayal of Frankie by his primitive friend Gypo and the Irish Underground's punitive measures; the "reaction," largely of Gypo's motivation and bewildered remorse. Since the last-mentioned elements, *plus* the Underground's vengeance, give the scenario its main interest, *The Informer* is primarily a "reaction picture."

This screenplay also performs the feat of turning an epic subject into a dramatic one. Most Hollywood epics, even good ones during World War II such as *The Story of G.I. Joe,* were episodic. By making closely related states of mind paramount in the picture, Ford and Nichols gave it not only a mature, psychological claim upon us but an emotional center that assured the numerous, rapidly changing screen images a strict *unity*. The elements of their screenplay have an undeviating relatedness, which is true "unity of action." It is the only unity that has ever mattered for the screen, and from it the other "unities" of time and place derive their only true reason and point. The events of *The Informer* transpire approximately in a single night; they end a little after daybreak. They occur in various parts of Dublin related in mood, symbolic value, and plot; and this, in true cinematic terms of mobile variety within the unity.

It is instructive to observe that the screenplay of *The Informer* never calls for a "fade-out" until the film reaches its conclusion. A "fade-out" is the momentary equivalent of a curtain at the end of an act of a stage play. Most pictures have several "fade-outs," but Nichols and Ford came to visualize their events as one uninterrupted experience. Most screenplays also employ numerous "dissolves" as divisions between scenes within an act. Most of Nichols' "dissolves" are synthesizing devices and are of psychological interest in relating objective events and mental images. They are so-called *Lap Dissolves,* one picture changing into another by means of double exposure of film strips, one scene "dissolving out" one image and simultaneously bringing into focus another one.

Although a screenplay is a species of play, it is not a stage-play any more than it is an epic, a novel, or a poem. The possibility of confusion with stage drama is the greatest, since both the "talking" scenario and the play employ dialogue. But the screenplay is a libretto for a different kind of theatre from the stage. The scenario can be equated with a stage play only if we imagine one written in the manner of a multi-scened Elizabethan drama divided into many more short scenes than *Antony and Cleopatra,* which has forty-two in standard editions, and with the scenes moving constantly. And even this description would be no more than an approximation, since the angle of vision is changed constantly in a film, and objects or parts of objects are seen at various distances and with different degrees of distinctness for description and for expressive purposes. The true screenplay takes account of the fundamental difference between stage and screen, as well as the difference between action caught by the moving camera and action by the stage actor, who can hardly play Proteus, Chimera, and vanishing Cheshire Cat.

It is apparent, too, that although we must acknowledge the screenplay to be a distinct, if rather recent, literary form, it is at least one step further removed from literature than a stage drama. We can, if we wish, read most of *Hamlet* as a supreme poem. Until such a time as screenwriters compose their film directions, as well as dialogue, in imperishable verse or prose, few critics will validate high literary claims for screenplays.

The literary flair of Dudley Nichols' writing makes his screenplay unusually rich in texture. Even he did not, however, write with a view to publication. When, and if, screenwriters come to regard themselves as men of letters writing for publication as well as for the picture studio, they may write down their final draft, or the copy they wish to preserve, in the best language at their command. It took playwrights a great deal of time to develop the habit of giving attention to descriptive directions. These were first made a literary part of the text of a play toward the end of the century when the advent of realism placed a strong emphasis on the role of environment in drama. Failure to provide description in a stage-play hardly matters in most instances, owing to the preponderant importance of dialogue in a play. In a screenplay, however, there is generally a preponderance of pictorial elements of action. When present in a screenplay, these would have to be rendered with considerably greater refinement than is usual, if the scenario is to make any claim to literary distinction.

SCREENWRITING AS PLAYWRITING

A major form of writing known as screenwriting has arisen in the past fifteen years. Although this type of literature has been exerting a great, if mainly deplorable, influence on our national life, since it is the basis of all talking movies, it is virtually unknown to the public. Unlike plays for the stage, which are published after, or even before, production, screenplays have rarely been revealed to the reading public.[1]

This is unfortunate for many reasons: While Hollywood has turned out some important films nearly every year, the public has had to rely on its fugitive impressions, except when a film is revived. Unlike the play-goer, the movie patron has been unable to refer to the text of the film-play as the playgoer refers to the published play. There have been virtually no possibilities of refreshing one's memory or of observing the dramatic sub-stance of the film at leisure for enjoyment or criticism; and it has not usually been possible to compare the scenario with the finished film as we compare a playscript with the kind of production it received. To discover the difference in effect between the writer's intention and the producer's work might well be revealing; we could use the comparison to challenge and perhaps, ultimately, correct flaws, whether deliberate or unintentional, in motion picture production. Lillian Hellman's public protest against the Lewis Milestone production of her screenplay, *The North Star,* gained considerable meaning after Viking Press published her film play. Screen-writers might arrive at the dignity of writers, acquiring the prerogatives and obligations of authors, if their contribution to a film were available to the interested part of the public instead of being hidden in a studio vault. Playwrights, besides, have learned a good deal of their craft from reading published plays. If screenwriters had been able to study screen-plays for which some merit is claimed, they might have learned something about their craft without being first twisted into an animated pretzel in the prisons for writers euphemistically known as Hollywood studios. They might have developed into playwrights for the screen rather than into overpaid hacks and been capable of original writing for the motion pic-

---

[1] Between 1942 and 1945, the author of this essay collaborated with Dudley Nichols in editing three collections of screenplays (*Twenty Best Film Plays, Best Film Plays of 1943-44,* and *Best Film Plays of 1945,* Crown Publishers), now out of print. Eight years have passed without any sequel to their efforts, except for the publication of *All About Eve* by Random House and the publication of Dudley Nichols' screenplay of *The Informer,* as edited by John Gassner, in the August, 1951, issue of *Theatre Arts Magazine.*

ture medium. In the long run, Hollywood itself might have benefited. Apart from these considerations, the screenplay holds interest as an example of the adaptation of dramatic form to modern times and to a mechanical medium, and as a new form of literature that has gradually developed a special structure. Playwriting has taken many forms in the course of the theatre's long history, as we can see by comparing the radically divergent examples of a Japanese Noh Play, a Greek tragedy, a Shakespearean drama, and a modern realistic play. And now we have the screenplay as a form of playwriting intended for a new modern medium. We have in screen-drama a new dramatic structure, multi-scened, remarkably fluid, and free to employ a large degree of visual symbolism without losing concrete reality for even the least sophisticated spectator, since a picture is a picture. (Most movie-goers are not even aware that their sensibilities are being constantly bombarded with symbols as they watch a film —even a very ordinary one.) Above all, the screenplay is playwriting possessing the mobility of the camera eye rather than playwriting limited to the comparatively static stage picture.

In the modern age, should everyone whose bent is dramatic pour his energies into the usually extremely limited medium of the stage when his subject matter and creative vision require the epic resources of motion picture art? I believe we should encourage an independent art—independent in the sense that the writer's work is not ordered but entirely initiated by himself, that the written screenplay, like the written play, goes in search of a producer rather than *vice versa,* and that the work could be published and would make good reading although nobody has as yet produced it. Somebody might take the initiative and write just such a screenplay and get it published even if nobody filmed it. It would be quixotic to do so, but, then, literature has never lacked Don Quixotes. As a matter of fact, one great writer came close to writing just such a screenplay, without knowing about the talking film: I refer to Thomas Hardy's *The Dynasts.* Ironically, this epic of the Napoleonic wars appeared in 1914, on the eve of the age of world wars which have more than equaled the epic character of Napoleon's ventures in world conflict. As a play, *The Dynasts* is a failure. It is substantially, however, a great screenplay that makes all our war films look absurdly insignificant. Hardy may not have known what medium he was writing for, but the medium now exists. It also has all the artists it needs in every department except writing. But it will never have great writing until writers have the boldness to compose screenplays without being first employed by a motion picture studio, writers who select the form of the screenplay because it enables them to have their say with maximum significance and force, writers who, moreover, use the form itself as a means of esthetic gratification.

Not to acknowledge the possibilities of a new form of playwriting that stems from the development of a remarkable machine-age form of theatre seems to me sheer snobbery—the snobbery of the litterateur—and sheer backwardness. And all the arguments that might be advanced against adopting the screenplay as a form of dramatic literature are fallacious. That most screenplays are unworthy of attention should not deter us. Most stage plays, too, are garbage. But there are worthy screenplays, just as there are worthy stage plays. The argument that the screenplay can give no pleasure to the reader is based on the erroneous assumption that there is only one format for screenwriting available to the writer—namely, that which consists of barbarously worded technical directions for the camera rendered in stenographic form. Actually, eminent screenwriters such as Dudley Nichols had dispensed with this format by 1940, and substituted descriptive directions. And these could be as well written, of course, as the author's talent and patience enabled him to write them. The labor of the file is not forbidden to the screenwriter. If he has not refined his style, the reasons have been economic (time is money in Hollywood) and artistic— that is, he has not written with a view to ultimate publication (neither did the writers of the medieval "tropes," the first form of playwriting in the Middle Ages), and working for a Hollywood studio has neither required nor promoted literary excellence. Some technical terminology and non-literary directions necessary to convey information or to indicate the nature of the motion-picture medium, moreover, can be retained in screenwriting without doing any more damage to readability and literary distinction than "Flourish, and enter the town," "Flourish. Exeunt," "Sound trumpets," and "Alarum. Excursions. Enter Pistol, French Soldier, Boy" in the Kittredge edition of Shakespeare's *Henry V*. There is no greater holiness about these practical notations than about "Dissolve to countryside—night" or "Ladies' Room—Stork Club" or "Eve's suite—Taft Hotel—Day" in the published screenplay of *All About Eve* by Joseph L. Mankiewicz.

The assumption that a screenplay could not be satisfactory literature because the motion picture is a visual medium is equally a fallacy. The stage, too, is a visual medium. Yet a considerable portion of the world's major literary achievements are in dramatic form, and correspond to the variable physical requirements of different stages and different modes of theatrical production that the world has known since the fifth century B.C. In fact, the more a play corresponds to the requirements of stage production, the better it is. The worst plays are those which do not possess this correspondence because the author was inept as a theatrician or did not intend to have the play staged and wrote "closet drama." The one exception with which I am familiar is *Samson Agonistes,* and it is not entirely an exception since Milton, too, had a theatrical frame of reference—

namely, the Greek theatre. Although Milton does not appear to have had much knowledge of that theatre or any strong intuition concerning the performance values of drama, he obviously did not write *Samson Agonistes* entirely without visualization, and he had an ear for the speaking value of many of the lines. Nor is the view that a screenplay has many more scenes than a play and is therefore choppy as description and narrative a valid argument against the possibilities of literary values in screenwriting. Not only is Shakespearean or Elizabethan drama multi-scened, but even a tightly knit one-set realistic play is actually composed of many short scenes whenever the work is theatrically effective. In our Anglo-American style of typing and printing a play, these scenes are not blocked out and titled Scene 1, Scene 2, Scene 3, and so forth, but in the French format the scenes, called *tableaux,* are plainly indicated and numbered. Quite a number of them, moreover, may not run much longer in the play-text than does a scene in a motion picture or in the screenplay. There are many such little scenes—and marvelously vivid they are, too—in poems, stories, and novels concerning whose literary merit there has been little or no dispute. Homer would have been a highly successful screenwriter, if Hollywood had employed him, and Cecil de Mille would have taken him to his bosom.

I trust that I am not laboring a point: But the epic poets and novelists of the past—from Homer up to the Joyce of *Ulysses*—all had superb cinematic sense. The epic and the novel have long been cinematic in the essentials of narration. They have consisted of episodes flowing into episodes; they have consisted of flashbacks, panoramic views, sharply noted tiny details that the camera catches better than the human eye, and mass-packed scenes. "Montage" has been a familiar device of narration in literature from the beginning of epic poetry. "Point of view" or "angle of narration" in fiction is not fundamentally different from the "camera angle" and the cinematic device of "shooting" from the observer to the observed object, and back again to the observer. Dialogue actually spoken and dialogue heard in the imagination have been used both in fiction and motion pictures. And both the novel and the film have focused on a small scene or the fragment of a scene as "close" as necessary, and then widened the view, moving from a close "shot" to a long one, "panned," "dollied," and so on. The fact is, of course, that both narrative and cinematic art have been thoroughly fluid.

Little imagination is needed to conceive the Homeric epics, the Norse sagas and Eddas, *The Song of Roland,* and *The Lay of the Nibelungs* as film plays. And it is almost as easy to perceive the cinematic qualities in novels such as *Gil Blas, Tom Jones, Charterhouse of Parma, Dead Souls, Salammbo, War and Peace, And Quiet Flows the Don, Growth of the Soil,*

Moby Dick, and *Huckleberry Finn,* not to mention such dramas as Shakespeare's chronicle plays. For cinematic writing, moreover, verse narration is actually exemplary, as Eisenstein noted when he picked out the following six lines concerning an execution from Pushkin's poem *Poltava*:

> "Too late," someone then said to them,
> And pointed finger to the field.
> Then the fatal scaffold was dismantled,
> A priest in cassock black was praying,
> And onto a wagon was being lifted
> By two Cossacks an oaken coffin.

My intention is not to point out "film properties" to Hollywood's story departments or dead authors to Hollywood's eager talent scouts. My point is that, if the cultural trends of democracy and of industrial society continue to exert their present pressures, and if the habit of reading literature declines more than it has already declined, the talent of the writer who has an epic imagination and a sense of drama could find expression in the screenplay. The novelist and poet would find an effective form in original writings for films; they could write directly for the visual translation of the poetic and narrative imagination.

Dramatic writing, in being cinematically employed, could become Shakespearian again; this, in every particular except the length of speeches that could be successfully assimilated by the film medium. And symbolism could become dramatically effective to a greater degree than it has been on the stage. The use of symbols as an integral element of cinematic narration has long been a remarkable feature of film art. Its expressiveness was evident, for example, in the recurrence of the century plant motif in Eisenstein's *Thunder Over Mexico,* and in the brilliant parallel drawn between routinized prison and factory life in René Clair's *A Nous la Liberté.* And one need hardly point out the enormous possibilities of deploying the sound-track expressively for speech, music, and sound effects.

Surely Pare Lorentz's *The River* and *The Fight for Life* and the Ford-Nichols film *The Informer,* based on Liam O'Flaherty's novel, revealed possibilities for dramatic effect that a stage director might well envy. In introducing the first of the three volumes of American-made talking pictures that Dudley Nichols and I edited, I noted some of these possibilities in greater detail:

> Objects extrapolated from their surroundings can be used with tremendous effect, and a part can speak eloquently for the whole, while routine exposition can be reduced to a flash. A separate "shot" of a

pen moving on a piece of paper or of a foot pushing against a door can create an instant sense of expectancy and suspense. A crumpled piece of paper clinging to a man who has sold his friend's life for a small reward may suggest the informer's troublesome conscience more eloquently than an extended verbal analysis. Seemingly unrelated "shots" of objects in quick succession, superimposed on each other or dissolving into each other, may establish a situation, enforce a comment, or convey the essence of an emotion in fresh and startling ways. A poetry of sensations or relations is often achieved by this kind of composition, for which the technical word is "montage." Speech can be shuttled back and forth, or can be supplemented and counter-pointed by picturized events, as well as alternated with effective silence while pantomime and visual backgrounds carry on the dialogue's content. The screenwriter knows that he can rely on the new technical resources of sound recording, described by Lewis Jacobs: "An art of sound devices now parallels the art of camera devices: the elimination of all but one voice or sound on the sound track parallels the camera close-up; the mingling of voices or noises corresponds to the double exposure; the traveling of sound is like the panning or dollying of the camera; the elongation of sound beyond normal parallels a lengthy still shot. The dissolve and the fade, the stop-voice and the play-back—these are other sound devices which approximate devices of the camera."

One written "shot" can follow another without preparation and intermission for a change of scene, as in a play; without delaying explanation of the transition, as in a novel. One accepts the convention as natural because films habituate us to freedom of movement in time and space. The viewpoint can also be tellingly differentiated for emphasis. The view can be expressively panoramic, distant and fully inclusive ("full shot"), fairly close and partially revealing ("medium shot"), or close and right on top of us (in a "close-up"). The view can also move to and fro, and up and down; it can expand or contract for revelation or emphasis; it can move with a character ("the camera pans with him" is the usual phrase) or precede him. The scene can "fade in" (generally conveying the start of a "sequence," a segment of the story), by the gradual materialization of a scene. It can "fade out," the gradual disappearance of the scene creating a sense of pause or of finality, generally suggesting the end of a sequence. It can dissolve quickly or lingeringly into another image, suggesting not merely a lapse of time but a special relationship with the image that follows. (A man's face is seen scowling, and as it "dissolves out," a picture of his being beaten as a child "dissolves in" simultaneously, creating an impression of psychological continuity and relationship.) The shot can "wipe off"—as though a tissue were being peeled off, giving place to another picture, like another, deeper layer of tissue. The scene can be "cut"—that is, concluded abruptly, changed before its logical termination to achieve some staccato effect. Scenes, moreover, can be presented from the viewpoint of different characters, enabling us to see an object or some transpiring action as some character—personally involved or affected—views it, objectively or subjectively.

The viewpoint of the camera excels that of the static spectator or reader, for it is all-seeing and omniscient. The composition of a screenplay is predicated on the fact that the camera can be moved in all directions and that the view on the screen is in continuous movement. The screenplay, too, is movement, of varying speed and duration. The actors are moving, the background is moving, objects are moving symbols are moving, the angles of vision are moving.

The resources of the motion picture are virtually inexhaustible, and the form and the detail of the screenplay correspond to them. Since the camera that takes the photographs corresponds to the eye of the observer, the "shooting script" visualizes the film for the reader. The shooting directions intended for those who make the film in the studios or "on location" become, in the reading of the script, "seeing" directions. They tell the reader what to see and imagine, or—if he has already seen the film—what to "re-see."

What I wrote in the above-quoted paragraphs, however, could be vastly extended, and this not merely by the film technician. There is surely no reason why the poet should permanently limit a fine imagination to a discourse with himself and a handful of poetry-readers; why the novelist should doggedly write novel after novel that is read only by a few thousand devotees; and why the playwright should always force himself into the tight confines of the realistic stage regardless of the demands of his subject and vision.

It is true, of course, that there are traps in cinematic art. They are many, even when we discount the demands of the merchants of film pabulum. There is the risk of becoming infected with the mechanism or the mechanical resources of the medium itself. We encounter a parallel in the theatre whenever some stage director or playwright falls in love with the electric switchboard, the turntable or revolving stage, constructivist ramps, treadmills *á la* Piscator, or steps *á la* Jessner. Reliance on the physical apparatus is dangerous for the playwright. It is dangerous, too, for the Hollywood scenarist; it may seduce even the screenwriter who may not be working for the moguls of Beverly Hills. The mechanism must be used, but the creator must not allow it to use him. Dudley Nichols was aware of the danger when he wrote in one of the Gassner-Nichols film books:

> This typewriter I am using converts finger-power into printed letters as its special function. If I am not careful my association with it will lead me into mechanical habits of writing, some of which may already be visible to the acute reader. Yes, the machine is a miraculous slave but a dangerous god.

These remarks were intended as a metaphor for succumbing to the machine of motion-picture production which Mr. Nichols noted in the case of the screen actor as well as the writer. "The machine has no imagination, neither errors nor inspirations. . . . Everything may get into the film of today or of tomorrow (if present conditions continue to prevail)— everything except the idiosyncrasy of the human soul, the kind of individuality that differentiates Chekhov from O'Henry or Shaw from Pinero."

Specific techniques capable of expressive employment may easily be used to suppress rather than express. The devices by means of which men can bankrupt their integrity are numberless, and the arts have as many on hand and give rise to as many as any other human enterprise. The quick effective curtain and the blackout often serve as such meretriciously managed devices in the theatre. Both "well-made play" fanciers (from the time of Scribe and Sardou to the latest writer of melodrama) and the modernist Expressionist playwrights have availed themselves of these dodges, while "Symbolists" have resorted to poetic suggestion and Craig-Appia atmosphere as a means of concealing unclear thinking, ambivalent emotion, and downright ineptitude. In the case of Hollywood motion pictures and the scenarios written for them, I noted other dodges when I wrote the following in *Best Film Plays, 1943-44*:

> What, with notable exceptions, is omitted by author or studio often comprises the most solid substance of plot and meaning. The logic of the resolution of a screenplay seems too often meager or hurried. The upshot of too many films is disproportionately small by comparison with the labor of preparation or the expository matter. The tendency is to follow the line of least resistance, or the line of least difficulty in comprehension, character analysis, and social import. For reasons that are generally ascribed to the Hays office but may also be attributed to the contagion of a lazy-minded attitude, to a flabby pursuit of the matter and idea, too much gets irretrievably lost in film-making.

The obituary notice on many a fine intention may well read *"spurlos versenkt."*

I cannot also avoid the suspicion that those excellent cinematic devices, the dissolve and the fade-out, serve as a seduction. Every craftsman will probably rise up in indignant protest against this amateur deduction, for without them cinematic art would be static, ponderous, and dull. Yet the temptation of evasion is always present in the technique. While writers for the stage are frequently guilty of relegating crucial events or decisions to the wings or to intermissions, those responsible for the final screenplay (the writer-producer-director-cutter combinations) seem too inclined to discharge an obligation by dissolving or "fading out" a scene and skipping to something else. This has never been the way of major art, which has invariably squeezed the last drop out of some matter. Take the example of *The Iliad, The Divine Comedy, Hamlet, War and Peace,* the Parthenon frieze, or the *St. Matthew's Passion.* Work of this order creates the impression that the inherent possibilities of the matter have been exhausted by the creator.

It is an impression, too, rarely given by [Hollywood-made] films, into which have gone vast expenditures of money and endeavor and the mechanical resources of the wonder-working machine age. No doubt Hollywood's more intelligent craftsmen could write a book-length explanation, citing all the intrinsic and extrinsic evils of a collaborative, constantly interrupted, star-harassed, censorship-ridden, commercialized mass production enterprise. My reference to dissolves and fade-outs is intended to be more metaphorical than literal. It is perhaps most apropos when considered as a symbol of evasion, and slickness, and sloth—of want or fear of concentration on the thing in hand, on the experience, whether serious or comic, to be evoked. That is the respect in which the facile and too-ready use of the dissolve and the fade-out appears to me an evil—a temptation too subverting and demoralizing. All the more so, since it is the essence of film art. All the more so because it is so easy to justify oneself, to wrap the robes of righteousness about oneself, and to proclaim that it was all done *pour l'art.* How often do we resort to the dissolve, for instance, *not* to make full use of the film medium, but to cheat on content and force?

That the filmic devices can be employed to master the material, to unfold its true substance, has already been too forcefully demonstrated for us to take excuses at their face value. We need only recall films like *Potemkin* or *Carnival in Flanders,* or, on home grounds, *The Informer.*

Risks, however, are always present, and evasions always tempting to all but the most dedicated and resolute individuals. Nor can we overlook the fact that even an entirely independent writer of a screenplay will want to see it filmed, and be subject, therefore, to pressures from producers and exhibitors of films. These may be less onerous as Hollywood learns, as it may well have to in competing with television, that only the superior motion picture can be expected to succeed. Now that television is here, art appears to be the only thing that "pays off" for Hollywood, maimed as that art is and may continue to be for a long time. The pressures of commerce have been less severe in the making of many foreign pictures, although the seeds of Mammon are seeds of Mammon anywhere. The pressures may be least—here as well as abroad—when films are made not for the entire population—for wit and half-wit, and for man, woman, and child—but for exhibition in special movie-houses. And the independent screenwriter (if he ever materializes) who writes his screenplay first and then sells it, instead of first selling himself and then writing a screenplay, may be able to withstand the publican best of all. In any case, this kind of screenwriter will at least start with one advantage—he will start by expressing his own intention instead of working on an assignment from an employer.

INDEX